Tennessee

W9-BBX-233

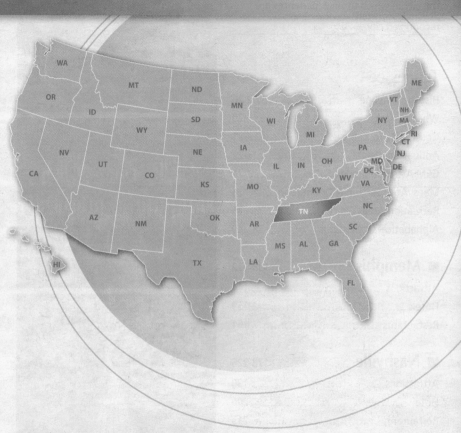

Published by AAA Publishing
1000 AAA Drive, Heathrow, FL 32746-5063
Copyright AAA 2015, All rights reserved

The publisher has made every effort to provide accurate, up-to-date information but accepts no responsibility for loss or injury sustained by any person using this book. TourBook® guides are published for the exclusive use of AAA members. Not for sale.

Advertising Rate and Circulation Information: (407) 444-8280

Printed in the USA by Quad/Graphics

This book is printed on paper certified by third-party standards for sustainably managed forestry and production.

Printed on recyclable paper.
Please recycle whenever possible.

Stock #4678 ◆ ◆

CONTENTS

Attractions, hotels, restaurants and other travel experience information are all grouped under the alphabetical listing of the city in which those experiences are physically located—or the nearest recognized city.

Tennessee

■ Memphis 133-172

■ Nashville 178-226

Featured Information

Dream.
Plan.
Go.

Picture yourself ...
- At your ideal destination
- In a comfortable hotel
- Eating your favorite meals
- Exploring the sights

Turn your dreams into reality
with **TripTik® Travel Planner**.

wavebreakmedia / Shutterstock.com

Online: AAA.com/ttp | On the go: AAA or CAA Mobile app

Going the Extra Mile

Every year AAA experts travel North America to check out places for members to see, stay, dine and play.

Professional Inspectors - conduct in-person hotel and restaurant evaluations, providing ratings, notes and tips to guide your decisions.

Seasoned Travel Writers - gather destination insight, providing itineraries and top picks including AAA GEM attractions.

A to Z City Listings

Cities and places are listed alphabetically within each state or province. Attractions, hotels and restaurants are listed once — under the city in which they are physically located.

Cities that are considered part of a larger destination city or area have an expanded city header. The header identifies the larger region and cross-references pages that contain shared trip planning resources:

- Destination map – outline map of the cities that comprise a destination city or area
- Attraction spotting map – regional street map marked with attraction locations
- Hotel/restaurant spotting map and index – regional street map numbered with hotel and restaurant locations identified in an accompanying index

Cities that are not considered part of a larger destination city or area but have a significant number of listings may have these resources within the individual city section:

- Attraction spotting map
- Hotel/restaurant spotting map and index

Location Abbreviations

Directions are from the center of town unless otherwise specified, using these highway abbreviations:

Bus. Rte.=business route
CR=county road
FM=farm to market
FR=forest road
Hwy.=Canadian highway
I=interstate highway
LR=legislative route
R.R.=rural route
SR/PR=state or provincial route
US=federal highway

Maps

Use the navigable road maps and accompanying legend in the Atlas Section for route planning. Check the destination maps for general location reference. In select cities only, refer to the mass transit overview maps to cross-reference station names and numbers. For attraction and hotel/restaurant spotting maps, see the legend below to identify symbols and color coding.

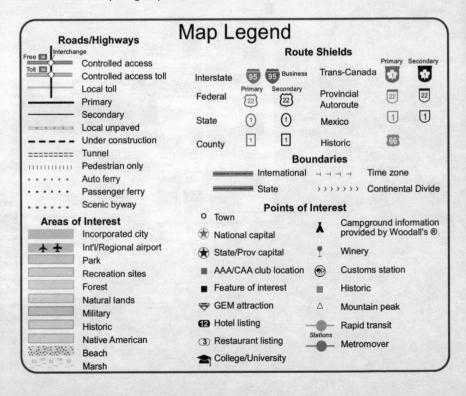

About Listed Establishments

AAA/CAA Approved hotels and restaurants are listed on the basis of merit alone after careful evaluation and approval by full-time, professionally trained AAA/CAA inspectors. An establishment's decision to advertise in the TourBook guide has no bearing on its evaluation or rating; nor does inclusion of advertising imply AAA endorsement of products and services.

Information in this guide was believed accurate at the time of publication. However, since changes inevitably occur between annual editions, please contact your AAA travel professional, visit AAA.com or download the AAA mobile app to confirm prices and schedules.

Attraction Listings

> **ATTRACTION NAME,** 3 mi. n. off SR 20A (Main Ave.), consists of 250 acres with Olmsted-designed gardens, a 205-foot marble and coquina bell tower and a Mediterranean-style mansion. One of the state's oldest attractions, the tower and gardens were dedicated to the American people in 1929 by President Calvin Coolidge on behalf of their founder, a Dutch immigrant.
>
> **Hours:** Gardens daily 8-6. Last admission 1 hour before closing. Visitor center daily 9-5. Estate tours are given at noon and 2. Carillon concerts are given at 1 and 3. Phone ahead to confirm schedule. **Cost:** $10; $3 (ages 5-12). Gardens and estate $16; $8 (ages 5-12). **Phone:** (555) 555-5555.
>
> GT ⏀ 🅿 Dupont Circle,13

AAA/CAA travel experts may designate an attraction of exceptional interest and quality as a AAA GEM — a *Great Experience for Members®. See GEM Attraction Index (listed on CONTENTS page) for a complete list of locations.*

Consult the online travel guides at AAA.com or visit AAA Mobile for additional things to do if you have time.

Cost

Prices are quoted without sales tax in the local currency (U.S. or Canadian dollars). Children under the lowest age specified are admitted free when accompanied by an adult. Most establishments accept credit cards, but a small number require cash, so please call ahead to verify.

Adventure Travel

Activities such as air tours, hiking, skiing and white-water rafting are listed to provide member information and do not imply AAA/CAA endorsement. For your safety, be aware of inherent risks and adhere to all safety instructions.

Icons

SAVE AAA Discounts & Rewards® member discount

◨ Electric vehicle charging station on premises. Domestic station information provided by the U.S. Department of Energy. Canadian station information provided by Plug'n Drive Ontario.

GT Guided Tours available

🅰 Camping facilities

⏀ Food on premises

🆇 Recreational activities

🐾 Pets on leash allowed

🅿 Picnicking allowed

In select cities only:

🚇 Mass transit station within 1 mile. Icon is followed by station name and AAA/CAA designated station number within listing.

Information-Only Attraction Listings

Bulleted listings, which include the following categories, are listed for informational purposes as a service to members:

- **Gambling establishments** (even if located in a AAA/CAA Approved hotel)
- **Participatory recreational activities** (those requiring physical exertion or special skills)
- **Wineries that offer tours and tastings**

Mobile Tags

Scan QR codes throughout the TourBook guide to see online offers, menus, videos and more on your smartphone or tablet. If you need a QR scanner app, download one for free from your app store.

If you see a non-QR code in an ad, check the nearby text for details on which app you'll need to scan it.

Hotel and Restaurant Listings

1 Diamond Rating – AAA/CAA Approved hotels and restaurants are assigned a rating of one to five Diamonds. Red Diamonds distinguish establishments that participate in the AAA/CAA logo licensing program. For details, see p. 11 or AAA.com/Diamonds.

[fyi] indicates hotels and restaurants that are not AAA/CAA Approved and/or Diamond Rated but are listed to provide additional choices for members:

- **Hotels** may be unrated if they are too new to rate, under construction, under major renovation or have not yet been evaluated; or if they do not meet all AAA requirements. Hotels that do not meet all AAA requirements may be included if they offer member value or are the only option; details are noted in the listing.
- **Restaurants** may be unrated if they have not yet been evaluated by AAA.

2 Classification or Cuisine Type – Noted after the Diamond Rating.

- **Hotel Classifications** indicate the style of operation, overall concept and service level. Subclassifications may also be added. (See p. 12.)
- **Restaurant Cuisine Types** identify the food concept from more than 100 categories. If applicable, a classification may also be added. (See p. 13.)

3 Dollar Amounts – Quoted without sales tax in the local currency (U.S. or Canadian dollars), rounded up to the nearest dollar. Most establishments accept credit cards, but a small number require cash, so please call ahead to verify.

- **Hotel Rates** indicate the publicly available two-person rate or rate range for a standard room, applicable all year.
- **Restaurant Prices** represent the minimum and maximum entrée cost per person. Exceptions may include one-of-a-kind or special market priced items.

4 Spotting Symbol – Ovals containing numbers correspond with numbered location markings on hotel and restaurant spotting maps.

5 Parking – Unless otherwise noted, parking is free, on-site self parking.

6 Hotel Value Nationwide – Blue boxes highlight member benefits available at AAA/CAA Approved locations across a hotel chain. (See Just For Members section for details.)

7 Hotel Unit Limited Availability – Unit types, amenities and room features preceded by "some" are available on a limited basis, potentially as few as one.

8 Hotel Terms – Cancellation and minimum stay policies are listed. Unless otherwise noted, most properties offer a full deposit refund with cancellations received at least 48 hours before standard check-in. Properties that require advance payment may not refund the difference for early departures. "Resort fee" indicates a charge may apply above and beyond the quoted room rate.

9 Hotel Check-in/Check-out – Unless otherwise noted, check-in is after 3 p.m. and check-out is before 10 a.m.

10 Restaurant Dress Code – Unless otherwise noted, dress is casual or dressy casual.

11 Restaurant Menu – Where indicated, menus may be viewed in a secure online environment at AAA.com or, if a mobile tag is provided, via the restaurant's website.

12 Hotel Icons – May be preceded by CALL and/or SOME UNITS.

Member Information:

[SAVE] Member rates: discounted standard room rate or lowest public rate available at time of booking for dates of stay.

[ECO] Eco-certified by government or private organization.

[⚡] Electric vehicle charging station on premises. Domestic station information provided by the U.S. Department of Energy. Canadian station information provided by Plug'n Drive Ontario.

[✕] Smoke-free premises

In select cities only:

[⊞] Mass transit station within 1 mile. Icon is followed by station name and AAA/CAA designated station number within listing.

Services:

[✈] Airport transportation

[🐾] Pets allowed (Call property for restrictions.)

[$🐾] Pets allowed (Call property for restrictions and fees.)

[🍴] Restaurant on premises

[🍴⁺] Restaurant off premises

[🍽] Room service for 2 or more meals

[🍸] Full bar

HOTEL LISTING

HOTEL NAME (555)555-5555 **50**

Hotel
$109-$199

LOGO **AAA Benefit:** Members save a minimum 5% off the best available rate.

Address: 300 Main St 55555 **Location:** I-275 exit 31 southbound; exit 30 northbound, 1.6 mi w on SR 688 (Oak Rd). Dupont Circle, 13. **Facility:** 149 units, some efficiencies. 3 stories, interior corridors. **Parking:** on-site (fee). **Terms:** check-in 4 pm, cancellation fee imposed, resort fee. **Amenities:** video games. **Pool(s):** heated outdoor. **Activities:** hot tub, exercise room. **Guest Services:** valet and coin laundry. **Featured Amenity:** continental breakfast.

RESTAURANT LISTING

RESTAURANT NAME 555/555-5555

Continental
Fine Dining
$15-$35

AAA Inspector Notes: *Historic.* A romantic aura punctuates the modern and casual dining room, which is accented with floral arrangements and dramatic, freshly cut branches. The menu features seasonal ingredients. The pastry chef's decadent creations are popular. Semiformal attire. **Features:** full bar, patio dining, happy hour. **Address:** 26 N Main St 55555 **Location:** SR A1A southbound, 2.7 mi s of jct SR 520. Dupont Circle, 13.

Menu on AAA.com

1 Child care
BIZ Business area
&M Accessible features (Call property for available services and amenities.)

Activities:
Full-service casino
Pool
Health club on premises

In-Room Amenities:
HS High-speed Internet service
SHS High-speed Internet service (Call property for fees.)
Wireless Internet service
Wireless Internet service (Call property for fees.)
No wireless Internet service
Pay movies
Refrigerator
Microwave
Coffee maker
AC No air conditioning
TV No TV
No telephones

13 Restaurant Icons
SAVE AAA Discounts & Rewards® member discount
ECO Eco-certified by government or private organization.
Electric vehicle charging station on premises. Domestic station information provided by the U.S. Department of Energy. Canadian station information provided by Plug'n Drive Ontario.
AC No air conditioning
&M Accessible features (Call property for available services and amenities.)
Designated smoking section
B Breakfast
L Lunch
D Dinner
24 Open 24 hours
LATE Open after 11 p.m.
Pet-friendly (Call property for restrictions.)

In select cities only:
Mass transit station within 1 mile. Icon is followed by station name and AAA/CAA designated station number within listing.

Just For Members

Understanding the Diamond Ratings

Hotel and restaurant evaluations are unscheduled to ensure our professionally trained inspectors encounter the same experience members do.

- When an establishment is Diamond Rated, it means members can expect a good fit with their needs. The inspector assigns a rating that indicates the type of experience to expect.
- While establishments at high levels must offer increasingly complex personalized services, establishments at every level are subject to the same basic requirements for cleanliness, comfort and hospitality. Learn more at AAA.com/Diamonds.

Hotels

Budget-oriented, offering basic comfort and hospitality.

Affordable, with modestly enhanced facilities, décor and amenities.

Distinguished, multifaceted with enhanced physical attributes, amenities and guest comforts.

Refined, stylish with upscale physical attributes, extensive amenities and high degree of hospitality, service and attention to detail.

Ultimate luxury, sophistication and comfort with extraordinary physical attributes, meticulous personalized service, extensive amenities and impeccable standards of excellence.

Restaurants

Simple, economical food, often self-service, in a functional environment.

Familiar food, often cooked to order, served in relaxed surroundings.

Popular cuisine, skillfully prepared and served, with expanded beverage options, in enhanced setting.

Imaginative, market-fresh food creatively prepared and skillfully served, often with wine steward, amid upscale ambience.

Cutting-edge cuisine of the finest ingredients, uniquely prepared by an acclaimed chef, served by expert service staff led by maître d' in extraordinary surroundings.

What's the difference?

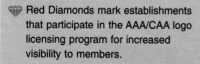 Red Diamonds mark establishments that participate in the AAA/CAA logo licensing program for increased visibility to members.

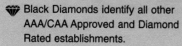 Black Diamonds identify all other AAA/CAA Approved and Diamond Rated establishments.

Hotel Classifications

Quality and comfort are usually consistent across each Diamond Rating level, but décor, facilities and service levels vary by classification.

Berry Manor Inn, Rockland, ME

Bed & Breakfast — Typically owner-operated with a high degree of personal touches. Guests are encouraged to interact during evening and breakfast hours. A continental or full, hot breakfast is included in the room rate.

Killarney Lodge, Algonquin Provincial Park, ON

Cabin — Often located in wooded, rural or waterfront locations. Freestanding units are typically rustic and of basic design. As a rule, essential cleaning supplies, kitchen utensils and complete bed and bath linens are supplied.

Hyatt Regency Clearwater Beach Resort & Spa, Clearwater Beach, FL

Condominium — Apartment-style accommodations of varying design or décor, units often contain one or more bedrooms, a living room, full kitchen and an eating area. As a rule, essential cleaning supplies, kitchen utensils and complete bed and bath linens are supplied.

Montpelier Plantation and Beach, St. Kitts and Nevis

Cottage — Often located in wooded, rural, or waterfront locations. Freestanding units are typically home-style in design and décor. As a rule, essential cleaning supplies, kitchen utensils and complete bed and bath linens are supplied.

Nottoway Plantation & Resort, White Castle, LA

Country Inn — Although similar in definition to a bed and breakfast, country inns are usually larger in scale with spacious public areas and offer a dining facility that serves breakfast and dinner.

The Shores Resort & Spa, Daytona Beach Shores, FL

Hotel — Typically a multistory property with interior room entrances and a variety of guest unit styles. The magnitude of the public areas is determined by the overall theme, location and service level, but may include a variety of facilities such as a restaurant, shops, a fitness center, a spa, a business center and meeting rooms.

All Star Vacation Homes, Kissimmee, FL

House — Freestanding units of varying home-style design. Typically larger scale, often containing two or more bedrooms, a living room, a full kitchen, a dining room and multiple bathrooms. As a rule, essential cleaning supplies, kitchen utensils and complete bed and bath linens are supplied.

Bryce View Lodge, Bryce Canyon City, UT

Motel — A one- or two-story roadside property with exterior room entrances and drive up parking. Public areas and facilities are often limited in size and/or availability.

Vista Verde Guest Ranch, Clark, CO

Ranch — Typically a working ranch featuring an obvious rustic, Western theme, equestrian-related activities and a variety of guest unit styles.

Hotel Subclassifications

These additional descriptives may be added to the classification for more information:

- **Boutique** — Often thematic, typically informal yet highly personalized; may have a luxurious or quirky style that is fashionable or unique.
- **Casino** — Extensive gambling facilities are available, such as blackjack, craps, keno and slot machines.
- **Classic** — Renowned and landmark properties, older than 50 years, well known for their unique style and ambience.
- **Contemporary** — Overall theme reflects characteristics of present mainstream trends.
- **Extended Stay** — Offers a predominance of long-term accommodations with a designated full-service kitchen area within each unit.
- **Historic** — More than 75 years old with one of the following documented historical features: Maintains the integrity of the historical nature, listed on the National Register of Historic Places, designated a National Historic Landmark or located in a National Register Historic District.
- **Resort** — Extensive recreational facilities and programs may include golf, tennis, skiing, fishing, water sports, spa

treatments or professionally guided activities.

- **Retro** — Overall theme reflects a contemporary design that reinterprets styles from a past era.
- **Vacation Rental** — Typically houses, condos, cottages or cabins; these properties are "home away from home" self-catering accommodations.
- **Vintage** — Overall theme reflects upon and maintains the authentic traits and experience of a past era.

Service Animals

Under the Americans with Disabilities Act (ADA), U.S. businesses that serve the public must allow people with disabilities to bring their service animals into all areas of the facility where customers are normally allowed to go.

Businesses may ask if an animal is a service animal and what tasks the animal has been trained to perform. Businesses may not ask about the person's disability, require special identification for the animal or request removal of the animal from the premises except in limited cases that require alternate assistance. Businesses may not charge extra fees for service animals, including standard pet fees, but may charge for damage caused by service animals if guests are normally charged for damage they cause.

Call the U.S. Department of Justice ADA Information Line: (800) 514-0301 or TTY (800) 514-0383, or visit ada.gov. Regulations may differ in Canada.

Restaurant Classifications

If applicable, in addition to the cuisine type noted under the Diamond Rating, restaurant listings may also include one or both classifications:

- **Classic** — Renowned and landmark operation in business for 25 plus years; unique style and ambience.
- **Historic** — Meets one of the following: Listed on National Register of Historic Places, designated a National Historic Landmark or located in a National Register Historic District.

AAA/CAA Approved Hotels

For members, AAA/CAA Approved means quality assured.

- Only properties that meet basic requirements for cleanliness, comfort and hospitality pass inspection.
- Approved hotels receive a Diamond Rating that tells members the type of experience to expect.

Guest Safety

Inspectors view a sampling of rooms during evaluations and, therefore, AAA/CAA cannot guarantee the presence of working locks and operational fire safety equipment in every guest unit.

Member Rates

AAA/CAA members can generally expect to pay no more than the maximum TourBook listed rate for a standard room. Member discounts apply to rates quoted within the rate range and are applicable at the time of booking. Listed rates are usually based on last standard room availability. Rates may fluctuate within the range and vary by season and room type. Obtain current AAA/CAA member rates and make reservations at AAA.com.

Exceptions

- Rates for properties operating as concessionaires for the U.S. National Park Service are not guaranteed due to governing regulations.
- Special advertised rates and short-term promotional rates below the rate range are not subject to additional member discounts.
- During special events, hotels may temporarily increase room rates, not recognize discounts or modify pricing policies. Special events may include Mardi Gras, the Kentucky Derby (including pre-Derby events), college football games, holidays, holiday periods and state fairs. Although some special events are listed in the TourBook guides and on AAA.com, it's always wise to check in advance with AAA travel professionals for specific dates.

If you are charged more than the maximum TourBook listed rate, question the additional charge. If an exception is not in effect and management refuses to adhere to the published rate, pay for the room and contact AAA/CAA. The amount paid above the stated maximum will be refunded if our investigation indicates an unjustified charge.

Reservations and Cancellations

When making your reservation, identify yourself as a AAA/CAA member and request written confirmation of your room type, rate, dates of stay, and cancellation and refund policies. At registration, show your membership card.

To cancel, contact the hotel, your AAA/CAA club office or AAA.com, depending on how you booked your reservation. Request a cancellation number or proof of cancellation.

If your room is not as specified and you have written confirmation of your reservation for a specific room type, you should be given the option of choosing a different room or receiving a refund. If management refuses to issue a refund, contact AAA/CAA.

Contacting AAA/CAA About Approved Properties

If your visit to a AAA/CAA Approved attraction, hotel or restaurant doesn't meet your expectations, please tell us about it — **during your visit or within 30 days**. Be sure to save your receipts and other documentation for reference.

Use the easy online form at AAA.com/TourBookComments to send us the details.

Alternatively, you can email your comments to: memberrelations@national.aaa.com or submit them via postal mail to: AAA Member Comments, 1000 AAA Dr., Box 61, Heathrow, FL 32746.

AAA/CAA Preferred Hotels

All AAA/CAA Approved hotels are committed to providing quality, value and member service. In addition, those designated as AAA/CAA Preferred Hotels also offer these extra values at Approved locations nationwide. Valid AAA/CAA membership required.

- **Best AAA/CAA member rates for your dates of stay**.
- **Seasonal promotions and special member offers.** Visit AAA.com to view current offers.
- **Member benefit.** See the blue boxes in hotel listings for the chains shown in the right-hand column below to find values offered at AAA/CAA Approved locations nationwide, subject to availability. Details valid at the time of publication and may change without notice.

- **Total satisfaction guarantee.** If you book your stay with AAA/CAA Travel and your stay fails to meet your expectations, you can apply for a full refund. Bring the complaint to the hotel's attention during the stay and request resolution; if the complaint is not resolved by the hotel, ask your AAA/CAA travel agent to request resolution through the AAA/CAA Assured Stay program.

DISCOUNTS >>REWARDS*
PREFERRED HOTELS

Rewards
PREFERRED HOTELS

ASSURED STAY
Total Satisfaction Guarantee

BW | Best Western. Hotels & Resorts	BEST WESTERN®, BEST WESTERN PLUS®, EXECUTIVE RESIDENCY, Vib, BEST WESTERN PREMIER® and BW Premier Collection℠
Hilton	Hilton Hotels & Resorts, Waldorf Astoria™ Hotels & Resorts, Conrad® Hotels & Resorts, Canopy by Hilton, Curio - A Collection by Hilton™, DoubleTree by Hilton™, Embassy Suites Hotels™, Hilton Garden Inn™, Hampton Inn™, Homewood Suites by Hilton™, Home2 Suites by Hilton™ and Hilton Grand Vacations™
HYATT®	Park Hyatt®, Andaz®, Grand Hyatt®, Hyatt Centric®, Hyatt®, Hyatt Regency®, Hyatt Place®, HYATT house®, Hyatt Zilara® and Hyatt Ziva®
Marriott.	JW Marriott®, Autograph Collection® Hotels, Renaissance® Hotels, Marriott Hotels®, Delta Hotels and Resorts®, Gaylord Hotels®, AC Hotels by Marriott®, Courtyard®, Residence Inn®, SpringHill Suites®, Fairfield Inn & Suites® and TownePlace Suites®
MGM RESORTS INTERNATIONAL®	Bellagio®, Aria®, Vdara®, MGM Grand®, The Signature at MGM Grand®, Mandalay Bay®, Delano™ Las Vegas, The Mirage®, Monte Carlo™, New York-New York®, Luxor®, Excalibur® and Circus Circus® Las Vegas
starwood Hotels and Resorts	St. Regis®, The Luxury Collection®, W®, Westin®, Le Méridien®, Sheraton®, Four Points® by Sheraton, Aloft®, element® and Tribute Portfolio™

Landry's Seafood House, The Crab House, Chart House, Oceanaire, Saltgrass Steak House, Muer Seafood Restaurants and Aquarium Restaurants

Member Discounts

Visit AAA.com/searchfordiscounts to find locations and available member discounts. Your AAA/CAA club may offer even greater discounts on theme park tickets. Amtrak and theme park discounts may be used for up to six tickets; restaurant savings may be used for up to six patrons. Other restrictions may apply. All offers subject to change. For complete restrictions, visit your AAA office or AAA.com/restrictions.

- Save 10% on food and nonalcoholic beverages at all of the above restaurants.

- Save 10% on merchandise at Aquarium, Downtown Aquarium and Rainforest Cafe restaurants.

ATTRACTIONS

Six Flags

- Save on admission at the gate, participating AAA/CAA offices or AAA.com/SixFlags.

- Save 10% on merchandise of $15 or more at in-park stores.

Universal Orlando Resort and Universal Studios Hollywood

- Save on tickets at select AAA/CAA offices or AAA.com/Universal. In-park savings available in FL.

- Save 10% on Blue Man Group tickets and at select food and merchandise venues at Universal CityWalk®.

DINING

Hard Rock Cafe

- Save 10% on food, nonalcoholic beverages and merchandise at all locations in the U.S. and Canada, plus select international locations. Visit AAA.com/HardRock for full listing.

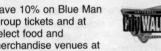

SHOPPING

adidas Outlet

- Save 20% on the entire purchase. Visit AAA.com/adidasoutlet for list of locations.

Reebok & Rockport Outlet

- Save 20% on the entire purchase. Visit AAA.com/Reebok for list of locations.

Tanger Outlet Centers

- Receive a free coupon book with discounts up to 50% at select merchants.

TRANSPORTATION

Amtrak

- Save 10% on rail fare booked at least three days in advance of travel date at AAA.com/Amtrak.

El Monte RV

- Save up to 10% on nightly rates booked at least 24 hours in advance of pickup at AAA.com/ElMonteRV or (800) 337-2156.

Hertz

- Save on daily, weekend, weekly and monthly rentals at AAA.com/Hertz or (800) 654-3080.

RACK UP
THE
REWARDS

Make membership an even more rewarding experience.

The AAA Member Rewards Visa® credit card lets you earn reward points on all of your purchases. Apply for an account today and let the rewards start rolling in!

 Earn 1 point for every $1 in purchases with your AAA Member Rewards Visa® card!*

 Earn 2X points for gas, grocery and drug store purchases!

 Earn 3X points on qualifying AAA and travel purchases!

 Redeem for cash or get a AAA Voucher that gives you up to 40% more value!**

 Exclusive rewards to make you smile!

VISIT AAA.com/creditcard   **STOP BY** any AAA branch

The Nashville skyline reflects in the Cumberland River

Tennessee

Why does Tennessee feel like home? Because the musicians and music many Americans listened to in their formative years started out in or came directly from Tennessee. Musically, we grew up here.

Stately Memphis was the early 20th-century "Home of the Blues." Colorful Beale Street still seems steeped in the humid refrains of W.C. Handy's music. Blues influenced the motion picture, swing, popular and symphonic music of the 1930s and '40s.

In the mid-20th century, Sun Studio reverberated with the rumbling monotone of Johnny Cash and the innovative rockabilly rhythms of Carl Perkins and Elvis Presley.

Nashville is home to The Grand Ole Opry, which began in the early 20th century and remains alive and pickin'. By the 1990s country recordings dominated the popular music industry.

Superstars sing of love, life and pickup trucks and warn of the consequences of not

A waterfall along the Motor Nature Trail

walking the line. And generations of teenagers listen and learn. Some aspect of the music that flows from Tennessee strikes a resonant chord in nearly everyone.

Exit Here for History

If your travels take you to Tennessee, you'll enjoy tranquil mountain vistas, elegant Southern mansions and pioneer settlements where history is relived on a daily basis. A good place to reflect is Shiloh National Military Park, which preserves the 1862 Civil War battlefield where close to 110,000 soldiers engaged in fierce combat. It's eerily peaceful now along this bend in the Tennessee River; the thunder of cannons long since silenced.

Continuing along the gently rolling terrain of middle Tennessee, you might decide to stop in Columbia, where—among an abundance of 19th-century residences—you'll find the ancestral home of President James K. Polk. And just north is the town of Franklin, where plantations and farmhouses were sites in the Battle of Franklin, serving as field hospitals, battlefields, headquarters and places of refuge during the Civil War.

Maybe it's time to take a break and wet your whistle at Jack Daniel's Distillery, just down the road in Lynchburg. You won't be able to sample the sour mash whiskey they've been producing in this holler since 1866 (the distillery is in a dry county), but a glass of lemonade will be offered at the completion of a guided tour.

Mountain Memories

As you journey farther east, take a worthwhile detour to the Museum of Appalachia in Clinton, akin to time traveling to an early 1800s mountain village. Come sit for a while and visit with the folks as they go about typical pioneer tasks. Reflect on how life has changed since the days of butter churns, looms and other "old-timey" tools.

A step even further back in Tennessee history can be experienced by a short excursion to Piney Flats. The year was 1791, and the settlement of Rocky Mount was the capital of the "Territory of the United States South of the Ohio River." On a high ridge with clear views of distant mountains and neighboring North Carolina, costumed interpreters welcome visitors into their rustic abodes, eager to share stories and demonstrate frontier crafts and skills.

And since you're in the neighborhood, swing through Great Smoky Mountains National Park, where there's an abundance of side trips to choose from. Roaring Fork Motor Nature Trail winds past falls and rapids as it makes its way through verdant wilderness areas, and the Sugarlands Motor Trail leads to spectacular views of Cades Cove.

Recreation

Tennessee's primary natural features afford unlimited options to outdoors enthusiasts, with the Appalachian Mountain chain defining the state's eastern boundary and the Cumberland River spilling from its Kentucky headwaters in the north-central region.

Boating and fishing are popular activities on the interconnected recreational lakes of the Cumberland system, while sailing and yachting are favorites on Old Hickory Lake, northeast of Nashville. Strange but true: Scuba diving is one of the most popular water sports at crystalline Dale Hollow Lake, reached via SRs 52 and 53 from Celina. The Willow Grove area contains underwater ruins of an abandoned village flooded when the lake was created in the 1940s.

The Cumberland is not the only river of opportunity in the state. J. Percy Priest Lake, southeast of Nashville, has four marinas and more than 15 recreation areas with launch ramps. The lake is stocked with rockfish, which can be caught April through October. Largemouth bass lurk in Cheatham Lake, 25 miles west of Nashville, while Kentucky Lake, a water playground forming the western boundary of the Land Between the Lakes National Recreation Area, is long on

both boating and fishing enjoyment.

All of the recreational lakes of the Cumberland system offer some type of camping; facilities range from primitive tent sites to developed areas for trailers. Center Hill Lake, in the rolling hills of central Tennessee east of Smithville, is surrounded with campgrounds furnished with electrical and water hookups. Edgar Evins State Park, near Center Hill Lake dam, has lakeside campsites nestled on wooded slopes. Family camping is especially fun near Cades Cove, one of the most idyllic places in the Smokies.

Horseback riders will find more than 300 miles of trails and a wrangler camp with water, electricity and bath facilities in Natchez Trace State Park northeast of Lexington. Chickasaw, off SR 100 near Henderson, is the only other state park with an equestrian campground.

The Appalachian Trail, accessible from several points in the Smokies, is the granddaddy of hiking paths in eastern Tennessee. Increasingly popular, Justin P. Wilson Cumberland Trail State Park was created in 1998 just for hiking and backpacking. Rocky terrain earns the Cumberland Mountain path a rating of difficult, but other trails of varying lengths and degrees also are open; the 10-mile hike offers views of the Powell River Valley.

Cast your line on Old Hickory Lake

Historic Timeline

1682	René-Robert Cavelier, Sieur de La Salle claims the region for France.
1739	The French build Fort Assumption to gain control over Chickasaw Indian lands.
1796	Tennessee becomes the 16th state to join the union.
1925	The WSM Barn Dance, later to become Grand Ole Opry, first broadcasts.
1942	Oak Ridge becomes a site of the Manhattan District atom bomb project.
1968	Civil rights leader Martin Luther King Jr. is assassinated in Memphis.
1982	Knoxville hosts the World's Fair.
1991	The city of Memphis elects its first African-American mayor.
1996	The Nobel Prize in physiology or medicine is awarded to a doctor from St. Jude Children's Research Hospital in Memphis.
2009	Great Smoky Mountains National Park celebrates its 75th anniversary.
2010	Torrential downpours in the South flood Nashville, causing one of the worst natural disasters in state history.

What To Pack

Temperature Averages Maximum/Minimum	JANUARY	FEBRUARY	MARCH	APRIL	MAY	JUNE	JULY	AUGUST	SEPTEMBER	OCTOBER	NOVEMBER	DECEMBER
Bristol	48/29	50/29	57/35	68/44	78/53	85/61	86/64	85/63	81/57	70/45	57/34	48/29
Chattanooga	51/32	54/34	61/39	72/48	81/56	88/65	90/68	89/67	84/60	74/48	61/37	52/32
Clarksville	45/25	51/29	61/36	71/44	79/54	86/63	90/68	89/65	83/58	72/45	62/36	49/29
Knoxville	50/32	53/32	60/38	71/48	80/56	87/65	90/68	89/67	84/61	73/49	59/37	50/32
Memphis	51/33	54/35	61/42	72/52	81/60	89/69	92/72	92/70	86/63	76/52	62/40	63/35
Nashville	49/31	51/33	59/39	71/48	80/57	88/66	91/70	90/68	85/61	74/49	59/38	50/32

From the records of The Weather Channel Interactive, Inc.

Good Facts To Know

ABOUT THE STATE

POPULATION: 6,346,105

AREA: 42,144 square miles; ranks 36th.

CAPITAL: Nashville.

HIGHEST POINT: 6,643 ft., Clingmans Dome.

LOWEST POINT: 178 ft., Mississippi River.

TIME ZONE(S): Eastern/Central. DST.

REGULATIONS

TEEN DRIVING LAWS: No more than one unrelated passenger is permitted unless one or more of the passengers is 21 or older and has a valid, unrestricted license. Driving is not permitted 11 p.m.-6 a.m. The minimum age for an unrestricted driver's license is 17. Phone (615) 251-5166 for more information.

SEAT BELT/CHILD RESTRAINT LAWS: Seat belts are required for driver and front-seat passengers ages 16 and over and for children ages 9-16. Booster seats are required for children ages 4-8 and under 57 inches tall. Child restraints are required for children under age 4. Children under age 9 must be in the rear seat. AAA recommends the use of seat belts or child restraints for driver and all passengers.

CELLPHONE RESTRICTIONS: Learner's permit or intermediate driver's license holders are not permitted to use cellphones while driving. All drivers are prohibited from text messaging while driving.

HELMETS FOR MOTORCYCLISTS: Required for all riders and passengers.

RADAR DETECTORS: Permitted. Prohibited for use by commercial vehicles.

MOVE OVER LAW: Driver required to slow down and vacate the lane nearest stopped police, fire and rescue vehicles using audible or flashing signals. Drivers also must move over for utility workers and tow truck drivers assisting motorists on the side of the road.

FIREARMS LAWS: Vary by state and/or county. Contact the Tennessee Department of Safety, 1150 Foster Ave., Nashville, TN 37243; phone (615) 251-5166.

HOLIDAYS

HOLIDAYS: Jan. 1 ▪ Martin Luther King Jr. Day, Jan. (3rd Mon.) ▪ Washington's Birthday/Presidents Day, Feb. (3rd Mon.) ▪ Good Friday ▪ Memorial Day, May (last Mon.) ▪ July 4 ▪ Labor Day, Sept. (1st Mon.) ▪ Columbus Day, Oct. (2nd Mon.) ▪ Veterans Day, Nov. 11 ▪ Thanksgiving, Nov. (4th Thurs.) ▪ Christmas, Dec. 25.

MONEY

TAXES: Tennessee's statewide sales tax is 7 percent, with cities and counties allowed to impose additional levies. Counties and cities also may levy Occupancy Taxes, which are typically 3 to 5 percent.

VISITOR INFORMATION

INFORMATION CENTERS: State welcome centers that provide details about attractions, accommodations, historic sites, parks and events are at Ardmore I-65S ▪ Bristol I-81S ▪ Chattanooga I-75S ▪ Clarksville I-24E ▪ Dyersburg I-155S ▪ Erwin I-26 (eastbound and westbound) ▪ Hartford I-40E ▪ Jellico I-75N ▪ Kingsport I-26 ▪ downtown Memphis near I-40 at Jefferson and Riverside Drive ▪ Mitchellville I-65N ▪ Smith County I-40 (eastbound and westbound) near New Middleton ▪ Nickajack Center, 3 miles north of the Tennessee/Alabama/Georgia line via I-24 and SR 59 ▪ and Tiftonia I-24E. Except for the downtown Memphis location, which is open daily 7 a.m.-10:30 p.m., all centers are open daily 24 hours. Lesser-equipped rest stops are I-40 at Camden ▪ I-40 at Carthage ▪ I-40 at Crossville ▪ I-40 at Dandridge ▪ I-40 at Dickson ▪ I-40 at Jackson ▪ US 51 at Henning ▪ I-24 at Monteagle and Jasper ▪ I-75 at Athens ▪ and I-81 west of Dandridge and Greeneville.

ROAD CONDITIONS: Information about road conditions or construction can be obtained from the Tennessee Department of Transportation; phone 511 or (877) 244-0065.

FURTHER INFORMATION FOR VISITORS:
Tennessee Department of Tourist Development
William Snodgrass/Tennessee Tower
312 Rosa L. Parks Ave., 13th floor
Nashville, TN 37243
(615) 741-2159

NATIONAL FOREST INFORMATION:
U.S. Forest Service—Cherokee National Forest
2800 Ocoee St. North
Cleveland, TN 37312
(877) 444-6777 (campground reservations)

FISHING AND HUNTING REGULATIONS:
Tennessee Wildlife Resources Agency
5107 Edmondson Pike
Nashville, TN 37211
(615) 781-6500

RECREATION INFORMATION:
Tennessee Department of Environment and Conservation
Division of State Parks
312 Rosa L. Parks Ave., 2nd floor
Nashville, TN 37243
(615) 532-0109
(888) 867-2757 (information)

Tennessee Annual Events

Please call ahead to confirm event details.

JANUARY

- Dr. Martin Luther King Jr. King Day Celebration Memphis 901-521-9699
- Elvis Presley Birthday Celebration / Memphis 800-238-2000
- Farm Expo / Kingsport 423-929-3115

FEBRUARY

- Saddle Up! Pigeon Forge Pigeon Forge 800-251-9100
- Winter Heritage Festival in the Smokies / Townsend 865-448-0044
- Antiques and Garden Show of Nashville / Nashville 615-352-1282

MARCH

- Daffodil Day / Bell Buckle 931-389-9663
- A Mountain Quiltfest Pigeon Forge 800-251-9100
- Winter Carnival of Magic Pigeon Forge 800-953-7469

APRIL

- World's Biggest Fish Fry Paris 731-642-3431
- National Cornbread Festival South Pittsburg 423-837-0022
- Spring Wildflower Pilgrimage / Gatlinburg 865-436-1290

MAY

- Tennessee Association of Craft Artists Spring Crafts Fair / Nashville 615-385-1904
- Memphis in May International Festival Memphis 901-525-4611
- Running of the Iroquois Memorial Steeplechase Nashville 615-322-4814

JUNE

- CMA Music Festival Nashville 615-259-4730
- Carnival Memphis Memphis 901-458-2500
- RC and MoonPie Festival Bell Buckle 931-389-9663

JULY

- Uncle Dave Macon Days Festival / Murfreesboro 615-893-6565
- Fourth of July Midnight Parade / Gatlinburg 800-568-4748
- Festival on the Fourth Knoxville 865-215-4248

AUGUST

- Cherokee Days of Recognition / Cleveland 423-478-0339
- Elvis Week / Memphis 901-332-3322
- Tennessee Walking Horse National Celebration Shelbyville 931-684-5915

SEPTEMBER

- Bristol Rhythm & Roots Reunion / Bristol 423-989-4850
- Sycamore Shoals Celtic Festival / Elizabethton 423-543-5805
- Tennessee State Fair Nashville 615-862-8980

OCTOBER

- Jack Daniel's World Championship Invitational Barbecue / Lynchburg 931-759-4111
- National Storytelling Festival Jonesborough 800-952-8392
- Tennessee Fall Homecoming / Clinton 865-494-7680

NOVEMBER

- Christmas Village / Nashville 615-256-2726
- Winter Magic Kickoff and Chili Cook-off / Gatlinburg 800-568-4748
- Blue & Gray Days / Franklin 615-794-0903

DECEMBER

- Christmas at Historic Rugby / Rugby 423-628-2441
- New Year's Eve Countdown on Beale Street / Memphis 901-526-0115
- Candlelight Christmas Piney Flats 423-538-7396

The Old Mill, Pigeon Forge

Fall Creek Falls State Park, Pikeville

B.B. King's Blues Club, Memphis

Elvis Presley's Graceland, Memphis

Discovery Park of America, Union City

Index: Great Experience for Members

AAA editor's picks of exceptional note

Hunter Museum of
American Art

Jack Daniel's
Distillery

Dollywood

Tennessee Museum
of Aviation

See Orientation map on p. 34 for corresponding grid coordinates, if applicable.

Get maps, travel information and road service with the AAA and CAA Mobile apps

Next Best Thing to a Personal Tour Guide

Going away? From drive trips and campouts to family getaways and world travel, your AAA/CAA office has the perfect travel guide to help with your planning and decision making — before you go and along the way.

Enjoy publications packed with vibrant maps and photos plus expert travel tips and recommendations you can trust, at discounted prices just for members.

Purchase at participating AAA/CAA club offices. Selections vary by location.

Tennessee
Atlas Section

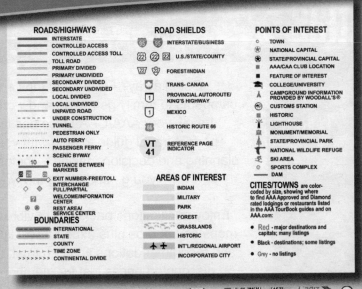

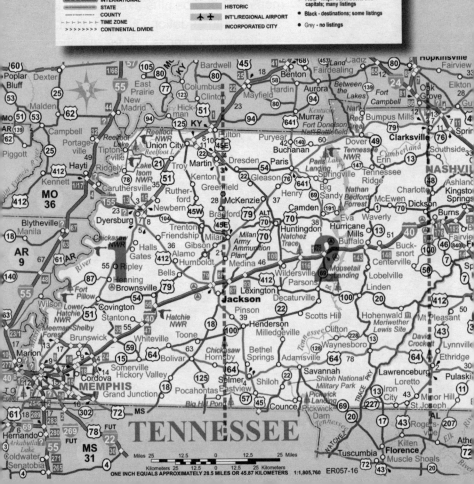

Use driving maps from the AAA Road Atlas to plan your itinerary and route. Purchase the complete 2016 AAA Road Atlas at participating AAA/CAA offices, retail stores and online booksellers.

EASTERN TENNESSEE

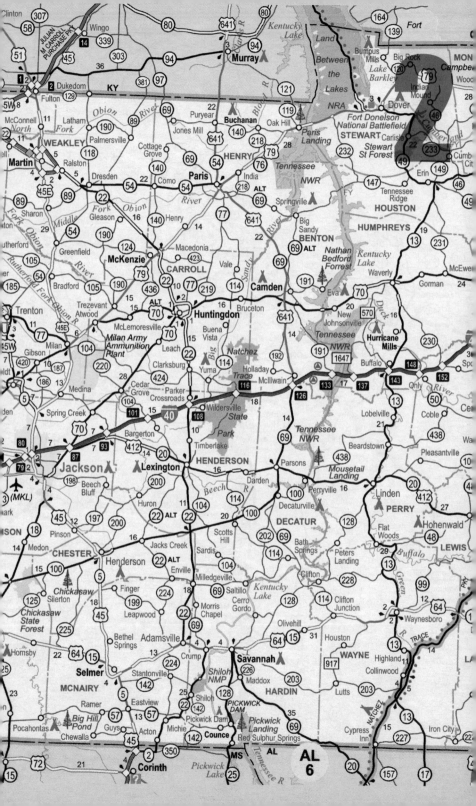

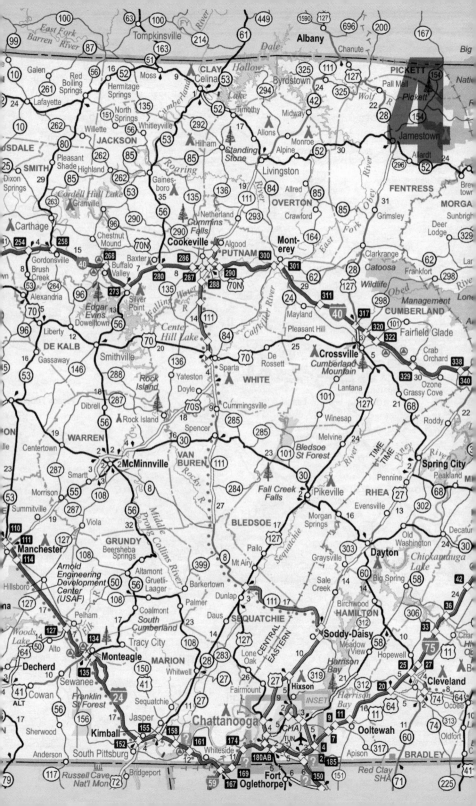

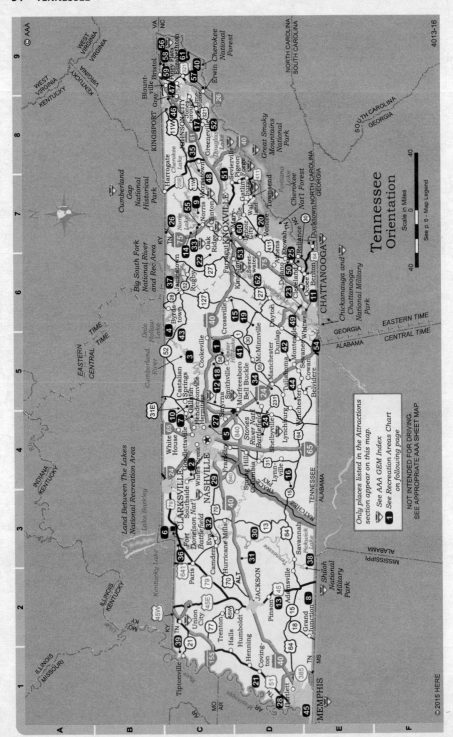

Tennessee
Orientation

Scale in Miles

See p. 6 · Map Legend

Only places listed in the Attractions
section appear on this map.

☆ See AAA GEM Index

■ See Recreation Areas Chart
on following page

NOT INTENDED FOR DRIVING.
SEE APPROPRIATE AAA SHEET MAP.

4013-16

© 2015 HERE

Recreation Areas Chart

The map location numerals in column 2 show an area's location on the preceding map.

	Map Location	Camping	Picnicking	Hiking Trails	Boating	Boat Ramp	Boat Rental	Fishing	Swimming	Pets on Leash	Bicycle Trails	Nature Progs.	Visitor Center	Lodge/Cabins	Food Service
NATIONAL PARKS *(See place listings.)*															
Great Smoky Mountains (D-8) 520,408 acres. Horse rental.		●	●	●				●				●	●	●	●
NATIONAL FORESTS *(See place listings.)*															
Cherokee (D-7) 650,000 acres. Eastern Tennessee. Historic. Horse rental.		●	●	●	●	●	●	●	●	●	●	●	●		
NATIONAL RECREATION AREAS *(See place listings.)*															
Big South Fork National River (B-6) 125,000 acres. Hunting, white-water rafting.		●	●	●	●	●	●	●	●	●	●	●	●		
Land Between the Lakes (B-3) 170,000 acres. Horseback riding; off-road vehicle trails.		●	●	●	●	●		●	●	●		●		●	
ARMY CORPS OF ENGINEERS															
Center Hill Lake (C-5) 38,551 acres 20 mi. e. of Smithville via US 70. Canoeing, hunting; marina.	❶	●	●	●	●	●	●	●	●	●				●	
Cheatham Lake (C-4) 10,727 acres 25 mi. w. of Nashville via SR 12. Canoeing, hunting.	❷	●	●	●	●	●	●	●	●	●					●
Cordell Hull Lake (C-5) 32,705 acres 50 mi. e. of Nashville off SR 85. Horse trails, hunting.	❸	●	●	●	●	●	●	●	●	●					
Dale Hollow Lake (C-6) 52,542 acres 3 mi. e. of Celina on SR 53. Canoeing, hunting, scuba diving. Horse trails.	❹	●	●	●	●	●	●	●	●	●				●	●
J. Percy Priest Lake (C-4) 14,200 acres 11 mi. e. of Nashville off I-40. Canoeing, hunting. Horse trails.	❺	●	●	●	●	●	●	●	●	●					
Lake Barkley (C-3) 69,626 acres off US 79 near Dover. Hunting, rock climbing, wildlife viewing.	❻	●	●	●	●	●	●	●	●	●				●	●
Old Hickory Reservoir (C-4) 22,500 acres 15 mi. n.e. of Nashville via US 31E. Archery, hunting, water skiing.	❼	●	●	●	●	●	●	●	●	●				●	
STATE															
Big Hill Pond (E-2) 5,000 acres 10 mi. w. of Eastview on SR 57. Boardwalk, horse trails, observation tower.	❽	●	●	●	●			●		●		●	●		
Big Ridge (C-7) 3,687 acres 14 mi. n.e. of Norris on SR 61. Basketball court, horseshoe pits, playground, softball field, tennis courts, volleyball court.	❾	●	●	●	●	●	●	●	●				●	●	
Bledsoe Creek (C-4) 164 acres 4 mi. e. of Gallatin off SR 25. Bird-watching.	❿	●	●	●	●	●		●		●		●			
Booker T. Washington (E-6) 353 acres 6 mi. n.e. of Chattanooga off SR 58. Bird-watching, water skiing; sports equipment rentals.	⓫	●	●	●	●	●	●	●					●		
Cedars of Lebanon (C-5) 900 acres 8 mi. s. of Lebanon on US 231. Baseball, disc golf, tennis, volleyball; horse rental, swimming pool.	⓬	●	●	●					●	●		●	●	●	
Chickasaw (D-2) 14,384 acres 7 mi. w. of Henderson on SR 100. Tennis; horse rental, playground.	⓭	●	●	●	●			●	●					●	
Cove Lake (C-7) 673 acres 1 mi. n. of Caryville on US 25W. Swimming pool.	⓮	●	●	●				●	●	●					●
Cumberland Mountain (D-6) 1,720 acres 5 mi. s. of Crossville on US 127. Bird-watching, golf (18 holes).	⓯	●	●	●	●	●	●		●			●	●	●	●
David Crockett (D-4) 1,083 acres 1 mi. w. of Lawrenceburg on US 64. Swimming pool, tennis court.	⓰	●	●	●	●			●	●				●		
Davy Crockett Birthplace (C-8) 105 acres 3 mi. e. of Limestone off US 11E. Historic. *(See Limestone p. 129.)*	⓱	●	●					●	●	●			●		
Edgar Evins (C-5) 6,000 acres n. of Smithville on SR 96. Bird-watching; marina.	⓲	●	●	●	●	●	●	●					●	●	
Fall Creek Falls (D-6) 22,477 acres 14 mi. n.w. of Pikeville off SR 30. Bird-watching, golf (18 holes), horseback riding.	⓳	●		●	●	●	●		●			●	●	●	●
Fort Loudoun (D-7) 1,200 acres 1 mi. n. of Vonore off US 411. Historic. Bird-watching. *(See Vonore p. 248.)*	⓴		●	●	●	●		●		●			●	●	
Fort Pillow (D-1) 1,642 acres 18 mi. w. of Henning off SR 87 via SR 207. Historic.	㉑	●	●		●	●		●		●		●	●		

Recreation Areas Chart

The map location numerals in column 2 show an area's location on the preceding map.

	MAP LOCATION	CAMPING	PICNICKING	HIKING TRAILS	BOATING	BOAT RAMP	BOAT RENTAL	FISHING	SWIMMING	PETS ON LEASH	BICYCLE TRAILS	NATURE PROGS.	VISITOR CENTER	LODGE/CABINS	FOOD SERVICE
Frozen Head (C-6) 13,122 acres 6 mi. e. of Wartburg off SR 62. Scenic. Bird-watching, horseback riding; amphitheater, horse trails, playground.	22	•	•	•				•	•	•	•	•	•		
Harrison Bay (D-6) 1,200 acres 10 mi. n.e. of Chattanooga off SR 58. Bird-watching, golf (18 holes); marina, playgrounds, swimming pool, tennis.	23	•	•	•	•	•	•	•	•	•		•			
Henry Horton (D-4) 1,141 acres 2 mi. s. of Chapel Hill on US 31 Alt. Historic. Bird-watching, disc golf, golf (18 holes); wildlife viewing; swimming pool, trap and skeet range.	24	•	•	•				•	•	•		•	•	•	•
Hiwassee & Ocoee Scenic River (D-6) 23-mile river section from the Tennessee-North Carolina state line to US 411 6 mi. n. of Benton. Horseback riding, white-water rafting; horse corral, playground.	25	•	•	•				•		•					
Indian Mountain (C-7) 200 acres off I-75 in Jellico. Bird-watching; playground.	26	•	•	•				•	•	•	•	•	•		
Long Hunter (C-4) 2,657 acres 13 mi. s.e. of Hermitage on SR 171, in four units around J. Percy Priest Lake. Scenic.	27		•	•	•	•		•		•		•			
Meeman-Shelby Forest (D-1) 13,467 acres 16 mi. n. of Memphis off US 51. Disc golf, horse rental, nature center.	28	•	•	•				•	•	•		•	•	•	
Montgomery Bell (C-4) 3,782 acres 8 mi. e. of Dickson on US 70. Golf (18 holes).	29	•	•	•	•	•	•	•	•	•		•		•	•
Mousetail Landing (D-3) 1,247 acres w. of Linden on SR 50. Beach.	30	•	•	•				•	•	•					
Natchez Trace (D-3) 48,000 acres 15 mi. n.e. of Lexington off I-40. Archery, basketball, softball, tennis, volleyball; horse rental, playground.	31	•	•	•	•	•	•	•	•	•		•	•	•	•
Nathan Bedford Forrest (C-3) 2,587 acres 2.3 mi. n.e. of Eva on SR 191. Historic. Backpacking, water skiing. *(See Eva p. 77.)*	32	•	•	•	•	•		•	•	•		•			
Norris Dam (C-7) 4,030 acres 6.6 mi. n. on US 441. Basketball, birding, tennis, volleyball; horse trails, interpretive programs, marina. *(See Norris p. 227)*	33	•	•	•	•	•	•	•	•	•		•	•	•	
Old Stone Fort (D-5) 876 acres 1.9 mi. n.w. of Manchester off US 41. Historic. Golf (nine-hole); museum. *(See Manchester p. 130)*	34	•	•	•				•		•		•	•		
Panther Creek (C-8) 1,435 acres 6 mi. w. of Morristown off US 11E. Bird watching, softball, tennis, volleyball; horse trails, interpretive programs, swimming pool.	35	•	•	•	•	•	•	•	•	•		•	•		
Paris Landing (C-3) 841 acres 16 mi. n.e. of Paris on US 79. Bird-watching, golf, tennis, water skiing; marina, playground, swimming pool.	36	•	•	•	•	•	•	•	•	•		•		•	•
Pickett (C-6) 19,200 acres 13 mi. n.e. of Jamestown on SR 154. Bird-watching, horseback riding, hunting, tennis; beach, interpretive programs.	37	•	•	•	•	•		•	•	•		•		•	
Pickwick Landing (E-3) 14,000 acres 15 mi. s. of Savannah off SR 128. Bird-watching, golf (18 holes), tennis; marina, swimming pools.	38	•	•	•	•	•	•	•	•	•		•		•	•
Reelfoot Lake (C-2) 25,000 acres 5 mi. e. of Tiptonville on SR 21. Tennis; bird-watching tour, boat cruise, museum, nature center.	39	•	•	•	•	•	•	•		•		•	•	•	
Roan Mountain (C-9) 2,006 acres 20 mi. s.e. of Elizabethton off US 19E via SR 143. Scenic. Basketball, softball, tennis; amphitheater, children's play area, museum, swimming pool.	40	•	•	•				•	•	•		•	•	•	
Rock Island (D-5) 883 acres at Rock Island off US 70S. Basketball, bird-watching, softball, tennis, volleyball; playground.	41	•	•	•	•	•		•	•	•					
South Cumberland (D-5) 16,000 acres 3 mi. e. of Monteagle on US 41. Scenic. Basketball, softball, tennis, volleyball; interpretive programs, museum, playground. *(See Monteagle p. 173)*	42	•	•	•				•		•		•	•		
Standing Stone (C-5) 11,000 acres 8 mi. n.w. of Livingston off SR 52. Basketball, bird-watching, softball, volleyball; amphitheater, swimming pool, tennis courts.	43	•	•	•	•	•		•	•	•		•		•	
Tims Ford (D-5) 10,700 acres 11 mi. w. of Winchester off SR 50W. Bird-watching, golf (18 holes); marina.	44	•	•	•	•	•	•	•	•	•		•	•	•	•

Recreation Areas Chart

The map location numerals in column 2 show an area's location on the preceding map.

	MAP LOCATION	CAMPING	PICNICKING	HIKING TRAILS	BOATING	BOAT RAMP	BOAT RENTAL	FISHING	SWIMMING	PETS ON LEASH	BICYCLE TRAILS	NATURE PROGS.	VISITOR CENTER	LODGE/CABINS	FOOD SERVICE
T.O. Fuller (E-1) 1,138 acres s.w. of Memphis off US 61. Bird-watching; swimming pool.	45	•	•	•					•	•			•	•	
Warriors' Path (C-8) 950 acres 5 mi. s.e. of Kingsport on SR 36. Bird-watching, disc golf, golf (18 holes); exhibits, horse rental, marina, playground, swimming pool.	46	•	•	•	•	•	•	•	•	•		•	•		
OTHER															
Boone Lake (C-9) 4,310 acres 12 mi. s.e. of Kingsport via SR 75. Wildlife viewing.	47	•	•		•	•		•	•	•			•		
Cherokee Lake (C-7) 30,300 acres 5 mi. n. of Jefferson City via SR 92. Bird-watching, hunting; swimming beach.	48	•	•	•	•	•	•	•	•	•			•		
Chickamauga Lake (D-6) 35,400 acres 5 mi. n. of Chattanooga off SR 153. Hunting.	49	•	•	•	•	•		•	•	•			•		
Chilhowee (D-6) 50 acres 17 mi. e. of Cleveland on US 64, then 7 mi. n.w. on FR 77. Amphitheater, sand beach.	50	•	•	•				•	•	•					
Douglas Lake (C-7) 30,400 acres 8 mi. n. of Sevierville via SR 66.	51	•	•	•	•	•		•	•	•			•		
Kinser Park (C-8) 225 acres 6 mi. s. of Greeneville off SR 70. Golf, miniature golf, softball, tennis; batting cages, playgrounds, waterslide.	52	•	•		•	•	•	•	•	•					
Melton Hill Lake (D-6) 5,690 acres 30 mi. w. of Knoxville off I-40. Hunting.	53	•	•	•	•	•		•	•	•			•		
Nickajack Lake (E-5) 10,370 acres 20 mi. w. of Chattanooga off I-24. Jet skiing, water skiing; horse stables.	54	•	•	•	•	•	•	•	•	•			•		
Norris Lake (C-7) 34,200 acres 7 mi. off I-75 near Norris. Horseback riding, hunting, water skiing; interpretive programs.	55	•	•	•	•	•	•	•	•	•		•	•	•	•
Observation Knob Park (C-9) 28 acres 13 mi. s. of Bristol off US 421. Jet skiing; playground.	56	•	•	•	•	•		•		•		•	•		
Rock Creek (C-9) 13 acres 5 mi. n.e. of Erwin off US 23. Steam-fed swimming pool.	57	•	•	•				•	•	•					
South Holston Lake (C-9) 7,580 acres 8 mi. s.e. of Bristol off US 421. Hunting.	58	•	•	•	•	•		•	•	•			•		
Steele Creek Park (C-9) 936 acres 3.5 mi. s.w. of Bristol via Volunteer Pkwy. and Broad St. Disc golf, golf (nine holes), miniature golf; paddleboats, swimming pools, train, waterslide.	59	•	•	•	•	•	•	•	•	•					
Tellico Lake (D-7) 15,900 acres 1 mi. s. of Lenoir City off US 321. Golf; horse trails, marinas.	60	•	•	•	•	•	•	•	•	•		•	•		
Watauga Lake (C-9) 6,430 acres 8 mi. s.e. of Elizabethton via US 321 and SR 67. Horseback riding.	61	•	•	•	•	•	•	•	•	•			•		
Watts Bar Lake (D-6) 39,000 acres 9 mi. s.e. of Spring City off SR 68.	62	•	•	•	•	•	•	•	•	•	•			•	•	•

ADAMSVILLE (D-2) pop. 2,207, elev. 518'

BUFORD PUSSER HOME AND MUSEUM is off US 64 to 342 Pusser St., following signs. This is the home of the sheriff known for his dogged pursuit of criminals; he was the subject of the "Walking Tall" movie trilogy. The house contains many original furnishings and features videos highlighting Pusser's career and an interview with his daughter, Dwana. On display is what remains of the 1974 Corvette the sheriff was driving at the time of his fatal crash.

Time: Allow 1 hour minimum. **Hours:** Mon.-Fri. 10-5, Sat. 9-5, Sun. 1-4, May-Aug.; Mon.-Tues. and Thurs.-Fri. 11-5, Sat. 10-4, Sun. 1-4, Mar.-Apr.; Mon.-Tues. and Thurs.-Sat. 10-4, Sun. 1-4, Sept.-Oct.; Mon.-Tues. and Thurs.-Fri. 11-4, Sat. 10-4, rest of year. Closed Easter, Thanksgiving, Christmas Eve and Christmas. **Cost:** $8; $5 (ages 55+ and military with ID); $3 (ages 6-18). **Phone:** (731) 632-4080 or (731) 632-1401.

ALCOA pop. 8,449

• Hotels & Restaurants map & index p. 117
• Part of Great Smoky Mountains National Park area — see map p. 97

CANDLEWOOD SUITES KNOXVILLE AIRPORT/ALCOA
865/233-4411 **54**

▼▼▼ **Extended Stay Hotel.** Rates not provided. **Address:** 176 Cusick Rd 37701 **Location:** US 129, just e. **Facility:** 81 efficiencies. 3 stories, interior corridors. **Pool(s):** outdoor. **Activities:** exercise room. **Guest Services:** complimentary laundry.

COMFORT SUITES   (865)984-9840 **56**

▼▼ **Hotel** $85-$99 **Address:** 140 Cusick Rd 37701 **Location:** US 129, just e. **Facility:** 59 units. 3 stories, interior corridors. **Amenities:** safes. **Pool(s):** heated indoor. **Activities:** hot tub, limited exercise equipment. **Guest Services:** coin laundry.

COUNTRY INN & SUITES BY CARLSON, KNOXVILLE AIRPORT   865/273-2800 **55**

▼▼ **Hotel.** Rates not provided. **Address:** 162 Cusick Rd 37701 **Location:** US 129, just e. **Facility:** 62 units. 3 stories, interior corridors. **Amenities:** Some: safes. **Pool(s):** heated indoor. **Activities:** hot tub, limited exercise equipment. **Guest Services:** coin laundry.

COURTYARD BY MARRIOTT KNOXVILLE AIRPORT ALCOA   (865)977-8333 **58**

▼▼▼ **Hotel** $99-$183 **Address:** 141 Furrow Way 37701 **Location:** US 129, just e. **Facility:** 95 units. 3 stories, interior corridors. **Activities:** hot tub, limited exercise equipment. **Guest Services:** valet and coin laundry, boarding pass kiosk, area transportation.

AAA Benefit:
Members save 5% or more!

HAMPTON INN-KNOXVILLE AIRPORT   (865)983-1101 **53**

▼▼▼▼ **Hotel** $79-$139 **Address:** 148 International Ave 37701 **Location:** US 129, just e. **Facility:** 118 units. 5 stories, interior corridors. **Terms:** 1-7 night minimum stay, cancellation fee imposed. **Pool(s):** outdoor. **Activities:** exercise room. **Guest Services:** valet laundry, area transportation.

AAA Benefit:
Members save up to 10%!

HILTON KNOXVILLE AIRPORT   (865)970-4300 **59**

▼▼▼ **Hotel** $120-$240 **Address:** 2001 Alcoa Hwy 37701 **Location:** US 129, just w. **Facility:** 236 units. 6 stories, interior corridors. **Terms:** 1-7 night minimum stay, cancellation fee imposed. **Pool(s):** heated indoor. **Activities:** hot tub, exercise room. **Guest Services:** valet laundry, area transportation.

AAA Benefit:
Members save 5% or more!

HOLIDAY INN EXPRESS & SUITES   (865)981-9008 **61**

▼▼▼ **Hotel** $99-$249 **Address:** 130 Associates Blvd 37701 **Location:** US 129, just s. **Facility:** 80 units. 3 stories, interior corridors. **Terms:** check-in 4 pm, cancellation fee imposed. **Pool(s):** heated indoor. **Activities:** limited exercise equipment. **Guest Services:** valet laundry.

LA QUINTA INN & SUITES KNOXVILLE AIRPORT   (865)984-9350 **57**

▼▼ **Hotel** $68-$196 **Address:** 126 Cusick Rd 37701 **Location:** US 129, just e. **Facility:** 89 units. 3 stories, interior corridors. **Terms:** check-in 4 pm. **Pool(s):** heated indoor. **Activities:** exercise room. **Guest Services:** valet and coin laundry, area transportation.

MAINSTAY SUITES   (865)379-7799 **60**

▼▼ **Extended Stay Hotel** $80-$120 **Address:** 361 Fountain View Cir 37701 **Location:** US 129, just n on SR 35, just se on Associates Blvd, then just w. **Facility:** 81 kitchen units. 3 stories, interior corridors. **Amenities:** safes. **Pool(s):** heated outdoor. **Activities:** limited exercise equipment. **Guest Services:** valet and coin laundry, area transportation.

QUALITY INN   (865)984-6800 **62**

▼▼ **Hotel** $77-$86 **Address:** 206 Corporate Pl 37701 **Location:** US 129, just s. **Facility:** 67 units. 3 stories, interior corridors. **Pool(s):** heated indoor. **Activities:** limited exercise equipment. **Guest Services:** valet and coin laundry.

WHERE TO EAT

EL SAZON MEXICANO RESTAURANT   865/681-8100 **30**

▼▼ Mexican. Casual Dining. $4-$25 **AAA Inspector Notes:** A little bit of Mexico in the center of town, this restaurant is just off the main strip. Festive decor, including hand-painted tables and chairs, lends to an upbeat setting for great Mexican fare. **Features:** full bar, happy hour. **Address:** 2650 Alcoa Hwy 37701 **Location:** US 129, just e.   L   D

(See map & index p. 117.)

MING TREE   865/984-3888

Asian. Casual Dining. $7-$26 **AAA Inspector Notes:** This restaurant has been dishing up consistently flavorful Thai and Chinese food for more than a decade. Some of the favorites featured here are pad thai, tom yum soup, hot and sour soup, mao pao tofu, and sweet and sour chicken. **Features:** beer only. **Address:** 2754 Alcoa Hwy 37701 **Location:** US 129, just e. [L] [D]

ANTIOCH

- **Hotels & Restaurants map & index p. 200**
- **Part of Nashville area — see map p. 179**

HAMPTON INN-HICKORY HOLLOW   (615)731-9911   **85**

Hotel
$99-$159

AAA Benefit: Members save up to 10%!

Address: 210 Crossings Pl 37013 **Location:** I-24 exit 60, 0.5 mi e. **Facility:** 85 units. 4 stories, interior corridors. **Terms:** 1-7 night minimum stay, cancellation fee imposed. **Pool(s):** outdoor. **Activities:** limited exercise equipment. **Guest Services:** valet laundry. **Featured Amenity: full hot breakfast.**

RODEWAY INN & SUITES   (615)641-7721   **86**

Motel $80-$176 **Address:** 13010 Old Hickory Blvd 37013 **Location:** I-24 exit 62, just ne. Located in a congested area. **Facility:** 135 units. 2 stories (no elevator), exterior corridors. **Pool(s):** outdoor. **Guest Services:** coin laundry.

WHERE TO EAT

BAILEY'S SPORTS GRILLE   615/731-4999

American. Casual Dining. $6-$16 **AAA Inspector Notes:** A classic pub decor of dark wood paneling and ceramic steins--with a modern American bar, where huge TV screens are tuned to sports in every possible spot, including the restrooms. You'll find the same mixing cultures evident on the menu; burgers, pizzas, and chicken wings sit beside fish 'n' chips, tortilla soup, fresh-baked pretzels, nachos, baby back ribs, and Texas-style brisket. **Features:** full bar, happy hour. **Address:** 5316 Mountain View Rd 37013 **Location:** I-24 exit 59 (Bell Rd), 0.6 mi e, then just s; in Bell Forge Square shopping plaza. [L] [D] [LATE] CALL

ATHENS (D-6) pop. 13,458, elev. 974'

Athens, founded in 1823, is an agricultural and manufacturing center for such local merchandise as timber products, farm implements and flour. Tennessee Wesleyan College is in the downtown area.

Athens Area Chamber of Commerce: 13 N. Jackson St., Athens, TN 37303. **Phone:** (423) 745-0334.

Shopping: The shops in historic Downtown Square specialize in antiques and regional crafts.

THE GARDENS OF SUNSHINE HOLLOW is 4 mi. n.w. of I-75 exit 42 on Riceville-Decatur Rd., 3 mi. s.w. on CR 82, then .5 mi. s.w. to 198 CR 52, following signs. Encompassing more than 20 acres, the site offers walking trails and foot bridges that

lead through the gardens and parts of the surrounding forest. Visitors can observe more than 1,750 varieties of cannas, dahlias, daylilies, hosta, roses and iris. Self-guiding tours are available.

Time: Allow 1 hour, 30 minutes minimum. **Hours:** Tues.-Sat. 8-4, mid-Apr. through July 31; by appointment rest of year. **Cost:** Donations. **Phone:** (423) 745-4289 or (800) 669-2005.

MAYFIELD DAIRY FARMS VISITOR CENTER is off I-75 exit 52, then 4.3 mi. e. to 4 Mayfield Ln. Visitors view a 10-minute video of company history and then take a 35-minute guided tour to see how the yellow milk jugs are made and learn how the milk and ice cream are produced, packaged and distributed. Tours include complimentary ice cream.

Time: Allow 1 hour minimum. **Hours:** Visitor center open Mon.-Fri. 10-4, Sat. 10-1. Last tour begins 1 hour before closing. Closed Jan. 1, July 4, Labor Day, Thanksgiving and Christmas. **Cost:** Visitor center free. Tours $4.50; $3.50 (ages 4-12). Prices may vary; phone ahead. **Phone:** (423) 649-2653.

McMINN COUNTY LIVING HERITAGE MUSEUM is at 522 W. Madison Ave. The museum features regional historical items. The Burns' Room contains a renovated 20th-century industrial exhibit and a general store. Other rooms contain arts and crafts; a display about transportation in the 1800s; children's toys, books and clothing dating 1850-1935; Native American artifacts; an early American church; and a pioneer log cabin. A 4-foot-long model of the USS *Ware* honors Charles R. Ware, for whom the ship was named, and the crewmen. **Time:** Allow 30 minutes minimum. **Hours:** Mon.-Fri. 10-5, Sat. 10-4. Closed major holidays. **Cost:** $5; $3 (ages 6-17 and 60+). **Phone:** (423) 745-0329.

COMFORT INN   (423)252-8030

Hotel $100-$140 **Address:** 2811 Decatur Pike 37303 **Location:** I-75 exit 49, just w. **Facility:** 68 units. 4 stories, interior corridors. **Pool(s):** heated indoor. **Activities:** hot tub, exercise room. **Guest Services:** valet and coin laundry.

HAMPTON INN   (423)745-2345

Hotel $114-$154 **Address:** 1821 Holiday Dr 37303 **Location:** I-75 exit 49, just e on SR 30, then just n. **Facility:** 70 units. 3 stories, interior corridors. **Terms:** 1-7 night minimum stay, cancellation fee imposed. **Pool(s):** outdoor. **Activities:** exercise room. **Guest Services:** valet laundry.

AAA Benefit: Members save up to 10%!

WHERE TO EAT

MICHAEL'S CASUAL DINING   423/649-0000

American. Casual Dining. $7-$18 **AAA Inspector Notes:** Enjoy hand-cut steaks, Angus burgers and hickory-smoked barbecue at this cozy eatery. Specialties include pork ribs and beef brisket, plus grilled steaks and coconut-fried chicken tenders. Also on the menu are sandwiches, salads, pasta and homemade chili. **Address:** 2011 Congress Pkwy 37303 **Location:** I-75 exit 49, 1.8 mi e on SR 30, then 0.5 mi s on US 11. [L] [D]

BARTLETT (D-1) pop. 54,613, elev. 285'

- Hotels p. 40 • Restaurants p. 40
- Hotels & Restaurants map & index p. 154
- Part of Memphis area — see map p. 134

DAVIES MANOR is 7.2 mi. e. on Stage Rd. (US 64), then 1.1 mi. n.w. to 9336 Davies Plantation Rd. A two-story plantation structure today, Davies Manor started out around 1830 as a one-room log cabin to which succeeding generations of the Davies family have added. Furnishings include family antiques and other period items. A doctor's office on the second floor was used by William Little Davies, who practiced medicine in the late 19th and early 20th centuries. A 7-minute video presentation offers a glimpse into the Davies family.

Time: Allow 1 hour minimum. **Hours:** Guided tours Tues.-Sat. noon-4, Apr. 1 to mid-Dec. Last tour begins at 3:30. Closed July 4, Thanksgiving and day after Thanksgiving. **Cost:** $5; $4 (ages 65+); $3 (ages 4-17 and students with ID). **Phone:** (901) 386-0715. [GT]

HAMPTON INN & SUITES   (901)382-2050 [62]

▼▼▼▼ **Hotel** $112-$137 **Address:** 2935 N Germantown Rd 38133 **Location:** I-40 exit 16 or 16B, 0.5 mi n. **Facility:** 125 units. 5 stories, interior corridors. **Terms:** check-in 4 pm, 1-7 night minimum stay, cancellation fee imposed. **Amenities:** video games. **Pool(s):** outdoor. **Activities:** limited exercise equipment. **Guest Services:** valet and coin laundry.

AAA Benefit: Members save up to 10%!

[icons] / SOME UNITS

WHERE TO EAT

COLETTA'S ITALIAN RESTAURANT   901/383-1122

▼▼ Italian Pizza. Casual Dining. $7-$24 **AAA Inspector Notes:** This locally owned favorite serves freshly made pasta dishes and a variety of pizzas. Specialty dishes include veal, chicken and eggplant Parmesan. **Features:** full bar. **Address:** 2850 Appling Rd 38133 **Location:** I-40 exit 15, 1 mi n. [L] [D] CALL

COLTON'S STEAKHOUSE & GRILL   901/383-8445

▼▼▼ Steak. Casual Dining. $6-$24 **AAA Inspector Notes:** Set in an Old-West atmosphere, this place offers patrons a variety of choices with salads, burgers and full entrees. A few favorites include their country fried steak, grilled pork chops or Hawaiian chicken. The menu also features some entrees under 700 calories. **Features:** full bar, happy hour. **Address:** 8030 Hwy 64 38133 **Location:** I-40 exit 18, 1.2 mi w. [L] [D]

DIXIE CAFE   901/377-2211

▼▼ Regional American. Family Dining. $6-$16 **AAA Inspector Notes:** Enjoy southern-style home cooking featuring chicken-fried steak, meat loaf, pork chops, turnip greens, mashed potatoes and fresh veggies. The restaurant's classic Norman Rockwell atmosphere makes it appealing to families. **Features:** early bird specials. **Address:** 2861 Bartlett Blvd 38134 **Location:** I-40 exit 12, 3 mi n on Sycamore View Rd. [L] [D]

FIREBIRDS WOOD FIRED GRILL   901/379-1300 [41]

▼▼▼ American. Casual Dining. $8-$36 **AAA Inspector Notes:** The restaurant re-creates the atmosphere of a mountain lodge. Hand-cut steaks and seafood dominate the menu, which also lists a few pork and chicken entrees, as well as elk tenderloin medallions and buffalo meatloaf. The kitchen uses wood grilling, and pizzas bake in a wood-burning oven. Flavorful food, enhanced presentations and a skilled, knowledgeable and attentive staff, together with distinctive physical elements, make this place appealing. **Features:** full bar, happy hour. **Reservations:** suggested. **Address:** 8470 Hwy 64 38133 **Location:** I-40 exit 18, 0.4 mi w. [L] [D] CALL

BELL BUCKLE (D-5) pop. 500, elev. 846'

A cryptic image of a bell and buckle, supposedly carved on a beech tree in the area, inspired the first settlers to name their community Bell Buckle in 1852. Among those who followed was W.R. Webb, nicknamed "Old Sawney" and distinguished as the father of preparatory school education in the South. Unsuccessful in persuading saloon keepers in Culleoka to stop selling whiskey to his students, Webb moved his school to Bell Buckle in 1886.

Sometimes implemented with the use of a rod, Webb's teaching methods were markedly effective. The Junior Room, the classroom where Webb taught, produced 10 Rhodes scholars and three state governors. Woodrow Wilson, as president of Princeton University, once said that "the best prepared boys we get come from a small school in Tennessee, known to its pupils as Old Sawney's."

Bell Buckle Chamber of Commerce: 4 Railroad Sq., P.O. Box 222, Bell Buckle, TN 37020. **Phone:** (931) 389-9663.

BELVIDERE (E-5) elev. 992'

FALLS MILL is 4 mi. w. on US 64, then 1 mi. n. on Salem-Lexie Rd. to Falls Mill Rd. Originally built as a woolen mill and cotton gin in 1873, the working gristmill features a 32-foot-tall water wheel. Locally grown corn and wheat are ground on the premises. Exhibits of various types of machinery are in the Museum of Power and Industry; a video presentation relates the history of the area and the role of the water wheel in its development.

Time: Allow 30 minutes minimum. **Hours:** Mill and museum Mon.-Tues. and Thurs.-Sat. 9-4. Closed Jan. 1-24, Thanksgiving and Dec. 24-31. **Cost:** $4; $3 (ages 60+); $2 (ages 4-13). **Phone:** (931) 469-7161.

BENTON (D-6) pop. 1,385, elev. 741'

RECREATIONAL ACTIVITIES
White-water Rafting

- **Ocoee Inn Rafting** is on US 64 at Lake Ocoee Marina. Other activities are offered. **Hours:** Rafting trips are offered Thurs.-Mon., late May-Aug. 31; Sat.-Sun., mid-Mar. through late May and early Sept.-Oct. 31. Dates and departure times vary depending on dam control; phone ahead. **Phone:** (423) 338-2064 or (800) 272-7238.

- **Ocoee Outdoors-Ocoee Outpost** is on US 64 5 mi. e. of jct. US 411. **Hours:** Ocoee River trips are offered Thurs.-Mon., June-Aug.; Sat.-Sun. and holidays, mid-Mar. through May 31 and Sept. 1-early Nov. Departure times vary; phone ahead. **Phone:** (423) 338-2438 or (800) 533-7767.

- **Outdoor Adventure Rafting** is at 629 Welcome Valley Rd. 2.5 mi. e. of jct. US 64 and US 411. Other activities are offered. **Hours:** Rafting trips are offered Thurs.-Mon., Memorial Day-Labor Day; Sat.-Sun., mid-Mar. through day before Memorial

Day and day after Labor Day-Oct. 31. Dates and departure times vary depending on dam control; phone ahead. **Phone:** (423) 338-5746 or (800) 627-7636.

BIG SOUTH FORK NATIONAL RIVER AND RECREATION AREA (B-6)

Approached by SR 297, US 27, US 127 and SR 52, Big South Fork National River and Recreation Area encompasses 125,000 acres on the Cumberland Plateau in northeastern Tennessee and southeastern Kentucky. Ninety miles of the Big South Fork River and its tributaries tumble through gorges carved over millions of years in the sandstone of the Cumberland Plateau. The area's eroded landscape—which contains scenic features such as natural arches, pinnacles, spires, sheer bluffs and huge sandstone overhangs—is said to have the most sandstone arches in the eastern United States.

Although much of the area has been logged, lush vegetation nurtured by the region's humid climate now covers ridges and encroaches on abandoned homesteads, logging camps and mining communities. The National Park Service manages the area for its scenic and recreational value.

General Information and Activities

The park has two visitor centers. The Bandy Creek Visitor Center is 15 miles west of Oneida at the Bandy Creek Campground off Leatherwood Ford Road (SR 297), where hiking trails, playing fields and horse stables are available. The recreation area, open all year, is entered from paved Leatherwood Ford Road or by gravel access roads. Blue Heron Mining Community Visitor Center is open seasonally and is on Mine 18 Road in Stearns, Ky. Within the park are miles of dirt back-country roads, 300 miles of horse trails and hiking trails, including sections of Sheltowee Trace Trail and John Muir National Recreation Trail. Phone (423) 286-7275 for the Bandy Creek Visitor Center or (606) 376-5073 for the Blue Heron Interpretive Center.

Nearly 100 miles of navigable waters, ranging in difficulty from those suitable for beginners to those that should be tried only by skilled white-water canoeists, attract paddlers. Sections of the Big South Fork are dangerous and remote, and canoeists and kayakers should plan their trips with care and prepare for emergencies. The visitor center provides the addresses of commercial rafting concessionaires offering trips on certain stretches of the river.

Other popular activities in the recreation area include swimming, hiking, back-country camping, mountain bike riding, and hunting and fishing in accordance with state and federal regulations. Trails, ranging in difficulty, wind past rock shelters, arches, waterfalls and impressive flora.

Pickett State Park and Forest, next to the national area's western boundary, also offers a broad range of facilities. *See Recreation Areas Chart.*

ADMISSION to the recreation area is free; however, camping fees are charged at all campgrounds. There is a fee for the required back-country camping permits.

PETS are permitted on leash.

ADDRESS inquiries to the Superintendent, Big South Fork National River and Recreation Area, 4564 Leatherwood Rd., Oneida, TN 37841; phone (423) 286-7275 or (423) 569-9778.

BLOUNTVILLE (C-9) pop. 3,074, elev. 1,596'

APPALACHIAN CAVERNS is 1.4 mi. s.e. on US 394, .1 mi. s. on Feathers Chapel Rd., 1.3 mi. e. on Buncombe Rd., then .5 mi. e. to 420 Cave Hill Rd. The 1-hour regular tour takes visitors along several levels of lighted walkways that traverse caverns filled with fragile mineral formations. Manganese, iron, copper and calcium deposits create vivid colors within the various rooms, with some chamber ceilings reaching 135 feet. More in-depth Explorer and Wild tours can be scheduled in advance. Gem mining and a climbing wall are available for an additional charge.

Time: Allow 1 hour minimum. **Hours:** Guided regular tours depart every 15 to 20 minutes Mon.-Sat. 9-6, Sun. 1-5, Apr.-Oct.; Mon.-Sat. 11-5, rest of year. Last tour begins 1 hour before closing. Closed Christmas. **Cost:** Regular tour $12; $10 (ages 60+); $7.50 (ages 4-11). Explorer Tour $20. Wild Tour $40. **Phone:** (423) 323-2337. 🅰️

WINERIES

- **Countryside Vineyards & Winery** is 1.5 mi. off I-81 exit 63 to 658 Henry Harr Rd. **Hours:** Mon.-Sat. 10-6, Sun. 1-6. Closed Jan. 1 and Christmas. **Phone:** (423) 323-1660. GT

... based on member priorities.

AAA.com/Diamonds

BRENTWOOD pop. 37,060
• Hotels & Restaurants map & index p. 200

BEST WESTERN BRENTWOOD (615)373-8585 **71**

Hotel
$109-$149

AAA Benefit: Save 10% or more every day and earn 10% bonus points!

Address: 5581 Franklin Pike Cir 37027 **Location:** I-65 exit 74A, just w, then just n. Located near Target Shopping Plaza. **Facility:** 46 units. 2 stories (no elevator), interior corridors. **Activities:** exercise room. **Featured Amenity: full hot breakfast.**

BRENTWOOD SUITES (615)277-4000 **75**

Hotel
$99-$199

Address: 622 Church St E 37027 **Location:** I-65 exit 74B, 0.5 mi w, 0.5 mi s on Franklin Rd (US 31), then 1 mi e. **Facility:** 56 units. 4 stories, interior corridors. **Terms:** cancellation fee imposed. **Activities:** exercise room. **Guest Services:** valet and coin laundry. **Featured Amenity: full hot breakfast.**

CANDLEWOOD SUITES 615/309-0600 **78**

Extended Stay Hotel. Rates not provided. **Address:** 5129 Virginia Way 37027 **Location:** I-65 exit 74B (SR 254 W), 0.3 mi s on Franklin Rd (US 31), 1.2 mi w on Maryland Way, just s on Ward Circle, then just s. **Facility:** 122 efficiencies. 3 stories, interior corridors. **Activities:** exercise room. **Guest Services:** complimentary and valet laundry.

COURTYARD BY MARRIOTT NASHVILLE BRENTWOOD
(615)371-9200 **74**

Hotel
$99-$269

COURTYARD Marriott
AAA Benefit: Members save 5% or more!

Address: 103 E Park Dr 37027 **Location:** I-65 exit 74B, 0.8 mi w on Old Hickory Blvd, then s. Located in a business park setting. **Facility:** 145 units. 3 stories, interior corridors. **Pool(s):** outdoor. **Activities:** exercise room. **Guest Services:** valet and coin laundry, boarding pass kiosk, area transportation.

FOUR POINTS BY SHERATON NASHVILLE-BRENTWOOD
(615)964-5500 **69**

Hotel
$99-$289

FOUR POINTS BY SHERATON
AAA Benefit: Members save up to 15%, plus Starwood Preferred Guest® benefits!

Address: 760 Old Hickory Blvd 37027 **Location:** I-65 exit 74A, just e. **Facility:** 212 units. 8 stories, interior corridors. **Amenities:** safes. **Pool(s):** outdoor. **Activities:** hot tub, exercise room. **Guest Services:** valet laundry, area transportation.

HAMPTON INN-BRENTWOOD (615)373-2212 **73**

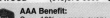 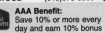
Hotel $119-$289 **Address:** 5630 Franklin Pike Cir 37027 **Location:** I-65 exit 74B, just w, then just n. **Facility:** 106 units. 5 stories, interior corridors. **Terms:** 1-7 night minimum stay, cancellation fee imposed. **Pool(s):** outdoor. **Activities:** exercise room. **Guest Services:** valet and coin laundry.

AAA Benefit: Members save up to 10%!

HILTON BRENTWOOD/NASHVILLE SUITES
(615)370-0111 **76**

Hotel
$115-$309

Hilton
HOTELS & RESORTS
AAA Benefit: Members save 5% or more!

Address: 9000 Overlook Blvd 37027 **Location:** I-65 exit 74B, 0.5 mi s on Franklin Rd (US 31), then e on Church St. **Facility:** 203 units. 4 stories, interior corridors. **Terms:** 1-7 night minimum stay, cancellation fee imposed. **Amenities:** safes. **Pool(s):** heated indoor. **Activities:** hot tub, exercise room. **Guest Services:** valet and coin laundry, area transportation.

HOLIDAY INN EXPRESS & SUITES BRENTWOOD NORTH-NASHVILLE AREA
(615)221-5001 **70**

Hotel $119-$199 **Address:** 5566 Franklin Pike Cir 37027 **Location:** I-65 exit 74A (SR 254 E), just n. Adjacent to Target shopping plaza. **Facility:** 110 units. 4 stories, interior corridors. **Terms:** cancellation fee imposed. **Activities:** hot tub, exercise room. **Guest Services:** valet and coin laundry, area transportation.

HOMEWOOD SUITES-BRENTWOOD (615)377-3332 **77**

Extended Stay Hotel $109-$209 **Address:** 5107 Peter Taylor Park Dr 37027 **Location:** I-65 exit 74B, 0.3 mi s on Franklin Rd (US 31), then 0.6 mi w on Maryland Way and Ward Cir. Located within a business park setting. **Facility:** 121 efficiencies, some two bedrooms. 3 stories, interior corridors. **Terms:** check-in 4 pm, 1-7 night minimum stay, cancellation fee imposed. **Pool(s):** outdoor. **Activities:** picnic facilities, exercise room. **Guest Services:** valet and coin laundry, area transportation.

AAA Benefit: Members save up to 10%!

HYATT PLACE NASHVILLE/BRENTWOOD
(615)661-9477 **72**

Hotel
$94-$209

HYATT PLACE®
AAA Benefit: Members save 10%!

Address: 202 Summit View Dr 37027 **Location:** I-65 exit 74A, just e. **Facility:** 124 units. 6 stories, interior corridors. **Terms:** cancellation fee imposed. **Amenities:** safes. **Pool(s):** outdoor. **Activities:** exercise room. **Guest Services:** valet laundry, area transportation. **Featured Amenity: breakfast buffet.** *(See ad p. 221.)*

(See map & index p. 200.)

RESIDENCE INN BY MARRIOTT NASHVILLE-BRENTWOOD

(615)371-0100 **79**

▽▽▽△△
Extended Stay Hotel
$109-$269

Residence Inn Marriott.

AAA Benefit: Members save 5% or more!

Address: 206 Ward Cir 37027 **Location:** I-65 exit 74B, 0.3 mi s on Franklin Rd (US 31), then 0.5 mi w on Maryland Way. Located in a business park. **Facility:** 110 units, some two bedrooms, efficiencies and kitchens. 2 stories (no elevator), interior/exterior corridors. **Terms:** check-in 4 pm. **Pool(s):** heated outdoor. **Activities:** hot tub, tennis, picnic facilities, exercise room. **Guest Services:** valet and coin laundry.

SAVE ⚓ ➤ BIZ 📶 ✕ 🅱 🖥 💻 / SOME UNITS 🛍

SLEEP INN

(615)376-2122

▽▽ **Hotel** $100-$180 **Address:** 1611 Galleria Blvd 37027 **Location:** I-65 exit 69, just w, then just n. **Facility:** 92 units. 4 stories, interior corridors. **Pool(s):** outdoor. **Activities:** limited exercise equipment. **Guest Services:** coin laundry.

➤ CALL 🅼 ⚓ BIZ 📶 ✕ 🅱 🖥 💻 / SOME UNITS 🛍

WHERE TO EAT

AMERIGO, AN ITALIAN RESTAURANT

615/377-7070

▽▽▽△ Italian. Fine Dining. $10-$33 **AAA Inspector Notes:** For starters, this trendy eatery serves a delicious artichoke cheese dip appetizer. Moving on to the entrées, you can't go wrong with the Tuscan chicken, served in a red wine sauce over angel-hair pasta. A professional and engaging staff completes an enjoyable evening. **Features:** full bar, early bird specials, Sunday brunch. **Reservations:** suggested. **Address:** 1656 Westgate Cir 37027 **Location:** I-65 exit 69 (SR 441), just e. ▣ L D CALL 🅼

FIREBIRDS WOOD FIRED GRILL

615/425-7240 **47**

▽▽△ American. Casual Dining. $11-$30 **AAA Inspector Notes:** The restaurant re-creates the atmosphere of a mountain lodge. Hand-cut steaks and seafood dominate the menu, which also lists a few pork and chicken entrees, as well as elk tenderloin medallions and buffalo meatloaf. The kitchen uses wood grilling, and pizzas bake in a wood-burning oven. Flavorful food, enhanced presentations and a skilled, knowledgeable and attentive staff, together with distinctive physical elements, make this place appealing. **Features:** full bar. **Reservations:** suggested. **Address:** 700 Old Hickory Blvd 37027 **Location:** I-65 exit 74A (Old Hickory Blvd), just e.

L D CALL 🅼

FULIN'S ASIAN CUISINE

615/377-9788 **46**

▽▽▽△ Asian. Casual Dining. $8-$22 **AAA Inspector Notes:** Here you'll explore a variety of delicious Asian dishes including ginger lobster, curry seafood Thai casserole, kung pao chicken and egg rolls. Order fresh-made sushi or sashimi with your dinner, or enjoy it at the sushi bar. **Features:** full bar, patio dining, happy hour. **Reservations:** suggested, weekends. **Address:** 782 Old Hickory Blvd, Suite 115 37027 **Location:** I-65 exit 74A (SR 254 E), just e; in Target shopping plaza. L D CALL 🅼 🐾

MEDITERRANEAN CUISINE

615/661-4100 **49**

▽ Mediterranean. Quick Serve. $5-$16 **AAA Inspector Notes:** This small restaurant prepares and delivers freshly made gyro sandwiches, hummus, Greek salad, falafel and more. You order at the counter and they bring it to you quickly with a friendly smile. **Features:** beer only, patio dining. **Address:** 214 Ward Cir 37027 **Location:** I-65 exit 74B, 0.3 mi s on Franklin Rd (US 31), 0.5 mi w on Maryland Way. L D 🐾

MERE BULLES

615/467-1945 **48**

▽▽▽▽ Southern American. Fine Dining. $11-$40 **AAA Inspector Notes:** This restaurant serves as a nice excuse to get dressed up and enjoy some food, wine and ambiance. In a restored Antebellum home, there is plenty to take in, from the original staircase upon entry to the Civil War depictions in the artwork. Lunch tends to be more casual with salads and sandwiches offered, while dinner offers more refined menu options such as phyllo-wrapped sea bass or veal chops with a mint risotto. Be sure to try the Charleston she-crab soup, a local favorite. **Features:** full bar, patio dining, senior menu, Sunday brunch, happy hour. **Reservations:** suggested. **Address:** 5201 Maryland Way 37027 **Location:** I-65 exit 74, 0.5 mi w, then 0.3 mi s. L D CALL 🅼

PUFFY MUFFIN

615/373-2741

▽▽ Breads/Pastries Sandwiches. Casual Dining. $8-$14 **AAA Inspector Notes:** The delectable and pretty pastries, cakes and cookies displayed in glass bakery cases are sure to make any diner save room for some dessert. Luckily the menu focuses on healthy and lighter sandwich selections to leave space for those tempting desserts. **Address:** 229 Franklin Rd 37027 **Location:** I-65 exit 74B, just e to US 31, then 0.5 mi s; in H.G. Hills Shopping Center.

B L CALL 🅼

SHOGUN JAPANESE STEAK, SEAFOOD AND SUSHI

615/377-7977

▽▽ Japanese Sushi Steak. Casual Dining. $9-$37 **AAA Inspector Notes:** A great spot for large groups, many celebrating special occasions, this lively restaurant offers a variety of Japanese options. Teppanyaki-style dishes are prepared at your table and there is also a mellower, quieter sushi bar. The experience is highlighted by the Asian garden and water feature outside, which is beautiful in springtime. **Features:** full bar. **Address:** 1638 Westgate Cir 37027 **Location:** I-65 exit 69 (US 441 E), just e, then 0.4 mi n. L D

SPORTSMAN'S LODGE TAVERN & GRILLE

615/373-1070

▽▽▽
American Casual Dining
$9-$28

AAA Inspector Notes: This local staple, since 1985, offers a rustic, lodge-style atmosphere perfect for relaxing and enjoying generous portions of traditional homemade food. Topping the list of favorites are fresh catfish, hand-packed burgers, fresh-cut fries, Prime steaks and chops, charbroiled salmon salad, filet or chicken Caesar and the eatery's famous barbecue on Cajun cornbread. **Features:** full bar, happy hour. **Address:** 1640 Westgate Cir 37027 **Location:** I-65 exit 69, 0.5 mi e, then just n; in Westgate Business Park. *Menu on AAA.com* L D CALL 🅼

BRISTOL (B-9) pop. 26,702, elev. 1,680'
• Hotels p. 44 • Restaurants p. 44

State Street, Bristol's main thoroughfare, is bisected by the Tennessee/Virginia border. The double yellow lines down the street's center denote the dividing line. Although each side has its own government and city services, together they form an important industrial center that manufactures metal goods, textiles and electronic products.

Evan Shelby, noted for battling Native Americans and founding what became the city of Bristol, built a stockade here in 1776. Daniel Boone and many other distinguished pioneers bartered in Bristol and planned the campaign that defeated the British at the Battle of Kings Mountain in South Carolina.

Congress declared Bristol the Birthplace of Country Music in 1998 because of the 1927 Bristol Sessions recordings that launched the careers of music legends Jimmie Rodgers and The Carter family. Today, Bristol hosts outdoor concerts between

April and October and an annual music festival, Bristol Rhythm and Roots Reunion, in September.

The city has a theater, an arts center and a ballet company. Recreational activities on the Tennessee BRISTOLside are provided by Steele Creek Park and South Holston Dam and Lake. Sugar Hollow Park is on the Virginia side. Both Steele Creek and Sugar Hollow parks provide miles of hiking, biking and walking trails. Area lakes and waterways offer opportunities for fishing and boating.

The Bristol Motor Speedway, a half-mile racetrack 5 miles south on US 11E in Tennessee, is on the NASCAR circuit; phone (423) 989-6900. Scenic I-81 passes through Bristol and continues 88 miles south to the I-40 junction.

Bristol Convention & Visitors Bureau: 20 Volunteer Pkwy., Bristol, TN 37620. **Phone:** (423) 989-4850.

THE BIRTHPLACE OF COUNTRY MUSIC MUSEUM is at 416 State St. The Smithsonian-affiliated museum features permanent and rotating exhibits documenting the impact of the 1927 Bristol Sessions recordings on country music. Themed display stations include interactive music-mixing and listening booths and a kiosk honoring Bristol native Tennessee Ernie Ford. Visitors can watch video profiles of important Appalachian musicians and also view signed instruments once owned by Ralph Stanley, Earl Scruggs and Bill Monroe.

A 70-seat theater screens the 14-minute orientation film "Bound for Bristol," while a 13-minute film about the influence of gospel music on the area's musical heritage is shown in a small second-floor chapel. Live performances and educational programming also are offered year-round at the state-of-the-art facility. **Time:** Allow 2 hours minimum. **Hours:** Tues.-Sat. 10-6, Sun. 1-5. Closed major holidays. **Cost:** $13; $11 (ages 6-17, military with ID and senior citizens). **Phone:** (423) 573-1927. GT

BRISTOL CAVERNS is 5.5 mi. s.e. on SR 435 and 2.5 mi. s. on US 421 to 1157 Bristol Caverns Hwy. The caverns have many unusual formations. A lighted asphalt trail traverses several levels, with guided 1-hour tours descending 180 feet below ground; visitors walk along the banks of an underground river. **Hours:** Tours are given every 20 minutes Mon.-Sat. 9-5, Sun. 12:30-5, Mar. 15-Oct. 31; Mon.-Sat. 10-4, Sun. 12:30-4, rest of year. Closed Easter, Thanksgiving, Christmas Eve and Christmas. **Cost:** $15; $14 (military with ID and ages 62+); $7.50 (ages 5-12). Prices may vary; phone ahead. **Phone:** (423) 878-2011.

HAMPTON INN (423)764-3600

Hotel $109-$399 **Address:** 3299 W State St 37620 **Location:** I-81 exit 74A, just w. **Facility:** 90 units. 5 stories, interior corridors. **Terms:** 1-7 night minimum stay, cancellation fee imposed. **Pool(s):** outdoor. **Activities:** limited exercise equipment. **Guest Services:** valet laundry.

AAA Benefit: Members save up to 10%!

WHERE TO EAT

FATZ 423/968-4498

Regional American. Casual Dining. $8-$19 **AAA Inspector Notes:** Friendly staff and appealing country decor help set the tone for a relaxed and enjoyable dining experience. It's not unusual for guests to wait to be seated at the popular spot, which earns raves for its well-prepared variations on chicken, steak, ribs and pasta, as well as salads and sandwiches. The signature Southern-style peach cobbler served with vanilla ice cream and walnuts is scrumptious. **Features:** full bar. **Address:** 1175 Volunteer Pkwy 37620 **Location:** Just s of center on US 11/19. L D CALL

STATE LINE BAR & GRILLE 423/652-0792

American. Casual Dining. $7-$15 **AAA Inspector Notes:** On the menu here are thick, juicy burgers, several sandwiches and salads and a wide choice of favorite appetizers, including nachos, chicken tenders and wings. **Features:** full bar, patio dining, happy hour. **Address:** 644 State St 37620 **Location:** Corner of State and 7th sts; downtown. **Parking:** street only. L D

Nearby Virginia

BRISTOL pop. 17,835, elev. 1,680'

BAYMONT INN & SUITES (276)669-9353

Hotel $58-$75 **Address:** 1014 Old Airport Rd 24201 **Location:** I-81 exit 7, just e. **Facility:** 123 units. 4 stories, exterior corridors. **Amenities:** video games. **Pool(s):** outdoor. **Activities:** exercise room. **Guest Services:** valet laundry. / SOME UNITS

BUDGET HOST INN (276)669-5187

Motel $58-$225

Address: 1209 W State St 24201 **Location:** I-81 exit 1, 2 mi s on SR 421. **Facility:** 23 units. 1 story, exterior corridors. **Terms:** 3 night minimum stay - seasonal, 7 day cancellation notice. SAVE / SOME UNITS

COURTYARD BY MARRIOTT (276)591-4400

Hotel $101-$166 **Address:** 3169 Linden Dr 24202 **Location:** I-81 exit 7, just w. **Facility:** 175 units. 5 stories, interior corridors. **Amenities:** video games. **Pool(s):** heated indoor. **Activities:** hot tub, exercise room. **Guest Services:** valet and coin laundry. / SOME UNITS

AAA Benefit: Members save 5% or more!

HOLIDAY INN HOTEL & SUITES   (276)466-4100

WWWW **Hotel** $99-$139 **Address:** 3005 Linden Dr 24202 **Location:** I-81 exit 7, just w. **Facility:** 226 units. 10 stories, interior corridors. **Pool(s):** heated outdoor. **Activities:** hot tub, exercise room. **Guest Services:** valet and coin laundry.

ECO 🍴 ♨ 🍸 CALL 🔥M 🏊 🛜 ✕ 🖥 🖨 🖵 / SOME UNITS 🆂🖥 HS

MOTEL 6 #4125   276/466-6060

W **Motel.** Rates not provided. **Address:** 21561 Clear Creek Rd 24202 **Location:** I-81 exit 7, 0.3 mi w. **Facility:** 53 units. 3 stories, interior corridors. **Guest Services:** coin laundry.

🍴➕ CALL 🔥M HS 🛜 🖥 🖨 / SOME UNITS 🐾

QUALITY INN   (276)669-8164

WW **Hotel** $70-$450 **Address:** 131 Bristol East Rd 24202 **Location:** I-81 exit 7 northbound, just w. **Facility:** 65 units. 3 stories, interior corridors. **Pool(s):** heated indoor. **Activities:** exercise room.

🍴➕ 🏊 HS 🛜 ✕ / SOME UNITS 🆂🖥 🖥 🖨 🖵

WHERE TO EAT

ATHEN'S STEAK HOUSE   276/466-8271

WW **Greek Steak.** Casual Dining. $7-$25 **AAA Inspector Notes:** The flavors of America and Greece mingle in selections on the restaurant's tempting menu. Most popular are the steaks and home-made desserts such as baklava and apple pie. Parquet and carpeted floors, along with candles and light music, create ambience. **Features:** full bar, patio dining. **Address:** 105 Goodson St 24201 **Location:** I-81 exit 3, 2.6 mi s to State St, 0.6 mi e, then just n. L D

LOS ARCOS RESTAURANT   276/591-3180

WW **Mexican Seafood.** Casual Dining. $6-$16 **AAA Inspector Notes:** Meticulously prepared Mexican cuisine is served with a smile and a heaping helping of piping hot chips and salsa. **Features:** full bar. **Address:** 3175 Linden Dr 24201 **Location:** I-81 exit 7, just w. L D

This ends the Bristol section and resumes the alphabetical city listings for Tennessee.

BROWNSVILLE pop. 10,292

BACK YARD BBQ   731/772-1121

W **Barbecue.** Casual Dining. $4-$11 **AAA Inspector Notes:** Huge pork and beef sandwiches and platters of ribs and beef are complemented with sides of beans and slaw, just what you would expect from this local favorite. **Address:** 703 E Main St 38012 **Location:** I-40 exit 56, 3.7 mi n, then just w. L D

BUCHANAN

THE RIVERBOAT AT PARIS LANDING STATE PARK
                                              731/642-4311

WW **American.** Family Dining. $6-$33 **AAA Inspector Notes:** Here you'll find great views of the lake and a buffet stocked with comfort foods. **Features:** beer & wine, early bird specials. **Address:** 400 Lodge Rd 38222 **Location:** Jct SR 119, just n on US 79, then just s; in Paris Landing State Park Inn. B L D

BULLS GAP pop. 738

QUALITY INN   (423)235-9111

WW **Hotel** $73-$106 **Address:** 50 Speedway Ln 37711 **Location:** I-81 exit 23, just w. **Facility:** 63 units. 4 stories, interior corridors. **Activities:** exercise room. **Guest Services:** coin laundry.

CALL 🔥M BIZ 🛜 🖵 / SOME UNITS 🆂🖥 🖥 🖨

BURNS pop. 1,468

MONTGOMERY BELL RESTAURANT   615/797-3101

WW WW **American.** Casual Dining. $6-$17 **AAA Inspector Notes:** Floor-to-ceiling windows provide a beautiful up-close view of Lake Acorn as you enjoy a menu of grilled steaks, crunchy catfish and hearty salads, plus a variety of buffet themes that change daily, such as "Seafood Fridays" and "Steak Saturdays." Other days offer a wider variety of common buffet items. An à la carte menu is always available. **Features:** beer & wine. **Address:** 1000 Hotel Ave 37029 **Location:** Jct SR 96, 3.7 mi e on US 70, then 1 mi s into Montgomery Bell State Park; in Montgomery Bell State Park Inn. B L D CALL 🔥M

BUTLER

IRON MOUNTAIN INN B & B AND CREEKSIDE CHALET
                                              423/768-2446

WWWW **Bed & Breakfast** $150-$400 **Address:** 268 Moreland Dr 37640 **Location:** 1.6 mi w on Pine Orchard Rd from SR 67 at Stout Store, follow signs; 13 mi w on SR 67 from US 421 in Mountain City, follow sign at Stout Store area; 15.1 mi from Shell station in Hampton to Pine Orchard Rd, 1.6 mi to Moreland Dr. **Facility:** A large log home offering picturesque views, the B&B features some antique furnishings as well as three units with additional steam showers. 5 units, some cabins. 2 stories (no elevator), interior/exterior corridors. **Terms:** 1-7 night minimum stay - seasonal and/or weekends, 14 day cancellation notice-fee imposed. **Activities:** fishing.

🛜 ✕ / SOME UNITS 🆂🖥 🏩 🌀 🖥 🖨 🖵

BYRDSTOWN (C-6) pop. 803, elev. 1,030'

CORDELL HULL BIRTHPLACE STATE PARK is at 1300 Cordell Hull Memorial Dr./SR 325, 1.5 mi. w. of SR 111. A museum displays memorabilia recalling the life of Cordell Hull, secretary of state under Franklin Delano Roosevelt. Hull received the Nobel Peace Prize in 1945 for his work toward establishing the United Nations. A replica of his log cabin birthplace is on the 58-acre site as well as a library archive that includes historic photographs and documents. A 2-mile nature trail leads to an overlook of Bunkum Cave. **Time:** Allow 30 minutes minimum. **Hours:** Daily 9-5, Apr.-Oct.; 9-4, rest of year. **Cost:** Free. **Phone:** (931) 864-3247. 🎫

CAMDEN (C-3) pop. 3,582, elev. 435'
• Hotels p. 46

Camden is known for its cultivation of freshwater pearls and production of sorghum. The juice of sorghum, a tropical grass, is cooked to produce a substance similar to cane syrup. In the past, entire communities turned out for "the cooking," often followed by a candy pull.

Kentucky Lake entices recreationalists with fishing, boating, swimming, skiing and other water sports. Hunters frequent the area for ducks, geese, deer and turkey.

The Patsy Cline Memorial on Mount Carmel Road marks the site of the 1963 airplane crash that killed Cline and other Grand Ole Opry performers.

Benton County/Camden Chamber of Commerce: 266 US 641 N., Camden, TN 38320. **Phone:** (731) 584-8395.

TENNESSEE RIVER FRESHWATER PEARL MUSEUM, FARM, TOUR AND PEARL JEWELRY SHOWROOM is off I-40 exit 133, then 9.2 mi. n. on SR 191. A tour of the freshwater pearl farm on Kentucky Lake allows guests to see the farm manager shuck mussels to reveal pearls in many shapes and colors. A 3- to 5-hour guided tour also includes lunch, an appearance by a diver and an expert-led discussion about mussels and pearls. A mini-tour, which lasts about 1 hour, also is available. Free 15-minute tours of a museum and showroom are offered to walk-in visitors. All tours begin with an orientation and video presentation.

Hours: Self-guiding tours of the museum are available every 15 minutes Mon.-Sat. 8-5, Sun. 1-4. Full and mini-tour departures require a minimum of 10 people and are available year-round. Closed Jan. 1, Thanksgiving and Christmas. **Cost:** Full tour (includes lunch) $55, mini-tour $39.50. Reservations are required for full and mini-tours. Walk-in tours and jewelry showroom are free. **Phone:** (731) 584-7880.

BEST WESTERN HOME PLACE INN   (731)584-2222

Motel
$100-$120

AAA Benefit:
Save 10% or more every day and earn 10% bonus points!

Address: 170 US Hwy 641 N 38320 **Location:** Jct US 70 business route, 0.4 mi n. Located in a quite rural area. **Facility:** 40 units. 2 stories (no elevator), exterior corridors. **Parking:** winter plug-ins. **Pool(s):** outdoor. **Guest Services:** valet and coin laundry.

CARYVILLE   pop. 2,297

HAMPTON INN-COVE LAKE   (423)562-9888

Hotel $129-$145 **Address:** 4459 Veterans Memorial Hwy 37714 **Location:** I-75 exit 134, just e. **Facility:** 62 units. 2 stories, interior corridors. **Terms:** 1-7 night minimum stay, cancellation fee imposed. **Pool(s):** heated outdoor. **Activities:** exercise room. **Guest Services:** coin laundry.

AAA Benefit:
Members save up to 10%!

HOLIDAY INN EXPRESS & SUITES CARYVILLE/I-75   (865)221-8002

Hotel $99-$199 **Address:** 154 John McGhee Blvd 37714 **Location:** I-75 exit 134, just e. **Facility:** 78 units. 4 stories, interior corridors. **Pool(s):** outdoor. **Activities:** limited exercise equipment. **Guest Services:** coin laundry.

WHERE TO EAT

RICKARD RIDGE BBQ AT COVE LAKE   423/907-8202

Barbecue. Family Dining. $6-$20 **AAA Inspector Notes:** At this family spot, you'll enjoy great down-home cooking and great views of Cove Lake State Park. **Address:** 131 Goose Ln 37714 **Location:** I-75 exit 134, just e, then 0.7 mi n on US 25 W; in Cove Lake State Park. L D

CASTALIAN SPRINGS (C-5) pop. 556, elev. 495'

CRAGFONT MUSEUM is 1.6 mi. w. on Hartsville Pike (SR 25), then .2 mi. n. to 200 Cragfont Rd. Built about 1800, the mansion was the home of Gen.

James Winchester, a Revolutionary War hero. It is furnished with antiques and handmade pioneer items. Guests at the Winchesters' home included Andrew Jackson and Sam Houston. A restored garden is on the grounds. **Hours:** Tues.-Sat. 10-5, Sun. 1-5, Apr. 15-Oct. 31. **Cost:** $5; $4 (ages 55+); $3 (ages 6-12). **Phone:** (615) 452-7070.

WYNNEWOOD is at 210 Old SR 25. Built in 1828, it served as a stagecoach inn and mineral springs resort. The 142-foot-long log structure contains period furnishings, including the bed that Jesse James slept on during his stay at the inn. **Time:** Allow 30 minutes minimum. **Hours:** Wed.-Sun. 10-4, Mar.-Nov.; by appointment rest of year. Closed major holidays. **Cost:** $5; $4 (ages 55+); $3 (ages 6-12). **Phone:** (615) 452-5463.

CHATTANOOGA (E-6) pop. 167,674, elev. 676'

Chattanooga began in 1815 as a small trading post started by Daniel and John Ross at what is now known as Ross's Landing (near the Tennessee Aquarium). It also served as one of the staging areas for the Cherokee relocation known as the Trail of Tears. Incorporated in 1839, Chattanooga's Creek Indian name means "rock coming to a point," in reference to 2,126-foot-high Lookout Mountain to the south.

During the Civil War Union forces occupied the city. Following this 1863 occupation Gen. William Tecumseh Sherman began his march from Chattanooga, through Georgia, to the sea. The Civil War battles of Lookout Mountain, Chickamauga and Missionary Ridge were fought near Chattanooga. Much of the historic area has been preserved in Chickamauga and Chattanooga National Military Park *(see place listing p. 63)*. Brochures detailing a driving tour of the Chickamauga Campaign Heritage Trail as well as sites along the Blue and Gray Trail and the Tennessee Civil War Trail can be obtained from the visitors bureau.

The Chattanooga National Cemetery was established in 1863 to contain the bodies of more than 12,000 Union soldiers who died in the area. The Andrews Raiders Monument marks the graves of the participants of the 1862 Andrews Raid—known as "The Great Locomotive Chase"—in which civilian James Andrews and his band of soldiers commandeered the *General* locomotive in an attempt to disrupt Confederate supplies by severing rail transportation. The monument depicts a replica of the train, which they piloted from Kennesaw to Ringgold, Ga., before being captured and hanged. Andrews' men were the first recipients of the Medal of Honor.

Chattanooga is the southern terminus of a scenic stretch of I-24, which runs 40 miles northeast to Monteagle at the SR 55 intersection.

Lookout Mountain is accessible by SRs 58 and 148 or by the Lookout Mountain Incline Railway *(see*

(See map & index p. 51.)

attraction listing p. 49). Point Park on Lookout Mountain overlooks Chattanooga, Moccasin Bend and the Tennessee River; a visitor center is available. Nearby are Chickamauga Dam and Lake and Nickajack Dam and Lake *(see Recreation Areas Chart).* Chickamauga Dam has a visitor lobby.

The Chattanooga riverfront has been revitalized and includes 129 acres of footpaths, pedestrian-bridges and a 160-foot lighted pier extending from Ross's Landing into the Tennessee River. At First and Market streets a walkway connects nearby attractions and is adorned with public art. The Passage, a pedestrian link along the riverfront, honors those Cherokees affected by the Trail of Tears with water features and six Native American clay symbols.

The restored 1909 Chattanooga Choo Choo train depot at 1400 Market St. contains a hotel, shops and restaurants. A free electric shuttle service provides transportation between the train station and the Tennessee Aquarium *(see attraction listing p. 50).*

In the Northshore district off Frazier Avenue, visitors enjoy the green, open space of Coolidge Park, which features a restored carousel and an interactive play fountain. Renaissance Park, offering 23 acres of wetland, is off Manufacturers Road and connected to Coolidge Park Landing, a shopping and entertainment complex. The legendary Delta Queen Steamboat now is moored as a hotel at 100 River St. in Coolidge Park Landing. Daily tours of the historic boat as well as entertainment are offered; phone (423) 468-4500.

Chattanooga Area Convention and Visitors Bureau: 736 Market St., Chattanooga, TN 37402. **Phone:** (423) 756-8687 or (800) 322-3344. *(See ad this page.)*

Shopping: Hamilton Place, just off I-75 exit 5 (Shallowford Road), is a mall with more than 175 stores, including Belk, Dillard's, JCPenney and Sears. Northgate Mall, north on SR 153 in Hixson, has more than 90 stores, including Belk and Sears.

Just across from downtown along the riverfront, the Northshore district includes eclectic, locally owned shops and eateries. The Southside district of Chattanooga has antiques, galleries and eateries, while the Central district is home to Warehouse Row's boutiques, fine dining and cultural attractions. Bluff View Art District, overlooking the Tennessee River, specializes in visual, culinary and landscape arts.

AUDUBON ACRES/THE ELISE CHAPIN SANCTUARY is off I-75 exit 3A, 1.1 mi. e. on E. Brainerd Rd. (SR 320), 1.1 mi. s. on Gunbarrel Rd., then .6 mi. s.w. to 900 N. Sanctuary Rd. Part of the Trail of Tears National Historic Trail, the 130-acre wildlife sanctuary includes a restored 18th-century log cabin and the archeological site of a Mississippian-era Native American village, 5 miles of hiking trails and a swinging bridge over South Chickamauga Creek.

More than 4 miles of trails and a visitor center with exhibits also are offered. **Hours:** Mon.-Sat. 9-5, Sun. 1-5. **Cost:** Grounds and trails $4; $3 (ages 60+); $2 (ages 5-12). Visitor center free. Prices may vary during special events. **Phone:** (423) 892-1499.

BESSIE SMITH CULTURAL CENTER is in the Heritage Center at 200 E. Martin Luther King Blvd. The museum houses educational, cultural and historical documents and artifacts that portray African-American contributions to Chattanooga and the nation; rotating exhibitions, musical performances and lectures are featured throughout the year. Of special interest is the exhibit about blues great Bessie

▼ See AAA listing this page ▼

(See map & index p. 51.)

Smith. **Time:** Allow 1 hour minimum. **Hours:** Mon.-Fri. 10-5, Sat. noon-4. Closed major holidays. **Cost:** $7; $5 (ages 56+ and students with ID); $3 (ages 6-12). **Phone:** (423) 266-8658.

CHATTANOOGA DUCKS is at 503 Market St. The 1-hour narrated tour takes visitors through downtown Chattanooga and along the Tennessee River aboard a World War II amphibious vehicle. The captain describes the city's history as well as Tennessee's Cherokee heritage. **Time:** Allow 1 hour minimum. **Hours:** Tours depart daily 10-dusk, Mar.-Oct. **Cost:** $22; $20 (ages 13-18, ages 62+ and military with ID); $11 (ages 3-12); $5 (ages 0-2). **Phone:** (423) 756-3825.

CHATTANOOGA RIVERBOAT CO. sails from Ross's Landing at 201 Riverfront Pkwy. The company offers 90-minute narrated sightseeing trips on the Tennessee River aboard the *Southern Belle* riverboat. Also offered are 2-hour family dinner cruises, as well as fall foliage cruises from October through November. Meals are available on the lunch and dinner cruises.

Hours: Sightseeing cruises depart daily, Apr.-Oct.; departure times vary. **Cost:** Sightseeing cruise $19.95; $10.95 (ages 3-12). Reservations are recommended. **Phone:** (423) 266-4488.

CREATIVE DISCOVERY MUSEUM is .1 mi. e. of US 27 exit 1C at 321 Chestnut St. Hands-on exhibits are geared for children under age 13 and include River Play, Excavation Station, Little Yellow House, Inventors' Clubhouse, Lookout Tower and Arts Alley. A dinosaur dig, netted climbing structure, water course, art lessons, infant garden and riverboat are popular. A second-floor gallery houses the rooftop Fun Factory and temporary exhibits.

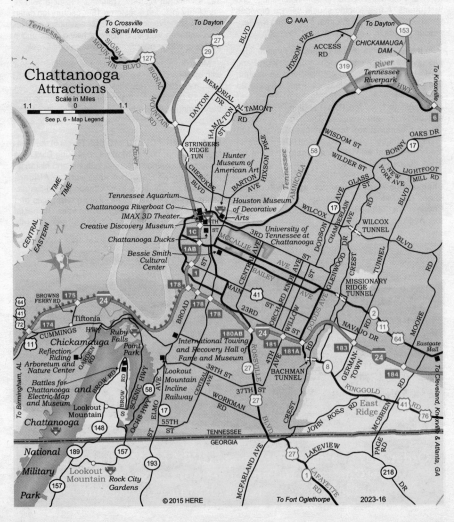

(See map & index p. 51.)

Time: Allow 2 hours minimum. **Hours:** Daily 9:30-5:30, mid-June to mid-Aug.; Mon.-Sat. 10-5, Sun. noon-5, Mar. 1 to mid-June and mid-Aug. through Labor Day; Mon.-Tues. and Thurs.-Sat. 10-5, Sun. noon-5, rest of year. Last admission 1 hour before closing. Closed Thanksgiving, Christmas Eve and Christmas. **Cost:** $12.95; $9.95 (active military with ID). Admission with Tennessee Aquarium ticket stub $10.95. **Phone:** (423) 756-2738.

HOUSTON MUSEUM OF DECORATIVE ARTS is at 201 High St. Decorative arts and antiques dating from the 18th century to the early 20th century are featured in a Victorian house. The collections were the lifework of Anna Safley Houston, an early 20th-century, unconventional antiques dealer and collector. Displays include furniture, textiles, glass, ceramics and music boxes. **Hours:** Guided tours Thurs.-Sun. noon-4, other days by appointment. Closed major holidays. **Cost:** $9; $3.50 (ages 4-17). **Phone:** (423) 267-7176. GT

HUNTER MUSEUM OF AMERICAN ART is off US 27N exit 1C; take 4th St. .5 mi. e., then High St. .3 mi. n. to 10 Bluff View. Perched on an 80-foot bluff overlooking the Tennessee River, the museum is noted for its permanent collection of American artwork from the 19th century to the present.

Both the lobby and sculpture garden provide panoramic views of the river and surrounding mountains. Works by Thomas Hart Benton, Winslow Homer, Thomas Sully and Andrew Wyeth can be seen. Permanent displays and changing exhibits are featured in spacious galleries, and an auditorium and art studios are included.

Time: Allow 1 hour minimum. **Hours:** Mon.-Tues. and Thurs.-Sat. 10-5 (also Thurs. 5-8), Wed. and Sun. noon-5. Closed Jan. 1, Thanksgiving and Christmas. **Cost:** $9.95; $4.95 (ages 3-17); free (to all first Sun. of the month). **Phone:** (423) 267-0968.

INTERNATIONAL TOWING AND RECOVERY HALL OF FAME AND MUSEUM is at 3315 Broad St. The museum displays restored antique tow trucks, industry-related collectible toys, tools, equipment and pictorial histories of manufacturers. Individuals who have contributed to the towing and recovery industry are recognized in the hall of fame. **Time:** Allow 1 hour minimum. **Hours:** Mon.-Sat. 9-5, Sun. 11-5, Mar.-Oct.; Mon.-Sat. 10-4:30, Sun. 11-5, rest of year. Closed major holidays. **Cost:** $10; $9 (ages 55+); $6 (ages 6-14). **Phone:** (423) 267-3132.

LOOKOUT MOUNTAIN INCLINE RAILWAY starts from St. Elmo Ave., about 3 mi. s. near SR 58S. One of the steepest railways in the world, its gradient reaches 72.7 percent. Views of the surrounding mountains and valleys can be enjoyed along the way. An observation deck at Lookout Mountain Station, the highest overlook on the mountain, also is

offered. A display depicts the history of the railway and other Lookout Mountain points of interest.

Time: Allow 1 hour minimum. **Hours:** Daily 8:30-8, Memorial Day weekend-Labor Day; 9-6, Mar. 1-day before Memorial Day weekend and day after Labor Day-Oct. 31; 10-6, rest of year. Last round-trip departure is 1 hour before closing. Closed Thanksgiving and Christmas. Phone ahead to confirm schedule.

Cost: Round-trip fare $15; $7 (ages 3-12); discounted fare for senior citizens available Dec.-Feb. Combination ticket with Rock City Gardens and Ruby Falls $48.90; $25.90 (ages 3-12). **Parking:** fee (meters at upper station, pay box at lower station). **Phone:** (423) 821-4224.

RACCOON MOUNTAIN CAVERNS is 4 mi. w. on I-24 to exit 174, then 1.3 mi. n.w. on US 41. Visitors may take a 45-minute guided Crystal Palace Tour past cave formations that include shields, three natural bridges, the Hall of Dreams, Grandfather Rock and cave beads, which are unusual stalactites. The underground temperature is a constant 60 F; a jacket and comfortable walking shoes are recommended. Overnight and 1- to 6-hour cave tours also are offered.

Time: Allow 1 hour, 45 minutes minimum. **Hours:** Guided tours Sun.-Fri. 9-5, Sat. 9-7. Last tour departs 1 hour before closing. **Cost:** $15.95; $13.95 (ages 65+); $7.50 (ages 5-12). **Phone:** (423) 821-9403 or (800) 823-2267. GT

RACCOON MOUNTAIN PUMPED STORAGE VISITORS CENTER is off I-24 exit 174, then n. on US 41 (Lookout Valley). The Tennessee Valley Authority power-generating plant is 1,160 feet inside Raccoon Mountain. A mountaintop visitor center offers exhibits about the plant and scenic views of the man-made lake. Mountain biking also can be enjoyed on more than 30 miles of trails, and a fishing area is near the mountain base.

Note: The visitors center is closed for renovations in 2015 and is scheduled to reopen in 2016; phone for updates. Bike trails will remain open during construction. **Hours:** Visitor center daily 9-5. Closed major holidays. **Cost:** Free. **Phone:** (423) 825-3100.

REFLECTION RIDING ARBORETUM AND NATURE CENTER is 4.5 mi. e. on US 41/SR 11, s. on Old Wauhatchie Pike, then s. to 400 Garden Rd. The center displays the area's flora and fauna and educates the public about the environment. Such native animals as endangered red wolves, red-tailed hawks, an American bald eagle and great horned owls can be seen. Visitors can walk, bike or drive along the Reflection Riding Loop, a 3-mile road through forests, gardens and wildflower meadows. A 1,400-foot-long boardwalk winds through a hardwood wetland to a tree house, and restored Native American log cabins are available to explore.

(See map & index p. 51.)

Pets are not permitted. **Time:** Allow 1 hour minimum. **Hours:** Mon.-Sat. 9-5 (also Sun. 1-5, Apr.-Oct.). Closed major holidays. **Cost:** $10; $7 (ages 4-11 and 65+). **Phone:** (423) 821-1160.

RUBY FALLS is 3 mi. s. on Lookout Mountain Scenic Hwy. (SR 148); from I-24 exit 174 or 178, follow signs to 1720 S. Scenic Hwy. Among the types of formations found along the cave's paved, level walkways are stalactites, stalagmites, columns, drapes and flowstone. The highlight is a 145-foot waterfall, which is 1,120 feet underground and said to be the largest underground waterfall accessible to the public in America. Lookout Mountain Tower at Ruby Falls Castle offers a panorama of the Tennessee River Valley. Fun Forest is a multilevel activity center for children.

Comfortable walking shoes are recommended for the tours. **Time:** Allow 1 hour, 30 minutes minimum. **Hours:** Guided tours lasting about 75 minutes depart daily every 15 minutes 8-8. Hours may vary; phone ahead to confirm schedule. Closed Christmas. **Cost:** $18.95; $10.95 (ages 3-12). Combination ticket with Lookout Mountain Incline Railway and Rock City Gardens $48.90; $25.90 (ages 3-12). **Phone:** (423) 821-2544. ᐅ GT

SIGNAL MOUNTAIN is 9 mi. n. off US 127. The mountain, the southernmost point on Walden's Ridge, got its name during the Civil War when it was used as a signaling point by the Union army; it had served a similar purpose for Native Americans. Signal Point and James Point offer views of the Tennessee River as it passes through the Tennessee River Gorge. **Phone:** (423) 886-2177.

TENNESSEE AQUARIUM is at 1 Broad St. On the banks of the Tennessee River, the aquarium highlights the voyage of a drop of water from its origin in the Appalachian Mountains to the Gulf of Mexico.

The River Journey building houses what is said to be the world's largest freshwater aquarium. Galleries include a mountain cove forest with river otters; a delta swamp with ducks, snapping turtles and alligators; and a world rivers gallery with piranhas, sturgeon and an electric eel.

The Ocean Journey building contains a stingray touch pool, jellyfish, sharks and a butterfly garden. In the Penguins' Rock gallery, Macaroni and Gentoo penguins waddle and dive into the water.

Free shuttle service from around town to the aquarium is available daily on CARTA. **Time:** Allow 2 hours, 30 minutes minimum. **Hours:** Daily 10-7:30. Last admission at 6 p.m. Guided behind-the-scenes aquarium tours are given daily. To take the guided tour, children must be accompanied by an adult, and under 10 are not permitted; reservations are recommended. Closed Thanksgiving and Christmas. **Cost:** $29.95; $18.95 (ages 3-12). IMAX 3D Theater $9.95; $8.50 (ages 3-12). Combination ticket with IMAX 3D Theater $35.95; $24.95 (ages 3-12). Guided behind-the-scenes aquarium tour $17 (plus admission). Prices may vary; phone ahead for current rates. **Phone:** (423) 265-0695 or (800) 262-0695. ᐅ

IMAX 3D Theater is at 201 Chestnut St. Larger-than-life films with digital surround sound are presented on a six-story screen, which is part of the Tennessee Aquarium. **Time:** Allow 1 hour minimum. **Hours:** Shows are offered daily 10-6 (also Fri.-Sat. 6-9 p.m.). Closed Thanksgiving and Christmas. **Cost:** $9.95; $8.50 (ages 3-12). Combination ticket with Tennessee Aquarium $35.95; $24.95 (ages 3-12). **Phone:** (423) 266-4629 or (800) 262-0695.

TENNESSEE VALLEY RAILROAD is at 4119 Cromwell Rd.; use the Jersey Pike exit off SR 153, near I-75. This historic railroad re-creates passenger train travel typical of the early 20th century. Locomotive crews wear overalls, and conductors punch each ticket. A vintage steam- or diesel-powered passenger train offers a 55-minute, 6-mile sightseeing trip over three bridges and through a Civil War railroad tunnel.

The East Chattanooga Station features a railroad yard with diesel engines, cars and a giant turntable. In mid-October the railroad also offers the Autumn Leaf Special, a mainline excursion to northwestern Georgia. Other excursions are offered. **Time:** Allow 2 hours minimum. **Hours:** Sightseeing trips depart daily 10-5, Memorial Day weekend to mid-Aug.; Mon.-Fri. 10-1:30, Sat.-Sun. 10-5, May 1-day before Memorial Day weekend; Tues.-Fri. 10-1:30, Sat.-Sun. 10-5, mid-Mar. through Apr. 30 and mid-Aug. through Oct. 31; limited schedule rest of year. Closed Easter and Thanksgiving. Phone ahead to confirm schedule. **Cost:** Sightseeing trip $17; $11 (ages 3-12). **Phone:** (423) 894-8028.

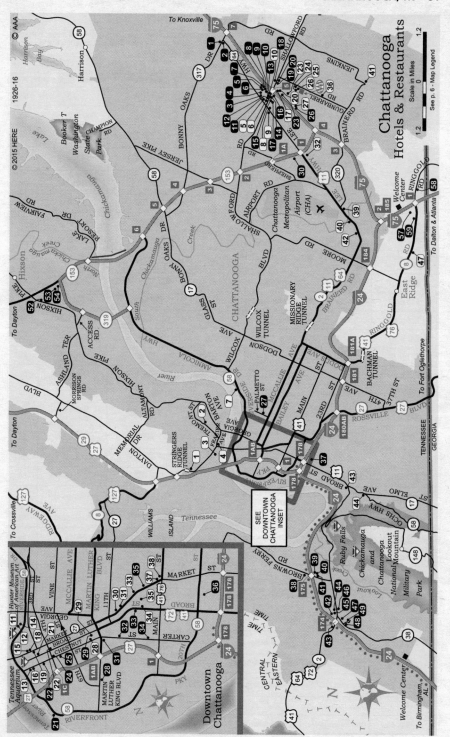

Chattanooga
Hotels & Restaurants

Downtown Chattanooga

Chattanooga and Vicinity

This index helps you "spot" where approved hotels and restaurants are located on the corresponding detailed maps. Hotel daily rate range is for comparison only. Restaurant price range is a combination of lunch and/or dinner. Turn to the listing page for more detailed rate and price information and consult display ads for special promotions.

CHATTANOOGA

Map Page	Hotels	Diamond Rated	Rate Range	Page
1 p. 51	Econo Lodge-Hamilton Mall Area	◈◈	$55	56
2 p. 51	BEST WESTERN Heritage Inn	◈◈	$60-$70 SAVE	55
3 p. 51	Residence Inn by Marriott Chattanooga near Hamilton Place	◈◈◈	$119-$249	58
4 p. 51	TownePlace Suites by Marriott Chattanooga near Hamilton Place	◈◈◈	$83-$125	59
5 p. 51	Country Inns & Suites By Carlson, Chattanooga at Hamilton Place Mall	◈◈◈	$119-$129 SAVE	56
6 p. 51	Super 8	◈◈	$50-$81	59
7 p. 51	Days Inn Chattanooga/Hamilton Place	◈◈	$79-$109	56
8 p. 51	Sleep Inn	◈◈	$67-$89 SAVE	59
9 p. 51	Fairfield Inn & Suites by Marriott Hamilton Place	◈◈◈	$83-$137 SAVE	57
10 p. 51	Hilton Garden Inn Chattanooga Hamilton Place	◈◈◈	$89-$149	57
11 p. 51	Hampton Inn Chattanooga Airport I-75	◈◈	$74-$99 SAVE	57
12 p. 51	Staybridge Suites-Hamilton Place	◈◈◈	$130-$260	59
13 p. 51	La Quinta Inn Chattanooga/Hamilton Place	◈◈	$64-$130	58
14 p. 51	Red Roof Inn Chattanooga Airport	◈	$39-$99 SAVE	58
15 p. 51	Homewood Suites by Hilton	◈◈◈	$129-$169	57
16 p. 51	MainStay Suites-Chattanooga	◈◈	$99-$129	58
17 p. 51	Holiday Inn Chattanooga at Hamilton Place	◈◈◈	Rates not provided SAVE	57
18 p. 51	Embassy Suites by Hilton Chattanooga-Hamilton Place	◈◈◈	$119-$229	56
19 p. 51	Wingate by Wyndham	◈◈◈	$129-$154 SAVE	59
20 p. 51	Quality Suites	◈◈	$70-$110 SAVE	58
21 p. 51	SpringHill Suites by Marriott Chattanooga Downtown/Cameron Harbor	◈◈◈	$118-$194 SAVE	59
22 p. 51	Hilton Garden Inn Chattanooga	◈◈◈	$139-$229	57
23 p. 51	Courtyard by Marriott Chattanooga I-75	◈◈◈	$79-$160 SAVE	56
24 p. 51	Hampton Inn & Suites Chattanooga/Downtown	◈◈◈	$129-$209	57
25 p. 51	DoubleTree by Hilton Hotel Chattanooga Downtown	◈◈◈	$149-$299	56
26 p. 51	Hampton Inn & Suites Chattanooga-Hamilton Place	◈◈◈	$89-$169	57
27 p. 51	The Mayor's Mansion Inn	◈◈◈◈	$129-$299 SAVE	58
28 p. 51	Holiday Inn Express Hotel & Suites	◈◈◈	Rates not provided	57
29 p. 51	The Read House Historic Inn & Suites	◈◈◈	$109-$219 SAVE	58
30 p. 51	Extended Stay America-Chattanooga-Airport	◈	Rates not provided	56
31 p. 51	Days Inn Rivergate	◈◈	$69-$125	56
32 p. 51	Chattanooga Marriott Downtown	◈◈◈	$104-$189 SAVE	55

CHATTANOOGA (cont'd)

Map Page	Hotels (cont'd)	Diamond Rated	Rate Range	Page
33 p. 51	**The Chattanoogan**	▽▽▽	$149-$259 SAVE	55
34 p. 51	Staybridge Suites	▽▽▽	$129-$199	59
35 p. 51	**Chattanooga Choo-Choo**	▽▽	$119-$229 SAVE	55
36 p. 51	La Quinta Inn Chattanooga	▽▽	$64-$163	58
37 p. 51	Comfort Inn Downtown-Lookout Mountain	▽▽	$69-$139	56
38 p. 51	**La Quinta Inn and Suites**	▽▽▽	$90-$213 SAVE	58
39 p. 51	**Quality Inn**	▽▽	$66-$150 SAVE	58
40 p. 51	**Comfort Inn & Suites**	▽▽	$100-$156 SAVE	55
41 p. 51	Econo Lodge Lookout Mountain, Chattanooga	▽▽	Rates not provided	56
42 p. 51	Hampton Inn Chattanooga West, Lookout Mountain	▽▽▽	$109-$179	57
43 p. 51	**Days Inn-Lookout Mountain/Tiftonia**	▽▽	$59-$85 SAVE	56
44 p. 51	**Clarion Inn**	▽▽	$79-$114 SAVE	55
45 p. 51	Fairfield Inn & Suites by Marriott Chattanooga I-24/Lookout Mountain	▽▽▽	$90-$148	56
46 p. 51	**BEST WESTERN Royal Inn**	▽▽	$75-$100 SAVE	55
47 p. 51	Red Roof Inn Chattanooga – Lookout Mountain	▽▽	Rates not provided	58
48 p. 51	Holiday Inn Express Hotel & Suites	▽▽▽	$99-$169	57
49 p. 51	Country Inn & Suites By Carlson, Chattanooga I-24 West	▽▽	$89-$169	56

Map Page	Restaurants	Diamond Rated	Cuisine	Price Range	Page
1 p. 51	Nikki's Drive-In	▽	Sandwiches	$7-$24	61
2 p. 51	Aretha Frankensteins	▽▽	Breakfast	$5-$10	59
3 p. 51	FoodWorks	▽▽	American	$8-$25	60
4 p. 51	**Japanese Restaurant Sushi Nabe**	▽▽▽	Japanese Sushi	$5-$19	61
5 p. 51	Armando's	▽	Sandwiches	$4-$8	59
6 p. 51	The Palms at Hamilton	▽▽	American	$12-$35	61
7 p. 51	Boathouse Rotisserie & Raw Bar	▽▽	Steak Seafood	$10-$28	60
8 p. 51	The Curry Pot	▽▽	Indian	$8-$15	60
9 p. 51	Rain Thai Bistro	▽▽	Thai Sushi	$8-$20	61
10 p. 51	Firebox Grill	▽	Sandwiches	$5-$10	60
11 p. 51	Back Inn Cafe'	▽▽▽	International	$14-$28	60
12 p. 51	Rembrandt's Coffee House	▽	Breads/Pastries	$7-$12	61
13 p. 51	The Blue Plate	▽▽	Comfort Food	$10-$30	60
14 p. 51	Tony's Pasta Shop and Trattoria	▽▽	Italian	$4-$15	62
15 p. 51	Sitar Indian Cuisine	▽▽	Indian	$9-$17	62
16 p. 51	Hennen's	▽▽▽	New American	$8-$32	60
17 p. 51	J. Alexander's Restaurant	▽▽▽	American	$10-$27	61
18 p. 51	**212 Market Restaurant**	▽▽▽	Continental	$12-$32	59

Map Page	Restaurants (cont'd)	Diamond Rated	Cuisine	Price Range	Page
19 p. 51	Thai Smile	▼▼	Thai	$8-$19	62
20 p. 51	The Acropolis	▼▼	Greek	$9-$27	59
21 p. 51	Bluewater Grille	▼▼	American	$9-$32	60
22 p. 51	Lupi's Pizza	▼	Pizza	$2-$20	61
23 p. 51	El Meson	▼▼	Mexican	$6-$11	60
24 p. 51	P.F. Chang's China Bistro	▼▼▼	Chinese	$8-$25	61
25 p. 51	Bonefish Grill	▼▼▼	Seafood	$14-$27	60
26 p. 51	Firebirds Wood Fired Grill	▼▼▼	American	$11-$30	60
27 p. 51	Big River Grille & Brewing Works	▼▼	American	$8-$27	60
28 p. 51	Innside Restaurant	▼	American	$4-$7	60
29 p. 51	Porter's Steakhouse	▼▼▼	American	$8-$72	61
30 p. 51	Tupelo Honey Cafe	▼▼	New Southern	$7-$23	62
31 p. 51	Public House	▼▼▼	American	$8-$26	61
32 p. 51	Seoul Restaurant	▼▼	Asian	$7-$20	62
33 p. 51	St. John's Restaurant	▼▼▼▼	New American	$27-$42	61
34 p. 51	Southern Star	▼▼	Southern American	$8-$16	62
35 p. 51	Urban Stack Burger Lounge	▼▼	Burgers	$7-$12	62
36 p. 51	Shogun of Chattanooga	▼▼	Japanese	$7-$31	62
37 p. 51	The Terminal Brewhouse	▼▼	American	$7-$14	62
38 p. 51	Alleia	▼▼▼	Traditional Italian	$15-$28	59
39 p. 51	Rib & Loin	▼	Barbecue	$6-$16	61
40 p. 51	Sweet Basil	▼▼	Thai	$6-$17	62
41 p. 51	Lupi's Pizza	▼	Pizza	$2-$20	61
42 p. 51	Ichiban Japanese Steak House & Sushi Bar	▼▼	Japanese	$9-$25	60
43 p. 51	Mt. Vernon Restaurant	▼▼	Southern	$9-$24	61
44 p. 51	Purple Daisy Picnic Cafe	▼	Sandwiches	$3-$8	61

HIXSON

Map Page	Hotels	Diamond Rated	Rate Range	Page
52 p. 51	Holiday Inn Express Hotel & Suites	▼▼▼	Rates not provided	105
53 p. 51	Hampton Inn-Hixson	▼▼▼	$114-$129	105
54 p. 51	Country Inn & Suites By Carlson, Chattanooga North at Hwy 153	▼▼	Rates not provided	105

EAST RIDGE

Map Page	Hotels	Diamond Rated	Rate Range	Page
57 p. 51	**Fairfield Inn & Suites by Marriott Chattanooga South/East Ridge**	▼▼▼	$76-$137 [SAVE]	75
58 p. 51	**BEST WESTERN PLUS Arbour Inn & Suites**	▼▼	$80-$160 [SAVE]	75
59 p. 51	Holiday Inn Express Hotel & Suites	▼▼▼	$90-$170	75

Map Page	Restaurant	Diamond Rated	Cuisine	Price Range	Page
47 p. 51	Armando's	▼	Burgers Sandwiches	$4-$9	75

(See map & index p. 51.)

BEST WESTERN HERITAGE INN   (423)899-3311

Motel
$60-$70

AAA Benefit:
Save 10% or more every day and earn 10% bonus points!

Address: 7641 Lee Hwy 37421 **Location:** I-75 exit 7B northbound; exit 7 southbound, just w. **Facility:** 100 units. 2 stories (no elevator), exterior corridors. **Terms:** check-in 4 pm, cancellation fee imposed. **Pool(s):** outdoor.

BEST WESTERN ROYAL INN   (423)821-6840

Motel
$75-$100

AAA Benefit:
Save 10% or more every day and earn 10% bonus points!

Address: 3644 Cummings Hwy 37419 **Location:** I-24 exit 174, 0.4 mi s. **Facility:** 53 units. 3 stories (no elevator), exterior corridors. **Pool(s):** outdoor. **Activities:** exercise room.

CHATTANOOGA CHOO-CHOO   (423)266-5000

Classic Historic Hotel
$119-$229

Address: 1400 Market St 37402 **Location:** I-24 exit 178 (Broad St) eastbound; exit Market St westbound, 0.5 mi n. **Facility:** This hotel is centered around an historic train terminal and rail yard. To get the best experience choose one of the rooms in the restored old railcars instead of a traditional room. 363 units. 1-5 stories, interior/exterior corridors. **Parking:** on-site (fee). **Terms:** cancellation fee imposed, resort fee. **Dining:** 3 restaurants. **Pool(s):** outdoor, heated indoor. **Activities:** hot tub, game room, limited exercise equipment. **Guest Services:** valet laundry. **Featured Amenity:** full hot breakfast.

CHATTANOOGA MARRIOTT DOWNTOWN   (423)756-0002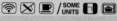

Hotel
$104-$189

AAA Benefit:
Members save 5% or more!

Address: 2 Carter Plaza 37402 **Location:** US 27 N exit 1A (Dr Martin Luther King Blvd), just e to Carter St, then just s. **Facility:** 343 units. 16 stories, interior corridors. **Parking:** on-site (fee) and valet. **Pool(s):** heated outdoor, heated indoor. **Activities:** sauna, exercise room. **Guest Services:** valet laundry, boarding pass kiosk, area transportation.

MARRIOTT
"This premier downtown hotel is within walking distance to Chattanooga's top attractions."

THE CHATTANOOGAN   (423)756-3400

Hotel
$149-$259

Address: 1201 Broad St 37402 **Location:** I-24 exit 178 (Market St), follow signs to Broad St/US 11, then 0.6 mi n. **Facility:** 199 units, some two bedrooms. 4 stories, interior corridors. **Parking:** on-site (fee) and valet. **Terms:** check-in 4 pm, cancellation fee imposed. **Amenities:** safes. **Dining:** 3 restaurants. **Pool(s):** heated indoor. **Activities:** sauna, hot tub, steamroom, spa. **Guest Services:** valet laundry, rental car service.

CLARION INN   (423)821-5500

Hotel
$79-$114

Address: 3641 Cummings Hwy 37419 **Location:** I-24 exit 174, just s. **Facility:** 91 units. 2 stories, interior corridors. **Pool(s):** outdoor. **Activities:** exercise room. **Guest Services:** valet laundry. **Featured Amenity:** continental breakfast.

COMFORT INN & SUITES   (423)822-7322

Hotel
$100-$156

Address: 3117 Parker Ln 37419 **Location:** I-24 exit 175, just s. **Facility:** 60 units. 4 stories, interior corridors. **Pool(s):** heated indoor. **Activities:** exercise room. **Guest Services:** coin laundry. **Featured Amenity:** continental breakfast.

(See map & index p. 51.)

COMFORT INN DOWNTOWN-LOOKOUT MOUNTAIN
(423)265-0077 **37**

◆◆ **Hotel** $69-$139 **Address:** 2420 Williams St 37408 **Location:** I-24 exit 178 (Market St), just s. **Facility:** 91 units. 3 stories, interior corridors. **Terms:** check-in 4 pm. **Pool(s):** outdoor. **Activities:** limited exercise equipment. **Guest Services:** coin laundry.

CALL &M ≋ BIZ ⚏ ▱ /SOME UNITS ≋ ▯ ▱

COUNTRY INN & SUITES BY CARLSON, CHATTANOOGA I-24 WEST
(423)825-6100 **49**

◆◆ **Hotel** $89-$169 **Address:** 3725 Modern Industries Blvd 37419 **Location:** I-24 exit 174, just s. **Facility:** 76 units. 3 stories, interior corridors. **Terms:** 2 night minimum stay - seasonal and/or weekends, cancellation fee imposed. **Activities:** limited exercise equipment. **Guest Services:** valet and coin laundry.

◀▶ CALL &M ≋ BIZ ⚏ ▯ ▱ /SOME UNITS ≋

COUNTRY INNS & SUITES BY CARLSON, CHATTANOOGA AT HAMILTON PLACE MALL
(423)899-2300 **5**

◆◆◆
Hotel
$119-$129

Address: 7051 McCutcheon Rd 37421 **Location:** I-75 exit 5 (Shallowford Rd), just w, then 0.5 mi n on Shallowford Village Dr. **Facility:** 82 units. 3 stories, interior corridors. **Pool(s):** heated indoor. **Activities:** recreation programs, limited exercise equipment. **Guest Services:** valet and coin laundry. **Featured Amenity: full hot breakfast.**

SAVE ✈ ◀▶ CALL &M ≋ BIZ HS ⚏ ▯ ▱ ▱

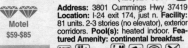

COURTYARD BY MARRIOTT CHATTANOOGA I-75
(423)499-4400 **23**

◆◆◆
Hotel
$79-$160

COURTYARD®
Marriott

AAA Benefit:
Members save 5% or more!

Address: 2210 Bams Dr 37421 **Location:** I-75 exit 5 (Shallowford Rd), 0.3 mi se. Adjacent to Hamilton Place Mall. **Facility:** 109 units. 2 stories (no elevator), interior corridors. **Pool(s):** outdoor. **Activities:** exercise room. **Guest Services:** valet and coin laundry, boarding pass kiosk.

SAVE ▯ Y CALL &M ≋ BIZ ⚏ ▱ ▱ /SOME UNITS ≋

DAYS INN CHATTANOOGA/HAMILTON PLACE
(423)664-1016 **7**

◆◆ **Hotel** $79-$109 **Address:** 2350 Shallowford Village Dr 37421 **Location:** I-75 exit 5 (Shallowford Rd), just w, then 0.3 mi n. **Facility:** 105 units. 3 stories, interior/exterior corridors. **Pool(s):** heated outdoor. **Guest Services:** valet laundry.

◀▶ CALL &M ≋ BIZ ⚏ ▱ ▯ ▱ ▱

DAYS INN-LOOKOUT MOUNTAIN/TIFTONIA
(423)821-6044 **43**

◆◆◆◆
Motel
$59-$85

Address: 3801 Cummings Hwy 37419 **Location:** I-24 exit 174, just n. **Facility:** 81 units. 2-3 stories (no elevator), exterior corridors. **Pool(s):** heated indoor. **Featured Amenity:** continental breakfast.

SAVE ◀▶ CALL &M ≋ ⚏ ✕ ▯ ▱ ▱ /SOME UNITS ≋

DAYS INN RIVERGATE
(423)266-7331 **31**

◆◆ **Motel** $69-$125 **Address:** 901 Carter St 37402 **Location:** US 27 exit 1A (Dr Martin Luther King Blvd), just e. **Facility:** 140 units. 3 stories, exterior corridors. **Amenities:** safes. **Pool(s):** outdoor. **Activities:** limited exercise equipment. **Guest Services:** coin laundry.

▯ Y ≋ HS ⚏ ▯ ▱ ▱

DOUBLETREE BY HILTON HOTEL CHATTANOOGA DOWNTOWN
(423)756-5150 **25**

◆◆◆ **Hotel** $149-$299 **Address:** 407 Chestnut St 37402 **Location:** US 27 exit 1C (4th St), just s. **Facility:** 186 units, some two bedrooms. 13 stories, interior corridors. **Parking:** on-site (fee) and valet. **Terms:** 1-7 night minimum stay, cancellation fee imposed. **Amenities:** safes. **Pool(s):** heated outdoor. **Activities:** exercise room. **Guest Services:** valet laundry.

AAA Benefit:
Members save 5% or more!

ECO ⬅ ▯ ⬆ Y CALL &M ≋ BIZ HS ⚏ ✕ ▯ ▱ ▱

ECONO LODGE-HAMILTON MALL AREA (423)499-9550 **1**

◆◆ **Motel** $55 **Address:** 7421 Bonny Oaks Dr 37421 **Location:** I-75 exit 7B northbound; exit 7 southbound, just w. **Facility:** 58 units. 2 stories (no elevator), exterior corridors. **Guest Services:** coin laundry. ◀▶ ≋ ⚏ ▱ ▱ /SOME UNITS ≋

ECONO LODGE LOOKOUT MOUNTAIN, CHATTANOOGA
(423)821-9000 **41**

◆◆ **Hotel.** Rates not provided. **Address:** 150 Brown Ferry Rd 37419 **Location:** I-24 exit 175, just s. **Facility:** 34 units. 3 stories, interior corridors. **Pool(s):** outdoor.

◀▶ ≋ HS ⚏ ▯ ▱ ▱

EMBASSY SUITES BY HILTON CHATTANOOGA-HAMILTON PLACE
(423)602-5100 **18**

◆◆◆ **Hotel** $119-$229 **Address:** 2321 Lifestyle Way 37421 **Location:** I-75 exit 5 (Shallowford Rd), just e. **Facility:** 203 units, some two bedrooms. 7 stories, interior corridors. **Terms:** 1-7 night minimum stay, cancellation fee imposed. **Amenities:** safes. **Pool(s):** indoor. **Activities:** exercise room. **Guest Services:** valet and coin laundry.

AAA Benefit:
Members save 5% or more!

▯ ⬆ Y CALL &M ≋ BIZ HS ⚏ ✕ ▯ ▱ ▱

EXTENDED STAY AMERICA-CHATTANOOGA-AIRPORT
(423)892-1315 **30**

◆ **Extended Stay Hotel.** Rates not provided. **Address:** 6240 Airpark Dr 37421 **Location:** SR 153 exit 1 (Lee Hwy), 0.3 mi s to Vance Rd, then just w to cul-de-sac. **Facility:** 120 efficiencies. 3 stories (no elevator), exterior corridors. **Guest Services:** coin laundry.
CALL &M ≋ ⚏ ▯ ▱ ▱ /SOME UNITS ≋

FAIRFIELD INN & SUITES BY MARRIOTT CHATTANOOGA I-24/LOOKOUT MOUNTAIN
(423)664-4222 **45**

◆◆◆ **Hotel** $90-$148 **Address:** 40 Starview Ln 37419 **Location:** I-24 exit 174, just s. **Facility:** 90 units. 4 stories, interior corridors. **Pool(s):** heated indoor. **Activities:** exercise room. **Guest Services:** valet and coin laundry.

AAA Benefit:
Members save 5% or more!

ECO ◀▶ CALL &M ≋ BIZ HS ⚏ ✕ ▯ ▱ ▱

(See map & index p. 51.)

FAIRFIELD INN & SUITES BY MARRIOTT HAMILTON PLACE
(423)499-3800

Hotel
$83-$137

AAA Benefit: Members save 5% or more!

Address: 2345 Shallowford Village Dr 37421 **Location:** I-75 exit 5 (Shallowford Rd), just w to Shallowford Village Dr, then just n. **Facility:** 108 units. 5 stories, interior corridors. **Amenities:** safes. **Pool(s):** outdoor. **Activities:** exercise room. **Guest Services:** valet and coin laundry.

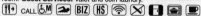

HAMPTON INN & SUITES CHATTANOOGA/DOWNTOWN
(423)693-0500

▼▲▼▲▼ **Hotel** $129-$209 **Address:** 400 Chestnut St 37402 **Location:** US 27 exit 1C (4th St), just e. **Facility:** 134 units. 5 stories, interior corridors. **Parking:** on-site (fee). **Terms:** check-in 4 pm, 1-7 night minimum stay, cancellation fee imposed. **Amenities:** safes. **Pool(s):** heated outdoor, heated indoor. **Activities:** exercise room. **Guest Services:** valet and coin laundry.

AAA Benefit: Members save up to 10%!

HAMPTON INN & SUITES CHATTANOOGA-HAMILTON PLACE
(423)602-7840

▼▲▼▲▼ **Hotel** $89-$169 **Address:** 2014 Hamilton Place Blvd 37421 **Location:** I-75 exit 5 (Shallowford Rd), just w, then 1 mi s; exit 4A northbound. **Facility:** 134 units. 6 stories, interior corridors. **Terms:** 1-7 night minimum stay, cancellation fee imposed. **Pool(s):** heated indoor. **Activities:** exercise room. **Guest Services:** valet and coin laundry.

AAA Benefit: Members save up to 10%!

HAMPTON INN CHATTANOOGA AIRPORT I-75
(423)855-0095

Hotel
$74-$99

AAA Benefit: Members save up to 10%!

Address: 7013 Shallowford Rd 37421 **Location:** I-75 exit 5 (Shallowford Rd), just w. **Facility:** 167 units. 2 stories, interior/exterior corridors. **Terms:** 1-7 night minimum stay, cancellation fee imposed. **Pool(s):** outdoor. **Activities:** exercise room. **Guest Services:** valet and coin laundry, area transportation.

HAMPTON INN CHATTANOOGA WEST, LOOKOUT MOUNTAIN
(423)602-5350

▼▲▼▲▼ **Hotel** $109-$179 **Address:** 74 Starview Ln 37419 **Location:** I-24 exit 174, just s. **Facility:** 94 stories, interior corridors. **Terms:** 1-7 night minimum stay, cancellation fee imposed. **Pool(s):** outdoor, heated indoor. **Activities:** exercise room. **Guest Services:** valet and coin laundry.

AAA Benefit: Members save up to 10%!

HILTON GARDEN INN CHATTANOOGA
(423)308-9000

▼▲▼▲▼ **Hotel** $139-$229 **Address:** 311 Chestnut St 37402 **Location:** US 27 exit 1C (4th St). **Facility:** 94 units. 6 stories, interior corridors. **Parking:** on-site (fee). **Terms:** 1-7 night minimum stay, cancellation fee imposed. **Amenities:** safes. **Pool(s):** heated indoor. **Activities:** hot tub, exercise room. **Guest Services:** valet and coin laundry.

AAA Benefit: Members save up to 10%!

HILTON GARDEN INN CHATTANOOGA HAMILTON PLACE
(423)308-4400

▼▲▼▲▼ **Hotel** $89-$149 **Address:** 2343 Shallowford Village Dr 37421 **Location:** I-75 exit 5 (Shallowford Rd), just w to Shallowford Village Dr, then just n. **Facility:** 112 units. 5 stories, interior corridors. **Terms:** 1-7 night minimum stay, cancellation fee imposed. **Pool(s):** heated indoor. **Activities:** exercise room. **Guest Services:** valet and coin laundry.

AAA Benefit: Members save up to 10%!

HOLIDAY INN CHATTANOOGA AT HAMILTON PLACE
423)485-1185

Hotel
Rates not provided

Address: 2232 Center St 37421 **Location:** I-75 exit 5 (Shallowford Rd), just w to Amin Dr, then just s. **Facility:** 137 units. 7 stories, interior corridors. **Terms:** check-in 4 pm. **Pool(s):** heated indoor. **Activities:** exercise room. **Guest Services:** valet and coin laundry.

HOLIDAY INN EXPRESS HOTEL & SUITES
(423)424-0125 **48**

▼▲▼▲▼ **Hotel** $99-$169 **Address:** 3710 Modern Industries Pkwy 37419 **Location:** I-24 exit 174, just e on US 41, then just sw on US 11. **Facility:** 92 units. 5 stories, interior corridors. **Terms:** cancellation fee imposed. **Pool(s):** heated indoor. **Activities:** limited exercise equipment. **Guest Services:** valet and coin laundry.

HOLIDAY INN EXPRESS HOTEL & SUITES
423/664-4321 **28**

▼▲▼▲▼ **Hotel.** Rates not provided. **Address:** 440 W Martin Luther King Blvd 37402 **Location:** US 27 exit 1A (Dr Martin Luther King Blvd), just w. **Facility:** 92 units. 5 stories, interior corridors. **Parking:** on-site (fee). **Pool(s):** heated indoor. **Activities:** limited exercise equipment. **Guest Services:** valet and coin laundry.

HOMEWOOD SUITES BY HILTON
(423)510-8020 **15**

▼▲▼▲▼ **Extended Stay Hotel** $129-$169 **Address:** 2250 Center St 37421 **Location:** I-75 exit 5 (Shallowford Rd), 0.5 mi w. **Facility:** 76 kitchen units, some two bedrooms. 4 stories, interior corridors. **Terms:** 1-7 night minimum stay, cancellation fee imposed. **Pool(s):** outdoor. **Activities:** exercise room. **Guest Services:** valet and coin laundry.

AAA Benefit: Members save up to 10%!

(See map & index p. 51.)

LA QUINTA INN AND SUITES   (423)551-4100 **38**

Hotel
$90-$213

Address: 311 Browns Ferry Rd 37419 **Location:** I-24 exit 175, just n. **Facility:** 49 units. 4 stories, interior corridors. **Pool(s):** outdoor. **Activities:** exercise room. **Guest Services:** coin laundry. **Featured Amenity: continental breakfast.**

SAVE ![] CALL ![] ![] ![] BIZ ![] ![] ![] ![] ![] ![] / SOME UNITS ![]

LA QUINTA INN CHATTANOOGA   (423)265-3151 **36**

Hotel $64-$163 **Address:** 100 W 21st St 37408 **Location:** I-24 exit 178 (Broad St) eastbound; exit Market St westbound, US 11 to Lookout Mountain, w to 20th St, w to Williams St, then w. Located in a commercial area. **Facility:** 103 units. 5 stories, interior corridors. **Pool(s):** outdoor. **Activities:** exercise room. **Guest Services:** coin laundry.

CALL ![] ![] BIZ ![] ![] ![] ![] / SOME UNITS ![] ![]

LA QUINTA INN CHATTANOOGA/HAMILTON PLACE   (423)855-0011 **13**

Motel $64-$130 **Address:** 7015 Shallowford Rd 37421 **Location:** I-75 exit 5 (Shallowford Rd), just w. **Facility:** 132 units. 2 stories (no elevator), exterior corridors. **Pool(s):** outdoor.

![] CALL ![] ![] ![] ![] / SOME UNITS ![] ![] ![]

MAINSTAY SUITES-CHATTANOOGA   (423)485-9424 **16**

Extended Stay Hotel $99-$129 **Address:** 7030 Amin Dr 37421 **Location:** I-75 exit 5 (Shallowford Rd), just w, then s. **Facility:** 77 efficiencies. 3 stories, interior corridors. **Amenities:** safes. **Activities:** exercise room. **Guest Services:** valet and coin laundry.

![] CALL ![] BIZ ![] ![] ![] ![] / SOME UNITS ![]

THE MAYOR'S MANSION INN   423/265-5000 **27**

Historic Bed & Breakfast
$129-$299

Address: 801 Vine St 37403 **Location:** Jct US 11 and Palmetto St, just n on Palmetto St to Vine St. **Facility:** Formerly a mayor's residence, the historic 1889 mansion is in the Fort Wood neighborhood, adjacent to the University of Tennessee at Chattanooga. 11 units. 3 stories (no elevator), interior corridors. **Terms:** check-in 4 pm, 2 night minimum stay - seasonal and/or weekends, 8 day cancellation notice-fee imposed, resort fee. **Activities:** massage. **Featured Amenity: full hot breakfast.**

SAVE ![] ![] ![] ![] / SOME UNITS ![]

QUALITY INN   (423)821-1499 **39**

Motel
$66-$150

Address: 3109 Parker Ln 37419 **Location:** I-24 exit 175, just s. **Facility:** 58 units. 2 stories (no elevator), exterior corridors. **Pool(s):** outdoor. **Guest Services:** coin laundry. **Featured Amenity: continental breakfast.**

SAVE ![] ![] BIZ ![] ![] ![] ![] / SOME UNITS ![]

QUALITY SUITES   (423)892-1500 **20**

Motel
$70-$110

Address: 7324 Shallowford Rd 37421 **Location:** I-75 exit 5 (Shallowford Rd), just e. **Facility:** 62 units. 2 stories (no elevator), exterior corridors. **Pool(s):** heated indoor. **Activities:** exercise room. **Guest Services:** valet and coin laundry. **Featured Amenity: continental breakfast.**

SAVE ![] ![] ![] BIZ ![] ![] ![] ![] ![] / SOME UNITS ![]

THE READ HOUSE HISTORIC INN & SUITES   (423)266-4121 **29**

Classic Historic Hotel
$109-$219

Address: 827 Broad St 37402 **Location:** US 27 exit 1A, just e; downtown. **Facility:** This classic property has been restored to its original elegance. The room décor leans to contemporary, yet the lobby maintains the ornate feel of the Gilded Age. 241 units. 6-10 stories, interior corridors. **Parking:** valet only. **Terms:** cancellation fee imposed. **Amenities:** video games. **Dining:** Porter's Steakhouse, see separate listing. **Pool(s):** heated indoor. **Activities:** exercise room. **Guest Services:** valet laundry.

SAVE ![] ![] ![] CALL ![] ![] BIZ ![] ![] ![] ![] ![] / SOME UNITS ![] ![]

RED ROOF INN CHATTANOOGA AIRPORT   (423)899-0143 **14**

Motel
$39-$99

Address: 7014 Shallowford Rd 37421 **Location:** I-75 exit 5 (Shallowford Rd), just w. **Facility:** 109 units. 2 stories (no elevator), exterior corridors.

SAVE ![] ![] / SOME UNITS ![] ![] ![] ![]

RED ROOF INN CHATTANOOGA – LOOKOUT MOUNTAIN   423/821-7162 **47**

Motel. Rates not provided. **Address:** 30 Birmingham Hwy 37419 **Location:** I-24 exit 174, just s. **Facility:** 75 units. 2 stories (no elevator), interior/exterior corridors. **Pool(s):** heated indoor. **Guest Services:** valet and coin laundry.

![] ![] ![] ![] ![] ![] / SOME UNITS ![]

RESIDENCE INN BY MARRIOTT CHATTANOOGA NEAR HAMILTON PLACE   (423)468-7700 **3**

Extended Stay Hotel $119-$249 **Address:** 2340 Center St 37421 **Location:** I-75 exit 5 (Shallowford Rd), 0.5 mi w to Lee Hwy, then just n. **Facility:** 109 units, some two bedrooms, efficiencies and kitchens. 5 stories, interior corridors. **Pool(s):** heated indoor. **Activities:** hot tub, exercise room. **Guest Services:** complimentary and valet laundry.

AAA Benefit: Members save 5% or more!

![] ![] CALL ![] ![] ![] ![] ![] ![] ![] ![] / SOME UNITS ![]

(See map & index p. 51.)

SLEEP INN
(423)894-5333 **8**

Hotel
$67-$89

Address: 2351 Shallowford Village Dr 37421 **Location:** I-75 exit 5 (Shallowford Rd), just w, then just e. **Facility:** 57 units. 3 stories, interior corridors. *Bath:* shower only. **Amenities:** safes. **Guest Services:** valet laundry.

SPRINGHILL SUITES BY MARRIOTT CHATTANOOGA DOWNTOWN/CAMERON HARBOR
(423)834-9300 **21**

Contemporary Hotel
$118-$194

AAA Benefit: Members save 5% or more!

Address: 495 Riverfront Pkwy 37402 **Location:** Waterfront. US 27 N exit 1A (Dr Martin Luther King Blvd), 0.5 mi w, then 0.3 mi n. **Facility:** 116 units. 5 stories, interior corridors. **Parking:** on-site (fee). **Pool(s):** heated indoor. **Activities:** hot tub, bicycles, exercise room. **Guest Services:** valet and coin laundry.

STAYBRIDGE SUITES
(423)267-0900 **34**

Extended Stay Hotel $129-$199 **Address:** 1300 Carter St 37402 **Location:** US 27 N exit 1A (Dr Martin Luther King Blvd), just e to Carter St, then 0.3 mi s. **Facility:** 124 efficiencies, some two bedrooms. 5 stories, interior corridors. **Parking:** on-site (fee). **Pool(s):** heated indoor. **Activities:** hot tub, exercise room. **Guest Services:** complimentary and valet laundry.

STAYBRIDGE SUITES-HAMILTON PLACE
(423)826-2700 **12**

Extended Stay Hotel $130-$260 **Address:** 7015 Shallowford Rd 37421 **Location:** I-75 exit 5 (Shallowford Rd), just w. **Facility:** 88 kitchen units, some two bedrooms. 6 stories, interior corridors. **Terms:** 2 night minimum stay - seasonal and/or weekends, cancellation fee imposed. **Pool(s):** heated indoor. **Activities:** hot tub, exercise room. **Guest Services:** complimentary and valet laundry.

SUPER 8
(423)490-8560 **6**

Hotel $50-$81 **Address:** 7024 McCutcheon Rd 37421 **Location:** I-75 exit 5 (Shallowford Rd), just w, then 0.3 mi n on Shallowford Village Dr. **Facility:** 51 units. 2 stories (no elevator), interior corridors. **Pool(s):** heated indoor.

TOWNEPLACE SUITES BY MARRIOTT CHATTANOOGA NEAR HAMILTON PLACE
(423)834-9444 **4**

Extended Stay Hotel $83-$125 **Address:** 7010 McCutcheon Rd 37421 **Location:** I-75 exit 5 (Shallowford Rd), 0.5 mi w to Lee Hwy, then just n. **Facility:** 87 efficiencies. 4 stories, interior corridors. **Pool(s):** heated indoor. **Activities:** exercise room. **Guest Services:** valet and coin laundry.

AAA Benefit: Members save 5% or more!

WINGATE BY WYNDHAM
(423)893-7400 **19**

Hotel
$129-$154

Address: 7312 Shallowford Rd 37421 **Location:** I-75 exit 5 (Shallowford Rd), just e. **Facility:** 82 units. 5 stories, interior corridors. **Amenities:** safes. **Activities:** hot tub, exercise room. **Guest Services:** valet and coin laundry. **Featured Amenity:** full hot breakfast.

HOLIDAY INN & SUITES-DOWNTOWN/RIVER FRONT
423/362-8555

[fyi] Not evaluated. **Address:** 434 Chestnut St 37402 **Location:** US 27 exit 1C (4th St), just s. Facilities, services, and décor characterize a mid-scale property.

WHERE TO EAT

212 MARKET RESTAURANT
423/265-1212 **18**

Continental Casual Dining
$12-$32

AAA Inspector Notes: Across from the Tennessee Aquarium, this green eatery is noteworthy for its focus on local ingredients. The creative cuisine features a range of international styles with some Southern influences. The menus change seasonally with daily specials. **Features:** full bar, patio dining, early bird specials, Sunday brunch, happy hour. **Address:** 212 Market St 37402 **Location:** US 27 N exit 1C (4th St), 0.3 mi e to Market St, then just n. **Parking:** on-site and street.

THE ACROPOLIS
423/899-5341 **20**

Greek. Casual Dining. $9-$27 **AAA Inspector Notes:** Guests can indulge in all their favorite Greek dishes at this casual spot, as well as some irresistible pastries. **Features:** full bar, patio dining, Sunday brunch, happy hour. **Address:** 2213 Hamilton Place Blvd 37421 **Location:** I-75 exit 5 (Shallowford Rd), just e, then just s.

ALLEIA
423/305-6990 **38**

Traditional Italian. Fine Dining. $15-$28 **AAA Inspector Notes:** The abundance of the season is precisely presented at this trendy hot spot. The contemporary ambiance is outdone only by the outstanding food prepared by the acclaimed chef and owner. The butternut squash ravioli, with fresh sage and brown butter, will melt in your mouth. All main courses are simply grilled, like the wagyu beef rib steak served with porcini vinaigrette. Individual gourmet pizzas are hand made and baked in the masonry oven. **Features:** full bar, patio dining, happy hour. **Reservations:** suggested. **Address:** 25 E Main St 37402 **Location:** Just s of Market St; downtown. **Parking:** valet and street only.

ARETHA FRANKENSTEINS
423/265-7685 **2**

Breakfast. Casual Dining. $5-$10 **AAA Inspector Notes:** Breakfast is the thing here and is served all day with blueberry pancakes being a must-do dish. Omelets are quite popular also. Lunch is offered and features quesadillas and burritos as well as sandwiches. Beers are available on tap and by the bottle. Be prepared to wait if dining during breakfast hours. **Features:** beer only, patio dining. **Address:** 518 Tremont St 37405 **Location:** Jct Frazier St, 0.5 mi e to Tremont St, 0.5 mi n; on north shore. **Parking:** on-site and street.

ARMANDO'S
423/855-0772 **5**

Sandwiches. Quick Serve. $4-$8 **AAA Inspector Notes:** Hamburgers (a Chattanooga favorite for years), BLTs, bison burgers, hot dogs, veggie burgers, fried bologna sandwiches and three types of grilled cheese sandwiches are just the tip of the iceberg at this place. You can also enjoy chicken finger and hamburger steak dinners here. Fried pickles are a great way to start, and a slice of pie is a fine way to finish. **Address:** 7032 Lee Hwy 37421 **Location:** I-75 exit 5 (Shallowford Rd), 0.5 mi w to Lee Hwy, then just n.

(See map & index p. 51.)

BACK INN CAFE'   423/265-5033   (11)
▼▼ International. Fine Dining. $14-$28 **AAA Inspector Notes:** *Historic.* A historic mansion houses this restaurant offering indoor and outdoor terrace seating with a fantastic view of the river. Thanks to the freshest seasonal foods available, a fine dining experience awaits you. **Features:** full bar, patio dining. **Reservations:** suggested. **Address:** 412 E 2nd St 37403 **Location:** 1 mi e on 4th St, just n on High St. (D)

BIG RIVER GRILLE & BREWING WORKS   423/553-7723   (27)
▼▼ American. Casual Dining. $8-$27 **AAA Inspector Notes:** A wide variety of classic American dishes such as grilled steaks and seafood are presented at this casual spot with earnest servers. Also offered in the comfortably elegant ambience are many appetizers, salads, pasta, pizza, burgers and sandwiches. A hand-crafted beer selection is a specialty of the house and includes seasonal offerings. **Features:** full bar, patio dining, Sunday brunch, happy hour. **Address:** 2020 Hamilton Place Blvd 37421 **Location:** I-75 exit 4, just e. (L)(D) CALL ⓖⓂ

THE BLUE PLATE   423/648-6767   (13)
▼▼ Comfort Food. Casual Dining. $10-$30 **AAA Inspector Notes:** The name says it all at this casual, family-friendly place where you'll find familiar dishes like meatloaf, fried chicken and burgers, all made with fresh, local ingredients. Breakfast here is very popular. The great location by the riverfront is close to all of the downtown attractions. **Features:** full bar, patio dining. **Address:** 191 Chestnut St, Unit B 37402 **Location:** Downtown; at Riverfront Pkwy. **Parking:** street only. (B)(L)(D) CALL ⓖⓂ

BLUEWATER GRILLE   423/266-4200   (21)
▼▼ American. Casual Dining. $9-$32 **AAA Inspector Notes:** Located across from the aquarium, the sea and water theme is carried out here both in blown-glass accessories and fresh seafood offerings. The eatery is casual with street side patio seating available, weather permitting. The large menu offers a huge selection with something for every appetite. **Features:** full bar, patio dining, Sunday brunch, happy hour. **Address:** 224 Broad St 37402 **Location:** Just n of 3rd Ave; downtown. **Parking:** on-site (fee).
(L)(D) CALL ⓖⓂ

BOATHOUSE ROTISSERIE & RAW BAR   423/622-0122   (7)
▼▼ Steak Seafood. Casual Dining. $10-$28 **AAA Inspector Notes:** Guests can check out the deck, settle back and enjoy the outstanding view of the Tennessee River while dining on raw oysters, grilled shrimp with island salad or smoked rib-eye. **Features:** full bar, patio dining, happy hour. **Address:** 1459 Riverside Dr 37406 **Location:** US 27 exit 1C (4th St), 0.5 mi n to Riverside Pkwy (which becomes Riverside Dr), then 1.7 mi e. (L)(D)

BONEFISH GRILL   423/892-3175   (25)
▼▼▼ Seafood. Fine Dining. $14-$27 **AAA Inspector Notes:** Fish is the house specialty, and the menu and nightly specials offer a variety of choices. Well-prepared food is cooked to perfection. Service is casual in nature, and the staff is skilled and attentive. **Features:** full bar. **Address:** 2115 Gunbarrel Rd 37421 **Location:** I-75 exit 4, just e to Gunbarrel Rd, then just n. (D) (LATE) CALL ⓖⓂ

THE CHOP HOUSE   423/892-1222
▼▼ Steak Seafood. Casual Dining. $7-$28 **AAA Inspector Notes:** Friendly servers hustle amid tables with preparations of quality aged meats, fresh seafood, chicken, lamb, pork and pasta. The restaurant is a popular spot for casually upscale dining. **Features:** full bar. **Address:** 2011 Gunbarrel Rd 37421 **Location:** I-75 exit 5 (Shallowford Rd), 0.5 mi to Gunbarrel Rd, then 0.5 mi s.
(L)(D)

THE CURRY POT   423/648-5069   (8)
▼▼ Indian. Casual Dining. $8-$15 **AAA Inspector Notes:** Goat, beef and lamb curry are specialties at this casual spot featuring simple service and atmosphere. Vegan and vegetarian options are offered along with both a lunch and dinner buffet. Free Wi-Fi is available. **Features:** beer & wine. **Address:** 6940 Lee Hwy 37421 **Location:** I-75 exit 5 (Shallowford Rd), 0.5 mi w to Lee Hwy, then just s. (L)(D)

EL MESON   423/894-8726   (23)
▼▼▼ Mexican. Casual Dining. $6-$11 **AAA Inspector Notes:** Chimichangas loaded with juicy fried meats and sizzling fajitas stuffed with veggies are sure to add a bit of spice to the dinner plans at this Mexican restaurant. **Features:** full bar, Sunday brunch, happy hour. **Address:** 2204 Hamilton Place Blvd 37421 **Location:** I-75 exit 5 (Shallowford Rd), 0.5 mi se; adjacent to Hamilton Place Mall.
(L)(D)

FIREBIRDS WOOD FIRED GRILL   423/308-1090   (26)
▼▼▼ American. Casual Dining. $11-$30 **AAA Inspector Notes:** The restaurant re-creates the atmosphere of a mountain lodge. Hand-cut steaks and seafood dominate the menu, which also lists a few pork and chicken entrees, as well as elk tenderloin medallions and buffalo meatloaf. The kitchen uses wood grilling, and pizzas bake in a wood-burning oven. Flavorful food, enhanced presentations and a skilled, knowledgeable and attentive staff, together with distinctive physical elements, make this place appealing. **Reservations:** suggested. **Address:** 2107 Gunbarrel Rd, Suite 101 37421 **Location:** I-75 exit 5 (Shallowford Rd), 0.4 mi e, then 0.4 mi s. (L)(D)

FIREBOX GRILL   423/899-7733   (10)
▼ Sandwiches. Quick Serve. $5-$10 **AAA Inspector Notes:** Sandwiches, sacks and salads are all popular items at this eatery. A great selection of these deli items includes tuna, turkey, roast beef, ham and the Reuben. Pita sacks, such as the Philly steak and grilled chicken, also hit the spot. The hamburgers are big sellers; the jalapeño-cheddar and mushroom versions are nice choices. Don't forget the shakes! **Address:** 7025 Shallowford Rd 37421 **Location:** I-75 exit 5 (Shallowford Rd), just w. (L)(D)

FOODWORKS   423/752-7487   (3)
▼▼ American. Casual Dining. $8-$25 **AAA Inspector Notes:** *Historic.* Mixed, casual fare is offered in this converted, historic knitting mill. On the menu you'll find steaks; a popular shrimp and grits dish; chicken piccata; seafood along the lines of salmon, crab and mahi; and pasta dishes such as lasagna and roasted red pepper Alfredo. There's also the ubiquitous burger. Beer lovers will find a wide variety of brews. During my visit it was apparent this is a very popular gathering spot. **Features:** full bar, patio dining, early bird specials, Sunday brunch, happy hour. **Address:** 205 Manufacturers Rd, Suite C 37421 **Location:** Jct Cherokee St, just w; in Knitting Mill. (L)(D) CALL ⓖⓂ

HENNEN'S   423/634-5160   (16)
▼▼▼ New American. Fine Dining. $8-$32 **AAA Inspector Notes:** With a cool, casual ambience, this innovative restaurant offers delightful, flavorful fare served by enthusiastic and professional staffers. Try the stone-seared salmon served with creamy spinach risotto, or the rack of lamb with herbed fingerling potatoes. The specialties of the house are the hand-cut Angus steaks; from that selection the most requested is the Delmonico. Whatever you choose, you won't be disappointed and the relaxing atmosphere invites you to linger. **Features:** full bar, patio dining, happy hour. **Reservations:** suggested. **Address:** 193 Chestnut St 37401 **Location:** Between Riverfront Pkwy and W Aquarium Way; downtown. **Parking:** on-site and street. (L)(D) CALL ⓖⓂ

ICHIBAN JAPANESE STEAK HOUSE & SUSHI BAR
423/892-0404   (42)
▼▼ Japanese. Casual Dining. $9-$25 **AAA Inspector Notes:** This eatery has been a long-time favorite with locals. Although some prefer ordering take-out, many eat in for the great show the talented chefs put on. Seafood and steaks are prepared hibachi-style and there is a full sushi bar. **Features:** full bar. **Address:** 5621 Brainerd Rd 37411 **Location:** I-24 exit 184, 1 mi ne on Moore Rd, then just se. (L)(D)

INNSIDE RESTAURANT   423/266-7687   (28)
▼ American. Casual Dining. $4-$7 **AAA Inspector Notes:** This downtown Chattanooga "greasy spoon" is quite popular with the local breakfast and lunch crowd. Daily vegetable plates come with one, three or four veggies, accompanied by chicken tenders or a hamburger steak if you so desire. The hamburgers are big sellers, as are sandwiches like tuna, turkey and grilled cheese. **Address:** 800 Chestnut St 37402 **Location:** US 27 exit 1A, just e. **Parking:** street only. (B)(L)

(See map & index p. 51.)

J. ALEXANDER'S RESTAURANT
423/855-5559 (17)

▼▼▼▼ American. Casual Dining. $10-$27 **AAA Inspector Notes:** The busy and casual restaurant prepares classic fare—including steak, grilled fish and prime rib—in the open kitchen. The dessert menu is excellent. **Features:** full bar, patio dining, Sunday brunch. **Address:** 2215 Hamilton Place Blvd 37421 **Location:** I-75 exit 5 (Shallowford Rd), just e to Hamilton Place Blvd, then just s.

L D CALL 💳M

JAPANESE RESTAURANT SUSHI NABE
423/634-0171 (4)

▼▼▼▼
Japanese
Sushi
Casual Dining
$5-$19

AAA Inspector Notes: This popular restaurant near the waterfront serves up ample portions of traditional Japanese dishes such as the flavorful chicken teriyaki but sushi reigns supreme here. The impressive sushi bar offers a wide range of market fresh fish and creative, expertly crafted rolls. **Features:** full bar, patio dining, happy hour. **Reservations:** suggested. **Address:** 110 River St 37405 **Location:** On north shore; in Coolidge Park. **Parking:** on-site (fee). L D

LUPI'S PIZZA
423/266-5874 (22)

▼ Pizza. Quick Serve. $2-$20 **AAA Inspector Notes:** This place offers a multitude of pizza toppings, including pesto, artichoke hearts, avocado, spicy chicken, roasted garlic, pineapple and smoked ham. Also on the menu you'll find calzones, bruschetta and lasagna. Fresh and local ingredients are used whenever possible. And beer lovers will enjoy the great selection of brews. Be sure to save room for a cookie or brownie. **Features:** beer & wine. **Address:** 406 Broad St, Suite A 37403 **Location:** US 27 exit 1C (4th St), just e; downtown. **Parking:** street only. L D

LUPI'S PIZZA
423/855-4104 (41)

▼ Pizza. Quick Serve. $2-$20 **AAA Inspector Notes:** Create your own combination pizza from a multitude of toppings. Some of these include pesto, artichoke hearts, avocado, spicy chicken, roasted garlic, pineapple and smoked ham. In addition to pizza you'll find calzones, bruschetta and lasagna on the menu. Fresh, local ingredients are used whenever possible. Be sure to save room for a cookie or brownie. Also, a great beer selection awaits you. **Features:** beer & wine, patio dining. **Address:** 1414 Jenkin's Rd 37421 **Location:** I-75 exit 3, 2 mi e. L D CALL 💳M

MT. VERNON RESTAURANT
423/266-6591 (43)

▼▼ Southern. Casual Dining. $9-$24 **AAA Inspector Notes:** Located near Ruby Falls, this eatery resembles a cozy living room with wooden tables and chairs and serves down-home Southern favorites. Try the crispy fried chicken, homemade turkey dressing and boneless rib-eye. The blueberry cheese pie is a can't-miss for dessert. The restaurant has been in the same family since the mid-50s. **Features:** full bar, happy hour. **Address:** 3535 Broad St 37409 **Location:** I-24 exit 178 (Market St), 2.5 mi e; at foot of Lookout Mountain. L D

NIKKI'S DRIVE-IN
423/265-9015 (1)

▼ Sandwiches. Casual Dining. $7-$24 **AAA Inspector Notes:** In continuous operation since 1941, this casual, busy diner has not changed its menu in more than 20 years. Along with favorites such as lightly breaded shrimp and huge, juicy burgers, the onion rings will be some of the best you've ever tasted. Want to hear some tunes? Drop a quarter in your table's mini jukebox. **Features:** beer only. **Address:** 899 Cherokee Blvd 37405 **Location:** Market St to Cherokee Blvd, n to jct US 27. B L D

THE PALMS AT HAMILTON
423/499-5055 (6)

▼▼ American. Casual Dining. $12-$35 **AAA Inspector Notes:** Eat, drink and be merry at The Palms. The main dining area is the Coconut Room, which also has a piano bar. You can also dine in the lounge or on the patio, which offers smoking and non-smoking areas. Entrées include 100% USDA Certified Angus beef, ahi tuna, Alaskan king crab legs and chicken Parmesan. The flaming chocolate fondue is a great finish. **Features:** full bar, patio dining, happy hour. **Address:** 6925 Shallowford Rd 37421 **Location:** I-75 exit 5 (Shallowford Rd), 0.3 mi w; in Hamilton Place. D CALL 💳M ✎

P.F. CHANG'S CHINA BISTRO
423/242-0045 (24)

▼▼▼ Chinese. Fine Dining. $8-$25 **AAA Inspector Notes:** Trendy, upscale decor provides a pleasant backdrop for New Age Chinese dining. Appetizers, soups and salads are a meal by themselves. Vegetarian plates and sides, noodles, chow meins, chicken and meat dishes are created from exotic, fresh ingredients. **Features:** full bar. **Address:** 2110 Hamilton Place Blvd 37421 **Location:** I-75 exit 5 (Shallowford Rd), just e, then 0.3 mi s; opposite Hamilton Place Mall. L D

PORTER'S STEAKHOUSE
423/643-1240 (29)

▼▼▼ American. Fine Dining. $8-$72 **AAA Inspector Notes:** This fine dining Chicago-style restaurant serves only USDA certified Prime or Black Angus beef. Pepperloin is a signature dish on a menu that also lists chops and seafood. **Features:** full bar. **Reservations:** suggested. **Address:** 827 Broad St 37402 **Location:** US 27 exit 1A (Dr Martin Luther King Blvd), just e; in The Read House Historic Inn & Suites. **Parking:** valet and street only.

B L D CALL 💳M

PUBLIC HOUSE
423/266-3366 (31)

▼▼▼ American. Casual Dining. $8-$26 **AAA Inspector Notes:** This downtown eatery offers a blend of stylish decor, high-quality food and expert service with a relaxed and comfortable atmosphere. The ever-changing menu of small plates, salads, sandwiches and entrees features local produce and market-fresh fish, as well as many creative interpretations of traditional comfort foods. **Features:** full bar, patio dining, happy hour. **Reservations:** suggested. **Address:** 1110 Market St, Unit 101 37402 **Location:** At Warehouse Row; center. **Parking:** on-site and street. L D CALL 💳M

PURPLE DAISY PICNIC CAFE
423/822-6477 (44)

▼ Sandwiches. Casual Dining. $3-$8 **AAA Inspector Notes:** Soups, salads, sandwiches and desserts are served at this cafe at the foot of Lookout Mountain. Fast and friendly servers dish up the restaurant's famous barbecue pork. **Address:** 4001 St. Elmo Ave 37409 **Location:** Jct 40th St; adjacent to Incline Railway parking lot. L D

RAIN THAI BISTRO
423/386-5586 (9)

▼▼▼ Thai Sushi. Casual Dining. $8-$20 **AAA Inspector Notes:** Stir-fry and noodle dishes are standouts as the kitchen shows their pride through flavorful sauces and the freshest spices in their foods. You'll find tried-and-true favorites like pad thai, tom yum goong (lemongrass soup with shrimp) and ginger chicken. The setting is cozy with a calming water feature along the wall. Not to be missed is the sushi bar, which has a variety of affordable favorites. **Features:** full bar, patio dining. **Address:** 6933 Lee Hwy, Suite 400 37421 **Location:** I-75 exit 5 (Shallowford Rd), 0.5 mi w to Lee Hwy (US 64 W), then just n. L D CALL 💳M

REMBRANDT'S COFFEE HOUSE
423/265-5033 (12)

▼ Breads/Pastries. Quick Serve. $7-$12 **AAA Inspector Notes:** This quaint, cozy coffeehouse's patio is perfect for enjoying a hot cup of cappuccino with a yummy, sweet-tooth-satisfying pastry. A selection of sandwiches is also offered. **Features:** patio dining. **Address:** 204 High St 37403 **Location:** US 27 exit 1C (4th St), 1 mi e, then just n; in Bluff View Arts District. B L D

RIB & LOIN
423/499-6465 (39)

▼ Barbecue. Casual Dining. $6-$16 **AAA Inspector Notes:** Folks with a hankering for delicious barbecue will be satisfied with a hearty rib meal or chicken with all the fixings at this casual spot. **Features:** beer only. **Address:** 5946 Brainerd Rd 37421 **Location:** I-24 exit 184, 1.5 mi e; I-75 exit 3B, 1.7 mi w, then just s. L D CALL 💳M

ST. JOHN'S RESTAURANT
423/266-4400 (33)

▼▼▼▼ New American. Fine Dining. $27-$42 **AAA Inspector Notes:** Housed in a historic hotel that once served as a brothel, this restaurant serves sophisticated, locally and seasonally inspired cuisine. Fresh fish, including Columbia River wild steelhead trout and Gulf red snapper, is flown in from around the country. Produce and meats are sourced from local farms. **Features:** full bar, happy hour. **Reservations:** suggested. **Address:** 1278 Market St 37402 **Location:** I-24 exit 178 (Broad St) eastbound; exit Market St westbound, 0.6 mi n. **Parking:** on-site and street. D

(See map & index p. 51.)

SEOUL RESTAURANT
423/855-9113 32

▼▼ Asian. Casual Dining. $7-$20 **AAA Inspector Notes:** The bibimbap here is a real treat as is the pho bulgogi and Korean stir-fry. Other Korean favorites are the casseroles (cod fish stew), kimchi jjigae and grilled beef short ribs. Some Vietnamese dishes, besides the pho, would be the vermicelli with shrimp, chicken, pork or vegetables. **Features:** beer only. **Address:** 6231 Perimeter Dr, Suite 199 37421 **Location:** SR 153 exit 1 (Lee Hwy), just s; in shopping plaza. L D

SHOGUN OF CHATTANOOGA
423/296-6500 36

▼▼ Japanese. Casual Dining. $7-$31 **AAA Inspector Notes:** People craving sushi can check out the variety of fresh offerings at this casual spot. Others can enjoy dinner and entertainment at the hibachi table. **Features:** full bar, early bird specials. **Address:** 1806 Gunbarrel Rd 37421 **Location:** I-75 exit 5 (Shallowford Rd), 1 mi e, then 2 mi s. L D

SITAR INDIAN CUISINE
423/894-9696 15

▼▼ Indian. Casual Dining. $9-$17 **AAA Inspector Notes:** The lunch buffet is quite popular and features a wide array of choices, such as chicken tandoori, pakora, goat curry, a couple of different types of chutney and, of course, fresh naan. Lamb specialties are a good option, and the vindaloo is a great way to go. Chicken tikka is a solid staple. Combination dinners are a nice way to sample several delights. **Features:** beer & wine. **Address:** 200A Market St 37402 **Location:** US 27 N exit 1C (4th St), 0.3 mi e to Market St, then just n. **Parking:** on-site (fee) and street. L D

SOUTHERN STAR
423/267-8899 34

▼▼ Southern American. Family Dining. $8-$16 **AAA Inspector Notes:** Tasteful and fresh dishes with an emphasis on Southern cuisine are offered at this eatery. Specialties include the delicious fried Gulf shrimp, baby back ribs and roasted pork chop. Check out the daily blue plate specials. **Features:** beer only, patio dining. **Address:** 1300 Broad St 37402 **Location:** At 13th Ave; center. **Parking:** on-site and street. L D CALL ♿M

STICKY FINGERS RIB HOUSE

▼▼ Barbecue. Family Dining. $8-$24 **AAA Inspector Notes:** Diners can put down their silverware and get their fingers ready for classic Carolina sweet ribs, as well as ribs cooked in the Texas and Tennessee styles. Hearty sides of baked beans and coleslaw complement the entrees. **Bar:** full bar. L D

For additional information, visit AAA.com
LOCATIONS:
Address: 420 Broad St 37402 **Location:** Between W 4th and 5th sts. **Phone:** 423/265-7427
Address: 2031 Hamilton Place Blvd 37402 **Location:** I-75 exit 5 (Shallowford Rd), just se, then 0.3 mi sw; opposite Hamilton Place Mall. **Phone:** 423/899-7427

SWEET BASIL
423/485-8836 40

▼▼ Thai. Casual Dining. $6-$17 **AAA Inspector Notes:** On the menu are traditional favorites such as pad thai, roast duck and three-flavored fish. **Features:** beer & wine. **Address:** 5845 Brainerd Rd 37411 **Location:** Jct SR 153, 2 mi s. L D CALL ♿M

THE TERMINAL BREWHOUSE
423/752-8090 37

▼▼ American. Casual Dining. $7-$14 **AAA Inspector Notes:** It goes without saying that a great way to start your time here is with a fresh-brewed beer. The American copper ale, west coast India pale and the oatmeal stout are good options. The ploughman's lunch (a cheese, fruit and bread plate) will go well with any of those brews. Other great choices are the salmon cakes, sandwiches, pizza and tender, tasty burgers. **Features:** full bar, patio dining, happy hour. **Address:** 6 E 14th St 37408 **Location:** I-24 exit 178 (Broad St) eastbound; exit Market St westbound, 0.5 mi n. **Parking:** street only. L D LATE ▥

THAI SMILE
423/266-2333 19

▼▼ Thai. Casual Dining. $8-$19 **AAA Inspector Notes:** The ambiance is airy, seating is limited and the service is spotty, but once you taste the food, the restaurant lives up to its name. Located near downtown venues, this place has been a local favorite since it opened. **Features:** beer & wine. **Address:** 219 Market St 37402 **Location:** US 27 N exit 1C (4th St), 0.3 mi e to Market St, then just n. **Parking:** on-site (fee). L D

TONY'S PASTA SHOP AND TRATTORIA
423/265-5033 14

▼▼ Italian. Casual Dining. $4-$15 **AAA Inspector Notes:** In the Bluff View Art District, this rustic, simple restaurant enables patrons to dine indoors or at the patio tables offering great river views. A range of fresh pasta and delicious sauces are featured as well as pizza, salads and traditional Italian entrées served with fresh baked bread. **Features:** beer & wine, patio dining. **Address:** 212 High St 37403 **Location:** US 27 exit 1C (4th St), 1 mi e, then just n; in Bluff View Arts District. L D ▥

TUPELO HONEY CAFE
423/779-0400 30

▼▼ New Southern. Casual Dining. $7-$23 **AAA Inspector Notes:** Traditional Lowcountry favorites such as fried green tomatoes and shrimp and grits are served in heaping portions. The menu always features twists on Southern staples, such as the nutty fried chicken served with smashed sweet potatoes, asparagus and a side of goat cheese grits. **Features:** full bar, patio dining. **Address:** 1110 Market St, Suite 121 37402 **Location:** US 27 N exit 1A (Dr Martin Luther King Blvd), just e to Market St, then just s. **Parking:** on-site and street. L D CALL ♿M

URBAN STACK BURGER LOUNGE
423/475-5350 35

▼▼ Burgers. Casual Dining. $7-$12 **AAA Inspector Notes:** They only have the good stuff here: hormone and antibiotic-free beef topped with premium artisan cheeses and creative toppings, and served on fresh locally baked rolls. Wash down one of these great burgers with something from the rotating craft beer list or the extensive whiskey selections. The setting, an 1867 railway baggage building, exudes rustic charm, but it also is a LEED-certified building in keeping with the owner's environmentally friendly approach to business. **Features:** full bar, patio dining. **Address:** 12 W 13th St 37402 **Location:** Between Market and Broad sts; downtown. **Parking:** street only. L D

CHEROKEE NATIONAL FOREST (D-7)

Elevations in the forest range from 739 ft. at the Ocoee River Dam to 6,286 ft. at Roan High Nob. Refer to AAA maps for additional information.

In eastern Tennessee, Cherokee National Forest is divided into two sections by the Great Smoky Mountains National Park *(see place listing p. 97)*. The 650,000 acres of thickly forested, mountainous terrain are punctuated by deep river gorges, streams and waterfalls. Dominant tree species are pine, hemlock, poplar and oak.

There are more than 200 recreational sites, 12 of which offer boating. More than 600 miles of trails, including the Appalachian Trail, traverse the forest. Activities and facilities include swimming, hiking, camping, horseback riding, interpretive trails, picnicking and wildlife viewing. White-water raft trips on the Ocoee River are offered by rafting operators based in Benton *(see place listing p. 40)*, Ducktown *(see place listing p. 74)* and Ocoee *(see place listing p. 229)*.

The Cherohala Skyway (SR 165), or Overhill Skyway, about 40 miles long, runs from Tellico Plains, Tennessee, east into Robbinsville, North Carolina. Following portions of what was once a Cherokee Indian trading route, the road meanders past the Tellico River and Bald River Falls, over rolling hills and through the Cherokee and Nantahala national forests. The road passes several scenic viewpoints.

For additional information contact the Forest Supervisor, Cherokee National Forest, 2800 N. Ocoee St., Cleveland, TN 37312; phone (423) 476-9700.

ROAN MOUNTAIN is just off US 19E via SR 143 between the town of Roan Mountain and N.C. SR 261. In mid-June the uncultivated Catawba rhododendron burst into bloom, forming one of the largest natural rhododendron gardens in the world, nearly 600 acres. Beneath the mountain's 6,327-foot peak, Roan Mountain State Park offers furnished cabins, recreational activities and spectacular views. *See Recreation Areas Chart.*

Hours: Visitor center daily 8:30-4. **Cost:** Free. Swimming pool $4 (per person, per day). **Phone:** (423) 772-0190 for park headquarters or (800) 250-8620. 🅐 🗙 🏠 🏤

CHICKAMAUGA AND CHATTANOOGA NATIONAL MILITARY PARK (E-6)
• Attractions map p. 48

Straddling the Georgia-Tennessee border, the 9,000-acre Chickamauga and Chattanooga National Military Park commemorates the September 1863 Battle of Chickamauga, the Battles for Chattanooga in November of that same year and 12,000 years of human history on Moccasin Bend. It is the oldest national military park administered by the U.S. National Park Service.

The Battle of Chickamauga occurred after Gen. William S. Rosecrans and 58,000 Union troops crossed the Tennessee River southwest of Chattanooga, forcing the Confederate troops of Gen. Braxton Bragg to abandon the city and move south to protect their Atlanta supply lines. Bragg obtained reinforcements and moved back northward hoping to retake Chattanooga. The two forces clashed at Chickamauga Creek near the Georgia-Tennessee line.

Although victorious, the Confederates suffered heavy losses. The Union forces withdrew to Chattanooga after suffering more than 16,000 casualties. The ensuing Confederate siege of the city almost subdued the Union army. However, bolstered by reinforcements and a new supply route, Union forces resumed the offensive by November.

The 3-day Battle of Chattanooga began Nov. 23, 1863, with Union forces driving the Confederates back to the base of Missionary Ridge and capturing Orchard Knob. When the Union troops assaulted the remaining Confederates in the Battle of Lookout Mountain the next day, the Confederates chose to evacuate the area rather than risk separation from their main line.

The decisive blow came a day later. Gen. Ulysses S. Grant directed the all-day Battle of Missionary Ridge, in which the Confederates were dislodged from strategic points and Union forces gained the steep slopes above the city. The Confederates withdrew after dark; their defeat opened the way to Atlanta and the heart of the Confederacy.

Much of the area in this beautiful park is kept in wartime condition. More than 1,600 markers, monuments, cannons and tablets indicate the battle lines

of both sides and recount the story of the area. Self-guiding tours enable visitors to explore the battlefields of Chickamauga, Lookout Mountain and Missionary Ridge.

Among the points of interest are Orchard Knob, Grant's headquarters during the Battle of Chattanooga; Crest Road, along Missionary Ridge; Wilder Brigade Monument, commanding a good view of the Chickamauga Battlefield and its surroundings; the Brotherton House, a reconstructed prewar farmhouse marking the spot where the Union line was broken; Snodgrass Hill, the scene of the last fighting at Chickamauga; and Snodgrass House, which served as a Union field hospital during the battle.

Chickamauga Battlefield grounds and monuments are open daily 6 a.m. to dusk. Visitor center open daily 8:30-5; closed Jan. 1 and Christmas. Free. Phone (706) 866-9241.

BATTLES FOR CHATTANOOGA ELECTRIC MAP AND MUSEUM is at 1110 E. Brow Rd., next to Point Park. A miniature battlefield display with more than 5,000 soldiers and cannons depicts the Battle of Chattanooga. A narrated video presentation describes the historic conflict. **Time:** Allow 1 hour minimum. **Hours:** Daily 9-6, Memorial Day weekend-Labor Day; 10-5, rest of year. Closed Christmas. **Cost:** $8; $6 (ages 6-12). **Phone:** (423) 821-2812.

CHICKAMAUGA VISITOR CENTER is 9 mi. s. of Chattanooga, Tenn., on US 27, near the n. end of the park on Chickamauga Battlefield. A museum has Civil War exhibits and the Fuller Gun Collection, a display of American military shoulder arms. Orientation programs are offered, including a fiber optic map and a video presentation depicting the Battle of Chickamauga. The park also offers maps and a cellphone tour of the battlefield (inquire at the information desk). **Hours:** Daily 8:30-5. Closed Jan. 1 and Christmas. **Cost:** Free. A CD narrating a self-guiding tour of the park is available for purchase at the bookstore. **Phone:** (706) 866-9241.

POINT PARK is on Lookout Mountain at 110 Point Park Rd. The park overlooks Chattanooga and the Moccasin Bend National Archeological District on the Tennessee River. The Ochs Memorial Museum and Observatory, the New York Peace Monument, Cravens House and Umbrella Rock are in the park. The Lookout Mountain Battlefield Visitor Center at the north end of E. Brow Road contains the restored James Walker painting "Battle of Lookout Mountain." **Hours:** Park open daily 9-dusk. Visitor center open daily 9-5. Closed Jan. 1 and Christmas. **Cost:** Admission, valid for 7 days, $5; free (ages 0-15). **Phone:** (423) 821-7786.

CLARKSVILLE (C-4) pop. 132,929, elev. 493'
• Hotels p. 64 • Restaurants p. 65

Founded in 1784, Clarksville was named for Gen. George Rogers Clark, an 18th-century frontier military leader and U.S. Indian commissioner.

The Clarksville Architectural District includes Public Square and Second, Commerce and Franklin streets. The area was destroyed by fire in 1878 and again by tornado in 1999, but many buildings have been restored.

Connecting to the historic district is Cumberland RiverWalk, a 1.7-mile riverfront promenade that highlights the city's river heritage with an interpretive exhibit as well as entertainment venues and overlooks.

Professional theater performances and community productions are offered at the 1947 Roxy Regional Theatre; phone (931) 645-7699. Concerts and stage shows find a venue at the Center of Excellence for the Creative Arts on the campus of Austin Peay State University; phone (931) 221-7876.

Fort Campbell, a military reservation near the Tennessee-Kentucky state line, is the home of the 101st Airborne Division of the U.S. Army.

Clarksville-Montgomery County Welcome Center: 180 Holiday Dr., Clarksville, TN 37040-5023. **Phone:** (931) 647-2331.

Self-guiding tours: Walking and driving tour maps are available from the convention and visitors bureau, the Customs House Museum and Cultural Center and RiverWalk.

CUSTOMS HOUSE MUSEUM AND CULTURAL CENTER is at 200 S. 2nd St. In the 1898 Old Post Office & Customs House, the museum's architecture consists of Italianate ornamentation, a pyramidal slate roof, Romanesque arches and guardian eagles. Permanent exhibits include a restored 1846 log house, a tobacco exhibit, children's hands-on exhibits, art galleries, a bubble cave and model train exhibits.

Time: Allow 1 hour minimum. **Hours:** Tues.-Sat. 10-5, Sun. 1-5. Model train runs Sun. 1-4. Closed major holidays. **Cost:** $7; $5 (ages 65+ and teachers and college students with ID); $3 (ages 6-18); free (to all second Sat. of the month). **Phone:** (931) 648-5780.

SMITH/TRAHERN MANSION is at 101 McClure St. Built 1858-59 for Christopher Smith, a wealthy tobacco grower, the house overlooks the Cumberland River. A curved staircase, a widow's walk and ornate woodwork are prominent features of the Greek Revival/Italianate-style mansion. **Time:** Allow 30 minutes minimum. **Hours:** Mon.-Fri. 9:30-2:30; otherwise by appointment. Closed Jan. 1 and Christmas. **Cost:** $2; free (ages 0-5). **Phone:** (931) 648-9998.

WINERIES

- **Beachaven Vineyards and Winery** is off I-24 exit 4 to 1100 Dunlap Ln. **Hours:** Mon.-Sat. 9-6, Sun. noon-5, Mar.-Oct.; Mon.-Sat. 9-5, Sun. noon-5, rest of year. Closed Jan. 1, Easter, Thanksgiving and Christmas. **Phone:** (931) 645-8867. GT

BAYMONT INN & SUITES (931)552-2255

▼▼ **Hotel** $105-$139 **Address:** 190 Holiday Dr 37040 **Location:** I-24 exit 4, just se. **Facility:** 77 units. 2 stories (no elevator), exterior corridors. **Terms:** cancellation fee imposed. **Amenities:** safes. **Pool(s):** outdoor. **Activities:** sauna, exercise room. **Guest Services:** valet and coin laundry.

CANDLEWOOD SUITES 931/906-0900

▼▼▼ **Extended Stay Hotel.** Rates not provided. **Address:** 3050 Clay Lewis Rd 37040 **Location:** I-24 exit 4, just s. **Facility:** 80 efficiencies. 4 stories, interior corridors. **Activities:** exercise room. **Guest Services:** complimentary and valet laundry.

COUNTRY INN & SUITES BY CARLSON (931)645-1400

▼▼ **Hotel** $99-$159 **Address:** 3075 Wilma Rudolph Blvd 37040 **Location:** I-24 exit 4, just s. **Facility:** 103 units. 4 stories, interior corridors. **Terms:** cancellation fee imposed. **Amenities:** Some: safes. **Pool(s):** heated indoor. **Activities:** exercise room. **Guest Services:** valet and coin laundry.

COURTYARD BY MARRIOTT - CLARKSVILLE (931)551-4480

▼▼▼ **Hotel** $111-$183 **Address:** 155 Fair Brook Pl 37040 **Location:** I-24 exit 4, just s, then just w at Westfield Ct. **Facility:** 91 units. 4 stories, interior corridors. **Pool(s):** heated indoor. **Activities:** hot tub, exercise room. **Guest Services:** valet and coin laundry, boarding pass kiosk.

> **AAA Benefit:** Members save 5% or more!

FAIRFIELD INN & SUITES BY MARRIOTT CLARKSVILLE (931)551-3200

▼▼▼ **Hotel** $97-$160 **Address:** 110 Westfield Ct 37040 **Location:** I-24 exit 4, just s. **Facility:** 75 units. 3 stories, interior corridors. **Pool(s):** heated indoor. **Activities:** exercise room. **Guest Services:** valet and coin laundry.

> **AAA Benefit:** Members save 5% or more!

HAMPTON INN & SUITES (931)378-6070

▼▼▼ **Hotel** $119-$159 **Address:** 3091 Clay Lewis Rd 37040 **Location:** I-24 exit 4, just se. **Facility:** 85 units. 4 stories, interior corridors. **Terms:** 1-7 night minimum stay, cancellation fee imposed. **Pool(s):** heated indoor. **Activities:** exercise room. **Guest Services:** coin laundry.

> **AAA Benefit:** Members save up to 10%!

HILTON GARDEN INN 931/647-1096

▼▼▼ **Hotel.** Rates not provided. **Address:** 290 Alfred Thun Rd 37040 **Location:** I-24 exit 4, just ne. **Facility:** 111 units. 5 stories, interior corridors. **Amenities:** safes. **Pool(s):** heated indoor. **Activities:** hot tub, exercise room. **Guest Services:** valet and coin laundry, area transportation.

> **AAA Benefit:** Members save up to 10%!

LA QUINTA INN & SUITES CLARKSVILLE (931)906-0606

▼▼▼ **Hotel** $75-$203 **Address:** 251 Holiday Dr 37040 **Location:** I-24 exit 4, just se. **Facility:** 82 units. 4 stories, interior corridors. **Pool(s):** heated indoor. **Activities:** hot tub, exercise room. **Guest Services:** coin laundry.

MAINSTAY SUITES (931)648-3400

◆◆◆◆ **Extended Stay Hotel** $70-$129 **Address:** 115 Fairbrook Pl 37043 **Location:** I-24 exit 4, just sw. **Facility:** 93 efficiencies. 4 stories, interior corridors. **Pool(s):** heated indoor. **Activities:** hot tub, exercise room. **Guest Services:** valet and coin laundry.

〔¶↑〕 CALL 〔&M〕 ⛄ 〔BIZ〕 〔HS〕 ⛅ ✕ ☐ 🖵 ▣ / SOME UNITS 〔S⬌〕

QUALITY INN-EXIT 4 (931)648-4848

◆◆◆◆
Hotel
$89-$99

Address: 3095 Wilma Rudolph Blvd 37040 **Location:** I-24 exit 4, just se. **Facility:** 143 units, some efficiencies. 2 stories (no elevator); exterior corridors. **Pool(s):** outdoor, heated indoor. **Activities:** sauna, hot tub, exercise room. **Guest Services:** valet and coin laundry. **Featured Amenity:** breakfast buffet.

〔SAVE〕 〔¶↑〕 〔⛏〕 〔Y〕 〔⛄〕 〔BIZ〕

〔HS〕 ⛅ ☐ 🖵 ▣ / SOME UNITS 〔S⬌〕

Clarksville's full service hotel. 5 time Choice Gold Award winner. Free buffet breakfast.

QUALITY INN

RED ROOF INN CLARKSVILLE (931)905-1555

◆◆ **Motel** $50-$119 **Address:** 197 Holiday Dr 37040 **Location:** I-24 exit 4, just s. **Facility:** 61 units. 2 stories (no elevator), exterior corridors. **Pool(s):** outdoor. **Guest Services:** valet and coin laundry. 〔¶↑〕 ⛄ ⛅ ☐ 🖵 / SOME UNITS 〔🐾〕 ▣

SUPER 8 CLARKSVILLE (931)645-6300

◆◆ **Motel** $65-$124 **Address:** 201 Holiday Dr 37040 **Location:** I-24 exit 4, just sw. **Facility:** 42 units. 2 stories (no elevator), exterior corridors. **Pool(s):** outdoor. **Guest Services:** coin laundry.

〔¶↑〕 ⛄ ⛅ ☐ 🖵 ▣

WHERE TO EAT

HARBOR CAFE 931/906-0188

◆◆ Steak Seafood. Casual Dining. $7-$22 **AAA Inspector Notes:** Pass by the chain restaurants and stop here instead; you won't be disappointed. A warm interior features rough-hewn log pillars, a river stone fireplace and a pressed tin ceiling. A wrap-around porch offers seating in pleasant weather. Steak and seafood are the specialty—the snow crab legs and steak combo is a local favorite. Oriental chicken, beef or burgers round out your options. **Features:** full bar, patio dining, happy hour. **Address:** 2131 Lowes Dr 37040 **Location:** I-24 exit 4, 2 mi w. 〔L〕 〔D〕 〔LATE〕 CALL 〔&M〕

CLEVELAND (D-6) pop. 41,285, elev. 864'
• Restaurants p. 66

In the foothills of the Smoky Mountains, Cleveland began in 1836 as a single cabin in the heart of the Cherokee Nation. Six years later, with a population of 400, the town was incorporated and named after Revolutionary War hero Col. Benjamin Cleveland. A reminder of the area's Native American heritage is downtown Johnston Park's "The Cherokee Chieftain," a large statue that is part of Peter Toth's "Trail of the Whispering Giants." Toth's sculptures honoring Native Americans are found in every state.

Cleveland/Bradley Chamber of Commerce: 225 Keith St. S.W., P.O. Box 2275, Cleveland, TN 37320-2275. **Phone:** (423) 472-6587.

Self-guiding tours: Brochures outlining a walking tour of the downtown district are available at the chamber. Points of interest along the route include the Gothic Revival-style St. Luke's Episcopal Church and what is said to be the oldest continuously operating bank building in the state.

RED CLAY STATE HISTORIC AREA is at 1140 Red Clay Park Rd. S.W. The 263-acre park preserves the site of the last Cherokee capital and council grounds before their relocation to Oklahoma via the Trail of Tears. A visitor center features 19th-century Cherokee artifacts and art. Replicas of a council house, Cherokee farmhouse, three sleeping huts, corn crib and barn are on the grounds, as are an amphitheater, nature trails and the Blue Hole spring. Weekend summer programs feature guided tours, nature walks, movies and demonstrations.

Time: Allow 1 hour, 30 minutes minimum. **Hours:** Park open daily 8-dusk, Mar.-Nov.; 8-4:30, rest of year. Visitor center open Tues.-Sat. 8-4:30, Sun.-Mon. 1-4:30, Mar.-Nov.; Mon.-Fri. 8-4:15, Sat.-Sun. 1-4:15, rest of year. Park closed Christmas. Visitor center closed Jan. 1 and Dec. 20-31. **Cost:** Free. **Phone:** (423) 478-0339. 〔⚷〕

BAYMONT INN & SUITES CLEVELAND (423)614-5583

◆◆ **Hotel** $69-$99 **Address:** 360 Paul Huff Pkwy 37312 **Location:** I-75 exit 27, 0.8 mi e. **Facility:** 60 units. 2 stories (no elevator), exterior corridors. **Pool(s):** outdoor. **Activities:** exercise room. **Guest Services:** valet laundry.

〔¶↑〕 CALL 〔&M〕 ⛄ ⛅ ☐ 🖵 ▣ / SOME UNITS 〔S⬌〕

CLARION INN (423)559-1001

◆◆ **Hotel** $69-$99 **Address:** 185 James Asbury Dr NW 37312 **Location:** I-75 exit 27, just w, then just s. **Facility:** 59 units. 2 stories, exterior corridors. **Pool(s):** outdoor. **Activities:** limited exercise equipment. **Guest Services:** valet laundry.

〔¶↑〕 CALL 〔&M〕 ⛄ 〔BIZ〕 ⛅ ▣

/ SOME UNITS 〔S⬌〕 ☐ 🖵

COMFORT INN & SUITES-CLEVELAND (423)339-1000

◆◆◆
Hotel
$75-$150

Address: 107 Interstate Dr NW 37312 **Location:** I-75 exit 25, just w, then just s. **Facility:** 90 units. 3 stories, interior corridors. **Pool(s):** outdoor. **Activities:** exercise room. **Guest Services:** coin laundry.

〔SAVE〕 〔¶↑〕 ⛄ 〔BIZ〕 ⛅ ✕ ☐ 🖵 ▣ / SOME UNITS 〔S⬌〕

DOUGLAS INN & SUITES (423)559-5579

◆◆◆
Hotel
$55-$115

Address: 2600 Westside Dr NW 37312 **Location:** I-75 exit 25, just e, then just n. **Facility:** 40 units, some kitchens. 2 stories, interior/exterior corridors. **Activities:** limited exercise equipment. **Guest Services:** valet and coin laundry. **Featured Amenity:** full hot breakfast.

〔SAVE〕 〔¶↑〕 CALL 〔&M〕 ⛅ ✕ ☐

🖵 ▣ / SOME UNITS 〔S⬌〕

FAIRFIELD INN & SUITES BY MARRIOTT CLEVELAND
(423)664-2501

 Hotel $90-$148 **Address:** 2815 Westside Dr NW 37312 **Location:** I-75 exit 25, just e, then just n. **Facility:** 82 units. 4 stories, interior corridors. **Pool(s):** heated indoor. **Activities:** exercise room. **Guest Services:** valet and coin laundry.

AAA Benefit:
Members save 5% or more!

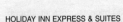

HAMPTON INN CLEVELAND
(423)458-1222

Hotel $109-$159 **Address:** 4355 Frontage Rd 37312 **Location:** I-75 exit 27, just w, then just n. **Facility:** 97 units. 4 stories, interior corridors. **Terms:** 1-7 night minimum stay, cancellation fee imposed. **Pool(s):** heated indoor. **Activities:** exercise room. **Guest Services:** valet and coin laundry.

AAA Benefit:
Members save up to 10%!

HOLIDAY INN EXPRESS & SUITES
423/790-1199

Hotel. Rates not provided. **Address:** 4355 Holiday Inn Express Way 37312 **Location:** I-75 exit 27, just e. **Facility:** 88 units. 4 stories, interior corridors. **Pool(s):** outdoor. **Activities:** exercise room. **Guest Services:** valet and coin laundry.

QUALITY INN
(423)478-5265

Hotel $65-$90 **Address:** 153 James Asbury Dr 37312 **Location:** I-75 exit 27, just w, then just s. **Facility:** 58 units. 2 stories (no elevator), interior/exterior corridors. **Amenities:** safes. **Pool(s):** outdoor.

SUPER 8
(423)476-5555

Motel $57-$141 **Address:** 163 Bernham Dr 37312 **Location:** I-75 exit 27, just w, then just s. **Facility:** 44 units. 2 stories (no elevator), interior/exterior corridors. **Amenities:** safes. **Pool(s):** outdoor.

WINGATE BY WYNDHAM
(423)478-1212

Hotel
$99-$119

Address: 110 Interstate Dr 37312 **Location:** I-75 exit 25, just s. **Facility:** 80 units. 4 stories, interior corridors. **Amenities:** safes. **Pool(s):** outdoor. **Activities:** exercise room. **Guest Services:** valet laundry. **Featured Amenity:** continental breakfast.

WHERE TO EAT

AUBREY'S
423/472-3030

American. Casual Dining. $9-$26 **AAA Inspector Notes:** This casual eatery's menu includes steaks, seafood pasta, and sandwiches, plus a short list of Southern specialties like pulled pork barbecue, buttermilk fried chicken, pot roast and peanut-crusted catfish. **Features:** full bar. **Address:** 275 Ocoee Crossing NW 37312 **Location:** I-75 exit 27, 1.5 mi e on Paul Huff Pkwy, 0.5 mi s on US 11, then just e.

BALD HEADED BISTRO
423/472-6000

American. Casual Dining. $17-$60 **AAA Inspector Notes:** The upscale Western-style dining room, complete with Wyoming timber and stone décor, has a rustic yet still sophisticated atmosphere. Wild game is a specialty with items such as elk and quail. Fresh seafood, beef and pasta also are on the menu. The staff is very professional, and special seasonal menus are offered. **Features:** full bar, happy hour. **Address:** 201 Keith St SW 37312 **Location:** Jct US 11 and SR 312; in Village Green.

EL CAZADOR MEXICAN RESTAURANT
423/790-0563

Mexican. Casual Dining. $5-$14 **AAA Inspector Notes:** Featuring many Mexican favorites at a good price, this family-friendly restaurant offers a large selection of combination platters including burritos, chalupas, enchiladas, tacos, quesadillas and nachos. Child- and senior-size plates also are available. Delicious chips and salsa are a great starter. **Features:** full bar, patio dining, senior menu, happy hour. **Address:** 2299 Keith St 37311 **Location:** At 23rd St.

GONDOLIER ITALIAN RESTAURANT AND PIZZA
423/472-4998

Italian Pizza. Casual Dining. $6-$13 **AAA Inspector Notes:** In addition to daily specials, diners can select from a tempting variety of calzones and such standards as spaghetti, manicotti and ravioli. Servers are fast and friendly. **Features:** beer only. **Address:** 3300 N Keith St NW 37312 **Location:** I-75 exit 25, 1.3 mi se on SR 60, then 0.6 mi n.

IMPERIAL GARDEN CHINESE RESTAURANT
423/559-9054

Chinese. Casual Dining. $8-$20 **AAA Inspector Notes:** At this casual café you'll savor traditional fare, including beef, chicken, pork and seafood dishes. Lunch specials include soup and an egg roll. **Address:** 217 Ocoee Crossing Way N 37312 **Location:** I-75 exit 27, 1.5 mi e on Paul Huff Pkwy, 0.5 mi s on US 11, then just e; in Ocoee Crossing Shopping Center.

JENKINS DELI & RESTAURANT
423/478-1648

American. Casual Dining. $6-$13 **AAA Inspector Notes:** Since 1976 this has been a locals' favorite for homemade soups and hearty sandwiches, such as the French dip and their signature chicken salad. Rounding out the offerings are a few pasta dishes and entrées along the lines of chicken fingers and hamburger steak. **Features:** full bar. **Address:** 88 Mouse Creek Rd 37312 **Location:** I-75 exit 27, 1.5 mi e on Paul Huff Pkwy, just s on US 11, then just e; in Cloverleaf Plaza.

THE OLD FORT RESTAURANT
423/339-0446

American. Family Dining. $5-$12 **AAA Inspector Notes:** For more than 50 years this family-owned café has been the locals' choice for down-home cooking. The menu features meat-and-vegetable plates, with entrées like meatloaf, ham and hamburger steak. Breakfast specialties include pancakes and fluffy biscuits, plus all the traditional sides. **Address:** 1422 25th St NW 37311 **Location:** I-75 exit 25, 0.4 mi e on SR 60.

CLINTON (C-7) pop. 9,841

GREEN MCADOO CULTURAL CENTER, 101 School St., chronicles the events leading to the desegregation of Clinton High School in 1956, a landmark event in the Civil Rights Movement. Exhibits include anti-integration propaganda from the period, recorded personal accounts and a CBS broadcast by Edward R. Murrow. **Time:** Allow 2 hours minimum. **Hours:** Tues.-Fri. 9-5, Sat. 11-4. **Cost:** Donations. **Phone:** (865) 463-6500. GT

MUSEUM OF APPALACHIA is off I-75 exit 122 at 2819 Andersonville Hwy. The village-farm complex includes dozens of log structures, exhibits with Civil War and Native American artifacts, gardens and free-roaming farm animals. Musicians perform seasonally, and demonstrations are offered during special events.

Also on the grounds is the Appalachian Hall of Fame, which pays tribute to the people of Appalachia. Among the hall's exhibits are Native American artifacts, quilts, baskets, folk art and early handmade musical instruments.

Time: Allow 2 hours minimum. **Hours:** Daily 9-6, May-Oct.; Mon.-Fri. 9-5, Sat.-Sun. 9-6, in Apr.; daily 9-5, rest of year. Closed Thanksgiving and Christmas. Phone ahead to confirm schedule. **Cost:** $18; $15 (ages 65+ and military with ID); $10 (ages 13-18); $6 (ages 5-12); $42 (family). Rates vary during special events. **Phone:** (865) 494-7680. 🍴

COMFORT INN-CLINTON   (865)457-2255
▼▼▼ **Hotel** $79-$116 **Address:** 120 Welcome Ln 37716 **Location:** I-75 exit 122, just w. **Facility:** 58 units. 2 stories (no elevator), interior corridors. **Pool(s):** heated outdoor. **Activities:** limited exercise equipment. **Guest Services:** coin laundry.

COUNTRY INN & SUITES BY CARLSON   (865)457-4311
▼▼▼ **Hotel** $89-$149 **Address:** 710 Park Pl 37716 **Location:** I-75 exit 122, just w. **Facility:** 63 units. 3 stories, interior corridors. **Terms:** 7 day cancellation notice-fee imposed. **Pool(s):** heated indoor. **Activities:** hot tub, exercise room. **Guest Services:** coin laundry.

HAMPTON INN CLINTON   (865)691-8070
▼▼▼ **Hotel** $119-$179 **Address:** 105 Hillvale Rd 37716 **Location:** I-75 exit 122, just w. **Facility:** 75 units. 4 stories, interior corridors. **Terms:** 1-7 night minimum stay, cancellation fee imposed. **Pool(s):** outdoor. **Activities:** exercise room.

AAA Benefit: Members save up to 10%!

HOLIDAY INN EXPRESS HOTEL & SUITES   (865)457-2233
▼▼▼ **Hotel** $99-$189 **Address:** 111 Hillvale Rd 37716 **Location:** I-75 exit 122, just w. **Facility:** 81 units. 4 stories, interior corridors. **Terms:** cancellation fee imposed. **Pool(s):** heated outdoor, heated indoor. **Activities:** hot tub, exercise room. **Guest Services:** coin laundry.

RED ROOF INN & SUITES-CLINTON   (865)457-9070
▼▼▼ **Hotel** $45-$99 **Address:** 141 Buffalo Rd 37716 **Location:** I-75 exit 122, just w. **Facility:** 47 units. 2 stories (no elevator), exterior corridors. **Pool(s):** outdoor. **Guest Services:** coin laundry.

WHERE TO EAT

GONDOLIER ITALIAN RESTAURANT AND PIZZA
                                       865/269-4767
▼▼ Italian Pizza. Casual Dining. $6-$13 **AAA Inspector Notes:** In addition to daily specials, diners can select from a tempting variety of calzones and such standards as spaghetti, manicotti and ravioli. Servers are fast and friendly. **Features:** beer only. **Address:** 116 Tanner Pl 37716 **Location:** I-75 exit 122, just n to Hillvale Rd, then just w. [L] [D] CALL 🅖🅜

HARRISON'S BAR & GRILL   865/463-6368
▼▼ American. Casual Dining. $8-$20 **AAA Inspector Notes:** This casual restaurant includes all the favorites, including burgers, barbecue and salads. **Features:** full bar. **Address:** 110 Hillvale Rd 37716 **Location:** I-75 exit 122, just n. [L] [D] CALL 🅖🅜

COLLIERVILLE pop. 43,965
- **Hotels & Restaurants map & index p. 154**
- **Part of Memphis area — see map p. 134**

HAMPTON INN COLLIERVILLE   (901)854-9400 ⑤⑨
▼▼▼ **Hotel** $99-$169 **Address:** 1280 W Poplar Ave 38017 **Location:** 0.9 mi w of jct CR 175 on US 72. **Facility:** 91 units. 3 stories, interior corridors. **Terms:** 1-7 night minimum stay, cancellation fee imposed. **Pool(s):** outdoor. **Activities:** exercise room. **Guest Services:** valet and coin laundry.

AAA Benefit: Members save up to 10%!

WHERE TO EAT

CAPTAIN JOHN'S OLD TYME PIT BARBECUE   901/853-8004
▼▼ Barbecue. Quick Serve. $5-$21 **AAA Inspector Notes:** Locals head here for slow-smoked beef and pork. Baked beans and coleslaw, either piled on the sandwich or on the side, are just a few of the sides offered. **Address:** 106 Hwy 72 E 38017 **Location:** Center; in Roseview Shopping Center. [B] [L] [D]

CORKY'S RIBS & BBQ   901/405-4999
▼▼ Barbecue. Casual Dining. $10-$28 **AAA Inspector Notes:** Here you'll enjoy good Southern fare in a causal, relaxed atmosphere. They have great-tasting ribs, chicken, beef, salads and homemade pies, which make this well-known barbecue restaurant a favorite stop in the city. It is also a great place to dine, whether for lunch or dinner, after a long day of enjoying all the attractions Memphis has to offer. **Features:** beer only. **Address:** 743 W Poplar Ave 38017 **Location:** Jct CR 175, just w on US 72. [L] [D] CALL 🅖🅜

EL PORTON   901/854-5770
▼▼ Mexican. Casual Dining. $5-$25 **AAA Inspector Notes:** Service is quick and friendly at this relaxed restaurant. The numerous Mexican dishes of fajitas, burritos, tacos and nachos should satisfy everyone. Fresh ingredients, authentic recipes and large portions make the meals tasty and a great value. **Features:** full bar, happy hour. **Address:** 1016 W Poplar Ave 38017 **Location:** 0.8 mi w of jct CR 175 on US 72. [L] [D] CALL 🅖🅜

FIREBIRDS WOOD FIRED GRILL   901/850-1603 ㊳
▼▼▼ American. Casual Dining. $11-$30 **AAA Inspector Notes:** The restaurant re-creates the atmosphere of a mountain lodge. Hand-cut steaks and seafood dominate the menu, which also lists a few pork and chicken entrees, as well as elk tenderloin medallions and buffalo meatloaf. The kitchen uses wood grilling, and pizzas bake in a wood-burning oven. Flavorful food, enhanced presentations and a skilled, knowledgeable and attentive staff, together with distinctive physical elements, make this place appealing. **Features:** full bar. **Reservations:** suggested. **Address:** 4600 Merchants Park Cir 38017 **Location:** SR 385 (Bill Morris Pkwy) exit S Houston Levee Rd, just s; in The Shops at Carriage Crossing. [L] [D]

COLUMBIA (D-4) pop. 34,681, elev. 656'
- **Hotels p. 68 • Restaurants p. 68**

The settlers who built Columbia on the low limestone bluffs of the Duck River in 1807 were a determined lot. A destructive flood, Native American threats and a series of earthquakes did not frighten them away.

In a region of fertile farmland, bluegrass meadows and wooded hills, Columbia boasts one of the state's richest collections of architecturally significant homes and plantations in five historic districts.

Maury County Convention & Visitors Bureau: Hunter Mathews Bldg., 8 Public Sq., Columbia, TN 38401. **Phone:** (931) 381-7176 or (888) 852-1860.

THE ATHENAEUM RECTORY is at 808 Athenaeum St. The 1835 house of Moorish-Gothic design has many original features and furnishings. The building was built by Samuel Walker, a nephew of President James K. Polk. It is all that remains of the Columbia Athenaeum, a nationally known women's college founded in 1852 by the Rev. Franklin Gillette Smith. **Time:** Allow 1 hour minimum. **Hours:** Tues.-Sat. 10-4, Feb.-Dec. Closed major holidays. **Cost:** $5. **Phone:** (931) 381-4822.

JAMES K. POLK HOME & MUSEUM is at 301 W. 7th St. The 1816 house is the only surviving residence of the 11th U.S. president besides the White House. It contains items and portraits belonging to the Polks along with many original furnishings from the White House. The adjacent Sisters' House exhibits political and Mexican War memorabilia as well as Mrs. Sarah Polk's jewelry and inaugural ball gown.

Note: Front entry into each building requires four steps; ramped entrances are available in the back. The Home Tour includes the upstairs (optional), where there are 20-30 steps up a staircase. **Time:** Allow 1 hour, 30 minutes minimum. **Hours:** Mon.-Sat. 9-5, Sun. 1-5, Apr.-Oct.; Mon.-Sat. 9-4, Sun. 1-5, rest of year. Closed Jan. 1, Thanksgiving, Christmas Eve and Christmas. **Cost:** $10; $8 (ages 60+); $7 (ages 13-18); $5 (ages 6-12); $25 (family). Combination ticket with Polk Presidential Hall $12; $10 (ages 60+); $9 (ages 13-18); $7 (ages 6-12); $35 (family). **Phone:** (931) 388-2354.

Polk Presidential Hall is on the grounds of the James K. Polk Home & Museum at 301 W. 7th St. This former 1882 church features original and changing exhibits related to the 11th U.S. president, his lifetime and the American presidency. **Hours:** Mon.-Sat. 9-5, Sun. 1-5, Apr.-Oct.; Mon.-Sat. 9-4, Sun. 1-5, rest of year. **Cost:** $5; $3 (ages 6-18). Combination ticket with James K. Polk Home & Museum $12; $10 (ages 60+); $9 (ages 13-18); $7 (ages 6-12); $35 (family). **Phone:** (931) 388-2354.

BAYMONT INN & SUITES COLUMBIA/MAURY   (931)388-3326

▼▼ **Hotel** $61-$99 **Address:** 715 S James M Campbell Blvd 38401 **Location:** Jct SR 50 and US 31, 0.9 mi w. Located in a commercial area. **Facility:** 55 units. 3 stories, interior corridors. **Terms:** cancellation fee imposed. **Pool(s):** outdoor. **Activities:** exercise room. **Guest Services:** valet laundry.

HAMPTON INN   (931)540-1222

▼▼▼▼ **Hotel** $109-$199 **Address:** 1551 Halifax Dr 38401 **Location:** I-65 exit 46, just w. **Facility:** 68 units. 3 stories, interior corridors. **Terms:** 1-7 night minimum stay, cancellation fee imposed. **Pool(s):** outdoor. **Activities:** exercise room. **Guest Services:** coin laundry.

AAA Benefit: Members save up to 10%!

HOLIDAY INN EXPRESS   931/380-2025

▼▼▼ **Hotel.** Rates not provided. **Address:** 1561 Halifax Dr 38401 **Location:** I-65 exit 46, just w. **Facility:** 73 units. 4 stories, interior corridors. **Pool(s):** heated indoor. **Activities:** exercise room. **Guest Services:** complimentary and valet laundry.

RICHLAND INN   931/381-4500

▼▼ **Motel** $75-$85 **Address:** 2405 Pulaski Hwy 38401 **Location:** Jct SR 50 and US 31, just s. Located in a commercial area. **Facility:** 74 units. 2 stories (no elevator), interior/exterior corridors. **Parking:** winter plug-ins. **Terms:** cancellation fee imposed.

WHERE TO EAT

BETTY'S PARKWAY RESTAURANT   931/388-5570

▼▼ ▼▼ American. Casual Dining. $5-$25 **AAA Inspector Notes:** Friendly service and excellent steaks make this is a popular spot. Other specialties include hand-formed gourmet burgers and a baked potato stuffed with secret ingredients. Breakfast is served all day. Tables with a river view are very popular. Inside, the jukebox takes center stage. **Features:** beer only, Sunday brunch. **Address:** 912 Riverside Dr 38401 **Location:** I-65 exit 46, 7.2 mi w on SR 99/US 412 (Bear Creek Pike), then 1 mi s.

LEGENDS STEAKHOUSE   931/380-1888

▼▼▼ Steak. Casual Dining. $7-$25 **AAA Inspector Notes:** In addition to the variety of steaks, which it is known for, this comfortable restaurant also serves tasty, freshly prepared dishes such as grilled chicken breast with wild rice and potato casserole. Melt-in-your-mouth hot rolls, heavily basted in butter and baked, are impossible to resist. **Features:** full bar, happy hour. **Address:** 2401 Pulaski Hwy 38401 **Location:** Jct US 31 and SR 50.

PUCKETT'S GRO. & RESTAURANT   931/490-4550

▼▼ Southern Barbecue. Casual Dining. $7-$26 **AAA Inspector Notes:** In business for more than 50 years, this is where everyone goes for live music and country cooking. Try the Elvis breakfast, their famous pork barbecue, or Southern fried chicken. Stay a while and enjoy singers, songwriters and local bands from all over the Music City region. Some live performances have a small cover charge. **Features:** full bar, patio dining, Sunday brunch, happy hour. **Reservations:** suggested, weekends. **Address:** 15 Public Square 38401 **Location:** In historic downtown. **Parking:** on-site and street.

SQUARE MARKET & CAFE   931/840-3636

▼▼▼ American. Casual Dining. $5-$11 **AAA Inspector Notes:** With more country charm than a summer Sunday picnic, this delightful market/deli will be your new downtown favorite. Literally tucked into a corner under the shadow of the downtown courthouse, try their famous chicken salad sandwich, a fresh cup of chunky tomato and artichoke soup or their famous Tennessee Hot Brown (baked with a fresh Alfredo sauce and cheddar cheese topping). Leave room for dessert; the chocolate decadence is sinful! Look for the red and white striped awning. **Features:** full bar, patio dining. **Reservations:** suggested, weekends. **Address:** 36 Public Square 38401 **Location:** In historic downtown; northwest corner behind courthouse. **Parking:** on-site and street.

STAN'S RESTAURANT   931/381-2234

▼ Southern American. Casual Dining. $5-$14 **AAA Inspector Notes:** Pull off the interstate to fuel up your car, and yourself. This no-frills restaurant, opened in 1947, is attached to a souvenir shop, a gas station and a car wash. **Features:** beer only, Sunday brunch. **Address:** 1555 Bear Creek Pike 38401 **Location:** I-65 exit 46, just w.

COOKEVILLE (C-5) pop. 30,435, elev. 1181'

COOKEVILLE DEPOT MUSEUM is at 116 W. Broad St. This 1909 former depot houses artifacts and photographs of the Tennessee Central Railroad. On the grounds are two cabooses and a 1913 10-wheeler steam locomotive. **Time:** Allow 1 hour minimum. **Hours:** Tues.-Sat. 10-4. Closed Jan. 1, Thanksgiving and Christmas. **Cost:** Donations. **Phone:** (931) 528-8570.

AMERICAS BEST VALUE INN   (931)526-9521

Motel
$50-$110

Address: 897 S Jefferson Ave 38501 **Location:** I-40 exit 287, just n. **Facility:** 78 units. 2 stories (no elevator), exterior corridors. **Terms:** cancellation fee imposed. **Pool(s):** outdoor. **Guest Services:** coin laundry. **Featured Amenity: continental breakfast.**

BEST WESTERN THUNDERBIRD MOTEL   (931)526-7115

Hotel
$63-$70

AAA Benefit:
Save 10% or more every day and earn 10% bonus points!

Address: 900 S Jefferson Ave 38501 **Location:** I-40 exit 287, just n. **Facility:** 76 units. 3 stories, exterior corridors. **Pool(s):** outdoor. **Activities:** limited exercise equipment. **Guest Services:** coin laundry.

COMFORT INN & SUITES   (931)372-0086

Hotel $80-$139 **Address:** 1045 Interstate Dr 38501 **Location:** I-40 exit 287, 0.3 mi n. **Facility:** 60 units. 3 stories, interior corridors. **Pool(s):** heated indoor. **Activities:** hot tub, limited exercise equipment. **Guest Services:** valet and coin laundry.

COMFORT SUITES   (931)372-1881

Hotel $89-$189 **Address:** 1035 Interstate Dr 38501 **Location:** I-40 exit 287, just n, then just w. **Facility:** 54 units, some two bedrooms. 3 stories, interior corridors. **Pool(s):** heated indoor. **Activities:** sauna, hot tub, limited exercise equipment. **Guest Services:** coin laundry.

COUNTRY INN & SUITES BY CARLSON COOKEVILLE   (931)525-6668

Hotel $99-$129 **Address:** 1151 S Jefferson Ave 38506 **Location:** I-40 exit 287, just s. **Facility:** 98 units. 5 stories, interior corridors. **Terms:** cancellation fee imposed. **Amenities:** safes. **Pool(s):** heated outdoor. **Activities:** limited exercise equipment. **Guest Services:** valet and coin laundry.

FAIRFIELD INN & SUITES BY MARRIOTT COOKEVILLE   (931)854-1050

Hotel $97-$160 **Address:** 1200 Sam's St 38506 **Location:** I-40 exit 287, just s on Jefferson Ave, then 0.3 mi w on Bunker Hill Rd. Opposite Sam's Club Shopping Center. **Facility:** 81 units.

AAA Benefit:
Members save 5% or more!

3 stories, interior corridors. **Pool(s):** heated indoor. **Activities:** hot tub, exercise room. **Guest Services:** valet and coin laundry.

HAMPTON INN   (931)651-1500

Hotel $114-$179 **Address:** 1025 Interstate Dr 38501 **Location:** I-40 exit 287, just n. **Facility:** 84 units. 4 stories, interior corridors. **Terms:** 1-7 night minimum stay, cancellation fee imposed. **Pool(s):** outdoor. **Activities:** exercise room. **Guest Services:** complimentary and valet laundry.

AAA Benefit:
Members save up to 10%!

HOLIDAY INN EXPRESS & SUITES   (931)881-2000

Hotel $119-$259 **Address:** 1228 Bunkerhill Rd 38506 **Location:** I-40 exit 287, just s. Across from Sam's Club. **Facility:** 93 units. 4 stories, interior corridors. **Terms:** 7 day cancellation notice. **Pool(s):** outdoor. **Activities:** exercise room. **Guest Services:** complimentary and valet laundry.

LA QUINTA INN & SUITES   (931)520-3800

Hotel $82-$214 **Address:** 1131 S Jefferson Ave 38506 **Location:** I-40 exit 287, just s. **Facility:** 66 units, some efficiencies. 3 stories, interior corridors. **Pool(s):** outdoor. **Activities:** limited exercise equipment. **Guest Services:** valet and coin laundry.

RED ROOF INN COOKEVILLE-TENNESSEE TECH.   (931)528-2020

Motel
$50-$125

Address: 1292 S Walnut Ave 38501 **Location:** I-40 exit 287, just n. **Facility:** 51 units. 2 stories (no elevator), exterior corridors. **Pool(s):** outdoor. **Guest Services:** complimentary laundry. **Featured Amenity: continental breakfast.**

 **WHERE TO EAT**

CRAWDADDY'S WEST SIDE GRILL   931/526-4660

Southern Cajun. Casual Dining. $9-$25 **AAA Inspector Notes:** *Historic.* Dine inside or outdoors on the patio of this restaurant, and enjoy such offerings as gator bites, crawfish pie and shrimp étouffée, or if you have a craving for steak, check out the rib-eye. **Features:** full bar, patio dining, Sunday brunch. **Address:** 53 W Broad St 38501 **Location:** In historic downtown. **Parking:** street only.

EL TAPATIO MEXICAN RESTAURANT   931/372-0246

Mexican. Casual Dining. $7-$13 **AAA Inspector Notes:** Mexican tapestries and paintings lend to the festive atmosphere at El Tapatio, where you simply have to try the chimichangas stuffed with savory chicken or beef. The delicious poblano peppers also are among the south-of-the-border fare offerings. **Features:** beer & wine. **Address:** 900 S Jefferson Ave 38501 **Location:** I-40 exit 287, just n.

MADDUX STATION   931/854-0883

American. Casual Dining. $8-$25 **AAA Inspector Notes:** This well-traveled chef returns to his roots and provides big-city excitement for the palate. Whether opting for a glass of wine and a small snack or dessert or choosing a full meal, the cuisine is sure to please the most sophisticated diner. The chef's daily offerings should not be overlooked. **Features:** full bar, Sunday brunch. **Address:** 319 E Spring St 38501 **Location:** Center; downtown square. **Parking:** street only.

THE ORIGINAL GONDOLA   931/854-1466

◆ Italian. Casual Dining. $7-$20 **AAA Inspector Notes:** Choose any of the numerous toppings for your pizza or calzone made from fresh dough at this family-style eatery. Baked manicotti, eggplant parmigiana and lasagna as well as sandwiches and a value-oriented lunch menu offer something for everyone. **Features:** beer only. **Address:** 1156 S Jefferson Ave 38506 **Location:** I-40 exit 287, just s.

[L] [D] CALL [&M]

CORDOVA

• Hotels & Restaurants map & index p. 154
• Part of Memphis area — see map p. 134

COMFORT SUITES   (901)213-3600   **45**

◆ Hotel $89-$149 **Address:** 2427 N Germantown Pkwy 38018 **Location:** I-40 exit 16 or 16A, just s, then just w on Rock Creek Cove. **Facility:** 60 units. 3 stories, interior corridors. **Pool(s):** heated indoor. **Activities:** exercise room. **Guest Services:** valet and coin laundry.

[¶] CALL [&M] [≈] [BIZ] [♀] [✕] [📶] [☐] [📺]

MICROTEL INN & SUITES BY WYNDHAM
                                      (901)213-4141   **46**

◆ Hotel $60-$130 **Address:** 2423 N Germantown Pkwy 38018 **Location:** I-40 exit 16 or 16A, just s, then just w on Rock Creek Cove. **Facility:** 63 units. 3 stories, interior corridors. **Guest Services:** coin laundry.

[¶] [♀] [📺] /SOME UNITS [🐾] [📶] [☐]

WINGATE BY WYNDHAM   (901)386-1110   **47**

◆ Hotel $90-$120 **Address:** 2270 N Germantown Pkwy 38016 **Location:** I-40 exit 16 or 16A, 0.4 mi s. **Facility:** 100 units. 3 stories, interior corridors. **Amenities:** safes. **Pool(s):** outdoor. **Activities:** exercise room. **Guest Services:** valet and coin laundry.

[¶] CALL [&M] [≈] [BIZ] [HS] [♀] [✕] [📶] [☐] [📺]

WHERE TO EAT

BOMBAY HOUSE   901/755-4114   **29**

◆ Indian. Casual Dining. $9-$18 **AAA Inspector Notes:** Flavorful, aromatic spices are the hallmarks of the traditional Indian fare served at this friendly, casual café. Enjoy classic dishes like tandoori chicken, chicken korma, lamb vindaloo and shrimp curry, plus many vegetarian dishes. Daily lunch buffet available. **Features:** beer & wine. **Address:** 1727 N Germantown Pkwy, Suite 101 38018 **Location:** I-40 exit 16 or 16A, 1.7 mi s; in The Commons at Dexter Lakes Shopping Center. [L] [D]

THE BUTCHER SHOP STEAKHOUSE   901/757-4244   **30**

◆ Steak. Casual Dining. $19-$50 **AAA Inspector Notes:** This casual steakhouse is a locals favorite for well-prepared, aged Prime beef grilled over hickory charcoal. You're given the option of preparing your own steak, but why would you want to? Sit back, relax, and enjoy the complimentary house salad while you wait for your order. The monstrous baked potato can be topped with anything you like, or you may opt for one of the vegetable sides. The house-made cashew-crunch cheesecake is a tempting delight. **Features:** full bar, patio dining. **Address:** 107 S Germantown Pkwy 38018 **Location:** I-40 exit 16 or 16A, 4.5 mi s. [D] CALL [&M]

CASABLANCA RESTAURANT   901/433-9712   **26**

◆ Moroccan. Casual Dining. $8-$20 **AAA Inspector Notes:** Transport yourself to exotic Morocco at this tiny café offering flavorful Middle Eastern fare in a charming setting. Enjoy lamb, beef and chicken kebabs, falafel, and shawarma (rotisserie-grilled meats served with pita). A few Greek specialties like spanakopita and moussaka are featured too, and baklava is a sweet way to end a meal. **Address:** 1890 N Germantown Pkwy, Suite 99 38016 **Location:** I-40 exit 16 or 16A, 1.4 mi s; in Briarwood Collection Shopping Center. [L] [D]

HUEY'S   901/754-3885   **27**

◆ Burgers Sandwiches. Casual Dining. $7-$12 **AAA Inspector Notes:** Craving a good burger and a beer in a funky, fun eatery? Check out this local chain, as famous for their juicy burgers as for the toothpicks stuck in the ceilings. The Huey burger is a true classic, but avocado, mushrooms, and barbecue sauce are topping options, too. For a healthier bent, swap beef for a turkey or veggie patty. The rest of the menu is lined with salads, sandwiches and bar munchies like onion rings, wings, fried pickles, and loaded nachos. Live music on Sundays. **Features:** full bar, patio dining, happy hour. **Address:** 1771 N Germantown Pkwy 38018 **Location:** I-40 exit 16 or 16A, 1.7 mi s; in Cordova Collection at Dexter Shopping Center.

[L] [D] [LATE]

JIM 'N NICK'S BAR-B-Q   901/388-0998

◆ Barbecue. Casual Dining. $7-$25 **AAA Inspector Notes:** Southern hospitality reigns at Jim 'N Nick's, where diners get neighborly treatment as they dig into huge portions of tasty lean sausage, fresh chili, juicy smoked beef and pork. A slice of sublime homemade pie ends the meal on a high note. **Features:** full bar, patio dining. **Address:** 2359 N Germantown Pkwy 38016 **Location:** I-40 exit 16 or 16A, just s. [L] [D] CALL [&M]

LA HACIENDA   901/624-2920   **28**

◆◆ Mexican. Casual Dining. $8-$15 **AAA Inspector Notes:** Family owned and operated, this restaurant serves huge portions at reasonable prices. Ten types of nachos, salads, eight types of burritos and just as many fajita selections await your dining pleasure. **Features:** full bar. **Address:** 1760 N Germantown Pkwy 38016 **Location:** I-40 exit 16 or 16A, 1.5 mi s. [L] [D]

SEKISUI   901/309-8800

◆ Japanese Sushi. Casual Dining. $7-$25 **AAA Inspector Notes:** Drop by this casual eatery for a tasty meal of traditional Japanese cuisine, including tempura and a lengthy list of sushi, with nigiri, sashimi and sushi rolls, both traditional and innovative. For a sweet treat, finish with green tea ice cream. **Features:** full bar, early bird specials, happy hour. **Address:** 1884 N Germantown Pkwy 38016 **Location:** I-40 exit 16A, 1.5 mi s. [L] [D] CALL [&M]

COUNCE

HAMPTON INN - PICKWICK DAM AT SHILOH FALLS
                                      (731)689-3031

◆◆ Hotel $99-$169 **Address:** 90 Old South Rd 38326 **Location:** Jct SR 128, 1.3 mi se on SR 57. **Facility:** 50 units. 3 stories, interior corridors. **Parking:** winter plug-ins. **Terms:** 1-7 night minimum stay, cancellation fee imposed. **Pool(s):** outdoor.

AAA Benefit: Members save up to 10%!

[≈] [BIZ] [♀] [📺] /SOME UNITS [HS] [☐] [📺]

PICKWICK LANDING STATE RESORT PARK INN
                                      731/689-3135

◆◆ Resort Hotel $74-$88 **Address:** 120 Playground Loop 38326 **Location:** Waterfront. Jct SR 128, just se on SR 57, then just e; in state park. **Facility:** Rooms have simple, modest décor and spacious bathrooms, plus balconies for views of the river and dam. Recreational activities abound. Pets are permitted in some rooms; phone for details. 124 units, some two bedrooms. 6 stories, interior corridors. **Parking:** winter plug-ins. **Terms:** check-in 4 pm, 3 day cancellation notice-fee imposed. **Dining:** Captain's Galley, see separate listing. **Pool(s):** outdoor, heated indoor. **Activities:** beach access, motor boats, marina, fishing, regulation golf, tennis, recreation programs in summer, playground, lawn sports, picnic facilities, trails, exercise room. **Guest Services:** coin laundry.

[¶] [♥] CALL [&M] [≈] [BIZ] [♀] [✕] [📺] /SOME UNITS [🐾] [☐] [📺]

WHERE TO EAT

CAPTAIN'S GALLEY   731/689-3135

♦♦ American. Family Dining. $8-$17 **AAA Inspector Notes:** A large lunch and dinner buffet-including salads and various chicken, beef, and ham dishes as well as tasty cobbler-is always part of the menu at this popular resort. A separate a la carte menu also is available. **Features:** full bar, patio dining. **Address:** 120 Playground Loop 38326 **Location:** Jct SR 128, just se on SR 57, then just e; in state park; in Pickwick Landing State Resort Park Inn.

[B] [L] [D] CALL 🛂M

FREDDY T'S   731/689-3099

♦♦ American. Casual Dining. $10-$27 **AAA Inspector Notes:** Here you'll unwind in a fun, casual, tropical atmosphere to sample chicken, fish, pasta and various seafood combinations. Take a seat at a picnic table or climb inside half of a speedboat. Enjoy a drink under the shade of a surfboard, then top it all off with a thick slice of cheesecake. **Features:** full bar, patio dining, happy hour. **Address:** 12750 Hwy 57 S 38326 **Location:** SR 57, 4.3 mi se of jct SR 128; at Pickwick Dam. [D] 🐾

COVINGTON (D-1) pop. 9,038, elev. 335'
• Part of Memphis area — see map p. 134

TIPTON COUNTY MUSEUM, 751 Bert Johnston Ave., features history exhibits of regional interest and a nature center with displays that highlight aspects of the West Tennessee ecosystem. The facility is in a forested 20-acre wildlife sanctuary and park with nature trails. **Time:** Allow 1 hour minimum. **Hours:** Tues.-Fri. 9-5, Sat. 9-3. Closed major holidays. **Cost:** Donations. **Phone:** (901) 476-0242.

DAYS INN   (901)475-1177

♦♦ Motel $70-$120 **Address:** 80 Deena Cove-Hwy 51 N 38019 **Location:** SR 59 W, 0.9 mi n. **Facility:** 35 units. 2 stories (no elevator), exterior corridors. **Parking:** winter plug-ins. **Terms:** 3 day cancellation notice-fee imposed. **Pool(s):** outdoor. **Guest Services:** coin laundry.

🍽️⁺ CALL 🛂M 🏊 [HS] 📶 🛗 🖼️

COWAN (D-5) pop. 1,737, elev. 978'

COWAN RAILROAD MUSEUM off US 64/41A at the railroad station, 108 Front St. S. Housed in a 1904 former railroad depot, the museum features an HO scale model railroad of the Cowan area, photographs, tools, old maps, control panels and figures in period costumes. On display in an outdoor park is a full-size train, including a 1920 Porter steam locomotive, a flat car, a caboose and a diesel electric locomotive. **Time:** Allow 30 minutes minimum. **Hours:** Thurs.-Sat. 10-4, Sun. 1-4, May-Oct. **Cost:** Free. **Phone:** (931) 967-3078.

CROSSVILLE (C-6) pop. 10,795
• Restaurants p. 72

HISTORIC HOMESTEADS HOUSE MUSEUM, 2611 Pigeon Ridge Rd., is one of more than 250 houses built 1937-38 during the Roosevelt-era Cumberland Homesteads project. The restored house includes furnishings from the 1930s and '40s that were made and used by early Homesteaders. **Hours:** Mon.-Sat. 1-5, Apr.-Oct. **Cost:** $2; $1 (ages 6-12). Combination ticket with Historic Homesteads Tower Museum $5; $2 (ages 6-12). **Phone:** (931) 456-9663.

HISTORIC HOMESTEADS TOWER MUSEUM is 4 mi. s. on US 127 at jct. US 127 and SR 68. The museum is in a stone tower built 1937-38 as the administrative offices for the Roosevelt-era Cumberland Homesteads project. More than 250 families participated in the "Showplace of the New Deal." The museum contains photographs, documents and items from the 1930s and '40s. Some of the original homesteads can be seen from the tower; one homestead is open to the public, the Historic Homesteads House Museum *(see attraction listing this page)*.

Time: Allow 30 minutes minimum. **Hours:** Mon.-Sat. 10-5, Sun. 1-5, Mar. to mid-Dec. Closed Easter and Thanksgiving. **Cost:** $4; $1 (ages 6-12). Combination ticket with Historic Homesteads House Museum $5; $2 (ages 6-12). **Phone:** (931) 456-9663.

WINERIES

• **Stonehaus Winery** is off I-40 exit 320 at 2444 Genesis Rd. **Hours:** Mon.-Sat. 9-7, Sun. noon-5. Closed major holidays. **Phone:** (931) 484-9463. [GT]

COMFORT SUITES   (931)707-8638

♦♦♦ Hotel $85-$114 **Address:** 2581 E 1st St 38555 **Location:** I-40 exit 322 (Peavine Rd), just s. **Facility:** 60 units. 3 stories, interior corridors. **Pool(s):** heated indoor. **Activities:** hot tub, exercise room. **Guest Services:** valet and coin laundry.

🍽️⁺ CALL 🛂M 🏊 [BIZ] [HS] 📶 ✕ 🛗 🖼️ ▢

HAMPTON INN CROSSVILLE   (931)707-7170

♦♦♦ Hotel $109-$249 **Address:** 64 Hospitality Dr 38555 **Location:** I-40 exit 322 (Peavine Rd), just s to 1st St. **Facility:** 72 units. 3 stories, interior corridors. **Terms:** 1-7 night minimum stay, cancellation fee imposed. **Pool(s):** outdoor. **Activities:** exercise room. **Guest Services:** valet laundry.

> **AAA Benefit:** Members save up to 10%!

🍽️⁺ CALL 🛂M 🏊 [BIZ] [HS] 📶 ✕ 🛗 🖼️ ▢

HOLIDAY INN EXPRESS HOTEL & SUITES   (931)707-1035

♦♦♦ Hotel $124-$138 **Address:** 560 Peavine Rd 38571 **Location:** I-40 exit 322 (Peavine Rd), just n. **Facility:** 67 units. 3 stories, interior corridors. **Terms:** cancellation fee imposed. **Pool(s):** heated indoor. **Activities:** hot tub, exercise room. **Guest Services:** valet and coin laundry.

🍽️⁺ CALL 🛂M 🏊 [BIZ] 📶 ✕ ▢ /SOME UNITS 🛗 🖼️

QUALITY INN CROSSVILLE   (931)484-1551

♦♦ Hotel $79-$129

Address: 4035 Hwy 127 N 38571 **Location:** I-40 exit 317 (US 127), just n. **Facility:** 64 units. 2 stories (no elevator), interior corridors. **Pool(s):** heated outdoor. **Activities:** exercise room. **Guest Services:** valet and coin laundry. **Featured Amenity:** full hot breakfast.

[SAVE] 🏊 [BIZ] 📶 ▢ /SOME UNITS 🍽️ 🛗 🖼️

Use travel time to share driving tips
and rules of the road with your teens

WHERE TO EAT

CANCUN MEXICAN RESTAURANT   931/707-5106
◈ Mexican. Casual Dining. $5-$20 **AAA Inspector Notes:** This restaurant focuses on Mexican standards, including burritos, enchiladas, fajitas and more. **Features:** patio dining. **Address:** 187 Peavine Rd 38558 **Location:** I-40 exit 322 (Peavine Rd), just s.
L D

CUMBERLAND MOUNTAIN STATE PARK RESTAURANT
                                             931/484-7186
◈ American. Casual Dining. $8-$12 **AAA Inspector Notes:** Inside park boundaries, this restaurant affords hard-to-beat views of the river and then ups the ante with a great buffet that varies its offerings of seafood, prime rib, pork chops and chicken, in addition to hot vegetables and salad fixings. And of course, you also have the option of ordering from the regular menu. On Fridays, it's hard to beat the park's pride selection: fried catfish. For dessert, the made-from-scratch banana pudding is a delicious treat. **Address:** Cumberland Mountain State Park 38555 **Location:** I-40 exit 317 (US 127), 9 mi s. L CALL M

LEFTY'S BAR-B-QUE   931/484-4205
◈ Barbecue. Casual Dining. $6-$18 **AAA Inspector Notes:** Friendly and helpful servers dish up wonderful smoked pulled pork, ribs, half-chicken or turkey as well as pork chops or pork tenderloin at this casual eatery. Freshly made fruit cobbler and fudge pie with a scoop of ice cream are great meal-enders. **Address:** 2565 Genesis Rd 38571 **Location:** I-40 exit 320, just n. L D

◆ GEM CUMBERLAND GAP NATIONAL HISTORICAL PARK (B-7)

Elevations in the park range from 1,600 ft. at the Cumberland Gap to 3,513 ft. at White Rocks. Refer to AAA maps for additional elevation information.

At the convergence of Kentucky, Tennessee and Virginia, Cumberland Gap National Historical Park covers 24,000 acres of heavily forested, rugged mountains honoring the historic pass.

The gap provides a natural doorway through the mountains. It was first used by migratory animals as a seasonal thoroughfare, then by Native Americans, whose footpaths followed buffalo and deer trails. The westward movement of settlers seemed barred by the Allegheny ridge until April 1750, when Dr. Thomas Walker discovered the gap while seeking the fabled land to the west, the "Kentucke" of Native American lore.

Daniel Boone passed through with a hunting party in 1769, and in 1775 he blazed the Wilderness Road. From 1775 to 1796 the gap could only be used by those on foot or horseback, and although no wagon passed over it during this period, more than 200,000 people made their way through the gap into Kentucky and beyond.

A strategic point during the Civil War, Cumberland Gap changed hands several times without any major battles. Some of the earthwork fortifications remain.

In the 1990s, the 4,600-foot-long Cumberland Gap Highway Tunnel was built; the project also included rerouting US 25E through the tunnel and the addition of new bridges, highway interchanges and parking areas. Although the final cost of this joint effort led by the National Park Service and the Federal Highway Administration was a staggering $265 million, the construction plan alleviated traffic problems and improved motorist safety while simultaneously restoring the historic appearance of the Cumberland Gap and the Wilderness Road.

General Information and Activities

At an elevation of 2,440 feet, Pinnacle Overlook provides a view into the gap as well as views of the mountain range and parts of three states. It is accessible via a 4-mile paved road from the visitor center. No trailers or vehicles more than 20 feet long are allowed. Shuttle service may be arranged for a small fee when staff is available; reservations are required.

Still a wild area, the park offers approximately 85 miles of hiking trails ranging from relatively easy nature trails to those requiring an overnight trek. Many park features, including Sand Cave, a multicolored sandstone overhang, and White Rocks, a prominent sandstone outcropping, can be reached only by trail. Ridge Trail, a 19-mile-long route offering panoramas of the valley, approaches five primitive campsites, all accessible by foot. The Wilderness Road Campground has 160 campsites, 41 of which have hookups.

Hensley Settlement is a reconstruction of a community that was occupied 1903-51. Reminiscent of a time much earlier than that from which it actually dates, Hensley seems like a community of the late 1700s or early 1800s. The settlement sits atop a mountain in the eastern end of the park. With more than 70 acres of land under cultivation, it has several reconstructed log houses, barns and outbuildings. The site can be reached by an all-day hike or, from mid-May through Oct. 31, via a guided tour that departs the park's visitor center daily. Building interiors may be seen during the 3.5- to 4-hour trip, which includes shuttle transportation to and from the settlement. The cost is $10; $5 (ages 0-12 and senior citizens). Phone (606) 248-2817, ext. 1075, for the shuttle tour schedule; reservations are recommended.

It is not advisable to hike alone; overnight camping requires a permit. Trail guides and other information can be obtained at the visitor center. The visitor center also contains a museum, which chronicles the rich history of the gap. Throughout the year ranger-led programs suitable for the entire family introduce visitors to the historical, cultural and natural aspects of the park; phone for a schedule of events.

The park is open daily. Some parking areas close before dusk. The visitor center at the park entrance is open daily 8-5, Memorial Day-Labor Day; otherwise varies rest of year. Closed Christmas.

ADMISSION to the park is free.

PETS must be restricted at all times, either in vehicles or by leash, and are not allowed in public buildings.

ADDRESS inquiries to the Superintendent, Cumberland Gap National Historical Park, 91 Bartlett Park Rd., Middlesboro, KY 40965; phone (606) 248-2817.

GAP CAVE is .25 mi. s. of Middlesboro, Ky., on US 25E. Two-hour guided tours of the cave, discovered in 1750, cover a 1.5-mile route and are conducted by lantern light. Rooms and walls are covered with stalactites and stalagmites. Wildlife, including bats and salamanders, can be seen, as can the names of Civil War soldiers carved on the walls.

Note: The guided tour's path includes 183 steps; visitors are advised to wear good walking shoes. No sandals or open-toed shoes are permitted. Due to the threat of white-nose syndrome to bats, visitors should not wear clothing and footwear that has been worn in other caves unless properly decontaminated.

Time: Allow 2 hours minimum. **Hours:** Tours are given daily at 10 and 2, Memorial Day-Labor Day; otherwise varies. Tickets may be purchased at the park visitor center or at Daniel Boone parking area 30 minutes in advance of the tour. Reservations are recommended, especially on weekends. **Cost:** $8; $4 (ages 5-12 and senior citizens with an interagency senior pass). Under 5 are not permitted on cave tours. **Phone:** (606) 248-2817. GT

DANDRIDGE pop. 2,812

HAMPTON INN DANDRIDGE   (865)940-1200

▼▼▼ **Hotel** $89-$145 **Address:** 126 Sharon Dr 37725 **Location:** I-40 exit 417, just s. **Facility:** 62 units. 3 stories, interior corridors. **Terms:** 1-7 night minimum stay, cancellation fee imposed. **Pool(s):** heated indoor. **Activities:** hot tub, exercise room. **Guest Services:** coin laundry.

AAA Benefit: Members save up to 10%!

CALL ⚑M 🏊 BIZ HS 🛜 ✕ 🖥 🖨 🖳

JEFFERSON INN   (865)940-5042

▼▼ **Hotel** $50-$110 **Address:** 127 Sharon Dr 37725 **Location:** I-40 exit 417, just s. **Facility:** 42 units. 2 stories (no elevator), interior corridors. **Terms:** cancellation fee imposed. **Pool(s):** outdoor. **Guest Services:** coin laundry.

🏊 BIZ HS 🛜 🖥 / SOME UNITS 🐕 🖨 🖳

SUPER 8   (865)397-1200

▼▼ **Hotel** $60-$70 **Address:** 125 Sharon Dr 37725 **Location:** I-40 exit 417, just s. **Facility:** 50 units. 2 stories (no elevator), interior corridors. **Pool(s):** outdoor. **Guest Services:** coin laundry.

🏊 BIZ 🛜 🖥 🖨 🖳 / SOME UNITS 🐕

DAYTON (D-6) pop. 7,191, elev. 703'

In the small town of Dayton during the summer of 1925 the basic principles of education were profoundly shaken. The eyes of the world were on the trial of John T. Scopes, a high-school science teacher accused of teaching evolution as fact rather than theory.

So great were the implications of this landmark case that the greatest legal minds of the day—William Jennings Bryan and Clarence Darrow—served as prosecution and defense attorneys, respectively. Darrow and Scopes lost, but the philosophy of education was never quite the same thereafter. Bryan died in town the Sunday following the verdict. In 1930 the small, Christian, liberal arts college of Bryan was founded in his honor.

The 7-day Tennessee Strawberry Festival in early May includes concerts, gospel singing, arts and crafts displays, sports events, parades, fireworks and strawberry foodstuffs.

Rhea Economic and Tourism Council: 107 Main St., Dayton, TN 37321. **Phone:** (423) 775-6171.

RHEA COUNTY COURTHOUSE & MUSEUM is at 1475 Market St. The Romanesque Revival-style courthouse was the site of the 8-day Scopes trial, the 1925 landmark case that pitted the Darwinian theory of evolution against Biblical creationism. The 1891 courtroom remains much as it was during the trial and is still used today. The Scopes Trial Museum, 2 floors below, contains articles relating to the trial and traces the proceedings from beginning to end. **Time:** Allow 30 minutes minimum. **Hours:** Mon.-Fri. 9-5. Closed major holidays. **Cost:** Free. **Phone:** (423) 775-7801.

BEST WESTERN DAYTON   (423)775-6560

Motel $65-$149

AAA Benefit: Save 10% or more every day and earn 10% bonus points!

Address: 7835 Rhea County Hwy 37321 **Location:** 1 mi n on US 27. **Facility:** 46 units. 2 stories (no elevator), exterior corridors. **Pool(s):** heated indoor. **Guest Services:** coin laundry.

SAVE 🏊 HS 🛜 🖥 🖨 🖳 / SOME UNITS 🐕

HOLIDAY INN EXPRESS   423/570-0080

▼▼▼ **Hotel.** Rates not provided. **Address:** 2650 Rhea County Hwy 37321 **Location:** 5 mi s on US 27. **Facility:** 66 units. 3 stories, interior corridors. **Pool(s):** indoor. **Activities:** exercise room. **Guest Services:** coin laundry.

CALL ⚑M 🏊 BIZ HS 🛜 ✕ 🖥 🖨 🖳

DECHERD pop. 2,361

QUALITY INN   (931)962-0130

▼▼▼ **Motel** $83-$85 **Address:** 1838 Decherd Blvd 37324 **Location:** Jct Main St and SR 41A, just s. **Facility:** 42 units. 2 stories (no elevator), exterior corridors. **Pool(s):** outdoor. **Activities:** limited exercise equipment.

🏊 BIZ 🛜 🖥 🖨 🖳 / SOME UNITS 🐕

DELANO (D-6) elev. 784'

WINERIES

- **Savannah Oaks Winery** is at 1817 Delano Rd. **Hours:** Mon.-Thurs. 10-5, Fri.-Sat. 10-6, Sun. 1-6. Closed Easter and Christmas. **Phone:** (423) 263-2762. GT

Keep your focus safely

on the road when driving

DICKSON pop. 14,538

BEST WESTERN EXECUTIVE INN   (615)446-0541

Hotel
$70-$100

AAA Benefit: Save 10% or more every day and earn 10% bonus points!

Address: 2338 Hwy 46 S 37055 **Location:** I-40 exit 172, just n. Located near railroad tracks. **Facility:** 60 units. 2 stories (no elevator), exterior corridors. **Pool(s):** outdoor. **Guest Services:** coin laundry. **Featured Amenity:** continental breakfast.

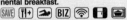

COMFORT INN   (615)740-1000

Hotel
$91-$199

Address: 1085 E Christi Dr 37055 **Location:** I-40 exit 172, just ne. Located in a busy commercial area. **Facility:** 67 units. 3 stories, interior corridors. **Pool(s):** heated indoor. **Activities:** limited exercise equipment. **Guest Services:** coin laundry. **Featured Amenity:** full hot breakfast.

HAMPTON INN   (615)446-1088

Hotel
$102-$350

AAA Benefit: Members save up to 10%!

Address: 1080 E Christi Rd 37055 **Location:** I-40 exit 172, just ne. **Facility:** 62 units. 3 stories, interior corridors. **Terms:** 1-7 night minimum stay, cancellation fee imposed. **Pool(s):** heated indoor. **Activities:** sauna, hot tub, exercise room. **Guest Services:** coin laundry. **Featured Amenity:** continental breakfast.

HOLIDAY INN EXPRESS & SUITES   615/446-2781
Hotel. Rates not provided. **Address:** 100 Barzani Blvd 37055 **Location:** I-40 exit 172, just se. **Facility:** 65 units. 3 stories, interior corridors. **Pool(s):** heated indoor. **Activities:** exercise room. **Guest Services:** coin laundry.

SUPER 8   (615)446-1923
Hotel $50-$100 **Address:** 150 Suzanne Dr 37055 **Location:** I-40 exit 172, just ne. **Facility:** 57 units. 2 stories, interior corridors. **Parking:** winter plug-ins. **Terms:** 3 day cancellation notice-fee imposed. **Pool(s):** heated indoor. **Guest Services:** coin laundry.

DUCKTOWN (E-7) pop. 475, elev. 1,720'

During the late 19th century in Ducktown copper ore was treated by roasting it on large piles of wood. The sulphur dioxide fumes given off and the felling of all surrounding trees resulted in a landscape similar to the Badlands of the West. Current reforestation practices have reclaimed much of the impacted area. In the vicinity today are many old buildings and abandoned mines. Scenic US 64 passes through Ducktown, running west through 20 miles of state and federal forestland before reaching the intersection with US 411 at Ocoee.

Ocoee Country Polk County, Tennessee Chamber of Commerce: 1697 Highway 64, P.O. Box 960, Benton, TN 37307. **Phone:** (423) 338-5040 or (877) 790-2157.

DUCKTOWN BASIN MUSEUM is on SR 68, .2 mi. n. of US 64 at 212 Burra Burra St. The museum presents 150 years of history in about an hour. Visitors can take a short journey through a century-and-a-half of copper mining and everyday life in the historic Copper Basin. View displays from the arrival of the area's oldest settlers through the closing of the last mine in 1987. **Hours:** Mon.-Sat. 10-4:30, Apr.-Oct.; Mon.-Sat. 9:30-4, Nov.-Dec.; Tues.-Sat. 9:30-4, rest of year. **Cost:** $5; $4 (ages 55+); $2 (ages 13-17); $1 (ages 0-12). **Phone:** (423) 496-5778.

RECREATIONAL ACTIVITIES
White-water Rafting

- **Ocoee Rafting Inc.** is at jct. US 64 and SR 68. **Hours:** Rafting trips are offered Thurs.-Mon., June-Aug.; Sat.-Sun., Apr.-May and Sept.-Oct. Departure times vary; phone ahead. **Phone:** (423) 496-3388 or (800) 251-4800.
- **Wildwater Ltd. Outdoor Adventures** is 3 mi. w. on US 64. Zipline activities also are available. **Hours:** Rafting trips are offered daily 9-5, May-Oct. Ziplining Mar.-Nov. Phone ahead to confirm schedule. **Phone:** (423) 496-4904 or (800) 451-9972.

DUNLAP (D-6) pop. 4,815, elev. 712'

HISTORIC DUNLAP COKE OVENS PARK is .75 mi. w. on Cherry St. to 350 Mountain View Cir. The 62-acre park features the remains of beehive coke ovens from the early 1900s and a museum with photos and artifacts from the early 20th century. The park is at the base of the Cumberland Plateau in the Sequatchie Valley. Visitors can hike the 3,900-foot incline to the top of Fredonia Mountain for views of the valley. **Time:** Allow 1 hour minimum. **Hours:** Park daily dawn-dusk. Museum Sat. 10-4, Sun. noon-4, Apr.-Oct.; by appointment rest of year. **Cost:** Free. **Phone:** (423) 949-3483.

DYERSBURG pop. 17,145

DAYS INN   (731)287-0888
Hotel $61-$84 **Address:** 2600 Lake Rd 38024 **Location:** I-155 exit 13, just s on SR 78. **Facility:** 57 units. 3 stories, interior corridors. **Parking:** winter plug-ins.

EXECUTIVE INN & SUITES   731/287-0044
Motel. Rates not provided. **Address:** 2331 Lake Rd 38024 **Location:** I-155 exit 13, 0.5 mi s on SR 78. **Facility:** 42 units. 2 stories (no elevator), exterior corridors.

HAMPTON INN
(731)285-4778

▼▼▼▼ Hotel $79-$119 Address: 2750 Mall Loop Rd 38024 Location: I-155 exit 13, just s on SR 78, then just e. Behind Dyersburg Mall. Facility: 60 units. 2 stories (no elevator), interior corridors. Terms: 1-7 night minimum stay, cancellation fee imposed. Pool(s): outdoor. Guest Services: valet laundry.

AAA Benefit: Members save up to 10%!

[icons]

HOLIDAY INN EXPRESS & SUITES
(731)286-1021

▼▼▼▼ Hotel $104-$124 Address: 822 Reelfoot Dr 38024 Location: I-155 exit 13, just s on SR 78, then just w. Facility: 63 units. 3 stories, interior corridors. Terms: cancellation fee imposed. Pool(s): heated indoor. Activities: picnic facilities, exercise room. Guest Services: complimentary and valet laundry.

[icons]

SLEEP INN & SUITES
(731)287-0248

▼▼▼ Hotel $75-$83 Address: 824 Reelfoot Dr 38024 Location: I-155 exit 13, just s on SR 78, then just w. Facility: 56 units. 3 stories, interior corridors. Pool(s): heated indoor. Guest Services: complimentary and valet laundry.

[icons]

WHERE TO EAT

ABE'S RIBEYE BARN
731/285-4648

▼▼▼ Steak Seafood. Casual Dining. $13-$37 AAA Inspector Notes: The restaurant's famous certified Angus rib-eye steaks are just the beginning of the tasty meats that are offered here. Other steaks include filet mignon, New York strip and porterhouse, as well as prime rib and pork chops. Seafood choices include lobster tail, salmon, halibut and shrimp. Great salads and desserts also are available. Features: full bar, happy hour. Address: 1130 Henry St 38024 Location: I-155 exit 13, 1 mi s on SR 78, then just s on US 51.

[D]

EL PATIO
731/287-9488

▼▼ Mexican. Casual Dining. $5-$14 AAA Inspector Notes: Hearty portions create a good value at this tastefully decorated establishment. The menu features traditional favorites, including enchiladas, fajitas and combination platters, plus specialties from the grill. The bar has a patio and a view of the TV, providing a variety of seating options. Features: full bar. Address: 1995 US 51 38024 Location: I-155 exit 13, 1 mi s on SR 78, then just s. [L] [D]

NEIL'S BARBEQUE & GRILL
731/285-2628

▼▼ Barbecue. Casual Dining. $7-$36 AAA Inspector Notes: Enjoy flavorful barbecue served in heaping portions under the watchful gaze of many a taxidermied creature at this country-rustic eatery. Pulled pork, ribs, beef brisket, turkey and chicken are featured, plus grilled steaks, fried catfish, fried chicken tenders and country fried steak. Prime rib is featured Friday and Saturday nights. Sandwiches, salads and stuffed baked potatoes will satisfy lighter appetites. Features: beer only. Address: 470 Mall Blvd, Suite A 38024 Location: I-155 exit 13, just s on SR 78, then just e; in Chandler Complex II. [L] [D]

AAA.com/ TourBook Comments

Let Your Voice Be Heard

EAST RIDGE pop. 20,979
• Hotels & Restaurants map & index p. 51

BEST WESTERN PLUS ARBOUR INN & SUITES
(423)893-7979 [58]

▼▼▼ Hotel $80-$160

 Best Western PLUS

AAA Benefit: Save 10% or more every day and earn 10% bonus points!

Address: 6710 Ringgold Rd 37412 Location: I-75 exit 1A (East Ridge) northbound; exit 1 southbound, just e. Facility: 110 units. 3 stories, interior corridors. Amenities: safes. Pool(s): outdoor. Activities: exercise room. Guest Services: valet laundry.

[icons]

FAIRFIELD INN & SUITES BY MARRIOTT CHATTANOOGA SOUTH/EAST RIDGE
(423)499-4080 [57]

▼▼▼ Hotel $76-$137

 FAIRFIELD INN & SUITES® Marriott.

AAA Benefit: Members save 5% or more!

Address: 1453 N Mack Smith Rd 37412 Location: I-75 exit 1 southbound; exit 1B northbound, just w. Facility: 79 units. 3 stories, interior corridors. Pool(s): heated indoor. Activities: hot tub, exercise room. Guest Services: valet and coin laundry. Featured Amenity: breakfast buffet.

[icons]

HOLIDAY INN EXPRESS HOTEL & SUITES
(423)308-0111 [59]

▼▼▼ Hotel $90-$170 Address: 1441 N Smith Rd 37412 Location: I-75 exit 1 southbound; exit 1B northbound, just w. Facility: 64 units. 3 stories, interior corridors. Terms: cancellation fee imposed. Pool(s): heated indoor. Activities: limited exercise equipment. Guest Services: valet and coin laundry.

[icons]

WHERE TO EAT

ARMANDO'S
423/867-5950 [47]

▼ Burgers Sandwiches. Quick Serve. $4-$9 AAA Inspector Notes: A wide selection of sandwiches includes turkey, roast beef, bologna or ham. The hamburgers are very popular, as are the hot dogs and Philly cheesesteak. Dinners also are available and include hamburger steaks and grilled chicken. Be sure to ask about the desserts as they vary from day to day. The atmosphere is simple and service is friendly. Address: 5700 Ringgold Rd 37412 Location: I-75 exit 1 southbound; exit 1B northbound, 1.1 mi w. [L] [D]

ELIZABETHTON (C-9) pop. 14,176, elev. 1,577'
• Restaurants p. 76

A bronze slab in front of the courthouse marks the spot where settlers formed the Watauga Association in 1772, the first independent government in America. The 1775 Transylvania Purchase—one of the largest land purchases in U.S. history—took place in Elizabethton. Fort Watauga, the focus of a major battle over Native American land rights in 1776, occupied a site near present-day Sycamore Shoals State Historic Area.

A covered bridge built in 1882 to allow for the town's expansion still carries pedestrian traffic across the Doe River. Other scenic areas include Watauga Lake (see Recreation Areas Chart) and Roan Mountain (see Cherokee National Forest p. 63).

Elizabethton/Carter County Chamber of Commerce: 500 Veterans Memorial Pkwy., P.O. Box 190, Elizabethton, TN 37644. **Phone:** (423) 547-3850.

Self-guiding tours: A brochure detailing a walking tour of the city's historical sites—including the Soldier's Monument and other notable spots—is available from the chamber of commerce.

SYCAMORE SHOALS STATE HISTORIC AREA is w. off US 321. The first permanent settlement outside the original American Colonies, the area contains a visitor center, museum, theater, hiking trails and a reconstruction of Fort Watauga. In 1780 the Overmountain Men departed the fort, crossed into North Carolina and later defeated the British at the Battle of King's Mountain in South Carolina. A re-enactment of the Siege of Fort Watauga takes place in May and the Overmountain Victory Trial Celebration takes place in September. The outdoor drama "Liberty: The Saga of Sycamore Shoals" is performed on the grounds evenings (Thurs.-Sat.) the last three weekends in July.

Time: Allow 1 hour minimum. **Hours:** Grounds daily dawn-dusk. Visitor center and museum Tues.-Sat. 9-4, Sun. 1-4:30. Closed Jan. 1, Easter, Thanksgiving and Christmas. **Cost:** Free. Admission to "Liberty: The Saga of Sycamore Shoals" $12; $10 (ages 55+); $9 (ages 6-17). **Phone:** (423) 543-5808. 🅰️

The John and Landon Carter Mansion is 3 mi. n. on the Broad St. Extension off US 321. Part of the historical area, this 1780 mansion is one of Tennessee's oldest frame houses and retains 90 percent of the original building material. John Carter and his son Landon were active in governmental and military affairs. **Time:** Allow 1 hour minimum. **Hours:** Wed.-Sun. 8-4:30, mid-May to mid-Aug. Hours may vary; phone ahead. Tours are offered by appointment only. Closed major holidays. **Cost:** Free. **Phone:** (423) 543-5808.

FATZ   423/547-0001
🔷🔷 Regional American. Casual Dining. $6-$18 **AAA Inspector Notes:** Friendly staff and appealing country decor help set the tone for a relaxed and enjoyable dining experience. It's not unusual for guests to wait to be seated at the popular spot, which earns raves for its well-prepared variations on chicken, steak, ribs and pasta, as well as salads and sandwiches. The signature Southern-style peach cobbler served with vanilla ice cream and walnuts is scrumptious. **Features:** full bar. **Address:** 980 Over Mountain Dr 37643 **Location:** Just w of center on US 321/SR 91.
[L] [D] CALL 🛗M

ERWIN (C-9) pop. 6,097, elev. 1,680'

Erwin is near the Nolichucky River in the northeast portion of the Cherokee National Forest (see place listing p. 62). The northern end of the Nolichucky Gorge, about 250 feet wide, borders the river for about 10 miles.

Until the 1950s a local pottery plant produced about 30,000 pieces of painted and underglazed pottery a day. Some of this pottery and other items of local interest are among the historical displays at the Unicoi County Heritage Museum, on the grounds of the Erwin National Fish Hatchery (see attraction listing).

Unicoi County-Erwin Chamber of Commerce: 100 S. Main St., P.O. Box 713, Erwin, TN 37650. **Phone:** (423) 743-3000.

ERWIN NATIONAL FISH HATCHERY is 2 mi. n. on SR 107 at 1715 Johnson City Hwy. The hatchery produces 15 million rainbow trout eggs from four different strains each year for distribution around the United States. Artificially fertilized eggs are incubated in jars and are later washed and sorted for shipping to other hatcheries. Growing fish are kept in rows of concrete tanks. All phases of the fish-breeding and rearing operations can be seen September through March. **Time:** Allow 1 hour minimum. **Hours:** Mon.-Fri. 7-3:30. Closed major holidays. **Cost:** Free. **Phone:** (423) 743-4712. 🅰️

RECREATIONAL ACTIVITIES
White-water Rafting
- **Cherokee Adventures** is 1.4 mi. n. of I-26 exit 37 on SR 81. Mountain biking, ropes courses and other activities are offered. **Hours:** Rafting trips are offered daily 8-8 and by reservation, June-Aug.; 9-4, Oct.-Mar. **Phone:** (423) 743-7733 for information, or (800) 445-7238 for reservations.
- **Nantahala Outdoor Center-Nolichucky Outpost** is e. off US 23 exit 15, then immediately .7 mi. s. on Temple Hill Rd., e. on River Rd. to stop sign at an unmarked road, e. on unmarked road, then s. 1.2 mi. to end of Jones Branch Rd. **Hours:** Rafting trips are offered daily, Mar.-Aug. Phone ahead to confirm schedule. **Cost:** Reservations are recommended. **Phone:** (828) 488-2175 for information, or (888) 905-7238 for reservations.

MOUNTAIN INN & SUITES   (423)743-4100
🔷🔷🔷 Hotel $85-$99 **Address:** 2002 Temple Hill Rd 37650 **Location:** I-26 exit 40, just e. **Facility:** 60 units. 4 stories, interior corridors. **Terms:** cancellation fee imposed. **Pool(s):** outdoor. **Activities:** hot tub, exercise room. **Guest Services:** coin laundry.
[📶+] CALL 🛗M 🛁 [BIZ] 📶 🔌 [🖥] / SOME UNITS 🍽

SUPER 8   (423)743-0200
🔷 Motel $50-$112 **Address:** 1101 N Buffalo St 37650 **Location:** I-26 exit 37, just w. **Facility:** 48 units. 2 stories (no elevator), interior corridors. [BIZ] 📶 🔌 🍽 [🖥] / SOME UNITS [HS]

ETOWAH (D-6) pop. 3,490, elev. 807'

L&N DEPOT MUSEUM is at 727 Tennessee Ave. (US 411). This restored 1906 depot presents historical collections of regional interest as well as local and traveling art shows.

A railroad caboose, a bandstand, a picnic area and a walking trail also are on the grounds. Half-day and full-day excursions on the Old Line depart from the Depot April through November; full-day excursions include a 2-hour lunch and a stop for shopping in Copperhill. **Hours:** Mon.-Fri. 8-4, Dec.-Mar; otherwise varies. Closed major holidays. Phone ahead to confirm schedule. **Cost:** Free. **Phone:** (423) 263-7840.

EVA (C-3) pop. 293

NATHAN BEDFORD FORREST STATE PARK is 2.3 mi. n.e. on SR 191, following signs. Within the 2,587-acre park, Pilot Knob overlooks the locale of the Battle of Johnsonville; in 1864 Confederate general Nathan Bedford Forrest destroyed Union boats and supplies with camouflaged artillery. A monument overlooks Kentucky Lake. Tennessee River Folklife Interpretive Center displays a variety of regional exhibits. Many recreational opportunities are available. *See Recreation Areas Chart.* **Hours:** Grounds daily dawn to dusk. Park office and interpretive center daily 8-11 and noon-4:30. **Cost:** Free. **Phone:** (731) 584-6356 for the park office, or (731) 584-2128 for the interpretive center.

FARRAGUT (D-7) pop. 20,676

FARRAGUT FOLKLIFE MUSEUM is in Farragut Town Hall at 11408 Municipal Center Dr. Artifacts and other memorabilia depict the history of the local East Tennessee community. The Adm. David Glasgow Farragut collection features personal belongings of the Civil War officer and U.S. Navy admiral. **Time:** Allow 45 minutes minimum. **Hours:** Mon.-Fri. 10-4:30. Closed major holidays. **Cost:** Free. **Phone:** (865) 966-7057.

AMERICAS BEST VALUE INN & SUITES-WEST KNOXVILLE/ TURKEY CREEK 865/288-3641
Motel. Rates not provided. **Address:** 11717 Campbell Lakes Dr 37934 **Location:** I-40/75 exit 373 (Campbell Station Rd), just s. **Facility:** 50 units. 2 stories (no elevator), exterior corridors. **Pool(s):** outdoor. **Guest Services:** coin laundry.

CLARION INN & SUITES (865)671-1010
Hotel $63-$110 **Address:** 11341 Campbell Lakes Dr 37934 **Location:** I-40/75 exit 373 (Campbell Station Rd), just s. **Facility:** 95 units. 3 stories, interior corridors. **Amenities:** safes. **Pool(s):** outdoor. **Activities:** limited exercise equipment. **Guest Services:** valet and coin laundry.

COMFORT SUITES (865)675-7585
Hotel $99-$160 **Address:** 811 N Campbell Station Rd 37932 **Location:** I-40/75 exit 373 (Campbell Station Rd), just n. **Facility:** 85 units. 3 stories, interior corridors. **Pool(s):** heated indoor. **Activities:** hot tub, exercise room. **Guest Services:** valet and coin laundry.

COUNTRY INN & SUITES BY CARLSON, KNOXVILLE WEST (865)675-9800
Hotel $79-$159 **Address:** 805 N Campbell Station Rd 37934 **Location:** I-40/75 exit 373 (Campbell Station Rd), just n. **Facility:** 57 units. 3 stories, interior corridors. **Pool(s):** heated indoor. **Activities:** hot tub, limited exercise equipment. **Guest Services:** coin laundry.

FAIRFIELD INN & SUITES BY MARRIOTT KNOXVILLE WEST (865)392-1122
Hotel $98-$199 **Address:** 11763 Snyder Rd 37932 **Location:** I-40/75 exit 373 (Campbell Station Rd), just n. **Facility:** 90 units. 4 stories, interior corridors. **Pool(s):** heated indoor. **Activities:** limited exercise equipment. **Guest Services:** valet and coin laundry.

AAA Benefit: Members save 5% or more!

HOLIDAY INN EXPRESS & SUITES (865)966-2500
Hotel $99-$179 **Address:** 816 N Campbell Station Rd 37932 **Location:** I-40/75 exit 373 (Campbell Station Rd), just n. **Facility:** 79 units. 3 stories, interior corridors. **Terms:** cancellation fee imposed. **Pool(s):** heated indoor. **Activities:** limited exercise equipment. **Guest Services:** valet and coin laundry. **Featured Amenity:** full hot breakfast.

SUPER 8 KNOXVILLE WEST (865)675-5566
Hotel $59-$83 **Address:** 11748 Snyder Rd 37932 **Location:** I-40/75 exit 373 (Campbell Station Rd), just ne. **Facility:** 60 units. 2 stories (no elevator), exterior corridors. **Pool(s):** outdoor. **Guest Services:** coin laundry, area transportation.

WHERE TO EAT

APPLE CAKE TEA ROOM 865/966-7848
American. Casual Dining. $8-$12 **AAA Inspector Notes:** Resembling an old log cabin, this charming eatery is decorated with oil lantern sconces, country quilts and folk art. Although the menu is limited, the selections such as homemade chicken salad, apple cake and bran muffins are attractive and tasty. **Address:** 11312 Station West Dr 37922 **Location:** I-40/75 exit 373 (Campbell Station Rd), just s; in Appalachian Log Square.

AUBREY'S 865/671-2233
Southern American. Casual Dining. $8-$20 **AAA Inspector Notes:** Diners savor traditional Texas barbecue in a family-friendly atmosphere. On the menu are beef ribs, baby back ribs, chicken, pulled pork, beef brisket, huge hamburgers and some Tex-Mex favorites including Baja fish tacos. **Features:** full bar. **Address:** 102 Campbell Station Rd 37922 **Location:** I-40/75 exit 373 (Campbell Station Rd), 1.5 mi s.

LAKESIDE TAVERN 865/671-2980
American. Casual Dining. $10-$29 **AAA Inspector Notes:** Inviting wooden décor, an open-air kitchen and picturesque marina views greet you at this restaurant, where menu offerings range from quality beef to fresh seafood. Desserts are prepared daily; don't miss the white chocolate cake. **Features:** full bar, patio dining, Sunday brunch, happy hour. **Address:** 10911 Concord Dr 37922 **Location:** I-140 exit 3, 2.5 mi w on Westland Dr, 0.5 mi n on Northshore Dr, then just e.

FAYETTEVILLE   pop. 6,827

BEST WESTERN FAYETTEVILLE INN   (931)433-0100

Hotel
$89-$119

AAA Benefit:
Save 10% or more every day and earn 10% bonus points!

Address: 3021 Thornton Taylor Pkwy 37334 **Location:** 0.7 mi e of US 431, on US 64 and 231 Bypass. **Facility:** 64 units. 2 stories (no elevator), exterior corridors. **Pool(s):** outdoor. **Guest Services:** coin laundry.

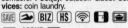

FORT DONELSON NATIONAL BATTLEFIELD (C-3)

On the Cumberland River near Dover, Fort Donelson National Battlefield embraces the area where the first major Federal victory of the Civil War was won. Gen. Ulysses S. Grant began the campaign in February 1862 to gain control of the Mississippi Valley and bisect the South.

When Grant moved 15,000 men up the Tennessee River to Fort Henry, the main Confederate garrison withdrew to Fort Donelson, leaving the remaining detachment to surrender after a short battle. Five days later, Grant moved against Fort Donelson, and a Feb. 13 skirmish had no clear outcome. The following day a Union gunboat attack failed, but Union reinforcements arrived and Grant's army swelled to 27,000 men.

Fearing entrapment, the Confederates rallied to clear the road to Nashville and steadily forced back the Union lines. Escape seemed sure until the Confederate commanders, in confusion, ordered their forces back to their trenches. Grant immediately ordered an advance and gained new ground.

Three Confederate officers with 1,500-2,000 troops managed to escape during the night of Feb. 15, but the following morning Grant issued his famous ultimatum, "No terms except unconditional and immediate surrender." Confederate Gen. Simon Buckner accepted and delivered approximately 13,000 troops as prisoners of war, at that time the largest number ever to surrender in North America.

This Confederate defeat resulted in the evacuation of Bowling Green, Ky., Columbus and Nashville, delivering Kentucky and most of middle and western Tennessee into Union hands.

The 554-acre park contains the Confederate-built fort, river batteries, outer defenses, the Dover Hotel where Buckner surrendered to Grant, and a national cemetery. Markers indicate all points of historical interest along a 6-mile driving tour.

FORT DONELSON VISITOR CENTER is on US 79, 1.5 mi. w. of the Cumberland River Bridge at Dover. The center offers exhibits and a 15-minute film describing the battle and campaign. **Time:** Allow 1 hour minimum. **Hours:** Visitor Center open daily 8-4:30.

Tour road open daily dawn-dusk for foot traffic, 8-4:30 for vehicles. Closed Jan. 1, Thanksgiving and Christmas. **Cost:** Free. **Phone:** (931) 232-5706.

FRANKLIN (C-4) pop. 62,487, elev. 646'
- Restaurants p. 81
- Hotels & Restaurants map & index p. 200

Satisfying both history buffs and casual sightseers, Franklin upholds small-town traditions as it continues to modernize. Innovative business ventures have breathed new life into many aging structures, including The Factory at Franklin, a complex of industrial buildings retrofitted into a mixed-use development. Here you'll enjoy antique shopping (there also are plenty of new goodies for sale), bars and restaurants, and live productions (the old boiler room now is home to Studio Tenn, a professional theater troupe).

High-tech, biodiesel-burning buses evocative of the community's former electric-powered trolleys also operate throughout the area. (Fixed route service is $1; 50c (ages 0-4 and 64+). Exact change is required.) Hop aboard and ride past Victorian architecture in the city's attractive downtown—a historic district now flourishing with chic boutiques and eateries that run the gamut from locally owned mom-and-pop operations to national vendors (yes, even Franklin's quaint Main Street has a Starbucks). Although it's a lively locale to explore any time of year, downtown Franklin lures more than 100,000 people in late April with its Main Street Festival. The long-time event offers a juried arts and crafts show, children's activities and live music.

You'll also discover several well-preserved sites in town, including Historic Carnton Plantation and The Carter House *(see attraction listings)*, both of which recall the Battle of Franklin, one of the Civil War's most decisive conflicts. On Nov. 30, 1864, 5 hours of fighting resulted in the death, wounding or capture of more than 6,000 Confederate and 2,000 Union soldiers. The Confederacy lost six generals; seven more were among those wounded or captured. Other reminders of the bloody encounter are the 1823 Masonic Hall, the first three-story building in Tennessee, on Second Avenue South, and the 1834 St. Paul's Episcopal Church at the corner of West Main Street and Fifth Avenue. Following the battle, both edifices were used as hospitals for injured troops.

While highly protective of their man-made treasures, Franklin residents also conserve plenty of green space. Nine scenic parks present visitors such amenities as nature trails and athletic playing fields. Encircled by a 1-mile paved track, Pinkerton Park on Murfreesboro Road connects to downtown Franklin via the Sue Douglas Berry Memorial Pedestrian Bridge. On Boyd Mill Avenue, 58-acre Jim Warren City Park features a 2.5-mile walking path, picnic tables and a catch-and-release fishing pond, along with a skate plaza for inline skaters and skateboarders.

Williamson County Convention & Visitors Bureau: 400 Main St., Suite 130, Franklin, TN 37064. **Phone:** (615) 591-8514 or (866) 253-9207.

(See map & index p. 200.)

Self-guiding tours: Brochures outlining a walking tour of Franklin's 15-block downtown historic district can be obtained at the visitor center. A self-guiding driving tour spotlighting Civil War sites also is available.

Shopping: The Factory at Franklin, 230 Franklin Rd., a collection of 12 restored Depression-era buildings, now houses shops, galleries and restaurants. Victorian buildings along Main Street have been restored and house antique shops, specialty stores and restaurants. A growing antique district surrounds the intersection of Second Avenue and South Margin Street.

THE CARTER HOUSE is at 1140 Columbia Ave. (US 31). Displays inside this 1830 brick farmhouse commemorate the Battle of Franklin. The house contains original and period furniture, and a museum has Civil War relics and a video about the Battle of Franklin. With more than 1,000 bullet holes, the farm office at Carter House is one of the most damaged Civil War buildings still standing.

   Time: Allow 1 hour minimum. **Hours:** Mon.-Sat. 9-5, Sun. 11-5. Closed major holidays. **Cost:** $15; $12 (ages 66+); $8 (ages 6-12). **Phone:** (615) 791-1861.

FRANKLIN ON FOOT offers guided walking tours of downtown Franklin. During the Classic Franklin Tour, guides escort guests around town on a 90-minute walk that features historic properties and areas. Bike tours and evening cemetery, crime and ghost tours also are offered. **Time:** Allow 1 hour, 30 minutes minimum. **Hours:** Classic Franklin Tour given daily at 10 or by appointment. Phone for other tour times. **Cost:** Classic Franklin Tour $15; $10 (ages 13-19); $5 (ages 6-12). Bike tour $35. Reservations are required. **Phone:** (615) 400-3808.

HISTORIC CARNTON PLANTATION AND MCGAVOCK CONFEDERATE CEMETERY is at 1345 Eastern Flank Cir. Confederate troops assembled on the property during the Battle of Franklin, a bloody 5-hour skirmish occurring on Nov. 30, 1864. The wounded and dying were brought to Carnton, which served as a field hospital. Adjacent to this elegant estate owners John and Carrie McGavock established a 1,500-grave cemetery. Released in 2005, the best-selling novel "The Widow of the South" is based on the life of Mrs. McGavock.

   Time: Allow 1 hour, 30 minutes minimum. **Hours:** Grounds Mon.-Sat. 9-5, Sun. 11-5. Closed Jan. 1, Easter, Thanksgiving, Christmas Eve and Christmas. **Cost:** $15; $12 (ages 65+); $8 (ages 6-12). Grounds tour $5. **Phone:** (615) 794-0903.

THE LOTZ HOUSE, A CIVIL WAR HOUSE MUSEUM is at 1111 Columbia Ave., just s. of Main St. A 1-hour guided tour of the 1855 home of German immigrant and master craftsman Johann Albert Lotz highlights the turbulent times as well as the owner's talents as a builder through remarkable features for

the period such as a wraparound staircase and hand-carved mantels, cartouches, millwork and finials.

   The home is furnished with fine antiques and artwork owned by the Lotz family. In addition, display cases house articles from the Civil War's Battle of Franklin in 1864. **Time:** Allow 1 hour minimum. **Hours:** Mon.-Sat. 9-5, Sun. 1-4. Closed major holidays. **Cost:** $10; $9 (ages 65+); $5 (ages 7-13). Reservations are recommended. **Phone:** (615) 790-7190.

ALOFT NASHVILLE-COOL SPRINGS   (615)435-8700

Hotel
$109-$209

AAA Benefit: Members save up to 15%, plus Starwood Preferred Guest® benefits!

Address: 7109 S Springs Dr 37067 **Location:** I-65 exit 68B, 0.4 mi w, 0.3 mi n on Mallory Ln, then just e. **Facility:** 143 units. 6 stories, interior corridors. *Bath:* shower only. **Amenities:** safes. *Some:* video games. **Pool(s):** heated indoor. **Activities:** exercise room. **Guest Services:** valet and coin laundry, area transportation.

BAYMONT INN & SUITES   (615)591-6660

Hotel
$63-$101

Address: 4202 Franklin Commons Ct 37067 **Location:** I-65 exit 65, just e. **Facility:** 66 units. 3 stories, interior corridors. **Terms:** 3 day cancellation notice. **Amenities:** safes. **Pool(s):** heated indoor. **Activities:** exercise room. **Guest Services:** valet and coin laundry. **Featured Amenity:** breakfast buffet.

BEST WESTERN FRANKLIN INN   (615)790-0570

Hotel
$84-$124

AAA Benefit: Save 10% or more every day and earn 10% bonus points!

Address: 1308 Murfreesboro Rd 37064 **Location:** I-65 exit 65, just w. Located in a busy commercial area. **Facility:** 132 units. 2 stories (no elevator), exterior corridors. **Pool(s):** outdoor. **Activities:** playground, exercise room. **Guest Services:** valet and coin laundry. **Featured Amenity:** full hot breakfast.

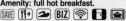

(See map & index p. 200.)

COMFORT INN
(615)791-6675

Motel $78-$105 **Address:** 4206 Franklin Commons Ct 37067 **Location:** I-65 exit 65, just e. **Facility:** 58 units. 2 stories (no elevator), exterior corridors. **Pool(s):** outdoor.

COUNTRY INN & SUITES BY CARLSON, COOL SPRINGS
(615)778-0321

Hotel $99-$309 **Address:** 7120 S Springs Dr 37067 **Location:** I-65 exit 68B, just w, 0.3 mi n on Mallory Ln, then just e. **Facility:** 64 units. 4 stories, interior corridors. **Terms:** cancellation fee imposed. **Pool(s):** heated indoor. **Activities:** exercise room. **Guest Services:** valet and coin laundry.

COURTYARD BY MARRIOTT FRANKLIN COOL SPRINGS
(615)778-0080

Hotel $119-$399 **Address:** 2001 Meridian Blvd 37067 **Location:** I-65 exit 68A, just e on Cool Springs Blvd, just n on Carothers Pkwy, then just w; in Meridian Cool Springs business park. **Facility:** 126 units. 4 stories, interior corridors. **Pool(s):** heated indoor. **Activities:** hot tub, exercise room. **Guest Services:** valet and coin laundry, boarding pass kiosk.

AAA Benefit: Members save 5% or more!

DRURY PLAZA HOTEL FRANKLIN
(615)771-6778

Hotel $120-$259 **Address:** 1874 W McEwen Dr 37067 **Location:** I-65 exit 67. 0.4 mi w. 338 units. 11 stories, interior corridors. **Terms:** cancellation fee imposed. **Pool(s):** heated outdoor, heated indoor. **Activities:** exercise room. **Guest Services:** valet and coin laundry, area transportation.

EMBASSY SUITES BY HILTON NASHVILLE SOUTH/COOL SPRINGS
(615)515-5151

Hotel $139-$249 **Address:** 820 Crescent Centre Dr 37067 **Location:** I-65 exit 68A, exit 68A to Carothers Rd. **Facility:** 250 units. 9 stories, interior corridors. **Parking:** on-site (fee) and valet. **Terms:** check-in 4 pm, 1-7 night minimum stay, cancellation fee imposed. **Pool(s):** heated indoor. **Activities:** sauna, hot tub, exercise room. **Guest Services:** valet and coin laundry, area transportation.

AAA Benefit: Members save 5% or more!

FRANKLIN MARRIOTT COOL SPRINGS
(615)261-6100

Hotel $125-$258 **Address:** 700 Cool Springs Blvd 37067 **Location:** I-65 exit 68A, just e. **Facility:** 300 units. 11 stories, interior corridors. **Terms:** check-in 4 pm. **Pool(s):** heated indoor. **Activities:** hot tub, exercise room. **Guest Services:** valet laundry, boarding pass kiosk, area transportation.

AAA Benefit: Members save 5% or more!

HAMPTON INN & SUITES
(615)771-7225

Hotel $89-$349 **Address:** 7141 S Springs Dr 37067 **Location:** I-65 exit 68B, just w, 0.3 mi n on Mallory Ln, then just se. **Facility:** 127 units, some efficiencies. 4 stories, interior corridors. **Terms:** 1-7 night minimum stay, cancellation fee imposed. **Pool(s):** outdoor. **Activities:** exercise room. **Guest Services:** valet and coin laundry.

AAA Benefit: Members save up to 10%!

HILTON GARDEN INN NASHVILLE/FRANKLIN/COOL SPRINGS
(615)656-2700

Hotel $109-$259 **Address:** 9150 Carothers Pkwy 37067 **Location:** I-65 exit 69 (SR 441), just e on Moores Ln, then just s. **Facility:** 131 units. 5 stories, interior corridors. **Terms:** 1-7 night minimum stay, cancellation fee imposed. **Pool(s):** heated indoor. **Activities:** hot tub, exercise room. **Guest Services:** valet and coin laundry.

AAA Benefit: Members save up to 10%!

HYATT PLACE NASHVILLE/FRANKLIN/COOL SPRINGS
(615)771-8900

Hotel $99-$249

HYATT PLACE
AAA Benefit: Members save 10%!

Address: 650 Bakers Bridge Ave 37067 **Location:** I-65 exit 69 (SR 441), 0.3 mi e to Carothers Pkwy, 0.5 mi s, then 0.3 mi w. **Facility:** 126 units. 6 stories, interior corridors. **Terms:** cancellation fee imposed. **Amenities:** safes. **Pool(s):** outdoor. **Activities:** exercise room. **Guest Services:** valet laundry, area transportation. **Featured Amenity:** breakfast buffet.

RAMADA FRANKLIN/COOL SPRINGS
(615)791-4004

Hotel $66-$88 **Address:** 6210 Hospitality Dr 37067 **Location:** I-65 exit 65, 0.5 mi e on US 96. **Facility:** 60 units. 3 stories, interior corridors. **Pool(s):** outdoor.

RESIDENCE INN BY MARRIOTT FRANKLIN COOL SPRINGS
(615)778-0002

Extended Stay Contemporary Hotel $129-$299 **Address:** 2009 Meridian Blvd 37067 **Location:** I-65 exit 68A, just e on Cool Springs Blvd, just n on Carothers Pkwy, then just w; in Meridian Cool Springs business park. **Facility:** 124 units, some two bedrooms, efficiencies and kitchens. 4 stories, interior corridors. **Pool(s):** heated indoor. **Activities:** hot tub, exercise room. **Guest Services:** valet and coin laundry.

AAA Benefit: Members save 5% or more!

(See map & index p. 200.)

TOWNEPLACE SUITES BY MARRIOTT FRANKLIN COOL SPRINGS   (615)861-1111

Extended Stay Hotel
$135-$229

TownePlace SUITES® Marriott

AAA Benefit: Members save 5% or more!

Address: 7153 S Springs Dr 37067 **Location:** I-65 exit 68B, just w, then just n; behind Cool Springs Galleria Mall. **Facility:** 120 efficiencies. 6 stories, interior corridors. **Pool(s):** heated indoor. **Activities:** limited exercise equipment. **Guest Services:** valet and coin laundry, area transportation. **Featured Amenity:** continental breakfast.

[SAVE] [📶] CALL [🛗M] [🏊] [BIZ] [📶] [✕] [🔌] [🧳] [🖥]
/ SOME UNITS [S🔒] [HS]

WHERE TO EAT

BASIL ASIAN BISTRO   615-771-0999
Asian. Casual Dining. $8-$27 **AAA Inspector Notes:** The abstract paintings and lemon-grass stained window lend to the dining room's Asian vibe. Furthering the feel are such menu choices as spring roll, lettuce wrap and crispy noodle appetizers, as well as Thai entrées of panang beef, basil duck or chicken, curried duck and spicy red snapper. **Features:** full bar. **Address:** 9040 Carothers Pkwy, Suite A201 37067 **Location:** I-65 exit 69 (SR 441), 0.3 mi e to Carothers Pkwy, then 0.6 mi s. [L] [D] CALL [🛗M]

CAJUN STEAMER - BAR & GRILL   615-435-3074
Cajun. Casual Dining. $9-$27 **AAA Inspector Notes:** This hopping restaurant offers such authentic and delicious fare as char-grilled oysters, steamed crawfish and farm-raised alligator with Gambino French bread for that chewy-yeasty flavor one used to only get in New Orleans. Gumbos, fried green tomatoes, crawfish étouffée and voodoo or Jamaican chicken are just a few items on the vast menu. Hot fresh beignets and Acadian bread pudding with wonderful bourbon caramel sauce are great endings for an experience you won't easily forget. **Features:** full bar, patio dining, happy hour. **Address:** 1175 Meridian Blvd, Suite 108 37067 **Location:** I-65 exit 68A, just e on Cool Springs Blvd, then just n on Carothers Pkwy.
[L] [D] CALL [🛗M] [🐾]

MERRIDEE'S BREADBASKET   615/790-3755
American. Casual Dining. $4-$8 **AAA Inspector Notes:** Natural ingredients go into homemade preparations of soup, sandwiches and sweets. Open for dinner Thursday through Saturday. **Address:** 110 4th Ave S 37064 **Location:** Center.
[B] [L]

NASHVILLE PIZZA COMPANY   615/591-7050   [57]
Pizza. Casual Dining. $6-$19 **AAA Inspector Notes:** Here you'll enjoy all your favorite pizza toppings including pepperoni, sausage and green peppers. Creative specialty pizzas include Harvey's special, topped with smoked turkey, jalapeños and two cheeses; there's even a vegetable medley pizza. Hungry for something different? Enjoy a fresh baked sandwich or zesty Greek salad. **Features:** beer only, happy hour. **Address:** 2176 Hillsboro Rd 37069 **Location:** 0.7 mi s; between Battlewood St and General N Forest Dr. [L] [D] CALL [🛗M]

RED PONY RESTAURANT   615/595-7669
Southern. Casual Dining. $16-$46 **AAA Inspector Notes:** The color red abounds at this restaurant—red walls, red ceiling, red menus and even a red name. Dishes, including fried green tomatoes, shrimp remoulade, crisp Mississippi catfish, grilled beef tenderloin and the most popular dish, the shrimp and grits with shrimp, apple bacon and wine over garlic cheese grits, have a Southern flair. A great wine list, extensive cocktail offerings and rich desserts complete the seasonally changing menu. **Features:** full bar, patio dining, happy hour. **Reservations:** suggested. **Address:** 408 Main St 37064 **Location:** Just w of 4th Ave and Main St; downtown. **Parking:** street only. [D] CALL [🛗M]

THE STOVE WORKS RESTAURANT   615/791-6065
American. Casual Dining. $8-$11 **AAA Inspector Notes:** Historic. The restaurant is in a restored warehouse with furniture stores and gift shops. On the menu are made-from-scratch soups, salads and sandwiches. **Features:** beer only, patio dining. **Address:** 230 Franklin Rd, Suite 11L 37064 **Location:** On US 31, 1.5 mi n.
[L] CALL [🛗M]

STROUD'S BARBEQUE   615/595-0200
Barbecue. Quick Serve. $5-$15 **AAA Inspector Notes:** This local family-run eatery specializes in hickory-smoked pork, beef, chicken and turkey; barbecue ribs are featured on weekends. Daily specials and family-size portions also are available. **Address:** 1010 Fulton Greer Ln 37064 **Location:** 3 mi n on Hillsboro Rd.
[B] [L] [D]

GALLATIN (C-4) pop. 30,278, elev. 521'

Founded in 1802 and named for Albert Gallatin, secretary of the treasury under Presidents John Adams and Thomas Jefferson, Gallatin is the industrial and agricultural marketplace for Sumner County. Tobacco and soybean farming, dairying and manufacturing farm products support the community. Nearby are Bledsoe Creek State Park (see Recreation Areas Chart) and Cages Bend Recreation Area.

Gallatin Chamber of Commerce: 118 Main St., Gallatin, TN 37066. **Phone:** (615) 452-4000.

Self-guiding tours: The Sumner County Courthouse and more than 30 restored buildings, many predating the Civil War, are included in a brochure outlining a historical walking tour of Gallatin's public square area. The square includes both shopping and dining opportunities. The brochure is available at the chamber of commerce.

SUMNER COUNTY MUSEUM is e. on US 25E to 183 W. Main St. Antique automobiles and rifles, Native American artifacts and re-creations of a pioneer kitchen and a tinsmith shop are among the many items contained within the museum. Guided tours available by appointment. **Hours:** Wed.-Sat. 9-4:30, Sun. 1-4:30, Apr.-Oct. Closed major holidays. **Cost:** Self-guiding tour $5; $3 (ages 6-12). **Phone:** (615) 451-3738.

BAYMONT INN & SUITES   (615)230-8300
Hotel $85-$179 **Address:** 354 Sumner Hall Dr 37066 **Location:** 1.5 mi s. **Facility:** 52 units. 2 stories (no elevator), exterior corridors. **Pool(s):** outdoor. **Activities:** exercise room. **Guest Services:** coin laundry.
[📶] CALL [🛗M] [🏊] [BIZ] [📶] [✕] [🔌] [🧳] [🖥]
/ SOME UNITS [S🔒]

HAMPTON INN GALLATIN   (615)206-9595
Hotel $114-$204 **Address:** 980 Village Green Crossing 37066 **Location:** 2 mi s on US 31 E. **Facility:** 64 units. 4 stories, interior corridors. **Terms:** 1-7 night minimum stay, cancellation fee imposed. **Pool(s):** outdoor. **Activities:** exercise room. **Guest Services:** valet and coin laundry.

AAA Benefit: Members save up to 10%!

[📶] CALL [🛗M] [🏊] [BIZ] [📶] [✕] [🎥] [🖥]
/ SOME UNITS [HS] [🔌] [🧳]

QUALITY INN OF GALLATIN   (615)451-4494

Hotel
$85

Address: 1001 Village Green Crossing 37066 **Location:** 2 mi s on US 31 E. **Facility:** 60 units. 2 stories (no elevator), exterior corridors. **Pool(s):** outdoor. **Activities:** picnic facilities, exercise room. **Guest Services:** valet and coin laundry.

GATLINBURG (D-7) pop. 3,944, elev. 1,292'
- **Hotels p. 89** • **Restaurants p. 92**
- **Attractions map p. 100**
- **Hotels & Restaurants map & index p. 84**
- **Part of Great Smoky Mountains National Park area — see map p. 97**

Stretching for 2 miles along the banks of the Little Pigeon River at the foot of Mount Le Conte, Gatlinburg is a popular mountain resort. Dogwood trees line the main street, which leads to the entrance of the Great Smoky Mountains National Park *(see place listing p. 97)*. Replicas of late 19th-century trolleys carry passengers in and around Gatlinburg from April through December with reduced winter hours.

Gatlinburg has become an important handicraft center for the Southern Highlands area. At a number of shops in the vicinity visitors can watch craftsmen displaying such outstanding skills as weaving, pottery, broom making, woodworking and furniture making.

Great Smoky Arts & Crafts Community, 3 miles east of downtown, began as a craft show in 1937 and now includes more than 120 craft shops along an 8-mile trail. Arrowmont School of Arts and Crafts offers various programs and courses throughout the year. The Gatlinburg Convention Center often hosts public events, including several craft fairs.

Gatlinburg Winter Magic, featuring an animated parade, a crafts show, a musical Nativity and a citywide display of LED lights, runs early November through February.

Of theatrical interest is Sweet Fanny Adams Theatre, which presents original comedy musicals and vaudeville-style shows from late April to December. Reservations are recommended; phone (865) 436-4039 or (877) 388-5784.

The 5-mile Roaring Fork Motor Nature Trail begins and ends in Gatlinburg, winding along Cherokee Orchard Road past mountain streams, trees, flowers and numerous homesteads.

Gatlinburg Convention and Visitors Bureau: 811 East Parkway, Gatlinburg, TN 37738. **Phone:** (865) 436-4178 or (800) 588-1817.

Shopping: An 8-mile loop centering on Glades Road features about 120 shops, studios and galleries where local artisans and craftspeople from Great Smoky Arts & Crafts Community sell their wares.

GATLINBURG SKY LIFT is at 765 Parkway. The cable chair takes visitors from the main street across the river and up the steep incline of 2,300-foot Crocket Mountain. **Time:** Allow 30 minutes minimum. **Hours:** Daily 9 a.m.-11 p.m., June-Aug.; 9 a.m.-10 p.m., Sept.-Oct.; 9-9, Apr.-May; hours vary rest of year. **Cost:** Round-trip fare $15; $11.25 (ages 3-11). One-day pass $18.75; $14.25 (ages 3-11). **Phone:** (865) 436-4307.

GUINNESS WORLD RECORDS MUSEUM is at 631 Parkway at Baskins Square Mall. Exhibits detail record-breaking phenomena and allow visitors to challenge records for block breaking, hopscotch, stretchy skin and fast texting. **Time:** Allow 1 hour minimum. **Hours:** Daily 10-9, Mar. 1-Memorial Day and Labor Day-Jan. 1; 10 a.m.-11 p.m., day after Memorial Day-day before Labor Day; 11-8, rest of year. **Cost:** $12.99; $7.99 (ages 6-11). **Phone:** (865) 430-7800.

HOLLYWOOD STAR CARS MUSEUM is at 914 Parkway. The museum houses more than 40 vehicles featured in movies and television shows. The collection includes the "Gone in 60 Seconds" Mustang Shelby GT 500, "The Fast and the Furious" Eclipse, the "Back to the Future" 1981 DeLorean time machine, the "Batman Returns" Batmobile, the "Days of Thunder" Mello Yello Chevrolet Lumina, the "Transformers" Bumblebee 1977 Chevrolet Camaro and five cars from "The Fast and the Furious." Vehicles owned by Bob Hope, Dolly Parton, Michael Jackson, Paul McCartney and Beach Boys drummer Dennis Wilson also are displayed. **Time:** Allow 1 hour minimum. **Hours:** Sun.-Thurs. 9-9, Fri.-Sat. 9 a.m.-10 p.m. **Cost:** $12.99; $6.99 (ages 6-12). **Parking:** Fee is charged. **Phone:** (865) 430-2200 for recorded information, or (865) 430-7900 for an operator.

OBER GATLINBURG is at 1339 Ski Mountain Rd., accessible via a narrow, steep, winding road off US 441 with limited parking at the main resort; recommended transportation is via the aerial tramway. This themed recreation complex on Mount Harrison includes an indoor ice-skating rink, winter skiing, an alpine slide, Wildlife Encounter, cafes, entertainment and a children's amusement area.

A sightseeing chairlift rises to the top of Mount Harrison (3,500 ft.). The view from the summit includes Gatlinburg, Pigeon Forge *(see place listing p. 230)* and Great Smoky Mountains National Park *(see place listing p. 97)*.

Time: Allow 30 minutes minimum. **Hours:** Chairlift Mon. and Fri.-Sun. 7:30-10:40; Tues.-Thurs. 9:30-9, rest of year. Last chairlift ride begins 1 hour before closing. Last activity ticket sold 15 minutes before closing. **Cost:** Free. Round-trip sightseeing chairlift $7; free (ages 0-4 with paid adult). Ice-skating $9. Wildlife Encounter $7; $5 (ages 5-11). Individual activity ticket $3.50; activities require 1-2 tickets each. Unlimited day pass $33; $28 (ages 5-11). **Phone:** (865) 436-5423, or (800) 251-9202 for snow updates.

(See map & index p. 84.)

Aerial Tramway departs from 1001 Parkway. The 120-passenger tram travels 2.2 miles between downtown and the amusement complex at Ober Gatlinburg, providing breathtaking views of the Great Smoky Mountains. **Time:** Allow 30 minutes minimum. **Hours:** Mon.-Thurs. 9:30 a.m.-9:40 p.m., Fri.-Sat. 7:30 a.m.-10:40 p.m., Sun. 7:30-6:20. **Cost:** Round-trip fare $12; $9.50 (ages 7-11). **Phone:** (865) 436-5423.

RIPLEY'S AQUARIUM OF THE SMOKIES is just off the Parkway at 88 River Rd. Boasting 100,000 square feet, the facility houses exotic aquatic life from around the world. Galleries include a simulated tropical rain forest, coral reef and the stingray bay, where visitors can touch stingrays.

On display are thousands of exotic sea creatures, including thousands of tropical fish, a giant octopus, sea turtles, giant spider crabs and horseshoe crabs. A submerged acrylic tunnel in the shark lagoon lets visitors get close to 11-foot-long sharks and other ocean predators via a moving glide path. The Penguin Playhouse features African blackfooted penguins in an indoor/outdoor habitat featuring clear underwater tunnels for visitors to view the whimsical birds.

Time: Allow 2 hours, 30 minutes minimum. **Hours:** Mon.-Thurs. 9 a.m.-10 p.m., Fri.-Sun. 9 a.m.-11 p.m. Memorial Day-Labor Day; Mon.-Thurs. 9-9, Fri.-Sun. 9 a.m.-10 p.m., day after Labor Day-Jan. 1; Mon.-Thurs. 9-8, Fri.-Sun. 9 a.m.-10 p.m., rest of year. **Cost:** $26.99; $15.99 (ages 6-11); $7.99 (ages 2-5). **Phone:** (865) 430-8808 or (888) 240-1358.

RIPLEY'S BELIEVE IT OR NOT! ODDITORIUM is at 800 Parkway. Interactive galleries feature natural oddities and bizarre artifacts from around the world, including wax figures of the Vampire Lady and Lizard Man, a shrunken head and a Transformer. **Time:** Allow 1 hour, 30 minutes minimum. **Hours:** Daily 9-11 p.m., day after Memorial Day to day before Labor Day; 9-9, Mar. to Memorial Day and Labor Day to New Year's Day; 10-8, rest of year. Phone ahead to confirm schedule. **Cost:** $16.99; $9.99 (ages 3-11). **Phone:** (865) 436-5096.

RIPLEY'S HAUNTED ADVENTURE is at 908 Parkway. Housed in the former Grimsby and Streaper Casket Co. building, this newly expanded haunted-house attraction features actors and special effects. **Time:** Allow 30 minutes minimum. **Hours:** Daily 10-11 p.m., day after Memorial Day to day before Labor Day; 10-9, Mar. to Memorial Day and Labor Day to Jan. 1; 10-8, rest of year. **Cost:** $13.99; $7.99 (ages 3-11). Under 6 are not permitted. **Parking:** Fee charged for area parking. **Phone:** (865) 430-9991.

WESTGATE'S WILD BEAR FALLS WATER PARK is at 915 Westgate Resort Rd. This 60,000-square-foot indoor/outdoor water park features slides, tube rides, dumping buckets, spray water devices and a retractable roof. **Time:** Allow 3 hours minimum. **Hours:** Daily 11-10, Memorial Day-Labor Day; Mon.-Thurs. 11-6, Fri.-Sun. 11-9, day after Labor Day to Jan. 1. Hours vary rest of year; phone ahead to confirm schedule. **Cost:** $18.95; free (ages 0-2). **Phone:** (865) 430-4800. 🍴

RECREATIONAL ACTIVITIES
White-water Rafting
- **Rafting in the Smokies** is off I-40E exit 447 (Hartford Rd.), then left at stop sign. Ziplines, sky bridges and a rope course also are available. Other activities are offered. **Hours:** Rafting trips are offered every 20 minutes Tues.-Thurs. and Sat. 11-4, May-Labor Day weekend. Schedule varies Mar.-May and day after Labor Day through Nov. 30; phone ahead. **Phone:** (865) 436-5008 or (800) 776-7238. 🎫

WINERIES
- **Smoky Mountain Winery** is .5 mi. n. of US 441 on US 321 at 450 Cherry St. **Hours:** Mon.-Sat.10-7, Sun. 10-6, Apr.-Dec.; Mon.-Sat. 10-5, Sun. 10-4, rest of year. Closed Christmas. **Phone:** (865) 436-7551. GT

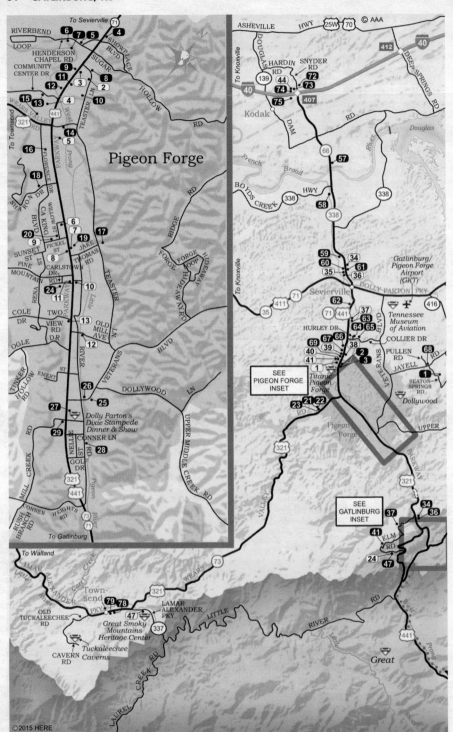

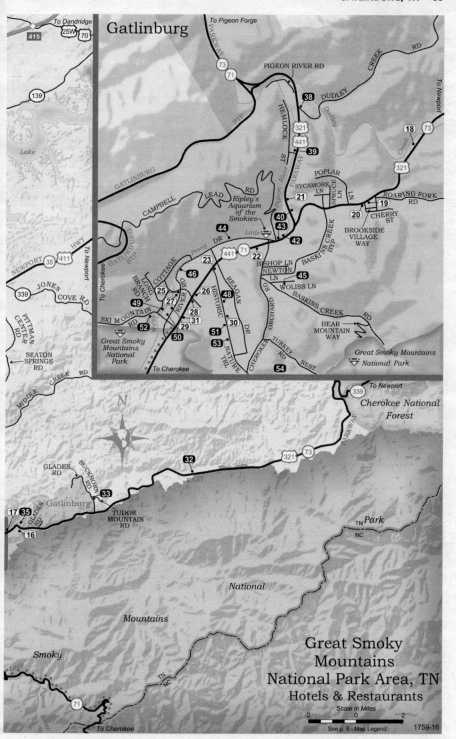

Gatlinburg

Great Smoky Mountains National Park Area, TN
Hotels & Restaurants

Scale in Miles

See p. 6 - Map Legend

1759-16

Great Smoky Mountains National Park Area, TN

This index helps you "spot" where approved hotels and restaurants are located on the corresponding detailed maps. Hotel daily rate range is for comparison only. Restaurant price range is a combination of lunch and/or dinner. Turn to the listing page for more detailed rate and price information and consult display ads for special promotions.

PIGEON FORGE

Map Page	Hotels	Diamond Rated	Rate Range	Page
1 p. 84	Berry Springs Lodge	◆◆◆	$205-$245	232
2 p. 84	Hampton Inn & Suites	◆◆◆	$99-$209	233
3 p. 84	Microtel Inn & Suites by Wyndham	◆◆	$45-$120	233
4 p. 84	**Ramada Pigeon Forge North**	◆◆	$50-$200 SAVE	234
5 p. 84	Holiday Inn Express Hotel & Suites	◆◆	$69-$189	233
6 p. 84	**Music Road Resort Hotel & Convention Center**	◆◆◆	$89-$199 SAVE	234
7 p. 84	Music Road Inn	◆◆◆	$89-$209	234
8 p. 84	Comfort Suites Pigeon Forge	◆◆◆	$89-$250	232
9 p. 84	**Econo Lodge Riverside**	◆◆	$49-$129 SAVE	233
10 p. 84	SpringHill Suites by Marriott	◆◆◆	$83-$194	234
11 p. 84	**The Inn at Christmas Place**	◆◆◆	$89-$429 SAVE	233
12 p. 84	The Inn on the River	◆◆	$79-$219	233
13 p. 84	**La Quinta Inn & Suites**	◆◆◆	$64-$268 SAVE	233
14 p. 84	Timbers Lodge	◆◆	Rates not provided	234
15 p. 84	**Clarion Inn Pigeon Forge**	◆◆◆	$79-$140 SAVE	232
16 p. 84	Shular Inn	◆◆	$60-$220	234
17 p. 84	Hampton Inn Pigeon Forge	◆◆◆	$99-$239	233
18 p. 84	Country Cascades	◆◆	Rates not provided	232
19 p. 84	Accommodations by Willow Brook Lodge	◆◆	$49-$260	232
20 p. 84	Super 8 Motel Pigeon Forge Near The Convention Center	◆	$45-$171	234
21 p. 84	Smoky Cove by Eden Crest Vacation Rentals	◆◆◆	Rates not provided	234
22 p. 84	Black Bear Ridge by Eden Crest Vacation Rentals	◆◆◆	Rates not provided	232
23 p. 84	Bear Creek Crossing by Eden Crest Vacation Rentals	◆◆	$100-$2500	232
24 p. 84	Holiday Inn Hotel & Convention Center	◆◆◆	$74-$220	233
25 p. 84	**RiverStone Resort & Spa**	◆◆◆	$110-$479 SAVE	234
26 p. 84	All Season Suites	◆◆	Rates not provided	232
27 p. 84	**BEST WESTERN Plaza Inn**	◆◆	$51-$162 SAVE	232
28 p. 84	Twin Mountain Inn II	◆◆	Rates not provided	234
29 p. 84	**BEST WESTERN Toni Inn**	◆◆	$52-$172 SAVE	232

Map Page	Restaurants	Diamond Rated	Cuisine	Price Range	Page
1 p. 84	Hard Rock Cafe	◆◆	American	$12-$24 SAVE	235
2 p. 84	Blue Moose Burgers & Wings	◆	Wings Burgers	$6-$10	235

Map Page	Restaurants (cont'd)	Diamond Rated	Cuisine	Price Range	Page
③ p. 84	Bullfish Grill	◈◈	American	$10-$25	235
④ p. 84	Smoky Mountain Brewery	◈◈	American	$8-$23	235
⑤ p. 84	Poynor's Pommes Frites	◈	German	$5-$8	235
⑥ p. 84	**Bennett's Pit Bar-B-Que**	◈◈	Barbecue Sandwiches	$7-$23	234
⑦ p. 84	**Big Daddy's Pizzeria**	◈◈	Pizza	$9-$22	234
⑧ p. 84	**Alamo Steakhouse**	◈◈	Steak Seafood	$7-$29	234
⑨ p. 84	**Mama's Farmhouse**	◈◈	Traditional Southern	$15-$18	235
⑩ p. 84	Red Rooster Pancake House	◈	Breakfast Sandwiches	$5-$12	235
⑪ p. 84	J. T. Hannah's Kitchen	◈◈	American	$8-$17	235
⑫ p. 84	The Old Mill Restaurant	◈◈	Southern	$7-$23	235
⑬ p. 84	Huck Finn's Restaurant	◈◈	American	$8-$20	235

GATLINBURG

Map Page	Hotels	Diamond Rated	Rate Range	Page
32 p. 84	**Cobbly Nob Rentals** (See ad p. 90, p. 98.)	◈◈◈	Rates not provided (SAVE)	90
33 p. 84	Buckhorn Inn	◈◈◈	$115-$195	90
34 p. 84	**Eight Gables Inn**	◈◈◈◈	$125-$205 (SAVE)	91
35 p. 84	Bluegreen Vacations Mountain Loft, an Ascend Resort Collection Member	◈◈◈	$129-$309	90
36 p. 84	**Westgate Smoky Mountain Resort & Spa**	◈◈◈	Rates not provided (SAVE)	92
37 p. 84	Outback Resort Rentals & Sales	◈◈◈	$100-$450	91
38 p. 84	**Fairfield Inn & Suites by Marriott-North Gatlinburg**	◈◈◈	$71-$160 (SAVE)	91
39 p. 84	**Baymont Inn & Suites on the River**	◈◈	$50-$110 (SAVE)	89
40 p. 84	**Crossroads Inn & Suites**	◈◈	Rates not provided (SAVE)	90
41 p. 84	**Foxtrot Bed & Breakfast**	◈◈◈	$190-$230 (SAVE)	91
42 p. 84	BEST WESTERN Twin Islands	◈◈	$69-$169 (SAVE)	89
43 p. 84	The Greystone Lodge on the River	◈◈	Rates not provided	91
44 p. 84	The Edgewater Hotel	◈◈	$70-$140	90
45 p. 84	**Baskins Creek Condominiums- Wyndham Vacation Rentals**	◈◈	Rates not provided (SAVE)	89
46 p. 84	Hilton Garden Inn Gatlinburg	◈◈◈	Rates not provided	91
47 p. 84	**The Lodge at Buckberry Creek**	◈◈◈◈	$205-$405 (SAVE)	91
48 p. 84	Gillette Motel	◈	$55-$120	91
49 p. 84	Travelodge Inn & Suites Gatlinburg	◈	$63-$109	92
50 p. 84	**Bearskin Lodge on the River**	◈◈	$79-$169 (SAVE)	89
51 p. 84	Holiday Inn Club Vacations-Smoky Mountain Resort	◈◈◈	Rates not provided	91
52 p. 84	Motel 6 Gatlinburg Smoky Mountains #4767	◈	Rates not provided	91
53 p. 84	**Glenstone Lodge**	◈◈	$69-$250 (SAVE)	91

GATLINBURG (cont'd)

Map Page	Hotels (cont'd)	Diamond Rated	Rate Range	Page
54 p. 84	**The Park Vista-a DoubleTree by Hilton Hotel Gatlinburg** *(See ad p. 92.)*	▽▽▽	$109-$269 SAVE	92

Map Page	Restaurants	Diamond Rated	Cuisine	Price Range	Page
16 p. 84	Greenbrier Restaurant	▽▽	American	$16-$44	93
17 p. 84	Mountain Lodge Restaurant	▽▽	Breakfast Sandwiches	$4-$7	93
18 p. 84	**Alamo Steakhouse & Saloon**	▽▽	Steak Seafood	$8-$30	92
19 p. 84	Flapjack's Pancake Cabin	▽	Breakfast	$6-$11	93
20 p. 84	Whole Earth Grocery Café	▽	Sandwiches Vegetarian	$5-$7	94
21 p. 84	The Smoky Mountain Trout House	▽▽	Seafood	$14-$20	93
22 p. 84	Pancake Pantry	▽▽	Breakfast	$7-$11	93
23 p. 84	Blaine's Grill & Bar	▽▽	American	$7-$21	93
24 p. 84	**The Restaurant at Buckberry Creek**	▽▽▽	Regional American	$26-$45	93
25 p. 84	**Bennett's Pit Bar-B-Que**	▽▽	Barbecue	$8-$22	93
26 p. 84	Best Italian Cafe & Pizzeria	▽▽	Italian	$8-$22	93
27 p. 84	**Big Daddy's Pizzeria**	▽▽	Pizza Sandwiches	$9-$22	93
28 p. 84	Cherokee Grill	▽▽	American	$10-$23	93
29 p. 84	The Peddler Steakhouse	▽▽	American	$21-$37	93
30 p. 84	Log Cabin Pancake House	▽	American	$4-$12	93
31 p. 84	The Park Grill	▽▽	American	$11-$42	93

SEVIERVILLE

Map Page	Hotels	Diamond Rated	Rate Range	Page
57 p. 84	La Quinta Inn & Suites Sevierville/Kodak	▽▽	$64-$187	240
58 p. 84	Clarion Inn Willow River	▽▽	$92-$155	239
59 p. 84	**Quality Inn & Suites River Suites**	▽▽	$60-$139 SAVE	240
60 p. 84	Econo Lodge	▽	$39-$139	239
61 p. 84	Hampton Inn	▽▽▽	$119-$179	240
62 p. 84	**BEST WESTERN Greenbrier Inn**	▽▽	$50-$120 SAVE	239
63 p. 84	Sleep Inn	▽▽	$45-$150	240
64 p. 84	Governor's Inn	▽▽	Rates not provided	240
65 p. 84	The Resort at Governor's Crossing	▽▽▽	$109-$249	240
66 p. 84	**Oak Tree Lodge**	▽▽	$50-$125 SAVE	240
67 p. 84	**Fairfield Inn & Suites by Marriott Pigeon Forge**	▽▽▽	$48-$139 SAVE	239
68 p. 84	Blue Mountain Mist Country Inn & Cottages	▽▽▽	Rates not provided	239
69 p. 84	**Comfort Inn Apple Valley** *(See ad p. 239.)*	▽▽▽	$59-$180 SAVE	239

Map Page	Restaurants	Diamond Rated	Cuisine	Price Range	Page
34 p. 84	Buddy's Bar-B-Q	▽	Barbecue	$6-$11	240

Map Page	Restaurants (cont'd)	Diamond Rated	Cuisine	Price Range	Page
㉟ p. 84	El Paso Mexican Restaurant	▽▽	Mexican	$7-$15	240
㊱ p. 84	Thai Basil	▽▽	Thai	$8-$17	241
㊲ p. 84	Flapjack's Pancake Cabin	▽	Breakfast	$6-$11	241
㊳ p. 84	Thai Palace	▽▽	Thai	$8-$16	241
㊴ p. 84	**Big Daddy's Pizzeria**	▽▽	Pizza Sandwiches	$9-$23	240
㊵ p. 84	**Applewood Farmhouse Grill**	▽▽	American	$9-$17	240
㊶ p. 84	**Applewood Farmhouse Restaurant**	▽▽	American	$8-$18	240

KODAK

Map Page	Hotels	Diamond Rated	Rate Range	Page
㉞ p. 84	Hampton Inn & Suites-Sevierville at Stadium Drive	▽▽▽	$109-$219	127
㉝ p. 84	Fairfield Inn & Suites by Marriott Sevierville Kodak	▽▽▽	$97-$160	127
㉔ p. 84	Holiday Inn Express & Suites-Sevierville/Kodak	▽▽▽	Rates not provided	127
㉕ p. 84	Comfort Suites Interstate	▽▽▽	$69-$149	127

Map Page	Restaurant	Diamond Rated	Cuisine	Price Range	Page
㊹ p. 84	Uncle Buck's Grill	▽▽	American	$10-$30	127

TOWNSEND

Map Page	Hotels	Diamond Rated	Rate Range	Page
㉘ p. 84	**BEST WESTERN Cades Cove Inn**	▽▽	$80-$130 [SAVE]	247
㉙ p. 84	Highland Manor Inn	▽	$60-$120	247

Map Page	Restaurant	Diamond Rated	Cuisine	Price Range	Page
㊼ p. 84	Carriage House Restaurant	▽▽	American	$5-$18	247

BASKINS CREEK CONDOMINIUMS- WYNDHAM VACATION RENTALS
844/798-5881 ㊺

▽▽▽
Vacation Rental Condominium
Rates not provided

Address: 215 Woliss Ln 37738 **Location:** Jct US 441, just e on Cherokee Orchard Rd at traffic light 6, then just n. **Facility:** Just off the main drag, but still within walking distance of the town. Nicely decorated two-bedroom condos with fireplaces, whirlpool bathtubs, well-equipped kitchens and covered parking. 60 condominiums. 5 stories, interior corridors. **Pool(s):** heated outdoor. **Activities:** hot tub, exercise room. **Guest Services:** complimentary laundry.

BAYMONT INN & SUITES ON THE RIVER
(865)436-5047 ㊴

▽▽
Motel
$50-$110

Address: 293 Parkway 37738 **Location:** On US 441, just n of traffic light 2. **Facility:** 67 units. 3 stories, exterior corridors. **Terms:** cancellation fee imposed. **Pool(s):** heated indoor. **Activities:** sauna, game room, exercise room. **Guest Services:** coin laundry. **Featured Amenity:** full hot breakfast.

BEARSKIN LODGE ON THE RIVER   (865)430-4330 ㊿

▽▽▽
Hotel
$79-$169

Address: 840 River Rd 37738 **Location:** US 441, just w at traffic light 10. **Facility:** 96 units. 5 stories, interior corridors. **Terms:** 2-3 night minimum stay - weekends, 30 day cancellation notice-fee imposed. **Pool(s):** heated outdoor. **Activities:** exercise room. **Featured Amenity:** continental breakfast.

BEST WESTERN TWIN ISLANDS   (865)436-5121 ㊷

▽▽
Motel
$69-$169

AAA Benefit:
Save 10% or more every day and earn 10% bonus points!

Address: 539 Parkway 37738 **Location:** On US 441; between traffic lights 3 and 5. **Facility:** 112 units. 1-2 stories (no elevator), exterior corridors. **Terms:** 2 night minimum stay - seasonal and/or weekends, 3 day cancellation notice-fee imposed, resort fee. **Pool(s):** heated outdoor. **Activities:** hot tub, fishing, playground. **Guest Services:** coin laundry.

    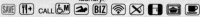

(See map & index p. 84.)

BLUEGREEN VACATIONS MOUNTAIN LOFT, AN ASCEND RESORT COLLECTION MEMBER (865)436-4367
 **Condominium** $129-$309 **Address:** 110 Mountainloft Dr 37738 **Location:** Jct US 441, 1.8 mi n on US 321. **Facility:** No matter which unit you choose in this condo complex, you'll be rewarded with awesome mountain views. Some accommodations are homey town houses, while others are like a high-rise apartment. 384 condominiums. 2-5 stories, exterior corridors. **Terms:** check-in 4 pm. **Pool(s):** heated outdoor, heated indoor. **Activities:** sauna, hot tub, recreation programs, playground, game room, exercise room. **Guest Services:** complimentary laundry.

BUCKHORN INN (865)436-4668
 Historic Country Inn $115-$195 **Address:** 2140 Tudor Mountain Rd 37738 **Location:** Jct US 441, 5.2 mi n on US 321, 0.6 mi w on Buckhorn Rd (SR 454), then just n. **Facility:** This 1938 inn, located on 28 scenic acres laced with walking trails, features cozy rooms, spacious suites and quaint cottages. 20 units, some cottages. 1-2 stories (no elevator), interior/exterior corridors. **Terms:** 2 night minimum stay - seasonal and/or weekends, 10 day cancellation notice-fee imposed. **Activities:** exercise room, massage.

 CALL   /SOME UNITS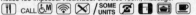

AAA.com/ TourBook Comments

Let Your Voice Be Heard

If your visit to a TourBook-listed property doesn't meet your expectations, tell us about it.

AAA.com/TourBookComments

CROSSROADS INN & SUITES 865/436-5661
 Motel
Rates not provided
Address: 440 Parkway 37738 **Location:** On US 441, just n of traffic light 3. **Facility:** 78 units, some two bedrooms and kitchens. 4 stories, exterior corridors. **Pool(s):** heated outdoor. **Activities:** exercise room. **Guest Services:** coin laundry. **Featured Amenity:** full hot breakfast.

SAVE

THE EDGEWATER HOTEL (865)436-4151
 Hotel $70-$140 **Address:** 402 River Rd 37738 **Location:** Jct US 441, veer just sw at traffic light 5. **Facility:** 205 units. 8 stories, interior corridors. **Terms:** check-in 4 pm, 3 day cancellation notice-fee imposed. **Pool(s):** heated outdoor, heated indoor. **Activities:** hot tub, game room, exercise room.

CALL

▼ See AAA listing this page ▼

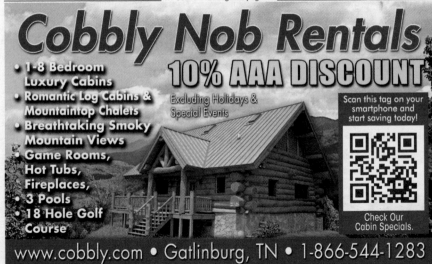

(See map & index p. 84.)

EIGHT GABLES INN

(865)430-3344 **34**

Bed & Breakfast
$125-$205

Address: 219 N Mountain Tr 37738 **Location:** US 441/321, just e on Little Smoky Rd. Located in a quiet area. **Facility:** This charming contemporary inn nestles comfortably in a wooded area. 22 units. 1-2 stories (no elevator), interior/exterior corridors. **Terms:** 2 night minimum stay - seasonal and/or weekends, age restrictions may apply, 14 day cancellation notice-fee imposed. **Activities:** exercise room, massage. **Featured Amenity: full hot breakfast.**

FAIRFIELD INN & SUITES BY MARRIOTT-NORTH GATLINBURG

(865)430-3659 **38**

Hotel
$71-$160

FAIRFIELD INN & SUITES Marriott.

AAA Benefit: Members save 5% or more!

Address: 168 Parkway 37738 **Location:** On US 441, just n of traffic light 1. **Facility:** 101 units. 3 stories, interior corridors. **Pool(s):** heated outdoor, heated indoor. **Activities:** hot tub, limited exercise equipment. **Guest Services:** coin laundry. **Featured Amenity: full hot breakfast.**

FOXTROT BED & BREAKFAST

(865)436-3033 **41**

Bed & Breakfast
$190-$230

Address: 1520 Garrett Ln 37738 **Location:** Jct US 441, 1.5 mi w on Ski Mountain Rd at traffic light 10, just n on Wiley Oakley Dr to 4-way stop, take sharp left switchback turn to stay on Wiley Oakley Dr another 0.8 mi, veer left onto Garrett Rd, then straight. **Facility:** On a crest overlooking the mountains, the inn offers tranquil rooms with king beds and spectacular views. A gourmet breakfast is served daily. 4 units. 2 stories (no elevator), interior corridors. **Terms:** 2 night minimum stay - seasonal and/or weekends, 15 day cancellation notice-fee imposed. **Featured Amenity: full hot breakfast.**

GILLETTE MOTEL   865/436-5601 **48**

Motel $55-$120 **Address:** 235 Airport Rd/Historic Nature Tr 37738 **Location:** 0.3 mi e of US 441 and traffic light 8. **Facility:** 80 units, some kitchens. 3 stories, exterior corridors. **Terms:** cancellation fee imposed. **Pool(s):** outdoor.

GLENSTONE LODGE

(865)436-9361 **53**

Hotel
$69-$250

Address: 504 Historic Nature Tr 37738 **Location:** 0.4 mi e of US 441 at traffic light 8. **Facility:** 215 units. 3-5 stories, interior/exterior corridors. **Terms:** 3 day cancellation notice-fee imposed. **Pool(s):** outdoor, heated indoor. **Activities:** hot tub. **Featured Amenity: breakfast buffet.**

THE GREYSTONE LODGE ON THE RIVER
865/436-5621 **43**

Hotel. Rates not provided. **Address:** 559 Parkway 37738 **Location:** Just w of jct US 441 at traffic light 5. **Facility:** 241 units, some two bedrooms. 2-5 stories, interior/exterior corridors. **Terms:** check-in 4 pm. **Pool(s):** heated outdoor. **Activities:** exercise room. **Guest Services:** coin laundry.

HILTON GARDEN INN GATLINBURG   865/436-0048 **46**

Hotel. Rates not provided. **Address:** 635 River Rd 37738 **Location:** US 441, 1.6 mi e at traffic light 5. **Facility:** 118 units. 5 stories, interior corridors. **Terms:** check-in 4 pm. **Pool(s):** heated indoor. **Activities:** hot tub, exercise room. **Guest Services:** valet and coin laundry.

AAA Benefit: Members save up to 10%!

HOLIDAY INN CLUB VACATIONS-SMOKY MOUNTAIN RESORT
865/908-1700 **51**

Vacation Rental Condominium. Rates not provided. **Address:** 404 Historic Nature Tr 37738 **Location:** Jct US 441, just e at traffic light 8. **Facility:** One- and two-bedroom condos with modern, attractive décor offer balconies, fireplaces and well-equipped kitchens. 105 condominiums. 10 stories, exterior corridors. **Terms:** check-in 4 pm. **Amenities:** safes. **Pool(s):** heated outdoor, heated indoor. **Activities:** hot tub, recreation programs, game room, exercise room, massage. **Guest Services:** complimentary laundry.

THE LODGE AT BUCKBERRY CREEK

(865)430-8030 **47**

Country Inn
$205-$405

Address: 961 Campbell Lead Rd 37738 **Location:** Jct US 441, 1.5 mi w on Ski Mountain Rd at traffic light 10, just n on Wiley Oakley Dr to 4-way stop, then just e. **Facility:** The Lodge recaptures the rustic charm of the classic Adirondack design with fireplaces in its spacious rooms and mountain views. 40 kitchen units. 3 stories (no elevator), exterior corridors. **Terms:** check-in 4 pm, 1-2 night minimum stay - seasonal and/or weekends, 7 day cancellation notice. **Dining:** The Restaurant at Buckberry Creek, see separate listing. **Activities:** fishing, recreation programs in summer, exercise room, massage. **Guest Services:** complimentary and valet laundry. **Featured Amenity: continental breakfast.**

MOTEL 6 GATLINBURG SMOKY MOUNTAINS #4767
865/436-7813 **52**

Motel. Rates not provided. **Address:** 309 Ownby St 37738 **Location:** Traffic light 10 (Ski Mountain Rd), 0.4 mi w. **Facility:** 53 units, some kitchens. 2 stories (no elevator), exterior corridors. **Pool(s):** heated outdoor.

OUTBACK RESORT RENTALS & SALES   865/430-9385 **37**

Vacation Rental House $100-$450 **Location:** Jct US 441 on north end of town at Great Smoky Mountains Welcome Center, 1 mi sw on Wiley Oakley Dr, then 0.5 mi w on N Woodland Dr. Located in a secluded mountain area. **Facility:** Guests will find these private, professionally decorated homes in an upscale, gated community with spectacular mountain views. 15 houses. 1-2 stories (no elevator), exterior corridors. **Terms:** 2 night minimum stay - seasonal, age restrictions may apply, 30 day cancellation notice-fee imposed, resort fee. **Amenities:** Some: video games. **Pool(s):** outdoor. **Guest Services:** complimentary laundry.

(See map & index p. 84.)

THE PARK VISTA-A DOUBLETREE BY HILTON HOTEL GATLINBURG
(865)436-9211   **54**

Hotel
$109-$269

AAA Benefit:
Members save 5% or more!

Address: 705 Cherokee Orchard Rd 37738 **Location:** Jct US 441, 0.6 mi e on Historic Nature Tr at traffic light 8. **Facility:** 300 units, some two bedrooms. 15 stories, interior corridors. **Terms:** check-in 4 pm, 1-7 night minimum stay, cancellation fee imposed. **Pool(s):** heated indoor. **Activities:** hot tub, playground, game room, exercise room. **Guest Services:** valet and coin laundry. *(See ad this page.)*

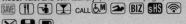

Spectacular views of the Smokies from your private balcony. On City of Gatlinburg's Trolley Route.

TRAVELODGE INN & SUITES GATLINBURG
(865)325-1516   **49**

Hotel $63-$109 **Address:** 218 Ski Mountain Rd 37738 **Location:** Traffic light 10 (Ski Mountain Rd), just n. **Facility:** 51 units. 6 stories, exterior corridors. **Pool(s):** outdoor.

WESTGATE SMOKY MOUNTAIN RESORT & SPA
865/430-4800   **36**

Vacation Rental
Condominium
Rates not provided

Address: 915 Westgate Resort Rd 37738 **Location:** Jct US 441, just e on Little Smoky Rd, then just s. Across from Gatlinburg Welcome Center. **Facility:** The resort features cabin-style duplexes, plus one- and two-bedroom condos that can be expanded to even larger units via connecting room doors. 866 condominiums. 1-5 stories, exterior corridors. **Terms:** check-in 4 pm. **Amenities:** safes. **Pool(s):** heated outdoor. **Activities:** hot tub, miniature golf, recreation programs, playground, game room, exercise room, spa. **Guest Services:** complimentary laundry.

OLD CREEK LODGE
865/430-7200

fyi Not evaluated. **Address:** 680 River Rd 37738 **Location:** Just w of US 441 at traffic light 9. Facilities, services, and décor characterize a mid-scale property.

WHERE TO EAT

ALAMO STEAKHOUSE & SALOON
865/436-9998   **18**

Steak
Seafood
Casual Dining
$8-$30

AAA Inspector Notes: This steakhouse offers friendly service in a Wild West atmosphere. The house specialty is tender, oak-fired Prime Black Angus steak. Choice cuts of beef and seafood include broiled lobster tail and grilled salmon. There is a one-pound burger for those with a big appetite. **Features:** full bar, patio dining. **Address:** 705 E Parkway 37738 **Location:** Jct US 441, 0.8 mi n on US 321. *Menu on AAA.com*

▼ See AAA listing this page ▼

YOUR VIEW OF THE SMOKY MOUNTAINS
STARTS HERE.

Contact us today to make reservations for a stay you will never forget.

Gatlinburg, TN 800-421-7275 www.parkvista.com

THE PARK VISTA
A DOUBLETREE BY HILTON

(See map & index p. 84.)

BENNETT'S PIT BAR-B-QUE
865/436-2400 (25)

Barbecue Family Dining
$8-$22

AAA Inspector Notes: Ribs, beef brisket and chicken are smoked over a wood fire to create this casual eatery's popular dishes. Other highlights include wings, burgers and sandwiches. The 40-item soup and salad bar is a meal in itself. At breakfast, the salad bar is converted into a breakfast buffet full of good eats to start the day off right. **Features:** full bar, patio dining. **Address:** 714 River Rd 37738 **Location:** Jct US 441, just w at traffic light 10 on Ski Mountain Rd, then just n. *Menu on AAA.com*

[B] [L] [D] CALL [&M]

BEST ITALIAN CAFE & PIZZERIA
865/430-4090 (26)

Italian. Casual Dining. $8-$22 **AAA Inspector Notes:** Among other offerings are specialty pizza, calzones, pasta dishes and salads. The hot garlic rolls are a local favorite. **Features:** full bar. **Address:** 968 Parkway, Suite 9 37738 **Location:** Just past traffic light 8; in Elks Plaza. **Parking:** on-site (fee). [L] [D]

BIG DADDY'S PIZZERIA
865/436-5455 (27)

Pizza Sandwiches Family Dining
$9-$22

AAA Inspector Notes: The specialty of the house is hand-tossed pizza baked in a wood-fired brick oven, available in a variety of flavors ranging from the unusual, like the Cuban with roast pork, ham, black beans and pickles, to the traditional, like the margherita with fresh mozzarella and roma tomatoes. Build-your-own is always an option too. For lighter appetites, the menu includes a few salads and sandwiches. **Features:** beer & wine, patio dining. **Address:** 714 River Rd 37738 **Location:** Jct US 441, just w at traffic light 10 on Ski Mountain Rd, then just n. *Menu on AAA.com* [L] [D]

BLAINE'S GRILL & BAR
865/430-1978 (23)

American. Casual Dining. $7-$21 **AAA Inspector Notes:** The hostess station and waiting area is on the first floor, but the dining space is on the second. There is no elevator access. The atmosphere is likened to that of a lively pub. **Features:** full bar, patio dining. **Address:** 812 Parkway, Suite 105 37738 **Location:** On US 441, at traffic light 8. **Parking:** on-site (fee). [L] [D] [LATE]

CALHOUN'S ON THE RIVER
865/436-4100

Regional American. Casual Dining. $9-$23 **AAA Inspector Notes:** Wrap yourself in genuine Southern hospitality from the minute you walk in the door. The decor is modern and upscale, and the service fast and friendly. The place has wonderful ribs, but it's hard to go wrong with the white bean chili either. **Features:** full bar. **Address:** 1004 Parkway 37738 **Location:** On US 441, just s of traffic light 10. [L] [D]

CHEROKEE GRILL
865/436-4287 (28)

American. Casual Dining. $10-$23 **AAA Inspector Notes:** With windows overlooking the main drag and a large stone fireplace, this steak house offers a cozy spot to people-watch and unwind with friends over well-prepared steaks, seafood, chicken, and sandwiches. Entrées include fried catfish, Maryland crab cakes and rotisserie chicken. On Fridays and Saturdays, prime rib is the specialty of the house. **Features:** full bar, happy hour. **Address:** 1002 Parkway 37738 **Location:** On US 441; between traffic lights 9 and 10. [L] [D]

FLAPJACK'S PANCAKE CABIN
865/430-3966 (19)

Breakfast. Family Dining. $6-$11 **AAA Inspector Notes:** Patrons can settle in for a hearty breakfast at this casual spot. The cozy cabin decor incorporates hunting and fishing items, and the flapjacks are superb. **Address:** 478 E Parkway, Hwy 321 37738 **Location:** 1.5 mi e on US 321. **Parking:** on-site (fee). [B]

GREENBRIER RESTAURANT
865/436-6318 (16)

American. Casual Dining. $16-$44 **AAA Inspector Notes:** A cozy atmosphere prevails in this 1939 log cabin, tucked away on a wooded knoll. House specialties are mountain trout, prime rib, filet mignon and chicken breast stuffed with crabmeat, as well as stuffed flounder and stuffed pork loin with apple dressing. **Features:** full bar. **Address:** 370 Newman Rd 37738 **Location:** Jct US 441, 1.4 mi n on US 321, then just e. [D]

LOG CABIN PANCAKE HOUSE
865/436-7894 (30)

American. Family Dining. $4-$12 **AAA Inspector Notes:** Two large fireplaces are stoked on chilly days to add to the coziness of the log cabin. Generous portions of breakfast items, such as pancakes, waffles and crepes, are served by a fast and friendly waitstaff. In season, lunch buffets are offered with a variety of Southern-style meats and vegetables. **Features:** senior menu. **Address:** 327 Historic Nature Tr 37738 **Location:** Jct US 441, just e at traffic light 8. [B] [L]

MOUNTAIN LODGE RESTAURANT
865/436-2547 (17)

Breakfast Sandwiches. Casual Dining. $4-$7 **AAA Inspector Notes:** The fast, friendly staff serves good home cooking. Locals frequent this popular spot, which prepares breakfast items until closing. **Address:** 913 E Parkway 37738 **Location:** Jct US 441 and 321, traffic light 3, 1.2 mi n on US 321. [B] [L]

NO WAY JOSE'S CANTINA
865/430-5673

Mexican. Casual Dining. $8-$13 **AAA Inspector Notes:** Diners who might think they have gone south of the border. Festive décor mingles with ample portions of fajitas, chimichangas and burritos, as well as many other mouthwatering entrées. **Features:** full bar, patio dining. **Address:** 555 Parkway 37738 **Location:** On US 441, at traffic light 5. [L] [D] CALL [&M]

PANCAKE PANTRY
865/436-4724 (22)

Breakfast. Family Dining. $7-$11 **AAA Inspector Notes:** These folks have perfected the pancake. Since 1960 the restaurant has offered an extensive pancake menu with more than 20 ingredient choices. You'll also find waffles and crepes. Those seeking a little protein can check out the egg menu, in addition to sides of bacon, sausage and ham. Patrons arriving at lunchtime can indulge in breakfast, or select from a number of gourmet sandwiches. **Address:** 628 Parkway 37738 **Location:** Between traffic lights 6 and 7. **Parking:** on-site (fee) and street. [B] [L]

THE PARK GRILL
865/436-2300 (31)

American. Casual Dining. $11-$42 **AAA Inspector Notes:** Log beams and high ceilings lend to the rustic feel at this restaurant. Special twists on favorite entrées include moonshine marinated chicken and beef. Entrées include an extensive salad bar. **Features:** full bar. **Address:** 1110 Parkway 37738 **Location:** On US 441, between traffic lights 9 and 10. [D] CALL [&M]

THE PEDDLER STEAKHOUSE
865/436-5794 (29)

American. Casual Dining. $21-$37 **AAA Inspector Notes:** Along the Little Pigeon River, this rustic log cabin house is a quaint place to enjoy aged beef and charcoal-grilled entrées, such as the rib-eye and marinated chicken. **Features:** full bar. **Address:** 820 River Rd 37738 **Location:** Just w of jct US 441 at traffic light 10, then just n. [D]

THE RESTAURANT AT BUCKBERRY CREEK
865/430-8030 (24)

Regional American Fine Dining
$26-$45

AAA Inspector Notes: The cozy lodge setting, which affords striking views of the mountains, sets the scene for an unforgettable dining experience. You can't miss with any of the flavorful dishes on the chef's seasonally changing menu. **Features:** full bar, patio dining. **Reservations:** suggested. **Address:** 961 Campbell Lead Rd 37738 **Location:** Jct US 441, 1.5 mi w on Ski Mountain Rd at traffic light 10, just n on Wiley Oakley Dr to 4-way stop, then just e; in The Lodge at Buckberry Creek. [B] [D] CALL [&M]

THE SMOKY MOUNTAIN TROUT HOUSE
865/436-5416 (21)

Seafood. Casual Dining. $14-$20 **AAA Inspector Notes:** This is the place for rainbow trout. It's raised on a local trout farm and served in 12 tasty ways, from fritters to fried with bacon, butter and sautéed onions. The specialty also spills into the décor, with wall mountings and antique fly rods. **Features:** beer & wine. **Address:** 410 N Parkway 37738 **Location:** On US 441, just n of traffic light 3. **Parking:** on-site (fee). [D]

(See map & index p. 84.)

WHOLE EARTH GROCERY CAFÉ   865/436-6967   **20**

Sandwiches Vegetarian. Quick Serve. $5-$7 **AAA Inspector Notes:** Inside Whole Earth Grocery, this café is a nice alternative for a healthful meal or snack. Many vegetarian and vegan selections are among options available for dining in or taking out. **Address:** 446 E Parkway, Unit 4 37738 **Location:** Jct US 441, 0.4 mi n on US 321; in Winery Square. [L]

GERMANTOWN pop. 38,844
- **Hotels & Restaurants map & index p. 154**
- **Part of Memphis area — see map p. 134**

COMFORT INN & SUITES-GERMANTOWN
    (901)757-7800   **52**

Hotel $89-$109 **Address:** 7787 Wolf River Blvd 38138 **Location:** I-40 exit 16A, 5.7 mi s on Germantown Pkwy, then just w. **Facility:** 81 units. 3 stories, interior corridors. **Pool(s):** heated indoor. **Guest Services:** coin laundry.

COURTYARD BY MARRIOTT MEMPHIS GERMANTOWN
    (901)751-0230   **51**

COURTYARD Marriott

Hotel $89-$183

AAA Benefit: Members save 5% or more!

Address: 7750 Wolf River Blvd 38138 **Location:** I-40 exit 16A, 5.7 mi s on Germantown Pkwy, then just w. **Facility:** 93 units. 3 stories, interior corridors. **Pool(s):** heated indoor. **Activities:** hot tub, exercise room. **Guest Services:** valet and coin laundry, boarding pass kiosk.

FAIRFIELD INN & SUITES BY MARRIOTT MEMPHIS GERMANTOWN
    (901)757-9100   **55**

Hotel $84-$171

FAIRFIELD INN & SUITES® Marriott

AAA Benefit: Members save 5% or more!

Address: 9320 Poplar Pike 38138 **Location:** SR 177 (Germantown Pkwy), 3 mi e on US 72 (Poplar Ave), just s on Forest Hill Irene Rd, then just e. **Facility:** 80 units. 3 stories, interior corridors. **Pool(s):** heated indoor. **Activities:** hot tub, limited exercise equipment. **Guest Services:** valet and coin laundry.

HOLIDAY INN EXPRESS & SUITES MEMPHIS-GERMANTOWN
    901/309-6700   **50**

Hotel. Rates not provided. **Address:** 7784 Wolf Trail Cove 38138 **Location:** I-40 exit 16, 5 mi s on Germantown Pkwy, then just w. **Facility:** 72 units. 3 stories, interior corridors. **Pool(s):** heated indoor. **Activities:** exercise room. **Guest Services:** valet and coin laundry.

Request roadside assistance in a click — online or using the AAA or CAA apps

HOMEWOOD SUITES BY HILTON-GERMANTOWN
    (901)751-2500   **53**

Extended Stay Hotel $109-$179 **Address:** 7855 Wolf River Blvd 38138 **Location:** I-40 exit 16, 5.7 mi s on Germantown Pkwy, then just e. **Facility:** 92 efficiencies. 3 stories, interior corridors. **Terms:** check-in 4 pm, 1-7 night minimum stay, cancellation fee imposed. **Pool(s):** outdoor. **Activities:** limited exercise equipment. **Guest Services:** valet and coin laundry, area transportation.

AAA Benefit: Members save up to 10%!

HYATT PLACE MEMPHIS/GERMANTOWN
    (901)759-1174   **56**

Hotel $89-$209

HYATT PLACE

AAA Benefit: Members save 10%!

Address: 9161 Winchester Rd 38138 **Location:** SR 177 (Germantown Pkwy), 3 mi e on US 72 (Poplar Ave), just s on Forest Hill Irene Rd, then just e. **Facility:** 127 units. 4 stories, interior corridors. **Terms:** cancellation fee imposed. **Pool(s):** outdoor. **Activities:** exercise room. **Guest Services:** valet and coin laundry, area transportation. **Featured Amenity:** breakfast buffet.

RESIDENCE INN BY MARRIOTT MEMPHIS/GERMANTOWN
    (901)752-0900   **54**

Extended Stay Hotel $104-$200 **Address:** 9314 Poplar Pike 38138 **Location:** SR 177 (Germantown Pkwy), 3 mi e on US 72 (Poplar Ave), just s on Forest Hill Irene Rd, then just e. **Facility:** 78 units, some two bedrooms, efficiencies and kitchens. 3 stories, interior corridors. **Pool(s):** outdoor. **Activities:** hot tub, tennis, exercise room. **Guest Services:** valet and coin laundry.

AAA Benefit: Members save 5% or more!

WHERE TO EAT

THE BELMONT GRILL GERMANTOWN   901/624-6001   **35**

American. Casual Dining. $8-$24 **AAA Inspector Notes:** This popular, local pub serves great burgers and house-smoked steaks. **Features:** full bar, happy hour. **Address:** 9102 Poplar Pike 38138 **Location:** Jct Forest Hill Irene Rd. [L] [D]

GERMANTOWN COMMISSARY   901/754-5540   **34**

Barbecue. Casual Dining. $6-$25 **AAA Inspector Notes:** Patrons start arriving at 9 am to pick up barbecue for their lunch get-togethers; the platters for lunch and dinner are huge, so guests will not go away hungry, and only the freshest made-from-scratch sides and desserts are allowed out of this restaurant. **Features:** beer only. **Address:** 2290 S Germantown Rd 38138 **Location:** Jct US 72 (Poplar Ave), 0.8 mi s on SR 177. [L] [D]

LAS TORTUGAS DELI MEXICANA   901/751-1200   **33**

Mexican. Quick Serve. $6-$19 **AAA Inspector Notes:** This modest-appearing restaurant, located on the end of a strip mall, serves great-tasting authentic cuisine. The dining area has limited seating and much of the experience is self-service, but the quality of food more than makes up for the lack of table service. They specialize in tortas, and their preparation skill and recipes come straight from their heritage in Mexico City. House-made salsas are a must-try. **Address:** 1215 S Germantown Rd 38138 **Location:** I-40 exit 16 or 16A, 5.7 mi s. [L] [D]

GOODLETTSVILLE (C-4) pop. 15,921, elev. 509'
- Hotels & Restaurants map & index p. 200
- Part of Nashville area — see map p. 179

HISTORIC MANSKER'S STATION FRONTIER LIFE CENTER is off I-65 exit 97, .5 mi. e. to Caldwell Dr., then .5 mi. s. to Moss-Wright Park. On the site of the Frontier Life Center is the two-story 1787 Bowen Plantation House as well as a reconstructed log station and fort. Interpreters in period costumes perform daily activities of the time; hands-on participation is encouraged for families with children.

Time: Allow 1 hour, 30 minutes minimum. **Hours:** Mon.-Fri. 9-4:30, early Mar.-early Dec. Last tour begins at 3:30. Closed major holidays. **Cost:** $8; $7 (ages 62+); $6 (ages 6-12). **Phone:** (615) 859-3678.

BEST WESTERN FAIRWINDS INN
(615)851-1067 **62**

Hotel
$70-$300

AAA Benefit: Save 10% or more every day and earn 10% bonus points!

Address: 100 Northcreek Blvd 37072 **Location:** I-65 exit 97 (Long Hollow Pike), just e, then just s. Located in a busy commercial area. **Facility:** 100 units. 3 stories, exterior corridors. **Terms:** cancellation fee imposed, resort fee. **Pool(s):** outdoor. **Featured Amenity:** continental breakfast.

AAA members 10% off. Free High Speed Wi-Fi. Free hot breakfast. Late check-out. Walk to restaurants

COMFORT SUITES
(615)448-2100 **66**

Hotel
$100-$150

Address: 621 Rivergate Pkwy 37072 **Location:** I-65 exit 96, just e. **Facility:** 80 units. 3 stories, interior corridors. **Pool(s):** heated indoor. **Activities:** hot tub, exercise room. **Guest Services:** valet and coin laundry.

COUNTRY INN & SUITES BY CARLSON (615)851-4444 **65**

Hotel $90-$250 **Address:** 641 Wade Cir 37072 **Location:** I-65 exit 96, just ne. **Facility:** 65 units, some kitchens. 3 stories, interior corridors. **Terms:** 5 day cancellation notice-fee imposed. **Pool(s):** heated indoor. **Activities:** exercise room. **Guest Services:** coin laundry.

COURTYARD BY MARRIOTT NASHVILLE GOODLETTSVILLE
(615)851-3000 **64**

Hotel
$89-$259

COURTYARD Marriott.

AAA Benefit: Members save 5% or more!

Address: 865 Conference Dr 37072 **Location:** I-65 exit 97 (Long Hollow Pike), just e, then s. **Facility:** 120 units. 4 stories, interior corridors. **Pool(s):** heated indoor. **Activities:** exercise room. **Guest Services:** valet and coin laundry, boarding pass kiosk.

HAMPTON INN NASHVILLE-GOODLETTSVILLE
(615)851-2828 **63**

Hotel $97-$110 **Address:** 202 Northgate Cir 37072 **Location:** I-65 exit 97 (Long Hollow Pike), 0.5 mi e to Conference Dr, then 0.5 mi s. **Facility:** 60 units. 3 stories, interior corridors. **Terms:** 1-7 night minimum stay, cancellation fee imposed. **Pool(s):** outdoor. **Activities:** exercise room. **Guest Services:** valet laundry.

AAA Benefit: Members save up to 10%!

WHERE TO EAT

BAILEY'S SPORTS GRILLE
615/851-9509

American. Casual Dining. $8-$16 **AAA Inspector Notes:** A classic pub decor of dark wood paneling and ceramic steins--with a modern American bar, where huge TV screens are tuned to sports in every possible spot, including the restrooms. You'll find the same mixing cultures evident on the menu; burgers, pizzas, and chicken wings sit beside fish 'n' chips, tortilla soup, fresh-baked pretzels, nachos, baby back ribs, and Texas-style brisket. **Features:** full bar, happy hour. **Address:** 786 Two Mile Pike, Suite 12 37072 **Location:** I-65 exit 97 (Long Hollow Pike), 0.5 mi w, then just n; across from Rivergate Mall.

BUCK'S BARBEQUE
615/855-6565 **39**

Barbecue. Quick Serve. $5-$12 **AAA Inspector Notes:** At the heart of the menu are hickory-smoked beef, pulled pork, turkey and fall-off-the-bone ribs. The daily specials are a great value for any barbecue enthusiast. **Address:** 327 N Cartwright St 37072 **Location:** I-65 exit 97 (Long Hollow Pike), just w.

CHEF'S MARKET CATERING & RESTAURANT
615/851-2433 **41**

American. Quick Serve. $9-$16 **AAA Inspector Notes:** Talented chefs at this hidden jewel prepare a variety of salads, sandwiches and desserts using fresh ingredients. Peer over a glass window and select your meal a la carte or try a daily special. Service is fast and friendly, regardless of whether you dine in or take out. **Features:** patio dining. **Address:** 900 Conference Dr 37072 **Location:** I-65 exit 97 (Long Hollow Pike), 1 mi e; in Music City Shopping Center.

Take Your
Imagination
to New Destinations

EL CHICO   615/859-1112 43

◈◈ ◈◈
Tex-Mex
Casual Dining
$6-$16

AAA Inspector Notes: Inside and out, the decor of the popular Mexican restaurant is inviting. The menu features traditional favorites such as enchiladas, tacos, burritos and fajitas. The broad menu also lists a few American classics. **Features:** full bar, happy hour. **Address:** 928 Rivergate Pkwy 37072 **Location:** I-65 exit 96, 1.5 mi e. L D CALL ⓜ

KABUTO   615/851-4004 40

◈◈ ◈◈ Japanese Sushi. Casual Dining. $8-$32 **AAA Inspector Notes:** Delicious entrées are cooked hibachi-style at this casual spot. You'll also find a great selection of sushi and sashimi offerings. **Features:** full bar. **Address:** 908 Conference Dr 37072 **Location:** I-65 exit 97 (Long Hollow Pike), just e. L D

PAINTURO'S   615/859-2522 38

◈◈ Italian Pizza. Quick Serve. $5-$22 **AAA Inspector Notes:** Freshly made thin-crust pizzas teem with an abundance of toppings such as flame-roasted peppers, spicy Italian sausage and chopped pepperoni. Stretched wafer thin, the light and airy farmhouse pizza truly differs from what's offered at major chains. Also on the extensive menu are fresh salads, baked pastas, calzones and assorted hot and cold sandwiches. **Features:** beer only. **Address:** 430 Long Hollow Pike, Suite C 37072 **Location:** I-65 exit 97 (Long Hollow Pike), 0.7 mi e; in Caldwell Square. L D CALL ⓜ

PANCHO VILLA GRILL   615/855-2955 42

◈◈ ◈◈ Mexican. Casual Dining. $6-$23 **AAA Inspector Notes:** Tasty traditional dishes are served in huge portions at this grill, where service is friendly and attentive. **Features:** full bar. **Address:** 233 Long Hollow Pike 37072 **Location:** I-65 exit 97 (Long Hollow Pike), just w. L D

GRAND JUNCTION (E-2) pop. 325, elev. 575'

NATIONAL BIRD DOG MUSEUM is at 505 W. SR 57, .7 mi. e. of jct. SR 18. The museum is dedicated to preserving the history and highlighting the talents of more than 40 breeds of sporting dogs. Paintings, photographs, sculptures and memorabilia depicting the most famous sporting dogs of the 19th and 20th centuries are featured.

In The Field Trial Hall of Fame more than 540 pointing, retrieving and flushing dogs and renowned field trial individuals are enshrined. **Time:** Allow 30 minutes minimum. **Hours:** Tues.-Fri. 9-4, Sat. 10-4, Sun. 1-4. Closed Jan. 1, Easter, Thanksgiving and Christmas. **Cost:** Donations. **Phone:** (731) 764-2058.

GRAY (C-8) pop. 1,222

ETSU NATURAL HISTORY MUSEUM AT GRAY FOSSIL SITE is at 1212 Suncrest Dr. In addition to a fossil collection, the museum features permanent and traveling exhibits, fossil preparation laboratory activities and on-site fossil excavations. **Time:** Allow 1 hour minimum. **Hours:** Tues.-Sat. 9-5. Closed Jan. 1, Thanksgiving, Christmas and university holidays. **Cost:** $6; $4 (ages 66+); $3 (ages 5-12). Special exhibit prices vary. **Phone:** (423) 439-3642 or (866) 202-6223. GT

GREAT SMOKY MOUNTAINS NATIONAL PARK (D-8)

• Attractions map p. 100

Elevations in the park range from 870 ft. along Abrams Creek to 6,643 ft. at Clingmans Dome. Refer to AAA maps for additional elevation information.

Divided between North Carolina and Tennessee, Great Smoky Mountains National Park covers more than 520,000 acres. A blue, smokelike haze hangs over the mountains, hence the name. Newfound Gap Road (US 441) bisects the park, which is 32 miles long and 70 miles wide.

Except for Mount Mitchell and Mount Craig, the highest mountain peaks in eastern North America are found in the Smokies—the most massive mountain uplift in the East and one of the oldest land areas on Earth. Sixteen summits rise more than 6,000 feet, and the main ridge does not drop below 5,000 feet for a distance of 36 miles.

Few places in the United States have such a variety of vegetation. Because the mountains catch the region's copious rainfall, they support an exceptionally wide variety of plant species, including more than 100 native trees. A fine stand of Eastern deciduous trees and a large tract of red spruce constitute the park's 120,000 acres of old-growth forest. Much of the remainder is second growth.

Northern conifers, mainly spruce and fir, dominate the higher elevations; at intermediate heights grow hardwoods typical of the Northeast. Some mountaintops are covered only with grass or shrubs and thus are known as "balds."

Many streams are bordered with rhododendron, and in certain areas, such as on Gregory Bald, flame azalea grows in profusion. Rhododendron and sand myrtle are scattered throughout the mountain summits and knife-edged ridges. Dogwood and innumerable wildflowers usually bloom from mid-March to mid-May; other blossoms create spectacular displays into July.

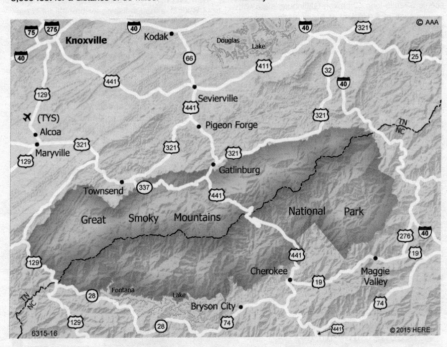

This map shows cities in Great Smoky Mountains National Park where you will find attractions, hotels and restaurants. Cities are listed alphabetically in this book on the following pages.

Wildlife was scarce when the park was established in 1934, but hunting has since been outlawed and many species are recovering. Deer often are observed in Cades Cove *(see attraction listing)*, and ruffed grouse, wild turkeys and bears live in the park.

General Information and Activities

The park is open all year. Headquarters and the Sugarlands Visitor Center are 2 miles south of Gatlinburg, Tenn., on US 441. Information about naturalist-led hikes, campfire programs and other park activities can be obtained at Sugarlands as well as at Oconaluftee Visitor Center, near the Cherokee, N.C., entrance.

Park information can be found at Cades Cove Visitor Center, 12 mi. s.w. of Townsend, Tenn. on Cades Cove Loop Road, and Clingmans Dome Visitor Center, 7 mi. s.w. of US 441 on Clingmans Dome Rd.

There are 238 miles of paved and 146 miles of gravel park roads. Newfound Gap Road (US 441), a scenic 33-mile-long Cherokee-Gatlinburg route with an elevation of 5,048 feet at the state line, crosses the park. The 469-mile scenic Blue Ridge Parkway in North Carolina links the park with Shenandoah National Park in Virginia. The Balsam Mountain Road, a 9-mile spur, branches off the parkway just north of the Cherokee Indian Reservation. Heintooga Ridge Road, a scenic loop drive, leads to an overlook.

The park has more than 850 miles of horse and foot trails. Leaflets are provided at the start of short self-guiding nature trails. The most heavily used path is the section of the Appalachian Trail that runs the length of the park. Back-country shelters and campsites along the trail are spaced a day's hike apart, and the camping limit is 1 day per site. All shelters and some campsites require reservations. Permits are required for all back-country camping

and can be obtained at Sugarlands Visitor Center; phone the backcountry office at (865) 436-1297 for more information.

Waterfalls are plentiful and welcome additions to the park's landscape. Although most require hikes of various lengths to reach, one can be enjoyed from the road: Meigs Falls is 13 miles west of the Sugarlands Visitor Center.

Saddle horses and guides can be obtained in the park. Horseback trails lead from concessionaire-operated stables at Smokemont, N.C., as well as Cades Cove and two stables near Gatlinburg.

The ascent of Mount Le Conte by foot from Gatlinburg offers awesome views. Lodging on the mountaintop is available by reservation. Also noted for spectacular views are Charlies Bunion, reached by the Appalachian Trail 4 miles east from Newfound Gap, and Tennessee's highest point, Clingmans Dome *(see attraction listing)*.

With 735 miles of streams available, fishing for trout is ideal, although fishing for brook trout is prohibited. Visitors fishing within the park must have a license from Tennessee or North Carolina; these cannot be purchased within the park. Fishing is permitted dawn to dusk; inquire for regulations at the park visitor center.

Most of the many developed campgrounds function on a first-come, first-served basis; however, reservations are recommended May 15-Oct. 31 at Cades Cove and Elkmont, Tenn., and at Smokemont, N.C. For reservations phone the National Park Reservation Service at (877) 444-6777. *See Recreation Areas Chart.*

ADMISSION to the park is free. Camping fees range from $14-$23. A permit fee of $4 per person per night is charged to camp overnight in the park's

▼ *See AAA listing p. 90* ▼

backcountry wilderness. Reservations can be made up to 30 days in advance.

PETS are permitted in the park's developed areas only if they are leashed, crated or otherwise physically restricted at all times. They are not permitted on trails.

ADDRESS inquiries to the Park Superintendent, Great Smoky Mountains National Park, 107 Park Headquarters Rd., Gatlinburg, TN 37738; phone (865) 436-1207 or (865) 436-1203.

CADES COVE, off Laurel Creek Rd. in Tennessee, is one of the park's scenic attractions as well as a historic area. An 11-mile, one-way loop road that circles a cove is popular with bicyclists and is therefore closed to all motor vehicles Saturday and Wednesday from dawn to 10 a.m., early May through late September. Park rangers conduct free tours of the mill area daily during the summer from the Cades Cove visitor center. **Time:** Allow 2 hours minimum. **Hours:** Daily dawn-dusk. **Cost:** Free. **Phone:** (865) 436-1200.

CATALOOCHEE is reached via US 276 through Cove Creek Gap, about 21 mi. n. of Waynesville, N.C. Formerly a remote but prosperous farming settlement, Cataloochee declined and its residents were displaced when the park was established in 1934. Several clues to the past remain, including a few homes, a school, a chapel and a cemetery. Elk, reintroduced to the park in 2001, now populate this highland valley known for its solitude, scenic vistas, good trout fishing and abundant wildlife. A self-guiding tour booklet detailing the area's history is available at a roadside box near the valley's entrance.

CLINGMANS DOME is 7 mi. s. of Newfound Gap on Clingmans Dome Rd. in Tennessee. Towering at 6,643 feet, it is Tennessee's highest point and the third tallest summit east of the Mississippi River. From the parking lot, an uphill, .5-mile paved trail leads to an observation tower, with a ramp spiraling up to the deck.

Several area trails afford recreational opportunities within the surrounding coniferous rain forest. **Time:** Allow 1 hour minimum. **Hours:** Daily 24 hours, Apr.-Nov. (weather permitting). **Cost:** Free. **Phone:** (865) 436-1200, option 2, for park road closure information.

NEWFOUND GAP is 16 mi. n. of Oconaluftee Visitor Center on Newfound Gap Rd. (US 441) or 13 mi. s. of Sugarlands Visitor Center on Newfound Gap Rd. in Tennessee. In 1940, President Franklin D. Roosevelt dedicated Great Smoky Mountains National Park at this site, which rests at the road's highest point. Visitors encounter spectacular views and can walk onto the Appalachian Trail. A sign indicates where one can stand to straddle the Tennessee-North Carolina border. **Note:** Newfound Gap Road is subject to closure due to weather conditions. **Time:** Allow 30 minutes minimum. **Hours:** Daily, weather permitting. **Cost:** Free. **Phone:** (865) 436-1291.

OCONALUFTEE VISITOR CENTER is at the south park entrance on Newfound Gap Rd. (US 441) near Cherokee, N.C. Exhibits and information about the park are provided. Next to the center is the Mountain Farm Museum, which captures the feel of a typical 1880s Southern Appalachian farm. A small farmhouse displays the essentials of a late 19th-century pioneer home. A barn, apple house, springhouse, smokehouse and working blacksmith shop also can be explored. **Hours:** Visitor center open daily; hours vary seasonally. Closed Christmas. **Cost:** Free. **Phone:** (828) 497-1900.

SUGARLANDS VISITOR CENTER is at jct. Newfound Gap Rd. (US 441) and Little River Rd. near park headquarters, 2 mi. s. of Gatlinburg, Tenn. This center provides information, DVDs and exhibits about native plant and animal life. A nature trail and theater also are on site. **Time:** Allow 30 minutes minimum. **Hours:** Visitor center open daily; hours vary seasonally. Closed Christmas. **Cost:** Free. **Phone:** (865) 436-1291.

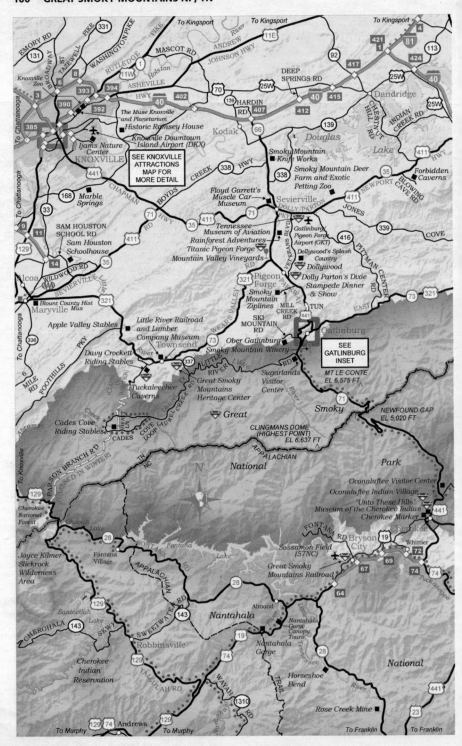

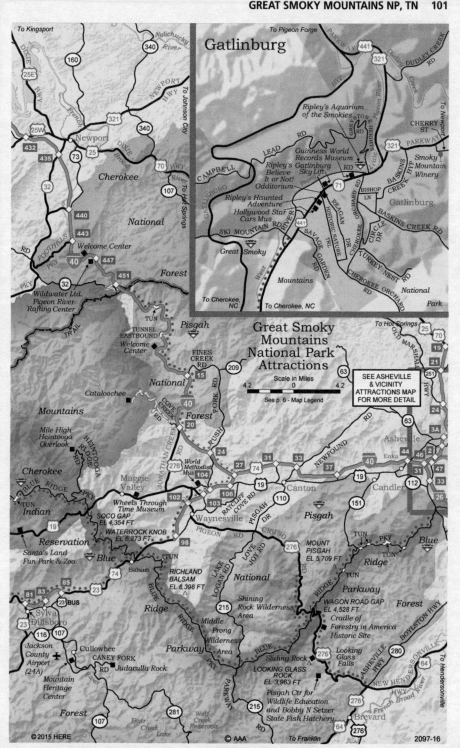

To Kingsport
Nolichucky River
340
160
25E
DIXIE HWY
25W
432
435
73
25
321
340
Newport
NEWPORT HWY
32
Cherokee
70 HWY
107
To Johnson City
To Hot Springs

Gatlinburg

To Pigeon Forge
441
321
PARKWAY
DUDLEY CREEK RD
Ripley's Aquarium of the Smokies
CHERRY ST
To Newport
LEAD RD
CAMPBELL
Guinness World Records Museum
321
PARKWAY
Smoky Mountain Winery
Ripley's Believe It or Not! Odditorium
71
BISHOP LN
Gatlinburg
Ripley's Haunted Adventure
REAGAN RD
Hollywood Star Cars Mus
441
BASKINS CREEK RD
CIRCLE DR
SKI MOUNTAIN RD
HISTORIC NATURE TRL
CHEROKEE
Great Smoky
SAVAGE GARDEN RD
TURKEY NEST RD
West PRONG RIVER
Mountains
CHEROKEE ORCHARD RD
National
To Cherokee, NC
To Cherokee, NC
Park

National
440
443
Welcome Center
FOOTHILLS PKY
40
447
32
451
Forest
Wildwater Ltd. Pigeon River Rafting Center
TRAIL
TUN
TUNNEL EASTBOUND
Welcome Center
Pisgah
To Hot Springs
25
70
FINES CREEK RD
209
19
21
HOLD MARSHALL HWY
251
Cataloochee
15
National
40
COVE CREEK RD
Forest
20
63
24
Mountains
Great Smoky Mountains National Park Attractions
Scale in Miles
4.2 0 4.2
See p. 6 - Map Legend
SEE ASHEVILLE & VICINITY ATTRACTIONS MAP FOR MORE DETAIL
Mile High Heintooga Overlook
HEINTOOGA RIDGE RD
RUSH FORK RD
27
31
33
NEWFOUND RD
63
3A
Asheville
Cherokee
276
World Methodist Mus
104
74
37
40
19
Enka
44
46
2
BLUE RIDGE PKY
TUN
Maggie Valley
102
106
19
Canton
31
47
Candler
112
33
Indian
Wheels Through Time Museum
103
RATCLIFF COVE RD
110
151
26
Reservation
19
SOCO GAP EL 4,354 FT
WATERROCK KNOB EL 6,273 FT
98
Waynesville
PISGAH DR
Pisgah
TUN
PKY
Blue
Santa's Land Fun Park & Zoo
Blue
74
TUN
PIGEON
CRUSO RD
MOUNT PISGAH EL 5,709 FT
TUN
Ridge
Balsam
RICHLAND BALSAM EL 6,398 FT
LAKE LOGAN RD
LOVE JOY RD
276
RIDGE RD
Parkway
81
83
85
23
National
WAGON ROAD GAP EL 4,528 FT
Forest
23 BUS
BLUE RIDGE
215
Shining Rock Wilderness Area
Cradle of Forestry in America Historic Site
280
ASHEVILLE HWY
Sylva
Dillsboro
23
116
107
Cullowhee
Middle Prong Wilderness Area
BLUE
Sliding Rock
276
Looking Glass Falls
NEW HENDERSONVILLE HWY
BOYLSTON HWY
To Hendersonville
Jackson County Airport (24A)
CANEY FORK RD
Judaculla Rock
Parkway
LOOKING GLASS ROCK EL 3,963 FT
64
Mountain Heritage Center
RIDGE
Pisgah Ctr for Wildlife Education and Bobby N Setzer State Fish Hatchery
Brevard
Forest
107
281
Wolf Creek Reservoir
215
PARKWAY RD
276
64
To Franklin
276

Bear Creek Lake

© 2015 HERE
© AAA
2097-16

GREENEVILLE (C-8) pop. 15,062, elev. 1,565'

From 1785 to 1788 Greeneville was the capital of the short-lived State of Franklin, which seceded from the state of North Carolina. Tennessee incorporated the town in 1817. A reconstruction of the capitol is on College Street between Church and Spencer streets. Big Spring, the center of the original town, is now a small park.

Named in honor of Revolutionary War general Nathanael Greene, Greeneville was the home of Andrew Johnson, 17th president of the United States. Davy Crockett, frontiersman and Alamo hero, also was born in Greene County. His birthplace is 15 miles northeast of town on US 11E in Davy Crockett Birthplace State Park *(see Limestone p. 129).* Also of interest is the Old Covered Bridge on Warrensburg Road via US 321.

The University of Tennessee Research & Education Center is nearby. Tusculum College, 5 miles east on US 11E, offers campus tours starting at the Simerly Student Union; phone (423) 636-7300 or (800) 729-0256 for reservations.

Greene County Partnership/Chamber of Commerce: 115 Academy St., Greeneville, TN 37743. **Phone:** (423) 638-4111.

Self-guiding tours: The Greene County Partnership/Chamber of Commerce offers a brochure detailing a self-guiding walking tour; highlights include the Andrew Johnson Tailor Shop and the 1850 St. James Episcopal Church. Pamphlets describing driving and biking tours of Greene County also are available.

ANDREW JOHNSON NATIONAL HISTORIC SITE is at 101 N. College St. The site, dedicated to Andrew Johnson, includes his early home, the Andrew Johnson Homestead and the national cemetery, where a monument at his gravesite symbolizes his adherence to the ideals of democracy. Two major achievements of his administration were the purchase of Alaska from Russia and his defense of the Constitution during his impeachment proceedings.

A museum contains a tailor shop in which Johnson worked. Tickets for a half-hour homestead tour, which includes a 14-minute film, are available at the nearby visitor center; visitors should sign up at least 15 minutes prior to tour start. **Note:** The site may be closed due to inclement weather in winter or extreme heat in summer months; phone ahead. **Time:** Allow 1 hour minimum. **Hours:** Visitor center daily 9-5. Homestead tours are given daily at 9:30, 10:30, 11:30, 1:30, 2:30, 3:30 and 4:30. Closed Jan. 1, Thanksgiving and Christmas. **Cost:** Donations. **Phone:** (423) 638-3551.

MAIN STREET TOURS departs from the General Morgan Inn, 111 N. Main St. A 90-minute tour of Tennessee's second-oldest town highlights architecture, notable residents and events, and historic sites. A tour of the 1821 Dickson-Williams Mansion, a Federal home furnished with period antiques, also is available. Walking tours are limited to 12 people.

Time: Allow 2 hours minimum. **Hours:** Walking tour Mon.-Sat. at 9:30, Apr.-Oct. Mansion tour daily at 1. Closed major holidays. **Cost:** Walking tour $5; free (ages 0-5). Mansion tour $10; $5 (ages 6-18). **Phone:** (423) 787-0500.

NATHANAEL GREENE MUSEUM is at 101 W. McKee St. at S. Main St. Named for the Revolutionary War general, the museum includes historical documents and items associated with President Andrew Johnson; Mordecai Lincoln, a Greene County leader and cousin of Abraham Lincoln; and Confederate general John Hunt Morgan. Additional highlights include the Cherokee Gallery, a military exhibit, antique furnishings and pioneer tools. **Time:** Allow 1 hour minimum. **Hours:** Tues.-Sat. 11-4, June-Aug.; Tues.-Sat. 11-5, rest of year. **Cost:** Donations. **Phone:** (423) 636-1558.

PRESIDENT ANDREW JOHNSON MUSEUM AND LIBRARY, on Gilland St. on the Tusculum College campus, contains approximately 100 items, including Johnson's top hat, political memorabilia and a copy of one of Abraham Lincoln's life masks. Johnson was a trustee of the college 1844-75. A student-created exhibit, "Reaper: Nettie Fowler McCormick and the Machine that Built Tusculum College," explores the impact of the mechanical harvest machine that built the McCormick fortune, and the contributions of philanthropist Nettie McCormick. In the library are more than 1,300 volumes that belonged to Tusculum's predecessor, Greeneville College, before their merger. **Time:** Allow 30 minutes minimum. **Hours:** Mon.-Fri. 9-5. Closed on college holidays. **Cost:** Free. **Phone:** (423) 636-7348. GT

HAMPTON INN   (423)638-3735

 Hotel $109-$189 **Address:** 3130 E Andrew Johnson Hwy 37745 **Location:** US 11 E Bypass, 3.6 mi ne. **Facility:** 67 units. 3 stories, interior corridors. **Terms:** 1-7 night minimum stay, cancellation fee imposed. **Pool(s):** outdoor. **Activities:** exercise room. **Guest Services:** valet and coin laundry.

> **AAA Benefit:** Members save up to 10%!

 CALL

QUALITY INN   (423)638-7511

 Hotel $85-$123 **Address:** 3160 E Andrew Johnson Hwy 37745 **Location:** US 11 E Bypass, 3.6 mi ne. **Facility:** 55 units. 3 stories, interior corridors. **Pool(s):** outdoor. **Activities:** exercise room.

WHERE TO EAT

FATZ   423/787-9090

 Regional American. Casual Dining. $6-$18 **AAA Inspector Notes:** Friendly staff and appealing country decor help set the tone for a relaxed and enjoyable dining experience. It's not unusual for guests to wait to be seated at the popular spot, which earns raves for its well-prepared variations on chicken, steak, ribs and pasta, as well as salads and sandwiches. The signature Southern-style peach cobbler served with vanilla ice cream and walnuts is scrumptious. **Features:** full bar. **Address:** 3140 E Andrew Johnson Hwy 37745 **Location:** Jct US 321 and 11 E, just e.

L   D   CALL

STAN'S BAR-B-QUE   423/787-0017

▼▼ ▼▼ Barbecue. Family Dining. $5-$20 **AAA Inspector Notes:** The smell of meat roasting on the open-pit barbecue draws hungry folks right in to this family spot. Tasty pulled pork, chicken and beef are served with a choice of homemade sides. **Features:** beer only, patio dining. **Address:** 2620 E Andrew Johnson Hwy 37743 **Location:** US 11 E, 2 mi e. [L] [D]

HALLS (C-1) pop. 2,255, elev. 312'

VETERANS' MUSEUM, 100 Veterans' Dr., is on the former Dyersburg Army Air Base and has a collection of military vehicles, weapons, uniforms and personal memorabilia from various conflicts. Exhibit topics include the role of the base as a training ground for B-17 aircraft crews 1942-45; the history of the *Memphis Belle*; and what life was like for women on the base. **Time:** Allow 1 hour, 45 minutes minimum. **Hours:** Mon.-Fri. 10-4, Sat.-Sun. 2-5. Closed major holidays. **Cost:** $5; $2 (ages 0-12 and military veterans). **Phone:** (731) 836-7400. [GT]

HARRIMAN pop. 6,350

COMFORT INN   (865)882-6600

▼▼ ▼▼ ▼▼
Hotel
$78-$124

Address: 1867 S Roane St 37748 **Location:** I-40 exit 347, just s on US 27/SR 61. **Facility:** 64 units. 3 stories, interior corridors. **Pool(s):** outdoor. **Activities:** exercise room. **Guest Services:** coin laundry.

DAYS INN HARRIMAN   (865)882-6200

▼▼ ▼▼ Motel $59-$70 **Address:** 120 Childs Rd 37748 **Location:** I-40 exit 347, just n on US 27. **Facility:** 50 units. 2 stories (no elevator), exterior corridors. **Activities:** exercise room.

HOLIDAY INN EXPRESS HOTEL & SUITES - HARRIMAN
                                           (865)295-0001

▼▼ ▼▼ ▼▼
Hotel
$89-$99

Address: 1885 S Roane St 37748 **Location:** I-40 exit 347, just s on US 27/SR 61. **Facility:** 68 units. 3 stories, interior corridors. **Pool(s):** heated indoor. **Activities:** exercise room. **Guest Services:** coin laundry.

WHERE TO EAT

LOS PRIMOS MEXICAN RESTAURANT   865/590-1300

▼▼ ▼▼ Mexican. Casual Dining. $5-$15 **AAA Inspector Notes:** This colorful cantina is a top pick by locals for its tasty Mexican fare, including quesadillas, fajitas, burritos, enchiladas and more. When the weather is nice, enjoy dining on the patio. **Features:** full bar, patio dining, happy hour. **Address:** 1712 S Roane St 37748 **Location:** I-40 exit 347, just n. [L] [D]

HARROGATE (C-7) pop. 4,389, elev. 1,315'

When plans to develop Harrogate as a health resort at the mouth of Cumberland Gap failed in 1888, the city turned to coal mining, which in turn attracted the railroads. Lincoln Memorial University, established in 1897, continues to shape the town's character and economy.

THE ABRAHAM LINCOLN LIBRARY AND MUSEUM is on the Lincoln Memorial University campus at 6965 Cumberland Gap Pkwy. The museum contains more than 30,000 items from Lincoln's life and the Civil War era. Of note is a bust of Lincoln by Gutzon Borglum and a life-size Jerome Uhl painting depicting Lincoln at the time of his debates with Stephen Douglas.

Time: Allow 1 hour minimum. **Hours:** Mon.-Fri. 10-5, Sat. noon-5, Sun. 1-5, Mar.-Oct.; Mon.-Fri. 10-5, Sat. noon-5, rest of year. Library by appointment Mon.-Fri. 9-4. Closed Jan. 1, Thanksgiving, Christmas and some university holidays. **Cost:** $5; $3.50 (ages 60+); $3 (ages 6-12). **Phone:** (423) 869-6235 or (800) 325-0900, , ext. 6235.

HARTFORD (D-8) elev. 1,260'
• Attractions map p. 100

RECREATIONAL ACTIVITIES
White-water Rafting
• **Wildwater Ltd. Pigeon River Rafting Center** is at 3555 Hartford Rd. Zipline activities also are available. **Hours:** Rafting trips are offered Tues.-Thurs. and Sat. 11-5, Memorial Day-Aug. 31. Phone ahead to confirm schedule. **Phone:** (423) 487-3307 or (800) 451-9972.

HENDERSONVILLE (C-4) pop. 51,372, elev. 485'

OLD HICKORY LAKE VISITOR CENTER is off Rockland Rd., 1 mi. s. of Gallatin Rd. (US 31E) at 5 Power Plant Rd. This center features interactive displays about Old Hickory Lake and the navigational lock and dam system. **Time:** Allow 30 minutes minimum. **Hours:** Mon.-Fri. 7:30-4. Closed major holidays. **Cost:** Free. **Phone:** (615) 822-4846.

ROCK CASTLE is at 139 Rock Castle Ln. This seven-level limestone Federal house dating from the late 18th century was built by Gen. Daniel Smith, a U.S. senator who, as a surveyor, drew the first map of Tennessee. A smokehouse and a lake are on the grounds. **Time:** Allow 30 minutes minimum. **Hours:** Tues.-Sat. 9-5, Sun. 1-5, Apr.-Nov. Guided tours offered Tues.-Sat. at 10, 11:30, 1:30 and 3, Sun. at 1:30 and 3. Closed Thanksgiving and Christmas. Phone ahead to confirm schedule. **Cost:** $7; $6 (ages 60+); $5 (ages 6-12); $20 (family); free (military with ID). **Phone:** (615) 824-0502. [GT]

(See map & index p. 200.)

HOLIDAY INN EXPRESS   615/824-0022

  Hotel. Rates not provided. Address: 615 E Main St 37075 **Location:** On US 31 E, 2 mi n. **Facility:** 93 units. 4 stories, interior corridors. **Pool(s):** heated outdoor. **Activities:** exercise room. **Guest Services:** valet and coin laundry.

HYATT PLACE NASHVILLE - NORTHEAST
     (615)826-4301   56

Hotel
$79-$209

▦ HYATT PLACE®
AAA Benefit: Members save 10%!

Address: 330 E Main St 37075 **Location:** US 31 E, 1 mi n. **Facility:** 98 units. 5 stories, interior corridors. **Terms:** cancellation fee imposed. **Pool(s):** outdoor. **Activities:** exercise room. **Guest Services:** valet laundry. **Featured Amenity:** breakfast buffet.

WHERE TO EAT

DEMOS' STEAK & SPAGHETTI HOUSE   615/824-9097

 American. Casual Dining. $5-$19 **AAA Inspector Notes:** This family-owned and -operated eatery offers well prepared traditional fare as well as specialties such as Mexican spaghetti. The cuisine is made from scratch. The atmosphere and service are casual and relaxed. **Features:** full bar. **Address:** 161 Indian Lake Blvd 37075 **Location:** Jct US 31 and Indian Lake Blvd.

FULIN'S ASIAN CUISINE   615/822-5000   35

 Asian. Casual Dining. $8-$25 **AAA Inspector Notes:** Here you can explore a variety of delicious Asian dishes, including ginger lobster, curry seafood Thai casserole, kung pao chicken and egg rolls. Order fresh-made sushi or sashimi with your dinner, or enjoy it at the sushi bar. **Features:** full bar, happy hour. **Reservations:** suggested, weekends. **Address:** 206 Anderson Ln N 37075 **Location:** Jct Indian Lake Blvd; in Walmart plaza.

HENNING (D-1) pop. 945, elev. 292'

Founded in 1873, Henning is a quiet, picturesque town of Victorian houses and late 19th-century storefronts. Nearby is Fort Pillow State Historic Park *(see Recreation Areas Chart).*

Self-guiding tours: Brochures and maps for self-guiding tours of Henning can be obtained at the Alex Haley Museum and Interpretive Center; the tour includes the town cemetery and the Haley family plots.

ALEX HALEY MUSEUM AND INTERPRETIVE CENTER is at 200 S. Church St. The former home of novelist Alex Haley is open to the public as a museum featuring Haley's work, childhood memorabilia and references to the people who inspired his characters in "Roots." From 1921 to 1929, and for many summers afterward, Haley lived here with his grandparents; he is buried in the front yard of the home.

The interpretive center focuses on the Pulitzer Prize-winning author's life and career. **Time:** Allow 1 hour minimum. **Hours:** Tues.-Sat. 10-5. Closed Jan. 1, Thanksgiving and Christmas. **Cost:** $6; $5 (ages 60+); $4 (ages 5-18). **Phone:** (731) 738-2240.

HERMITAGE (C-4) elev. 758'

- Hotels & Restaurants map & index p. 200
- Part of Nashville area — see map p. 179

THE HERMITAGE is at 4580 Rachel's Ln. The two-story Greek Revival mansion was the home of Andrew Jackson, seventh president of the United States. The house originally was built as a brick Federal-style structure 1819-21 and was greatly expanded in 1831. Following a fire in 1834, it was rebuilt in the Greek Revival style, with six massive Corinthian columns lining the front. Following his presidency, Jackson returned to the house and lived here until his death in 1845.

Costumed guides lead visitors through the mansion, which houses original Jackson family pieces. Log cabins where slaves lived and formal gardens where the Jacksons are buried are on the 1,120-acre grounds. A 20-minute film about the president is shown in the visitor center, which also houses exhibits related to the Jackson presidency and the history of the slave population that lived on the property. Audio tours interpret more than 40 sites throughout the grounds and visitor center. A multimedia presentation focusing on the historical and archeological significance of the mansion and grounds is available for an additional charge. Seasonal farm and garden tours and interpretive horse-drawn wagon rides also are offered.

Time: Allow 2 hours minimum. **Hours:** Daily 8:30-5, mid-Mar. to mid-Oct.; 9-4, rest of year. Closed third week of Jan., Thanksgiving and Christmas. **Cost:** Grounds, visitor center and film presentation $20; $17 (ages 65+); $15 (ages 13-18); $10 (ages 6-12); free (active military with ID); $54 (family, including 2 adults and 2 children ages 0-17). Self-guiding multimedia presentation additional $8. **Phone:** (615) 889-2941.

NASHVILLE SHORES LAKESIDE RESORT, 4001 Bell Rd. on Percy Priest Lake, features a marina and water park. Water activities include a lazy river, a wave pool, waterslides, kayaks and a swimming beach with a beach volleyball area. On shore, Treetop Adventure Park offers rope courses for climbing and ziplining.

Hours: Water park open early May-early June and late July to mid-Sept. Treetop Adventure Park open early Apr.-late Nov. Hours may vary; phone ahead. **Cost:** Water park $36.99; $28.99 (under 52 inches tall, ages 62+ and military with ID); free (ages 0-2). Treetop Adventure Park $24.99-$49.99. **Parking:** $9. **Phone:** (615) 889-7050.

(See map & index p. 200.)

SUPER 8

Motel
$70-$100

Address: 1414 Princeton Pl 37076 **Location:** I-40 exit 221 (Old Hickory Blvd) westbound; exit 221B eastbound, just n. **Facility:** 60 units. 2-3 stories, exterior corridors. **Pool(s):** heated outdoor, heated indoor. **Activities:** limited exercise equipment. **Guest Services:** coin laundry. **Featured Amenity:** full hot breakfast.

(615)871-4545   82

WHERE TO EAT

HERMITAGE HOUSE SMORGASBORD   615/883-9525   54

Southern American. Family Dining. $11-$15 **AAA Inspector Notes:** A local standby for years, the restaurant features a variety of home-cooked food ranging from carrots, green beans and corn to fried chicken, breaded fish and mashed potatoes. Salads and desserts, like cobblers, apple fritters and ice cream, complete the meal. **Address:** 3131 Lebanon Pike 37214 **Location:** I-40 exit 219 (Stewarts Ferry Pike), 2 mi n, then 2 mi e.

HERMITAGE STEAKHOUSE   615/872-9535   52

Steak. Casual Dining. $17-$76 **AAA Inspector Notes:** Judge a book by its cover and you'll miss out on a delicious steak. This unimposing yet cozy restaurant offers a unique dining experience. The salad bar is quite popular and frequently offers items such as smoked oysters and fresh asparagus. **Features:** full bar. **Reservations:** suggested, weekends. **Address:** 4342 Lebanon Pike 37076 **Location:** I-40 exit 221, 2 mi n on Old Hickory Blvd, then 0.8 mi e on US 70.

SAKURA JAPANESE STEAK HOUSE   615/883-1498   53

Japanese. Casual Dining. $9-$29 **AAA Inspector Notes:** Delicious entrées are cooked hibachi style. Guests can choose from among all the standards, as well as sushi bar offerings made right before their eyes. **Features:** full bar. **Address:** 3451 Lebanon Pike 37076 **Location:** I-40 exit 219 (Stewarts Ferry Pike), 2 mi n, then 3 mi e.

HIXSON
• Hotels & Restaurants map & index p. 51

COUNTRY INN & SUITES BY CARLSON, CHATTANOOGA NORTH AT HWY 153   423/308-2333   54

Hotel. Rates not provided. **Address:** 5000 New Country Dr 37343 **Location:** Jct SR 319 and 153, just e. **Facility:** 81 units. 3 stories, interior corridors. **Pool(s):** heated indoor. **Activities:** limited exercise equipment. **Guest Services:** valet and coin laundry.

HAMPTON INN-HIXSON   (423)877-3100   53

Hotel. $114-$129 **Address:** 1920 Hamill Rd 37343 **Location:** Jct SR 319 and 153, just e. Opposite Northgate Mall. **Facility:** 59 units. 3 stories, interior corridors. **Terms:** 1-7 night minimum stay, cancellation fee imposed. **Pool(s):** outdoor. **Activities:** exercise room. **Guest Services:** valet and coin laundry.

AAA Benefit: Members save up to 10%!

HOLIDAY INN EXPRESS HOTEL & SUITES   423/877-6464   52

Hotel. Rates not provided. **Address:** 4820 Hixson Pike 37343 **Location:** SR 153 and Hixson Pike, just s. **Facility:** 70 units. 3 stories, interior corridors. **Pool(s):** heated indoor. **Activities:** hot tub, exercise room. **Guest Services:** valet and coin laundry.

WHERE TO EAT

GLEN GENE DELI   423/877-9997

Sandwiches. Quick Serve. $2-$8 **AAA Inspector Notes:** Deli sandwiches and salads are popular items at this eatery. The great selection of sandwiches includes tuna, turkey, roast beef, ham and the Reuben. Pita sacks, such as the Philly steak and grilled chicken, also hit the spot. Hamburgers are big sellers; choose from the jalapeño-cheddar burger, the mushroom burger and more. And of course you'll want to order one of the delicious shakes. **Features:** senior menu. **Address:** 5748 Hwy 153 37343 **Location:** 1.5 mi w of jct SR 319 and 153; in Oak Park Town Center.

HUMBOLDT (D-2) pop. 8,452, elev. 364'

WEST TENNESSEE REGIONAL ART CENTER is at 1200 Main St. Housed in Humboldt's former city hall, the Caldwell Collection features portraits, landscapes and contemporary artwork representing such styles as impressionism, abstract expressionism and folk art. African sculptures also are part of the permanent collection, while rotating exhibitions are presented in a downstairs gallery. **Time:** Allow 1 hour minimum. **Hours:** Mon.-Fri. 9-4:30. Closed major holidays. **Cost:** Donations. **Phone:** (731) 784-1787.

HUNTINGDON pop. 3,985

HERITAGE INN   (731)986-2281

Motel. $78-$83 **Address:** 11790 Lexington St 38344 **Location:** Jct US 70, just n on SR 22 business route. Located in a quiet rural area. **Facility:** 26 units. 1 story, exterior corridors. **Parking:** winter plug-ins. **Pool(s):** outdoor.

HURRICANE MILLS (C-3) elev. 400'
• Hotels p. 106

Hurricane Mills is commonly associated with country star Loretta Lynn, who has a ranch in town. Each year in early August the ranch is the setting of the Amateur National Motocross Championship.

LORETTA LYNN'S RANCH, MUSEUM AND HOME is off SR 13 at I-40 exit 143, following signs to 44 Hurricane Mills Rd. The 18,000-square-foot Coal Miner's Daughter Museum contains singer Loretta Lynn's country-western memorabilia and costumes. Guided tours include her plantation home, a simulated coal mine, a grist mill and a replica Butcher Holler house. Concerts are offered in the summer.

Time: Allow 1 hour minimum. **Hours:** Daily 9-5, Mar.-Oct.; 9-4, rest of year. Guided tours depart on the hour. Last tour begins 1 hour before closing. **Cost:** Plantation home or museum $12.50, free (ages 0-9). Tour including plantation home and museum $20; free (ages 0-9). Tour including plantation home, Butcher Holler house and simulated coal mine $25; free (ages 0-9). Prices may vary; phone ahead. **Phone:** (931) 296-7700.

BEST WESTERN OF HURRICANE MILLS   (931)296-4251

Hotel
$100-$120

 AAA Benefit: Save 10% or more every day and earn 10% bonus points!

Address: 15542 Hwy 13 S 37078 **Location:** I-40 exit 143, just n. **Facility:** 89 units. 2 stories (no elevator), exterior corridors. **Pool(s):** outdoor. **Activities:** playground. **Guest Services:** coin laundry. **Featured Amenity:** continental breakfast.

HOLIDAY INN EXPRESS   931/296-2999

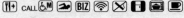 **Hotel.** Rates not provided. **Address:** 15368 Hwy 13 S 37078 **Location:** I-40 exit 143, 0.4 mi n. **Facility:** 50 units. 2 stories, interior corridors. **Pool(s):** outdoor. **Activities:** exercise room. **Guest Services:** coin laundry.

JACKSON   (D-2) pop. 65,211, elev. 425'

Once part of the Chickasaw Indians' hunting grounds, the area opened for settlement in 1818. Early residents set aside 30 acres for the city in 1822, naming it in honor of war hero and future U.S. president Andrew Jackson. The frontier town was laid out with broad streets, and when lots were auctioned off, the county court allocated $20 worth of whiskey to enliven the bidding.

Jackson grew rapidly into a railroading center—particularly for cotton—by the 1850s and was a critical supply depot during the Civil War. After both Union and Confederate occupations, Jackson surrendered to Union general John P. Hatch in July 1863.

Jackson Convention & Visitors Bureau: 197 Auditorium St., Jackson, TN 38301. **Phone:** (731) 425-2200 or (800) 498-4748.

CASEY JONES HOME & RAILROAD MUSEUM is off I-40 exit 80A on US 45 bypass in Casey Jones Village, 30 Casey Jones Ln. This is the home of John Luther "Casey" Jones, a 19th-century railroad engineer whose heroic actions during a train wreck were memorialized in "The Ballad of Casey Jones." The home, where Jones lived with his wife and three children, is decorated with period furniture.

A replica of his engine, "Old 382," is in the museum, which also displays assorted railroad memorabilia, including a baggage car and caboose. The Train Station addition re-creates an 1890s-era train station. Displays in the Jackson Room focus on the town's rich railroad history. A 9-minute video portrays Jones' story. Self-guiding tours are available.

Time: Allow 1 hour, 15 minutes minimum. **Hours:** Mon.-Sat. 9-5, Sun. noon-5, Mar.-Sept.; Mon.-Sat. 10-5, Sun. 1-5, rest of year. Closed Jan. 1, Easter, Thanksgiving and Christmas. Phone ahead to confirm schedule. **Cost:** $6.50; $5.50 (ages 60+); $4.50 (ages 6-12). **Phone:** (731) 668-1222.

CYPRESS GROVE NATURE PARK is at 866 Airways Blvd. on US 70W, 1.4 mi. w. of jct. US 45 bypass. A 6,000-foot-long boardwalk winds through this 165-acre cypress forest, which is a haven for birds, deer, rabbits, squirrels, minks, raccoons, frogs and turtles. The raptor sanctuary houses bald eagles, owls and hawks. A three-story wildlife observation tower overlooks a 25-acre lake. Fishing is allowed from the boardwalk. **Time:** Allow 1 hour minimum. **Hours:** Daily 8 a.m.-dusk. **Cost:** Free. **Phone:** (731) 425-8316.

INTERNATIONAL ROCK-A-BILLY HALL OF FAME & MUSEUM is at 105 N. Church St. The resource center presents memorabilia relating to rockabilly music—an early style of rock 'n' roll influenced by country, swing, and rhythm and blues. Clothing, instruments, records and photographs are on display. An art exhibit features 16 life-size oil portraits of genre icons, and a large mural pays tribute to Carl Perkins and Paul McCartney. The museum hosts live music and dance performances. **Time:** Allow 45 minutes minimum. **Hours:** Mon.-Thurs. 10-5, Fri.-Sat. 10-2. Closed major holidays. **Cost:** Guided tours $10; free (ages 0-12). **Phone:** (731) 427-6262.

BEST WESTERN CARRIAGE HOUSE INN & SUITES
(731)664-3030

Motel
$85-$100

 AAA Benefit: Save 10% or more every day and earn 10% bonus points!

Address: 1936 Hwy 45 Bypass 38305 **Location:** I-40 exit 80A, just s. Located in a congested area. **Facility:** 48 units. 2 stories (no elevator), exterior corridors. **Pool(s):** outdoor.

COMFORT SUITES   (731)868-1700

Hotel $109-$165 **Address:** 61 Casey Jones Ln 38305 **Location:** I-40 exit 80A, just s on US 45 Bypass, then just w. **Facility:** 70 units. 3 stories, interior corridors. **Amenities:** safes. **Pool(s):** heated indoor. **Activities:** hot tub, limited exercise equipment. **Guest Services:** valet and coin laundry.

COURTYARD BY MARRIOTT   (731)422-1818

Hotel $118-$209 **Address:** 200 Campbell Oaks Dr 38305 **Location:** I-40 exit 83, just s on Campbell St, then just w. **Facility:** 94 units. 4 stories, interior corridors. **Pool(s):** heated indoor. **Activities:** hot tub, exercise room. **Guest Services:** valet and coin laundry.

AAA Benefit: Members save 5% or more!

Remember, car seats, booster seats
and seat belts save lives

DOUBLETREE BY HILTON HOTEL JACKSON   (731)664-6900

▼▼ **Hotel** $99-$139 **Address:** 1770 Hwy 45 Bypass 38305 **Location:** I-40 exit 80A, 0.5 mi s. **Facility:** 166 units. 5 stories, interior corridors. **Terms:** 1-7 night minimum stay, cancellation fee imposed. **Pool(s):** heated outdoor, heated indoor. **Guest Services:** valet laundry.

AAA Benefit:
Members save 5% or more!

ⒺⒸⓄ ⏐⏐ 👤 Ⓨ CALL ⑤Ⓜ 🏊 BIZ 🛜 ✕ 🖥
🖥 / SOME UNITS 🖨

HAMPTON INN & SUITES   (731)427-6100

▼▼▼ **Hotel** $129-$209 **Address:** 150 Campbell Oaks Dr 38305 **Location:** I-40 exit 83, just s on Campbell St, then just w. **Facility:** 83 units. 4 stories, interior corridors. **Terms:** 1-7 night minimum stay, cancellation fee imposed. **Pool(s):** outdoor. **Activities:** exercise room. **Guest Services:** valet laundry.

AAA Benefit:
Members save up to 10%!

CALL ⑤Ⓜ 🏊 BIZ ⒽⓈ 🛜 🖥 🖥 🖥 / SOME UNITS 🐾

HOLIDAY INN EXPRESS & SUITES   731/736-1174

▼▼▼▼ **Hotel.** Rates not provided. **Address:** 55 Parkstone Pl 38305 **Location:** I-40 exit 85, just s on Dr F.E. Wright Dr, then just e. Across from Pringles Park Athletic Complex. **Facility:** 92 units. 5 stories, interior corridors. **Pool(s):** heated outdoor. **Activities:** exercise room. **Guest Services:** valet and coin laundry.

⏐⏐ CALL ⑤Ⓜ 🏊 BIZ ⒽⓈ 🛜 ✕ 🖥 🖥 🖥

HOWARD JOHNSON - JACKSON   (731)660-8651

▼▼▼ **Hotel** $89-$109 **Address:** 1292 Vann Dr 38305 **Location:** I-40 exit 80B, just n on US 45 Bypass, then 0.6 mi w. Across from The Columns Shopping Center. **Facility:** 67 units. 3 stories, interior corridors. **Terms:** cancellation fee imposed. **Pool(s):** outdoor. **Activities:** limited exercise equipment. **Guest Services:** valet laundry.

⏐⏐ 🏊 ⒽⓈ 🛜 🖥 🖥 🖥 / SOME UNITS 🔁

RESIDENCE INN BY MARRIOTT JACKSON   (731)935-4100

▼▼▼ **Extended Stay Hotel** $118-$194 **Address:** 126 Old Medina Crossing 38305 **Location:** I-40 exit 83, just ne. Located in a quiet area. **Facility:** 92 units, some two bedrooms, efficiencies and kitchens. 4 stories, interior corridors. **Pool(s):** heated indoor. **Activities:** hot tub, picnic facilities, exercise room. **Guest Services:** valet and coin laundry.

AAA Benefit:
Members save 5% or more!

🏊 BIZ ⒽⓈ 🛜 ✕ 🖥 🖥 🖥 / SOME UNITS 🔁

WHERE TO EAT

ASIA GARDEN   731/668-9024

▼▼ Asian. Casual Dining. $5-$16 **AAA Inspector Notes:** For more than 25 years, this simple, casual café has been the locals' choice for traditional Chinese and Japanese fare. The menu features such classic dishes as sweet and sour chicken, orange beef and shrimp with garlic sauce, along with teriyaki and tempura fare, plus a lengthy list of sushi rolls and sashimi. **Features:** full bar. **Address:** 581-C Old Hickory Blvd 38305 **Location:** I-40 exit 80A, 0.4 mi s on US 45 Bypass, then just e; in Hamilton Hills Shopping Center.

Ⓛ Ⓓ

CATFISH CABIN   731/422-1001

▼▼ Seafood. Casual Dining. $6-$30 **AAA Inspector Notes:** Settle in at this rustic log cabin with planked floors and hunting and fishing décor on the walls. Dig into large baskets of hot hushpuppies and creamy coleslaw before your meal. Lunch is also available Friday through Sunday. **Features:** early bird specials, senior menu. **Address:** 1290 S Highland Ave 38301 **Location:** Jct US 70, 2.5 mi s on US 45. Ⓓ

FUJI YAMA JAPANESE STEAKHOUSE AND SUSHI BAR   731/664-8889

▼▼ Japanese. Casual Dining. $7-$35 **AAA Inspector Notes:** Lots of sushi and sashimi offerings, as well as noodle and hibachi dinner entrees, are cooked right before diners' eyes. Skilled Japanese chefs show their mastery with spatulas flying and quick speed of hand. **Features:** beer & wine. **Address:** 10 Stonebridge Blvd, Suite E 38305 **Location:** I-40 exit 80B, 0.5 mi n on US 45, just e on Vann Dr, then just n; in Towne Center Shopping Center.

Ⓛ Ⓓ CALL ⑤Ⓜ

OLD COUNTRY STORE IN CASEY JONES VILLAGE   731/668-1223

▼ American. Family Dining. $6-$12 **AAA Inspector Notes:** Country antiques from the late 1800s and early 1900s decorate this family-friendly restaurant. Known primarily for its extensive buffet, the eatery also features an old-fashioned ice cream parlor and a variety of Southern-style dinners. Before or after your meal, wander the spacious general store and discover hundreds of yesteryear treasures. **Features:** early bird specials, senior menu. **Address:** 56 Casey Jones Ln 38305 **Location:** I-40 exit 80A, just s on US 45 Bypass, then just w. 🍽 Ⓑ Ⓛ Ⓓ

OLD TOWN SPAGHETTI STORE   731/668-4937

▼▼ Italian. Casual Dining. $6-$33 **AAA Inspector Notes:** Zesty spaghetti, ravioli, veal, seafood, chicken and Certified Angus Beef steaks are served in an open dining area that evokes the feel of an Italian villa. Try a freshly made soup or homemade dessert. **Features:** full bar, patio dining, happy hour. **Address:** 550 Carriage House Dr 38305 **Location:** I-40 exit 80A, just s on US 45 Bypass, then just e. Ⓛ Ⓓ CALL ⑤Ⓜ 🐾

PICASSO BISTRO & PIZZERIA   731/664-5070

▼▼ Pizza. Casual Dining. $8-$36 **AAA Inspector Notes:** This popular, family-owned eatery offers creative gourmet pizzas, artfully named then handcrafted and baked in a traditional Italian hearth oven. "Master Pizzas" such as Rockin' Lobster, Black and Bleu, and Caribbean Jerk are definitely not your ordinary pizza—and that's what sets this place apart. Salad, pasta, wraps and sandwiches (on fresh-baked focaccia bread) are other great choices. **Features:** full bar, patio dining, happy hour. **Address:** 10 Stonebridge Blvd, Suite A 38305 **Location:** I-40 exit 80B, 0.5 mi n on US 45 Bypass, just e on Vann Dr, then just n; in Towne Center Shopping Center.

Ⓛ Ⓓ CALL ⑤Ⓜ

REDBONE'S GRILL & BAR   731/660-3838

▼▼ American. Casual Dining. $6-$27 **AAA Inspector Notes:** Friendly service and a laid-back vibe welcome patrons to this casual eatery. The lengthy menu offers many Cajun-influenced dishes, such as red beans and rice, gumbo and fried gator bites. Rounding out the menu are steaks, seafood, chicken, ribs, pasta, burgers and sandwiches. Live music is featured Wednesday through Sunday nights. **Features:** full bar, happy hour. **Address:** 584 Carriage House Dr 38305 **Location:** I-40 exit 80A, just s on US 45 Bypass, then just e. Ⓛ Ⓓ

JAMESTOWN   (C-6) pop. 1,959, elev. 1,698'

Jamestown is the county seat of predominantly rural Fentress County. From this agricultural landscape emerged two notable figures. John Clemens, father of Samuel Clemens (better known as Mark Twain), arrived in Jamestown with his family in 1827 and served as the county's first circuit court clerk and also as attorney general. During his tenure he drew plans for the first courthouse and jail and established the town's first post office.

The region's most famous native son was Sgt. Alvin C. York, the World War I hero awarded the Medal of Honor and described by Gen. John J. Pershing as "the greatest soldier of the war." Trapped by the Germans in a forest in Argonne, France, York single-handedly fought a battalion of machine gunners until they surrendered. He later marched the 132 prisoners to the American line.

York and members of his family are buried in the Wolf River Cemetery, 10 miles north on US 127. The gristmill York operated in Pall Mall, 4 miles north of the cemetery on US 127, is a state historic area. The Alvin C. York Homeplace is open for tours. The General Store, which operated after World War I, now functions as a visitor center and is the starting point for tours of the mill, cemetery and home; phone (931) 879-6456.

A 60-foot waterfall, hemlock trees, pink and white rhododendron and mountain laurel, high cliffs and rock houses once inhabited by cliff-dwelling Native Americans characterize Colditz Cove State Natural Area, about 1.5 miles off SR 52 via Northrup Falls Road near Allardt. Horse trails are plentiful.

Jamestown serves as headquarters for what is known as the World's Longest Yard Sale, a 4-day event in early August that draws thousands of buyers and sellers along US 127 from Addison, Mich., to Gadsden, Ala.

Fentress County Chamber of Commerce: 114 Central Ave. W., P.O. Box 1294, Jamestown, TN 38556. **Phone:** (931) 879-9948.

WINERIES

- **Highland Manor Winery** is 3.5 mi. s. on US 127S. **Hours:** Mon.-Sat. 9-5, Sun. 11-5. **Phone:** (931) 879-9519. GT

JOHNSON CITY (C-9) pop. 63,152, elev. 1,631'

Nestled in the scenic northeastern corner of Tennessee 96 miles from Knoxville, Johnson City was known by at least five other names prior to its 1869 incorporation. Johnson City has grown from a community surrounding the 18th-century St. John's Mill into the largest of the Tri-Cities, which include Bristol and Kingsport.

Along with its historical and agricultural orientation, Johnson City claims a college-town atmosphere. Washington Academy, established in 1780, is the state's oldest educational institution. During the Civil War, Union troops used the school as a stable and as officers' quarters. Also in Johnson City are East Tennessee State University, Milligan College and the Emmanuel School of Religion.

A short distance from the city are two Tennessee Valley Authority recreation areas, Boone Lake *(see Recreation Areas Chart)* and Fort Patrick Henry Lake. Buffalo Mountain Park and Winged Deer Park offer miles of hiking trails; phone (423) 283-5815.

A particularly scenic segment of US 23 runs concurrent with I-181, passing through Johnson City before ending 15 miles northwest at the junction with I-81. A scenic stretch of US 321 winds 26 miles east from Johnson City to the North Carolina line.

Johnson City Chamber of Commerce/ Convention and Visitors Bureau: 603 E. Market St., P.O. Box 180, Johnson City, TN 37605. **Phone:** (423) 461-8000 or (800) 852-3392.

HANDS ON! REGIONAL MUSEUM is at 315 E. Main St. Entertaining and educational interactive exhibits are featured. Visitors can fly an airplane, visit a coal mine and perform a science experiment. **Time:** Allow 2 hours minimum. **Hours:** Mon.-Fri. 9-6, Sat. 10-5, Sun. 1-5, in Mar. and June-Aug.; Tues.-Fri. 9-5, Sat. 9-6, Sun. 1-5, rest of year. Closed major holidays. **Cost:** $8; $7 (ages 65+ and military with ID); free (ages 0-2). **Phone:** (423) 928-6508.

REECE MUSEUM is at jct. Stout Dr. and Gilbreath Cir. on the East Tennessee State University campus. Changing exhibits focus on aspects of Appalachian history, art and culture. A permanent exhibit on regional music features interactive audiovisual recordings of Appalachian musicians, past and present. **Time:** Allow 1 hour minimum. **Hours:** Mon.-Fri. 9-4:30. **Cost:** Free. **Phone:** (423) 439-4392.

TIPTON-HAYNES STATE HISTORIC SITE is 1.8 mi. s.e. to 2620 S. Roan St. In 1788 the farm was the site of the Battle of the Lost State of Franklin, which led to its collapse. The farmhouse was enlarged in the early 19th century by John Tipton Jr.; it encases a 1798 log house built by his father, Col. John Tipton. The surroundings include a large barn, corn crib, Landon Carter Haynes' law office, nature trails, a woodworking shop, period gardens and the law office of Landon Carter Haynes, a Confederate senator. There is also a small museum with a permanent exhibit about the site.

Time: Allow 1 hour minimum. **Hours:** Tues.-Sat. 9-4, Mar. to late Nov.; Tues.-Sat. 9-3, rest of year. Closed Jan. 1-8, Thanksgiving, day after Thanksgiving and Dec. 21-31. Phone ahead to confirm schedule. **Cost:** $5; $2.50 (ages 4-12). **Phone:** (423) 926-3631.

CARNEGIE HOTEL
(423)979-6400

Hotel
$135-$144

Address: 1216 W State of Franklin Rd 37604 **Location:** I-26 exit 24, 2.2 mi se on US 321 S. **Facility:** Restored to its former turn-of-the-century grandeur, Carnegie Hotel guests enjoy the elegance of a bygone era but with all of the attention and amenities expected of a great hotel today. 137 units. 6 stories, interior corridors. **Terms:** cancellation fee imposed. **Amenities:** safes. **Dining:** Wellington's Restaurant, see separate listing. **Pool(s):** heated outdoor. **Activities:** exercise room, spa. **Guest Services:** valet laundry.

COMFORT SUITES
(423)610-0010

Hotel $99-$130 **Address:** 3118 Browns Mill Rd 37604 **Location:** I-26 exit 19, just e, then just n. **Facility:** 80 units. 4 stories, interior corridors. **Amenities:** safes. **Pool(s):** outdoor. **Activities:** exercise room. **Guest Services:** valet laundry.

COURTYARD BY MARRIOTT JOHNSON CITY
(423)262-0275

Hotel $97-$148 **Address:** 4025 Hamilton Pl 37604 **Location:** I-26 exit 19, 1.7 mi e on State of Franklin Rd to Med Tech Dr, just n, then just w. **Facility:** 90 units. 3 stories, interior corridors. **Pool(s):** outdoor. **Activities:** exercise room. **Guest Services:** valet and coin laundry.

AAA Benefit: Members save 5% or more!

DOUBLETREE BY HILTON HOTEL JOHNSON CITY
(423)929-2000

Hotel $99-$179 **Address:** 211 Mockingbird Ln 37604 **Location:** I-26 exit 20A westbound; exit 20 eastbound, just w on N Roan St. **Facility:** 184 units. 5 stories, interior corridors. **Terms:** 1-7 night minimum stay, cancellation fee imposed. **Pool(s):** heated outdoor, heated indoor. **Activities:** exercise room. **Guest Services:** valet laundry.

AAA Benefit: Members save 5% or more!

HAMPTON INN
(423)929-8000

Hotel $109-$499 **Address:** 508 N State of Franklin Rd 37604 **Location:** I-26 exit 19, 3.4 mi sw. Across from Johnson City Medical Center and East Tennessee State University. **Facility:** 77 units. 3 stories, interior corridors. **Terms:** 1-7 night minimum stay, cancellation fee imposed. **Pool(s):** outdoor. **Activities:** exercise room. **Guest Services:** valet laundry.

AAA Benefit: Members save up to 10%!

HOLIDAY INN EXPRESS-JOHNSON CITY
(423)328-0500

Hotel $108-$275 **Address:** 2 Orr Ct 37615 **Location:** I-26 exit 17, just s. **Facility:** 81 units. 4 stories, interior corridors. **Terms:** 14 day cancellation notice. **Pool(s):** heated indoor. **Activities:** hot tub, limited exercise equipment. **Guest Services:** valet laundry.

HOLIDAY INN-JOHNSON CITY
(423)282-4611

Hotel $91-$210 **Address:** 101 W Springbrook Dr 37604 **Location:** I-26 exit 20A eastbound; exit 20 eastbound, just e on N Roan St, then just n. **Facility:** 206 units. 6 stories, interior corridors. **Terms:** check-in 4 pm. **Pool(s):** heated outdoor. **Activities:** exercise room. **Guest Services:** valet and coin laundry.

QUALITY INN
(423)282-0488

Motel
$76-$78

Address: 119 Pinnacle Dr 37615 **Location:** I-26 exit 17, just w on CR 354, then just s. Located behind Cracker Barrel. **Facility:** 60 units. 2 stories (no elevator), exterior corridors. **Pool(s):** outdoor. **Activities:** exercise room. **Featured Amenity:** full hot breakfast.

RED ROOF INN-JOHNSON CITY
(423)282-3040

Motel
$50-$100

Address: 210 Broyles Dr 37601 **Location:** I-26 exit 20A westbound; exit 20 eastbound, just w on N Roan St. **Facility:** 115 units. 3 stories, exterior corridors. **Amenities:** video games, safes.

SLEEP INN & SUITES
(423)915-0081

Hotel $70-$106 **Address:** 2020 Franklin Terrace Ct 37604 **Location:** I-26 exit 19, just n, then just n, follow signs; entrance on Oakland Ave at light. **Facility:** 70 units. 3 stories, interior corridors. **Activities:** exercise room. **Guest Services:** valet laundry.

SUPER 8 MOTEL JOHNSON CITY
(423)282-8818

Motel $54-$81 **Address:** 108 Wesley St 37601 **Location:** I-26 exit 20A westbound; exit 20 eastbound, just e on N Roan St, then just s on E Spring Brook Dr. **Facility:** 56 units. 3 stories (no elevator), interior corridors. **Guest Services:** coin laundry.

WHERE TO EAT

ALTA CUCINA ITALIAN RESTAURANT
423/928-2092

Italian. Casual Dining. $10-$35 **AAA Inspector Notes:** Much of the food at this intimate restaurant is homemade, from soups and sauces to breads and desserts. The owner/chef is noted for creating attractively presented Sicilian specialties. Fresh flowers on the tables are a nice touch. **Features:** beer & wine, patio dining. **Address:** 1200 N Roan St 37601 **Location:** I-26 exit 22, just s on W Unalaka Ave, then just w.

ANGKOR BISTRO
423/929-1001

Asian. Quick Serve. $8-$16 **AAA Inspector Notes:** The chow's pretty good at this small restaurant, which serves Thai and Cambodian food in a cafeteria setting. **Features:** patio dining. **Address:** 600 N State of Franklin Rd, Suite 1 37604 **Location:** I-26 exit 19, 3.5 mi sw.

BABYLON
423/282-9600

▼ Mediterranean. Casual Dining. $8-$21 **AAA Inspector Notes:** Middle Eastern and Mediterranean flavors are an exotic departure from Southern cuisine. Features are lamb shank that is fall-off-the-fork tender, shawarma bathed in flavorful juices and baklava made with pistachios. **Features:** patio dining. **Address:** 2122 N Roan St, Suite 8 37601 **Location:** I-26 exit 20A westbound; exit 20 eastbound, just w. L D

BELLA VITA
423/282-8600

▼▼ Italian. Casual Dining. $8-$20 **AAA Inspector Notes:** Creamy garlic soup. Homemade Italian sausage with smooth marinara sauce. Thin-crust pizza that's crunchy on the outside and chewy on the inside. Comfort food really doesn't get any better than this. The building is tucked away, but well worth finding. **Features:** full bar. **Reservations:** suggested. **Address:** 2927 N Roan St, Suite 2 37601 **Location:** I-26 exit 20A westbound; exit 20 eastbound, 1 mi e. L D

CAFE ONE 11
423/283-4633

▼▼ Asian. Casual Dining. $8-$23 **AAA Inspector Notes:** Here you'll find a lovely fusion of neo-Asian cuisine and a hip and trendy setting. You step into a dimly lit room with contemporary, colorful drapes and light fixtures mixed with tables and chairs from Asia. The restaurant is closed between lunch and dinner. **Features:** full bar. **Reservations:** suggested. **Address:** 111 Broyles St 37601 **Location:** I-26 exit 20A westbound; exit 20 eastbound, 0.5 mi w on N Roan St; in Holiday Plaza. L D

THE FIREHOUSE RESTAURANT
423/929-7377

▼▼ Barbecue. Casual Dining. $7-$22 **AAA Inspector Notes:** The staff is uniformed for a fire at the laid-back restaurant. Guests who need to get in and out in a hurry can order from the guest computer and have their food delivered to the table, but there's always the option of doing it the old-fashioned way, in which a server takes down the order. The barbecue is tasty and the desserts a delight. **Address:** 627 W Walnut St 37604 **Location:** I-26 exit 24, 2 mi se on US 321 S, then just w. L D

MING'S ASIAN CUISINE
423/328-7173

▼▼ Asian Sushi. Casual Dining. $6-$16 **AAA Inspector Notes:** The restaurant features tasty sushi, sashimi and maki and other Japanese dishes along with well-executed Chinese specialties. The Chinese eggplant dish and the spicy tuna roll were standouts! **Features:** full bar. **Address:** 1045 Hamilton Place Dr 37604 **Location:** I-26 exit 19, 1.7 mi e on State of Franklin Rd to Med Tech Dr, just n, then just w; in Hamilton Place at Market Center. L D CALL M

THE PEERLESS
423/282-2351

▼▼ American. Casual Dining. $10-$30 **AAA Inspector Notes:** An established family business since 1938, this restaurant feels warm and homey thanks in part to knowledgeable, friendly servers and an attractive lobby with a fireplace. A wide selection of meat, seafood and pasta shows quality in its preparation. Features: early bird specials, happy hour. **Address:** 2531 N Roan St, Suite 1 37601 **Location:** I-26 exit 20A westbound; exit 20 eastbound, just e. D

TUPELO HONEY CAFE
828/202-9740

▼▼ New Southern. Casual Dining. $7-$23 **AAA Inspector Notes:** In the old train depot, you'll enjoy traditional Lowcountry favorites, such as fried green tomatoes and shrimp and grits, served in heaping portions. The menu always features twists on Southern staples. Try the nutty fried chicken served with smashed sweet potatoes, asparagus and a side of goat cheese grits. **Features:** full bar, patio dining. **Address:** 300 Buffalo St 37604 **Location:** Jct Cherry St, just w; downtown; in train depot. L D CALL M

WELLINGTON'S RESTAURANT
423/979-6401

▼▼▼▼ **AAA Inspector Notes:** Try the braised lamb shanks served with white bean cassoulet or the wild mushroom beef stroganoff. The wine selection here is superb. The dining room has quiet, traditional décor. **Features:** full bar. **Reservations:** suggested. **Address:** 1216 W State of Franklin Rd 37604 **Location:** I-26 exit 24, 2.2 mi se on US 321 S; in Carnegie Hotel. B L D

Continental
Fine Dining
$8-$35

JONESBOROUGH (C-8) pop. 5,051, elev. 1,691'

The oldest town in Tennessee, Jonesborough was founded in 1779 as the seat of Washington County, an area of North Carolina that encompassed all of present-day Tennessee. In 1784 North Carolina ceded its lands west of the mountains to the United States, and the settlers in Washington County were left without a government. A convention met in Jonesborough in 1785 and created the State of Franklin, with John Sevier as its first and only governor.

Although Franklin was never approved by Congress and it only existed for a few years, the state was the first to be created after the Thirteen Colonies. The constitutional convention and the first two meetings of the General Assembly were held in Jonesborough before the capital was relocated to Greeneville.

Today Jonesborough is the seat of a much smaller Washington County. Main Street has a 19th-century atmosphere, with many restored brick stores, four historic churches, brick sidewalks and street lamps that resemble gaslights.

Jonesborough is the home of the International Storytelling Center, which sponsors the National Storytelling Festival the first Friday, Saturday and Sunday in October. During the festival renowned practitioners of this folk art hold visitors spellbound with tales that range from fairy to tall; phone (423) 753-2171 or (800) 952-8392. The visitor center offers guided walking/storytelling tours of home and church interiors by appointment.

Historic Jonesborough Visitor Center: 117 Boone St., Jonesborough, TN 37659. **Phone:** (423) 753-1010 or (866) 401-4223.

Self-guiding tours: The visitor center has free brochures outlining walking tours of Jonesborough's historic district.

JONESBOROUGH-WASHINGTON COUNTY HISTORY MUSEUM is off US 11E at 117 Boone St. in the Historic Jonesborough Visitor Center. Exhibits focus on 200 years of history in Tennessee's oldest town. **Time:** Allow 30 minutes minimum. **Hours:** Mon.-Fri. 9-5, Sat.-Sun. 10-5. Closed Jan. 1, Easter, Thanksgiving and Christmas. **Cost:** Donations. **Phone:** (423) 753-9580.

AMERICINN LODGE & SUITES OF JONESBOROUGH
423/753-3100

▼▼ Hotel. Rates not provided. **Address:** 376 E Jackson Blvd 37659 **Location:** I-26 exit 17 (Boones Creek Rd). **Facility:** 60 units. 3 stories, interior corridors. **Pool(s):** heated indoor. **Activities:** hot tub, limited exercise equipment. **Guest Services:** coin laundry.

HISTORIC EUREKA INN
423/913-6100

▼▼ Historic Hotel. Rates not provided. **Address:** 127 W Main St 37659 **Location:** Downtown. **Facility:** This quaint, historical hotel located in the middle of downtown offers cozy rooms with a mix of period pieces. The lobby area, with a small sitting area by a fireplace, beckons the weary. 13 units. 2 stories (no elevator), interior corridors. **Amenities:** safes.

WHERE TO EAT

MAIN STREET CAFE & CATERING　　　423/753-2460

 American. Quick Serve. $4-$8 **AAA Inspector Notes:** *Historic.* Deli-style sandwiches piled high with fresh meat are the specialty at this quaint diner. A glass display case filled with delicious deli meats and homemade desserts welcomes guests at the front. Try the tangy Key lime pie and The Breezy sandwich, a specialty. **Features:** beer & wine. **Address:** 117 W Main St 37659 **Location:** Downtown.

KIMBALL pop. 1,395

COMFORT INN　　　(423)837-2478

Hotel
$55-$125

Address: 205 Kimball Crossing 37347 **Location:** I-24 exit 152B, 0.3 mi n. **Facility:** 72 units. 2 stories (no elevator), interior corridors. **Pool(s):** outdoor. **Activities:** limited exercise equipment. **Guest Services:** valet laundry. **Featured Amenity:** full hot breakfast.

HAMPTON INN　　　(423)228-4270

Address: 100 Hampton Dr 37380 **Location:** I-24 exit 152B. Located in a busy commercial area. **Facility:** 80 units. 3 stories, interior corridors. **Terms:** 1-7 night minimum stay, cancellation fee imposed. **Pool(s):** outdoor. **Activities:** exercise room. **Guest Services:** valet and coin laundry.

AAA Benefit:
Members save up to 10%!

HOLIDAY INN EXPRESS HOTEL & SUITES　　　(423)837-1500

Hotel $79-$119 **Address:** 300 Battle Creek Rd 37380 **Location:** I-24 exit 152, just n to Battle Creek Rd, then just w. **Facility:** 59 units. 3 stories, interior corridors. **Pool(s):** outdoor. **Activities:** exercise room. **Guest Services:** valet laundry.

SUPER 8 - KIMBALL　　　(423)837-7185

Hotel
$63-$102

Address: 395 Main St 37347 **Location:** I-24 exit 152, 0.5 mi n. **Facility:** 64 units. 2 stories (no elevator), exterior corridors. **Pool(s):** outdoor. **Activities:** picnic facilities. **Guest Services:** coin laundry. **Featured Amenity:** full hot breakfast.

KINGSPORT (C-8) pop. 48,205
• Hotels p. 112 • Restaurants p. 112

Led by Dr. Thomas Walker in 1750, the first organized expedition into northeastern Tennessee followed a well-marked Native American path that crossed the Holston River at Long Island and continued through what is now Kingsport. This was the trail Daniel Boone used in 1769 to mark the beginning of the Wilderness Road to Kentucky.

Native American uprisings halted many attempts to settle the area until 1776, when the Cherokee were defeated in the Battle of Island Flats. Incorporated in 1822, Kingsport was known as Boat Yard because of its many wagon and flatboat freighting agencies. Dramatic growth began in 1909 when the railroad linked the town to the Great Lakes and the Atlantic. During World War I a planned industrial city was built next to old Kingsport.

The Tennessee Eastman Co. (now Eastman Chemical Co.) was among the city's first businesses and is still operating. Eastman is one of the state's largest industrial employers, with a labor force of 7,000.

Surrounded by the Blue Ridge, Cumberland, Clinch and nearby Bays mountains, Kingsport has several parks. Boatyard-Riverfront Park, on the banks of the north and south forks of the Holston River, includes riverfront paths, a swinging bridge and the historic Netherland Inn. Fishing piers, picnic shelters and playgrounds also are available; phone (423) 229-9457.

Nearby Warrior's Path State Park *(see Recreation Areas Chart)* is on the lake formed by Fort Patrick Henry Dam. More than 8 miles long, The Greenbelt is a linear park system with paved paths for walkers, joggers and cyclists. A 3-mile segment wanders through Boatyard-Riverfront Park.

The Kingsport Renaissance Center, 1200 E. Center St., contains an art gallery and a 350-seat theater, and is the home of the Symphony of the Mountains and the Arts Council of Greater Kingsport as well as the Kingsport Theatre Guild, Art Guild and Senior Center. The renovated 1927 school building is centered on a three-story atrium; phone (423) 392-8427.

Scenic US 23 runs 15 miles southeast from the I-81 junction at the Kingsport city limits to Johnson City.

Kingsport Area Chamber of Commerce: 400 Clinchfield St., Kingsport, TN 37660. **Phone:** (423) 392-8800 or (800) 743-5282.

BAYS MOUNTAIN PARK & PLANETARIUM is 2 mi. w. of I-26 exit 3 on Meadowview Pkwy./Reservoir Rd., then 1.4 mi. n. to 853 Bays Mountain Park Rd., following signs. Programs about the area's ecology are presented at the 3,500-acre nature preserve. The visitor center houses a planetarium and nature and astronomy exhibits. The park also offers 37 miles of hiking trails, where fauna and more than 60 different types of wildflowers can be seen, as well as barge trips, native animal habitats and a variety of other live animal displays.

Pets on leash and fishing are permitted in some areas. **Hours:** Nature center open Mon.-Fri. 8:30-5 (also 5-6, June-Aug.), Sat.-Sun. 11-5 (also 5-6, Mar.-Oct.). Park grounds Mon.-Sat. 8:30-8, Sun. 11-8, Mar.-Oct.; Mon.-Sat. 8:30-5, Sun. 11-5, rest of year. Closed Jan. 1, Thanksgiving, Christmas Eve and Christmas. Phone ahead to confirm schedule. **Cost:** Park admission $4 (per private vehicle). Planetarium $4; free (ages 0-5). Barge ride $3. Nature program $2. Prices are subject to change; phone ahead for updates. **Phone:** (423) 229-9447.

HAMPTON INN-KINGSPORT　　　　(423)247-3888

▼▼▼ **Hotel** $99-$144 **Address:** 2000 Enterprise Pl 37660 **Location:** I-26 exit 4, just n on SR 93. **Facility:** 115 units. 4 stories, interior corridors. **Terms:** 1-7 night minimum stay, cancellation fee imposed. **Pool(s):** valet laundry. **Activities:** limited exercise equipment. **Guest Services:** valet laundry.

AAA Benefit: Members save up to 10%!

[icons]

HOLIDAY INN EXPRESS HOTEL & SUITES　　423/723-2300

▼▼▼ **Hotel.** Rates not provided. **Address:** 1217 Stewball Cir 37660 **Location:** I-26 exit 4, just n. **Facility:** 79 units. 5 stories, interior corridors. **Pool(s):** heated indoor. **Activities:** exercise room. **Guest Services:** valet and coin laundry.

[icons]

LA QUINTA INN & SUITES KINGSPORT TRI-CITIES AIRPORT　　(423)323-0500

▼▼▼ **Hotel** $64-$284 **Address:** 10150 Airport Pkwy 37663 **Location:** I-81 exit 63, just e. **Facility:** 118 units. 5 stories, interior corridors. **Pool(s):** outdoor. **Activities:** limited exercise equipment. **Guest Services:** coin laundry.

[icons]

MEADOWVIEW MARRIOTT CONFERENCE RESORT & CONVENTION CENTER　　(423)578-6600

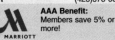

Resort Hotel $112-$194

AAA Benefit: Members save 5% or more!

MARRIOTT

Address: 1901 Meadowview Pkwy 37660 **Location:** I-26 exit 3, just e. **Facility:** Nestled in the foothills of the Blue Ridge Mountains, this updated resort offers a championship 18-hole golf course and a restaurant that serves a wide variety of Continental cuisine. 305 units. 5-7 stories, interior corridors. **Parking:** on-site and valet. **Terms:** check-in 4 pm. **Pool(s):** heated indoor. **Activities:** hot tub, regulation golf, exercise room. **Guest Services:** valet and coin laundry.

[icons]

QUALITY INN　　　　(423)230-0534

▼▼▼ **Hotel** $94-$129 **Address:** 3004 Bay Meadow Pl 37664 **Location:** I-26 exit 4, just n. **Facility:** 55 units. 3 stories, interior corridors. **Pool(s):** outdoor. **Activities:** exercise room.

[icons]

SLEEP INN　　　　(423)279-1811

▼▼▼ **Hotel** $80-$90 **Address:** 200 Hospitality Pl 37663 **Location:** I-81 exit 63, just s. **Facility:** 70 units. 3 stories, interior corridors. **Activities:** limited exercise equipment.

[icons]

THE CHOP HOUSE　　　　423/247-1704

▼▼ Steak Seafood. Casual Dining. $10-$34 **AAA Inspector Notes:** Friendly servers hustle amid tables with preparations of quality aged meats, fresh seafood, chicken, lamb, pork and pasta. The restaurant is a popular spot for casually upscale dining. **Features:** full bar, patio dining. **Address:** 1704 N Eastman Rd 37660 **Location:** 0.5 mi sw of jct US 11 W. [L] [D]

FATZ　　　　423/392-9885

▼▼ Regional American. Casual Dining. $6-$19 **AAA Inspector Notes:** Friendly staff and appealing country decor help set the tone for a relaxed and enjoyable dining experience. It's not unusual for guests to wait to be seated at the popular spot, which earns raves for its well-prepared variations on chicken, steak, ribs and pasta, as well as salads and sandwiches. The signature Southern-style peach cobbler served with vanilla ice cream and walnuts is scrumptious. **Features:** full bar. **Address:** 2610 W Stone Dr 37660 **Location:** I-26 exit 1, 1.6 mi w on US 11. [L] [D]

GIUSEPPE'S　　　　423/288-5265

▼▼ Italian. Casual Dining. $9-$44 **AAA Inspector Notes:** This family-owned and -operated eatery prepares made-to-order cuisine using only the freshest ingredients and home-grown herbs. Taking center stage on the menu are chicken cacciatore, veal Sorrentina and several seafood selections such as mussels marinara, tilapia francese and Giuseppe's seafood combo platter. A few Italian specialties also are sure to delight the appetite. **Features:** full bar. **Address:** 2539 E Stone Dr 37660 **Location:** Just e of John B Dennis Hwy. [L] [D]

POP'S RESTAURANT　　　　423/288-1171

◆◆◆
American Casual Dining $6-$19

AAA Inspector Notes: A casual and comfortable restaurant liked by the locals, this casual spot dishes up many comfort foods. **Address:** 3016 John B Dennis Hwy 37660 **Location:** I-26 exit 4, 5.1 mi n on SR 93. [B] [L] [D]

SAGEBRUSH STEAKHOUSE　　　　423/245-0067

▼▼ Steak. Casual Dining. $5-$23 **AAA Inspector Notes:** Born from the spirit of Texas cattle drives, the restaurant presents a menu of hearty steaks, prime rib, chicken, seafood and baby back ribs. Yummy desserts merit a splurge. Guests can call ahead to facilitate seating. **Features:** full bar. **Address:** 1600 E Stone Dr 37660 **Location:** I-81 exit 55 (US 11 W), 4 mi e. [L] [D] CALL [&M]

KINGSTON (D-6) pop. 5,934, elev. 787'

Kingston had two brushes with fame. The first came in 1797 when the Duke of Orléans, later to become Louis Philippe of France, passed through en route to Nashville on a trip organized by President George Washington. Though it is said the prince enjoyed the wilderness journey, he found it difficult to adapt to frontier living, especially the food served at inns along the way. The second instance occurred when the city was the capital of Tennessee for a day on Sept. 21, 1807.

Covering 39,000 acres, Watts Bar Lake *(see Recreation Areas Chart)* is a popular destination for water sports.

Roane County Visitors Bureau: 1209 N. Kentucky St., Kingston, TN 37763. **Phone:** (865) 376-5572.

FORT SOUTHWEST POINT is at 1226 S. Kentucky St. The site of this former frontier outpost overlooks the confluence of the Tennessee and Clinch rivers. Built in 1797, the fort played an important role in the protection of the frontier and served as an Indian Agency headquarters.

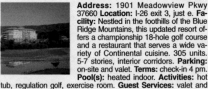

Restoration of the fort buildings on their original foundations is ongoing. To date, visitors can see a blockhouse, a barracks, a blacksmith shop, a Cherokee cabin and 250 feet of palisades while enjoying views from the bluff. The self-guiding tour departs from the visitor center, which features exhibits of artifacts excavated from the site, reproductions of period costumes, weapons and a model of the fort. **Time:** Allow 30 minutes minimum. **Hours:** Tues.-Sat. 10-4. Closed Jan. 1, Thanksgiving and Christmas. **Cost:** Donations. **Phone:** (865) 376-3641.

MOTEL 6 #4403   (865)376-2069

▼ **Motel** $43-$90 **Address:** 495 Gallaher Rd 37763 **Location:** I-40 exit 356, just n. **Facility:** 42 units. 2 stories (no elevator), exterior corridors. **Guest Services:** coin laundry.

WHITESTONE COUNTRY INN   (865)376-0113

▼▼▼ ▼▼▼
Country Inn
$165-$325

Address: 1200 Paint Rock Rd 37763 **Location:** I-40 exit 352, 6.5 mi s on SR 58, 5 mi e on SR 72, then 4 mi n. **Facility:** This 275-acre contemporary estate overlooks a scenic lake and serves as a popular Christian spiritual retreat. Spacious guest rooms feature gas fireplaces. 22 units, some kitchens. 2-3 stories (no elevator), interior/exterior corridors. **Terms:** 14 day cancellation notice-fee imposed, resort fee. **Activities:** fishing, tennis, spa. **Featured Amenity: full hot breakfast.**

WHERE TO EAT

RED BONES ON THE RIVER   865/376-9696

▼▼ American. Casual Dining. $7-$17 **AAA Inspector Notes:** Enjoy friendly, down-home service and a menu of steaks, seafood, pasta and more at this casual eatery that overlooks the river. Enjoy such entrées as pasta Alfredo, fish and chips, baby back ribs, crab legs and prime rib. Exotic entrées include the gator po' boy or fried frog legs. The upstairs lounge and deck are a great place to relax with friends over a drink and grab a tasty bite. **Features:** full bar. **Address:** 316 W Race St 37763 **Location:** I-40 exit 352, 1 mi s on SR 58, then 0.5 mi e on US 70. [L] [D]

KINGSTON SPRINGS pop. 2,756

BEST WESTERN HARPETH INN   (615)952-3961

▼▼▼ ▼▼▼
Hotel
$60-$120

Best Western
AAA Benefit:
Save 10% or more every day and earn 10% bonus points!

Address: 116 Luyben Hills Rd 37082 **Location:** I-40 exit 188, just n. **Facility:** 44 units. 2 stories (no elevator), exterior corridors. **Pool(s):** outdoor. **Featured Amenity: continental breakfast.**

Enjoy great member rates and benefits at AAA/CAA Preferred Hotels

---

KNOXVILLE (C-7) pop. 178,874, elev. 936'
• **Hotels p. 121** • **Restaurants p. 124**
• **Attractions map p. 114**
• **Hotels & Restaurants map & index p. 117**

At the close of the 18th century a flood of settlers burst into Tennessee, transforming the Knoxville outpost on the Tennessee River into a gateway to the West. In 1791 the first territorial governor, William Blount, chose James White's Fort *(see attraction listing)* as the capital of the territory and renamed it for Secretary of War Henry Knox.

Earlier that year the chiefs of the Cherokee Nation had met along the Tennessee River and ceded all claims in the wilderness valley to the United States. Knoxville was the territorial capital 1792-96 and the state capital 1796-1811, and again in 1817.

During the Civil War Knoxville was occupied by both Confederate and Union armies. The only major engagement was in 1863, when rebel forces led by Gen. James Longstreet failed to regain the city from Gen. Ambrose E. Burnside's Union troops.

The elegant Mabry-Hazen House, 1711 Dandridge Ave., an 1858 Italianate frame house that served as headquarters for both sides during the Civil War, is furnished with original artifacts such as china, silver, crystal and antique furniture. It is open for tours by appointment; phone (865) 522-8661.

During Reconstruction, Knoxville recovered rapidly and has since become the business center of the rich East Tennessee Valley. Knoxville was host of the 1982 World's Fair, a tribute to its emergence as a major metropolis. Today, the city is home to many art galleries, including the Arts & Culture Alliance at 100 Gay St., phone (865) 523-7543; The Ewing Gallery, on the University of Tennessee campus at 1715 Volunteer Blvd., phone (865) 974-3200; and the University Downtown Gallery, 106 S. Gay St., phone (865) 673-0802.

The Beck Cultural Exchange Center, (865) 524-8461, is a museum for the research, preservation and display of the achievements of Knoxville's African-Americans in east Tennessee, the Southeast and across the country from the early 1800s to the present. The collections include photography, sketches, fine art, newspapers and books.

In Haley Heritage Square, at the corner of Dandridge and Hazen avenues, is a larger-than-life bronze statue of Pulitzer Prize winner Alex Haley holding a copy of his book "Roots." Haley is buried on the grounds of his boyhood home in Henning. Old Gray Cemetery at 543 North Broadway is named for English poet Thomas Gray, who wrote the poem "Elegy Written in a Country Churchyard." The cemetery was established in the 1850s as part of the Rural Cemetery Movement and contains many examples of Victorian art and architecture.

Two major institutions have helped shape modern Knoxville: the University of Tennessee and the Tennessee Valley Authority (TVA). The federal government chose the city as the headquarters of the TVA, which oversees a regional network of dams.

(See map & index p. 117.)

The 400-acre University of Tennessee campus plays a vital role in the city's cultural life with its many museums, sports facilities and professional complexes. Thompson-Boling Arena is the university's basketball facility and sports arena, while Neyland Stadium is the site of football games and other entertainment for students and townspeople alike.

Knoxville Trolley Lines provides free transportation aboard red trolley buses among various downtown attractions, including the Governor William Blount Mansion, the Knoxville Museum of Art and the Women's Basketball Hall of Fame *(see attraction listings)*. Trolley stops for both the trolley system's orange and blue lines are scattered throughout downtown; phone (865) 637-3000.

Volunteer Landing, along the Tennessee River, consists of a 1-mile landscaped walkway, historical markers, waterfalls, fountains and observation decks.

More than 60 miles of marked dogwood trails weave through several of the city's neighborhoods. During the Dogwood Arts Festival in April bus tours of the trails depart from Market Square. Complementing the dogwood trails are garden paths and marked auto routes in neighborhoods with especially colorful floral displays; for more information phone (865) 637-4561.

Knoxville is the southern terminus of a scenic stretch of I-75, which runs 45 miles north, intersecting with SR 9 before entering Kentucky. A scenic portion of I-40 also begins at Knoxville, running 30 miles east to the I-81 intersection. Knoxville has easy access to 800 miles of trout streams and seven major TVA lakes.

Knoxville Tourism & Sports Corporation Visitor Center: 301 S. Gay St., Knoxville, TN 37902. **Phone:** (865) 523-7263 or (800) 727-8045.

Self-guiding tours: Brochures available from the Knoxville Tourism Corporation outline the Cradle of Country Music downtown walking tour and a Knoxville Civil War driving tour.

Shopping: Major shopping malls include Knoxville Center, north off I-640 exit 8 at 3001 Knoxville Center Dr.; West Town Mall, 7600 Kingston Pike off the I-40 West Hill exit; and Turkey Creek, off the I-40 Lovell Rd. exit.

Market Square, downtown between Gay and Walnut streets, offers boutiques, eateries and galleries. At Jackson Avenue and Central Street, the Old City is a vibrant neighborhood featuring renovated 19th-century brick warehouses containing shops, art galleries, coffee houses, antiques stores, restaurants and nightclubs. The District in Bearden, just outside of downtown, has locally owned, upscale specialty shops.

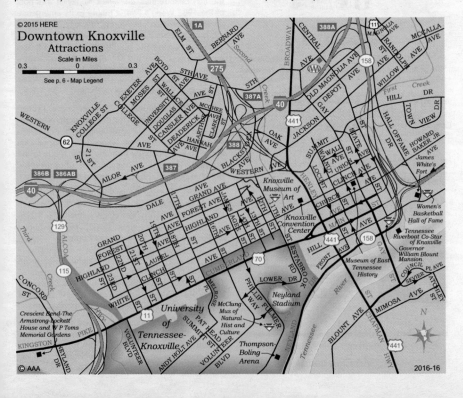

© 2015 HERE
Downtown Knoxville
Attractions

Scale in Miles
See p. 6 - Map Legend

© AAA

2016-16

(See map & index p. 117.)

CRESCENT BEND—THE ARMSTRONG-LOCKETT HOUSE AND W.P. TOMS MEMORIAL GARDENS is 1.4 mi. s.w. on Cumberland Ave., then .5 mi. s.w. to 2728 Kingston Pike. This is one of Knoxville's oldest continuously occupied houses. It was built in 1834 by Drury Paine Armstrong to serve as the centerpiece of his 600-acre farm. The restored house showcases 18th-century American and English furniture, decorative arts and a 1610-1820 collection of English silver.

The W.P. Toms Memorial Gardens, terraced Italianate gardens with fountains, descend to the river. During April some 20,000 tulips are in bloom. **Time:** Allow 30 minutes minimum. **Hours:** Wed.-Fri. 10-4, Sat. 10-1, Mar.-Dec. (when wedding not in session). Closed major holidays. Phone ahead to confirm schedule. **Cost:** House and gardens $7; $5 (students with ID and senior citizens); free (ages 0-12). **Phone:** (865) 637-3163. GT

GOVERNOR WILLIAM BLOUNT MANSION is at 200 W. Hill Ave. One of the first frame houses west of the Alleghenies, the circa 1792 house is furnished with original and period pieces. The State of Tennessee came into being in the office of William Blount, governor of the Territory South of the River Ohio and a signer of the U.S. Constitution. **Time:** Allow 1 hour minimum. **Hours:** Tues.-Fri. 10-5; Sat. 10-2. Guided tours offered on the hour; last tour begins 1 hour before closing. Closed major holidays. **Cost:** $7; $6 (ages 65+); $5 (ages 6-17). **Phone:** (865) 525-2375. GT

HISTORIC RAMSEY HOUSE is 4 mi. e. off I-40 exit 394 on Asheville Hwy., s. on John Sevier Hwy. (SR 168), then .2 mi. e. to 2614 Thorngrove Pike. This two-story house was built 1795-97 using local pink and blue limestone. Exterior highlights include quoins and keystone arches; inside, the home contains 18th-century furniture. Pets on leash allowed on the grounds. **Time:** Allow 1 hour minimum. **Hours:** Wed.-Sat. 10-4. Last tour departs at 3. Closed major holidays. **Cost:** $7; $5 (ages 6-12). **Phone:** (865) 546-0745.

IJAMS NATURE CENTER is at 2915 Island Home Ave. Encompassing 300 acres along the Tennessee River, this park and environmental education center features 12 miles of multiuse trails, meadows, marble quarries, ponds, woodlands and a treetop zipline course. Bike, canoe, kayak and paddleboard rentals are available.

A visitor center houses the Lost Species exhibit, a bird nest and aquatic animal displays. **Time:** Allow 2 hours minimum. **Hours:** Grounds daily 8-dusk. Visitor center Mon.-Sat. 9-5, Sun. 11-5. **Cost:** Donations. **Phone:** (865) 577-4717. 🐾 🎍

JAMES WHITE'S FORT is at 205 E. Hill Ave. between Neyland Dr. and Hall of Fame Dr. The fort was the first settlement in this area and was the home of Gen. James White, who founded Knoxville

in 1786. The fort consists of seven log houses, each containing pioneer articles and furnishings. Self-guiding tours are available.

Time: Allow 1 hour minimum. **Hours:** Mon.-Sat. 10-3, Jan.-Mar.; 9:30-4, rest of year. Last tour begins at closing. Closed major holidays and during University of Tennessee football games. **Cost:** $7; $3 (ages 5-17). **Phone:** (865) 525-6514.

KNOXVILLE MUSEUM OF ART is at 1050 World's Fair Park Dr. in World's Fair Park. The fine arts museum focuses on the art and artists of east Tennessee as well as contemporary art. Housed in a three-story glass and pink Tennessee marble building, the museum includes five galleries; gardens; Creative Corner, which features child-friendly activities; and the Great Hall overlooking World's Fair Park, the site of the 1982 World's Fair.

Don't miss the museum's collection of Mrs. James Ward Thorne miniature rooms. Lectures, walking tours, concerts and art workshops are offered. **Time:** Allow 1 hour minimum. **Hours:** Tues.-Sat. 10-5, Sun. 1-5. Closed major holidays. **Cost:** Free. **Phone:** (865) 525-6101.

KNOXVILLE ZOO is 2.5 mi. e. off I-40 exit 392 (Knoxville Zoo Dr./Rutledge Pike), following signs to 3500 Knoxville Zoo Dr. The 53-acre zoo houses more than 800 animals, many in natural habitats. Special exhibits include The Ann and John Schaad Family Lion Courtyard, Clayton Safari Splash, The Williams Family Giraffe Encounter, The Boyd Family Red Panda Village, Grasslands Africa, Black Bear Falls, Chimp Ridge, Penguin Rock and Birds of Central America. Activities for children include the Clayton Family Kids Cove, Nature Play, WeePlay Adventure and interactive animal exhibits.

The zoo also features camel rides, a carousel, an animal show, an elephant preserve and a reptile exhibit. **Time:** Allow 2 hours minimum. **Hours:** Daily 10-4:30. Last admission 1 hour before closing. Closed Christmas. **Cost:** $19.95; $16.95 (ages 2-12 and 65+). Tickets bought after 3 p.m. provide free admission the following operating day. **Parking:** $5. **Phone:** (865) 637-5331.

MARBLE SPRINGS is 7 mi. s. on US 129, then 6 mi. e. to 1220 W. Gov. John Sevier Hwy. (US 168). The last residence of John Sevier, first governor of Tennessee, stands on a 35.5-acre tract. Hiking trails and picnic facilities are on the grounds. **Time:** Allow 1 hour minimum. **Hours:** Wed.-Sat. 10-5, Sun. noon-5, Mar.-Dec.; phone ahead to confirm schedule Jan.-Feb. Last tour begins 1 hour before closing. **Cost:** Free. Guided tour $5; $4 (ages 5-17 and military and senior citizens with ID); free (ages 0-4). Prices may vary for special events; phone ahead. **Phone:** (865) 573-5508.

McCLUNG MUSEUM OF NATURAL HISTORY AND CULTURE is at 1327 Circle Park Dr. on the University of Tennessee campus. On display are geological, anthropological, ancient Egyptian, archeological, decorative arts, local history and

(See map & index p. 117.)

natural history collections. Exhibits about the Tennessee River Valley include specimens of marine fossils and 12,000-year-old artifacts of early Native American cultures.

Galleries focusing on ancient Egypt present funeral objects, mummies, clothing, jewelry and pottery. The Native Peoples of Tennessee exhibit contains a scale model of a 600-year-old village complete with fiber optic lights. Temporary exhibits are offered.

Parking passes good Mon.-Fri. are available at the campus information booth; passes are not required Sat.-Sun. **Time:** Allow 1 hour minimum. **Hours:** Mon.-Sat. 9-5, Sun. 1-5. Closed major holidays. **Cost:** Free. **Phone:** (865) 974-2144.

THE MUSE KNOXVILLE AND PLANETARIUM is at 516 N. Beaman St. in Chilhowee Park. The 4,000 square-foot facility features hands-on exhibits and activities that focus on science, technology, engineering, math and the arts. An outdoor play area includes a playground. **Time:** Allow 1 hour, 30 minutes minimum. **Hours:** Center Tues.-Fri. 9-5, Sat. 10-5, Mon. 9-noon. Planetarium shows are given every hour. Closed major holidays. Phone ahead to confirm schedule. **Cost:** Museum $5; $4 (ages 2-18 and 65+). Planetarium $2. **Phone:** (865) 594-1494.

MUSEUM OF EAST TENNESSEE HISTORY is downtown at 601 S. Gay St. in the East Tennessee History Center. The museum is dedicated to researching, preserving, interpreting and presenting the region's history and culture through permanent and temporary exhibits. The Voices of the Land exhibit explores three centuries of life and culture in the area. **Time:** Allow 1 hour minimum. **Hours:** Mon.-Fri. 9-4, Sat. 10-4, Sun. 1-5. Closed Jan. 1,

Easter, Thanksgiving, Christmas Eve and Christmas. **Cost:** $5; $4 (ages 55+); free (ages 0-15). **Phone:** (865) 215-8830.

TENNESSEE RIVERBOAT CO.—STAR OF KNOXVILLE is off I-40 exit 388A Business Loop to 300 Neyland Dr. Sightseeing cruises lasting 1-2 hours are offered along urban and rural sections of the Tennessee River. Lunch and dinner cruises also are available. **Hours:** Sightseeing cruises are offered year-round. Phone ahead to confirm schedule. **Cost:** Sightseeing cruise $13.50-17; $10.75-$12.50 (ages 5-11). Lunch or dinner cruise $22.75-$39.75; $14.95-$19.90 (ages 5-11). Reservations are required. **Phone:** (865) 525-7827 or (800) 509-2628.

WOMEN'S BASKETBALL HALL OF FAME is at 700 Hall of Fame Dr. A giant, 30-foot-wide basketball greets visitors at the north end of the building. In the south rotunda, a bronze sculpture of three female players represents the past, present and future of the sport. A historical timeline recounts the first 100 years of women's basketball, and a video presentation provides further history.

The Senda Berenson Diorama features an animatronic player that discusses the benefits of physical education. In a simulated locker room, visitors can listen to a recording of a coach discussing strategy.

An exhibit honors the 1936-86 All American Red Heads, a professional traveling team. The Hall of Honor highlights the achievements of inductees, and the Winners' Wall displays photographs of national champions.

Time: Allow 2 hours minimum. **Hours:** Mon.-Sat. 10-5, May 1-Labor Day; Tues.-Fri. 11-5, Sat. 10-5, rest of year. Closed major holidays. **Cost:** $7.95; $5.95 (ages 6-15 and 62+). **Phone:** (865) 633-9000.

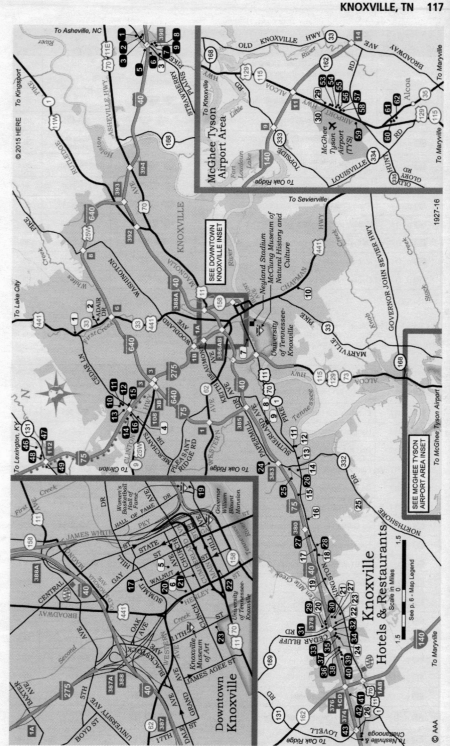

McGhee Tyson Airport Area

Knoxville
Hotels & Restaurants

Downtown Knoxville

© 2015 HERE

© AAA

1927-16

✈ Airport Hotels

Map Page	MCGHEE TYSON (Maximum driving distance from airport: 2.2 mi)	Diamond Rated	Rate Range	Page
54 p. 117	Candlewood Suites Knoxville Airport/Alcoa, 1.3 mi	▽▽▽	Rates not provided	38
56 p. 117	Comfort Suites, 1.2 mi	▽▽	$85-$99	38
55 p. 117	Country Inn & Suites By Carlson, Knoxville Airport, 1.3 mi	▽▽	Rates not provided	38
58 p. 117	Courtyard by Marriott Knoxville Airport Alcoa, 1.2 mi	▽▽▽	$99-$183	38
53 p. 117	Hampton Inn-Knoxville Airport, 1.5 mi	▽▽▽	$79-$139	38
59 p. 117	Hilton Knoxville Airport, 0.5 mi	▽▽▽	$120-$240	38
61 p. 117	Holiday Inn Express & Suites, 2.1 mi	▽▽▽	$99-$249	38
57 p. 117	La Quinta Inn & Suites Knoxville Airport, 1.2 mi	▽▽	$68-$196	38
60 p. 117	MainStay Suites, 2.2 mi	▽▽	$80-$120	38
62 p. 117	Quality Inn, 2.2 mi	▽▽	$77-$86	38

Knoxville and Vicinity

This index helps you "spot" where approved hotels and restaurants are located on the corresponding detailed maps. Hotel daily rate range is for comparison only. Restaurant price range is a combination of lunch and/or dinner. Turn to the listing page for more detailed rate and price information and consult display ads for special promotions.

KNOXVILLE

Map Page	Hotels	Diamond Rated	Rate Range	Page
1 p. 117	Holiday Inn Express Knoxville-East	▽▽▽	Rates not provided	123
2 p. 117	Econo Lodge Inn & Suites-East Knoxville	▽▽	$51-$65	122
3 p. 117	Hampton Inn Knoxville East	▽▽▽	$99-$169	123
5 p. 117	Red Roof Inn & Suites Knoxville-East	▽▽	$49-$119	124
6 p. 117	Fairfield Inn & Suites by Marriott Knoxville/East	▽▽▽	$76-$125	122
7 p. 117	Comfort Suites	▽▽▽	$89-$149	121
8 p. 117	**BEST WESTERN PLUS Strawberry Inn & Suites**	▽▽▽	$70-$149 [SAVE]	121
9 p. 117	La Quinta Inn & Suites Knoxville Strawberry Plains	▽▽	$64-$163	123
10 p. 117	Hampton Inn & Suites Knoxville North I-75	▽▽▽	$89-$169	122
11 p. 117	**BEST WESTERN Knoxville Suites**	▽▽	$74-$170 [SAVE]	121
12 p. 117	Quality Inn Merchants Dr	▽▽	$59-$79	124
13 p. 117	Comfort Suites North	▽▽▽	$75-$165	121
14 p. 117	The Clarion Inn	▽▽	$55-$155	121
15 p. 117	**MainStay Suites Knoxville**	▽▽	$79-$109 [SAVE]	123
16 p. 117	Econo Lodge-North	▽▽	$40-$150	122
17 p. 117	**Crowne Plaza Knoxville**	▽▽▽	$99-$399 [SAVE]	122
19 p. 117	Marriott Knoxville Hotel	▽▽▽	$110-$396	124
20 p. 117	Holiday Inn World's Fair Park	▽▽▽	Rates not provided	123
21 p. 117	**Hilton Knoxville Downtown**	▽▽▽	$99-$299 [SAVE]	123

KNOXVILLE (cont'd)

Map Page	Hotels (cont'd)	Diamond Rated	Rate Range	Page
22 p. 117	Hampton Inn & Suites Downtown Knoxville	▽▽▽	$129-$299	122
23 p. 117	**Four Points by Sheraton Knoxville Cumberland House Hotel**	▽▽▽	$129-$499 [SAVE]	122
24 p. 117	La Quinta Inn & Suites Papermill	▽▽▽	$92-$367	123
25 p. 117	Hampton Inn & Suites Knoxville Papermill	▽▽▽	$99-$169	122
26 p. 117	Courtyard by Marriott-Knoxville West/Bearden	▽▽▽	$118-$194	121
27 p. 117	Ramada	▽▽	$64-$140	124
28 p. 117	Extended Stay America Knoxville-West Hills	▽	Rates not provided	122
29 p. 117	Country Inn & Suites By Carlson, West Knoxville/Cedar Bluff	▽▽▽	Rates not provided	121
30 p. 117	Hampton Inn-Knoxville West at Cedar Bluff	▽▽▽	$109-$169	123
31 p. 117	**Holiday Inn Cedar Bluff**	▽▽▽	$109-$169 [SAVE]	123
32 p. 117	**Red Roof Inn Knoxville-University of Tennessee**	▽▽	$50-$120 [SAVE]	124
33 p. 117	Baymont Inn Knoxville/Cedar Bluff, TN	▽▽	$74-$179	121
34 p. 117	Rodeway Inn & Suites West	▽▽	$59-$99	124
35 p. 117	Hilton Garden Inn Knoxville West/Cedar Bluff	▽▽▽	$129-$199	123
36 p. 117	Extended Stay America Knoxville-Cedar Bluff	▽▽	Rates not provided	122
37 p. 117	**BEST WESTERN PLUS Cedar Bluff Inn**	▽▽▽	$94-$189 [SAVE]	121
38 p. 117	Courtyard by Marriott Knoxville Cedar Bluff	▽▽▽	$107-$194	121
39 p. 117	Residence Inn by Marriott Knoxville Cedar Bluff	▽▽▽	$125-$206	124
40 p. 117	Embassy Suites by Hilton Knoxville West	▽▽▽	$129-$209	122
41 p. 117	Candlewood Suites-Knoxville	▽▽	$95-$125	121
42 p. 117	Homewood Suites by Hilton	▽▽▽	$109-$199	123
43 p. 117	SpringHill Suites by Marriott Knoxville at Turkey Creek	▽▽▽	$119-$197	124

Map Page	Restaurants	Diamond Rated	Cuisine	Price Range	Page
1 p. 117	Litton's Market, Restaurant & Bakery	▽▽	Burgers Desserts	$12-$25	125
2 p. 117	Rita's Bakery	▽	Breads/Pastries	$1-$28	126
3 p. 117	Golden Wok Chinese Restaurant & Gift Shop	▽	Chinese	$5-$13	125
4 p. 117	Nixon's Deli	▽	Deli	$5-$9	126
5 p. 117	Tupelo Honey Cafe	▽▽	New Southern	$8-$18	126
6 p. 117	Chesapeake's	▽▽	Seafood	$9-$40	125
7 p. 117	Copper Cellar & Cumberland Grill	▽▽	Steak Sandwiches	$10-$35	125
8 p. 117	Holy Land Market & Deli	▽	Middle Eastern Deli	$7-$15	125
9 p. 117	Gosh Ethiopian Restaurant	▽▽	Ethiopian	$8-$25	125
10 p. 117	Buddy's Bar-B-Q	▽	Barbecue	$6-$10	124
11 p. 117	**The Orangery**	▽▽▽	Continental	$12-$46	126

Map Page	Restaurants (cont'd)	Diamond Rated	Cuisine	Price Range	Page
⑫ p. 117	**Naples Italian Restaurant**	▽▽	Italian	$8-$23	126
⑬ p. 117	Buddy's Bar-B-Q	▽	Barbecue	$6-$10	124
⑭ p. 117	Surin of Thailand	▽▽	Thai Sushi	$10-$24	126
⑮ p. 117	P.F. Chang's China Bistro	▽▽▽	Chinese	$8-$25	126
⑯ p. 117	Copper Cellar West	▽▽	Steak Seafood	$7-$34	125
⑰ p. 117	Chez Guevara	▽▽	Mexican	$9-$17	125
⑱ p. 117	Bida Saigon	▽▽	Vietnamese	$7-$12	124
⑲ p. 117	Woodlands	▽▽	Indian	$9-$16	127
⑳ p. 117	Lemon Grass Thai, Hibachi & Sushi Bar	▽▽	Thai Sushi	$7-$12	125
㉑ p. 117	Taste of Thai	▽▽	Thai	$8-$17	126
㉒ p. 117	Puleo's Grille	▽▽	American	$8-$25	126
㉓ p. 117	Altruda's	▽▽	Italian	$11-$23	124
㉔ p. 117	Parkside Grill	▽▽	American	$9-$25	126
㉕ p. 117	Sullivan's Fine Foods	▽▽	American	$8-$20	126
㉖ p. 117	**Connors Steak & Seafood**	▽▽▽	Steak Seafood	$9-$40	125
㉗ p. 117	Viet Taste	▽▽	Vietnamese	$7-$12	127

POWELL

Map Page	Hotels	Diamond Rated	Rate Range	Page
㊻ p. 117	Comfort Inn	▽▽▽	$84-$149	236
㊼ p. 117	Country Inn & Suites By Carlson	▽▽	$75-$155	236
㊽ p. 117	Holiday Inn Express	▽▽▽	Rates not provided	236
㊾ p. 117	Super 8 of Powell	▽▽	$60-$80	236

ALCOA

Map Page	Hotels	Diamond Rated	Rate Range	Page
㊾... 53 p. 117	Hampton Inn-Knoxville Airport	▽▽▽	$79-$139	38
54 p. 117	Candlewood Suites Knoxville Airport/Alcoa	▽▽▽	Rates not provided	38
55 p. 117	Country Inn & Suites By Carlson, Knoxville Airport	▽▽	Rates not provided	38
56 p. 117	Comfort Suites	▽▽	$85-$99	38
57 p. 117	La Quinta Inn & Suites Knoxville Airport	▽▽	$68-$196	38
58 p. 117	Courtyard by Marriott Knoxville Airport Alcoa	▽▽▽	$99-$183	38
59 p. 117	Hilton Knoxville Airport	▽▽▽	$120-$240	38
60 p. 117	MainStay Suites	▽▽	$80-$120	38
61 p. 117	Holiday Inn Express & Suites	▽▽▽	$99-$249	38
62 p. 117	Quality Inn	▽▽	$77-$86	38

Map Page	Restaurants	Diamond Rated	Cuisine	Price Range	Page
㉙ p. 117	Ming Tree	▽▽	Asian	$7-$26	39
㉚ p. 117	El Sazon Mexicano Restaurant	▽▽	Mexican	$4-$25	38

(See map & index p. 117.)

BAYMONT INN KNOXVILLE/CEDAR BLUFF, TN
(865)531-7444 **33**

WWW Hotel $74-$179 **Address:** 209 Market Place Blvd 37922 **Location:** I-40/75 exit 378 (Cedar Bluff Rd), then just s to N Peters Rd, then just w. **Facility:** 122 units. 3 stories, interior corridors. **Pool(s):** outdoor. **Activities:** exercise room.

[icons] / SOME UNITS

BEST WESTERN KNOXVILLE SUITES
(865)687-9922 **11**

Hotel
$74-$170

AAA Benefit:
Save 10% or more every day and earn 10% bonus points!

Address: 5317 Pratt Rd 37912 **Location:** I-75 exit 108 (Merchants Dr), just e, then n. **Facility:** 58 units. 4 stories, interior corridors. **Terms:** cancellation fee imposed. **Pool(s):** heated indoor. **Activities:** hot tub, limited exercise equipment. **Guest Services:** coin laundry.

[SAVE] [icons]
[icons]
/ SOME UNITS [HS]

BEST WESTERN PLUS CEDAR BLUFF INN
(865)539-0058 **37**

Hotel
$94-$189

AAA Benefit:
Save 10% or more every day and earn 10% bonus points!

Address: 420 N Peters Rd 37922 **Location:** I-40/75 exit 378 (Cedar Bluff Rd), just s to N Peters Rd, then 0.5 mi w. **Facility:** 95 units. 3 stories, interior corridors. **Pool(s):** outdoor. **Activities:** exercise room. **Guest Services:** valet and coin laundry. **Featured Amenity:** breakfast buffet.

[SAVE] [icons]
/ SOME UNITS [HS]

BEST WESTERN PLUS STRAWBERRY INN & SUITES
(865)544-7737 **8**

Hotel
$70-$149

AAA Benefit:
Save 10% or more every day and earn 10% bonus points!

Address: 7260 Saddlerack St 37914 **Location:** I-40 exit 398 (Strawberry Plains Pike), just s, then just e. **Facility:** 64 units. 3 stories, interior corridors. **Terms:** cancellation fee imposed. **Pool(s):** heated indoor. **Activities:** hot tub, exercise room. **Guest Services:** valet and coin laundry. **Featured Amenity:** full hot breakfast.

[SAVE] [icons]
[icons] / SOME UNITS

CANDLEWOOD SUITES-KNOXVILLE (865)777-0400 **41**

WW Extended Stay Hotel $95-$125 **Address:** 10206 Parkside Dr 37922 **Location:** I-40/75 exit 374 (Lovell Rd), 0.5 mi s, then 1 mi e. **Facility:** 98 efficiencies. 3 stories, interior corridors. **Activities:** exercise room. **Guest Services:** complimentary and valet laundry.

[icons]

THE CLARION INN (865)687-8989 **14**

WWW Hotel $55-$155 **Address:** 5634 Merchants Center Blvd 37912 **Location:** I-75 exit 108 (Merchants Dr), just w, then just n. Located in a commercial area. **Facility:** 123 units. 5 stories, interior corridors. **Pool(s):** outdoor. **Guest Services:** valet and coin laundry.

[icons]
/ SOME UNITS [icons]

COMFORT SUITES (865)246-2426 **7**

WWW Hotel $89-$149 **Address:** 7230 Regions Ln 37914 **Location:** I-40 exit 398 (Strawberry Plains Pike), just s, then 0.3 mi n. **Facility:** 68 units. 4 stories, interior corridors. **Pool(s):** heated indoor. **Activities:** limited exercise equipment. **Guest Services:** coin laundry. [icons]

COMFORT SUITES NORTH (865)342-0373 **13**

WWW Hotel $75-$165 **Address:** 5466 Central Ave Pike 37912 **Location:** I-75 exit 108 (Merchants Dr), just e, then n. **Facility:** 72 units. 5 stories, interior corridors. **Pool(s):** heated indoor. **Activities:** hot tub, exercise room. **Guest Services:** valet and coin laundry.

[icons]

COUNTRY INN & SUITES BY CARLSON, WEST KNOXVILLE/ CEDAR BLUFF 865/693-4500 **29**

WWW Hotel. Rates not provided. **Address:** 9137 Cross Park Dr 37923 **Location:** I-40/75 exit 378 (Cedar Bluff Rd), just e. **Facility:** 89 units. 5 stories, interior corridors. **Amenities:** safes. **Pool(s):** heated indoor. **Activities:** hot tub, exercise room. **Guest Services:** complimentary and valet laundry.

[icons]
/ SOME UNITS [icons]

COURTYARD BY MARRIOTT KNOXVILLE CEDAR BLUFF
(865)539-0600 **38**

WWW Hotel $107-$194 **Address:** 216 Langley Pl 37922 **Location:** I-40/75 exit 378 (Cedar Bluff Rd), just s, then 1 mi w on N Peters Rd. **Facility:** 78 units. 3 stories, interior corridors. **Pool(s):** heated indoor. **Activities:** hot tub, exercise room. **Guest Services:** valet and coin laundry, boarding pass kiosk.

AAA Benefit:
Members save 5% or more!

[icons]
/ SOME UNITS [icons]

COURTYARD BY MARRIOTT-KNOXVILLE WEST/BEARDEN
(865)690-7680 **26**

WWW Hotel $118-$194 **Address:** 250 Brookview Centre Way 37919 **Location:** I-40/75 exit 383 (Papermill Dr NW), just w, just s on N Northshore Dr, then just n. **Facility:** 124 units. 6 stories, interior corridors. **Pool(s):** heated indoor. **Activities:** exercise room. **Guest Services:** valet and coin laundry, boarding pass kiosk.

AAA Benefit:
Members save 5% or more!

[icons]

(See map & index p. 117.)

CROWNE PLAZA KNOXVILLE (865)522-2600 **17**

Hotel
$99-$399

Address: 401 W Summit Hill Dr 37902 **Location:** Corner of Walnut St; downtown. **Facility:** 197 units, some two bedrooms and efficiencies. 12 stories, interior corridors. **Parking:** on-site (fee) and valet. **Terms:** cancellation fee imposed. **Pool(s):** heated indoor. **Activities:** exercise room. **Guest Services:** valet laundry.

SAVE | CALL | BIZ | SOME UNITS

CROWNE PLAZA
KNOXVILLE
Award winning service in the heart of downtown Knoxville's business and entertainment district.

ECONO LODGE INN & SUITES-EAST KNOXVILLE
(865)932-1217 **2**

Motel $51-$65 **Address:** 7424 Strawberry Plains Pike 37924 **Location:** I-40 exit 398 (Strawberry Plains Pike), just n. **Facility:** 72 units. 2 stories (no elevator), exterior corridors. **Pool(s):** heated outdoor. **Guest Services:** coin laundry.

ECONO LODGE-NORTH
(865)687-5680 **16**

Motel $40-$150 **Address:** 5505 Merchants Center Blvd 37912 **Location:** I-75 exit 108 (Merchants Dr), just w, then just n. Located in a commercial area. **Facility:** 37 units. 2 stories (no elevator), exterior corridors.

EMBASSY SUITES BY HILTON KNOXVILLE WEST
(865)246-2309 **40**

Hotel $129-$209 **Address:** 9621 Parkside Dr 37922 **Location:** I-40 exit 378A (N Cedar Bluff Rd), just s, then 1.1 mi w on N Peters Rd (which becomes Parkside Dr). **Facility:** 140 units.

AAA Benefit: Members save 5% or more!

6 stories, interior corridors. **Terms:** 1-7 night minimum stay, cancellation fee imposed. **Pool(s):** heated indoor. **Activities:** sauna, hot tub, exercise room. **Guest Services:** valet and coin laundry.

EXTENDED STAY AMERICA KNOXVILLE-CEDAR BLUFF
865)769-0822 **36**

Extended Stay Motel. Rates not provided. **Address:** 214 Langley Pl 37922 **Location:** I-40/75 exit 378 (Cedar Bluff Rd), just s, then 1 mi w on N Peters Rd. **Facility:** 96 efficiencies. 3 stories, exterior corridors. **Guest Services:** coin laundry.

Trust the recommendations of AAA/CAA travel experts to make a good trip great

EXTENDED STAY AMERICA KNOXVILLE-WEST HILLS
865/694-4178 **28**

Extended Stay Hotel. Rates not provided. **Address:** 1700 Winston Rd 37919 **Location:** I-40/75 exit 380 (West Hills), just w on Kingston Pike, then just s. **Facility:** 72 kitchen units. 3 stories (no elevator), interior corridors. **Pool(s):** outdoor. **Guest Services:** coin laundry.

FAIRFIELD INN & SUITES BY MARRIOTT KNOXVILLE/EAST
(865)971-4033 **6**

Hotel $76-$125 **Address:** 1551 Cracker Barrel Ln 37914 **Location:** I-40 exit 398 (Strawberry Plains Pike), just s, then just w. **Facility:** 105 units. 3 stories, interior corridors. **Pool(s):** heated indoor. **Activities:** exercise room. **Guest Services:** coin laundry.

AAA Benefit: Members save 5% or more!

FOUR POINTS BY SHERATON KNOXVILLE CUMBERLAND HOUSE HOTEL
(865)971-4663 **23**

Hotel
$129-$499

FOUR POINTS BY SHERATON

AAA Benefit: Members save up to 15%, plus Starwood Preferred Guest® benefits!

Address: 1109 White Ave 37916 **Location:** Jct 11th St. Across from World's Fair Park. **Facility:** 129 units. 7 stories, interior corridors. **Parking:** on-site (fee). **Activities:** exercise room. **Guest Services:** valet and coin laundry.

SAVE | CALL | BIZ | SOME UNITS | HS

HAMPTON INN & SUITES DOWNTOWN KNOXVILLE
(865)522-5400 **22**

Hotel $129-$299 **Address:** 618 W Main St 37902 **Location:** Corner of Henley and W Main sts; downtown. **Facility:** 85 units. 6 stories, interior corridors. **Terms:** 1-7 night minimum stay, cancellation fee imposed. **Amenities:** safes. **Pool(s):** heated indoor. **Activities:** exercise room. **Guest Services:** valet and coin laundry.

AAA Benefit: Members save up to 10%!

ECO | CALL | BIZ | HS

HAMPTON INN & SUITES KNOXVILLE NORTH I-75
(865)689-1011 **10**

Hotel $89-$169 **Address:** 5411 Pratt Rd 37912 **Location:** I-75 exit 108 (Merchants Dr), just e to Pratt Rd, then just n. **Facility:** 102 units. 4 stories, interior corridors. **Terms:** 1-7 night minimum stay, cancellation fee imposed. **Pool(s):** heated indoor. **Activities:** exercise room. **Guest Services:** valet and coin laundry.

AAA Benefit: Members save up to 10%!

CALL | BIZ

HAMPTON INN & SUITES KNOXVILLE PAPERMILL
(865)693-5400 **25**

Hotel $99-$169 **Address:** 601 N Weisgarber Rd 37919 **Location:** I-40 exit 383 (Papermill Dr NW), just w. **Facility:** 108 units. 6 stories, interior corridors. **Terms:** 1-7 night minimum stay, cancellation fee imposed. **Amenities:** safes. **Pool(s):** heated indoor. **Activities:** exercise room. **Guest Services:** valet and coin laundry.

AAA Benefit: Members save up to 10%!

CALL | BIZ | HS | SOME UNITS

(See map & index p. 117.)

HAMPTON INN KNOXVILLE EAST   (865)525-3511   **3**

▼▼▼ **Hotel** $99-$169 **Address:** 7445 Sawyer Ln 37924 **Location:** I-40 exit 398 (Strawberry Plains Pike), 0.4 mi n, just e on Huckleberry Springs Rd, then just s. **Facility:** 81 units. 5 stories, interior corridors. **Terms:** 1-7 night minimum stay, cancellation fee imposed. **Pool(s):** heated indoor. **Activities:** exercise room. **Guest Services:** valet and coin laundry.

AAA Benefit: Members save up to 10%!

[icons]

HAMPTON INN-KNOXVILLE WEST AT CEDAR BLUFF   (865)693-1101   **30**

▼▼▼ **Hotel** $109-$169 **Address:** 9128 Executive Park Dr 37923 **Location:** I-40/75 exit 378 (Cedar Bluff Rd) eastbound; exit 378B westbound, just n. **Facility:** 175 units. 3-6 stories, interior corridors. **Terms:** 1-7 night minimum stay, cancellation fee imposed. **Pool(s):** outdoor. **Activities:** exercise room. **Guest Services:** valet and coin laundry.

AAA Benefit: Members save up to 10%!

[icons]

HILTON GARDEN INN KNOXVILLE WEST/CEDAR BLUFF   (865)690-6511   **35**

▼▼▼ **Hotel** $129-$199 **Address:** 216 Peregrine Way 37922 **Location:** I-40/75 exit 378 (Cedar Bluff Rd), just s to N Peters Rd, then just w. **Facility:** 118 units. 4 stories, interior corridors. **Terms:** 1-7 night minimum stay, cancellation fee imposed. **Pool(s):** heated indoor. **Activities:** hot tub, exercise room. **Guest Services:** valet and coin laundry.

AAA Benefit: Members save up to 10%!

[icons]

HILTON KNOXVILLE DOWNTOWN   (865)523-2300   **21**

▼▼▼ Hotel $99-$299

AAA Benefit: Members save 5% or more!

Address: 501 W Church Ave 37902 **Location:** Between Locust and Walnut sts; downtown. **Facility:** 320 units. 18 stories, interior corridors. **Parking:** on-site (fee). **Terms:** 1-7 night minimum stay, cancellation fee imposed. **Amenities:** video games, safes. **Pool(s):** outdoor. **Activities:** exercise room. **Guest Services:** valet laundry.

[icons]

HOLIDAY INN CEDAR BLUFF   (865)693-1011   **31**

▼▼▼ Hotel $109-$169

Address: 9134 Executive Park Dr 37923 **Location:** I-40/75 exit 378 (Cedar Bluff Rd) eastbound; exit 378B westbound, just n to Executive Park Dr. **Facility:** 222 units. 5 stories, interior corridors. **Terms:** cancellation fee imposed. **Pool(s):** outdoor, heated indoor. **Activities:** hot tub, exercise room. **Guest Services:** valet and coin laundry, area transportation.

[icons]

HOLIDAY INN EXPRESS KNOXVILLE-EAST   865/525-5100   **1**

▼▼▼ **Hotel.** Rates not provided. **Address:** 730 Rufus Graham Rd 37924 **Location:** I-40 exit 398 (Strawberry Plains Pike), just n. **Facility:** 77 units. 4 stories, interior corridors. **Pool(s):** heated indoor. **Activities:** exercise room. **Guest Services:** coin laundry.

[icons]

HOLIDAY INN WORLD'S FAIR PARK   865/522-2800   **20**

▼▼▼ **Hotel.** Rates not provided. **Address:** 525 Henley St 37902 **Location:** Corner of Clinch Ave; downtown. **Facility:** 286 units, some two bedrooms. 11 stories, interior corridors. **Parking:** on-site (fee). **Pool(s):** heated indoor. **Activities:** exercise room. **Guest Services:** valet and coin laundry, area transportation.

[icons]

HOMEWOOD SUITES BY HILTON   (865)777-0375   **42**

▼▼▼ **Extended Stay Hotel** $109-$199 **Address:** 10935 Turkey Dr 37922 **Location:** I-40/75 exit 374 (Lovell Rd), just s to Parkside Dr, then 0.5 mi n on Snow Goose Dr. **Facility:** 103 efficiencies, some two bedrooms. 4 stories, interior corridors. **Terms:** check-in 4 pm, 1-7 night minimum stay, cancellation fee imposed. **Pool(s):** outdoor. **Activities:** hot tub, exercise room. **Guest Services:** valet and coin laundry.

AAA Benefit: Members save up to 10%!

[icons]

LA QUINTA INN & SUITES KNOXVILLE STRAWBERRY PLAINS   (865)633-5100   **9**

▼▼ **Hotel** $64-$163 **Address:** 7210 Saddlerack St 37914 **Location:** I-40 exit 398 (Strawberry Plains Pike), just s, just e on Region Ln, then just se on Shumard Ave. **Facility:** 65 units, some two bedrooms. 3 stories, interior corridors. **Amenities:** safes. **Pool(s):** heated indoor. **Activities:** exercise room. **Guest Services:** coin laundry.

[icons]

LA QUINTA INN & SUITES PAPERMILL   (865)321-1840   **24**

▼▼▼ **Hotel** $92-$367 **Address:** 1317 Kirby Rd 37909 **Location:** I-40 exit 383 (Papermill Dr NW), just w. **Facility:** 96 units. 4 stories, interior corridors. **Pool(s):** outdoor. **Activities:** trails, limited exercise equipment. **Guest Services:** coin laundry.

[icons]

MAINSTAY SUITES KNOXVILLE   (865)247-0222   **15**

Extended Stay Hotel $79-$109

Address: 144 Merchants Dr 37912 **Location:** I-75 exit 108 (Merchants Dr), just n. **Facility:** 86 efficiencies. 5 stories, interior corridors. **Activities:** exercise room. **Guest Services:** coin laundry. **Featured Amenity:** full hot breakfast.

[icons]

Visit AAA.com/searchfordiscounts
to save on travel, shopping,
dining and attractions

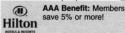

(See map & index p. 117.)

MARRIOTT KNOXVILLE HOTEL (865)637-1234 19

WWW Hotel $110-$396 Address:
500 E Hill Ave 37915 Location: I-40
exit 388A, 0.5 mi s on James White
Pkwy. Adjacent to Civic Coliseum. Facility: 378 units. 11 stories, interior cor-
ridors. Pool(s): heated outdoor. Activities: exercise room. Guest
Services: valet laundry.

AAA Benefit:
Members save 5%
or more!

QUALITY INN MERCHANTS DR (865)342-3701 12

WWW Motel $59-$79 Address: 117 Cedar Ln 37912 Location:
I-75 exit 108 (Merchants Dr), just e. Located in a commercial area.
Facility: 128 units. 3 stories, exterior corridors. Amenities: safes.
Pool(s): outdoor. Guest Services: valet and coin laundry.

RAMADA (865)690-0034 27

WWW Hotel $64-$140 Address: 7737 Kingston Pike 37919 Location: I-40/75 exit 380 (West Hills), just w. Across from West Town
Mall. Facility: 82 units. 4 stories, interior corridors. Terms: 3 day cancellation notice. Amenities: safes. Pool(s): outdoor. Activities:
sauna, limited exercise equipment. Guest Services: valet and coin
laundry.

RED ROOF INN & SUITES KNOXVILLE-EAST (865)546-5700 5

WWW Hotel $49-$119 Address: 7525 Crosswood Blvd 37924
Location: I-40 exit 398 (Strawberry Plains Pike), just n, then w. Facility: 56 units. 2 stories (no elevator), interior corridors. Pool(s):
heated indoor. Activities: exercise room. Guest Services: coin
laundry.

RED ROOF INN KNOXVILLE-UNIVERSITY OF TENNESSEE (865)691-1664 32

Motel
$50-$120

Address: 209 Advantage Pl 37922 Location: I-40/75 exit 378 (Cedar Bluff
Rd), just s to N Peters Rd, then w. Facility: 110 units. 3 stories, exterior corridors. Amenities: safes.

RESIDENCE INN BY MARRIOTT KNOXVILLE CEDAR BLUFF (865)539-5339 39

WWW Extended Stay Hotel
$125-$206 Address: 215 Langley Pl
37922 Location: I-40/75 exit 378 (Cedar
Bluff Rd), just s, then 1 mi w on N Peters
Rd. Facility: 78 units, some two bed-
rooms, efficiencies and kitchens. 3 stories, interior corridors. Terms:
check-in 4 pm. Pool(s): outdoor. Activities: hot tub, exercise room.
Guest Services: valet and coin laundry.

AAA Benefit:
Members save 5%
or more!

Ask about on-the-spot
vehicle battery testing and replacement

RODEWAY INN & SUITES WEST (865)531-1900 34

WW Hotel $59-$99 Address: 208 Market Place Ln 37922 Location: I-40/75 exit 378 (Cedar Bluff Rd), just s to N Peters Rd, then
just w. Facility: 135 units. 2 stories (no elevator), interior corridors.
Pool(s): heated outdoor. Activities: hot tub, exercise room. Guest
Services: valet and coin laundry.

SPRINGHILL SUITES BY MARRIOTT KNOXVILLE AT TURKEY CREEK (865)966-8888 43

WWW Hotel $119-$197 Address:
10955 Turkey Dr 37934 Location:
I-40/75 exit 374 (Lovell Rd), just s to
Parkside Dr, then 0.5 mi n on Snow
Goose Dr. Facility: 103 units. 4 stories,
interior corridors. Terms: check-in 4 pm. Pool(s): heated indoor. Activities: exercise room. Guest Services: valet and coin laundry.

AAA Benefit:
Members save 5%
or more!

THE OLIVER HOTEL 865/521-0050

[fyi] Hotel Address: 407 Union Ave 37902 Location: Jct Market
Square; downtown. Facilities, services, and décor characterize a mid-
scale property. Newly remodeled, this historic hotel in the heart of
downtown features rooms with 300-thread-count bedding, down duvets, velvet headboards and satellite HDTVs.

WHERE TO EAT

ALTRUDA'S 865/690-6144 23

WW Italian. Casual Dining. $11-$23 AAA Inspector Notes:
Leave the chain restaurants behind and enjoy real Italian cooking at
this eatery. The garlic bread knots are delicious. The endless variety
of meats and seafood, as well as chicken and veal, is complemented
by their fresh-made tomato and cream sauces. Features: full bar.
Address: 125 N Peters Rd 37923 Location: Jct Kingston Pike; in
The Commons Center. D

BAILEY'S SPORTS GRILLE 865/531-2644

WW American. Casual Dining. $7-$20 AAA Inspector Notes:
A classic decor of dark wood paneling and ceramic steins--with a
modern American bar, where huge TV screens are tuned to sports in
every possible spot, including the restrooms. You'll find the same
mixing cultures evident on the menu; burgers, pizzas, and chicken
wings sit beside fish 'n' chips, tortilla soup, fresh-baked pretzels, nachos, baby back ribs, and Texas-style brisket. Features: full bar. Address: 250 N Seven Oaks Dr 37922 Location: I-40/75 exit 378
(Cedar Bluff Rd), 0.6 mi s, 0.8 mi w on Kingston Pike, then just s.
L D LATE

BIDA SAIGON 865/694-5999 18

WW Vietnamese. Casual Dining. $7-$12 AAA Inspector
Notes: The basic storefront on this small strip plaza restaurant
doesn't give a clue to the great flavors inside. The owner/chef sim-
mers beef bones for the flavorful beef pho and chicken for the pho ga
(chicken soup). Spring rolls overflow with minced meat, mushrooms
and shrimp. The menu is limited to the more classic comfort food
dishes. Every item is scrumptious. Features: beer only. Address:
8078 Kingston Pike, Suite 165 & 167 37919 Location: I-40/75 exit
380, just s, then 0.5 mi w; in The Plaza. L D

BUDDY'S BAR-B-Q 865/579-1747 10

W Barbecue. Quick Serve. $6-$10 AAA Inspector Notes: This
restaurant prepares great pit barbecue, including beef, ribs, chicken,
pulled pork and even a sampling of it all. Patrons can round out a
meal with sides of corn on the cob and slaw. Features: patio dining,
senior menu. Address: 4401 Chapman Hwy 37920 Location: 3.5 mi
s. L D

BUDDY'S BAR-B-Q 865/588-0528 13

W Barbecue. Quick Serve. $6-$10 AAA Inspector Notes: This
restaurant prepares great pit barbecue, including beef, ribs, chicken,
pulled pork and even a sampling of it all. Patrons can round out a
meal with sides of corn on the cob and slaw. Address: 5806
Kingston Pike 37919 Location: I-40/75 exit 380 (West Hills), just w.
L D

(See map & index p. 117.)

CALHOUN'S ON THE RIVER

▼▼ Regional American. Casual Dining. $9-$22 **AAA Inspector Notes:** Wrap yourself in genuine Southern hospitality from the minute you walk in the door. The decor is modern and upscale, and the service fast and friendly. The place has wonderful ribs, but it's hard to go wrong with the white bean chili either. **Bar:** full bar. L D

For additional information, visit AAA.com

LOCATIONS:

Address: 10020 Kingston Pike 37923 **Location:** I-40/75 exit 376B, 0.5 mi s on Mabry Hood Rd, then 0.3 mi e on US 11 and 70.
Phone: 865/673-3444

Address: 400 Neyland Dr 37902 **Location:** US 129 S/SR 115 S/73 S exit 386B, 1 mi s on Airport/Smoky Mts, then 2.6 mi e on SR 158.
Phone: 865/673-3355

CHESAPEAKE'S   865-673-3433 6

▼▼ Seafood. Casual Dining. $9-$40 **AAA Inspector Notes:** A popular spot among travelers and college students, this is a great place to relax and dine on an array of tasty seafood. The aroma of steamed Maine lobsters and Maryland-style crab cakes fills the nautical-themed dining room. **Features:** full bar, patio dining, Sunday brunch, happy hour. **Reservations:** suggested. **Address:** 500 Henley St 37902 **Location:** I-40 exit 388, 1 mi s, then just e.

⊟ L D 🐾

CHEZ GUEVARA   865/690-5250 17

▼▼ Mexican. Casual Dining. $9-$17 **AAA Inspector Notes:** More than 1,000 photographs of a hip-swiveling Elvis decorate the walls of this lively, funky café. Tender beef enchiladas are served with frijoles and rice, and such seafood choices as king crab, grilled salmon and varied shrimp dishes also are scrumptious. **Features:** full bar, patio dining. **Address:** 8023 Kingston Pike, Suite 4 37919 **Location:** I-40/75 exit 380 (West Hills), 0.4 mi sw on US 11 and 70; at Suburban Shopping Center. D ✂

THE CHOP HOUSE   865/531-2467

▼▼ Steak Seafood. Casual Dining. $8-$28 **AAA Inspector Notes:** Friendly servers hustle amid tables with preparations of quality meats, fresh seafood, chicken, lamb, pork and pasta. The restaurant is a popular spot for casually upscale dining. **Features:** full bar. **Address:** 9700 Kingston Pike 37922 **Location:** I-40/75 exit 378 (Cedar Bluff Rd), 1 mi s to Kingston Pike, then 2 mi w. L D

CONNORS STEAK & SEAFOOD   865/966-0933 26

▼▼▼▼
Steak
Seafood
Casual Dining
$9-$40

AAA Inspector Notes: The menu lists dry-aged steak, prime rib, New York strip, rib-eye and filet, in addition to selections of fresh seafood flown in daily from around the world. Connors offers a casual, friendly atmosphere for celebrating, gathering or catching up. **Features:** full bar, happy hour. **Reservations:** suggested. **Address:** 10915 Turkey Dr 37922 **Location:** I-40/75 exit 374 (Lovell Rd), just s to Parkside Dr, just n to Turkey Dr, then w. L D CALL ♿M

COPPER CELLAR & CUMBERLAND GRILL
                                   865/673-3411 7

▼▼ Steak Sandwiches. Casual Dining. $10-$35 **AAA Inspector Notes:** If you're in the mood for an intimate experience, the restaurant's downstairs dining room suits a refined meal of fresh fish or other seafood, prime rib or steak. For a more casual outing, head upstairs, where you'll find menu choices along the lines of distinctive appetizers, salads, sandwiches and burgers. Treat yourself to one of the homemade desserts, which are prepared daily. **Features:** full bar, Sunday brunch. **Address:** 1807 W Cumberland Ave 37916 **Location:** I-40 exit 386B (Kingston Pike), 1 mi s, then just e.

L D

COPPER CELLAR WEST   865/673-3422 16

▼▼ Steak Seafood. Casual Dining. $7-$34 **AAA Inspector Notes:** A local following frequents the casual restaurant, known for its fresh seafood , crab bisque and prime rib. A copper-topped bar, booths and lighting all contribute to the romantic, cozy atmosphere. **Features:** full bar, Sunday brunch. **Reservations:** suggested. **Address:** 7316 Kingston Pike 37919 **Location:** I-40/75 exit 380 (West Hills), just s, then 0.6 mi e on US 70. L D

EL CHICO   865/687-4242

▼▼ Tex-Mex. Casual Dining. $8-$18 **AAA Inspector Notes:** Inside and out, the decor of the popular Mexican restaurant is inviting. The menu features traditional favorites such as enchiladas, tacos, burritos and fajitas. The broad menu also lists a few American classics. **Features:** full bar. **Address:** 116 Cedar Ln 37912 **Location:** I-75 exit 108 (Merchants Dr), just e. L D CALL ♿M

GATTI'S PIZZA

▼ Pizza. Family Dining. $6-$16 **AAA Inspector Notes:** Diners find great value for the dollar at the casual eatery, where the extensive salad and pizza bar includes a variety of dessert pizzas.

L D

For additional information, visit AAA.com

LOCATIONS:

Address: 6909 Kingston Pike 37919 **Location:** I-40/75 exit 380 (West Hills), just e. **Phone:** 865/558-8899

Address: 6903 Maynardville Pike 37918 **Location:** Corner of Neal Rd and Maynardville Pike; between Crippen Rd and Fountain Valley Dr. **Phone:** 865/922-5519

GOLDEN WOK CHINESE RESTAURANT & GIFT SHOP
                                   865/633-9618 3

▼ Chinese. Casual Dining. $5-$13 **AAA Inspector Notes:** At this eatery, Chinese food is served buffet style, or can be ordered directly from the menu. The simple dining room has a relaxed feel. **Features:** beer only. **Address:** 7116 Strawberry Plains Pike 37914 **Location:** I-40 exit 398 (Strawberry Plains Pike), just s. L D

GONDOLIER ITALIAN RESTAURANT AND PIZZA
                                   865/693-0999

▼▼ Italian Pizza. Casual Dining. $6-$17 **AAA Inspector Notes:** In addition to daily specials, diners can select from a tempting variety of calzones and such standards as spaghetti, manicotti and ravioli. Servers are fast and friendly. **Features:** beer & wine. **Address:** 1063 N Cedar Bluff Rd 37932 **Location:** I-40/75 exit 378 (Cedar Bluff Rd) or 378B, 2.2 mi n. L D

GOSH ETHIOPIAN RESTAURANT   865/544-4475 9

▼▼ Ethiopian. Casual Dining. $8-$25 **AAA Inspector Notes:** Always flavorful, this food is also fun to eat! Entrées come with traditional flat bread (injera), useful when scooping up stews and sopping up every last drop. Along with lamb, beef and chicken, the cuisine typically has numerous vegetarian offerings. **Features:** beer only. **Address:** 3609 Sutherland Ave 37919 **Location:** I-40/75 exit 383 eastbound, 1.5 mi e on Papermill Dr NW, just s on Hollywood Rd, then just e; exit 386B westbound, 2.5 mi sw. D

HOLY LAND MARKET & DELI   865/525-4659 8

▼ Middle Eastern Deli. Casual Dining. $7-$15 **AAA Inspector Notes:** If you're new to dining in a deli, Walter (the owner) will make a point to welcome you! The staff is friendly and will describe all of the dishes and ingredients. You'll find standards, such as hummus and gyros, but make sure to read the specials board for delectables like lentil soup and lamb kabobs. **Address:** 3601 Sutherland Ave 37919 **Location:** I-40/75 eastbound, exit 383, 1.5 mi e on Papermill Dr NW, just s on Hollywood Rd, then just e; exit 386B westbound 2.5 mi sw.

L D CALL ♿M

LEMON GRASS THAI, HIBACHI & SUSHI BAR
                                   865/539-8059 20

▼▼ Thai Sushi. Casual Dining. $7-$12 **AAA Inspector Notes:** In a nondescript strip mall, this spot is worth seeking out. Whether you sit under the pagoda at the sushi bar, or choose a booth, the friendly owners will help you choose a tasty meal. On the menu you'll find traditional Thai favorites as well as hibachi dishes. **Features:** beer & wine. **Address:** 9117 Executive Park Dr 37923 **Location:** Jct N Cedar Bluff Rd, 0.5 mi ne; in Cedar Bluff Center. L D

LITTON'S MARKET, RESTAURANT & BAKERY
                                   865/688-0429 1

▼▼▼ Burgers Desserts. Family Dining. $12-$25 **AAA Inspector Notes:** You'll get lost in the 1950s at this upbeat restaurant, where meat coolers line a wall, a dessert cooler with baked goods abuts another, and hardwood floors recall a bygone era. Thick steaks and succulent hamburgers are prepared simply, but with good flavor and at a fair price. **Features:** beer only. **Address:** 2803 Essary Dr 37918 **Location:** I-640 exit 6, 1.3 mi n on Broadway Rd; corner of Broadway Rd and Essary Dr. L D

(See map & index p. 117.)

NAPLES ITALIAN RESTAURANT 865/584-5033 ⑫

Italian
Casual Dining
$8-$23

AAA Inspector Notes: This restaurant offers well-prepared Italian fare, served in a comfortable, casual atmosphere. Start with the Asiago olives, an unexpected treat of black olives with Asiago cheese—breaded, fried and served with a roasted red bell pepper sour cream. For an entrée try one of the seafood specials, such as scallops pan-seared with lemon-garlic butter, and served over capellini with fresh spinach and pine nuts. A nice wine selection is available. Lunch is served Tuesday through Friday. **Features:** full bar. **Address:** 5500 Kingston Pike 37909 **Location:** I-40 exit 383 (Papermill Rd), 0.3 mi s, 0.3 mi se to Northshore Dr, then 0.5 mi e. *Menu on AAA.com* L D CALL M

NIXON'S DELI 865/687-7444 ④

Deli. Quick Serve. $5-$9 **AAA Inspector Notes:** Enjoy your favorite made-to-order sandwiches including the Italian sub, steak hoagie, corned beef and pizza hoagie. Some diners may want to satisfy their hunger with a salad or a slice of pie or banana pudding. **Address:** 508 Merchants Dr 37912 **Location:** I-75 exit 108 (Merchants Dr), just s. L D

THE ORANGERY 865/588-2964 ⑪

Continental
Fine Dining
$12-$46

AAA Inspector Notes: Luxurious décor and comfortable seating add to the appeal of the dimly lit, romantic dining room. Fresh salmon made with asparagus is a shining example of the well-prepared cuisine. Blue cheese crumbles, walnuts and sweet raspberry vinaigrette garnish the house salad. On Sunday, the restaurant is only open for brunch. **Features:** full bar, Sunday brunch, happy hour. **Reservations:** suggested. **Address:** 5412 Kingston Pike 37919 **Location:** I-40/75 exit 383 (Papermill Rd), follow Northshore Dr, 0.4 mi s to US 11 and 70, then 0.5 mi ne. L D

PARKSIDE GRILL 865/862-5358 ㉔

American. Casual Dining. $9-$25 **AAA Inspector Notes:** Choose from a variety of menu options in this casual tavern with stonework accents and dark wood trim. From some tables you can watch as chefs work behind the glass window preparing some of the favorite tavern classics: specialty salads, burgers, steaks, seafood and more. This is the sister restaurant to Riverside Tavern. **Features:** full bar. **Reservations:** suggested. **Address:** 338 N Peters Rd 37923 **Location:** I-40/75 exit 378 (Cedar Bluff Rd), just s, then just w. L D

P.F. CHANG'S CHINA BISTRO 865/212-5514 ⑮

Chinese. Fine Dining. $8-$25 **AAA Inspector Notes:** Trendy, upscale decor provides a pleasant backdrop for New Age Chinese dining. Appetizers, soups and salads are a meal by themselves. Vegetarian plates and sides, noodles, chow meins, chicken and meat dishes are created from exotic, fresh ingredients. **Features:** full bar. **Address:** 6741 Kingston Pike 37919 **Location:** Corner of Kingston Pike and Papermill Rd. L D

PULEO'S GRILLE 865/673-9101

American. Casual Dining. $8-$25 **AAA Inspector Notes:** If you crave Prime cut steaks, Italian specialties or Southern comfort foods, look no further. An extensive menu includes many favorites, such as maple-glazed pork chops with sweet potatoes and kale greens. **Features:** full bar. **Address:** 7224 Region Ln 37914 **Location:** I-40 exit 398 (Strawberry Plains Pike), just s. L D CALL M

PULEO'S GRILLE 865/691-1960 ㉒

American. Casual Dining. $8-$25 **AAA Inspector Notes:** If it's Prime-cut steaks, Italian specialties or Southern comfort foods you crave, look no further. An extensive menu includes many favorites such as maple-glazed pork chops with sweet potatoes and kale greens. **Features:** full bar, Sunday brunch. **Address:** 260 N Peters Rd 37922 **Location:** I-40/75 exit 378 (Cedar Bluff Rd), just s to N Peters Rd, then e. L D CALL M

RITA'S BAKERY 865/688-5484 ②

Breads/Pastries. Quick Serve. $1-$28 **AAA Inspector Notes:** This local bakery has been a family-owned business for more than 15 years. There are delicious brownies, cookies, fruit and custard pies as well as specialty sheet cakes and 10 different cheesecakes. The sticky buns are the best I have ever tasted—pair with a cup of hot coffee to complete the experience. **Address:** 3023 Tazewell Pike 37918 **Location:** Jct Tazewell Pike and Jacksboro Pike NE (SR 331). B L

S & S CAFETERIA 865/584-5191

Southern Comfort Food. Cafeteria. $4-$10 **AAA Inspector Notes:** A longtime favorite for comfort food, the family-owned cafeteria invites diners to load a plate with traditionally prepared chicken, beef, vegetables, salad and dessert. **Address:** 4808 Kingston Pike 37919 **Location:** Jct US 70 and 11, 0.4 mi w. L D

SMOKY MOUNTAIN BREWERY & RESTAURANT 865/288-5500

Steak Wings. Gastropub. $8-$25 **AAA Inspector Notes:** Handcrafted Tennessee microbrews pair with choices such as wild naked wings, old-fashioned griddle-cooked burgers, appetizers, salads and sandwiches at this family-friendly restaurant. Big-screen TVs allow you to watch just about any possible sporting event. **Features:** full bar. **Address:** 11308 Parkside Dr 37934 **Location:** I-40/75 exit 374 (Lovell Rd), just s, then 1.4 mi n; in Turkey Creek Colonial Promenade. L D LATE CALL M

SONNY'S REAL PIT BAR-B-Q 865/692-9941

Barbecue. Family Dining. $7-$14 **AAA Inspector Notes:** Bearing the name after its founder, Floyd "Sonny" Tillman, this barbecue restaurant first opened its doors circa 1968 in Gainesville, Florida and has since spawned over 150 more throughout the Southeast. The menu is steeped in finger lickin' favorites such as ribs, pulled pork, beef brisket, burgers, catfish, shrimp and char-grilled chicken. Let's not forget about the fried okra, which is the perfect starter dish, and their homemade baked beans. **Features:** beer only. **Address:** 350 N Peters Rd 37922 **Location:** I-40/75 exit 378 (Cedar Bluff Rd), just s to N Peters Rd, then w. L D

SULLIVAN'S FINE FOODS 865/694-9696 ㉕

American. Casual Dining. $8-$20 **AAA Inspector Notes:** This trendy family dining spot is housed in a modern building near a shopping area. Creative cuisine at this casual eatery includes such dishes as Caribbean chicken, Southwestern entrées, pasta and seafood. **Features:** full bar, patio dining. **Address:** 7545 Northshore Dr 37919 **Location:** I-40/75 exit 383, just sw on Papermill Rd, then 3 mi s; at Rocky Hill Shopping Center. L D

SURIN OF THAILAND 865/330-0007 ⑭

Thai Sushi. Casual Dining. $10-$24 **AAA Inspector Notes:** One can find traditional Thai favorites such as pad Thai and tom yum soup, but for the more adventurous, try the roasted shrimp and scallops with asparagus made with chili sauce or the sea bass! The setting is intimate, with canopies of bamboo alongside a huge Buddha. A sushi menu is half off after 5:30 p.m. **Features:** full bar, patio dining. **Address:** 6213 Kingston Pike 37919 **Location:** I-40 exit 383 (Weisgarber Rd), 1 mi s, then just w; north side of Kingston Pike. L D CALL M

TASTE OF THAI 865/691-4442 ㉑

Thai. Casual Dining. $8-$17 **AAA Inspector Notes:** Here you'll find all the favorites: steamed dumplings, fresh rolls, tom yum soup, pad thai and cashew chicken among other tasty curries. This newer restaurant is tucked away between Best Buy and Lowe's. **Features:** full bar, patio dining, Sunday brunch. **Address:** 8926 Town and Country Cir 37923 **Location:** I-40/75 exit 378 (Cedar Bluff Rd), just s to N Peters Rd, 1 mi e, then just n. L D CALL M

TUPELO HONEY CAFE 865/522-0004 ⑤

New Southern. Casual Dining. $8-$18 **AAA Inspector Notes:** Traditional Lowcountry favorites such as fried green tomatoes and shrimp and grits are served in heaping portions. The menu always features twists on Southern staples, such as the nutty fried chicken served with smashed sweet potatoes, asparagus and a side of goat cheese grits. **Features:** full bar, patio dining. **Address:** 1 Market Sq 37902 **Location:** Jct Union Ave; downtown; adjacent to The Oliver Hotel. **Parking:** street only. B L D

(See map & index p. 117.)

VIET TASTE   865/249-8424   (27)

♦♦♦ Vietnamese. Casual Dining. $7-$12 **AAA Inspector Notes:** If you've never tried this cuisine, the folks at this place will walk you through the menu. For others in the know, anything you choose from the healthy "street food" menu (try the pho, bún or bánh mì) will be sure to please. **Features:** beer only. **Address:** 213 N Peters Rd 37923 **Location:** I-40 exit 378 (Cedar Bluff Rd), just s, then just w on N Peters Rd; in Dick's Sporting Goods Center.

[L] [D] CALL [⑤M]

WOODLANDS   865/670-2878   (19)

♦♦♦ Indian. Casual Dining. $9-$16 **AAA Inspector Notes:** A nice variety of Indian and Indonesian specialties are cooked to perfection using just the right amount of spice. Numerous vegetarian dishes are offered and all of the proteins are halal. A buffet is a huge draw for the lunchtime crowds. Dosa specials are offered on Tuesday. **Features:** beer only. **Address:** 8520 Kingston Pike 37919 **Location:** I-40 exit 379A, just e, then just s. [L] [D]

KODAK

- **Hotels & Restaurants map & index p. 84**
- **Part of Great Smoky Mountains National Park area — see map p. 97**

COMFORT SUITES INTERSTATE   (865)933-3131   (75)

♦♦♦ Hotel $69-$149 **Address:** 161 W Dumplin Valley Rd 37764 **Location:** I-40 exit 407, just s, then 0.3 mi w on Winfield Dunn Pkwy. **Facility:** 74 units. 4 stories, interior corridors. **Pool(s):** heated indoor. **Activities:** hot tub, exercise room. **Guest Services:** valet and coin laundry.

[⑪] CALL [⑤M] [≈] [BIZ] [HS] [⑨] [✕] [▮] [▤] [▰]

FAIRFIELD INN & SUITES BY MARRIOTT SEVIERVILLE KODAK   (865)933-3033   (73)

♦♦♦ Hotel $97-$160 **Address:** 3620 Outdoor Sportsman Pl 37764 **Location:** I-40 exit 407, just n, then w on Bass Pro Dr. **Facility:** 91 units. 4 stories, interior corridors. **Pool(s):** heated indoor. **Activities:** hot tub, exercise room. **Guest Services:** valet and coin laundry.

AAA Benefit: Members save 5% or more!

[⬛] [⑪] CALL [⑤M] [≈] [BIZ] [HS] [⑨] [✕] [▰] / SOME UNITS [▮] [▤]

HAMPTON INN & SUITES-SEVIERVILLE AT STADIUM DRIVE   (865)465-0590   (72)

♦♦♦ Hotel $109-$219 **Address:** 105 Stadium Dr 37764 **Location:** I-40 exit 407, just n. Next to Stadium Park. **Facility:** 87 units. 4 stories, interior corridors. **Terms:** 1-7 night minimum stay, cancellation fee imposed. **Pool(s):** outdoor. **Activities:** exercise room. **Guest Services:** coin laundry.

AAA Benefit: Members save up to 10%!

[⑪] CALL [⑤M] [≈] [BIZ] [HS] [⑨] [✕] [🎬] [▮] [▤] [▰]

HOLIDAY INN EXPRESS & SUITES-SEVIERVILLE/KODAK   865/933-0087   (74)

♦♦♦ Hotel. Rates not provided. **Address:** 3526 Outdoor World Dr 37764 **Location:** I-40 exit 407, just n, then w on Bass Pro Dr. **Facility:** 91 units. 4 stories, interior corridors. **Pool(s):** heated indoor. **Activities:** exercise room. **Guest Services:** valet and coin laundry.

[⬛] [⑪] CALL [⑤M] [≈] [BIZ] [HS] [⑨] [✕] [▮] [▤] [▰]

Keep your focus safely on the road when driving

THE CHOP HOUSE   865/932-5198

♦♦♦ Steak Seafood. Casual Dining. $10-$34 **AAA Inspector Notes:** Friendly servers hustle amid tables with preparations of quality aged meats, fresh chicken, lamb, pork and pasta. The restaurant is a popular spot for casually upscale dining. **Features:** full bar, patio dining. **Address:** 3609 Outdoor Sportsman Pl 37764 **Location:** I-40 exit 407, just n, then just w; in Bass Pro Shopping Center. [L] [D]

UNCLE BUCK'S GRILL   865/932-5500   (44)

♦♦♦ American. Casual Dining. $10-$30 **AAA Inspector Notes:** The boathouse theme and colorful wall-size aquarium would have you think you're right at the ocean; but, this fresh seafood restaurant is set inside a large Bass Pro Shop at the edge of the Smoky Mountains. Seafood of all types abounds as well as some "land" choices, including chicken, steak and ribs. **Features:** full bar, patio dining. **Address:** 3629 Outdoor Sportsman Pl 37764 **Location:** I-40 exit 407, just n to E Dumplin Valley Rd, then just w; in Bass Pro Shopping Center. [L] [D] CALL [⑤M]

LAND BETWEEN THE LAKES NATIONAL RECREATION AREA (B-3)

Between Barkley and Kentucky lakes in western Kentucky and Tennessee, Land Between The Lakes National Recreation Area can be reached from I-24W exit 31 by taking SR 453 south to Woodlands Trace National Scenic Byway and following signs. The 170,000-acre wooded peninsula is managed by the USDA Forest Service.

More than 200 miles of hiking, mountain biking and horseback riding trails lead to points of natural and historic interest. Dozens of elk and bison roam a 700-acre restored prairie in the Kentucky portion of the area. Fishing, boating, camping, picnicking and hunting are popular activities. The Turkey Bay Off Highway Vehicle Area offers 100 miles of designated trails.

The recreation area is served by three visitor centers. The North Welcome Station, near Grand Rivers, and the South Welcome Station, near Dover, Tenn., provide visitor information, including trail maps. The Golden Pond Visitor Center, centrally located at Woodlands Trace and US 68/SR 80, has visitor information and maps, interpretive displays, audiovisual orientation programs and a planetarium *(see attraction listing)*.

The recreation area is accessible daily 24 hours. The North and South welcome stations are open daily 9-5, Apr.-Oct.; Wed.-Sun. 9-5 in Mar. and Nov. The Golden Pond Visitor Center is open daily 9-5. Closed Jan. 1, Thanksgiving and Christmas. Some activities free. For additional information phone (270) 924-2000 or (800) 525-7077. *See Recreation Areas Chart.*

ELK & BISON PRAIRIE is 1 mi. n. on Woodlands Trace National Scenic Byway from jct. US 68/SR 80. This 700-acre area re-creates the vast prairie that existed here 200 years ago. By prescribed burns and reintroducing plant and animal species that once thrived in the area, the grassland habitat is slowly being reestablished.

Bison, elk, wild turkeys, rabbits, raccoons, hawks, owls and songbirds can be seen. A 3.5-mile paved loop road allows guests to see the prairie from their car and visit interactive interpretive stops. **Time:** Allow 30 minutes minimum. **Hours:** Daily dawn-dusk. **Cost:** $5 per private vehicle. **Phone:** (270) 924-2000 or (800) 525-7077.

GOLDEN POND PLANETARIUM, in the Golden Pond Visitor Center, at the jct. of Woodlands Trace National Scenic Byway and US 68/SR 80, presents shows on a 40-foot-diameter dome screen. An observatory has telescopes available for stargazing June through August. **Time:** Allow 1 hour minimum. **Hours:** Shows daily at 10, noon, 1, 2, 3 and 4. Evening show hours vary; phone ahead to confirm schedule. Visitor Center daily 9-5. Closed Jan. 1, Thanksgiving and Christmas. **Cost:** $5; $3 (ages 5-12). **Phone:** (270) 924-2233 or (800) 525-7077.

THE HOMEPLACE, 15 mi. s. on Woodland Trace National Scenic Byway from jct. US 68/SR 80, re-creates the lifestyle and farming practices of a mid-1800s family living between the Cumberland and Tennessee rivers. Interpreters dressed in period clothing talk with guests and perform daily activities. Buildings include 16 restored log structures, some relocated from the surrounding area. The interpretive center has an audiovisual presentation and exhibits about farm life. Special events, programs and festivals are held throughout the season.

   Time: Allow 1 hour minimum. **Hours:** Daily 10-5, Apr.-Oct.; Wed.-Sun. 10-5 in Mar. and Nov. Last admission 1 hour before closing. **Cost:** $5; $3 (ages 5-12). **Phone:** (270) 924-2000 or (800) 525-7077.

WOODLANDS NATURE STATION, n. on Woodlands Trace National Scenic Byway, then e. on Mulberry Flat Rd. following signs, has live animal exhibits, seasonal canoe and kayak rentals, trails and interpretive programming. The Nature Station, within the 5,000-acre Woodlands Nature Watch Area on Lake Barkley, enables visitors to observe wildlife in a natural setting. Special events, programs and festivals are offered weekends March through November, and bald eagle viewing excursions are available during the winter.

   Time: Allow 1 hour minimum. **Hours:** Daily 10-5, Apr.-Oct.; Wed.-Sun. 10-5 in Mar. and Nov. Closed Thanksgiving. **Cost:** $5; $3 (ages 5-12). **Phone:** (270) 924-2000 or (800) 525-7077.

LA VERGNE pop. 32,588
• Hotels & Restaurants map & index p. 200

QUALITY INN & SUITES   (615)793-9999   **59**
▼▼▼ Hotel $79-$129 **Address:** 110 Enterprise Blvd 37086 **Location:** I-24 exit 64, just e. Located in a busy commercial area. **Facility:** 54 units. 3 stories, interior corridors. **Pool(s):** heated indoor. **Activities:** exercise room. **Guest Services:** coin laundry.

LAWRENCEBURG pop. 10,428

AMERICAS BEST VALUE INN   (931)762-4467
▼▼ **Motel** $70-$80 **Address:** 1940 N Locust Ave 38464 **Location:** Jct US 43 and 64, 1.6 mi n. **Facility:** 50 units. 2 stories (no elevator), exterior corridors. **Terms:** cancellation fee imposed. **Guest Services:** coin laundry.

RICHLAND INN   931/762-0061
▼▼ **Motel.** Rates not provided. **Address:** 2125 N Locust Ave 38464 **Location:** On US 43, 2.3 mi n of jct US 64. **Facility:** 55 units. 2 stories (no elevator), interior/exterior corridors. **Parking:** winter plug-ins. **Guest Services:** valet laundry.

WHERE TO EAT

DAVID CROCKETT STATE PARK RESTAURANT   931/762-9541
▼ Southern American. Family Dining. $7-$15 **AAA Inspector Notes:** After exploring the lush park surroundings, you can look forward to country home cooking and Southern hospitality. Regulars drive in from near and far just for the rotating buffet offerings. Don't miss the crispy, warm apple cobbler. Vaulted ceilings and panoramic windows surround the dining room, bringing the outdoors in. **Features:** Sunday brunch. **Address:** 1400 W Gaines St 38464 **Location:** 1.4 mi w, jct US 64 (Gaines St) and 43 (Locust St), 2.4 mi n into park. L D CALL 🅶🅼

LEBANON pop. 26,190
• Hotels & Restaurants map & index p. 200

COMFORT SUITES   (615)443-0027
▼▼▼ Hotel $75-$160 **Address:** 904 Murfreesboro Rd 37090 **Location:** I-40 exit 238, just s. **Facility:** 87 units. 3 stories, interior corridors. **Pool(s):** heated indoor. **Activities:** sauna, hot tub, limited exercise equipment. **Guest Services:** valet and coin laundry.

ECONO LODGE   (615)444-1001
▼▼ **Motel** $55-$95 **Address:** 829 S Cumberland St 37087 **Location:** I-40 exit 238, just n. **Facility:** 76 units. 2 stories (no elevator), exterior corridors. **Pool(s):** outdoor. **Activities:** sauna, exercise room. **Guest Services:** valet and coin laundry.

HAMPTON INN & SUITES   (615)444-3445
▼▼▼ Hotel $119-$209 **Address:** 1065 Franklin Rd 37090 **Location:** I-40 exit 236 (S Hartman Dr), 0.4 mi n. **Facility:** 80 units. 4 stories, interior corridors. **Terms:** 1-7 night minimum stay, cancellation fee imposed. **Pool(s):** outdoor. **Activities:** exercise room. **Guest Services:** complimentary and valet laundry.

AAA Benefit: Members save up to 10%!

HOLIDAY INN EXPRESS HOTEL & SUITES   (615)994-3225
▼▼▼ Hotel $129-$149 **Address:** 826 S Cumberland St 37087 **Location:** I-40 exit 238, just n. **Facility:** 87 units. 5 stories, interior corridors. **Terms:** resort fee. **Pool(s):** heated indoor. **Activities:** exercise room. **Guest Services:** valet and coin laundry.

SLEEP INN & SUITES-LEBANON/NASHVILLE   (615)449-7005   **45**
▼▼ Hotel $74-$139 **Address:** 150 S Eastgate Ct 37090 **Location:** I-40 exit 232, just n. **Facility:** 73 units. 3 stories, interior corridors. **Amenities:** safes. **Pool(s):** heated indoor. **Activities:** picnic facilities, exercise room. **Guest Services:** valet and coin laundry.

(See map & index p. 200.)

WHERE TO EAT

DEMOS' STEAK & SPAGHETTI HOUSE   615/443-4600
⬙⬙ American. Family Dining. $6-$18 **AAA Inspector Notes:** This family-owned and -operated eatery offers well prepared traditional fare as well as specialties such as Mexican spaghetti. The cuisine is made from scratch. The atmosphere and service are casual and relaxed. **Features:** full bar. **Address:** 130 Legends Dr 37087 **Location:** I-40 exit 238, 0.3 mi n, then just e. L D CALL ⬙M

LENOIR CITY (D-7) pop. 8,642, elev. 798'

Lenoir City is named after William Lenoir who participated in the Battle of Kings Mountain, a decisive victory for Colonial troops during the Revolutionary War. Later awarded the rank of general, he also served as speaker of the North Carolina senate and as a member of its state convention, which rejected the United States Constitution in 1788 but then ratified it the following year.

As an award for his military service, Lenoir received from the state of North Carolina a tract of land that is now present-day Lenoir City. In 1810 his son William Ballard Lenoir moved there. The city's name also commemorates the younger Lenoir for his political and commercial contributions to the locale.

Loudon County Visitors Bureau: 1075 US 321N, Lenoir City, TN 37771. **Phone:** (865) 986-6822.

Self-guiding tours: Brochures detailing a walking tour of important sites and buildings within the downtown district can be obtained at the visitor bureau. Pamphlets also are available at the Lenoir City Museum, which is housed in a Victorian cottage at 110 Depot St. Guided tours also are available by appointment; phone (865) 986-9169 or (865) 693-3664.

COMFORT INN   (865)988-8880
⬙⬙⬙ Hotel $89-$119 **Address:** 150 Interchange Park Ln 37772 **Location:** I-75 exit 81, just w. **Facility:** 48 units. 3 stories, interior corridors. **Pool(s):** outdoor. **Guest Services:** coin laundry.
ⓘ⫶ CALL ⬙M ⟿ BIZ 🛜 🏠 🖥 🖥 / SOME UNITS HS

DAYS INN   (865)986-2011
⬙⬙ Hotel $50-$90 **Address:** 1110 Hwy 321 N 37771 **Location:** I-75 exit 81, just e. **Facility:** 80 units. 2 stories (no elevator), exterior corridors. **Pool(s):** outdoor. **Guest Services:** coin laundry.
ⓘ⫶ ⟳ ⟿ 🛜 🖥 🖥 🖥 / SOME UNITS S⬙

ECONO LODGE   (865)986-0295
⬙⬙
Hotel
$59-$89
Address: 1211 Hwy 321 N 37771 **Location:** I-75 exit 81, just w. **Facility:** 41 units. 2 stories (no elevator), exterior corridors. **Pool(s):** outdoor. **Featured Amenity: continental breakfast.**
SAVE ⓘ⫶ ⟿ 🛜 🖥 🖥
/ SOME UNITS S⬙

HAMPTON INN KNOXVILLE/LENOIR CITY   (865)988-2000
⬙⬙⬙ Hotel $99-$159 **Address:** 585 Fort Loudon Medical Center Dr 37772 **Location:** I-75 exit 81, just e. Next to a hospital. **Facility:** 81 units. 4 stories, interior corridors. **Terms:** 1-7 night minimum stay, cancellation fee imposed. **Pool(s):** outdoor. **Activities:** exercise room. **Guest Services:** valet laundry.

> **AAA Benefit:**
> Members save up to 10%!

🖥 ⓘ⫶ CALL ⬙M ⟿ BIZ HS 🛜 ❌ 🎥 🖥
🖥 🖥

HOLIDAY INN EXPRESS HOTEL & SUITES   865/635-0070
⬙⬙⬙ Hotel. Rates not provided. **Address:** 1112 Hwy 321 N 37771 **Location:** I-75 exit 81, just e. **Facility:** 71 units. 3 stories, interior corridors. **Pool(s):** heated indoor. **Activities:** limited exercise equipment. **Guest Services:** valet and coin laundry.
ⓘ⫶ CALL ⬙M ⟿ BIZ HS 🛜 ❌ 🖥 🖥 🖥

WHERE TO EAT

AUBREY'S   865/986-3113
⬙⬙ American. Casual Dining. $7-$22 **AAA Inspector Notes:** Diners savor traditional Texas barbecue in a family-friendly atmosphere. On the menu are beef ribs, baby back ribs, chicken, pulled pork, beef brisket, huge hamburgers and some Tex-Mex favorites including Baja fish tacos. **Features:** full bar. **Address:** 401 E Town Center Rd 37772 **Location:** I-75 exit 81, just e; next to hospital.
L D CALL ⬙M

CALHOUN'S ON THE RIVER   865/988-9838
⬙⬙⬙ Regional American. Casual Dining. $9-$22 **AAA Inspector Notes:** Wrap yourself in genuine Southern hospitality from the minute you walk in the door. The decor is modern and upscale, and the service fast and friendly. The place has wonderful ribs, but it's hard to go wrong with the whole bean chili either. **Features:** full bar, patio dining. **Address:** 4550 City Park Dr 37772 **Location:** I-75 exit 81, 3.5 mi n to Lenoir City Park, follow signs to marina. 🖥 L D

GONDOLIER ITALIAN RESTAURANT AND PIZZA
865/986-6668
⬙⬙ Italian Pizza. Casual Dining. $7-$20 **AAA Inspector Notes:** In addition to daily specials, diners can select from a tempting variety of calzones and such standards as spaghetti, manicotti and ravioli. Servers are fast and friendly. **Features:** beer only. **Address:** 744 Hwy 321 N 37771 **Location:** I-75 exit 81, 1.3 mi e. L D

LEXINGTON pop. 7,652

DAYS INN OF LEXINGTON   (731)968-1997
⬙⬙ Motel $70-$77 **Address:** 41 W Church St 38351 **Location:** Jct SR 22, just w on US 412. **Facility:** 41 units. 2 stories (no elevator), exterior corridors. **Amenities:** safes. **Pool(s):** outdoor.
ⓘ⫶ CALL ⬙M ⟿ BIZ HS 🛜 🖥 🖥 🖥

LIMESTONE (C-8) elev. 1,388'

DAVY CROCKETT BIRTHPLACE STATE PARK, 1245 Davy Crockett Park Rd., preserves the birthplace of Davy Crockett and interprets the life of the hunter, hero, businessman and politician. The site includes a museum with exhibits; a replica log cabin near the spot where Crockett's original cabin once stood; and 105 acres with campgrounds, picnic facilities, a boat launch and a swimming pool. *See Recreation Areas Chart.*

Time: Allow 45 minutes minimum. **Hours:** Daily 8-dusk. Closed Jan. 1, Thanksgiving and Christmas. **Cost:** Park and museum free. Fees are charged for camping and other day use. **Phone:** (423) 257-2167.
🔺 ❌ 🏕

LOUDON pop. 5,381

COUNTRY INN & SUITES BY CARLSON   (865)657-0050

Hotel
$95-$130

Address: 12400 Hwy 72 N 37774 **Location:** I-75 exit 72, just e. **Facility:** 66 units. 3 stories, interior corridors. **Terms:** 3 day cancellation notice-fee imposed. **Pool(s):** heated indoor. **Activities:** hot tub, exercise room. **Guest Services:** valet and coin laundry. **Featured Amenity:** full hot breakfast.

LYNCHBURG (D-5)

Lynchburg is virtually synonymous with Jack Daniel, who built a distillery next to Cave Spring in the 1860s. Along with the well-known distillery, Miss Mary Bobo's Boarding House on Main Street has been a Lynchburg landmark since it opened in 1908. For 77 years Miss Bobo won regional acclaim for her bountiful noontime meal attended by guests such as Jack Daniel and other prominent residents. The traditional dinner is served by reservation only; phone (931) 759-7394.

Lynchburg-Moore County Welcome Center: 10 Mechanic St. P.O. Box 421, Lynchburg, TN 37352. **Phone:** (931) 759-4111.

JACK DANIEL'S DISTILLERY is at 182 Lynchburg Hwy. (SR 55). This is the nation's oldest registered distillery, dating from 1866. On hour-long guided tours, visitors can observe each step of the Tennessee whiskey-making art, including Jack Daniel's charcoal-mellowing process, originally perfected here by Mr. Jack Daniel more than a century ago. A sampling tour allows visitors to taste the final product. Portions of the distillery tour are outdoors and include walking and stairs. Visitors should wear comfortable shoes. **Hours:** Guided tours daily 9-4:30. Closed Jan. 1, Thanksgiving, Christmas Eve, Christmas and Dec. 31. **Cost:** One-hour tour free. Sampling tour $10.95 (ages 21+). **Phone:** (931) 759-6357. GT

LYNNVILLE (D-4) pop. 287, elev. 751'

Townsfolk always leave a light on for visitors in Lynnville, a small town whose 59-building historic district harks back to the days of five-and-dimes, family picnics and hometown holiday parades. Antique shops, a restored pharmacy with a 1940s soda fountain, mom-and-pop-style restaurants and a railroad depot add to the old-fashioned charm exuded here.

One of Giles County's most notable residents was Frank C. Mars, creator of the Mars candy brand. After successfully launching the Milky Way candy bar in the 1920s, Mars relocated from Chicago and established a large dairy farm named Milky Way. The farm also raised Thoroughbreds, one of which won the Kentucky Derby in 1940. An exhibit about Milky Way Farm is featured at the Lynnville Railroad Museum *(see attraction listing)*.

LYNNVILLE RAILROAD MUSEUM is at 162 Mill St. The museum is housed in a replica L&N depot and contains a collection of railroad memorabilia and a scale model railroad. Outside, visitors may tour a non-operational 1927 Baldwin 2-6-2 steam locomotive, a caboose, a flatcar and a passenger coach. One rail car features an exhibit about Milky Way Farms, founded in the 1920s by candy manufacturer Frank C. Mars. **Time:** Allow 30 minutes minimum. **Hours:** Daily 8-4. Closed major holidays. **Cost:** Donations. **Phone:** (931) 478-0880.

MANCHESTER (D-5) pop. 10,102

OLD STONE FORT STATE ARCHAEOLOGICAL PARK is off I-24 exit 110; take SR 53 1 mi. s., then Murfreesboro Hwy. (US 41) .5 mi. n.w., following signs to 732 Stone Fort Dr. The structure is a 2,000-year-old ceremonial site. Cliffs and waterfalls of two rivers have set apart a promontory on which Native Americans constructed a 1.25-mile perimeter, 50-acre enclosure consisting of long, wall-like mounds. A museum orients visitors to the mound site and its builders.

Recreational activities include hiking, fishing and golf. *See Recreation Areas Chart.* **Time:** Allow 1 hour minimum. **Hours:** Grounds daily 8-dusk. Museum daily 8-4:30. Closed Thanksgiving and Christmas. **Cost:** Free. **Phone:** (931) 723-5073.

COMFORT SUITES   (931)728-1301

Hotel $109-$139 **Address:** 152 Hospitality Blvd 37355 **Location:** I-24 exit 114, just e. **Facility:** 77 units. 4 stories, interior corridors. **Pool(s):** heated indoor. **Activities:** exercise room. **Guest Services:** valet and coin laundry.

HOLIDAY INN EXPRESS & SUITES MANCHESTER
931/728-9383

Hotel. Rates not provided. **Address:** 111 Hospitality Blvd 37355 **Location:** I-24 exit 114, just e. **Facility:** 80 units. 3 stories, interior corridors. **Terms:** check-in 4 pm. **Pool(s):** heated indoor. **Activities:** hot tub, exercise room. **Guest Services:** valet laundry.

/ SOME UNITS HS

MICROTEL INN & SUITES BY WYNDHAM MANCHESTER
(937)723-7001

Hotel $67-$250 **Address:** 201 Expressway Dr 37355 **Location:** I-24 exit 114, just w, then just n. **Facility:** 62 units. 3 stories, interior corridors. **Amenities:** safes. **Pool(s):** outdoor.

/ SOME UNITS

SLEEP INN & SUITES   (931)954-0580

Hotel
$75-$350

Address: 84 Relco Dr 37355 **Location:** I-24 exit 114, just e. **Facility:** 76 units. 3 stories, interior corridors. **Pool(s):** heated indoor. **Activities:** exercise room. **Guest Services:** valet and coin laundry. **Featured Amenity:** full hot breakfast.

 / SOME UNITS

COFFEE CAFE   931/954-0440

▼▼ American. Casual Dining. $5-$9 **AAA Inspector Notes:**
The comfortable small town atmosphere is obvious at this casual spot
as locals greet one another upon entering. Freshly ground coffee is
the signature drink along with the rotating daily hot lunch special. Also
offered are a wide variety of hot and cold sandwiches, wraps and
burgers. Dinner is an additional option Thursday-Saturday. **Features:**
Sunday brunch. **Address:** 108 W McLean St 37355 **Location:** Between Spring St and Murfreesboro Hwy; in historic downtown.
Parking: street only. [L]

POTRILLOS MEXICAN RESTAURANT   931/728-7000

▼▼ Mexican. Casual Dining. $5-$15 **AAA Inspector Notes:**
Mild or spicy is the order, and guests are encouraged to ask servers
for recommendations at this eatery. Many types of nachos, fajitas,
quesadillas and seafood dinners are available. Delicious flan or tres
leches are great choices for dessert. **Features:** beer & wine, happy
hour. **Address:** 177 Relco Dr 37355 **Location:** I-24 exit 114, 2 mi se;
in Walmart Shopping Mall. [L] [D]

RAFAEL'S PIZZERIA & ITALIAN RESTAURANT   931/728-1228

▼ Italian Pizza. Casual Dining. $5-$19 **AAA Inspector Notes:**
Family- and personal-size pizzas at this casual eatery are crafted with
homemade dough, 100-percent real cheese and fresh toppings. Other
highlights include traditional Italian pasta dishes, calzones and subs.
Features: beer only. **Address:** 2161 Hillsboro Blvd 37355 **Location:**
I-24 exit 114, 0.5 mi w; in Whispering Pines Plaza. [L] [D]

MARTIN pop. 11,473

HAMPTON INN   (731)587-5800

▼▼▼ Hotel $104-$124 **Address:**
5575 Skyhawk Pkwy 38237 **Location:**
Jct SR 22, 1.5 mi s on SR 43. **Facility:**
67 units. 3 stories, interior corridors.
Parking: winter plug-ins. **Terms:** 1-7

AAA Benefit:
Members save up to
10%!

night minimum stay, cancellation fee imposed. **Pool(s):** heated indoor. **Activities:** exercise room. **Guest Services:** valet and coin
laundry.

CALL [&M] [⇆] [BIZ] [HS] [🛜] [🎞] [▣] /SOME UNITS [🍴] [🖨]

MARYVILLE (D-7) pop. 27,465, elev. 945'
• **Part of Great Smoky Mountains National Park
area — see map p. 97**

In 1785 Scot-Irish farmers from Virginia settled
along Pistol Creek in the shadow of the Great
Smoky Mountains. The settlement was named
Maryville, after Gov. William Blount's wife, Mary,
when it became the seat of newly carved Blount
County 10 years later. Agriculture, lumber production and textile milling sustained the community
throughout the 19th century; the economy was
boosted considerably in 1914 when the Aluminum
Company of America opened a plant nearby, creating hundreds of jobs for area residents.

Maryville is home to Maryville College, a private
liberal arts school founded in 1819. The entrance to
Great Smoky Mountains National Park *(see place
listing p. 97)* is 20 miles east via US 321.

**Smoky Mountain Convention and Visitors Bu-
reau:** 201 S. Washington St., Maryville, TN 37804.
Phone: (865) 983-2241 or (800) 525-6834.

BLOUNT COUNTY HISTORICAL MUSEUM, 1006
E. Lamar Alexander Pkwy., covers Blount County
history with displays about the Civil War, agriculture
and settlement geography. A Model T Ford and a
1926 American LaFrance fire engine can be seen.

Hours: Tues.-Sat. 10-3. **Cost:** Donations. **Phone:**
(865) 454-4256. [GT]

SAM HOUSTON SCHOOLHOUSE is 2.6 mi. n.e. on
Wildwood Rd., then .4 mi. n. on Old Sam Houston
School Rd. to 3650 Sam Houston Schoolhouse Rd.
This log cabin schoolhouse was built in 1794, two
years before Tennessee became a state. Sam
Houston, later commander of the Army of Texas,
governor of Tennessee and Texas, and president of
the Republic of Texas, taught area residents here
when he was 18 years old. Displays relate to
Houston and local history. **Hours:** Tues.-Sat. 10-5,
Sun. 1-5, Feb.-Dec. Closed Thanksgiving,
Christmas Eve and Christmas. **Cost:** $3; free (ages
0-9). **Phone:** (865) 983-1550. [🏛]

LUXBURY INN & SUITES   (865)983-9839

▼ Motel $55-$159 **Address:** 805 Foothills Mall Dr 37801 **Location:** Jct US 321 (Lamar Alexander Pkwy). **Facility:** 32 units, some
two bedrooms, efficiencies and kitchens. 2 stories (no elevator), exterior corridors. **Terms:** 2-3 night minimum stay - seasonal, cancellation fee imposed. **Guest Services:** coin laundry.

[🍴] CALL [&M] [HS] [🛜] [🖥] [📷] [▣] /SOME UNITS [🍴]

AUBREY'S   865/379-8800

▼▼ Southern American. Casual Dining. $9-$26 **AAA Inspector Notes:** Diners savor traditional Texas barbecue in a family-
friendly atmosphere. On the menu are beef ribs, baby back ribs,
chicken, pulled pork, beef brisket, huge hamburgers and some
Tex-Mex favorites including Baja fish tacos. **Features:** full bar. **Address:** 909 W Lamar Alexander Pkwy 37801 **Location:** US 321 S
(Lamar Alexander Pkwy); at Foothills Mall Dr. [L] [D]

GATTI'S PIZZA   865/981-9999

▼ Pizza. Family Dining. $4-$10 **AAA Inspector Notes:** Diners
find great value for the dollar at the casual eatery, where the extensive
salad and pizza bar includes a variety of dessert pizzas. **Address:**
1616 W Broadway Ave 37801 **Location:** Corner of Foothills Mall Dr
and Broadway Ave (US 129); just s of jct US 129/411. [L] [D]

GONDOLIER ITALIAN RESTAURANT AND PIZZA
865/982-7444

▼▼ Italian Pizza. Casual Dining. $6-$13 **AAA Inspector
Notes:** In addition to daily specials, diners can select from a tempting
variety of calzones and such standards as spaghetti, manicotti and
ravioli. Servers are fast and friendly. **Features:** beer & wine. **Address:** 2632 US Hwy 411 S 37801 **Location:** Jct US 321 (Lamar Alexander Pkwy), 3 mi s on US 129/411. [L] [D] [◥]

MASON pop. 1,609
• **Part of Memphis area — see map p. 134**

BOZO'S HOT PIT BAR-B-Q   901/294-3400

▼▼ Barbecue. Casual Dining. $5-$16 **AAA Inspector Notes:**
Established in 1923, they must be doing something right here. This
barbecue restaurant features pulled pork shoulder, vinegar-based
slaw and delicious sweet baked beans—that's what the regulars
order. Numerous sauces are available to add a kick or sweetness.
Address: 342 Hwy 70 W 38049 **Location:** Downtown. [L] [D]

McKENZIE pop. 5,310

BEST WESTERN MCKENZIE (731)352-1083

Motel
$77-$84

AAA Benefit: Save 10% or more every day and earn 10% bonus points!

Address: 16180 N Highland Ave 38201 **Location:** Jct SR 22, 1 mi s on US 79. **Facility:** 27 units. 2 stories (no elevator), exterior corridors. **Parking:** winter plug-ins. **Terms:** 3 day cancellation notice-fee imposed. **Pool(s):** outdoor. **Featured Amenity:** continental breakfast.

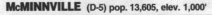

McMINNVILLE (D-5) pop. 13,605, elev. 1,000'

McMinnville was settled on an old Native American war trace between southeastern Tennessee and Kentucky. The Trail of Tears brought almost 10,000 Cherokee through the area in 1838. Native American mounds are found throughout the area. The "Birthing Tree" on the trail received its name from tales of pioneer women—members of traveling wagon trains—giving birth under its branches.

The town's W.S. "Dad" Lively Southern School of Photography, attended by students from all over the country, operated until it was destroyed by fire in 1929. The school drew considerable attention in the early 1900s for its use of a giant camera that required negative plates 60 inches long and 30 inches wide.

Lively's students need not have gone far to find interesting subjects to photograph. Magnificent scenery abounds at nearby Rock Island State Park (see Recreation Areas Chart).

McMinnville-Warren County Chamber of Commerce: 110 S. Court Sq., P.O. Box 574, McMinnville, TN 37111. **Phone:** (931) 473-6611.

CUMBERLAND CAVERNS is 6 mi. s.e. off SR 8 at 1437 Cumberland Caverns Rd. The caverns feature one of the largest cave rooms in the eastern United States. Visitors also see waterfalls, pools, a ¾-ton chandelier, a historic saltpeter mine and unusual rock formations. The scenic walking tour includes the underground light-and-sound presentation "God of the Mountain." A monthly bluegrass show is broadcast from the Volcano Chamber.

Hours: Guided 90-minute tours depart daily on the hour 9-5. Last tour begins at 5 p.m. Closed Jan. 1, Thanksgiving, Christmas Eve and Christmas. **Cost:** $19; $12 (ages 6-12); $50 (family). **Phone:** (931) 668-4396.

FALCON REST MANSION & GARDENS is 1.3 mi. n. of US 70S bypass at 2645 Faulkner Springs Rd. Tour guides relate the history of the home, a solid-brick, 10,000-square-foot Victorian mansion built in 1896 by local entrepreneur Clay Faulkner. **Time:** Allow 1 hour minimum. **Hours:** Guided tours and Victorian Tea Room daily 9-5. Closed Jan. 1, Thanksgiving, Christmas and Dec. 31. **Cost:** $12; $6 (ages 4-12). **Phone:** (931) 668-4444.

BEST WESTERN TREE CITY INN 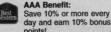 (931)473-2159

Hotel
$73-$81

AAA Benefit: Save 10% or more every day and earn 10% bonus points!

Address: 809 Sparta St 37110 **Location:** Jct US 70 S Bypass and Red Rd, 1 mi s, follow signs. **Facility:** 41 units. 2 stories (no elevator), exterior corridors. **Pool(s):** heated indoor. **Activities:** hot tub, exercise room. **Guest Services:** coin laundry. **Featured Amenity:** full hot breakfast.

Memphis

Then & Now

Beale Street at night. The garish hues of neon-lit signs. The mouthwatering scent of barbecue. The touch of a breeze off the Mississippi. But most of all the sounds, the music. The thrum of an electric guitar, visceral drum beats, a saxophone's mellow moan. And mixed in, the rich, layered tones of human voices expressing joy, sorrow or hope for something better.

Of course, the musical style most at home on Beale Street is the blues. Here in 1909 bandleader and classically trained musician W.C. Handy published one of the first and most popular blues songs, "The Memphis Blues." A statue of the Father of the Blues holding his trumpet presides over Beale Street in W.C. Handy Performance Park.

It's hard to believe that bustling Beale's historic buildings were virtually abandoned due to hard times in the 1960s and '70s. But thanks to a 1980s redevelopment project, the district is one of the city's most visited attractions. Blues legend B.B. King, who saw the rise, fall and rebirth of Beale Street, started here in the 1940s. His flagship club's massive guitar-shaped sign is topped by a golden crown—he was the King of the Blues after all.

Another of Memphis' musical royal family also holds court on Beale. A statue of a guitar-wielding, hip-thrusting Elvis Presley captures the King of Rock 'n' Roll in mid-song, eye closed, lips apart; you can almost hear adoring teenage girls screaming. Some credit him with not only popularizing rock music, but helping to invent the genre—as an unknown 19-year-old he recorded "That's All Right" in a small Memphis studio.

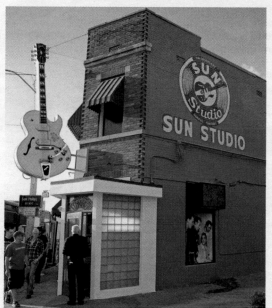

Now a museum near the Beale Street Historic District, Sun Studio is hallowed ground to Elvis fans, but it's also where music legends B.B. King, Johnny Cash, Carl Perkins and Jerry Lee Lewis began their recording careers.

What Beale Street is to blues lovers, Graceland is to King devotees. Modest by today's standards, Elvis' home is the centerpiece of a complex covering many aspects of his life, including his military service, film career and automobile collection. Tours conclude at his gravesite after visiting rooms frozen in 1977, the year of his death. And yes, the Jungle Room is as kitschy as you've heard, with green shag carpeting and Polynesian decor.

The city's contribution to American music continues at Memphis Rock 'n' Soul Museum, with its comprehensive music history exhibits. The name Stax comes up a lot in those exhibits, and for good reason. Stax Records developed the Southern Soul sound and was home to greats like Otis Redding, Isaac Hayes and Booker T. & the MGs. The Stax Museum of American Soul Music, on the

Sun Studio

(Continued on p. 135.)

Destination Memphis

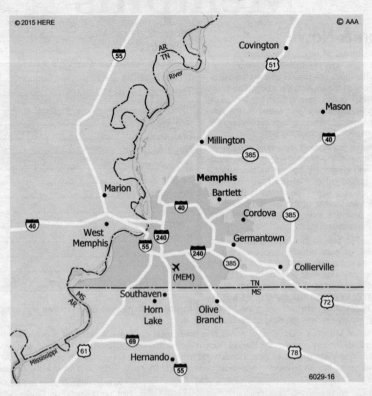

This map shows cities in the Memphis vicinity where you will find attractions, hotels and restaurants. Cities are listed alphabetically in this book on the following pages.

Fast Facts

ABOUT THE CITY

POP: 646,889 ▪ **ELEV:** 337 ft.

MONEY

SALES TAX: State sales tax is 7 percent; occupancy tax is 6 percent; and Memphis sales tax is 2.25 percent, for a combined lodging tax of 15.25 percent.

WHOM TO CALL

EMERGENCY: 911

POLICE (non-emergency): (901) 545-2677

TIME AND TEMPERATURE: (901) 526-5261

HOSPITALS: Baptist Memorial Hospital, (901) 226-5000 ▪ Delta Medical Center, (901) 410-4676 ▪ Methodist North Hospital, (901) 516-5200 ▪ Methodist South Hospital, (901) 516-3700 ▪ Regional Medical Center at Memphis, (901) 545-7100 ▪ Saint Francis Hospital, (901) 765-1000.

WHERE TO LOOK AND LISTEN

NEWSPAPERS: Memphis has two daily newspapers, *The Commercial Appeal* and *The Daily News*; one weekday-only paper, the *Evening Times*; three weeklies, *The Memphis Flyer, Memphis Business Journal* and *Tri-State Defender;* and the monthly *Memphis Key* magazine.

RADIO: Memphis radio station WKNO (91.1 FM) is a member of National Public Radio.

VISITOR INFORMATION

Memphis/Shelby County Visitors Center: 12036 Arlington Tr., Arlington, TN 38002. The center is open daily 9-6, Apr.-Sept.; 9-5, rest of year. **Phone:** (901) 543-5333 or (888) 633-9099.

Memphis Visitors Center: 3205 Elvis Presley Blvd., Memphis, TN 38116. **Phone:** (901) 543-5333 or (888) 633-9099.

The Tennessee State Welcome Center, 119 N. Riverside Dr. (at Jefferson), can provide maps, brochures, calendars of events and area attraction information; phone (901) 543-5333 or (888) 633-9099.

TRANSPORTATION

AIR TRAVEL: Domestic and foreign airlines serve Memphis International Airport (MEM), off I-240 exit 23 (Airways Boulevard). Taxis to major downtown hotels are available for about $30.

RENTAL CARS: Discounts are offered to AAA members by Hertz, (901) 345-5680 or (800) 654-3131.

RAIL SERVICE: Amtrak offers passenger service from Central Station, 545 S. Main St.; phone (901) 526-0052 or (800) 872-7245.

BUSES: The Greyhound bus station is at 3033 Airways Blvd.; phone (800) 231-2222.

TAXIS: The major company is Yellow Cab, (901) 577-7777. Fares are metered, with the basic rate $3.80 for the first mile, then $1.80 for each additional mile. One dollar is added for each additional passenger. A $3 surcharge is added to fares originating from the airport.

PUBLIC TRANSPORTATION: Memphis Area Transit Authority (MATA) buses operate Mon.-Fri. 4:30 a.m.-11:15 p.m., Sat. 5 a.m.-10 p.m., Sun. and holidays 8-6:15. Base fare is $1.75, with increases for zones outside city limits; a day pass can be purchased for $3.50, and covers unlimited bus rides. Ages 65+, students and the physically impaired pay reduced rates with a special MATA ID card. Park 'n' Ride service is available at multiple locations within the city. Not all routes operate nights and Sundays.

(Continued from p. 133.)
site of the old Stax Records building, is crammed with memorabilia from the golden age of Memphis soul music.

But Memphis' music heritage lives on outside museum display cases. Memphis in May International Festival, a month-long event beginning with the Beale Street Music Festival, draws thousands to outdoor stages on the banks of the Mississippi as international and hometown acts treat crowds to a spectrum of musical styles. Memphis in May's finale, Sunset Symphony, is a day of music and entertainment climaxing with fireworks synchronized to a performance of the Memphis Symphony Orchestra.

And the World Championship Barbecue Cooking Contest pits teams such as the Natural Born Grillers, Aporkalypse Now and The Hogfather vying to win thousands of dollars. Despite the lighthearted names, barbecue in Memphis is serious business and as much a part of the culture as the blues.

Memphis-style ribs and soul-stirring blues go well together, and several Beale Street clubs serve both. But Memphis isn't all about music. It has its share of cultural institutions like Memphis Brooks Museum of Art and The National Civil Rights Museum at the former Lorraine Motel, site of Martin Luther King's 1968 assassination, now a moving, powerful tribute to the civil rights struggles of the 20th century.

Must Do: AAA Editor's Picks

- Cut your own record at **Sun Studio,** said to be the birthplace of rock 'n' roll; this is the small, unimposing studio where a young Elvis Presley, Jerry Lee Lewis and Johnny Cash first recorded their now signature sounds.

- Shop for kitschy Elvis souvenirs at the museumlike **A. Schwab Dry Goods Store,** or just peruse everything from voodoo potions to vintage clothes; in operation at the same location on Beale since 1876, its creaky wood floors hold tables loaded with fascinating knickknacks.

- Ply the muddy waters of the Mississippi River on the *Memphis Queen*—choosing from narrated sightseeing cruises or evening cruises featuring a barbecue dinner and music—with **Sightseeing Cruises Aboard the Memphis Riverboats.**

- Catch live music in any number of clubs on legendary **Beale Street,** on which W.C. Handy, Louis Armstrong, Muddy Waters and B.B. King introduced the world to the Memphis blues. Although the city was declared "Home of the Blues" in 1977, once vibrant Beale had by then lost much of its appeal, with most of its music halls, saloons, pawnshops and stores shuttered; see why—after a 1980s makeover—it remains a Memphis focal point. Expect street performers entertaining as visitors go hopping from jazzy blues emporiums to lively rock clubs, and neon signs keep pointing to shops and cafes.

- Chow down on Memphis' famed dry ribs at the bare-bones, basement-style **Rendezvous** barbecue joint. (A heads-up: The waitstaff prides itself on being curt.) Or try a slow-cooked, hand-pulled pork sandwich (topped with coleslaw, of course) at one of the area **Corky's Ribs & BBQ** barbecue emporiums.

- Check out colorful, homespun works in the folk art gallery, examine historic photographs and attend a jazz, soul, gospel or blues concert at the **Center for Southern Folklore.**

- Pay homage to the civil rights movement and to Dr. Martin Luther King Jr. at the site of his assassination, the Lorraine Motel, and visit ▽ **The National Civil Rights Museum,** which will leave you in a contemplative mood.

- Join the pilgrims at ▽ **Elvis Presley's Graceland** for a tour of the King's retro-style **Graceland Mansion.** Check out the King's airplanes; his 1955 pink Cadillac; his flashy, custom-made clothing; view home movies; and visit his gravesite while exploring the compound.

- Learn the history of soul music at **Stax Museum of American Soul Music,** on the site of the original Stax Records, where you can see Isaac Hayes' blue '72 Cadillac, Ike Turner's Fender guitar and a century-old church from the Mississippi Delta.

- Experience the scope of Memphis' music history at the ▽ **Memphis Rock 'n' Soul Museum,** where exhibits include B.B. King's "Lucille" guitar and costumes worn by Johnny Cash and Elvis.

- Peruse paintings from the Italian Renaissance, British portraiture and Baroque, French Impressionist and contemporary collections at ▽ **Memphis Brooks Museum of Art;** the museum's 1916 Beaux Arts building in Overton Park is a work of art itself.

- Explore the history of Memphis and the Mid-South (cultural as well as natural) at ▽ **Memphis Pink Palace Museum** and become part of the action at the museum's IMAX theater and planetarium. (And, yes, the museum earns its name—its exterior is pink marble.)

- Cross a bridge or take a monorail by the riverfront to reach ▽ **Mud Island River Park;** be sure to check out the two full-size boat replicas at the **Mississippi River Museum** and the River Walk, a scale model of every curve of the Mississippi as it flows from Cairo, Ill., to the Gulf of Mexico.

- Enjoy the elaborate ceremony as the five resident ducks at the **Peabody Memphis,** one of the city's most posh hotels, take an elevator from their rooftop palace to the lobby, waddle across a red carpet to a marble fountain and float for 6 hours before repeating the process in reverse.

Pay homage at The National Civil Rights Museum

Memphis 1-day Itinerary

AAA editors suggest these activities for a great short vacation experience. Those staying in the area for a longer visit can access a 3-day itinerary at AAA.com/TravelGuide.

Morning

- Memphis is known for its music and its smoky, slow-cooked barbecue. Today's agenda, centered in the downtown area, introduces you to the city's blues and rock 'n' roll heritage and that aforementioned smoked pork.

- Begin your Memphis musical journey at the **W.C. Handy Memphis Home & Museum.** The celebrated music pioneer, the "Father of the Blues," lived in this unassuming wood-frame shotgun house when he wrote "Beale Street Blues" and "Memphis Blues."

- Derived from the mournful tunes of slaves and sharecroppers, the blues was a major influence on early rock 'n' roll musicians. The **Memphis Rock 'n' Soul Museum** traces rock from its rural Mississippi roots through rockabilly, rhythm and blues, and soul. The rock 'n' roll revolution began here when Elvis Presley recorded his first song at Sun Studio. Instruments, costumes and memorabilia document this musical genre's development.

- For a building that played such a pivotal role in rock 'n' roll history, **Sun Studio** is remarkably small. An amazing number of future stars recorded in the studio's three-rooms. In addition to Elvis, Jerry Lee Lewis, Carl Perkins, B.B. King, Johnny Cash and Roy Orbison began their careers at this landmark. Drop in for a guided tour.

Afternoon

- If you're in the mood for comfort food, head to **Blue Plate Café,** where you can indulge in the Southern tradition of "meat and three" (a meat entrée and three home-style side dishes). Or choose breakfast items; the café is renowned for its biscuits and gravy, omelets and waffles. Regardless, you won't leave hungry.

- Walk off those calories at **Gibson Guitar Factory Tours** where luthiers handcraft Gibson's acclaimed instruments. Watch artisans trim, shape, lacquer and tune a block of wood into one of the company's guitars.

- Eclectic describes the **Center for Southern Folklore.** Folk art, crafts and photography document the Southern experience, and visitors can watch shows filmed by the center about the artists and musicians who have kept these regional traditions alive.

- Memphis' musical heritage also includes soul. **Stax Museum of American Soul Music** sits on the site of the former Stax Records, which launched the careers of Isaac Hayes, Otis Redding, Wilson Pickett and Booker T. & the MG's. Displays feature costumes, instruments and photographs, including one of Tina Turner's

Grab a souvenir from A. Schwab Dry Goods Store

sequined dresses and Isaac Hayes' '72 "Superfly" Cadillac Eldorado.

- A visit to Memphis isn't complete without stopping at **A. Schwab Dry Goods Store,** a Beale Street institution since 1876. The dry goods store, still owned by the same family, retains its squeaky floors and aisles stocked with voodoo supplies, size 74 overalls, lye soap and top hats. If you rummage around, you'll also find reasonably priced Elvis souvenirs.

Evening

- Start your evening with a tradition begun in 1933. The elegant **Peabody Memphis** hotel's marble fountain is the site of a twice-daily ritual—the march of the hotel's resident ducks, who travel with their Duckmaster from their rooftop suite to the lobby, waddle across a red carpet to John Philip Sousa's "King Cotton March" and plop into the fountain where they float from 11 until 5, when the ceremony is repeated in reverse. Get there early; the ritual is wildly popular, and crowds congregate.

- For dinner sample some of Memphis' famous barbecue. The **Rendezvous'** grill has been smoking since 1948. The restaurant is known for its "dry" ribs, a Memphis specialty (pork ribs are massaged with a special blend of dry spices before being placed on the grill). The restaurant's walls are covered with memorabilia; it can be crowded; and the waiters are characters in their own right.

- For a perfect end to your evening, head to **Beale Street** or return to the Peabody for a nightcap in the hotel's classy lobby bar.

Top Picks for Kids

Under 13

- Imaginative minds will discover all sorts of fun at **The Children's Museum of Memphis** as they play in an indoor tree house, shop for groceries in a pint-sized store, watch honeybees in action and drive a sheriff's car—virtually, of course. In summer, the H2Oh! Splash Park provides plenty of opportunities to burn off extra energy.

- Young firefighters-in-training will beg for a visit to the **Fire Museum of Memphis.** Located in a historic fire house, the museum encourages children to climb on and through real fire trucks and slide down a brass fireman's pole. High-tech exhibits like a fire simulation room and an animatronic firehouse horse teach fire safety.

- Kids can run, slide and climb their way around Woodland Discovery Playground, an innovative play space within **Shelby Farms** in East Memphis. The playground includes sand play areas, a grassy lawn and giant slides and rope nets. After playtime, check out the other things to do at Shelby Farms urban park—there are miles of trails, a zipline course and even a buffalo range to explore.

- Offering much more than just plants, **Memphis Botanic Garden** features a kid-friendly zone called My Big Backyard with more than 15 themed play areas and educational activities. From tunnels and rope bridges to puppet shows and whimsical playhouses, kids and families will love playing together at this garden.

Teens

- The **Slave Haven Underground Railroad Museum** is a great experience for teens with an interest in history. Guides take visitors on a narrated tour through the antebellum home of Jacob Burkle, a German immigrant who provided refuge to runaway slaves. The home was a stop on the Underground Railroad; a hidden cellar, trap doors and an escape route reveal its remarkable past.

- Did you know Memphis is home to a guitar factory? Get a behind-the-scenes tour of the facility with **Gibson Guitar Factory Tours.** If you're lucky, you'll get to watch as luthiers—the skilled artisans who make the guitars—transform simple blocks of wood into beautiful instruments. The guided tour ends in the factory store where you can play on the finished guitars or pick one out to take home.

- Spend a few hours immersed in history at **The National Civil Rights Museum,** housed in the Lorraine Hotel where Dr. Martin Luther King, Jr. was assassinated in 1968. The museum includes interactive exhibits and a film that tells the story of the African American experience from slavery through the Civil Rights Movement. Emotional—and sometimes graphic—displays bring history to life and encourage discussion.

- The summer music concert series at **Overton Park** is well-loved by both Memphis residents and visitors. Beginning in late May, free outdoor concerts are offered Thursday through Sunday at the band shell, with shaved ice vendors and food trucks providing snacks and sweet treats. Be sure to bring a blanket and arrive early for a good seat on the lawn.

All Ages

- Lions and tigers and meerkats—oh my! The **Memphis Zoo** entertains visitors of all ages with animal shows and more than 3,500 animal residents. Hands-on opportunities include a stingray touch tank, giraffe feedings and camel rides. Be sure to visit the giant panda exhibit where "YaYa" and "Le Le" live among authentic Chinese gardens and architecture.

- No trip to Beale Street is complete without a stop at **A. Schwab.** Part general store, part soda fountain, the shop has been a Memphis institution since 1876. Tables are filled with an assortment of voodoo potions, knickknacks, t-shirts and Moon Pies, and an old-fashioned soda fountain serves up milkshakes, sundaes and made-to-order sodas.

- A good time is guaranteed when dining at **Huey's Downtown,** where patrons are allowed (and encouraged!) to blow frilled toothpicks through a straw into the ceiling while they wait. Ask your server to demonstrate their best toothpick-shootin' technique, then nosh on tasty burgers, onion rings, fried pickles and other favorites.

Enjoy the fresh scent of flowers at Memphis Botanic Garden

Arriving
By Car

Except for the downtown business core flanking the river, Memphis is circled by a controlled-access highway, I-240, which intersects with all major approach routes. I-40 is the primary east-west route, linking Memphis with Jackson and Nashville to the east and Little Rock and Fort Smith, Ark., and Oklahoma City to the west. As a bypass it runs convergent with I-240 around the northern edge of the metropolitan area, intersecting with Austin Peay Highway (SR 14) from the northeast and Danny Thomas Boulevard (US 51) from the north.

A freeway extension of the eastern portion of I-40 penetrates inside the I-240 loop as far as Highland Avenue, where it is shunted over to Summer Avenue (US 64/70/79) for a straight westward run toward downtown. On the west, I-40 interchanges with Arkansas-Riverside Drive, Second Street, Third Street and Front Street, the most direct entrances to the downtown area.

The major north-south corridor is I-55. From Jackson, Miss., and other points south it connects with the western leg of I-240, loops around the southwest part of the city and then, having picked up US 61, veers west at an interchange with E.H. Crump Boulevard. From St. Louis and points north, I-55 runs southward along the west bank of the Mississippi River, absorbing US 63 traffic from the northwest.

At West Memphis, Ark., I-55 joins briefly with I-40 before the two divide again to cross the Mississippi and circumnavigate Memphis. US 61 brings light traffic through the southern countryside from Vicksburg, Miss., and US 51 repeats the leisurely pace from Kentucky on the north.

The only other major approach routes are US 72 and US 78. The former provides access from Huntsville and Florence, Ala., angling into the heart of the city via Poplar Avenue. US 78 from Birmingham and Tupelo, Miss., enters Memphis as Lamar Avenue. It interchanges twice with I-240—once at the circumferential highway's southern segment and again on the western leg at E.H. Crump Boulevard.

Getting Around
Street System

As did nearly every facet of the city, Memphis' street plan developed with the river as a focus. Streets form a compass-oriented grid, running parallel or perpendicular to the Mississippi. Major arterials follow a more or less diagonal course as they radiate from the downtown business section.

Except for downtown, where Front, Main and Second through Seventh streets (all parallel to the Mississippi River) march inland, most streets and avenues are named. Although Madison divides north from south and Main and Florida separate east from west, compass designations are rarely used in Memphis addresses.

Unless posted otherwise, the downtown speed limit is 25 mph. The speed limit is 35 mph on major thoroughfares. Turning right at a red light after

Gibson Beale Street Showcase Retail Center

coming to a complete stop is legal unless otherwise posted. Similarly, so is turning left from one one-way street onto another. Pedestrians always have the right-of-way, particularly at marked crosswalks. Driving during rush hours, 6:30-9 a.m. and 4-6:30 p.m., should be avoided if possible.

Parking

As in any big city, parking downtown or near the major attractions is often at a premium. On-street parking, when a space can be found, is governed by meters. Commercial garages and parking lots are scattered throughout downtown. Rates average $2-$4 per hour, $7-$15 for all day.

Shopping

Beale Street, with its raucous blues clubs and brilliant neon signs, is the heart of downtown Memphis' tourist district and the place to go for Blues City T-shirts, Elvis refrigerator magnets and postcards of Graceland and the Peabody Memphis hotel. First-time visitors may be surprised at how compact the district is—it's really just a couple blocks along Beale—so you could conceivably hit all the stores here within a single afternoon. But first on your list should be **A. Schwab Dry Goods Store,** a Beale Street institution since 1876.

Yes, they have Memphis souvenirs here. They also have just about anything else you can imagine: sun hats, calendars, clothing, coffee mugs, shampoo, collectible figurines and other knickknacks, Elvis biographies, toys, costume jewelry, candy, hardware, tools and even some voodoo paraphernalia. On the second floor, there's a museum of sorts where you can handle antique items from the old-fashioned general store's past, including ancient-looking adding machines, mysterious iron kitchen gadgets, photos, ledgers and high school yearbooks. Just 5 minutes of sensory overload here and you'll know why the store's motto is, "If you can't find it at A. Schwab, you're better off without it!"

Other shops on Beale worth noting: **Tater Red's** under the neon sign of a skull with hypnotic eyes wearing a top hat. This purveyor of lucky mojos and voodoo dolls will also sell you signed photographs of blues and rock 'n' roll stars and an array of other music collectibles in addition to souvenirs emblazoned with the creepy cartoon image of the store's death's-head logo.

Strange Cargo, across the street, has novelty items, some of which are on the risqué side, while nearby **Memphis Music** specializes in blues recordings and music-themed gifts. For rock 'n' roll merchandise, head to [SAVE] **Hard Rock Cafe** at 126 Beale. A block south of Beale is the **Gibson Beale Street Showcase Retail Center** at the Gibson Guitar Factory *(see attraction listing p. 151),* a fun place to browse if you're in the market for a new guitar or just enjoy looking at the beautifully crafted instruments.

Head a few blocks north to the historic Peabody Memphis hotel to check out the elegantly appointed lobby—famous for its twice daily duck parade to and from the centerpiece marble fountain—and the Peabody's upscale gift shops and clothing stores. Foremost among these is another Memphis institution: **Lansky Brothers,** a men's clothier since the late 1940s known for its famous clientèle, which has included Elvis Presley as well as Johnny Cash, B.B. King, Isaac Hayes and Jerry Lee Lewis among

Grab a bite at the Arcade Restaurant

others. Even if the prices are out of your range, the wall-mounted guitars autographed by various recording stars are worth a look in their own right.

Memphis' historic commercial district along **Main Street** has struggled for a long time, and the smattering of clothing stores, art galleries and furniture stores does not exactly qualify the district as a shopping mecca, but getting around couldn't be easier thanks to the historic trolleys running up and down its length. Adding to this pleasant environment: the street is closed to car traffic between Market Street and Union Avenue, and the early 20th-century buildings are well maintained and many have lovely, ornate facades.

One local favorite on Main Street is **The Peanut Shoppe,** a tiny store that's hard to miss thanks to its 2-story-high "Peanuts" sign in the shape of an arrow pointing to its front door. The clerks here will explain the health benefits associated with each kind of nut (their selection is in no way limited to just peanuts), but for candy lovers, they also have an assortment of caramel- and chocolate-covered nuts as well. Munching on a bag of fresh roasted pecans while strolling through this pedestrian-friendly district is a great way to experience downtown Memphis once you've seen the sights along Beale Street.

At the southern end of the trolley line near The National Civil Rights Museum *(see attraction listing p. 150),* you'll find what's become known in recent years as the **South Main Street Arts District.** Art galleries, trendy clothing boutiques featuring local designers and shops selling hand-crafted jewelry give the district a more urban, sophisticated vibe than you'll experience elsewhere on Main Street. Coffee shops offer a quick cup of your favorite blend or if you have time for a sit-down meal, check out the **Arcade Restaurant** at the corner of Main and G.E. Patterson, Memphis' oldest café, serving Southern home cooking since 1919.

Housed in a pyramid-shaped building just north of downtown, **Bass Pro Shops at the Pyramid** is a sprawling complex featuring an 84,000-gallon alligator swamp, duck aviary, waterfowling museum, bowling alley and a glass-floored observation deck.

If you venture outside of downtown, the **Cooper-Young** neighborhood in **Midtown** just a few miles east of the city center is known for antiques and secondhand clothing shops. Most of the antique stores are along Central Avenue between Cooper Street and East Parkway, a stretch of busy four-lane road not at all inviting to pedestrians. On one side of Central is **Market Central Antiques and Gardens,** a large warehouse divided into dozens of display spaces filled with tasteful arrangements of high-end antiques and galleries showcasing local artists. While you probably won't be shopping for massive water features while in town, the fountain showroom at Water Works next door is a fun place to wander through just to see the huge variety of bubbling, splashing waterfalls and basins for sale.

Across Central Avenue and down a couple blocks toward East Parkway is **Flashback,** a large store specializing in 1950s-era housewares, knickknacks and furniture with a small area for vintage clothing off to one side. You'll find several styles and decades represented here, but mid-century modern rules, so if you're in the market for a kidney-shaped coffee table, a starburst wall clock or a chrome dinette, this is the place to go.

The epicenter of the Cooper-Young District—no surprise here—is the intersection of Cooper Street and Young Avenue a couple blocks south of Central. With trees, Victorian houses, narrower streets and crosswalks, this part of the district offers a more pedestrian-friendly environment, so you'll find it easier (not to mention less hazardous) to browse among the locally owned shops selling used records, used books and funky clothing. The area's also known for its coffee houses and trendy restaurants where you can pause to take stock of your purchases.

Just east of Midtown in the area known as **East Memphis,** two shopping centers worth noting face each other across busy Poplar Avenue. **Oak Court Mall** is anchored by Macy's and Dillard's, while **Laurelwood Shopping Center** features high-end clothing boutiques, art and interior design galleries, jewelry stores, a stationery shop and **The Booksellers at Laurelwood,** an independent book store.

If you continue east on Poplar Avenue, you'll come across a retail landmark of sorts in the Memphis suburb of **Germantown. The Shops of Saddle Creek,** at Poplar and West Street/West Farmington Boulevard, was one of the first lifestyle shopping centers—typified by open-air plazas and immaculate landscaped areas connecting stores rather than enclosed corridors—when it was built in 1987. Burbling fountains and a thick tree canopy provide a lovely setting for the trendy, upscale shops that include Free People, J. Crew, Madewell, Lucky Brand Jeans and Talbots.

Nightlife

Since an act of Congress in 1977, Memphis has officially been known as the "Home of the Blues," and **Beale Street** has been the cherished front door of that home from the beginning, when musical pioneers such as W.C. Handy composed some of the earliest blues songs here in the early 1900s. Originally a bustling commercial district with African-American-owned businesses of all kinds, Beale Street fell on hard times until a 1980s revitalization project created the neon-lit, tourist-friendly and some would say sanitized version of today.

Crowds still make the pilgrimage to Beale seeking that soulful sound, but now they are just as likely to come for the various restaurants, shops and bars occupying the renovated brick buildings between **Main and Fourth.** On any given night you might hear rock 'n' roll, jazz, funk and the latest dance club music along with the home-grown blues style so closely associated with Memphis and Beale.

Enjoying a prominent corner on Beale and Second, this location of the **B.B. King's Blues Club** chain, 143 Beale St., might disappoint blues purists

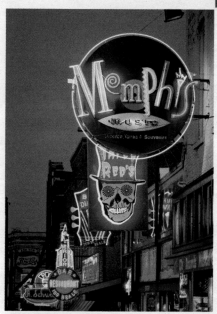

Enjoy a night out on Beale Street

since the house band is as likely to play rock and funk as traditional blues, despite the name of the legendary guitarist and King of the Blues over the door. But anyone hankering for tasty Southern cooking and a lively atmosphere steeped in blues imagery is bound to leave this Beale Street landmark happy, and that's not to mention the frequent appearances by big-name blues acts. Phone (901) 524-5464.

Across the street, **Club 152** adds something different to the Beale Street scene by being both a blues venue, as you might expect, as well as an urban-style dance club. You'll find the main stage on the first floor, which is the venue for both live music and DJ-mixed dance tunes. Phone (901) 544-7011.

Just down the block, at the corner of Beale and Third, is **Rum Boogie Café,** which has a reputation for rum drinks (hence the name), a respectable beer selection, Memphis-style barbecue ribs, and red beans and rice. Even if you skip the Southern cuisine you can still have a blast grooving to the blues and rock bands playing nightly or ogling the décor, which includes more than a hundred autographed guitars suspended from the ceiling and mounted on the walls. Look for the prized scribbles of George Thorogood, Stevie Ray Vaughn, Sting, Henry Rollins, Kenny Loggins and bands like Aerosmith and The B-52s. Phone (901) 528-0150.

Probably the most eye-catching establishment on Beale, which is saying a lot considering the gaudy neon signage competing for your attention, is **Silky O'Sullivan's Irish Bar,** across the street from Rum Boogie Café. Massive steel beams support an elaborate three-story brick façade, all that remains of a 19th-century hotel, saloon and gambling den known as the Gallina Building. The old reinforced façade is now the entrance to a festive patio, scene of dueling pianos nightly, while blues bands play indoors. This is Beale Street, after all, and even Irish pubs host the blues. O'Sullivan's other claim to fame? A gallon-bucket-sized cocktail called "The Diver," to be shared, of course. Phone (901) 522-9596.

Find a seat on the second-floor patio at **Alfred's On Beale** across Third Street from Silky O'Sullivan's at 197 Beale St., and you'll have a nice view of the goings-on along Beale. And you can enjoy good Southern comfort food while you people watch. Alfred's books a variety of musical acts but focuses on classic rock 'n' roll and Top 40 faves from the past. On weekends, the large dance floor stays busy late into the night. Phone (901) 525-3711.

If you're looking for a place to relax and enjoy a cold one, then walk on over to nearby **Flying Saucer Draught Emporium**, 130 Peabody Pl., which has what can only be called an encyclopedic beer selection. A bank of windows on two sides opens up to create something like a patio when the weather is nice, and the spacious brew pub has pool tables and dartboards that will help you pass the time with friends. Scores of plates displayed on the walls honor local beer connoisseurs—members of the "UFO Club"—who have managed to sample the Flying Saucer's entire beer menu. Phone (901) 523-8536.

The **Peabody Memphis** hotel, 149 Union Ave., famous for its twice daily duck march through its lobby, is a favorite with tourists. Once you've seen the ducks waddle into the elevator to return to their rooftop pen around 5 p.m., step over to the lobby bar for a martini and a chance to take in the elegant setting without the crowds. Phone (901) 529-4000.

Watch the ducks march at Peabody Memphis

If you're hungry, exit the Peabody and cross Second Street to **Huey's Downtown**, 77 S. Second St., home of juicy, award-winning hamburgers and delectable onion rings. And you can hone your skill at blowing frilled toothpicks through a straw and into the ceiling, an activity the management surprisingly encourages; your waiter will show you the best technique. On Sunday evenings Huey's features live bands playing blues, rock and soul. Phone (901) 527-2700.

If you want a taste of Memphis beyond the usual tourist haunts downtown, drive or catch a cab to **Midtown's Cooper-Young District**, an eclectic neighborhood popular with Memphians looking for innovative cuisine and cool, laidback hangouts closer at hand than the party dens of Beale Street. **Celtic Crossing**, 903 S. Cooper St., is one such gathering place, an Irish bar with a tree-shaded patio and live music outside on Sundays when weather permits. Phone (901) 274-5151.

And just off the intersection of Cooper and Young that gives the district its name, **Young Avenue Deli**, 2119 Young Ave., brings local bands to its stage several nights a week. What's more, the deli's better-than-average pub fare includes several vegetarian options as well as tasty beer batter fried pickles and homemade french fries. The deli's combination of good food, a large beer selection and live alternative rock, pop and country music is a winning one. Phone (901) 278-0034.

Not long ago another exciting nightlife option appeared on the southern horizon when rural Tunica County, Miss., transformed itself virtually overnight into a 24-hour, Las Vegas-style gambling mecca. Less than an hour south of Memphis, the huge casino resorts along the Mississippi River boast headline entertainment, live music and comedy acts along with all the slot machines and poker, blackjack, roulette and craps tables you'd find on the Vegas Strip. Phone the Tunica Convention & Visitors Bureau, (662) 363-3800 or (888) 488-6422.

Big Events

Memphis kicks off the year by honoring the birth of its favorite sons. Fans from around the world flock to the ⚐ **Elvis Presley Birthday Celebration.** The festival, which spans several days surrounding January 8, includes a concert of the King's tunes performed by the Memphis Symphony Orchestra and an Elvis Presley Day Ceremony, complete with birthday cake.

In mid-January, the city honors another King. The **Dr. Martin Luther King Jr. Day Celebration** features speakers, forums and concerts to honor the civil rights leader on his birthday.

It wouldn't be Memphis without the sultry sounds emanating from Beale Street, and the **Beale Street Music Festival** in May highlights blues, rock, gospel, R&B, alternative and soul artists from around the country. The 3-day, Mardi Gras-like celebration brings throngs of partiers to the street, and more than 60 musical acts take to stages set up in Tom Lee Park, where Beale meets the Mississippi River.

The music festival is part of the city's most well-known event, the ▽ **Memphis in May International Festival.** This monthlong event focuses on a different country and its culture every year. Highlights include the **World Championship Barbecue Cooking Contest,** known as the Super Bowl of Swine, where grill masters gather under a cloud of hickory smoke and compete to prepare the tastiest pork barbecue. The **Sunset Symphony,** a bring-a-picnic event, features an air show as well as performances by the Memphis Symphony Orchestra on the banks of the Mississippi.

Summer is ushered in with the **FedEx St. Jude Classic,** a key PGA Tour event in June. The city rallies in mid-August to pay tribute to Memphis' hip-shaking, lip-curling king during **Elvis Week.** The weeklong, all-Elvis festival includes more than 30 events: bus and house tours, tribute concerts, dance parties, karaoke nights, trivia competitions and a candlelight vigil are some of the highlights. This event attracts loyal fans from all over the world.

Music is again the focus of celebration during the **Memphis Music and Heritage Festival,** held over Labor Day weekend; local and noted personalities perform blues, jazz, country, pop and bluegrass music on various downtown stages. Dance, poetry and spoken word performances also are featured.

With more than 300 booths with art, crafts and gourmet food, the **Pink Palace Crafts Fair,** set in Audubon Park in early October, also is a big draw.

When the holidays approach, Graceland celebrates in style with the **Christmas at Graceland** event. Running from late November to early January, it displays decorations that Elvis himself used when he resided here.

There's no better spot to ring in the New Year than where the blues began. Attend the **New Year's Eve Countdown on Beale Street** for a Guitar Drop and a merry good time.

Sports & Rec

With more than 160 parks, Memphis has the space and facilities to provide recreation for its citizens and visitors. Sprawling 350-acre **Overton Park** contains the Memphis Brooks Museum of Art *(see attraction listing p. 148)* and Memphis Zoo *(see attraction listing p. 149)* as well as a nine-hole **golf** course, a lake, picnic grounds and walking trails.

Golfers have a choice of public golf courses, including Cordova Club, 7400 E. Cordova Club Dr. in Cordova, (901) 758-8188; Galloway, 3815 Walnut Grove Rd., (901) 685-7805; Quail Ridge, 4055 Altruria Rd., (901) 386-6951; and Stonebridge, 3049 Davies Plantation Rd. in Lakeland, (901) 382-1886. Also in Memphis are more than 100 public **tennis** courts, including Leftwich Tennis Center, 4145 Southern Ave., (901) 685-7907.

The city's premier recreation area is the Meeman-Shelby Forest State Park *(see Recreation Areas Chart),* north of town near Millington. Opportunities for **biking, horseback riding, swimming, boating, camping** and **hiking** are all available. Lakeland

The FedEx St. Jude Classic

Park, 7 miles east of Memphis via I-40, is popular for camping, **fishing** and picnicking.

The 1,138-acre T.O. Fuller State Park *(see Recreation Areas Chart)* is at the southern city limits. This park has a swimming pool, a picnic area and self-guiding nature trails; for more information phone (901) 543-7581.

Shelby Farms, a 4,500-acre park northeast of Memphis off I-40 at 7171 Mullins Station Rd., offers biking, fishing and horseback riding and has nature paths, paddleboats and an 18-hole disc golf course; phone (901) 767-7275.

Live and simulcast greyhound and Thoroughbred **racing** can be found at Southland Park Gaming and Racing, 1550 N. Ingram Blvd. in West Memphis, Ark. (pari-mutuel betting is illegal in Tennessee); phone 800-467-6182.

Although not a spectator sport, another form of betting has become a popular recreational activity with Memphians. Many citizens enjoy traveling just south of town to Tunica, Miss., off US 61, where a small city of casinos, some dockside, offers gambling and entertainment.

The **baseball** tradition is upheld by the Memphis Redbirds, a farm club of the St. Louis Cardinals. The Redbirds play at AutoZone Park at 200 Union Ave.; phone (901) 721-6000. Major sports facilities include the Liberty Bowl Memorial Stadium and Fairgrounds, (901) 729-4344, and Landers Center in Southaven, Miss., home to the Mississippi RiverKings of the Southern Professional Hockey League; for ticket information phone (662) 342-1755.

The NBA's Memphis Grizzlies and University of Memphis Tigers play **basketball** at the FedExForum

Arena, 191 Beale St. at Third Street. For Grizzlies tickets phone (800) 462-2849; for Tigers tickets phone (901) 678-2331.

Performing Arts

Memphis offers a variety of cultural activities—ballet, opera, dance, the symphony and professional theater. The arts are supported by several colleges and professional organizations. Many touring companies play Memphis, and there are eight local theater groups.

The Playhouse on the Square, at 66 S. Cooper in Overton Square, offers professional live theater throughout the year; phone (901) 726-4656.

The Orpheum Theatre, 203 S. Main St. at the corner of Beale, was one of the South's grandest vaudeville and movie palaces. Built in 1928, it has its original Wurlitzer organ and offers a variety of musical and theatrical productions, including Broadway road shows, throughout the year; phone (901) 525-3000. Also performing at the Orpheum is **Opera Memphis,** which offers a limited season from October to April; phone (901) 257-3100 for ticket or performance information. **The Memphis Symphony Orchestra** performs at **The Cannon Center for the Performing Arts,** Poplar Avenue and N. Main Street; phone (800) 726-0915 for the Cannon Center or (901) 537-2500 for symphony tickets.

Memphis also has a number of repertory theaters, including the **Circuit Playhouse,** 51 S. Cooper, (901) 726-4656, and **Theatre Memphis,** 630 Perkins Extended, (901) 682-8323.

Big-name bands play at the **Memphis Cook Convention Center.** Other headliners appear at **Mud Island Amphitheater.**

Check out the bike gate at Overton Park

ATTRACTIONS

THE ART MUSEUM OF THE UNIVERSITY OF MEMPHIS (AMUM) is on the University of Memphis campus in the Communication and Fine Arts Building at 3750 Norriswood Ave. Permanent displays feature Egyptian and African art, while changing exhibitions focus primarily on contemporary art. **Hours:** Mon.-Sat. 9-5. Closed university holidays and between exhibitions. **Cost:** Free. **Phone:** (901) 678-2224.

BELZ MUSEUM OF ASIAN AND JUDAIC ART is at 119 S. Main St. in the Pembroke Sq. Bldg. Works exemplify 19th-century Chinese art and reflect the opulence of Imperial China during the Qing Dynasty 1644-1911. Many of the elaborate jade sculptures, intricate ivory carvings, period furnishings and textiles have symbolic meanings. Rare minerals, fossils, Russian lacquer boxes and an extensive contemporary Judaic art collection also are showcased. Photographs, testimonials and artifacts from survivors, refugees, and liberators of Holocaust survivors living in Tennessee are on display in the Holocaust Memorial Gallery.

Time: Allow 30 minutes minimum. **Hours:** Tues.-Fri. 10-5:30, Sat.-Sun. noon-5. Last admission 30 minutes before closing. Closed major holidays. **Cost:** $6; $5 (ages 55+); $4 (ages 5+ and students with ID). **Phone:** (901) 523-2787.

CENTER FOR SOUTHERN FOLKLORE is at 119 S. Main St. (Peabody Place trolley stop). Exhibits, music, events and tours offer visitors a "Southern experience." The center houses folk art and photography displays as well as a performance area inside the Folklore storeroom that is the site of blues, jazz, soul, gospel, rockabilly, country and folk music concerts.

Hours: Folklore storeroom Mon.-Fri. 11-6, Fri. 11-10, Sat. noon-midnight, Sun. noon-6 p.m. Folklore Hall schedule may vary; phone ahead to confirm schedule. Closed Jan. 1, Labor Day, Thanksgiving and Christmas. **Cost:** $10. Fees are charged for special programs and tours. **Phone:** (901) 525-3655.

THE CHILDREN'S MUSEUM OF MEMPHIS is at the Katherine and John Dobbs Family Center next to the Liberty Bowl Memorial Stadium and Fairgrounds at 2525 Central Ave. The 33,500-square-foot museum offers children the chance to explore and discover a cityscape with hands-on exhibits. Tykes can climb inside an indoor tree house, virtually drive a fire engine or sheriff's car, shop for groceries, dance in a disco, watch live honeybees or cash a check at a bank.

Going Places, a flight exhibit, features a simulator, a real airplane cockpit and a package loading conveyor system. In summer months the H2Oh! Splash water park keeps kids cool while they learn about plants, sun and water safety. **Time:** Allow 2 hours minimum. **Hours:** Museum daily 9-5. Water park daily 10-4, Memorial Day-Labor Day. Closed Easter, Thanksgiving and Christmas. **Cost:** Museum or water park $12; free (ages 0-1). Combination museum and water park one-day admission $20; free (ages 0-1). **Phone:** (901) 458-2678.

C.H. NASH MUSEUM AT THE CHUCALISSA ARCHAEOLOGICAL SITE is off I-55 exit 9, .25 mi. e. on Mallory Ave. to Riverport Rd., 4 mi. s.w. to T.O. Fuller State Park entrance, then s. into park to 1987 Indian Village Dr. Also known as the C.H. Nash Museum at Chucalissa, the facility is on the site of a settlement that flourished about A.D. 1000-early 1500s; among the exhibits are prehistoric artifacts, Native American cultural heritage items and hands-on laboratory displays. The village consists of earthen mounds, an interpretive trail and an arboretum.

T.O. Fuller State Park *(see Recreation Areas Chart)* offers camping, golfing and swimming. **Time:** Allow 1 hour minimum. **Hours:** Park open 8-dusk. Museum open Tues.-Sat. 9-5, Sun. 1-5. Last admission 30 minutes before closing. Closed major holidays. **Cost:** $5; $3 (ages 4-11 and 60+). **Phone:** (901) 785-3160. 🏕

THE COTTON MUSEUM AT THE MEMPHIS COTTON EXCHANGE is at 65 Union Ave. The history of the cotton trade and its influence on regional culture is explored through artifacts, interpretive exhibits, educational programs and multimedia displays. The Cotton Museum Hall of Fame celebrates the achievements of people involved in the world's cotton industry. **Time:** Allow 1 hour minimum. **Hours:** Mon.-Sat. 10-5, Sun. noon-5. Closed major holidays. **Cost:** $10; $9 (ages 55+ and students with ID); $8 (military with ID); $7 (ages 6-12). **Phone:** (901) 531-7826.

THE DANNY THOMAS/ALSAC PAVILION is at 332 N. Lauderdale St. on the grounds of St. Jude Children's Research Hospital. Reflecting the cultural heritage of its benefactors, the American Lebanese Syrian Associated Charities, the pavilion features terrazzo flooring, a brilliant cupola and arched panels inscribed with Arabic calligraphy.

Exhibits detail the hospital's history and Danny Thomas' show business career and humanitarian work. Thomas and his wife Rose Marie are entombed in the adjoining memorial garden. **Time:**

Downtown
Memphis
Attractions

Scale in Miles

0.2   0   0.2

See p. 6 - Map Legend

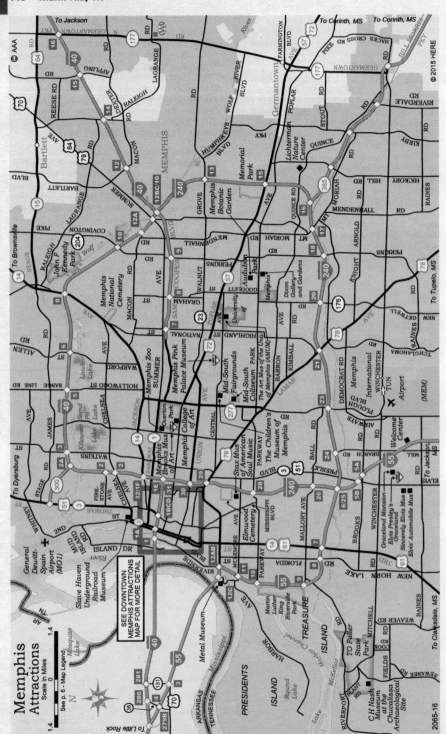

Memphis Attractions

Allow 1 hour minimum. **Hours:** Pavilion daily 8-4. Garden daily 8-5. **Cost:** Free. **Phone:** (901) 595-4414 or (800) 877-5833.

DIXON GALLERY AND GARDENS is across from Audubon Park at 4339 Park Ave. Amid 17 acres of formal and informal gardens, this former private estate displays American and French impressionist and post-impressionist paintings, the Stout Collection of 18th-century porcelain and changing exhibits. **Hours:** Tues.-Fri. 10-5 (also 5-8 third Thurs. of the month), Sat. 10-5, Sun. 1-5. Closed major holidays. **Cost:** $7; $5 (ages 65+ and students with ID); $3 (ages 7-17); by donation (Tues. 10-4); free (to all Sat. 10-noon). **Phone:** (901) 761-5250.

ELMWOOD CEMETERY, at 824 S. Dudley St., is the oldest active cemetery in Memphis. This well-kept Victorian-era garden cemetery and arboretum covers 80 acres and includes hundreds of examples of Victorian cemetery art. Audio tours and tour maps of the cemetery tell about local history and many of the notable Civil War soldiers, politicians, musicians and civil rights activists buried here. **Time:** Allow 1 hour minimum. **Hours:** Grounds daily 8-4:30. Office Mon.-Fri. 8-4:30, Sat. 8-noon. **Cost:** Free. Audio tours and maps are available for a fee. **Phone:** (901) 774-3212.

ELVIS PRESLEY'S GRACELAND is off I-55 exit 5B (Elvis Presley Blvd. S.), 1.5 mi. s. of I-240 at 3717 Elvis Presley Blvd. (US 51S). The Graceland complex is made up of the 14-acre Presley estate, museums and an entertainment facility with eateries and shops.

The Platinum Tour includes an iPad tour of Graceland Mansion, the Graceland Archives Experience, the "I Shot Elvis" exhibit and other plaza attractions.

Allow 3 hours, 30 minutes minimum for the Platinum Tour. **Hours:** Mansion and plaza attractions open Mon.-Sat. 9-5, Sun. 10-4 (also Sun. 9-10 a.m., June-Aug.), Mar.-Oct.; daily 10-4, in Nov.; mansion open Wed.-Mon. 10-4, plaza attractions daily 10-4, rest of year. Closed Thanksgiving and Christmas. **Cost:** Platinum Tour $40; $36 (ages 62+ and students with ID); $19 (ages 7-12). Prices may vary; phone ahead. Reservations are suggested and can be made 2 hours to 6 months in advance with payment. **Parking:** $10 (per private vehicle); $15 (oversized vehicles). **Phone:** (901) 332-3322 or (800) 238-2000. *(See ad this page.)*

Elvis' Automobile Museum, off Elvis Presley Blvd., highlights Elvis' renowned collection of vehicles. His 1955 pink Cadillac, two Stutz Blackhawks, a six-door Mercedes Benz limousine and a 1975 Dino Ferrari are among the automobiles displayed.

Time: Allow 30 minutes minimum. **Hours:** Mon.-Sat. 10-5, Sun. 10-4, Mar.-Oct.; daily 11-4, rest of year. Closed Thanksgiving and Christmas. **Cost:** $12; $10.80 (ages 13-18, ages 62+ and students with ID); $5.50 (ages 7-12). Rates may vary. **Phone:** (901) 332-3322 or (800) 238-2000.

Graceland Mansion is at 3764 Elvis Presley Blvd. The mansion and the grounds are accessible on an interactive iPad tour, narrated by actor John Stamos, featuring commentary by Elvis and his daughter Lisa Marie. Visitors can see the Jungle Room, pool room, living areas, kitchen, business office and racquetball facility. Guests also can tour the trophy building, which displays Elvis' gold and platinum records, memorabilia and clothing. The tour ends in the Meditation Garden, where Elvis and family members are buried.

Time: Allow 1 hour minimum. **Hours:** Mon.-Sat. 9-5, Sun. 9-4, Mar.-Oct.; daily 10-4, in Nov.; Mon. and Wed.-Sun. 10-4, rest of year. Closed Thanksgiving and Christmas. **Cost:** $36; $32.40 (ages 13-18, ages 62+ and students with ID); $16 (ages 7-12). Entrance is timed. Rates may vary; phone ahead. **Phone:** (901) 332-3322 or (800) 238-2000.

Sincerely Elvis Museum, off Elvis Presley Blvd., features a rotating exhibit which focuses on different eras of Elvis' personal life as well as his life on the road. **Time:** Allow 30 minutes minimum. **Hours:** Mon.-Sat. 10-5, Sun. 10-4, Mar.-Oct.; daily 11-4, rest of year. Closed Jan. 1, Thanksgiving and Christmas. **Cost:** $11; $9.90 (ages 13-18, ages 62+ and students with ID); $4.50 (ages 7-12). **Phone:** (901) 332-3322 or (800) 238-2000.

FIRE MUSEUM OF MEMPHIS is at 118 Adams Ave. Housed in the 1910 Fire Engine House No. 1, the museum is filled with interactive exhibits and displays of historic firefighting equipment, including early 20th-century fire trucks and a horse-drawn steam fire engine. Toys on Fire displays nearly 1,000 firefighting toys and collectibles, and an animatronic firehouse horse describes how fires were fought in years past. The virtual reality Fire Room lets visitors experience a simulated residential fire. The Memorial Wall commemorates fallen firefighters.

Time: Allow 1 hour minimum. **Hours:** Mon.-Sat. 9-6, Sun. 1-6, Memorial Day-Labor Day; Mon.-Sat. 9-4:30, Sun. 1-4:30, rest of year. Last admission is 1 hour before closing. Closed Jan. 1, July 4, Thanksgiving, Christmas Eve and Christmas. **Cost:** $10; $8 (ages 3-18, ages 60+ and military with ID); $30 (family of four). **Phone:** (901) 636-5650.

HEALTH SCIENCES PARK is bounded by Union Ave., Manassas St., Madison Ave. and Dunlap St. The park contains a memorial to Gen. Nathan Bedford Forrest, Confederate hero and resident of Memphis. **Hours:** Daily 6 a.m.-8 p.m., mid-Mar. to Oct. 31; 6-6, rest of year. **Cost:** Free. **Phone:** (901) 576-4200.

LICHTERMAN NATURE CENTER is at 5992 Quince Rd. This 65-acre park and environmental education facility features a visitor center, a special events pavilion, accessible nature trails, a lake, meadow, forest, boardwalks, a greenhouse and the Backyard Wildlife Center. **Time:** Allow 2 hours minimum. **Hours:** Tues.-Thurs. 10-3, Fri.-Sat. 10-4. Last admission 1 hour before closing. Closed Jan. 1, Thanksgiving, Christmas Eve and Christmas. **Cost:** $6; $5.50 (ages 60+); $4.50 (ages 3-12); free (to all Tues. 1-3). **Phone:** (901) 767-7322.

MEMORIAL PARK is at 5668 Poplar Ave. (US 72). This suburban cemetery contains the Crystal Shrine Grotto, a man-made crystal cavern. Mexican artist Dionicio Rodriguez scooped out part of the hillside and made a cave of natural rock, quartz crystal and other semiprecious stones from the Ozark Mountains. The life of Jesus Christ is depicted. **Hours:** Daily 8-4. **Cost:** Free. **Phone:** (901) 767-8930.

MEMPHIS BOTANIC GARDEN is in Audubon Park at 750 Cherry Rd. Home of the Goldsmith Civic Garden Center, the garden has more than 23 specialty gardens with roses, irises, wildflowers and magnolias as well as Audubon Lake and a visitor center with changing monthly art exhibits. The Japanese Garden of Tranquility features Red Drum Bridge and Moongazing Pavilion; My Big Backyard includes open play areas and educational activities for children and The Nature Photography Garden is designed to attract wildlife and provides photo opportunities.

Time: Allow 1 hour minimum. **Hours:** Daily 9-6, mid-Mar. to early Nov.; 9-4:30, rest of year. Closed Jan. 1, Thanksgiving and Christmas. **Cost:** $8; $6.50 (ages 62+); $5 (ages 2-12). **Phone:** (901) 636-4100.

MEMPHIS BROOKS MUSEUM OF ART is in Overton Park just w. of East Pkwy. at 1934 Poplar Ave. Founded in 1916, the museum is said to

Take a tour of Elvis Presley's Graceland

be one of the largest in the South. A permanent collection of more than 8,000 works as well as traveling exhibitions spans antiquity to the present. The core of the collection includes Italian Renaissance, Northern Renaissance and Baroque paintings; 18th- and 19th-century English and American portraits; works by French Impressionists; American paintings and sculptures; decorative arts; and an African art survey.

An audio tour is available. **Time:** Allow 1 hour minimum. **Hours:** Wed.-Fri. 10-4 (also Thurs. 4-8), Sat. 10-5, Sun. 11-5. Last admission 30 minutes before closing. Closed Jan. 1, July 4, Thanksgiving and Christmas. **Cost:** $7; $6 (ages 65+); $3 (ages 7-17 and students with ID). Audio tour free. **Phone:** (901) 544-6200.

MEMPHIS COLLEGE OF ART is in Overton Park at 1930 Poplar Ave. The Rust Hall Galleries feature 10 to 12 changing exhibits annually by contemporary artists as well as students, faculty and alumni. The downtown Hyde Gallery, at 477 S. Main St., houses special exhibitions and showcases the work of graduate students. **Time:** Allow 1 hour minimum. **Hours:** Rust Hall Galleries Mon.-Fri. 8:30-5, Sat. 9-4, Sun. noon-4; Hyde Gallery Mon.-Fri. noon-5 (also last Fri. of the month 6-9 p.m.), Sat. noon-7. Closed major holidays. Phone ahead to confirm schedule. **Cost:** Free. **Phone:** (901) 272-5151.

MEMPHIS PARK is on Front St. at Court Ave. The park, formerly known as Confederate Park, preserves ramparts used in defense against Federal gunboats in 1862. Facing Front Street is a statue of Confederacy President Jefferson Davis, who lived in Memphis following his internment after the Civil War. **Time:** Allow 30 minutes minimum. **Hours:** Daily dawn-dusk. **Phone:** (901) 312-9190.

MEMPHIS PINK PALACE MUSEUM is at 3050 Central Ave. The museum's name refers to the pink marble used in its construction. The 1920s estate was to be the home of entrepreneur Clarence Saunders, founder of Piggly Wiggly grocery stores. It now contains exhibits about life in Memphis through the 20th century; displays about dinosaurs, birds, mammals, insects, fossils and geology; and pioneer-era, 19th-century and Civil War memorabilia.

In addition the museum houses a life-size replica of the first self-serve Piggly Wiggly store; the Clyde Parke Miniature Circus; the Sharpe Planetarium; and a hall for traveling exhibits. IMAX films also are presented in the CTI 3D Giant Theater.

Time: Allow 1 hour minimum. **Hours:** Museum and 3D theater Mon.-Sat. 9-5, Sun. noon-5. Planetarium shows offered Tues.-Sat.; phone for schedule. **Cost:** Museum exhibits only $12.75; $12.25 (ages 60+); $7.25 (ages 3-12); free (to all Tues. 1-5). Exhibits and planetarium $15.25; $14.25 (ages 60+); $9.25 (ages 3-12). Museum, 3D theater and planetarium $19.75; $18.25 (ages 60+); $12.25 (ages 3-12). Prices may vary; phone ahead. **Phone:** (901) 636-2362.

Visit the Memphis Zoo

MEMPHIS ROCK 'N' SOUL MUSEUM is 1 blk. s. of Beale St. at the FedExForum Plaza. The museum examines the lives of such legends as Elvis Presley and B.B. King as well as the city's musical heritage and its contributions to blues, country, rock 'n' roll and soul music.

Photographs, costumes and instruments shed light on rural sharecroppers' musical experiences and the sounds of Sun, Stax and Hi Records performers. Collections showcase the stories of musical pioneers in seven themed areas, including the Social Changes, Soul Music and Rural Music galleries.

A 15-minute orientation film and an audio self-guiding tour of the museum are included with admission. **Time:** Allow 1 hour minimum. **Hours:** Daily 10-7. Last admission 45 minutes before closing. Closed Jan. 1, Thanksgiving, Christmas Eve and Christmas. **Cost:** $12; $9 (ages 5-17). **Phone:** (901) 205-2533.

MEMPHIS ZOO is in Overton Park at 2000 Prentiss Pl. The 70-acre zoo is one of only four in the country where giant pandas reside. Home to more than 3,500 animals representing more than 500 species, the zoo has an aquarium, a tropical birdhouse, an interactive farm, a primate exhibit and shows. The 3-acre Northwest Passage exhibit features polar bears, sea lions and bald eagles. Cat Country is a 4-acre natural exhibit with lions, tigers, cheetahs and meerkats. Stingray Bay is a seasonal interactive exhibit where visitors can touch stingrays and sharks. The live bird show "Memphis Zoo Takes Flight" is included with admission.

Hours: Daily 9-5, Mar. 1-Oct. 26; 9-4, rest of year. Live bird show Mon.-Fri. at 10:30 and 4 (also Sat. at

12:30). Closed Thanksgiving, Christmas Eve and Christmas. **Cost:** $15; $14 (ages 60+); $10 (ages 2-11). **Parking:** $5. **Phone:** (901) 333-6500.

METAL MUSEUM is .4 mi. s.w. off I-55N exit 12C (Metal Museum Dr.). The museum is devoted to the preservation of fine metalwork and the promotion of metalworking. Historic and contemporary metal objects are exhibited. The museum's 3-acre grounds have an outdoor sculpture garden, a picnic area and a river-bluff pavilion built from a salvaged 19th-century Beale Street building. Metalworking demonstrations are regularly conducted in the Schering-Plough Smithy and Lawler Foundry, also on the grounds.

Time: Allow 30 minutes minimum. **Hours:** Tues.-Sat. 10-5, Sun. noon-5. Closed Jan. 1, Easter, Thanksgiving, Christmas Eve, Christmas, day after Christmas, New Year's Day and during exhibit installations. **Cost:** $6; $5 (ages 62+); $4 (ages 5-18 and college students with ID). **Phone:** (901) 774-6380 or (877) 881-2326.

MUD ISLAND RIVER PARK is downtown on the Mississippi River; it is reached by an automobile bridge or a pedestrian bridge/monorail accessed from 125 N. Front St. Completed in 1982, the park occupies the southern tip of a peninsula—it's not really an island—separating the Mississippi River from the downtown area. The park's main feature is the Mississippi River Museum *(see attraction listing),* which occupies most of the five-story building you enter once you step off the covered pedestrian Skybridge or the monorail suspended beneath the bridge. On the island you'll have a fantastic view of the Memphis skyline and the double arches of the Hernando de Soto Bridge carrying I-40 traffic over the Mississippi into Arkansas.

Outside the museum is the River Walk, a half-mile-long concrete scale model of the Lower Mississippi complete with flowing water, inlaid street maps of major towns and a 1-acre pond representing the Gulf of Mexico. The detailed model depicts Ole Man River's every serpentine twist and turn. It is constructed of layered slabs with each 1-inch layer representing 5 feet of depth. Each 30-inch step you take corresponds to a mile, making you feel like a giant as you walk all the way from Cairo, Ill., to New Orleans. Signs placed at regular intervals describe interesting landmarks, historic sites and natural features.

Besides splashing barefoot through the River Walk, you can listen to music during concerts held in the park's 5,000-seat amphitheater.

Hours: Tues.-Sun. 10-5, mid-Apr. to Oct. 31. Last admission 1 hour before closing. **Cost:** Free. Round-trip monorail ride fee $4. Combination ticket including entrance to the Mississippi River Museum, a guided River Walk tour and monorail fare $10; $9 (ages 60+); $7 (ages 5-11). **Phone:** (901) 576-7241 or (800) 507-6507. GT

Mississippi River Museum is inside the River Center Building at Mud Island River Park. The museum has 18 galleries with more than 5,000 artifacts

and a 4,000-gallon freshwater aquarium. Exhibits detail the valley's creation and settlement from Native American inhabitants to European explorers; transportation on the river, with a replica of an 1870s steamboat; the Civil War, with a full-scale Union gunboat; and the development of Delta music from early blues to rock 'n' roll.

Time: Allow 1 hour minimum. **Hours:** Tues.-Sun. 10-5, Apr.-Oct. Last admission 1 hour before closing. Phone ahead to confirm schedule. **Cost:** (includes a guided River Walk tour and monorail fare) $10; $9 (ages 60+); $7 (ages 5-11). **Phone:** (901) 576-7230.

THE NATIONAL CIVIL RIGHTS MUSEUM is between Huling and G.E. Patterson aves. at 450 Mulberry St. Housed in two buildings, interpretive exhibits and audiovisual displays tell of the key events in the civil rights movement from the early days of slavery to the present. Interactive exhibits, short films, recorded oral histories and artifacts evoke tensions and emotions prevalent during the period. Housed in the Lorraine Motel, where Martin Luther King Jr. was assassinated, the museum features dramatic exhibits that immerse visitors in pivotal moments of the history of civil rights in America, from the first anti-slavery movements to the present day.

Time: Allow 2 hours minimum. **Hours:** Mon. and Wed.-Sat. 9-6, Sun. 1-6, Memorial Day-Labor Day; Mon. and Wed.-Sat. 9-5, Sun. 1-5, rest of year. Closed major holidays. **Cost:** $15; $14 (ages 55+ and students with ID); $12 (ages 4-17). **Phone:** (901) 521-9699.

SLAVE HAVEN UNDERGROUND RAILROAD MUSEUM, 826 N. Second St., preserves the 1856 home of Jacob Burkle, a German immigrant who provided refuge to runaway slaves. Visitors tour his seven-room house, which served as a way station on the Underground Railroad. A hidden cellar and trap doors reveal the slaves' escape route. **Hours:** Mon.-Sat. 10-5, June-Aug.; Mon.-Sat. 10-4, rest of year. Closed Thanksgiving and Christmas. **Cost:** $10; $9 (ages 65+); $8 (ages 4-17). **Phone:** (901) 527-3427. GT

STAX MUSEUM OF AMERICAN SOUL MUSIC is at 926 E. McLemore Ave. More than 17,000 square feet of exhibit space contains some 2,000 artifacts that outline the roots of American soul music. Isaac Hayes' gold-trimmed, blue 1972 Cadillac El Dorado, Ike Turner's Fender guitar and Otis Redding's suede jacket are among memorabilia on display. Interactive computer exhibits and photographs round out the collection.

Time: Allow 1 hour minimum. **Hours:** Tues.-Sat. 10-5, Sun. 1-5. Closed Jan. 1, Easter, Thanksgiving and Christmas. **Cost:** $13; $12 (ages 62+ and students and active military with ID); $10 (ages 9-12). **Phone:** (901) 261-6338 or (888) 942-7685.

SUN STUDIO is at 706 Union Ave. The small recording facility is where such music legends as

Johnny Cash, B.B. King, Jerry Lee Lewis, Roy Orbison and Elvis Presley began their recording careers. Blues, rock 'n' roll and country music memorabilia are on display. A guided tour features recorded music and stories relating to the history of the studio.

Time: Allow 1 hour minimum. **Hours:** Daily 10-6. Guided 45-minute tours depart 30 minutes after the hour. Last tour begins 30 minutes before closing. Closed Thanksgiving and Christmas. **Cost:** $12; free (ages 5-11). Under 5 are not permitted on the tour. **Phone:** (901) 521-0664 or (800) 441-6249.

W.C. HANDY MEMPHIS HOME & MUSEUM is at 352 Beale St. Items that belonged to Handy are featured in the turn-of-the-20th-century frame house where he lived while composing "Memphis Blues" and "St. Louis Blues." **Time:** Allow 30 minutes minimum. **Hours:** Tues.-Sat. 10-5, June-Aug.; Tues.-Sat. 11-4, rest of year. **Cost:** $6; $4 (ages 4-17). **Phone:** (901) 527-3427 or (901) 522-1556.

WOODRUFF-FONTAINE HOUSE is in the Victorian Village area at 680 Adams Ave. A fine example of French Victorian style and craftsmanship, this 1870 house is restored and furnished with antiques. Changing exhibits often feature antique clothing. **Time:** Allow 1 hour minimum. **Hours:** Wed.-Sun. noon-4. Last tour departs at 3:15. Closed major holidays. **Cost:** $10; $8 (ages 65+); $6 (students grades 1-12); free (ages 0-6). **Phone:** (901) 526-1469.

Sightseeing
Boat Tours

SIGHTSEEING CRUISES ABOARD THE MEMPHIS RIVERBOATS depart from 251 Riverside Dr. at the foot of Beale St. A guide narrates the history of the area as visitors enjoy views of the Memphis skyline from the Mississippi River. Dinner and holiday cruises also are offered.

Inquire about refund and weather policies. **Hours:** Ninety-minute sightseeing cruises depart Mon.-Fri. at 2:30, Sat.-Sun. at 2:30 and 5, May-Aug.; daily at 2:30, Mar.-Apr. and Sept.-Oct.; Sat.-Sun. at 2:30, in Nov. Boarding times are 1 hour before departure. Phone ahead to confirm schedule.

Cost: Sightseeing cruise $20; $17 (ages 13-17, ages 60+ and military and students with ID); $10 (ages 4-12); $5 (ages 2-3). Reservations are recommended. **Phone:** (901) 527-2628.

Bus and Carriage Tours

Horse-drawn carriage tours of the city are available through Carriage Tours of Memphis, 393 N. Main St., (901) 527-7542. Blues City Tours, 325 Union St., offers bus tours of Graceland, downtown Memphis, Beale Street and Mud Island; a riverboat tour also is available. Phone (901) 522-9229.

Industrial Tours

GIBSON GUITAR FACTORY TOURS is 1 blk. s. of Beale St. at 145 Lt. George W. Lee Ave. Visitors go behind the scenes at a Gibson facility that manufactures some of the company's award-winning guitars. Called luthiers, the artisans who make the stringed instruments can sometimes be viewed as they transform simple blocks of wood into guitars. A tour guide leads the walking tour of the factory, outlining the production process along the way.

Time: Allow 1 hour minimum. **Hours:** Tours are given Mon.-Sat. on the hour 11-4, Sun. noon-4. Closed major holidays. **Cost:** $10. Children under 5 are not permitted on tour. Phone ahead to confirm tour availability. Reservations are recommended. **Phone:** (901) 544-7998.

Walking Tours

There are several sightseeing areas in Memphis, including Victorian Village, Beale Street and Elmwood Cemetery *(see attraction listing p. 147)*. Victorian Village is a collection of 19th-century buildings centering on the 600 block of Adams Avenue. Of the nine churches nearby, the oldest is Calvary Episcopal Church, which dates from 1832. Brochures describing a self-guiding walking tour through Victorian Village are available at the Woodruff-Fontaine House *(see attraction listing)*.

Beale Street, the birthplace of the blues, now features restaurants, shops and music clubs in a three-block entertainment district.

Docent-led walking tours of Elmwood Cemetery are available by appointment; phone (901) 774-3212.

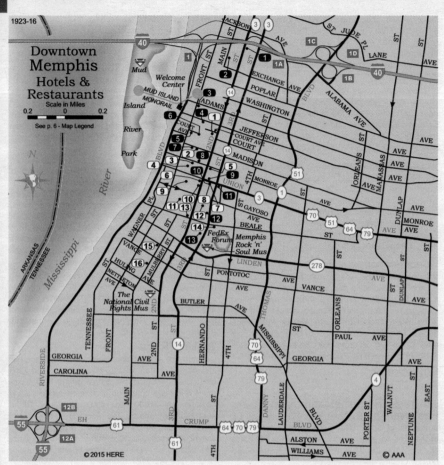

Downtown Memphis
Hotels & Restaurants
Scale in Miles
0.2 0 0.2
See p. 6 - Map Legend

1923-16

© 2015 HERE   © AAA

Downtown Memphis

This index helps you "spot" where approved hotels and restaurants are located on the corresponding detailed maps. Hotel daily rate range is for comparison only. Restaurant price range is a combination of lunch and/or dinner. Turn to the listing page for more detailed rate and price information and consult display ads for special promotions.

DOWNTOWN MEMPHIS

Map Page		Hotels	Diamond Rated	Rate Range	Page
1	this page	**Crowne Plaza Memphis Downtown**	▽▽▽	$119-$299 SAVE	159
2	this page	**Sheraton Memphis Downtown Hotel**	▽▽▽	$109-$349 SAVE	161
3	this page	**Comfort Inn Downtown**	▽▽▽	$159-$259 SAVE	159
4	this page	Courtyard by Marriott Downtown Memphis	▽▽▽	$139-$229	159
5	this page	Sleep Inn at Court Square	▽▽	$124-$224	161
6	this page	SpringHill Suites by Marriott Memphis Downtown	▽▽▽	$125-$206	161
7	this page	**Madison Hotel**	▽▽▽▽	$189-$379 SAVE	160
8	this page	Residence Inn by Marriott Memphis Downtown	▽▽▽	$167-$312	161
9	this page	**Holiday Inn Downtown Memphis** (See ad p. 160.)	▽▽▽	$149-$339 SAVE	160

DOWNTOWN MEMPHIS (cont'd)

Map Page	Hotels (cont'd)	Diamond Rated	Rate Range	Page
10 p. 152	Peabody Memphis	▽▽▽▽	Rates not provided [SAVE]	160
11 p. 152	DoubleTree by Hilton Hotel Memphis Downtown	▽▽▽	$159-$229 [SAVE]	159
12 p. 152	Hampton Inn & Suites at Beale Street	▽▽▽	$169-$229 [SAVE]	159
13 p. 152	The Westin Memphis Beale Street	▽▽▽▽	$159-$399 [SAVE]	161

Map Page	Restaurants	Diamond Rated	Cuisine	Price Range	Page
① p. 152	Blue Plate Cafe	▽▽	Southern American	$5-$10	161
② p. 152	eighty3 food & drink	▽▽▽	American	$8-$48	161
③ p. 152	Flight Restaurant and Wine Bar	▽▽▽	Continental Small Plates	$8-$34	161
④ p. 152	Deja Vu	▽▽	Soul Food	$11-$26	161
⑤ p. 152	Rendezvous	▽▽	Barbecue	$5-$20	162
⑥ p. 152	Huey's Downtown	▽▽	Burgers Sandwiches	$6-$11	162
⑦ p. 152	**Chez Philippe**	◆▽▽▽	Continental	$80-$175	161
⑧ p. 152	Capriccio Grill	▽▽▽	Italian	$12-$42	161
⑨ p. 152	Local Gastropub	▽▽	American	$10-$19	162
⑩ p. 152	Kooky Canuck	▽▽	American	$7-$30	162
⑪ p. 152	The Majestic Grille	▽▽▽	American	$8-$48	162
⑫ p. 152	Texas de Brazil	▽▽▽	Brazilian Steak	$25-$43	162
⑬ p. 152	Hard Rock Cafe	▽▽	American	$12-$24 [SAVE]	162
⑭ p. 152	Dyer's Burgers	▽	Burgers	$7-$17	161
⑮ p. 152	Pearl's Oyster House	▽▽	Southern Seafood	$8-$39	162
⑯ p. 152	SOB - South of Beale	▽▽▽	American	$9-$21	162

© AAA

© 2015 HERE

Meeman-Shelby Forest State Park

SEE DOWNTOWN MEMPHIS ACCOMMODATIONS MAP FOR MORE DETAIL

General Dewitt-Spain Airport (MO1)

Mud Island River Park Welcome Center

Memphis Brooks Museum of Art

PRESIDENTS ISLAND

MEMPHIS

Harbor Channel

Lake McKellar

TREASURE ISLAND

TO Fuller State Park

Elvis Presley's Graceland

Memphis Int'l Airport (MEM)

Memphis and Vicinity
Hotels & Restaurants

Scale in Miles
1.5   0   1.5

See p. 6 - Map Legend

1922-16   To Clarksdale   Southeaven   To Jackson

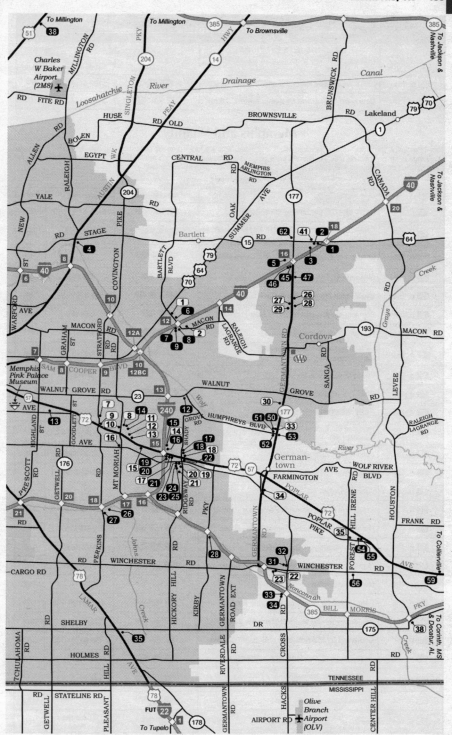

✈ Airport Hotels

	MEMPHIS INTERNATIONAL (Maximum driving distance from airport: 3.6 mi)	Diamond Rated	Rate Range	Page
Map Page				
30 p. 154	BEST WESTERN Executive Inn, 2.9 mi	▽▽	$109-$114 SAVE	162
29 p. 154	Courtyard by Marriott Memphis Airport, 3.6 mi	▽▽▽	$102-$177 SAVE	163

Memphis and Vicinity

This index helps you "spot" where approved hotels and restaurants are located on the corresponding detailed maps. Hotel daily rate range is for comparison only. Restaurant price range is a combination of lunch and/or dinner. Turn to the listing page for more detailed rate and price information and consult display ads for special promotions.

MEMPHIS

Map Page	Hotels	Diamond Rated	Rate Range	Page
1 p. 154	BEST WESTERN Galleria Inn & Suites	▽▽▽	$100-$199 SAVE	162
2 p. 154	Fairfield Inn & Suites by Marriott Memphis East/Galleria	▼▼▼	$98-$260	163
3 p. 154	Holiday Inn & Suites Memphis-Wolfchase Galleria	▼▼▼	Rates not provided	165
4 p. 154	Sleep Inn	▼▼	$58-$120	167
5 p. 154	Hyatt Place Memphis/Wolfchase Galleria	▽▽▽	$84-$189 SAVE	166
6 p. 154	Baymont Inn & Suites Memphis East	▼▼	$59-$79	162
7 p. 154	Fairfield Inn & Suites by Marriott Memphis	▼▼	$83-$137	163
8 p. 154	La Quinta Inn & Suites Memphis East-Sycamore View	▽▽▽	$64-$240 SAVE	166
9 p. 154	Econo Lodge Inn & Suites	▼▼	$60-$94	163
10 p. 154	River Inn of Harbor Town	▽▽▽▽	$215-$635 SAVE	167
11 p. 154	BEST WESTERN PLUS Gen X Inn	▽▽▽	$99-$149 SAVE	163
12 p. 154	Hampton Inn Memphis-Walnut Grove/Baptist Hospital East	▼▼▼	$109-$139	165
13 p. 154	Holiday Inn-University of Memphis	▼▼▼	$139-$169	165
14 p. 154	DoubleTree by Hilton Hotel Memphis	▼▼▼	$109-$199	163
15 p. 154	Hilton Memphis	▼▼▼	$109-$299	165
16 p. 154	Staybridge Suites Memphis-Poplar Ave East	▼▼▼	$129-$189	167
17 p. 154	Hampton Inn & Suites Memphis-Shady Grove	▼▼▼	$109-$169	164
18 p. 154	Embassy Suites by Hilton Memphis	▼▼▼	$139-$289	163
19 p. 154	Homewood Suites by Hilton Memphis-Poplar	▼▼▼	$129-$159	165
20 p. 154	Marriott Memphis East	▽▽▽	$99-$298 SAVE	167
21 p. 154	Four Points by Sheraton Memphis East	▽▽▽	$109-$199 SAVE	163
22 p. 154	Residence Inn by Marriott Memphis East	▽▽▽	$99-$206 SAVE	167
23 p. 154	Courtyard by Marriott Memphis East/Park Ave	▽▽▽	$99-$178 SAVE	163
24 p. 154	La Quinta Inn & Suites-Memphis Primacy Parkway	▼▼▼	$71-$203	167
25 p. 154	Hyatt Place-Memphis/Primacy Parkway (See ad p. 166.)	▽▽▽	$89-$219 SAVE	166
26 p. 154	Crowne Plaza Memphis East	▼▼▼	$109-$189	163
27 p. 154	The Inn at Thousand Oaks	▼▼	Rates not provided	166

MEMPHIS (cont'd)

Map Page	Hotels (cont'd)	Diamond Rated	Rate Range	Page
28 p. 154	Courtyard by Marriott Memphis East/Bill Morris Parkway	▼▼▼	$99-$183	163
29 p. 154	**Courtyard by Marriott Memphis Airport**	▼▼▼	$102-$177 [SAVE]	163
30 p. 154	**BEST WESTERN Executive Inn**	▼▼	$109-$114 [SAVE]	162
31 p. 154	Homewood Suites by Hilton Southwind-Hacks Cross	▼▼▼	$109-$299	165
32 p. 154	Hampton Inn Memphis-Southwind	▼▼	$109-$199	164
33 p. 154	Holiday Inn Express & Suites Memphis Southwind	▼▼▼	Rates not provided	165
34 p. 154	**Four Points by Sheraton Memphis-Southwind**	▼▼▼	Rates not provided [SAVE]	164
35 p. 154	Travelers Inn and Suites	▼▼	Rates not provided	167

Map Page	Restaurants	Diamond Rated	Cuisine	Price Range	Page
① p. 154	Cajun Catfish Company	▼▼	Cajun	$7-$17	167
② p. 154	La Playita Mexican Restaurant	▼▼	Mexican	$6-$18	168
③ p. 154	**Paulette's Restaurant**	▼▼▼	Regional American	$10-$35	169
④ p. 154	Bogie's Delicatessen	▼	Deli	$6-$12	167
⑤ p. 154	The Second Line	▼▼	Regional American	$12-$18	169
⑥ p. 154	Central BBQ in Memphis	▼	Barbecue	$4-$25	167
⑦ p. 154	Old Venice Pizza Company	▼▼	Italian	$7-$18	168
⑧ p. 154	Interim Restaurant & Bar	▼▼▼	American	$11-$30	168
⑨ p. 154	Jim's Place Restaurant & Bar	▼▼▼	American	$12-$29	168
⑩ p. 154	Folk's Folly Prime Steak House	▼▼▼	Traditional Steak	$26-$67	168
⑪ p. 154	Napa Cafe	▼▼▼	Continental	$13-$32	168
⑫ p. 154	Hog & Hominy	▼▼	Fusion Comfort Food	$14-$18	168
⑬ p. 154	Marciano Mediterranean & Italian Restaurant	▼▼	Mediterranean	$14-$28	168
⑭ p. 154	Rooks Corner	▼▼	American	$10-$38	169
⑮ p. 154	Buckley's	▼▼	American	$12-$26	167
⑯ p. 154	Patrick's Restaurant	▼▼	American	$8-$26	168
⑰ p. 154	River Oaks	▼▼▼	Continental	$15-$28	169
⑱ p. 154	Owen Brennan's Restaurant	▼▼	Cajun	$9-$33	168
⑲ p. 154	Wang's Mandarin House	▼▼	Chinese	$7-$25	169
⑳ p. 154	Amerigo, An Italian Restaurant	▼▼▼	Italian	$9-$32	167
㉑ p. 154	Happy Mexican	▼▼	Mexican	$6-$20	168
㉒ p. 154	The Half Shell	▼▼	Seafood	$7-$37	168
㉓ p. 154	Huey's	▼▼	American	$6-$11	168

MILLINGTON

Map Page	Hotel	Diamond Rated	Rate Range	Page
38 p. 154	Plantation Oaks Suites & Inn	▼▼	Rates not provided	172

WEST MEMPHIS, AR

Map Page	Hotels	Diamond Rated	Rate Range	Page
41 p. 154	Ramada	▼▼	$79-$109	169
42 p. 154	**BEST WESTERN West Memphis Inn**	▽▽	$80-$225 [SAVE]	169
43 p. 154	Days Inn West Memphis	▼▼	$53-$80	169

CORDOVA

Map Page	Hotels	Diamond Rated	Rate Range	Page
45 p. 154	Comfort Suites	▼▼	$89-$149	70
46 p. 154	Microtel Inn & Suites by Wyndham	▼▼	$60-$130	70
47 p. 154	Wingate by Wyndham	▼▼▼	$90-$120	70

Map Page	Restaurants	Diamond Rated	Cuisine	Price Range	Page
26 p. 154	Casablanca Restaurant	▼▼	Moroccan	$8-$20	70
27 p. 154	Huey's	▼▼	Burgers Sandwiches	$7-$12	70
28 p. 154	La Hacienda	▼▼	Mexican	$8-$15	70
29 p. 154	Bombay House	▼▼	Indian	$9-$18	70
30 p. 154	The Butcher Shop Steakhouse	▼▼	Steak	$19-$50	70

GERMANTOWN

Map Page	Hotels	Diamond Rated	Rate Range	Page
50 p. 154	Holiday Inn Express & Suites Memphis-Germantown	▼▼▼	Rates not provided	94
51 p. 154	**Courtyard by Marriott Memphis Germantown**	▽▽▽	$89-$183 [SAVE]	94
52 p. 154	Comfort Inn & Suites-Germantown	▼▼▼	$89-$109	94
53 p. 154	Homewood Suites by Hilton-Germantown	▼▼▼	$109-$179	94
54 p. 154	Residence Inn by Marriott Memphis/Germantown	▼▼▼	$104-$200	94
55 p. 154	**Fairfield Inn & Suites by Marriott Memphis Germantown**	▽▽▽	$84-$171 [SAVE]	94
56 p. 154	**Hyatt Place Memphis/Germantown**	▽▽▽	$89-$209 [SAVE]	94

Map Page	Restaurants	Diamond Rated	Cuisine	Price Range	Page
33 p. 154	Las Tortugas Deli Mexicana	▼	Mexican	$6-$19	94
34 p. 154	Germantown Commissary	▼▼	Barbecue	$6-$25	94
35 p. 154	The Belmont Grill Germantown	▼▼	American	$8-$24	94

COLLIERVILLE

Map Page	Hotel	Diamond Rated	Rate Range	Page
59 p. 154	Hampton Inn Collierville	▼▼▼	$99-$169	67

Map Page	Restaurant	Diamond Rated	Cuisine	Price Range	Page
38 p. 154	Firebirds Wood Fired Grill	▼▼▼	American	$11-$30	67

BARTLETT

Map Page	Hotel	Diamond Rated	Rate Range	Page
62 p. 154	Hampton Inn & Suites	▼▼▼	$112-$137	40

Map Page	Restaurant	Diamond Rated	Cuisine	Price Range	Page
41 p. 154	Firebirds Wood Fired Grill	▼▼▼	American	$8-$36	40

DOWNTOWN MEMPHIS

COMFORT INN DOWNTOWN   (901)526-0583

Hotel
$159-$259

Address: 100 N Front St 38103 **Location:** Jct Adams Ave. **Facility:** 71 units. 7 stories, interior corridors. **Parking:** on-site (fee). **Amenities:** safes. **Pool(s):** outdoor. **Activities:** exercise room. **Guest Services:** valet laundry. **Featured Amenity:** full hot breakfast.

COURTYARD BY MARRIOTT DOWNTOWN MEMPHIS   (901)522-2200

Hotel $139-$229 Address: 75 Jefferson Ave 38103 **Location:** Jct Main St. **Facility:** 131 units. 8 stories, interior corridors. **Parking:** on-site (fee) and valet. **Amenities:** safes. **Activities:** hot tub, exercise room. **Guest Services:** valet and coin laundry, boarding pass kiosk.

AAA Benefit:
Members save 5% or more!

CROWNE PLAZA MEMPHIS DOWNTOWN   (901)525-1800

Hotel
$119-$299

Address: 300 N 2nd St 38105 **Location:** I-40 exit 1A westbound; exit 1 eastbound, just s. **Facility:** 230 units. 11 stories, interior corridors. **Parking:** on-site (fee). **Terms:** check-in 4 pm, cancellation fee imposed. **Pool(s):** outdoor. **Activities:** exercise room. **Guest Services:** valet laundry.

DOUBLETREE BY HILTON HOTEL MEMPHIS DOWNTOWN   (901)528-1800

Hotel
$159-$229

AAA Benefit:
Members save 5% or more!

Address: 185 Union Ave 38103 **Location:** Jct 3rd St. **Facility:** 280 units. 10 stories, interior corridors. **Parking:** on-site (fee) and valet. **Terms:** 1-7 night minimum stay, cancellation fee imposed. **Pool(s):** outdoor. **Activities:** exercise room. **Guest Services:** valet laundry.

HAMPTON INN & SUITES AT BEALE STREET   (901)260-4000

Hotel
$169-$229

AAA Benefit:
Members save up to 10%!

Address: 175 Peabody Pl 38103 **Location:** Jct 3rd St. Across from Beale Street entertainment district. **Facility:** 144 units, some efficiencies. 7 stories, interior corridors. **Parking:** on-site (fee). **Terms:** check-in 4 pm, 1-7 night minimum stay, cancellation fee imposed. **Pool(s):** heated indoor. **Activities:** hot tub, exercise room. **Guest Services:** valet and coin laundry.

Get maps, travel information
and road service with the
AAA and CAA Mobile apps

(See map & index p. 152.)

HOLIDAY INN DOWNTOWN MEMPHIS

(901)525-5491 [9]

Hotel
$149-$339

Address: 160 Union Ave 38103 **Location:** Jct 2nd St. **Facility:** 192 units. 14 stories, interior corridors. **Parking:** on-site (fee) and valet. **Terms:** check-in 4 pm, cancellation fee imposed. **Pool(s):** heated outdoor. **Activities:** exercise room. **Guest Services:** valet laundry. *(See ad this page.)*

[SAVE] [▯] [▯] [▯] [▯] [BIZ]
[▯] [✕] [▯] / SOME UNITS [▯] [▯]

Holiday Inn

Next to AutoZone Baseball Pk. Walking distance to Historic Beale St, Restaurants & Attractions.

Recommend places
you'd like us to inspect at
AAA.com/TourBookComments

MADISON HOTEL

(901)333-1200 [7]

Boutique Hotel
$189-$379

Address: 79 Madison Ave 38103 **Location:** Jct Main St, just w. **Facility:** Stylish, jazzy décor adds to the intimate ambiance at this boutique hotel, a former bank. Check out the fitness center, where the inner workings of the original vault are on display. 110 units, some two bedrooms. 17 stories, interior corridors. **Parking:** valet only. **Terms:** 3 day cancellation notice-fee imposed. **Amenities:** safes. **Dining:** eighty3 food & drink, see separate listing. **Pool(s):** heated indoor. **Activities:** exercise room. **Guest Services:** valet laundry.

[SAVE] [▯] [▯] [▯] CALL [▯] [▯]

[BIZ] [HS] [▯] [✕] [▯] [▯] / SOME UNITS [▯]

PEABODY MEMPHIS

901/529-4000 [10]

Historic Hotel
Rates not provided

Address: 149 Union Ave 38103 **Location:** Jct 2nd St. **Facility:** The grand, impressive lobby is popular for afternoon tea, cocktails and watching the daily parade of ducks to the fountain. The stylish, elegant rooms offer a modern take on old Hollywood glamor. 464 units. 12 stories, interior corridors. **Parking:** on-site (fee) and valet. **Terms:** check-in 4 pm. **Amenities:** video games, safes. **Dining:** Capriccio Grill, Chez Philippe, see separate listings, entertainment. **Pool(s):** heated indoor. **Activities:** sauna, hot tub, steamroom, spa. **Guest Services:** valet laundry. Affiliated with Preferred Hotels & Resorts.

[SAVE] [▯] [▯] [▯] [▯] [▯] [▯] [BIZ] [▯] [✕] [▯]
/ SOME UNITS [▯] [▯] [▯] [▯]

(See map & index p. 152.)

RESIDENCE INN BY MARRIOTT MEMPHIS DOWNTOWN
(901)578-3700

▼▼▼▼ **Historic Extended Stay Hotel** $167-$312 **Address:** 110 Monroe Ave 38103 **Location:** Jct Main St. **Facility:** Spacious studio and one- and two-bedroom suites with modern décor

AAA Benefit: Members save 5% or more!

and kitchenettes are housed in a historic hotel. The rooftop patio provides a great view. 90 units, some two bedrooms, efficiencies and kitchens. 11 stories, interior corridors. **Parking:** on-site (fee) and valet. **Activities:** exercise room. **Guest Services:** valet and coin laundry.

SHERATON MEMPHIS DOWNTOWN HOTEL
(901)527-7300 ②

▼▼▼▼
Hotel
$109-$349

Sheraton
HOTELS & RESORTS

AAA Benefit: Members save up to 15%, plus Starwood Preferred Guest® benefits!

Address: 250 N Main St 38103 **Location:** I-40 exit 1A westbound; exit 1 eastbound, just s. Across from Memphis Cook Convention Center. **Facility:** 600 units. 14-19 stories, interior corridors. **Parking:** valet only. **Terms:** check-in 4 pm. **Amenities:** video games. **Pool(s):** heated indoor. **Activities:** exercise room. **Guest Services:** complimentary and valet laundry, boarding pass kiosk.

SLEEP INN AT COURT SQUARE
(901)522-9700 ⑤

▼▼ **Hotel** $124-$224 **Address:** 40 N Front St 38103 **Location:** Jct Madison Ave, just n. **Facility:** 118 units. 6 stories, interior corridors. **Parking:** on-site (fee) and valet. **Amenities:** safes. **Activities:** exercise room. **Guest Services:** valet laundry.

SPRINGHILL SUITES BY MARRIOTT MEMPHIS DOWNTOWN
(901)522-2100 ⑥

▼▼▼ **Hotel** $125-$206 **Address:** 85 W Court Ave 38103 **Location:** Jct Madison Ave, just n. **Facility:** 147 units. 7 stories, interior corridors. **Parking:** valet only. **Amenities:** safes. **Pool(s):**

AAA Benefit: Members save 5% or more!

outdoor. **Activities:** hot tub, exercise room. **Guest Services:** complimentary and valet laundry.

THE WESTIN MEMPHIS BEALE STREET
(901)334-5900 ⑬

▼▼▼▼
Hotel
$159-$399

WESTIN
HOTELS & RESORTS

AAA Benefit: Members save up to 15%, plus Starwood Preferred Guest® benefits!

Address: 170 Lt. George W. Lee Ave 38103 **Location:** Jct S 3rd St. Across from FedEx Forum. **Facility:** Adjacent to the famous and historic Beale Street entertainment district, this upscale hotel offers stylish rooms in minimalist tones of beige and gray. 203 units. 9 stories, interior corridors. **Parking:** on-site (fee) and valet. **Amenities:** safes. **Activities:** exercise room. **Guest Services:**

valet laundry.

 WHERE TO EAT

BLUE PLATE CAFE
901/523-2050 ①

▼▼ Southern American. Casual Dining. $5-$10 **AAA Inspector Notes:** This cafe is known for its wonderful made-from-scratch breakfasts of buttermilk pancakes with any of eight toppings, as well as the legendary waffles and omelets. For lunch, patrons can order a daily hot meal special with two sides, juicy meatloaf, turkey and dressing, or any of numerous sandwiches and soups. **Address:** 113 S Court Square 38103 **Location:** Just w of jct 2nd St.

CAPRICCIO GRILL
901/529-4199 ⑧

▼▼▼▼ Italian. Fine Dining. $12-$42 **AAA Inspector Notes:** This restaurant features all Prime-grade beef, starting with filet mignon, porterhouse and New York strip and, for that special occasion, their own 24-ounce signature rib-eye steak. Fresh seafood includes numerous specials of the day as well as New Zealand lobster tail. An extensive pasta bar is offered at lunchtime as an alternative for people who are pressed for time at the noon hour. Leave room for one of the signature dessert shooters. **Features:** full bar, Sunday brunch, happy hour. **Address:** 149 Union Ave 38103 **Location:** Jct 2nd St; in Peabody Memphis. **Parking:** on-site (fee) and valet.

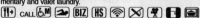

CHEZ PHILIPPE
901/529-4188 ⑦

▼▼▼▼
Continental Fine Dining
$80-$175

AAA Inspector Notes: This innovative menu incorporates such dishes as a juicy petite filet, succulent monkfish and a wonderful rack of lamb cooked to perfection and served with a steamed vegetable medley. Formally dressed servers anticipate each diner's every need or want. The entire experience is exceptional. **Features:** full bar. **Reservations:** suggested. Semiformal attire. **Address:** 149 Union Ave 38103 **Location:** Jct 2nd St; in Peabody Memphis. **Parking:** on-site (fee) and valet.

DEJA VU
901/505-0212 ④

▼▼ Soul Food. Casual Dining. $11-$26 **AAA Inspector Notes:** Don't let the small exterior fool you. Here you'll be transported to New Orleans and enjoy tasty food served by a super-friendly staff. Menu highlights include seafood gumbo, jambalaya, Creole-style shrimp and alligator stew, plus some vegetarian and vegan options. **Features:** beer & wine. **Address:** 51 S Main St 38103 **Location:** Between Monroe and Union aves. **Parking:** street only.

DYER'S BURGERS
901/527-3937 ⑭

▼ Burgers. Quick Serve. $7-$17 **AAA Inspector Notes:** *Classic.* Since 1912, this quick serve has followed the distinctive cooking style of submerging hamburgers in a skillet of grease. Order the chili with cheese and onions-a large chunk of melted cheese over the top of rings of onions. **Features:** beer only. **Address:** 205 Beale St 38103 **Location:** Jct 3rd St, just e. **Parking:** no self-parking.

EIGHTY3 FOOD & DRINK
901/333-1224 ②

▼▼▼ American. Casual Dining. $8-$48 **AAA Inspector Notes:** The trendy, upscale eatery is a favorite among the theater crowd. Entrées include aged beef tenderloin, tempura soft-shell crab and lamb with roasted vegetables. A specialty is martinis served in special glassware. Delicious desserts conclude the offerings. **Features:** full bar, Sunday brunch, happy hour. **Address:** 83 Madison Ave 38103 **Location:** Jct Main St, just w; in Madison Hotel. **Parking:** valet only.

FLIGHT RESTAURANT AND WINE BAR
901/521-8005 ③

▼▼▼ Continental Small Plates. Fine Dining. $8-$34 **AAA Inspector Notes:** As the name suggests, the menu features "flights" for your courses. A trio of dishes, plus a trio of wines to go with them, it's a great way to explore the menu. A popular choice is the "feathered flight" with chicken breast, quail and duck breast. For dessert, the cupcake flight is a nice choice. **Features:** full bar, patio dining. **Reservations:** suggested. **Address:** 39 S Main St 38103 **Location:** Jct Monroe Ave. **Parking:** street and on-site.

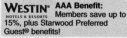

(See map & index p. 152.)

HARD ROCK CAFE
901/529-0007 ⬟13

▽▽ American. Casual Dining. $12-$24 **AAA Inspector Notes:** Rock 'n' roll memorabilia decorates the walls of the popular theme restaurant. Live music on the weekends contributes to the bustling atmosphere. On the menu is a wide variety of American cuisine—from burgers and sandwiches to seafood, steaks and pasta. **Features:** full bar. **Address:** 126 Beale St 38103 **Location:** Jct Handy Cir. **Parking:** on-site (fee) and street.
⬜SAVE⬜ ⬜L⬜ ⬜D⬜ CALL ⬜&M⬜

HUEY'S DOWNTOWN
901/527-2700 ⬟6

▽▽ Burgers Sandwiches. Casual Dining. $6-$11 **AAA Inspector Notes:** Craving a good burger and a beer in a funky, fun eatery? Check out this local chain, as famous for their juicy burgers as for the toothpicks stuck in the ceilings. The Huey burger is a true classic, but avocado, mushrooms, and barbecue sauce are topping options, too. For a healthier option, swap beef for a turkey or veggie patty. The rest of the menu is lined with salads, sandwiches and bar munchies like onion rings, wings, fried pickles, and loaded nachos. **Features:** full bar. **Address:** 77 S 2nd St 38103 **Location:** Jct Union Ave. **Parking:** on-site and street. ⬜L⬜ ⬜D⬜ ⬜LATE⬜

KOOKY CANUCK
901/578-9800 ⬟10

▽▽ American. Casual Dining. $7-$30 **AAA Inspector Notes:** Deep in the heart of the city, this Canadian-style lodge is home of the four-pound Sasquatch burger. Those who need a little less substance might opt for a prime rib sandwich, fried ham and cheese or Asian egg roll salad. Diners can complete their lodge experience by preparing s'mores right at the table. **Features:** full bar, happy hour. **Address:** 97 S 2nd St 38103 **Location:** Jct Union Ave, just s. **Parking:** street only. ⬜L⬜ ⬜D⬜ ⬜LATE⬜ CALL ⬜&M⬜

LOCAL GASTROPUB
901/473-9573 ⬟9

▽▽ American. Gastropub. $10-$19 **AAA Inspector Notes:** At this downtown hot spot, the creative pub fare includes entrées like Dr Pepper-marinated short rib tacos, lobster BLT, fried catfish and Gouda grits, and goat cheese and crab enchiladas. Bar munchies, such as the smoked duck quesadilla, are a departure from the ordinary. Though you'll also find the usual calamari and wings, plus warm, hand-crafted pretzels with beer-cheese fondue. The bar features hand-crafted cocktails and a changing selection of seasonal beers. **Features:** full bar, patio dining, Sunday brunch, happy hour. **Address:** 95 S Main St 38103 **Location:** Jct Union Ave, just s. **Parking:** on-site (fee) and street. ⬜L⬜ ⬜D⬜ ⬜LATE⬜

THE MAJESTIC GRILLE
901/522-8555 ⬟11

▽▽▽ American. Casual Dining. $8-$48 **AAA Inspector Notes:** This former movie palace retains many of its Beaux Arts architectural flourishes, and stills shows vintage movies as part of the dining room's backdrop. Enjoy fresh, flavorful cuisine that runs the gamut from flatbread pizzas with toppings both traditional and inventive, to aged steaks, grilled seafood, and pasta. Hearty sandwiches and fresh salads round out the menu. Brunch is served weekends. Convenient parking in the Peabody Tower Garage at 110 Peabody Place. **Features:** full bar, patio dining, Sunday brunch. **Address:** 145 S Main St 38103 **Location:** Jct Peabody Pl, just n. **Parking:** on-site (fee) and street. ⬜L⬜ ⬜D⬜

PEARL'S OYSTER HOUSE
901/522-9070 ⬟15

▽▽ Southern Seafood. Casual Dining. $8-$39 **AAA Inspector Notes:** An L-shaped bar serves as the focal point for this lively, upbeat eatery. Large windows offer a glimpse of passing trolley cars along Main Street. On the menu you'll find a variety of chicken, beef and seafood dishes; blackened catfish is a local favorite. **Features:** full bar, Sunday brunch, happy hour. **Address:** 299 S Main St 38103 **Location:** Jct Beale St, just s. ⬜L⬜ ⬜D⬜

RENDEZVOUS
901/523-2746 ⬟5

▽▽ Barbecue. Casual Dining. $5-$20 **AAA Inspector Notes:** Since 1948, the restaurant's ribs have been legendary in this city along with its pork entrées. Slow-cooked beans and mustard-based coleslaw complete your hog-heaven dinner. **Features:** full bar. **Address:** 52 S 2nd St 38103 **Location:** Jct Union Ave, just n; in General Washburn Alley. **Parking:** street only. ⬜D⬜

SOB - SOUTH OF BEALE
901/526-0388 ⬟16

▽▽▽ American. Gastropub. $9-$21 **AAA Inspector Notes:** Seared duck and bone-in rib-eye isn't your typical bar food and SOB isn't your typical bar. The strong emphasis on food includes a variety of wonderful dishes, including pecan-crusted pumpkin ravioli, red snapper and seared scallops. Desserts even keep with the pub theme and include beer and pretzel cheesecake drizzled with Guinness syrup. **Features:** full bar, patio dining, Sunday brunch, happy hour. **Address:** 361 S Main St 38103 **Location:** Jct Beale St, just s. ⬜L⬜ ⬜D⬜ ⬜LATE⬜ ⬜🐾⬜

THE SPAGHETTI WAREHOUSE
901/521-0907

▽▽ Italian. Casual Dining. $7-$16 **AAA Inspector Notes:** The Italian-style restaurant chain sustains a festive family atmosphere. All entrees include bottomless tossed salad or soup. Patrons enjoy plentiful portions of such classic dishes as ravioli, lasagna, baked penne or the richly flavored cannelloni Florentine. Splurging on one of the many desserts, such as tiramisu, espresso mousse cake or carrot cake, is worthwhile. **Features:** full bar. **Address:** 40 W Huling Ave 38103 **Location:** Jct Beale St, just s on Main St, then just w. ⬜L⬜ ⬜D⬜

TEXAS DE BRAZIL
901/526-7600 ⬟12

▽▽▽ Brazilian Steak. Casual Dining. $25-$43 **AAA Inspector Notes:** "Gauchos" bring skewered meat selections directly to the table at the Brazilian-style steakhouse, and diners use a small colored coaster to let the server know when they are ready for another selection of beef, chicken, pork or lamb. The extensive salad bar gets meals off to the right start. Desserts are worthy of serious consideration. **Features:** full bar, Sunday brunch, happy hour. **Address:** 150 Peabody Pl, Suite 103 38103 **Location:** Jct Union Ave and 2nd St. **Parking:** on-site (fee) and street. ⬜D⬜ CALL ⬜&M⬜

MEMPHIS (E-1)

BAYMONT INN & SUITES MEMPHIS EAST
(901)377-2233 ⬟6

▽▽ Hotel $59-$79 **Address:** 6020 Shelby Oaks Dr 38134 **Location:** I-40 exit 12, just n, then just e. **Facility:** 97 units. 3 stories, interior corridors. **Pool(s):** outdoor. **Activities:** exercise room.
⬜📶⬜ ⬜🏊⬜ ⬜BIZ⬜ ⬜📶⬜ ⬜▦⬜ / SOME UNITS ⬜🛎⬜ ⬜🍴⬜ ⬜▦⬜

BEST WESTERN EXECUTIVE INN
(901)312-7000 ⬟30

▽▽ Motel $109-$114

AAA Benefit:
Save 10% or more every day and earn 10% bonus points!

Address: 3105 Millbranch Rd 38116 **Location:** I-240 exit 24, just s. **Facility:** 60 units. 2 stories (no elevator), exterior corridors. **Pool(s):** outdoor. **Activities:** limited exercise equipment. **Guest Services:** valet and coin laundry. **Featured Amenity:** breakfast buffet.
⬜SAVE⬜ ⬜🍴⬜ ⬜🏊⬜ ⬜BIZ⬜ ⬜HS⬜ ⬜📶⬜ ⬜🍴⬜ ⬜▦⬜ ⬜▦⬜

BEST WESTERN GALLERIA INN & SUITES
(901)372-0000 ⬟1

▽▽▽ Hotel $100-$199

AAA Benefit:
Save 10% or more every day and earn 10% bonus points!

Address: 8635 Hwy 64 38133 **Location:** I-40 exit 18, just w on US 64, then just s. **Facility:** 108 units. 5 stories, interior corridors. **Activities:** exercise room. **Guest Services:** coin laundry.
⬜SAVE⬜ ⬜📶⬜ CALL ⬜&M⬜ ⬜BIZ⬜ ⬜📶⬜ ⬜✕⬜ ⬜🍴⬜ ⬜▦⬜ ⬜▦⬜ / SOME UNITS ⬜HS⬜

(See map & index p. 154.)

BEST WESTERN PLUS GEN X INN (901)692-9136 **11**

Hotel
$99-$149

AAA Benefit: Save 10% or more every day and earn 10% bonus points!

Address: 1177 Madison Ave 38104 **Location:** I-240 exit 30 southbound, just e; exit northbound, just n on Waldran Blvd, just e on Monroe Ave, just n on Bellevue Blvd, then just w. **Facility:** 32 units. 5 stories, interior corridors. **Terms:** cancellation fee imposed. **Activities:** limited exercise equipment.

COURTYARD BY MARRIOTT MEMPHIS AIRPORT
(901)396-3600 **29**

Hotel
$102-$177

COURTYARD *Marriott*

AAA Benefit: Members save 5% or more!

Address: 1780 Nonconnah Blvd 38132 **Location:** I-240 exit 24, just s, then just e. **Facility:** 145 units. 3 stories, interior corridors. **Pool(s):** outdoor. **Activities:** exercise room. **Guest Services:** valet and coin laundry.

COURTYARD BY MARRIOTT MEMPHIS EAST/BILL MORRIS PARKWAY
(901)365-6400 **28**

Hotel $99-$183 **Address:** 3076 Kirby Pkwy 38115 **Location:** Jct SR 385, just s. **Facility:** 93 units. 3 stories, interior corridors. **Pool(s):** outdoor. **Activities:** hot tub, picnic facilities, exercise room. **Guest Services:** valet and coin laundry, boarding pass kiosk, area transportation.

AAA Benefit: Members save 5% or more!

COURTYARD BY MARRIOTT MEMPHIS EAST/PARK AVE
(901)761-0330 **23**

Hotel
$99-$178

COURTYARD *Marriott*

AAA Benefit: Members save 5% or more!

Address: 6015 Park Ave 38119 **Location:** I-240 exit 15 (Poplar Ave), just s, just s on Ridgeway Rd, then just w. **Facility:** 146 units. 3 stories, interior corridors. **Pool(s):** outdoor. **Activities:** picnic facilities, exercise room. **Guest Services:** valet and coin laundry, boarding pass kiosk.

CROWNE PLAZA MEMPHIS EAST (901)362-6200 **26**

Hotel $109-$189 **Address:** 2625 Thousand Oaks Blvd 38118 **Location:** I-240 exit 18, just se. **Facility:** 319 units. 12 stories, interior corridors. **Terms:** cancellation fee imposed. **Pool(s):** outdoor, heated indoor. **Activities:** hot tub, exercise room. **Guest Services:** valet and coin laundry, luggage security pick-up.

DOUBLETREE BY HILTON HOTEL MEMPHIS
(901)767-6666 **14**

Hotel $109-$199 **Address:** 5069 Sanderlin Ave 38117 **Location:** I-240 exit 15 (Poplar Ave), 1 mi w, 0.5 mi n on White Station Rd, then just w. **Facility:** 263 units. 8 stories, interior corridors. **Terms:** 1-7 night minimum stay, cancellation fee imposed. **Amenities:** Some: safes. **Pool(s):** heated outdoor, heated indoor. **Activities:** exercise room. **Guest Services:** valet laundry, area transportation.

AAA Benefit: Members save 5% or more!

ECONO LODGE INN & SUITES (901)385-1999 **9**

Hotel $60-$94 **Address:** 6045 Macon Cove Rd 38134 **Location:** I-240 exit 12, just s on Sycamore View Rd, then just w. **Facility:** 37 units. 4 stories, exterior corridors. **Pool(s):** outdoor. **Activities:** limited exercise equipment.

EMBASSY SUITES BY HILTON MEMPHIS
(901)684-1777 **18**

Hotel $139-$289 **Address:** 1022 S Shady Grove Rd 38120 **Location:** I-240 exit 15 (Poplar Ave), 0.5 mi e, then n. **Facility:** 220 units, some two bedrooms. 5 stories, interior corridors. **Terms:** 1-7 night minimum stay, cancellation fee imposed. **Pool(s):** heated indoor. **Activities:** hot tub, game room, exercise room. **Guest Services:** valet and coin laundry, area transportation.

AAA Benefit: Members save 5% or more!

FAIRFIELD INN & SUITES BY MARRIOTT MEMPHIS
(901)384-0010 **7**

Hotel $83-$137 **Address:** 6010 Macon Cove Rd 38134 **Location:** I-40 exit 12, just s, then just w. **Facility:** 63 units. 3 stories, interior corridors. **Pool(s):** heated indoor. **Activities:** hot tub, limited exercise equipment. **Guest Services:** valet and coin laundry.

AAA Benefit: Members save 5% or more!

FAIRFIELD INN & SUITES BY MARRIOTT MEMPHIS EAST/GALLERIA
(901)381-0085 **2**

Hotel $98-$260 **Address:** 8489 Hwy 64 38133 **Location:** I-40 exit 18 (US 64), 0.4 mi w, then just s. **Facility:** 62 units. 3 stories, interior corridors. **Pool(s):** heated indoor. **Activities:** hot tub, exercise room. **Guest Services:** valet and coin laundry.

AAA Benefit: Members save 5% or more!

FOUR POINTS BY SHERATON MEMPHIS EAST
(901)767-6300 **21**

Hotel
$109-$199

FOUR POINTS BY SHERATON

AAA Benefit: Members save up to 15%, plus Starwood Preferred Guest® benefits!

Address: 5877 Poplar Ave 38119 **Location:** I-240 exit 15A (Poplar Ave), just e. **Facility:** 124 units. 5 stories, interior corridors. **Terms:** cancellation fee imposed. **Amenities:** safes. **Pool(s):** outdoor. **Activities:** exercise room. **Guest Services:** valet and coin laundry, area transportation.

(See map & index p. 154.)

FOUR POINTS BY SHERATON MEMPHIS-SOUTHWIND
901/309-3020

Hotel
Rates not provided

AAA Benefit: Members save up to 15%, plus Starwood Preferred Guest® benefits!

Address: 4090 Stansell Ct 38125 **Location:** I-240 exit 16, 4 mi e on SR 385 E exit Hacks Cross Rd, then just s. **Facility:** 93 units. 4 stories, interior corridors. **Amenities:** safes. **Pool(s):** heated indoor. **Activities:** hot tub, exercise room. **Guest Services:** valet and coin laundry, luggage security pick-up, area transportation.

THE GUEST HOUSE AT GRACELAND
877/777-0606

[fyi] Hotel Under construction, scheduled to open November 2016. **Address:** 3600 Elvis Presley Blvd 38116 **Location:** I-55 S exit 5B, s on Elvis Presley Blvd to 4th traffic light. **Planned Amenities:** 450 units, restaurant, coffeemakers, refrigerators, pool. *(See ad this page.)*

HAMPTON INN & SUITES MEMPHIS-SHADY GROVE
(901)762-0056

Hotel $109-$169 **Address:** 962 S Shady Grove Rd 38120 **Location:** I-240 exit 15 (Poplar Ave), 0.5 mi e. **Facility:** 130 units, some efficiencies. 5 stories, interior corridors. **Terms:** check-in 4 pm, 1-7 night minimum stay, cancellation fee imposed. **Pool(s):** outdoor. **Activities:** exercise room. **Guest Services:** valet and coin laundry, area transportation.

AAA Benefit: Members save up to 10%!

HAMPTON INN MEMPHIS-SOUTHWIND
(901)754-8454

Hotel $109-$199 **Address:** 3579 Hacks Cross Rd 38125 **Location:** I-240 exit 16, 4 mi e on SR 385 E, then 1 mi n. **Facility:** 133 units. 4 stories, interior corridors. **Terms:** check-in 4 pm, 1-7 night minimum stay, cancellation fee imposed. **Pool(s):** outdoor. **Activities:** exercise room. **Guest Services:** valet and coin laundry, area transportation.

AAA Benefit: Members save up to 10%!

▼ *See AAA listing this page* ▼

INTRODUCING A NEW HOTEL EXPERIENCE
IN THE HEART OF ELVIS PRESLEY'S GRACELAND

THE GUEST HOUSE
AT
Graceland

OPENING IN MEMPHIS, FALL 2016
Visit Graceland.com/Guesthouse

Request roadside assistance in a click —
online or using the AAA or CAA apps

(See map & index p. 154.)

HAMPTON INN MEMPHIS-WALNUT GROVE/BAPTIST
HOSPITAL EAST   (901)747-3700   12

▼▼▼ **Hotel** $109-$139 **Address:**
33 Humphreys Center Dr 38120 **Loca-**
tion: I-240 exit 13 (Walnut Grove E), just
e. Adjacent to Humphreys Center and
Baptist East Memorial Hospital. **Facility:**
121 units. 4 stories, interior corridors. **Terms:** 1-7 night minimum stay,
cancellation fee imposed. **Pool(s):** outdoor. **Activities:** exercise
room. **Guest Services:** valet laundry.

> **AAA Benefit:**
> Members save up to
> 10%!

[icons]

HILTON MEMPHIS   (901)684-6664   15

▼▼▼ **Hotel** $109-$299 **Address:**
939 Ridge Lake Blvd 38120 **Location:**
I-240 exit 15 (Poplar Ave), just e, then n
under overpass. **Facility:** 405 units. 27
stories, interior corridors. **Parking:** on-
site and valet. **Terms:** 1-7 night minimum stay, cancellation fee imposed. **Amenities:** video games, safes. **Dining:** Rooks Corner, see
separate listing. **Pool(s):** outdoor. **Activities:** hot tub, exercise room.
Guest Services: valet laundry, area transportation.

> **AAA Benefit:**
> Members save 5%
> or more!

[icons]

HOLIDAY INN & SUITES MEMPHIS-WOLFCHASE GALLERIA
                                                 901/266-1952   3

▼▼▼ **Hotel.** Rates not provided. **Address:** 2751 New Bruns-
wick Rd 38133 **Location:** I-40 exit 18, just w on US 64, then just s.
Facility: 133 units. 6 stories, interior corridors. **Pool(s):** heated indoor. **Activities:** hot tub, exercise room. **Guest Services:** valet and
coin laundry.

[icons]

HOLIDAY INN EXPRESS & SUITES MEMPHIS SOUTHWIND
                                                 901/309-6474   33

▼▼▼ **Hotel.** Rates not provided. **Address:** 4068 Stansell Ct
38125 **Location:** I-240 exit 16, 4 mi e on SR 385 E exit Hacks Cross
Rd, then just s. **Facility:** 89 units. 3 stories, interior corridors. **Pool(s):**
outdoor. **Activities:** exercise room. **Guest Services:** valet and coin
laundry, area transportation.

[icons]

HOLIDAY INN-UNIVERSITY OF MEMPHIS
                                                 (901)678-8200   13

▼▼▼ **Hotel** $139-$169 **Address:** 3700 Central Ave 38152 **Lo-**
cation: Jct Goodlett St, 0.7 mi w. **Facility:** 82 units. 4 stories, interior
corridors. **Terms:** 3 day cancellation notice-fee imposed. **Activities:**
exercise room. **Guest Services:** valet and coin laundry, luggage security pick-up, area transportation.

[icons]

HOMEWOOD SUITES BY HILTON MEMPHIS-POPLAR
                                                 (901)763-0500   19

▼▼▼ **Extended Stay Hotel**
$129-$159 **Address:** 5811 Poplar Ave
38119 **Location:** I-240 exit 15 (Poplar
Ave), just e. **Facility:** 140 efficiencies,
some two bedrooms. 2-3 stories,
interior/exterior corridors. **Terms:** 1-7 night minimum stay, cancellation fee imposed. **Amenities:** video games. **Pool(s):** outdoor. **Activ-**
ities: picnic facilities, exercise room. **Guest Services:** valet and coin
laundry.

> **AAA Benefit:**
> Members save up to
> 10%!

[icons]

HOMEWOOD SUITES BY HILTON SOUTHWIND-HACKS
CROSS   (901)758-5018   31

▼▼▼ **Extended Stay Hotel**
$109-$299 **Address:** 3583 Hacks Cross
Rd 38125 **Location:** I-240 exit 16, 4 mi e
on SR 385, then 1 mi n. **Facility:** 123 efficiencies. 4 stories, interior corridors.
Terms: check-in 4 pm, 1-7 night minimum stay, cancellation fee imposed. **Pool(s):** outdoor. **Activities:** exercise room. **Guest Services:**
valet and coin laundry, area transportation.

> **AAA Benefit:**
> Members save up to
> 10%!

[icons]

(See map & index p. 154.)

HYATT PLACE-MEMPHIS/PRIMACY PARKWAY
(901)680-9700 **25**

Hotel
$89-$219

⊞ HYATT PLACE®

AAA Benefit: Members save 10%!

Address: 1220 Primacy Pkwy 38119 **Location:** I-240 exit 15 (Poplar Ave), 0.5 mi e, s on Ridgeway Rd, just w, then just s. **Facility:** 126 stories, interior corridors. **Terms:** cancellation fee imposed. **Amenities:** safes. **Pool(s):** outdoor. **Activities:** exercise room. **Guest Services:** valet and coin laundry, area transportation. **Featured Amenity:** breakfast buffet.

(See ad this page.)

[SAVE] [📶] [🍴] [🍸] CALL [👓M] [🏊] [BIZ] [📶] [✕] [🦮] [🔌]
[💻] /SOME UNITS [📶] [HS]

HYATT PLACE MEMPHIS/WOLFCHASE GALLERIA
(901)371-0010 **5**

Hotel
$84-$189

⊞ HYATT PLACE®

AAA Benefit: Members save 10%!

Address: 7905 Giacosa Pl 38133 **Location:** I-40 exit 16 or 16B, just n on Germantown Rd, then just w. **Facility:** 126 units. 6 stories, interior corridors. **Terms:** cancellation fee imposed. **Amenities:** safes. **Pool(s):** outdoor. **Activities:** exercise room. **Guest Services:** valet and coin laundry. **Featured Amenity:** breakfast buffet.

[SAVE] [📶] [🍸] CALL [👓M] [🏊] [BIZ]
[HS] [📶] [✕] [🔌] [💻] /SOME UNITS [📶]

THE INN AT THOUSAND OAKS
901/367-1234 **27**

▼▼▼ **Hotel.** Rates not provided. **Address:** 2700 Perkins Rd S 38118 **Location:** I-240 exit 18, just se. **Facility:** 130 units. 5 stories, interior corridors. **Amenities:** video games. **Pool(s):** outdoor. **Activities:** limited exercise equipment. **Guest Services:** valet laundry.

[✈] [📶] CALL [👓M] [🏊] [BIZ] [📶] [🦮]
/SOME UNITS [📶] [🔌] [💻]

LA QUINTA INN & SUITES MEMPHIS EAST-SYCAMORE VIEW
(901)381-0044 **8**

▼▼▼
Hotel
$64-$240

Address: 6069 Macon Cove 38134 **Location:** I-40 exit 12, just s, then just w. **Facility:** 64 units. 4 stories, interior corridors. **Activities:** exercise room. **Guest Services:** coin laundry. **Featured Amenity:** continental breakfast.

[SAVE] [📶] CALL [👓M] [BIZ] [HS] [📶]
[✕] [🔌] [🖨] [💻] /SOME UNITS [🦮]

▼ See AAA listing this page ▼

(See map & index p. 154.)

LA QUINTA INN & SUITES-MEMPHIS PRIMACY PARKWAY
(901)374-0330

▼▼▼ **Hotel** $71-$203 **Address:** 1236 Primacy Pkwy 38119 **Location:** I-240 exit 15 (Poplar Ave), 0.5 mi e, just s on Ridgeway Rd, just w on Park Ave, then just s. **Facility:** 131 units. 6 stories, interior corridors. **Pool(s):** outdoor. **Activities:** hot tub, exercise room. **Guest Services:** valet and coin laundry.

[🍴] CALL [👤M] [🚲] [BIZ] [📶] [✕] [🖨] / SOME UNITS [🐾] [🔒] [🍽]

MARRIOTT MEMPHIS EAST   (901)682-0080 **20**

▼▼▼
Hotel
$99-$298

AAA Benefit: Members save 5% or more!

MARRIOTT

Address: 5795 Poplar Ave 38119 **Location:** I-240 exit 15 (Poplar Ave), just e. **Facility:** 232 units. 10 stories, interior corridors. **Pool(s):** heated indoor. **Activities:** hot tub, exercise room. **Guest Services:** valet and coin laundry, boarding pass kiosk, area transportation.

[SAVE] [✈] [🍴] [👤] [Y] CALL [👤M] [🚲] [BIZ] [SHS] [📶] [✕] [🔒] [🖨] [🍽]

RESIDENCE INN BY MARRIOTT MEMPHIS EAST
(901)685-9595 **22**

▼▼▼
Extended Stay Hotel
$99-$206

Residence Inn Marriott

AAA Benefit: Members save 5% or more!

Address: 6141 Poplar Pike 38119 **Location:** I-240 exit 15 (Poplar Ave), 0.5 mi e. **Facility:** 105 units, some two bedrooms, efficiencies and kitchens. 4 stories, interior corridors. **Pool(s):** outdoor. **Activities:** picnic facilities, exercise room. **Guest Services:** valet and coin laundry.

[SAVE] [🍴] CALL [👤M] [🚲] [BIZ] [📶] [✕] [🔒] [🖨] [🍽] / SOME UNITS [🍽]

RIVER INN OF HARBOR TOWN   (901)260-3333 **10**

▼▼▼ ▼▼▼
Boutique Hotel
$215-$635

Address: 50 Harbor Town Square 38103 **Location:** I-40 exit 1D eastbound; exit 1B westbound, just n on Danny Thomas Blvd, 1 mi w on A.W. Willis Ave, just n on Island Dr, then just e. **Facility:** Located in the upscale Harbor Town area, this boutique hotel offers European charm and Memphis hospitality. The well-appointed rooms and suites offer wonderful views of the mighty Mississippi River. 28 units. 4 stories, interior corridors. **Terms:** cancellation fee imposed, resort fee. **Amenities:** safes. **Dining:** 2 restaurants, also, Paulette's Restaurant, see separate listing. **Activities:** limited exercise equipment. **Guest Services:** valet laundry. **Featured Amenity:** full hot breakfast.

[SAVE] [🍴] [👤] [Y] CALL [👤M] [BIZ] [HS] [📶] [✕] [🔒]

SLEEP INN   (901)312-7777 **4**

▼▼ **Hotel** $58-$120 **Address:** 2855 Old Austin Peay Hwy 38128 **Location:** I-40 exit 8 or 8A, 0.8 mi ne. **Facility:** 70 units. 3 stories, interior corridors. **Parking:** winter plug-ins. **Amenities:** safes. **Pool(s):** heated indoor. **Activities:** limited exercise equipment. **Guest Services:** coin laundry.

CALL [👤M] [🚲] [HS] [📶] [🔒] [🖨] [🍽] / SOME UNITS [🍽]

STAYBRIDGE SUITES MEMPHIS-POPLAR AVE EAST
(901)682-1722 **16**

▼▼▼ **Extended Stay Hotel** $129-$189 **Address:** 1070 Ridge Lake Blvd 38120 **Location:** I-240 exit 15 (Poplar Ave), just e, then n under overpass. **Facility:** 114 efficiencies. 4 stories, interior corridors. **Terms:** cancellation fee imposed. **Pool(s):** outdoor. **Activities:** exercise room. **Guest Services:** complimentary and valet laundry, area transportation.

[✈] [🍴] CALL [👤M] [🚲] [BIZ] [📶] [✕] [🔒] [🖨] [🍽] / SOME UNITS [🍽]

TRAVELERS INN AND SUITES   901/363-8430 **35**

▼ **Motel.** Rates not provided. **Address:** 5024 Lamar Ave (US Hwy 78) 38118 **Location:** I-240 exit 21 (US 78), 5 mi s. Located in a commercial area. **Facility:** 52 units. 2 stories (no elevator), exterior corridors. **Pool(s):** outdoor. **Guest Services:** coin laundry.

[🍴] [🚲] [BIZ] [📶] [🔒] [🖨] [🍽] / SOME UNITS [🍽] [HS]

WHERE TO EAT

AMERIGO, AN ITALIAN RESTAURANT   901/761-4000 **20**

▼▼▼ Italian. Fine Dining. $9-$32 **AAA Inspector Notes:** Drift off to a Florence-inspired café, where the staff is friendly and cordial, and the aroma of freshly cooked pizza and pasta fills the air. Start your meal with the signature "Amerigo" bruschetta or a cup of the delicious gumbo soup. Tuscan crab cakes, wood-fired pizza and the must-try veal piccata are popular options as well. **Features:** full bar, early bird specials, Sunday brunch. **Reservations:** suggested. **Address:** 1239 Ridgeway Rd 38119 **Location:** I-240 exit 15 (Poplar Ave), 0.4 mi e, then just s; in Park Place Center.

[L] [D] CALL [👤M]

BOGIE'S DELICATESSEN   901/272-0022 **4**

▼ Deli. Quick Serve. $6-$12 **AAA Inspector Notes:** Made-to-order deli sandwiches of Reubens, roast beef and Italian varieties are some of the local favorites, and the muffuletta is a meal in itself. For a delicious dessert, try the homemade Black Forest cake or Key lime square. **Features:** beer only, patio dining. **Address:** 2098 Lasalle Pl 38104 **Location:** Just nw of jct Madison Ave and Cooper St; in Overton Square. [B] [L] [D]

BUCKLEY'S   901/683-4538 **15**

▼▼ American. Casual Dining. $12-$26 **AAA Inspector Notes:** Don't let the modest exterior fool you, as this local favorite has great-tasting steaks, pasta, fish and chicken. Rag's cheese bread and sizzling stuffed mushrooms are great starters. The cow chip dessert is a luscious ending to the meal. **Features:** full bar. **Address:** 5355 Poplar Ave 38119 **Location:** I-240 exit 15A (Poplar Ave), 0.5 mi w. [D] CALL [👤M]

CAJUN CATFISH COMPANY   901/383-8958 **1**

▼▼ Cajun. Casual Dining. $7-$17 **AAA Inspector Notes:** As the name implies, the many different ways to enjoy the best in catfish are numerous and delicious. Fried, blackened, grilled and with various toppings is just the beginning. Shrimp, oysters, sandwiches and great tasting hush puppies are just a few other menu items available. **Features:** beer & wine, patio dining, happy hour. **Address:** 1616 Sycamore View Rd 38134 **Location:** I-40 exit 12, 0.4 mi n. [L] [D]

CENTRAL BBQ IN MEMPHIS   901/272-9377 **6**

▼ Barbecue. Quick Serve. $4-$25 **AAA Inspector Notes:** Since opening in 2002, this family restaurant has built quite the local following and has won numerous awards for their barbecue, ribs and wings. When ordering a sandwich ask for the sauce on the side to make it easier to eat. **Features:** beer only, patio dining. **Address:** 2249 Central Ave 38104 **Location:** Between S Cooper St and E Parkway S. [L] [D] [🐾]

CORKY'S RIBS & BBQ   901/685-9744

▼▼ Barbecue. Casual Dining. $10-$28 **AAA Inspector Notes:** Top-notch barbecue, such as succulent dry-rubbed ribs, never disappoint at this casual restaurant. You may have to wait for it as this place often cannot contain the crowds that come to dine here. The atmosphere is delightfully rustic. **Features:** beer only. **Address:** 5259 Poplar Ave 38119 **Location:** I-240 exit 15 (Poplar Ave W), 0.8 mi w. [L] [D]

(See map & index p. 154.)

DIXIE CAFE   901/683-7555

▼▼ ▼▼ Regional American. Family Dining. $6-$12 **AAA Inspector Notes:** Enjoy southern-style home cooking featuring chicken-fried steak, meat loaf, pork chops, turnip greens, mashed potatoes and fresh veggies. The restaurant's classic Norman Rockwell atmosphere makes it appealing to families. **Features:** early bird specials, senior menu. **Address:** 4699 Poplar Ave 38111 **Location:** I-240 exit 15 (Poplar Ave), 2 mi w. L D

FOLK'S FOLLY PRIME STEAK HOUSE   901/762-8200   10

▼▼▼ ▼▼▼ Traditional Steak. Fine Dining. $26-$67 **AAA Inspector Notes:** The bustling steakhouse's several private rooms make this place an elegant favorite for special occasions. Fresh seafood and prime steaks, including grilled filet mignon, are good choices, as is the chocolate fudge brownie with vanilla ice cream. **Features:** full bar. **Reservations:** suggested. **Address:** 551 S Mendenhall Rd 38117 **Location:** I-240 exit 15 (Poplar Ave W), 1.8 mi w, then just n. **Parking:** on-site and valet. D

THE HALF SHELL   901/737-6755   22

▼▼ ▼▼ Seafood. Casual Dining. $7-$37 **AAA Inspector Notes:** The restaurant offers fresh seafood, including numerous types of oysters and toppings, jumbo shrimp, Gulf amberjack and Alaskan king crab legs. Also on the menu are aged, hand-carved steaks of premium beef and signature salads. Inside, you'll find this is a quaint getaway during the day for lunch, or for dinner. With its proximity to FedEx's world headquarters, this restaurant is frequented by both locals and business travelers, and has an active bar scene. **Features:** full bar, Sunday brunch. **Address:** 7825 Winchester Rd 38125 **Location:** I-240 exit 16, 4 mi e on SR 385, 0.8 mi n on Hacks Cross Rd, then just w. L D LATE CALL M

HAPPY MEXICAN   901/683-0000   21

▼▼ ▼▼ Mexican. Casual Dining. $6-$20 **AAA Inspector Notes:** Festive décor and lively music set the theme for your favorite Mexican dishes. **Features:** full bar. **Address:** 6080 Primacy Pkwy 38119 **Location:** I-240 exit 15 (Poplar Ave), 0.5 mi e, just s on Ridgeway Rd, then just w. L D

HOG & HOMINY   901/207-7396   12

▼▼ ▼▼ Fusion Comfort Food. Casual Dining. $14-$18 **AAA Inspector Notes:** In this former ranch home you'll find funky décor, friendly service and an innovative menu of Southern cuisine with an Italian flair. Brick oven thin-crust pizzas, the house specialty, are topped with gourmet ingredients like pickled peppers, marinated olives, and speck, a juniper-flavored Italian ham. The dinner menu includes creative dishes like duck sausage with Brussels sprouts slaw, and poutine (fries topped with gravy and cheese curd). **Features:** full bar, patio dining. **Address:** 707 W Brookhaven Cir 38117 **Location:** I-240 exit 15 (Poplar Ave), 1 mi w, then just n. **Parking:** on-site and street. L D CALL M

HUEY'S   901/624-8911   23

▼▼ ▼▼ American. Casual Dining. $6-$11 **AAA Inspector Notes:** Casual theme with plenty of barstools, TVs and memorabilia. I enjoyed the Texas toast burger loaded with pepper jack cheese, onions and jalapeños. **Features:** full bar. **Address:** 7825 Winchester Rd 38125 **Location:** 0.4 mi e of jct Bill Morris Pkwy. L D LATE

INTERIM RESTAURANT & BAR   901/818-0821   8

▼▼▼ ▼▼▼ American. Fine Dining. $11-$30 **AAA Inspector Notes:** Enjoy fresh, creative fare that includes seafood, beef, chicken and more on a seasonally changing menu in a casually elegant dining room. Entrées may include dishes like braised pork shank with collard greens and smoked paprika sauce, or pecan-crusted salmon with carrot-ginger butter. Lunch features crisp salads, gourmet sandwiches, and a few entrées. The state-of-the-art kitchen is in full view, so it's almost like having a front row seat at a cooking show. **Features:** full bar, Sunday brunch. **Reservations:** suggested. **Address:** 5040 Sanderlin Ave 38117 **Location:** I-240 exit 15 (Poplar Ave), 1.4 mi w, just n on S Mendenhall Rd, then just e; in Sanderlin Place. L D

JIM'S PLACE RESTAURANT & BAR   901/766-2030   9

▼▼▼ ▼▼▼ American. Casual Dining. $12-$29 **AAA Inspector Notes:** This family-owned spot has been a fixture in the Memphis dining scene since 1921, offering menu items that range from Greek moussaka to New Orleans gumbo. Grilled or broiled beef and seafood are the house specialties—try the charcoal-grilled lamb chops, filet mignon or red snapper. Classic fare includes fried oysters, chopped sirloin, and grilled liver and onions. For dessert, the caramel fudge pecan pie is a decadent temptation. **Features:** full bar, happy hour. **Address:** 518 Perkins Ext 38117 **Location:** I-240 exit 15 (Poplar Ave), 2.2 mi w. L D

LA PLAYITA MEXICAN RESTAURANT   901/377-2282   2

▼▼ ▼▼ Mexican. Family Dining. $6-$18 **AAA Inspector Notes:** You cannot go wrong with this tucked-away restaurant. Traditional selections such as tacos, burritos, enchiladas and quesadillas are served in a relaxed family atmosphere. Draft beer and margaritas are offered. **Features:** full bar. **Address:** 6194 Macon Rd 38134 **Location:** I-40 exit 12, just s on Sycamore View Rd, then just e. L D

MARCIANO MEDITERRANEAN & ITALIAN RESTAURANT
                                                       901/682-1660   13

▼▼ ▼▼ Mediterranean. Casual Dining. $14-$28 **AAA Inspector Notes:** Though this cozy bistro's focus is on Italian and Greek fare, you'll also find a few Turkish and Moroccan-inspired dishes on the menu. Classics like veal marsala, chicken piccata, and fettuccine Bolognese are featured, plus there's pizza and specialties like Turkish chicken split pea stew and grilled rack of lamb. **Features:** full bar, happy hour. **Address:** 780 E Brookhaven Cir 38117 **Location:** I-240 exit 15 (Poplar Ave), 1 mi w, then just n. D

NAPA CAFE   901/683-0441   11

▼▼▼ ▼▼▼ Continental. Fine Dining. $13-$32 **AAA Inspector Notes:** Rich shrimp bisque, lump meat crab cakes and aged beef are just a few delights that await you at the friendly and relaxed café. Many seafood offerings of salmon, tilapia, yellowfin tuna and halibut are cooked to perfection. Rich and artistic desserts complete the meal. As the name suggests, the restaurant takes pride in its extensive, award-winning wine list. **Features:** full bar, patio dining. **Address:** 5101 Sanderlin Ave, Suite 122 38117 **Location:** I-240 exit 15 (Poplar Ave), 1 mi w, 0.5 mi n on White Station Rd, then just w; in Sanderlin Centre. L D CALL M

OLD VENICE PIZZA COMPANY   901/767-6872   7

▼▼ ▼▼ Italian. Casual Dining. $7-$18 **AAA Inspector Notes:** Calzones, salads and inventive pizzas are all available at this Memphis hot spot. Hit their Burgundy Room for a drink and try one of the many enjoyable appetizers. **Features:** full bar. **Address:** 368 S Perkins Ext 38119 **Location:** I-240 exit 15 (Poplar Ave), 2.4 mi w, then just n. L D

OWEN BRENNAN'S RESTAURANT   901/761-0990   18

▼▼▼ ▼▼▼ Cajun. Fine Dining. $9-$33 **AAA Inspector Notes:** The décor transports diners to New Orleans, as do made-from-scratch recipes that appeal to the Cajun connoisseur. Piquant flavors infuse seafood, fowl and beef. Signature desserts are well worth trying. **Features:** full bar, patio dining, Sunday brunch. **Address:** 6150 Poplar Ave, Suite 150 38119 **Location:** I-240 exit 15 (Poplar Ave), 0.5 mi e; in Regalia Shopping Plaza. L D CALL M

PATRICK'S RESTAURANT   901/682-2852   16

▼▼ ▼▼ American. Casual Dining. $8-$26 **AAA Inspector Notes:** For nearly 20 years Patrick's has served a variety of Southern-style dishes, including barbecue ribs, meatloaf, steaks and daily lunch plate specials, but it's the burgers that draw the crowds. Their sandwiches aren't too shabby, either. Only the really disciplined could resist the mempho, a stack of mac-n-cheese, pulled pork and caramelized onions between two slices of white bread. Discipline is over rated anyway. **Features:** full bar, patio dining, happy hour. **Address:** 4972 Park Ave 38117 **Location:** Just w of jct Mt Moriah Rd. L D LATE

AAA Vacations® packages ...
exciting itineraries and exclusive values

(See map & index p. 154.)

PAULETTE'S RESTAURANT   901/260-3300   ③

Regional
American
Casual Dining
$10-$35

AAA Inspector Notes: Colorful presentations and rich flavors mark the seasonally changing menu at this popular bistro decorated in French country style. Classic dishes such as filet mignon, grilled salmon, coq au vin and Low-country crab cakes are often featured, along with tasty homemade soups. Give the dessert crêpes a try to appease the sweet tooth. **Features:** full bar, Sunday brunch, happy hour. **Reservations:** suggested. **Address:** 50 Harbor Town Square 38103 **Location:** I-40 exit 1D eastbound; exit 1B westbound, just n on Danny Thomas Blvd, 1 mi w on A.W. Willis Ave, just n on Island Dr, then just e; in River Inn of Harbor Town. Ⓑ Ⓛ Ⓓ

RIVER OAKS   901/683-9305   ⑰

▽▽▽ Continental. Fine Dining. $15-$28 **AAA Inspector Notes:** At this upscale and trendy restaurant, New American cuisine is prepared with a French twist. Menu offerings include Camembert cheese beignets and jicama lobster tacos. **Features:** full bar, happy hour. **Reservations:** suggested. **Address:** 5871 Poplar Ave 38119 **Location:** I-240 exit 15A (Poplar Ave), just e.

Ⓛ Ⓓ CALL⅏

ROOKS CORNER   901/684-6664   ⑭

▽▽▽ American. Casual Dining. $10-$38 **AAA Inspector Notes:** The casually upscale restaurant is great for special or business occasions, with a tranquil view of the pond with fountain. The menu features steaks, seafood and pasta, plus sandwiches and salads. **Features:** full bar. **Reservations:** suggested, for dinner. **Address:** 939 Ridge Lake Blvd 38120 **Location:** I-240 exit 15 (Poplar Ave), just e, then n under overpass; in Hilton Memphis.

Ⓑ Ⓛ Ⓓ CALL⅏

THE SECOND LINE   901/590-2829   ⑤

▽ Regional American. Casual Dining. $12-$18 **AAA Inspector Notes:** In a vibrant atmosphere you'll feast on traditional New Orleans favorites like po'boys and seafood plates. Lunch is only available on Saturday and Sunday. **Features:** full bar. **Address:** 2144 Monroe Ave 38104 **Location:** Jct Cooper St. **Parking:** street only. Ⓓ

SEKISUI   901/725-0005

▽▽ Japanese Sushi. Casual Dining. $9-$27 **AAA Inspector Notes:** The main dining room at this casual spot offers a quiet and relaxed setting while the sushi bar features a bustling, high-energy atmosphere. Crunchy shrimp rolls and stir-fried teriyaki chicken are popular samplings. Finish with green tea ice cream for an unusual, sweet treat. **Features:** full bar. **Address:** 25 S Belvedere Blvd 38104 **Location:** I-240 exit 30 (Union Ave) northbound; exit 29 southbound, 1 mi e, then just n. Ⓛ Ⓓ

WANG'S MANDARIN HOUSE   901/685-9264   ⑲

▽▽ Chinese. Casual Dining. $7-$25 **AAA Inspector Notes:** Since 1983, this locals' favorite for flavorful, classic Chinese fare has won many local best-of-awards. The charming dining room offers an intimate setting for a leisurely lunch or dinner. Friendly servers are happy to make menu suggestions to suit your tastes. Favorites include Singapore rice noodles, General Tso's chicken, Szechuan beef, and twice-cooked pork. Peking duck and crispy whole fish are specialties. A small lunch buffet is available weekdays. **Features:** full bar, happy hour. **Address:** 6065 Park Ave 38119 **Location:** I-240 exit 15 (Poplar Ave), 0.5 mi e, just s on Ridgeway Rd, then just w; in Park Place Center. Ⓛ Ⓓ

RESTAURANT IRIS   901/590-2828

ⓕⓨⓘ Not evaluated. In a restored Victorian house, this lovely setting prepares you for a journey that tantalizes your taste buds with dishes such as shrimp with Delta Grind grits, gulf mahi mahi with Creole mustard beurre blanc, and hickory house-smoked moulard breast with dirty rice and maple-bourbon glaze. Don't leave without trying their specialty bread pudding. **Address:** 2146 Monroe Ave 38104 **Location:** Just e of Cooper St.

Choose real ratings you can trust from

professional inspectors who've been there

Nearby Arkansas

MARION   pop. 12,345

• Part of Memphis area — see map p. 134

HAMPTON INN   870/739-2800

ⓕⓨⓘ Hotel. Rates not provided. Too new to rate, opening scheduled for January 2015. **Address:** 310 Angelo's Grove Rd 72364 **Location:** I-55 exit 10. **Amenities:** 80 units, coffeemakers, refrigerators, pool, exercise facility.

AAA Benefit:
Members save up to 10%!

WHERE TO EAT

COLTON'S STEAKHOUSE & GRILL   870/739-1900

▽▽ Steak. Casual Dining. $7-$24 **AAA Inspector Notes:** Set in an Old-West atmosphere, this place offers patrons a variety of choices with salads, burgers and full entrees. A few favorites include their country fried steak, grilled pork chops or Hawaiian chicken. The menu also features some entrees under 700 calories. **Features:** full bar. **Address:** 303 Angelo's Grove 72364 **Location:** I-55 exit 10, just w on US 64, then just s. Ⓛ Ⓓ

WEST MEMPHIS   pop. 26,245

• Hotels & Restaurants map & index p. 154
• Part of Memphis area — see map p. 134

BEST WESTERN WEST MEMPHIS INN   (870)735-7185   ㊷

▽▽ Hotel
$80-$225

AAA Benefit:
Save 10% or more every day and earn 10% bonus points!

Address: 3401 Service Loop Rd 72301 **Location:** I-55 exit 4, just nw. **Facility:** 39 units. 2 stories (no elevator), interior corridors. **Pool(s):** outdoor.

SAVE ⓘⓕ➕ CALL⅏ 〰 BIZ 📶 🛏 ◻ ◻ / SOME UNITS Ⓗ

DAYS INN WEST MEMPHIS   (870)735-8600   ㊸

▽▽ Hotel $53-$80 **Address:** 1100 Ingram Blvd 72301 **Location:** I-40 exit 279A, just n. **Facility:** 145 units, some two bedrooms and kitchens. 2 stories (no elevator), exterior corridors. **Pool(s):** outdoor. **Guest Services:** coin laundry.

ⓘⓕ➕ CALL⅏ 〰 BIZ 📶 🛏 ◻ ◻ / SOME UNITS 🔌

RAMADA   (870)732-1102   ㊶

▽▽ Hotel $79-$109 **Address:** 2003 E Service Rd 72301 **Location:** I-40 exit 279A, just s. **Facility:** 76 units. 2 stories (no elevator), interior corridors. **Pool(s):** outdoor. **Activities:** exercise room. **Guest Services:** valet and coin laundry.

ⓘⓕ➕ CALL⅏ 〰 BIZ 📶 ◻ / SOME UNITS 🛏 ◻

Nearby Mississippi

HERNANDO   pop. 14,090

• Part of Memphis area — see map p. 134

SASSAFRAS INN BED & BREAKFAST   662/429-5864

▽▽ Bed & Breakfast $110-$245 **Address:** 785 Hwy 51 S 38632 **Location:** I-55 exit 184, just w, then 2.3 mi s. Located in a rural area. **Facility:** Surrounded by a large yard in a nicely forested area, this serene home features traditional décor, including lace and beaded lamp shades. Some rooms have a skylight and modern conveniences. 4 units, some cottages. 1-2 stories (no elevator), interior/exterior corridors. **Terms:** 7 day cancellation notice-fee imposed. **Pool(s):** heated indoor. **Activities:** hot tub, game room.

〰 📶 ✖ 🚭 🛏 / SOME UNITS ◻

HORN LAKE pop. 26,066
• Part of Memphis area — see map p. 134

BEST WESTERN PLUS GOODMAN INN & SUITES
(662)510-6999

Hotel
$109-$209

AAA Benefit: Save 10% or more every day and earn 10% bonus points!

Address: 6910 Windchase Dr 38637 **Location:** I-55 exit 289, just w, then just s. **Facility:** 70 units. 4 stories, interior corridors. **Pool(s):** heated indoor. **Activities:** hot tub, exercise room. **Guest Services:** valet and coin laundry.

[SAVE] [tt+] CALL [&M] [≥] [BIZ] [HS]
[⌂] [♦] [▭] [▢] / SOME UNITS [🛏]

COMFORT INN
(662)349-3493

Hotel $84-$105 **Address:** 801 Desoto Cove 38637 **Location:** I-55 exit 289, just w, then just n. **Facility:** 49 units. 3 stories, interior corridors. **Amenities:** safes. **Pool(s):** outdoor. **Activities:** exercise room. **Guest Services:** valet and coin laundry.

[tt+] CALL [&M] [≥] [BIZ] [⌂] [♦] [▭] [▢] / SOME UNITS [🛏]

DRURY INN & SUITES-MEMPHIS SOUTH
(662)349-6622

Hotel $90-$169 **Address:** 735 Goodman Rd W 38637 **Location:** I-55 exit 289, just w, then just s. **Facility:** 159 units. 6 stories, interior corridors. **Terms:** cancellation fee imposed. **Pool(s):** heated outdoor, heated indoor. **Activities:** hot tub, exercise room. **Guest Services:** valet and coin laundry.

[tt+] CALL [&M] [≥] [BIZ] [⌂] [✕] [♦] [▭] [▢] / SOME UNITS [🛏]

LA QUINTA INN & SUITES HORN LAKE SOUTHAVEN
(662)510-6500

Hotel $82-$196 **Address:** 721 Southwest Dr 38637 **Location:** I-55 exit 289, just sw. **Facility:** 65 units. 3 stories, interior corridors. **Pool(s):** heated indoor. **Activities:** hot tub, exercise room. **Guest Services:** valet and coin laundry.

CALL [&M] [≥] [BIZ] [HS] [⌂] [✕] [♦] [▭] [▢] / SOME UNITS [🐕]

WHERE TO EAT

EL CHARRO
662/280-2610

Tex-Mex. Casual Dining. $5-$12 **AAA Inspector Notes:** This cozy Mexican restaurant has a standard menu, but the food is consistently good. Among traditional favorites are tacos and burritos. **Features:** full bar, happy hour. **Address:** 1651 Goodman Rd W 38637 **Location:** I-55 exit 289, 1.1 mi w. [L] [D] [N]

OLIVE BRANCH pop. 33,484
• Part of Memphis area — see map p. 134

A fast-growing suburb of Memphis, Olive Branch borders the Mississippi-Tennessee state line and offers convenient access to Memphis International Airport. The city's charming Old Towne area near Pigeon Roost and Goodman roads features antique stores and gift shops and hosts a series of festivals and concerts throughout the year.

BEST WESTERN PLUS OLIVE BRANCH HOTEL & SUITES
(662)892-2680

Hotel
$80-$150

AAA Benefit: Save 10% or more every day and earn 10% bonus points!

Address: 10915 Business Center Dr 38654 **Location:** US 78 exit 6 (Bethel Rd), just n. **Facility:** 65 units, some efficiencies. 3 stories, interior corridors. **Pool(s):** heated outdoor. **Activities:** exercise room. **Guest Services:** valet and coin laundry.

[SAVE] [tt+] CALL [&M] [≥] [BIZ] [HS]
[⌂] [♦] [▭] [▢]

CANDLEWOOD SUITES
(662)890-7491

Extended Stay Hotel $89-$169 **Address:** 7448 Craft Goodman Rd 38654 **Location:** US 78 exit 1 westbound, 0.5 mi se; exit 2 (SR 302) eastbound, 1.4 mi ne. **Facility:** 70 efficiencies. 3 stories, interior corridors. **Terms:** cancellation fee imposed. **Activities:** exercise room. **Guest Services:** valet and coin laundry.

CALL [&M] [BIZ] [HS] [⌂] [♦] [▭] [▢] / SOME UNITS

FAIRFIELD INN & SUITES BY MARRIOTT MEMPHIS OLIVE BRANCH
(662)892-4469

Hotel $78-$137 **Address:** 7044 Hacks Cross Rd 38654 **Location:** SR 302 exit Hacks Cross Rd, just n. **Facility:** 109 units. 3 stories, interior corridors. **Pool(s):** outdoor. **Activities:** hot tub, exercise room. **Guest Services:** valet and coin laundry, area transportation.

AAA Benefit: Members save 5% or more!

[✈] [tt+] CALL [&M] [≥] [BIZ] [⌂] [✕] [🎦] [♦] [▭]
[▢]

HAMPTON INN
(662)893-7600

Hotel
$104-$179

AAA Benefit: Members save up to 10%!

Address: 6830 Crumpler Blvd 38654 **Location:** US 78 exit 2 (SR 302), just w, then just s. **Facility:** 111 units. 3 stories, interior corridors. **Terms:** 1-7 night minimum stay, cancellation fee imposed. **Pool(s):** heated indoor. **Activities:** hot tub, exercise room. **Guest Services:** valet and coin laundry. **Featured Amenity:** breakfast buffet.

[SAVE] [tt+] CALL [&M] [≥] [BIZ] [⌂]
[✕] [🎦] [♦] [▭] [▢] / SOME UNITS [HS]

HOLIDAY INN EXPRESS HOTEL & SUITES
662/893-8700

Hotel. Rates not provided. **Address:** 8900 Expressway Dr 38654 **Location:** US 78 exit 4, just n, then just w. **Facility:** 80 units. 3 stories, interior corridors. **Pool(s):** outdoor. **Activities:** recreation programs, exercise room. **Guest Services:** valet and coin laundry.

[tt+] CALL [&M] [≥] [BIZ] [⌂] [✕] [🎦] [♦] [▭] [▢]

MAGNOLIA INN & SUITES
(662)895-4545

Hotel $65-$180 **Address:** 6935 W Hamilton Cir 38654 **Location:** US 78 exit 2 (SR 302), 0.5 mi w. **Facility:** 51 units, some efficiencies. 3 stories, interior corridors. **Pool(s):** outdoor. **Activities:** limited exercise equipment. **Guest Services:** coin laundry.

[✈] CALL [&M] [≥] [BIZ] [HS] [⌂] [♦] [▭] [▢]
/ SOME UNITS [🛏]

WHISPERING WOODS HOTEL AND CONFERENCE CENTER
(662)895-2941

▼▼▼ **Resort Hotel** $79-$109 **Address:** 11200 E Goodman Rd 38654 **Location:** US 78 exit 2 (SR 302), 3.6 mi e. **Facility:** Nestled in the northern pines, the resort provides a retreat from the bustle of nearby Memphis, with expansive facilities and sports fields. 180 units. 4 stories, interior corridors. **Terms:** 3 day cancellation notice-fee imposed. **Pool(s):** outdoor. **Activities:** exercise room. **Guest Services:** coin laundry.

WHERE TO EAT

CASA MEXICANA
662/890-7174

▼▼▼ Mexican. Casual Dining. $5-$14 **AAA Inspector Notes:** Diners can expect a south-of-the-border experience for the senses at this casual spot: Savory aromas, colorful, festive decor and background music set the stage for flavorful Mexican cuisine. **Features:** full bar. **Address:** 7565 Goodman Rd 38654 **Location:** Just w of US 78 on SR 302. L D

COLTON'S STEAKHOUSE & GRILL
662/890-4142

▼▼▼ Steak. Casual Dining. $7-$24 **AAA Inspector Notes:** Set in an Old-West atmosphere, this place offers patrons a variety of choices with salads, burgers and full entrees. A few favorites include their country fried steak, grilled pork chops or Hawaiian chicken. The menu also features some entrees under 700 calories. **Features:** full bar, happy hour. **Address:** 8051 Goodman Rd 38654 **Location:** US 78, just e on SR 302. L D CALL

DANVER'S RESTAURANT
662/890-6364

▼ American. Casual Dining. $4-$11 **AAA Inspector Notes:** For a fast meal at an economical price, diners can step inside and grab something to eat or pull through the drive-through. In addition to burgers and sandwiches, the menu lists steak, chicken, shrimp and catfish. **Address:** 7406 Hacks Cross Rd 38654 **Location:** US 78 exit 2 (SR 302), 3 mi e, then 0.5 mi n. B L D CALL

KYOTO JAPANESE STEAKHOUSE & SUSHI BAR
662/895-8780

▼▼ Japanese. Casual Dining. $8-$32 **AAA Inspector Notes:** In addition to hibachi meals that feature entertainment such as shrimp flying through the air and landing on a plate, diners can opt for a more subdued meal, perhaps sushi or another Japanese classic, at a standard table or at the sushi bar. **Features:** full bar, early bird specials, happy hour. **Address:** 6399 Goodman Rd 38654 **Location:** Just w of US 78 on SR 302. L D

OLD STYLE BAR-B-QUE
662/895-9932

▼ American. Family Dining. $2-$19 **AAA Inspector Notes:** Friendly servers have delivered down-home country cooking at this informal eatery for some 30 years. Patrons can savor slow-cooked barbecue in a kitchen-style atmosphere. **Address:** 8920 Expressway Dr 38654 **Location:** US 78 exit 4, just e. B L D

OSAKA JAPANESE CUISINE
662/890-9312

▼▼ Japanese. Casual Dining. $7-$25 **AAA Inspector Notes:** Traditional Asian dishes served in the sleek, contemporary Oriental setting include hibachi, sushi and teriyaki options. **Features:** full bar. **Address:** 7164 Hacks Cross Rd 38654 **Location:** US 78 exit 2 (SR 302), 3 mi e, then just n. L D CALL

SOUTHAVEN pop. 48,982
• Restaurants p. 172
• Part of Memphis area — see map p. 134

The third largest city in Mississippi, Southaven is a Memphis suburb just inside the Mississippi state line and only a couple miles from Memphis International Airport. Southaven was the boyhood home of best-selling author John Grisham, whose legal thrillers are often set in the area.

Shopping: Southaven Towne Center, at Airways Boulevard and Marathon Way, features more than 40 retail stores in an open-air mall setting. A Tanger Outlet at Airways Boulevard and Church Road is scheduled to open in winter 2015.

COMFORT SUITES SOUTHAVEN
(662)349-0100

▼▼▼ Hotel $89-$169 **Address:** 7075 Moore Dr 38671 **Location:** I-55 exit 289, just e. **Facility:** 73 units. 4 stories, interior corridors. **Pool(s):** outdoor. **Activities:** exercise room. **Guest Services:** valet and coin laundry.

COURTYARD BY MARRIOTT MEMPHIS SOUTHAVEN
(662)996-1480

▼▼▼ Hotel $97-$160 **Address:** 7225 Sleepy Hollow Dr 38671 **Location:** I-55 exit 289, just e, just n on Southcrest Pkwy, then w on Market Plaza. **Facility:** 85 units. 3 stories, interior corridors. **Pool(s):** heated indoor. **Activities:** hot tub, exercise room. **Guest Services:** valet and coin laundry, area transportation.

> **AAA Benefit:**
> Members save 5% or more!

FAIRFIELD INN & SUITES BY MARRIOTT MEMPHIS SOUTHAVEN
(662)349-6640

▼▼▼ Hotel $83-$149 **Address:** 7149 Sleepy Hollow Dr 38671 **Location:** I-55 exit 289, just e, just n on Southcrest Pkwy, then w on Market Plaza. **Facility:** 92 units. 3 stories, interior corridors. **Pool(s):** outdoor. **Activities:** exercise room. **Guest Services:** valet and coin laundry, area transportation.

> **AAA Benefit:**
> Members save 5% or more!

HAMPTON INN
(662)349-8855

▼▼▼ Hotel $124-$179 **Address:** 390 Goodman Rd W 38671 **Location:** I-55 exit 289, just e, just n on Southcrest Pkwy, then w on Market Plaza. **Facility:** 86 units. 3 stories, interior corridors. **Terms:** 1-7 night minimum stay, cancellation fee imposed. **Pool(s):** outdoor. **Activities:** exercise room. **Guest Services:** valet and coin laundry.

> **AAA Benefit:**
> Members save up to 10%!

HILTON GARDEN INN MEMPHIS/SOUTHAVEN, MS
(662)349-0277

▼▼▼ Hotel $129-$199 **Address:** 6671 Towne Center Loop 38671 **Location:** I-55 exit 289, just e to Southcrest Pkwy, then just s; in Towne Center Plaza. **Facility:** 117 units. 3 stories, interior corridors. **Terms:** 1-7 night minimum stay, cancellation fee imposed. **Amenities:** video games. **Pool(s):** heated indoor. **Activities:** hot tub, exercise room. **Guest Services:** valet and coin laundry, area transportation.

> **AAA Benefit:**
> Members save up to 10%!

HOLIDAY INN SOUTHAVEN
(662)349-0444

▼▼▼ Hotel $99-$229 **Address:** 280 Marathon Way 38671 **Location:** I-55 exit 289, 0.7 mi e, then just s on Hospitality Ln. **Facility:** 121 units. 5 stories, interior corridors. **Terms:** cancellation fee imposed. **Pool(s):** heated indoor. **Activities:** exercise room. **Guest Services:** valet and coin laundry.

MAGNOLIA INN & SUITES (662)280-5555

▼▼▼ **Hotel** $50-$95 **Address:** 5069 Pepper Chase Dr 38671 **Location:** I-55 exit 287, just w. **Facility:** 27 units, some efficiencies. 1 story, interior corridors. **Terms:** cancellation fee imposed.

[icons]

RESIDENCE INN BY MARRIOTT MEMPHIS SOUTHAVEN
(662)996-1500

▼▼▼ **Extended Stay Hotel** $101-$186 **Address:** 7165 Sleepy Hollow Dr 38671 **Location:** I-55 exit 289, just e, just n on Southcrest Pkwy, then w on Market Plaza. **Facility:** 78 units,

AAA Benefit: Members save 5% or more!

some efficiencies and kitchens. 3 stories, interior corridors. **Pool(s):** outdoor. **Activities:** exercise room. **Guest Services:** valet and coin laundry, area transportation.

[icons]

WHERE TO EAT

ABBAYS 662/510-5532

▼ Southern American. Quick Serve. $6-$18 **AAA Inspector Notes:** This restaurant prides itself on how "the South does fast food." It is a great option for a quick lunch and is reasonably priced with a variety of convenience-food options such as beef tips, chicken and dumplings, and homemade corn bread. It also offers veggie and side items that complement the entrées. **Address:** 7084 Southcrest Pkwy 38671 **Location:** I-55 exit 289, just e. [L] [D] CALL [icon]

THE BOILING POINT SEAFOOD & OYSTER BAR
662/280-7555

▼▼ Seafood. Casual Dining. $8-$40 **AAA Inspector Notes:** This popular eatery has an abundant variety of seafood selections as well as daily fresh-catch items. Lots of fried options, po'boys, stuffed crab and grilled salmon and steak also are offered. **Features:** full bar. **Address:** 4975 Pepperchase Dr 38671 **Location:** I-55 exit 287, just w. [L] [D] [icon]

DALE'S RESTAURANT 662/393-2060

▼▼ Southern Comfort Food. Family Dining. $6-$23 **AAA Inspector Notes:** Since 1966, this family-owned restaurant has provided down-home country cooking, including fabulous homemade pies. Start your meal with Dale's sampler platter to try a variety of the appetizers all at once. Enjoy the fried catfish platter, which is one of the signature dishes and also quite delicious. **Address:** 1226 Main St 38671 **Location:** I-55 exit 291, 0.5 mi w. [L] [D]

JIM NEELY'S INTERSTATE BARBECUE 662/393-5699

▼ Barbecue. Casual Dining. $7-$21 **AAA Inspector Notes:** If you've heard of the other Neely's, then you'll be happy to know that Interstate Barbecue gave birth to the award-winning hickory-smoked barbecue that is sold across the nation today. The ribs, barbecue nachos and, yes, even the barbecue spaghetti are the hot sellers at this location, but prep your palate because items here run a little on the spicy side. **Address:** 150 E Stateline Rd 38671 **Location:** I-55 exit 291, 0.5 mi e. [L] [D] [icon]

LA HACIENDA MEXICAN RESTAURANT 662/349-4484

▼▼ Mexican. Casual Dining. $7-$13 **AAA Inspector Notes:** Located in a bustling shopping area, this restaurant serves up the type of Mexican food that should delight those looking for an experience more on par with visiting a restaurant closer to the border. Fajitas and tacos can be had anywhere, so be a little adventurous and try the mole, chile verde or one of the other house specialties. The chiles rellenos are as close as you can get to homemade. **Features:** full bar. **Address:** 175 B Goodman Rd 38671 **Location:** I-55 exit 289, just e; in South Lake Shopping Center. [L] [D] [icon]

LOST PIZZA COMPANY 662/892-8684

▼ Pizza. Quick Serve. $5-$10 **AAA Inspector Notes:** Besides creating your own pizza at this eclectic spot, you can choose from a variety of creations, including one with pulled pork and another Southwest-inspired one with ground beef and salsa. A few subs and pasta dishes also are served. You can bring your own wine for a small corkage fee. **Features:** beer only, patio dining. **Address:** 5960 Getwell Rd, Suite 108 38672 **Location:** I-55 exit 289, 3.6 mi e, then 1 mi s. [L] [D] [icon]

MESQUITE CHOP HOUSE 662/890-2467

▼▼▼ Steak. Fine Dining. $23-$55 **AAA Inspector Notes:** Combining a classical steakhouse feel with upscale, contemporary design, the exterior of the restaurant resembles a warehouse, and the interior showcases local and regional artwork, all blending to create a hip, yet sophisticated, atmosphere. Signature dishes combine such classics as Caesar salad, shrimp cocktail and Prime, aged, hand-cut steaks with more contemporary dishes such as mesquite-grilled quail, free-range chicken, Maytag bleu cheese-stuffed filet and green apple-stuffed pork chops. **Features:** full bar, Sunday brunch. **Address:** 5960 Getwell Rd, Suite 119 38672 **Location:** I-55 exit 289, 3.6 mi e on Goodman Rd (SR 302), 1 mi s. [D] CALL [icon]

MILANO'S NY PIZZA RESTAURANT 662/349-8111

▼ Pizza. Quick Serve. $7-$10 **AAA Inspector Notes:** Crispy, thin-crust pizza is the specialty on a menu that also lists pasta dinners, calzones, stromboli, sandwiches and salads. Guests can top it all off with either tiramisu or cannoli. Take-out is a popular option. **Features:** beer only. **Address:** 7065 Airways Blvd, Suite 121 38671 **Location:** I-55 exit 289, just e, then just n on Moore Dr. [L] [D]

This ends the Memphis section and resumes the alphabetical city listings for Tennessee.

MILLINGTON pop. 10,176
• Hotels & Restaurants map & index p. 154
• Part of Memphis area — see map p. 134

DAYS INN - MILLINGTON (901)872-3335

▼▼ **Motel** $65-$99 **Address:** 7763 Hwy 51 N 38053 **Location:** SR 385, 0.5 mi n. **Facility:** 34 units. 2 stories (no elevator), exterior corridors. [icons]

HAMPTON INN & SUITES (901)872-4435

▼▼▼ **Hotel** $109-$149 **Address:** 8838 Hwy 51 N 38053 **Location:** SR 385, 3.8 mi n. **Facility:** 81 units. 4 stories, interior corridors. **Terms:** 1-7 night minimum stay, cancellation fee imposed.

AAA Benefit: Members save up to 10%!

Pool(s): outdoor. **Activities:** exercise room. **Guest Services:** valet and coin laundry.

[icons]

HOLIDAY INN EXPRESS & SUITES 901/872-3640

▼▼▼ **Hotel.** Rates not provided. **Address:** 5090 Copper Creek Blvd 38053 **Location:** SR 385, 3.5 mi n on US 51, then just w. **Facility:** 98 units. 4 stories, interior corridors. **Pool(s):** heated indoor. **Activities:** exercise room. **Guest Services:** valet and coin laundry.

[icons]

PLANTATION OAKS SUITES & INN 901/872-8000 [38]

▼▼ **Motel.** Rates not provided. **Address:** 6656 Hwy 51 N 38053 **Location:** SR 385, 2.4 mi s. **Facility:** 93 units, some two bedrooms and kitchens. 2 stories (no elevator), interior/exterior corridors. **Pool(s):** outdoor. **Activities:** limited exercise equipment. **Guest Services:** coin laundry.

[icons]

WHERE TO EAT

EXLINE'S PIZZA 901/873-1944

▼ Pizza. Casual Dining. $6-$14 **AAA Inspector Notes:** Pizza crust that is crisper than most, plenty of gooey cheese and a variety of fresh toppings have kept this regional chain going since 1974. **Features:** full bar. **Address:** 8507 Hwy 51 N 38053 **Location:** Jct SR 385, 3.5 mi n. [L] [D]

MONTEAGLE (D-5) pop. 1,192, elev. 1,931'

For nearly a century the Monteagle Chautauqua Assembly has been a part of this summer resort in the Cumberland Mountains. Lectures, concerts and art classes are held from June to August.

The visitor center of the South Cumberland State Park (see Recreation Areas Chart), a 24,550-acre park composed of nine separate areas, is 3 miles east on US 41. Interpretive exhibits depict the park's many natural attractions, including the Great Stone Door, a 150-foot-high rock crevice in the Savage Gulf Natural Area, and the historic Lone Rock Coke Ovens, which converted locally mined coal to coke, in the Grundy Lakes Recreation Area.

Other features in the park include the Sewanee Natural Bridge, a gracefully curved stone arch 27 feet high; Foster Falls, near Grundy Lakes, which is 60 feet high; and the Lost Cove Caves in the Carter Natural Area.

Scenic I-24 passes through Monteagle at the intersection with SR 56, continuing 40 miles southeast to Chattanooga.

South Cumberland State Park Visitors Center: 16 Dixie Lee Ave., P.O. Box 353, Monteagle, TN 37356. **Phone:** (931) 924-2980.

EDGEWORTH INN (931)924-4000

Historic Bed & Breakfast $139-$225 **Address:** 19 Wilkins Ave 37356 **Location:** I-24 exit 134, 0.4 mi e on SR 41A. Located within historic Monteagle Assembly. **Facility:** Full of Southern charm and Mayberry character, this restored former boarding house dates to 1896. Wicker chairs line a wrap-around porch while towering trees provide comfortable shade. 10 units, some two bedrooms and kitchens. 3 stories (no elevator), interior corridors. **Terms:** check-in 4 pm, 7 day cancellation notice-fee imposed. **Pool(s):** outdoor. **Activities:** tennis, recreation programs in summer, playground, lawn sports, picnic facilities, trails.

MONTEAGLE INN & RETREAT CENTER (931)924-3869

Contemporary Bed & Breakfast $165-$275 **Address:** 204 W Main St 37356 **Location:** I-24 exit 134, 0.4 mi e on US 41A. **Facility:** From the moment you arrive to the minute you reluctantly leave, you'll be planning your return. Original art and authentic Italian décor create an elegant, comfortable and relaxing atmosphere. 13 units, some cottages. 2 stories (no elevator), interior/exterior corridors. **Terms:** 2 night minimum stay - seasonal and/or weekends, 15 day cancellation notice-fee imposed, resort fee.

THE SMOKE HOUSE LODGE & CABINS (931)924-2268

Hotel $80-$110

Address: 844 W Main St 37356 **Location:** I-24 exit 134, just s. Located on a quiet, wooded property of 20 acres. **Facility:** 105 units, some kitchens, houses and cabins. 2 stories (no elevator), exterior corridors. **Terms:** cancellation fee imposed. **Dining:** Jim Oliver's Smoke House Restaurant, see separate listing. **Pool(s):** outdoor. **Activities:** fishing, tennis, playground, lawn sports, picnic facilities, trails.

WHERE TO EAT

HIGH POINT RESTAURANT 931/924-4600

Steak Seafood. Fine Dining. $22-$45 **AAA Inspector Notes:** Historic. Local legend claims that this charming and intimate restaurant was once a stone compound built by gangster Al Capone. It is rumored to have rooftop escape hatches and underground tunnels, which were thought to be used to run bootleg liquor during Prohibition. Many original features remain, including fireplaces and staircases. The current owners maintain the essence of the intrigue with audio and visual elements. **Features:** full bar, patio dining. **Reservations:** suggested. **Address:** 224 E Main St 37356 **Location:** I-24 exit 134, 0.6 mi n on Dixie Lee Hwy; jct US 41.

JIM OLIVER'S SMOKE HOUSE RESTAURANT 931/924-2091

Southern Barbecue Family Dining $8-$20

AAA Inspector Notes: It's a down-home mountain getaway at the Smoke House Restaurant and Trading Post. Make your way through the store—past a wall covered with country artists photos; buckets of salt-water taffy; shelves stocked with homemade barbecue sauces, jams and jellies; display cases full of nostalgic knick-knacks, soda pops and old-time candies—and say "hello" to a welcoming hostess who will show you to a table, where you can relax and enjoy a mouth-watering barbecue. **Features:** beer only, patio dining, Sunday brunch. **Address:** 850 W Main St 37356 **Location:** I-24 exit 134, just s; adjacent to Smoke House Lodge. Menu on AAA.com

Homemade Pies, Ice Cream, Fudge; Open 6am-10pm everyday

MONTEREY pop. 2,850

CUP & SAUCER RESTAURANT 931/839-6149

American. Casual Dining. $5-$12 **AAA Inspector Notes:** Located on the main street, this quaint diner offers original home-style cooking. **Address:** 118 E Commercial Ave 38574 **Location:** I-40 exit 300, 1 mi n, then just e on US 62.

MORRISTOWN (C-8) pop. 29,137, elev. 1,283'
• Hotels p. 174 • Restaurants p. 174

CROCKETT TAVERN MUSEUM is at 2002 Morningside Dr. Featured is the reconstructed boyhood home of Davy Crockett, a wagoner's inn his family ran in the 1790s. A basement contains period artifacts. **Time:** Allow 1 hour minimum. **Hours:** Tues.-Sat. 11-5, May to late Oct. **Cost:** $5; $4.50 (ages 65+); $1 (ages 5-18). **Phone:** (423) 587-9900.

ROSE CENTER is at 442 W. 2nd North St. Housed in a restored 1892 school building, this cultural, educational and historical center has a period classroom exhibit and children's touch museum. The Hal Noe Gallery has a collection of old photographs, Civil War artifacts, a Melville Murrell flying machine exhibit and area historical memorabilia. The Edith Davis Gallery offers monthly changing exhibits of local and regional artists' works. Monthly concerts by regional artists also are featured. **Time:** Allow 1 hour minimum. **Hours:** Mon.-Fri. 9-5, Sat. 10-2. Closed major holidays. **Cost:** Free. **Phone:** (423) 581-4330.

BEST WESTERN PLUS MORRISTOWN CONFERENCE CENTER HOTEL
(423)587-2400

Hotel
$115-$200

AAA Benefit: Save 10% or more every day and earn 10% bonus points!

Address: 130 Cracker Rd 37813 **Location:** I-81 exit 8, just w. **Facility:** 112 units, some efficiencies. 3 stories, interior corridors. **Pool(s):** outdoor. **Activities:** exercise room. **Guest Services:** valet and coin laundry.

DAYS INN
(423)587-2200

Motel $55-$145 **Address:** 2512 E Andrew Johnson Hwy 37814 **Location:** I-81 exit 8, 6 mi n on US 25 E to exit 2B (Greeneville-Morristown), then just w. **Facility:** 65 units. 2 stories (no elevator), exterior corridors. **Parking:** winter plug-ins. **Terms:** 3 day cancellation notice. **Pool(s):** outdoor. **Guest Services:** coin laundry.

HAMPTON INN
(423)587-0952

Hotel $120-$264 **Address:** 3750 W Andrew Johnson Hwy 37814 **Location:** 3 mi w on US 11 E. **Facility:** 82 units. 3 stories, interior corridors. **Terms:** 1-7 night minimum stay, cancellation fee imposed. **Pool(s):** heated outdoor. **Activities:** exercise room. **Guest Services:** valet and coin laundry.

AAA Benefit: Members save up to 10%!

HOLIDAY INN EXPRESS HOTEL & SUITES
(423)307-1111

Hotel $114-$118 **Address:** 2903 Millers Pointe Dr 37813 **Location:** I-81 exit 8, 6.5 mi n on US 25 E exit 2A (US 11 E), then just w; in Millers Landing. **Facility:** 80 units. 4 stories, interior corridors. **Terms:** cancellation fee imposed. **Pool(s):** heated indoor. **Activities:** exercise room. **Guest Services:** valet and coin laundry.

SUPER 8
(423)318-8888

Motel $50-$102 **Address:** 5400 S Davy Crockett Pkwy 37813 **Location:** I-81 exit 8, just n. **Facility:** 49 units. 2 stories (no elevator), interior corridors. **Guest Services:** coin laundry.

WHERE TO EAT

LITTLE DUTCH RESTAURANT
423/581-1441

American. Casual Dining. $7-$25 **AAA Inspector Notes:** In continuous operation since 1939, this restaurant is as comfortable as an old shoe. The expanded menu lists Italian, seafood and beef selections. **Features:** beer only. **Address:** 115 S Cumberland St 37814 **Location:** Center.

SAGEBRUSH STEAKHOUSE
423/586-7493

Steak. Casual Dining. $7-$24 **AAA Inspector Notes:** Born from the spirit of Texas cattle drives, the restaurant presents a menu of hearty steaks, prime rib, chicken, seafood and baby back ribs. Yummy desserts merit a splurge. Guests can call ahead to facilitate seating. **Features:** full bar. **Address:** 2323 E Morris Blvd 37814 **Location:** Jct US 25 E/11 E, 0.4 mi s on US 11 E.

MOUNT JULIET   pop. 23,671
• Hotels & Restaurants map & index p. 200

COMFORT SUITES
(615)206-3310   48

Hotel
$99-$189

Address: 600 Red Ink Dr 37122 **Location:** I-40 exit 226, just n, then just e. **Facility:** 73 units. 4 stories, interior corridors. **Pool(s):** heated indoor. **Activities:** hot tub, exercise room. **Guest Services:** valet and coin laundry. **Featured Amenity:** full hot breakfast.

HAMPTON INN & SUITES
(615)553-5900   52

Hotel $114-$229 **Address:** 5001 Crossings Cir 37122 **Location:** I-40 exit 226A eastbound; exit 226 westbound, just s. **Facility:** 108 units. 5 stories, interior corridors. **Terms:** 1-7 night minimum stay, cancellation fee imposed. **Pool(s):** heated indoor. **Activities:** hot tub, exercise room. **Guest Services:** valet and coin laundry.

AAA Benefit: Members save up to 10%!

HOLIDAY INN EXPRESS HOTEL & SUITES, MT. JULIET
(615)553-5200   53

Hotel
$114-$179

Address: 565 S Mt. Juliet Rd 37122 **Location:** I-40 exit 226, 0.3 mi s. Next to Providence Marketplace Outdoor Shopping Plaza. **Facility:** 81 units. 3 stories, interior corridors. **Amenities:** Some: safes. **Pool(s):** heated indoor. **Activities:** exercise room. **Guest Services:** valet and coin laundry. **Featured Amenity:** continental breakfast.

QUALITY INN & SUITES
(615)773-3600   51

Hotel $70-$120 **Address:** 1000 Hershel Dr 37122 **Location:** I-40 exit 226A eastbound; exit 226 westbound, just s. **Facility:** 85 units. 3 stories, interior corridors. **Pool(s):** outdoor. **Guest Services:** coin laundry.

WHERE TO EAT

CORI'S DOGHOUSE
615/758-6960   32

Hot Dogs Sandwiches. Quick Serve. $4-$8 **AAA Inspector Notes:** The bun may remind you of Texas toast, but it really comes from the lobster roll made famous in New England—thick sided and grilled to golden perfection. Here the dogs are named after American cities and states. "Eat your way across the USA" and they'll add your photo to the wall of wieners, proudly declaring your tail-waggin' achievement. With more than 38 toppings and 50 menu items, it may take you a road trip or two to find your favorite. **Features:** patio dining. **Address:** 401 S Mt. Juliet Rd, Suite 360 37122 **Location:** I-40 exit 226, 0.6 mi s; in Providence Marketplace.

Upgrade to Plus or Premier membership
for *more* of the benefits you need most

MURFREESBORO (D-5) pop. 108,755, elev. 573'

• Hotels p. 176 • Restaurants p. 177

Despite its central location and its tenure as the state capital 1819-26, Murfreesboro lost the seat of government to Nashville by one vote. A 26-foot obelisk, 3 miles from the public square on Old Lascassas Pike, indicates the geographic center of Tennessee.

The 1859 Rutherford County Courthouse on E. Main Street was the site of a dawn attack by Gen. Nathan Bedford Forrest and his Confederate cavalry on Union troops encamped within. About 3 miles northwest of town the Battle of Stones River was fought in late December and early January 1862-63 (see Stones River National Battlefield p. 244).

During the 🚂 Uncle Dave Macon Days Festival in July, nearly 45,000 people flock to Cannonsburgh Village for three days of arts and crafts, old-time music, dancing and specialty foods. More than 450 Tennessee walking horses are on parade during the International Pleasure and Colt Grand Championship Horse Show in late July.

Rutherford County Convention and Visitors Bureau: 3050 Medical Center Pkwy., Murfreesboro, TN 37129. Phone: (615) 893-6565 or (800) 716-7560. (See ad this page.)

Self-guiding tours: The battlefield and other places of interest in Rutherford County are linked by a 4.5-mile trail used by bicyclists, hikers and joggers.

BRADLEY ACADEMY MUSEUM AND CULTURAL CENTER is just s. on Broad St. to 415 S. Academy St. The academy is housed in a restored, two-story building where African-Americans were formally educated 1918-55. Many exhibits explore the history of 19th-century Rutherford County, the academy and the Civil War, including an exhibit about the recruitment of African-Americans into the Union Army. Tour guides tell the story of the Underground Railroad and show visitors through a restored classroom. **Time:** Allow 1 hour, 30 minutes minimum. **Hours:** Tues.-Sat. 10-4. Closed major holidays. **Cost:** $5; $3 (ages 66+ and students with ID); $1 (ages 5-12). **Phone:** (615) 867-2633.

CANNONSBURGH VILLAGE is at 312 S. Front St. Reconstructed and restored Middle Tennessee buildings depict aspects of early Southern life. Included are a blacksmith's shop, log home, church, one-room schoolhouse, general store, gristmill and chapel. **Time:** Allow 30 minutes minimum. **Hours:** Grounds daily dawn-dusk, year-round. Village Tues.-Sat. 9-4, Sun. 1-4, May-Nov. Closed Jan. 1, Easter, Thanksgiving and Christmas. **Cost:** Free. **Phone:** (615) 890-0355.

DISCOVERY CENTER is at 502 S.E. Broad St. The hands-on museum features a fire truck; a 2½-story slide; a "creation station," where children can paint, sculpt and draw; the Nissan Super Center where children can use tools to work on a car; and interactive

▼ See AAA listing this page ▼

exhibits focusing on arts, culture, health and the environment. Some 20 acres of wetlands can be explored on boardwalks. Inhabitants of this area include blue herons, muskrats and river otters. **Time:** Allow 1 hour, 30 minutes minimum. **Hours:** Mon.-Sat. 10-5, Sun. 1-5. Closed major holidays. **Cost:** $6; free (ages 0-1). Prices are subject to change; phone ahead for current rates. **Phone:** (615) 890-2300.

FORTRESS ROSECRANS is off Old Fort Pkwy. (SR 96) in Old Fort Park. These are the remnants of the largest earthen fort built during the Civil War. **Time:** Allow 30 minutes minimum. **Hours:** Daily dawn-dusk. Closed Christmas. **Cost:** Free. **Phone:** (615) 893-9501.

HERITAGE CENTER, 225 W. College St., offers exhibits about the Civil War, the jazz era and notable citizenry. Also available are guided town walking tours that feature historic and architecturally interesting sites. **Time:** Allow 1 hour minimum. **Hours:** Mon.-Fri. 10-3. Guided tours available on the hour. Closed major holidays. **Cost:** Free. **Phone:** (615) 217-8013.

OAKLANDS HISTORIC HOUSE MUSEUM is at 900 N. Maney Ave. Home of the Maney family from about 1815-84, Oaklands evolved from a two-room brick cabin to the stately Italianate mansion visitors see today. During the Civil War, on July 13, 1862, Confederate cavalrymen under Gen. Nathan Bedford Forrest defeated Union forces encamped on the grounds of the plantation.

   Time: Allow 1 hour minimum. **Hours:** Guided tours Tues.-Sat. 10-4, Sun. 1-4. Last tour begins 1 hour before closing. Closed Jan. 1, Easter, Thanksgiving and Christmas. **Cost:** $15; $12 (ages 65+ and military with ID); $6 (ages 6-17 and college students with ID). **Phone:** (615) 893-0022. GT

STONES RIVER NATIONAL BATTLEFIELD—see place listing p. 244.

BAYMONT INN & SUITES   (615)896-1172
 Motel $69-$109 **Address:** 2230 Armory Dr 37129 **Location:** I-24 exit 78B, just n. **Facility:** 108 units, some efficiencies. 2 stories (no elevator), exterior corridors. **Terms:** cancellation fee imposed. **Pool(s):** outdoor. **Activities:** exercise room. **Guest Services:** valet and coin laundry.

BEST WESTERN CHAFFIN INN   (615)895-3818

Motel
$60-$160

| Best Western | **AAA Benefit:** Save 10% or more every day and earn 10% bonus points! |

Address: 168 Chaffin Pl 37129 **Location:** I-24 exit 78B, just s. **Facility:** 51 units. 2 stories (no elevator), exterior corridors. **Pool(s):** outdoor. **Guest Services:** coin laundry.

COMFORT SUITES   (615)869-0950

Hotel
$90-$251

Address: 226 N Thompson Ln 37129 **Location:** I-24 exit 78B, just ne. **Facility:** 82 units. 4 stories, interior corridors. **Amenities:** safes. **Pool(s):** outdoor. **Activities:** hot tub, exercise room. **Guest Services:** coin laundry. **Featured Amenity:** full hot breakfast.

DOUBLETREE BY HILTON HOTEL MURFREESBORO
                                        (615)895-5555

Hotel
$119-$179

| DOUBLETREE BY HILTON | **AAA Benefit:** Members save 5% or more! |

Address: 1850 Old Fort Pkwy 37129 **Location:** I-24 exit 78B, 0.6 mi ne. **Facility:** 168 units. 5 stories, interior corridors. **Terms:** 1-7 night minimum stay, cancellation fee imposed. **Pool(s):** heated outdoor, heated indoor. **Activities:** trails, limited exercise equipment. **Guest Services:** valet laundry, area transportation.

EMBASSY SUITES BY HILTON MURFREESBORO-HOTEL AND
CONFERENCE CENTER   (615)890-4464
 Hotel $149-$189 **Address:** 1200 Conference Center Blvd 37129 **Location:** I-24 exit 76, 0.4 mi e, then just s. **Facility:** 283 units. 10 stories, interior corridors. **Terms:** 1-7 night minimum stay, cancellation fee imposed. **Amenities:** safes. **Pool(s):** heated indoor. **Activities:** hot tub, exercise room, spa. **Guest Services:** valet and coin laundry, area transportation.

| | **AAA Benefit:** Members save 5% or more! |

FAIRFIELD INN & SUITES BY MARRIOTT MURFREESBORO
                                        (615)849-1150
Hotel $130-$200 **Address:** 175 Chaffin Pl 37129 **Location:** I-24 exit 78B, just e, then just s. Located in a busy commercial area. **Facility:** 69 units. 4 stories, interior corridors. **Pool(s):** heated indoor. **Activities:** exercise room. **Guest Services:** complimentary and valet laundry.

| | **AAA Benefit:** Members save 5% or more! |

HAMPTON INN & SUITES   (615)890-2424
Hotel $129-$189 **Address:** 325 N Thompson Ln 37129 **Location:** I-24 exit 78B, just ne. **Facility:** 101 units. 4 stories, interior corridors. **Terms:** 1-7 night minimum stay, cancellation fee imposed. **Pool(s):** heated outdoor. **Activities:** limited exercise equipment. **Guest Services:** valet and coin laundry.

| | **AAA Benefit:** Members save up to 10%! |

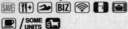

HILTON GARDEN INN MURFREESBORO   (615)225-2345

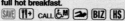 **Hotel** $129-$199 **Address:** 1335 Conference Center Blvd 37129 **Location:** I-24 exit 76, just e, then just s. Located within walking distance to conference center. **Facility:** 100 units. 4 stories, interior corridors. **Terms:** 1-7 night minimum stay, cancellation fee imposed. **Activities:** exercise room. **Guest Services:** valet and coin laundry.

AAA Benefit: Members save up to 10%!

HOLIDAY INN EXPRESS   615/849-9000

Hotel. Rates not provided. **Address:** 165 Chaffin Pl 37129 **Location:** I-24 exit 78B, just e, then just s. Located in a busy commercial area. **Facility:** 86 units. 4 stories, interior corridors. **Pool(s):** outdoor. **Activities:** exercise room. **Guest Services:** complimentary and valet laundry.

QUALITY INN MURFREESBORO   (615)890-1006

Hotel
$72-$250

Address: 2135 S Church St 37130 **Location:** I-24 exit 81, e on US 231 E. **Facility:** 83 units. 4 stories, interior corridors. **Pool(s):** outdoor. **Activities:** limited exercise equipment. **Guest Services:** coin laundry. **Featured Amenity:** full hot breakfast.

RESIDENCE INN BY MARRIOTT-MURFREESBORO   (615)225-9250

Extended Stay Hotel $152-$194 **Address:** 1409 Conference Center Blvd 37129 **Location:** I-24 exit 76, just e. Located within walking distance to conference center. **Facility:** 112 units, some two bedrooms, efficiencies and kitchens. 4 stories, interior corridors. **Terms:** check-in 4 pm. **Pool(s):** outdoor. **Activities:** miniature golf, picnic facilities, exercise room. **Guest Services:** valet and coin laundry.

AAA Benefit: Members save 5% or more!

SLEEP INN   (615)396-3000

Hotel $75-$115 **Address:** 193 Chaffin Pl 37129 **Location:** I-24 exit 78B, just s. **Facility:** 83 units. 4 stories, interior corridors. **Bath:** shower only. **Pool(s):** outdoor. **Activities:** limited exercise equipment. **Guest Services:** valet and coin laundry.

SUPER 8   (615)867-5000

Motel
$90-$105

Address: 127 Chaffin Pl 37129 **Location:** I-24 exit 78B, just e, then just s. **Facility:** 51 units, some kitchens. 2 stories (no elevator), exterior corridors. **Pool(s):** outdoor. **Featured Amenity:** continental breakfast.

 **WHERE TO EAT**

THE CLAY PIT   615/904-6262

Indian. Quick Serve. $8-$15 **AAA Inspector Notes:** Order at the counter from the menu or have one of the staff members assist you with the buffet. Guests are invited to enjoy authentic dishes, spiced to the requested level, that include chicken, lamb, goat and seafood specialties, as well as vegetarian selections. The staff is knowledgeable about menu preparations. The dining area is limited and the décor basic. Food is served on plastic plates and a cafeteria tray. **Features:** beer only. **Address:** 1813 Memorial Blvd 37129 **Location:** I-24 exit 78, 2.7 mi e, then ne, via Old Fort Pkwy/Memorial Blvd. L D

DEMOS' STEAK & SPAGHETTI HOUSE   615/895-3701

American. Casual Dining. $8-$18 **AAA Inspector Notes:** This family-owned and -operated eatery offers well prepared traditional fare as well as specialties such as Mexican spaghetti. The cuisine is made from scratch. The atmosphere and service are casual and relaxed. **Features:** full bar. **Address:** 1115 NW Broad St 37129 **Location:** I-24 exit 78, 2 mi e on US 96, then 2 blks n. L D CALL

KLEER-VU LUNCHROOM   615/896-0520

Soul Food. Quick Serve. $5-$10 **AAA Inspector Notes:** Every home-cooked Southern-style dish is made from scratch at this classic mom-and-pop, meat-and-three dining room, which was once a neighborhood grocery store. Friendly cafeteria-line attendants serve up hearty portions of steaming hot foods flavored with lots of butter and bacon. **Address:** 226 S Highland Ave 37130 **Location:** Jct Highland Ave and Vine St, just s. L D

MARINA'S ON THE SQUARE   615/849-8881

Italian. Casual Dining. $6-$16 **AAA Inspector Notes:** This family-owned and -operated restaurant provides authentic pasta dishes, pizza, calzones and everyone's favorite, lasagna. The made-from-scratch pizza is the most popular, but eggplant Parmesan and stuffed shells also are featured. **Features:** beer & wine. **Address:** 125 N Maple St 37130 **Location:** Center. L D

PARTHENON GRILLE   615/895-2665

Continental. Casual Dining. $10-$40 **AAA Inspector Notes:** A good mix of Mediterranean cuisine, much of which is made to order, characterizes the varied menu at this restaurant. The filet Diane is seared with a splash of cognac and wine, then spiced with a touch of Dijon mustard. Also on the menu you'll find a good selection of fish. Cocktails are crafted with care, and make a nice addition to any meal. **Features:** full bar, patio dining, Sunday brunch, happy hour. **Address:** 1962 S Church St 37130 **Location:** I-24 exit 81, 0.5 mi ne. L D

THROUGH THE GRAPEVINE   615/890-7346

American. Casual Dining. $7-$10 **AAA Inspector Notes:** Simple, savory foods, such as garlic-roasted potato soup and chicken salad on a croissant, are typical of the charming tearoom offerings. If a dessert sounds tempting, order it early; the excellent homemade sweet treats often sell out. **Address:** 630 Broadmor Blvd, Suite 190 37129 **Location:** Jct Ridgely Rd and Memorial Blvd. L CALL

TOOT'S RESTAURANT   615/898-1301

Wings Burgers. Casual Dining. $5-$16 **AAA Inspector Notes:** Even though 'Elvis' has gone on to iguana heaven, people still come from near and far to have good food and good fun. This was the first restaurant in middle Tennessee to offer buffalo wing appetizers. As one can imagine, the wing flavors range from mild to napalm. Other menu highlights include half-pound burgers and sandwiches of rib, catfish, Reuben and Philly cheese steak. Seafood offerings include shrimp, oysters on the half shell and snow crab legs. Lunch menu available for a bargain meal. **Features:** full bar, happy hour. **Address:** 860 NW Broad St 37129 **Location:** I-24 exit 78B, 2.5 mi e, then just n on US 70 S. L D LATE

Nashville

Then & Now

The barroom is quiet, save for the persistent sounds of clinking bottles and shuffling boots, and when the young man on stage clears his throat, the gruff sound startles him a bit. His eyes are closed as his lips part, but then the lyrics barrel out from somewhere deep inside in his chest, knocking him out of his nervous haze. Finally, with the last strum of his guitar hanging in the air, his long lashes flutter apart, allowing for a few precious glimpses of a thoroughly captivated audience.

This is Nashville, though the songs aren't always upbeat and triumphant finales don't befall every would-be musician. While health care and publishing are two of the city's chief industries, the lifeblood of the community is music— whether it's belted out by rhinestone-adorned country stars, opera divas or wailing rock gods.

Though millions of visitors arrive each year seeking out Music City's harmonious core, a few other nicknames suit the Tennessee capital just fine. Home to more than 700 churches, Nashville—flush with pristine steeples and exquisite stained glass windows—is sometimes referred to as the "Buckle of the Bible Belt." Both the United Methodist Publishing House and the Southern Baptist Convention are headquartered here, along with one of the world's largest publishers of Bibles, Thomas Nelson Publishers.

As the "Athens of the South," the city's architecture often reflects a strong preference for Greek symmetry. Case in point: the full-size replica of the Parthenon. An impressive classical clone, the columned building is the centerpiece of lush Centennial Park, where paired Canadian geese and their fluffy brood ply the waters of Lake Watauga. Nashville boasts several edifying institutions, including Vanderbilt University, founded in 1873, and Fisk University, well-known for its renowned African-American ensemble, first organized in 1871.

Still, most everyone comes to town to experience the thrill of at least one live performance: an impromptu session in a rustic honky-tonk or a well-oiled revue in a nicely equipped theater. The city's most recognizable tabernacle remains the Ryman Auditorium, or, more appropriately, the "Mother Church of Country Music," where fans seated in restored 19th-century pews now worship the likes of Alison Krauss and Vince Gill.

Revelers roam the entertainment district surrounding the Ryman nightly, eyeballing raucous bands hard at work inside the string of honky-tonks lining Broadway. Along this historic thoroughfare peppered with Western shops and neon signs, street performers pose for

Honky-tonks lining Broadway

(Continued on p. 180.)

Destination Nashville

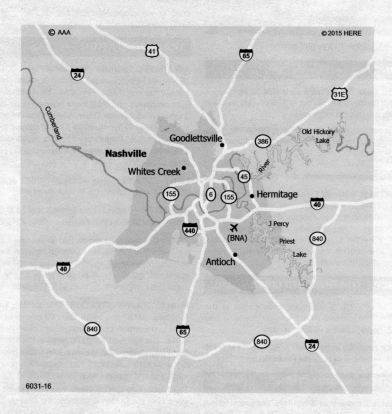

This map shows cities in the Nashville vicinity where you will find attractions, hotels and restaurants. Cities are listed alphabetically in this book on the following pages.

Fast Facts

ABOUT THE CITY

POP: 601,222 ▪ **ELEV:** 597 ft.

MONEY

SALES TAX: Tennessee's statewide sales tax is 7 percent; Nashville's sales tax is 2.25 percent, and the city has a 6 percent lodging tax.

WHOM TO CALL

EMERGENCY: 911

POLICE (non-emergency): (615) 862-8600

HOSPITALS: Nashville General Hospital at Meharry, (615) 341-4000 ▪ Saint Thomas Midtown Hospital, (615) 284-5555 ▪ Saint Thomas West Hospital, (615) 222-2111 ▪ TriStar Southern Hills Medical Center, (615) 781-4000 ▪ TriStar Summit Medical Center, (615) 316-3000 ▪ Vanderbilt University Medical Center, (615) 322-5000.

WHERE TO LOOK AND LISTEN

NEWSPAPERS: Nashville's daily paper is the morning *Tennessean*. The *Nashville Scene,* a free weekly paper, offers a visitors' section.

RADIO: Nashville radio station WPLN (90.3 FM, 1430 AM) is a member of National Public Radio.

VISITOR INFORMATION

Nashville Convention & Visitors Bureau: 150 4th Ave. N., Suite G-250, Nashville, TN 37219. **Phone:** (615) 259-4730 or (800) 657-6910.

The visitors bureau has two information centers; one is in the glass tower of the Bridgestone Arena, at 5th Avenue and Broadway, and is open daily; phone (615) 259-4747. A second is on the corner of 4th Avenue North and Commerce Street in the Regions Bank building and is open Monday through Friday; phone (615) 259-4730.

TRANSPORTATION

AIR TRAVEL: Nashville International Airport (BNA) is 15 minutes from downtown. Gaylord Opryland *(see attraction listing p. 193)* offers commuter shuttle service from the airport, and most major hotels provide airport courtesy cars. Jarmon Transportation provides airport shuttle service to downtown for $14 per person; round-trip fare is $25. Rates vary to major hotels outside downtown. Shuttle service runs 4 a.m.-11 p.m.; phone (615) 275-0146.

RENTAL CARS: Hertz, (615) 275-2600 or (800) 654-3131, offers discounts to AAA members.

BUSES: The Greyhound bus terminal is at 1030 Charlotte Ave.; phone (615) 255-3556 or (800) 231-2222.

TAXIS: Cab fare is $3 to start and $2 per mile ▪ a $25 flat fee is charged for transportation between the airport and downtown. Cabs are not easy to hail outside downtown, but they can be ordered by phone. The major cab company is Yellow, (615) 256-0101.

PUBLIC TRANSPORTATION: Metropolitan Transit Authority (MTA) has more than 40 city routes, including an airport connection. Exact change is required. The fare is $1.70; $1.00 (ages 5-19); 85c (ages 65+). Day passes also are available. Buses generally run daily 5:15 a.m.-11:15 p.m., depending upon the route. For information phone (615) 862-5950.

The Music City Circuit offers free bus service with stops near the Ryman Auditorium, the Country Music Hall of Fame, Bridgestone Arena and other downtown restaurants, attractions and landmarks. The Blue Circuit runs north to south between Bicentennial Capitol Mall and the Schermerhorn Symphony Center. The Green Circuit runs east to west from Riverfront Station to the Gulch. Both routes operate Monday through Saturday.

(Continued from p. 178.)

photos with rockabilly-loving tourists and captivated grade-schoolers. Well-traveled retirees barhop from Tootsie's Orchid Lounge to Legends Corner to Robert's Western World—memorabilia-crammed establishments where great country artists continue to stir things up.

A nondescript, concrete block building on Roy Acuff Place serves as a shrine to Nashville's storied musical past, smack-dab in the middle of the city's $5 billion entertainment industry. State-of-the-art for its time, RCA Studio B was built in 1957 in a burgeoning district quickly emerging as *the* place to record—Music Row.

Tours of the "Home of 1,000 Hits" are available through the Country Music Hall of Fame and Museum, where song plays a part in, well, everything. Visitors drool over Mother Maybelle Carter's Gibson L-5 and the 1928 Weymann strummed by Jimmie Rodgers, "The Father of Country Music." In the stately hall of fame, bronze likenesses of bygone Grand Ole Opry stars enthrall groups who, just the evening prior, were wowed by contemporary acts at the stage show that first aired on Nov. 28, 1925.

Inspired by Nashville's long broadcasting history, a steel, triangular-braced tower attached to the Bridgestone Arena rises more than 200 feet high; its elliptical 100-foot base recalls an angled spotlight lighting a stage. The arena exemplifies the city's melodic roots with its music box-style roof, left ajar to allow the sounds of shows to resonate through downtown.

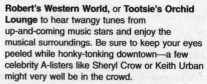

Must Do: AAA Editor's Picks

- Attend a production of the legendary 🎵 **Grand Ole Opry.** Launched in Nashville in 1925, the live radio broadcast continues to introduce many a country musician hopeful to the world. If you're a big fan, sign up for a guided tour of the Grand Ole Opry House; besides learning about the history of the 4,400-seat venue, you'll have the chance to stand at center stage, on the round 6-foot piece of oak wood typically occupied by regulars like Loretta Lynn and Brad Paisley. Taken from the show's previous home, the Ryman Auditorium, the circle memorializes such Opry royalty as Roy Acuff and Minnie Pearl.

- Take a drive through **Music Row,** the hub of the country music recording industry. Centered between 16th and 17th avenues and Division and Grand streets, the tree-lined business district currently embraces hundreds of major record labels, music publishing firms, booking agencies and high-tech recording studios.

- Locate signs of the Dolly Parton incident—the day the buxom songstress drove her car into **RCA Studio B** while en route to a recording session—during your Music Row expedition. The small and now *slightly* dented building built in 1957 saw the likes of the King of Rock 'n' Roll as well as such country and pop icons as Eddy Arnold, Jim Reeves, Willie Nelson, the Everly Brothers and Roy Orbison.

- Spend a neon-illuminated night gallivanting through **Lower Broadway,** Nashville's top spot for live music. Duck into **Legends Corner,** **Robert's Western World,** or **Tootsie's Orchid Lounge** to hear twangy tunes from up-and-coming music stars and enjoy the musical surroundings. Be sure to keep your eyes peeled while honky-tonking downtown—a few celebrity A-listers like Sheryl Crow or Keith Urban might very well be in the crowd.

- Sign up for a line-dancing lesson at the **Wildhorse Saloon,** a three-level, rowdy, boot-scootin' saloon that marked its 1994 opening with a cattle stampede presided over by Reba McEntire. Yee-haw!

- Look through scores of country records and CDs at **Lawrence Record Shop** or the original **Ernest Tubb Record Shop** on Broadway. A second Ernest Tubb Record Shop location on Music Valley Drive is next door to the **Texas Troubadour Theatre,** where the Midnite Jamboree radio broadcast takes place every Saturday night.

- Settle into an oak pew and enjoy a show at the "Mother Church of Country Music," the 🎵 **Ryman Auditorium.** The home of the Grand Ole Opry 1943-74, the storied venue often praised for its stellar acoustics now hosts musical theater performances as well as concerts— everything from bluegrass to gospel to jazz. Get a behind-the-scenes look at the dressing rooms and more on a backstage tour.

- Wander the expansive **Gaylord Opryland Resort,** where nearly 3,000 guestrooms, pulsing nightclubs and several stylish eateries intermingle with 9 acres of lush indoor gardens and waterways. When you're tired of exploring on foot, hop aboard the *General Jackson Showboat,* a four-deck paddlewheeler that plies the Cumberland River.

- Peruse exhibits at the 🎵 **Country Music Hall of Fame and Museum,** chock-full of glittery stage costumes, treasured instruments and all things in between. On top of its eye-catching collection of gold records, interactive displays and relics, the attraction regularly schedules panel discussions with movers and shakers in the music business.

- Discover the prestigious **Belle Meade** neighborhood, home to impressive estates owned by recording stars and other affluent Music City residents. Located about 5 miles southwest of downtown, the posh area boasts elegant remnants from the past, including **Belle Meade Plantation** and **Cheekwood Botanical Garden & Museum of Art.**

Wander the expansive Gaylord Opryland Resort

Nashville 1-day Itinerary

AAA editors suggest these activities for a great short vacation experience. Those staying in the area for a longer visit can access a 3-day itinerary at AAA.com/TravelGuide.

Morning

- Begin your Music City adventure by visiting the ▽ **Ryman Auditorium,** home to the Grand Ole Opry from 1943 until 1974, when the show relocated to its present 4,400-seat performance house at Gaylord Opryland. Take a daytime tour of the Ryman to learn all about the "Mother Church of Country Music," which originated in the late 1800s as a tabernacle for Christian revivals.

- Walk to the nearby ▽ **Country Music Hall of Fame and Museum** to peruse all kinds of glitzy paraphernalia, from cherished Gibsons to fringed leather jackets. The museum also offers tours of legendary letterpress shop Hatch Show Print as well as Music Row's historic RCA Studio B, where Elvis Presley, Willie Nelson, Roy Orbison and countless others cut singles before the recording facility ceased operation in the late '70s.

Afternoon

- Enjoy a casual lunch in **Lower Broadway**—the spirited historic heart of downtown where you'll find yourself singing along with street musicians while simultaneously storing a long mental list of honky-tonks you want to check out after dusk. As for chowing down, you'll have your pick of restaurants along Second Avenue and Broadway (the area's main thoroughfares), though natives usually pack **Jacks Bar-B-Que,** established in 1976.

- Downtown's many souvenir stores house a wealth of country music-themed wares. But if you want something more memorable than a magnet or a commemorative shot glass—or even if you're just window-shopping—two venerable businesses nearby are worth a peek inside. At the original **Ernest Tubb Record Shop** opened in the 1940s, you can score some rare vinyl, along with hard-to-find CDs. Or, you could spend your hard-earned cash on a concert poster reprint from Nashville's historic **Hatch Show Print.** The cool turn-of-the-20th-century letterpress print shop has created custom designs for everyone from Bob Dylan to Elvis Presley and now resides inside the Country Music Hall of Fame and Museum.

- Other points of interest to include on your afternoon itinerary are the **Tennessee State Museum,** the **State Capitol** and **Bicentennial Capitol Mall State Park**—all three are clustered a few blocks north of the ▽ **Ryman Auditorium.** Or, head west on Broadway to the **Frist Center for the Visual Arts.** The former Art Deco post office building now houses an impressive collection of art from local, regional and international artists.

Gold and platinum albums at the Country Music Hall of Fame

Evening

- Dine at the expansive ▽ **Gaylord Opryland** complex. After eating, you can wander the botanical garden of the **Gaylord Opryland Resort** or take a 15-minute flatboat ride along canals in the atrium. And, when you're ready to kick up your cowboy boots, the sophisticated multifaceted leisure development once again delivers: Several bars and dance halls, including **Fuse Sports Club** and a **Wildhorse Saloon,** are on-site.

- If you've already seen the ▽ **Grand Ole Opry,** you could opt for a melodious Cumberland River voyage aboard the *General Jackson* *Showboat,* which departs from Gaylord Opryland. The surrounding Music Valley area also offers plenty in the way of live entertainment. Enjoy the dinner show at **Nashville Palace** or take in the popular (and free!) Midnite Jamboree, an enduring radio show broadcast from the **Texas Troubadour Theatre** every Saturday evening.

- For late-night revelers who instead choose to prowl Lower Broadway, the Second Avenue **Wildhorse Saloon** is always a good bet. You can take a few lessons in two-stepping at the three-level restaurant, concert hall and dance club before hitting up such celebrated honky-tonks as **Legends Corner, Robert's Western World** and **Tootsie's Orchid Lounge.** If you're hungry for some fancy vittles, try the upstairs dining room at **Merchants,** located in a 19th-century hotel on Broadway that once accommodated such country greats as Roy Acuff, Dolly Parton and Hank Williams.

Top Picks for Kids

Under 13

- Animal viewing isn't the only thing to do at **Nashville Zoo at Grassmere.** The 66,000-square-foot Jungle Gym calls to little ones who like to slide, climb and crawl. This community-built playground probably doesn't look like the one at school; it has a 35-foot-tall tree house, a dancing water fountain and a large snake tunnel. Check out the carousel, train, animal shows and keeper talks, too.

- Water play. Need we say more? When the weather is nice, water parks are a sure bet for active youngsters. **Wave Country** and **Nashville Shores Lakeside Resort,** in nearby **Hermitage,** offer slides, pools and water activities. The former has fewer attractions than Nashville Shores but is closer to downtown.

- Enjoy simple pleasures at **Cumberland Park.** The 6.5-acre riverfront site entices kids with its climbing wall, oversize slide, spray fountains, misting areas and rain curtains. There also are walking trails and picnic areas. Take the elevator or stairs up to the pedestrian bridge. The former roadway over the Cumberland River was spared demolition and is now a walkway with great city views and nighttime illumination.

Teens

- You don't need to be an avid history or art fan to appreciate **The Parthenon**—a full-scale replica of the ancient Greek temple. The interior holds a nice art collection, but the highlight is the 42-foot statue of the goddess Athena, a re-creation of the one Phidias sculpted in the 5th century B.C.

Enjoy the tunes from the Grand Ole Opry

- Learn about Taylor Swift and other country superstars at the ⇒ **Country Music Hall of Fame and Museum.** Historical audio recordings and performances along with instruments, costumes and automobiles tell the history of this music genre.

All Ages

- Amble down Broadway's large thoroughfare between Second Avenue and the Bridgestone Arena. This lively downtown historic area is *the* place for live music. You don't have to frequent the bars and honky-tonks to hear it, either; most doors are propped wide open to allow the sounds to spill out into the street, and there are plenty of street performers to wow budding musicians. Enjoy the old architecture, duck into souvenir shops and poll the group about which neon sign is their favorite. Walk by ⇒ **Ryman Auditorium,** the Grand Ole Opry's home 1943-74.

- Create some family bonding time by seeing a ⇒ **Grand Ole Opry** performance; the radio show that began in 1925 made country music famous. These 2-hour shows welcome a mix of legendary artists, current hit makers and newbies to the stage. The several hundred Opry members and guest artists include Garth Brooks, Jewel, Lady Antebellum, Loretta Lynn, Tim McGraw, Willie Nelson and Dolly Parton.

- Have a meal at **Aquarium Restaurant** (at the Opry Mills mall), where each table has a view of the 200,000-gallon aquarium, home to fish, sharks, stingrays and other marine life. The decor and lighting enhance the aquatic theme. The menu has a large seafood section and plenty of chicken and beef options along with a fun underwater-themed kids' menu. Stop by The LEGO Store before leaving the mall.

- Experience science out of the classroom at ⇒ **Adventure Science Center** with interactive exhibits or kick back at a planetarium show. Dozens of activities provide practical, relevant and fun ideas related to science topics like health, energy, sound, light, air and space.

- Visit the atrium at **Gaylord Opryland Resort** to see three indoor gardens—the Garden Conservatory, the Cascades and the Delta—and two 25-minute fountain shows—"Aqua" and "International Waters"—at the Delta Fountain. A waterfall at the lush Cascades is a highlight, and the Delta offers guided flatboat rides.

- If your trip coincides with the holiday season, experience ⇒ **Gaylord Opryland's A Country Christmas.** The resort's fountain shows don't run, but the indoor gardens are dressed with beautiful holiday decor, and carriage rides show off the grounds' 2 million lights and an impressive nativity display. Get tickets to see ice sculptures at ICE!, or make plans to glide around the ice skating rink under the stars.

Arriving
By Car

Three major interstates pass through Nashville. Near the heart of the city these highways combine to form a near circle around downtown. Convenient exits provide easy access to major city streets.

The main north-south route is I-65. Closely parallel is the US 31 corridor, which divides into US 31E and US 31W north of Nashville, US 31 and Alt. US 31 to the south, and I-24 to the west.

East-west access comes primarily from transcontinental I-40. A close companion is US 70, another route that spans a considerable portion of the nation; east of Nashville it splinters into US 70N and US 70S.

I-24 runs on a northwest-southeast axis, bringing traffic from other routes in Chattanooga and southern Illinois. A close relative on part of its journey is US 41 and Alt. US 41.

SR 155 (Briley Parkway/Thompson Lane/Woodmont Boulevard/White Bridge Road), a bypass, encircles Nashville and connects all major interstates running through the city.

Getting Around
Street System

Nashville is a fairly easy city in which to navigate, given that the downtown area is ringed by five major interstates: 40, 65, 440, 24 and 840, an outer bypass. The key to deciphering the street system is to remember that the Cumberland River runs north to south, bisecting the heart of the city. The numbered *avenues* run north to south, *west* of and parallel to

Pick up a pair of new cowboy boots at Boot Barn

the river. The numbered *streets* run north to south, *east* of and parallel to the river. East-west streets are generally perpendicular to the river on both sides.

Three vehicular bridges connect the east and west sections of downtown: the Victory Memorial Bridge, Woodland Street Bridge and Jefferson Street Bridge. Broadway (US 70) and Charlotte, Church and Jefferson streets are the principal crosstown routes. The Shelby Avenue bridge—once scheduled for destruction—has been preserved as the John Seigenthaler Pedestrian Bridge, one of the longest pedestrian bridges in the world.

US 41 is the main north-south thoroughfare, though it is separated by the James Robertson Parkway for about a half-mile in the area around the State Capitol. James Robertson Parkway also is the link with Victory Memorial Bridge. South of Demonbreun Street, US 41 (also called 8th Avenue) divides, and the 8th Avenue S. part of the fork becomes US 31. US 41 continues south as Lafayette Street.

Broadway and Jefferson, Charlotte, Church and Demonbreun streets are all downtown access exits off the I-40 loop of the circumferential highway. On the eastern side of the river, Jefferson, Main and Woodland streets and Shelby Avenue are exits off the I-24 loop of the highway.

The average speed downtown is 30-35 mph. Right turns at red lights are legal unless otherwise posted.

Parking

On-street parking is convenient at meters, with an hourly rate of $1.50 in the Central Business District and $1 in all others. Parking garages and outdoor parking lots average $2-$3 for each half-hour or $12-$14 per day. Valet parking is common for downtown restaurants and hotels.

Shopping

Before you start collecting mementos from your trip to Music City, kick things off with some fancy footwear. Several boot dealers operate in downtown Nashville. Stock up on cowboy boots at **Boot Barn,** 318 Broadway, or **Boot Country,** 304 Broadway, where there's always a buy-one-get-two-free deal going on. Ladies will love the fashionable boot selection at **Betty Boots,** 321 Broadway. Once you're outfitted, break in your new gear rambling past honky-tonks and crooning street musicians in the Lower Broadway district between Second Avenue and the Bridgestone Arena.

Stores housed in late-19th-century commercial structures along Broadway and Second Avenue peddle souvenir magnets and colorful guitar picks, assorted packages of Goo Goo Clusters (made by a local candymaker, the old-school chocolates have nourished sweet-toothed Southerners since 1912) and bold Johnny Cash T-shirts that most often come in black (naturally!). **Opry Originals,** 300 Broadway, stocks music-themed merchandise and souvenirs, as does the **Ryman Auditorium Store,** 116 Fifth Ave. N. You'll find rock 'n' roll merchandise at ⟨SAVE⟩ **Hard Rock Cafe,** 100 Broadway.

If you're decked out in a glittery ten-gallon hat or a fringe-riffic suit with nowhere to go, pick up a few sing-along-perfect tunes at the **Ernest Tubb Record Shop.** In 1947 singer-songwriter Tubb opened the longtime Broadway business, which still holds the stage formerly used during radio broadcasts of the "Midnite Jamboree." The CD-, music DVD- and record-crammed space also showcases a variety of country music memorabilia, as does a secondary Music Valley Drive location next to the **Texas Troubadour Theatre** *(see attraction listing p. 194),* current home of the enduring "Jamboree."

Visitors crane their necks perusing the placarded walls of **Hatch Show Print,** in the lobby of the Country Music Hall of Fame and Museum building at 224 Fifth Ave. S., one of the country's oldest working letterpress print shops. Reproduction posters promoting past performances by such stars as B.B. King, Willie Nelson and Elvis Presley are up for sale, as are t-shirts and coffee mugs emblazoned with memorable Hatch designs. You can even watch posters coming off the presses in the production shop or take a tour to create your own print.

Just a short drive southwest on Broadway is **Hillsboro Village.** This bohemian neighborhood abutting Vanderbilt University features a small shopping and dining district centered on 21st Avenue South. After filling up on sweet potato flapjacks at the **Pancake Pantry,** comb neatly marked shelves in **BookMan/BookWoman.** The bookstore boasts more than 90,000 new and gently used titles, with many shelves packed two-books-deep. Nearby, walls covered with decorative mirrors and Mexican folk art dazzle customers browsing at **Pangaea,** which also sells clothing, handmade jewelry, candles and quirky knickknacks. Score a few more unconventional goodies—from distinctive greeting cards to contemporary art pieces—at **A Thousand Faces,** a local favorite.

Less than 2 miles from Hillsboro Village you'll find merchants and eateries scattered along 12th Avenue South, between Wedgewood Avenue and Gale Lane, in an up-and-coming neighborhood known as **12South.** Trade your air guitar for the real deal at **Corner Music,** 2705 12th Ave. S., *the* place for acoustic essentials since 1976. Continue your 12South shopping spree with a well-caffeinated stop at **Frothy Monkey,** 2509 12th Ave. S., then head next door to **MODA Boutique,** where a well-curated selection of designer clothing and jewelry awaits. A short walk away is **Cadeau,** 2308 12th Ave. S., a fun spot to browse for home decor, gifts and candles.

But dressing up in Opry-worthy duds from Panhandle Slim, Rockmount or Skully won't land anyone a contract on Music Row. The first step is to trade your air guitar for the real deal at **Corner Music,** 2705 12th Ave. S., *the* place for acoustic essentials since 1976. Continue your 12South shopping spree with a well-caffeinated stop at **Frothy**

Music lives at the Ernest Tubb Record Shop

Monkey, 2509 12th Ave. S., then head next door to **MODA Boutique,** where a well-curated selection of designer clothing and jewelry awaits. A short walk away is **Cadeau,** 2308 12th Ave. S., a fun spot to browse for home decor, gifts and candles.

Nashvillians who prefer indie wails to Southern twangs score vinyl and hard-to-find CDs at **Grimey's New & Preloved Music,** 1604 Eighth Ave. S., where albums from bands such as The White Stripes, the Meat Puppets, and Nick Cave & The Bad Seeds occupy every available nook and cranny. New and vintage stringed instruments await the next great pickers, fiddlers and strummers at **Gruhn Guitars,** 2120 Eighth Ave. S., in business since 1970. Both music shops are in the vicinity of **Eighth Avenue South,** a district known for its antique shops. Closer to downtown but still on Eighth Avenue, **Carter Vintage Guitars,** 625 Eighth Ave. S., offers even more stringed instruments for serious collectors (the price tags are pretty serious, too).

Opry Mills, an outlet mall located on the site of the former Opryland USA theme park, suffered heavy flood damage in 2010, but reopened in 2012 with a new layout. Retailers include Coach Factory Store, Fossil Outlet, Polo Ralph Lauren Factory Store, Forever 21, H&M and J. Crew Factory Store.

Fashionistas aching for a no-holds-barred shopping spree should head to **The Mall at Green Hills,** 8 miles southwest of downtown at 2126 Abbott Martin Rd. Anchored by Dillard's and Macy's, the pristine, skylight-capped shopping center offers more than 100 specialty stores (upscale merchants include Burberry, Tiffany & Co. and Williams-Sonoma) and eateries.

Close by, hip urbanites linger inside such shops as Anthropologie, Johnston & Murphy, Vineyard Vines and West Elm at **Hill Center Green Hills,** an open-air, main street-style shopping village. The daughter of Hank Williams Jr. owns the nearby boutique **H. Audrey,** 4027 Hillsboro Pike, a popular spot for celebrity sightings.

Also serving Nashville-area mall rats are **River-Gate Mall,** on Rivergate Parkway off I-65 in Goodlettsville and home to Dillard's, JCPenney, Macy's and Sears; and **Lebanon Premium Outlets,** 25 miles east at the junction of I-40 and SR 231 in Lebanon, featuring 50-plus merchants, including Coach, Brooks Brothers and Polo Ralph Lauren. A suburban retail paradise, **CoolSprings Galleria** and **CoolSprings Crossings,** off I-65 at Moores Lane in Franklin, lure patrons with five department stores and more than 165 specialty shops, including an American Girl store.

After hitting the CoolSprings shopping hub, check out **The Factory at Franklin,** 230 Franklin Rd., a complex of Depression-era factory buildings first built for a stove manufacturing company. While the cavernous space retains its industrial look, patrons of art galleries, restaurants, and clothing and gift boutiques now swarm the site. Though it surely will be tempting, *don't* shop 'til you drop—more vendors await you less than a mile away in Franklin's quaint 15-block historic downtown district. Wooden planters and canvas awnings line **Main Street,** along which you'll find fine teas, chic accessories and campy toys as well as local lollygaggers enjoying the sights, sounds and smells of their charming burg. If you love rummaging through collections of rare books, oil paintings and pretty china

Enjoy live music at Robert's Western World

sets, walk to **Second Avenue and South Margin Street,** where a handful of antique dealers operate.

If what you really enjoy is haggling over prices, don't miss the **Nashville Flea Market** at the **Tennessee State Fairgrounds,** held the fourth weekend of each month (held the third weekend in December). One mile south of downtown Nashville at 500 Wedgewood Ave., the fair attracts bargain hunters in search of arts and crafts, furniture and collectibles.

Nightlife

They don't call the Tennessee capital NashVegas for nothin'. Serving as kitschy homing beacons for party-going natives, neon signs illuminate Broadway, otherwise known as the "**Honky Tonk Highway.**" Though smaller and more countrified than Nevada's exotic, well-lit strip, Music City's main drag remains a heady setting for both seasoned bar hoppers and those more accustomed to an 8 o'clock bedtime. Singing everything from country to rockabilly to bluegrass, bands crank up the volume at such down-home bars as **The Stage on Broadway, Layla's Bluegrass Inn** and **Legends Corner;** outside, the harmonies continue as street performers serenade kid-toting couples and photo-happy grandparents. Phone (615) 726-0504 for The Stage, (615) 726-2799 for Layla's or (615) 248-6334 for Legends Corner.

While exploring Broadway (where the action is centered between the Cumberland River and Fifth Avenue), experience the winning combination of Pabst Blue Ribbon, fried bologna sandwiches and live music at **Robert's Western World,** a former apparel store that's often heralded as one of the city's best honky-tonks; phone (615) 244-9552. Afterward, sidle up to one of three bars at **Tootsie's Orchid Lounge**—long the watering hole of choice for Nashville hit makers, Grand Ole Opry icons and up-and-coming talents. With multiple floors and multiple bands playing each night, you're sure to stumble on something good; phone (615) 726-0463.

Along Second Avenue (between Union Street and Broadway), techno-blaring dance clubs and themed bars lure raucous twentysomethings looking to let the good times roll. Hit the dance floor at **B.B. King's Blues Club** or pick up a few new moves at the **Wildhorse Saloon,** which offers line dancing lessons most nights. Phone (615) 256-2727 for B.B. King's Blues Club, (615) 902-8200 for the Wildhorse Saloon. **Acme Feed & Seed** is a relative newcomer to the Broadway scene and offers three floors of dining and entertainment, including a first floor honky-tonk, a second floor hipster-chic lounge, and a rooftop bar overlooking the city; phone (615) 915-0888.

Vestiges of a naughty past linger in **Printers Alley.** Long the hub of Nashville's printing industry, the alley also became home to speakeasies, gambling halls and other underground establishments around the turn of the 20th century. Though raids by billy club-bearing police officers have slowed since Prohibition ended, late-night debauchery endures in this historic quarter. (Needless to say, infamous

Printers Alley isn't for everyone.) Located between Third and Fourth avenues and Union and Church streets, the alley includes nightspots like the **Bourbon Street Blues and Boogie Bar**—where artists such as James Brown, Matt "Guitar" Murphy and Magic Slim have jammed; phone (615) 242-5837.

If you've had your fill of Lower Broadway nightlife, choose from the selection of classy restaurants and saloons at the Gaylord Opryland Resort *(see attraction listing p. 193)*, less than 20 minutes northeast of downtown Nashville. After dinner and drinks at the stunning hotel, mosey next door for some good old-fashioned entertainment and watch the show that helped define American country music: the **Grand Ole Opry.** Since Nov. 28, 1925, the live radio broadcast has enchanted audiences with nimble banjo players and tuned-in singer-songwriters. Fans of stars such as Dolly Parton, Alan Jackson and Martina McBride will no doubt be pleased by the show's ever-changing lineup; however, even those who aren't big country music lovers will likely consider their Opry pilgrimage to be a hoot. While songs about achy, breaky hearts and wanderlust-driven outlaws reign supreme, you'll also hear crossover artists' pop-infused melodies and amusing one-liners ("Always drink upstream from the herd!") delivered by droll cowpokes.

Stay up late and be part of the "Ernest Tubb Midnite Jamboree." If you've already spent all your dough on a pair of rhinestone cowboy boots or a Gibson Firebird electric guitar, don't worry; you still can join the live, toe-tapping studio audience at the **Texas Troubadour Theatre** *(see attraction listing p. 194)* on Music Valley Drive. Airing every Saturday at 12 o'clock following the Grand Ole Opry, the country's second-longest running live radio show won't cost you a dime to enjoy.

Also free is Writers' Night, held every Sunday at 8 p.m. at **The Bluebird Cafe,** 4104 Hillsboro Pike. The show features between nine and 12 up-and-comers—who each play three original songs—as well as a guest performance by an experienced Nashville hit maker. Just keep in mind, mum's the word during the gig (The Bluebird's unofficial slogan is "Shhh!"). Also, since seating is first-come, first-served, you'll need to arrive early to snag a spot inside the tiny listening room. If you can't get in on a Sunday, take note of the determined amateurs who take the stage during Monday's open mike night. In addition, reservations are generally accepted Tuesdays through Saturdays, when esteemed country and acoustic musicians make appearances at the intimate venue; phone (615) 383-1461.

In Nashville's **Gulch district,** an old-school sign outside **The Station Inn,** 402 12th Ave. S., (615) 255-3307, points out all you need to know about this spartan local institution, a mecca for true bluegrass aficionados:

- Live Acoustic Music
- Open at 7 p.m. – Music at 9 p.m.
- Pizza/Beer/Snacks

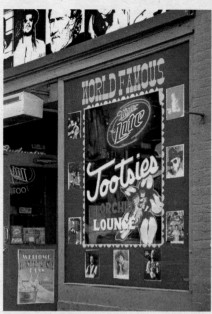
Grab a barstool at Tootsie's Orchid Lounge

Though physically close to The Station Inn, **Sambuca,** 601 12th Ave. S., is on the opposite end of the nightlife spectrum in every other way. Surrounded by velvet draperies, plump leather seats and ornate candelabras, stylish patrons sip martinis inside this sexy restaurant and lounge as musicians ranging from jazz crooners to classic rock 'n' rollers take the stage. Enjoy some lobster enchiladas or a flat-iron steak served with a side of quesadillas, then head up to Sambuca's posh rooftop patio for after-dinner cocktails and impressive views of Nashville's twinkling skyline; phone (615) 248-2888.

Just a twist, shimmy and knee slide away, **The Mercy Lounge** at One Cannery Row draws hipsters and wailing front men to a former food-canning factory. In the '80s and '90s, riotous crowds went hoarse cheering on acts such as Iggy Pop, Lenny Kravitz and Jane's Addiction in this retrofitted warehouse; these days, the intimate second-floor venue packs 'em in with local and nationally touring buzz bands as well as such regular events as 8 off 8th, a showcase for fledgling artists still unaccustomed to groupies and throngs of Zippo-brandishing fans. On the ground floor is the **Cannery Ballroom,** which hosts larger concerts. Phone (615) 251-3020.

If you find yourself standing in a long line outside the **Exit/In,** 2208 Elliston Pl., scan the wall of fame by the entrance. Odds are you'll recognize more than just a few of the names scribbled haphazardly on the side of the building. Since the club's opening in 1971, R.E.M., Johnny Cash, Kings of Leon, Willie Nelson and Bon Iver are just a few who've brought down the house in this dark, standing-room-only dive; phone (615) 321-3340. But, before all the headbanging and fist pumping action starts, grab a bite and a few longnecks nearby.

With Vanderbilt University as a neighbor, it's no wonder **Elliston Place** (a.k.a. the "Rock Block") and the surrounding area are home to a number of quirky taverns and restaurants. Mellow hole-in-the-wall **The Gold Rush,** 2205 Elliston Pl., baits hordes of hungry, college-going night owls with happy hour specials and bar grub, while sorority sisters and biker babes clink suds-capped mugs at the **Broadway Brewhouse,** 1900 Broadway. Phone (615) 321-1160 for The Gold Rush or (615) 340-0089 for the Broadway Brewhouse.

Big Events

As is befitting, music celebrations abound in Music City, USA. During the ◄► **CMA Music Festival** in early June, barbecues, exhibits and general fanfare envelop downtown Nashville. But let's not forget the live music: Huge crowds of fans pack outdoor and arena concerts given by country music's biggest celebrities.

The **Tin Pan South Songwriters Festival,** named after New York's Tin Pan Alley, attracts hundreds of songwriters who perform in venues throughout the city in late March. Catch the acts of both legendary and up-and-coming musicians.

Each March 15th, ◄► **The Hermitage** celebrates the **Anniversary of Andrew Jackson's Birthday** with a grand display. Folks flock to the president's antebellum mansion for tours of the home and 1,120-acre grounds, where the president and his wife are buried.

Montgomery Bell State Park

Spring also welcomes the **Nashville Film Festival** in mid-April, during which well-known and promising film producers present their works. Cinemas host screenings, and festivalgoers can attend film-related seminars and forums.

One of Nashville's finest traditions is the **Running of the Iroquois Memorial Steeplechase.** This classic event, held the second Saturday in May, has been a major festivity since 1941 and is said to be one of the longest-running steeplechases in the country. Attracting the city's elite, the steeplechase features seven races and is held in **Percy Warner Park.**

The **Tennessee State Fair** in September offers carnival rides, performances, art exhibits, competitions, performances and pageants. In October, attend the **Celebration Nashville Cultural Festival,** an ethnic festival with food, exhibits, crafts and over 60 music and dance performances on seven different stages.

Holiday events take place at **Cheekwood Botanical Garden & Museum of Art,** the **Belle Meade Plantation,** the ◄► **Country Music Hall of Fame and Museum,** and **Loews Vanderbilt Hotel Nashville,** but ◄► **Gaylord Opryland's A Country Christmas,** an event draped in almost 2 million lights, is tough to top. The celebration runs from mid-November to early January and features a living nativity, carriage rides and a craft and gift fair. **ICE!,** a frozen wonderland built around life-size ice sculptures, also is a cool part of the celebration.

Sports & Rec

Stroll through **Riverfront Park,** sandwiched between Lower Broadway and the Cumberland River, for views of **Nissan Stadium,** 1 Titans Way, where vociferous natives cheer on their gridiron darlings: the National **Football** League's **Tennessee Titans.** For tickets phone (615) 565-4200 or (888) 313-8326. Vanderbilt University's football team, the **Commodores,** has attracted a faithful crowd to **Vanderbilt Stadium** for years; phone (615) 322-4653 or (877) 448-2639 for tickets.

Both the women's and men's Vanderbilt Commodores **basketball** teams are usually contenders in their conferences, making tickets a valuable commodity; phone (615) 322-3544.

Baseball fans root for the **Nashville Sounds,** a Triple-A minor league team affiliated with the Milwaukee Brewers. Tickets to their games at First Tennessee Park, 401 Jackson St., are available; phone (615) 690-4487.

Watch streaks of navy blue, gold and white—a.k.a. the National **Hockey** League's **Nashville Predators**—whiz past opponents at the **Bridgestone Arena,** downtown at Fifth Avenue and Broadway. Phone (615) 770-2000 for Predators ticket information.

The **J. Percy Priest** and **Old Hickory** reservoirs (*see Recreation Areas Chart*) and a network of inner-city parks are the mainstay of many sports and leisure activities around Nashville. Family-oriented

Cumberland Park includes an open lawn, a river walk, landscaped gardens and play equipment for children. Centennial Park offers picnic areas, a short trail and a dog park. Wooded trails provide shade to joggers and walkers at Edwin and Percy Warner Parks (see attraction listing p. 192). Radnor Lake State Natural Area, south of Nashville off I-65, has 10 hiking trails of various levels of difficulty, as well as nature walks and plenty of opportunities for wildlife viewing.

Bicycling is enjoyable on the 26-mile Music City Bikeway between Percy Warner Park and J. Percy Priest Dam. The trail, which consists of greenway bike paths, shared street routes as well as designated bike lanes, offers scenic views of the Cumberland River, Nissan Stadium and Bicentennial Capitol Mall State Park. Mountain bike trails are located in Percy Warner Park.

Bike equipment rentals are available from Nashville's GreenBikes, a no-cost bicycle-sharing program. Check out bikes from various stations along the Music City Bikeway, including stations in Riverfront Park and Shelby Bottoms Nature Center. Phone (615) 625-2153 for more information. Another bicycle-sharing option is Nashville B-Cycle. Two-wheelers may be rented and returned at self-service kiosks found throughout the city. A 24-hour pass costs $5, which includes rides of up to 1 hour. Additional fees are charged for longer rides. Phone (615) 625-2153 for Nashville B-Cycle information.

The J. Percy Priest and Old Hickory reservoirs are popular spots for boating, water skiing, swimming and other water sports. Children can cool off at Cumberland Park's water play area featuring an interactive splash pad, water jets and rain curtains. Indoor swimming is offered at Centennial Sportsplex; phone (615) 862-8480 for the Aquatics Department. Metro Parks and Recreation maintains both outdoor and indoor pools for public use at locations throughout Nashville; phone (615) 862-8400.

The Harpeth Scenic River, southwest of the city off US 70, welcomes canoes and kayaks. For information on canoeing trips in the Nashville vicinity contact the Tennessee Department of Tourist Development, 312 Rosa L. Parks Ave.; phone (615) 741-2159.

Fishing for crappie, bass, catfish and sunfish in the lakes and reservoirs around Nashville is a favorite pastime. For fishing license information, contact the Tennessee Wildlife Resources Agency, phone (615) 781-6622. Licenses also are available at discount stores and sporting goods stores, bait shops and marinas.

Indoor and outdoor tennis courts are available at Centennial Sportsplex Tennis Center, across from Centennial Park. Metro Parks and Recreation offers free public courts on a first-come, first-served basis; phone (615) 862-8490 for Centennial and Metro Parks. Courts also are available at local high schools and universities.

Nine-hole golf courses open to the public include Percy Warner, (615) 352-9958, and Little Course at

Schermerhorn Symphony Center

Aspen Grove, (615) 790-0222, in nearby Franklin. For 18-hole courses head to Harpeth Hills, (615) 862-8493, in Percy Warner Park; Nashboro Golf Club, (615) 367-2311; Ted Rhodes, (615) 862-8463, on the banks of the Cumberland River; Two Rivers, (615) 889-2675, near the Grand Ole Opry; or Shelby, (615) 862-8474, in East Nashville.

Just northeast of town in Old Hickory you'll find 18-hole Riverside, (615) 847-5074, and Hermitage Golf Club, (615) 847-4001. Golfing options in Franklin include Forrest Crossing, (615) 794-9400, and Vanderbilt Legends Club of Tennessee, (615) 791-8100. McCabe Golf Course in West Nashville offers 27 holes; (615) 862-8491.

Performing Arts

One of the most important events in Nashville's history was the building of the Ryman Auditorium (see attraction listing p. 194). The home of the Grand Ole Opry for 31 years, the stage of the Ryman Auditorium also has been graced by the likes of Enrico Caruso, Katharine Hepburn, Helen Keller and Harry Houdini. In 1994 an $8 million renovation and restoration project once again put the Ryman in the spotlight as the city's premier cultural venue; audiences enjoy concerts, musicals and award shows there. The facility also serves as a daytime museum, documenting the Ryman's past through a variety of exhibits and videos.

Built in east Nashville along the Cumberland River in 1974, the Grand Ole Opry House in Gaylord Opryland is a center for country music shows. For those who prefer down-home cookin' with their music, Nashville Nightlife Dinner Theater fills the bill daily; phone (615) 885-4747 or (800) 573-7973 for schedule information.

In the heart of town the **Tennessee Performing Arts Center (TPAC)** has four showcases for top shows and artists: the **Andrew Jackson Hall** for concerts, operas and touring Broadway shows; the Andrew **Johnson Theater** for theater-in-the-round; the **James K. Polk** Theater for theatrical productions, operettas, dance and chamber concerts; and the **War Memorial Auditorium** for orchestral and theatrical shows.

Nashville Ballet presents classical and contemporary works at the Tennessee Performing Arts Center as well as at The Martin Center for Nashville Ballet, 3630 Redmon St.

The **Nashville Symphony** performs September through May in the **Schermerhorn Symphony Center,** one of only a few major concert halls in North America to use natural lighting; phone (615) 687-6400 for information and reservations.

Colleges and universities in Nashville also offer their share of music, dance and drama productions. Some of the programs are free and many are performed at Vanderbilt University's **Blair School of Music,** (615) 322-7651. The **Nashville Children's Theater,** 25 Middleton St., specializes in children's

productions; phone (615) 252-4675. **Chaffin's Barn Dinner Theatre,** 8204 Hwy. 100, presents comedies and musicals. On the main stage, a platform descends from the ceiling at the start of each show. Performances are offered year-round; phone (615) 646-9977 or (800) 282-2276.

Concerts take place on weekends, mid-May through September at **Centennial Park** and other area parks; for more information phone (615) 862-8424.

Downtown art galleries host receptions and art openings during the **First Saturday Art Crawl,** held on the first Saturday of the month at venues along Fifth Avenue.

ATTRACTIONS

ADVENTURE SCIENCE CENTER is reached via I-40 exit 210C (2nd and 4th aves.) or off the I-65S Wedgewood exit, following signs to 800 Fort Negley Blvd. Interactive exhibits and programs explore astronomy, the physical sciences, natural history and human health.

Space Chase is an interactive sky and space exhibit hall featuring Moonwalker, a simulated walk on

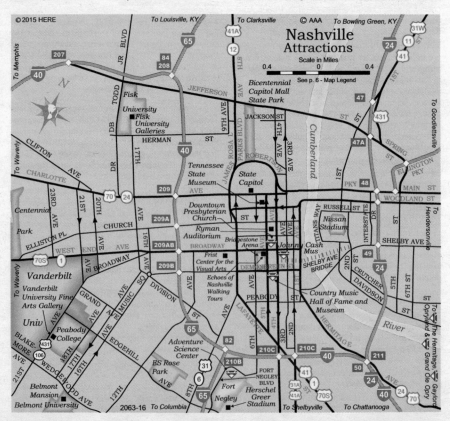

the moon, and Cosmic Ray's, where visitors can play interactive galactic games. Other permanent displays include BodyQuest, which helps visitors better understand the functions of human body systems, and BlueMax, a full-motion flight simulator that children can pilot. The seven-story Adventure Tower climbing structure offers more than 75 hands-on activities. Sudekum Planetarium features full-dome digital projection and stadium seating.

Time: Allow 2 hours minimum. **Hours:** Daily 10-5. Closed Thanksgiving and Christmas. **Cost:** $14; $11 (ages 2-12, 65+ and college students and military with ID). Planetarium show $6. Laser show $8. BlueMax ride $5.50. Prices may vary. **Phone:** (615) 862-5160.

BELLE MEADE PLANTATION is 7 mi. s.w. on US 70S at 5025 Harding Pike. Guides in period costumes conduct tours of an 1853 Greek Revival mansion noted for its cantilevered staircase, 14-foot ceilings and classic proportions. It originally was the centerpiece of a 5,400-acre working plantation and Thoroughbred farm. The site also includes a winery, an 1890 carriage house displaying antique carriages, a 1790 log cabin, an 1820 smokehouse, an 1840 mausoleum and an 1884 creamery.

Time: Allow 1 hour minimum. **Hours:** Guided tours daily 9-5. Last tour begins at 4. Closed Jan. 1, Easter, Thanksgiving, Christmas Eve and Christmas. **Cost:** $18; $16 (ages 65+); $12 (ages 13-18); $10 (ages 6-12); $50 (family, two adults and up to four children ages 6-18). A free wine-tasting opportunity at the winery may be available with adult (ages 21+) admission; phone ahead. Grounds only $10. **Phone:** (615) 356-0501 or (800) 270-3991. (GT) (†1)

BELMONT MANSION is on the Belmont University campus at 1700 Acklen Ave. The ornate Italianate villa was built in the 1850s as a summer home for Adelicia Acklen, one of the country's wealthiest women of the mid-19th century. Exterior features include elaborate cast-iron balconies and an octagonal cupola. Guided 1-hour tours visit such spacious rooms as an arched-ceiling ballroom. The grand staircase, marble mantels, period furnishings and artwork are notable.

Time: Allow 1 hour minimum. **Hours:** Guided tours Mon.-Sat. 10-4, Sun. 1-4. Last tour departs at 3:30. Closed major holidays. **Cost:** $12; $11 (ages 65+ and military with ID); $3 (ages 6-12). **Phone:** (615) 460-5459. (GT)

BICENTENNIAL CAPITOL MALL STATE PARK is off James Robertson Pkwy. between 6th and 7th aves. The 19-acre park was completed in 1996 to commemorate the 200th year of Tennessee statehood. A granite map of Tennessee is imbedded in the concrete plaza; the state's rivers are represented by fountains.

A 2,000-seat amphitheater provides dramatic views of the Capitol to the south, while a plaza contains the Tennessee World War II Memorial. A 95-bell carillon plays Tennessee-themed songs on the

The Parthenon

hour. Adjacent to the park on 7th Avenue is the Nashville Farmers' Market, open daily 8-6. Access to a multi-use greenway path is available on the 6th Avenue side of the park. **Time:** Allow 30 minutes minimum. **Hours:** Daily 6 a.m.-10 p.m. **Cost:** Free. **Phone:** (615) 741-5280. (🏕)

CENTENNIAL PARK is at West End and 25th aves. The site of the 1897 Tennessee Centennial Exposition, the 132-acre park features grassy areas, sunken gardens, a dog park, a playground, a 1-mile walking trail around Lake Watauga and The Parthenon *(see attraction listing)*, which houses an art museum. "If Trees Could Sing," an interactive outdoor exhibit, features 18 video presentations by Nashville celebrities that can be accessed by smartphone. Centennial Art Center displays works of art by local and regional artists. Free outdoor music concerts are held at the band shell on Saturday afternoons during Musicians Corner, May-June and Sept.-Oct. **Hours:** Grounds daily dawn-11 p.m. Art center Mon.-Thurs. 9-5. **Cost:** Free. **Phone:** (615) 862-8400, or (615) 862-8442 for Art Center. (🏕)

The Parthenon is in Centennial Park at West End and 25th aves. This is a full-size replica of the Parthenon on the Acropolis in Athens, Greece. The only such replica in the world, the Nashville Parthenon is home to the city of Nashville's permanent art collection. Inside is a 42-foot-high sculpture of Athena, the goddess of wisdom. **Time:** Allow 1 hour minimum. **Hours:** Tues.-Sat. 9-4:30, Sun. 12:30-4:30. Closed Jan. 1, July 4, Thanksgiving, Christmas Eve and Christmas. Phone ahead to confirm schedule. **Cost:** $6; $4 (ages 4-17 and 62+). **Phone:** (615) 862-8431.

CHEEKWOOD BOTANICAL GARDEN & MUSEUM OF ART is 8 mi. s.w. on Harding Rd., s.e. on Belle Meade Blvd., then s. on Page Rd. to 1200 Forrest Park Dr. This 55-acre estate was built by the family of the Maxwell House Coffee fortune and is an example of the Country Place Era of landscape design. An herb garden, a Japanese garden, a water garden and a wildflower garden constitute the botanical area. The Museum of Art, housed in a Georgian-style mansion, includes collections of American and contemporary painting and sculpture, English and American decorative arts and traveling exhibitions.

The 1-mile Carell Woodland Sculpture Trail features works by national and international artists among native trees, shrubs and wildflowers. Seasonal events include Cheekwood in Bloom, a spring festival featuring a display of more than 100,000 tulips. **Time:** Allow 2 hours minimum. **Hours:** Tues.-Sun. 9-5. Closed major holidays. **Cost:** $14; $12 (ages 65+); $10 (college students with ID); $7 (ages 3-17 and active military with ID). Reservations are required for tours. **Parking:** $3. **Phone:** (615) 356-8000. (GT) (¶)

COUNTRY MUSIC HALL OF FAME AND MUSEUM, 222 5th Ave. S., celebrates the origins and heritage of country music—even before you set foot inside. Look closely as you approach the striking edifice and you'll spot a 1950s Cadillac fin (the arch on the structure's right side) and black piano keys (the tall, slim windows along the front). Emerging from the Hall of Fame Rotunda, a diamond-shaped tower recalls Nashville's WSM AM radio antenna.

Cheekwood Botanical Garden & Museum of Art

Once indoors, you'll discover film and audio clips, interactive displays and trivia games, glittery costumes worn by Carrie Underwood and Taylor Swift, and well-traveled instruments that bring history to life in the museum's permanent exhibits. Inside a replica tour bus you'll be able to record your own country track to send to friends and family. Temporary exhibitions, performances, songwriting and instrument demonstrations, celebrity audio tours and bus tours to Music Row's Historic RCA Studio B are available.

Time: Allow 1 hour, 30 minutes minimum. **Hours:** Museum daily 9-5, Mar.-Dec.; Wed.-Mon. 9-5, rest of year. Studio B tours depart daily 10:30-2:30. Closed Jan. 1, Thanksgiving and Christmas. **Cost:** Museum $24.95; $22.50 (ages 60+ and college students with ID); $21.50 (military with ID); $14.95 (ages 6-12). Celebrity audio tour and Studio B tour fees vary; phone ahead. **Phone:** (615) 416-2001. (¶)

DOWNTOWN PRESBYTERIAN CHURCH is at 154 5th Ave. N. An example of the Egyptian Revival style popular during the 19th century, this 1851 church served as a Union hospital during the Civil War. **Time:** Allow 30 minutes minimum. **Hours:** Self-guiding tours Mon.-Fri. 9-3 during office hours. Services Sun. at 11 a.m. Closed major holidays. **Cost:** Free. **Phone:** (615) 254-7584.

EDWIN AND PERCY WARNER PARKS are 9 mi. s.w. via US 70S and SR 100. Encompassing over 3,100 acres of rugged hills, hollows, meadows and fields, the two parks, known collectively as The Warner Parks, are a wildlife sanctuary. A nature center features a natural history museum, an organic garden, a wildflower garden and several nature trails of varying lengths and difficulties. There are also athletic fields and two golf courses. Scenic drives and trails for hiking, mountain biking and horseback riding can be traveled; horse rentals are not available.

Picnic facilities include shelters and tables. **Hours:** Parks open daily dawn-11 p.m. Nature center open Tues.-Sat. 9-4; closed major holidays. **Cost:** Free. **Phone:** (615) 370-8051 for the park, or (615) 352-6299 for the nature center. (🏕)

FISK UNIVERSITY GALLERIES are on the Fisk University campus near the corner of Jackson St. and Dr. D.B. Todd Jr. Blvd. The university library houses The Aaron Douglas Gallery, which features changing exhibitions of African, African-American and European paintings, photographs, prints, sculpture and folk art. Every two years the adjacent Carl Van Vechten Gallery houses a rotating exhibit of the Stieglitz Collection including works by Paul Cézanne, Georgia O'Keeffe, Pablo Picasso and Pierre-Auguste Renoir.

Hours: Galleries open Mon.-Fri. 10-5, May 7-Aug. 14; Tues.-Sat. 10-5, rest of year. Closed university holidays. **Cost:** $10; $6 (ages 60+); $5 (college students with ID); free (ages 0-17). **Phone:** (615) 329-8720, or (615) 329-8685 for the library gallery.

FRIST CENTER FOR THE VISUAL ARTS is at 919 Broadway; the parking lot is entered from either Broadway or Demonbreun St. In an impressive Art Deco structure that once housed the Nashville post office, the center offers changing exhibits featuring local, national and international art spanning many time periods. The second floor includes Martin Art-Quest, an interactive children's play area with hands-on art stations.

Time: Allow 1 hour minimum. **Hours:** Mon.-Sat. 10-5:30 (also Thurs.-Fri. 5:30-9), Sun. 1-5:30. Docent-led tours are offered Mon.-Fri. at 1:30pm and on select weekends. Architecture tours offered the first Sat. of the month at 4:30. Closed Jan. 1, Thanksgiving and Christmas. **Cost:** $12; $9 (ages 65+ and college students with ID); $7 (active military with ID); free (ages 0-18). iPod audio tour $3. **Parking:** $3 for 2 hours (bring ticket inside for validation). **Phone:** (615) 244-3340, or (615) 744-3247 for tour schedule information.

 GAYLORD OPRYLAND is 10 mi. n.e. via the Opryland and Music Valley Dr. interchanges on Briley Pkwy., which connects I-40 and I-65, following signs. The complex, which incorporates a collection of entertainment, hospitality, shopping and broadcasting attractions, includes the Grand Ole Opry; the *General Jackson* showboat; Opry Mills Mall; the Gaylord Opryland Resort; and Gaylord Spring Golf Links. **Phone:** (615) 889-1000.

Gaylord Opryland Resort is 10 mi. n.e. via Music Valley Dr. interchange (exit 12) on Briley Pkwy. The hotel features three interior garden spaces under glass roofs: The Garden Conservatory is a botanical garden with more than 10,000 tropical plants; the Cascades is a lushly planted area with waterfalls and fountains; and the Delta covers 4.5 acres and is highlighted by a water system with flatboats.

Gaylord Opryland's A Country Christmas celebrates the holiday season from mid-November to late December with spectacles such as ICE! and its huge ice sculptures. **Phone:** (615) 889-1000.

Grand Ole Opry shows are performed in the Grand Ole Opry House, 2804 Opryland Dr., for most of the year or downtown at the Ryman Auditorium, 116 Fifth Ave. N., during the winter. Since 1925, country's best have mesmerized audiences at the Opry, the live radio show that made country music famous. While performances from both legendary honky-tonk entertainers and the latest country music acts are the norm, if you go (and while in Nashville, you really *must*), you'll also enjoy bluegrass bands, comedians and gospel artists.

The list of current Grand Ole Opry members includes such stars as the Charlie Daniels Band, Loretta Lynn, Brad Paisley, Connie Smith and Carrie Underwood, all of whom return regularly to sing on the same spot—a round, 6-foot piece of oak wood at center stage. Cut from the Ryman Auditorium *(see attraction listing p. 194)*, the show's home 1943-74,

the circle pays tribute to the Opry's storied existence and its bygone talents—everyone from Roy Acuff to Patsy Cline.

Guided backstage tours of the Grand Ole Opry House, which was refurbished after a May 2010 flood, offer visitors an up-close look at the celebrated venue and its 18 themed dressing rooms. **Hours:** Shows are given Tues. and Fri.-Sat. at 7 p.m. (also Wed. at 7 p.m., mid-Jun. to early Aug.), Mar.-Oct.; Fri. and Sat. at 7 p.m., in Feb. Backstage tours offered daily. Show and tour times vary; phone ahead to confirm schedule. **Cost:** Reserved performance seating varies by seat location and range $32-$72.50; free (ages 0-3). Daily backstage tour $22; $17 (ages 4-11). Other tour prices vary. **Phone:** (615) 871-6779 or (800) 733-6779.

THE HERMITAGE—see Hermitage p. 104.

 JOHNNY CASH MUSEUM is downtown at 119 3rd Ave. S. The museum features the largest archive of Johnny Cash memorabilia in the world. It showcases items documenting his childhood, his service in the U.S. Air Force, his earliest steps entering the country music industry, personal items and an entire stone wall from his Tennessee home. Rare items include handwritten lyrics to "Folsom Prison Blues" and "I Walk the Line."

Listening stations feature music spanning six decades of his music, and a theater shows a short video chronicling his involvement in the entertainment industry outside of country music. One of two videos that can't be missed includes a dramatic reading of "This Ragged Old Flag." Then before you exit, there's Cash's Grammy-winning cover of "Hurt," his version of a tune so rife with painful lyrics they could have easily been taken from the pages of his life.

Time: Allow 1 hour minimum. **Hours:** Daily 8-7. Closed Thanksgiving and Christmas. **Cost:** $16; $15 (military with ID and senior citizens); $12 (ages 6-15). **Parking:** $7-$16. **Phone:** (615) 256-1777.

LANE MOTOR MUSEUM is .3 mi. s. off I-24 exit 212 on Fessler's Ln., then .4 mi. s.e. to 702 Murfreesboro Pike. The collection of more than 150 automobiles and motorcycles, including amphibious, competition and military vehicles, are displayed in rotating exhibits in a former commercial bakery. Primarily arranged by country of origin, the mainly European collection features older vehicles such as a 1924 Citroën 5CV as well as recent additions, including a 2007 Renault Mégane. An art gallery and children's play area also are on-site.

Time: Allow 1 hour minimum. **Hours:** Thurs.-Mon. 10-5. Closed Jan. 1, Thanksgiving and Christmas. **Cost:** $9; $6 (ages 65+); $3 (ages 6-17). **Phone:** (615) 742-7445.

NASHVILLE SHORES LAKESIDE RESORT—see Hermitage p. 104.

NASHVILLE ZOO AT GRASSMERE is 2 mi. e. off I-65 exit 78A (Harding Pl.), then just n. to 3777 Nolensville Pike. The 180-acre zoo features global wildlife, including African elephants, Bengal tigers, Eurasian lynx, hyacinth macaws, red river hogs and African crested porcupines. A giant anaconda and poison arrow frogs are among the creatures in the Unseen New World exhibit area. Historic home tours, carousel rides and a 66,000-square-foot play area for children also are available.

Time: Allow 2 hours minimum. **Hours:** Daily 9-6, mid-Mar. to mid-Oct.; 9-4, rest of year. Closed Jan. 1, Thanksgiving and Christmas. **Cost:** $15; $13 (ages 65+); $10 (ages 2-12). **Parking:** $5. **Phone:** (615) 833-1534.

OPRYLAND—see Gaylord Opryland p. 193.

RYMAN AUDITORIUM is at 116 5th Ave. N. Built as the Union Gospel Tabernacle in 1892 by riverboat captain Thomas Ryman, the auditorium was named in his honor posthumously. The Ryman is most famous for being home to the Grand Ole Opry live radio show from 1943-74.

Daytime tours offer a chance to walk around the 2,362-seat auditorium, fully restored after an $8 million renovation in the 1990s. Displays and exhibits highlight the building's storied history and feature costumes worn by Ryman performers. Year-round concerts are offered. Opry at the Ryman shows are offered during the winter season (Nov.-Jan.).

Guided backstage tours are available. **Time:** Allow 1 hour, 15 minutes minimum. **Hours:** Self-guiding tours daily 9-4. Opry at the Ryman shows are given Tues. and Fri.-Sat. at 7 p.m. (also Sat. at 9:30 p.m.), Nov.-Jan. Closed Jan. 1, Thanksgiving and Christmas. **Cost:** Standard tour $20; $15 (ages 4-11). Backstage tour additional $7.50. Opry at the Ryman ticket prices vary by seat location and range $32-$72.50. **Phone:** (615) 889-3060. GT Y1

STATE CAPITOL is at 600 Charlotte Ave; entrance is on the west side of the building. A fine example of Greek Revival architecture designed by William Strickland, this 1859 building has been renovated to reflect the period. Guided and self-guiding tours allow access to the House and Senate chambers, the Governor's Reception Room and the restored State Library room, which features an original spiral staircase and detailed iron railings.

Statues and markers on the grounds include an equestrian statue of Andrew Jackson and statues of Sam Davis and Alvin York. Also on the grounds are the tombs of 11th president James K. Polk and his wife. **Note:** A photo ID is required for entry. All visitors must pass through metal detectors; bags and packages are subject to hand inspection. **Time:** Allow 30 minutes minimum. **Hours:** Mon.-Fri. 9-4.

Guided tours depart on the hour 9-3. Last tour begins at closing. Closed major holidays. **Cost:** Free. **Phone:** (615) 741-0830 or (800) 407-4324. GT

TENNESSEE STATE MUSEUM, housed in the lower levels of the James K. Polk Cultural Center at 5th Ave. and Deaderick St., includes permanent collections and changing exhibits on three floors. The museum's interpretive collection begins 15,000 years ago with prehistoric humans and continues through the early 1900s with special selections featuring Native Americans, explorers, pioneers, the antebellum age, the Civil War and the New South.

Highlights include special displays of Tennessee-made furniture, silver, weapons, quilts and paintings. The museum's extensive Civil War collection include uniforms, battle flags and weapons. Visitors also will see replicas of an 18th-century printing press, a Conestoga wagon, an antebellum parlor and a frontier mill, as well as one-of-a-kind items like a musket belonging to Daniel Boone and a top hat worn by President Andrew Jackson at his inauguration. **Time:** Allow 1 hour minimum. **Hours:** Tues.-Sat. 10-5, Sun. 1-5. Closed Jan. 1, Easter, Thanksgiving and Christmas. **Cost:** Free. **Phone:** (615) 741-0830 or (800) 407-4324.

TEXAS TROUBADOUR THEATRE is off Briley Pkwy. exit 12, in the Music Valley Village at 2416 Music Valley Dr. The Saturday late-night radio country music show "Ernest Tubb Midnight Jamboree" is broadcast from the theater, as is the Sunday morning gospel music show "Nashville Cowboy Church" featuring Johnny Cash's sister Joanne Cash. **Hours:** Jamborees take place Sat. at midnight. "Nashville Cowboy Church" Sun. at 10 a.m. **Cost:** Free. **Phone:** (615) 889-2474 for general information, jamboree and church information, or (615) 758-0098 for musical production reservations.

TRAVELLERS REST PLANTATION AND MUSEUM is 6 mi. s. on I-65 to exit 78B (Harding Pl.), .25 mi. w. to Franklin Rd., .5 mi. s. to Lambert Dr., then e. following signs to 636 Farrell Pkwy. Although it was later expanded, the original four-room house was built in 1799 by John Overton, a Tennessee Supreme Court judge and a presidential advisor to Andrew Jackson. During the Civil War Battle of Nashville, the estate served as headquarters for the Confederate army. The grounds include both formal and herb gardens.

Time: Allow 1 hour minimum. **Hours:** Mon.-Sat. 10-4:30 (also Sun. 1-4:30, Mar.-Nov.). Phone ahead to confirm schedule. Last tour begins 1 hour before closing. Closed Jan. 1, Easter, Thanksgiving and Christmas. Phone ahead to confirm schedule. **Cost:** House, grounds and exhibits $12; $11 (ages 65+ and military with ID); $10 (ages 6-17). Grounds and exhibits $5; free (ages 0-6). **Phone:** (615) 832-8197.

VANDERBILT UNIVERSITY FINE ARTS GALLERY is at 1220 21st Ave. S. The gallery's collection encompasses more than 6,000 pieces of African, American, Asian, Egyptian, Etruscan, European,

Greek, Oceanic and Pre-Columbian art. While many exhibitions feature works from this collection, traveling exhibits often are presented throughout the year. **Time:** Allow 1 hour minimum. **Hours:** Mon.-Fri. 11-4, Sat.-Sun. 1-5, Sept.-Apr.; Tues.-Fri. noon-4, Sat. 1-5, rest of year. Closed school holidays. Phone ahead to confirm schedule. **Cost:** Free. **Phone:** (615) 322-0605.

WAVE COUNTRY, 2320 Two Rivers Pkwy., offers three water flumes, two speed slides, a children's pool and a playground. Waves are periodically sent through the park's main pool. **Hours:** Fri.-Sat. 10-6 (also Memorial Day, July 4 and Labor Day), Mon.-Thurs. 11-5, Sun. 11-6, late May-early Aug.; Sat. 10-6, Sun. 11-6, early Aug.-Labor Day weekend. **Cost:** $12; $10 (ages 3-12). **Phone:** (615) 885-1052.

Sightseeing
Boat Tours

GENERAL JACKSON SHOWBOAT departs from Gaylord Opryland's Cumberland River dock. The four-deck paddle-wheel riverboat offers midday, dinner and Sunday brunch cruises featuring live entertainment. **Hours:** Midday cruises depart Fri.-Sat. at noon; dinner cruises depart Sat. at 7 p.m.; brunch cruises depart Sun. at 11 a.m., Mar.-Dec. Boarding begins 30 minutes before departure. Phone ahead to confirm schedule. **Cost:** Brunch or midday cruise with meal and show $64.46; $40.58 (ages 4-11). Brunch or midday cruise with show only $45; $30 (ages 4-11). Dinner cruise with meal $99.06; $65.26 (ages 4-11). Other cruise fares vary; phone ahead for details. Reservations are recommended. **Phone:** (615) 458-3900 or (866) 567-5225.

Bus Tours

Sightseeing excursions with stops at the major attractions and/or tours of the stars' homes are offered by several companies, including NashTrash Tours, (615) 226-7300 or (800) 342-2132.

GRAY LINE TOURS picks up passengers from area hotels. A 3.5-hour all-inclusive Discover Nashville tour includes such landmarks as Honky Tonk Row, Bicentennial Capitol Mall State Park, Music Row and The Parthenon as well as entrance to the Ryman Auditorium and the Country Music Hall of Fame and Museum. A variety of other tours is available. **Time:** Allow 4 hours minimum. **Hours:** Departures daily at 9 and 1:30. Phone ahead to confirm schedule. **Cost:** Fare $55; $28 (ages 6-11). **Phone:** (615) 883-5555 or (800) 251-1864.

Walking Tours

ECHOES OF NASHVILLE WALKING TOURS departs from 501 Broadway; meet under the Bridgestone Arena digital sign. Guided, comfortably paced walking tours offer a detailed look at Nashville's history long before it was Music City, USA. You'll hear how Broadway got its name, where Nashville's first settlers lived and why the city once wanted to be known as the "Athens of the South."

Other highlights include stops at the Riverfront, the Tennessee State Capitol grounds, the original site of the Maxwell House Hotel and the historic Ryman Auditorium. **Time:** Allow 1 hour, 30 minutes minimum. **Hours:** Tours depart Wed.-Sat. at 10 and 1, Sun. at 1, or by appointment. **Cost:** $15; $8.50 (ages 6-12). Reservations are recommended. **Phone:** (615) 554-0053 or (615) 576-0804.

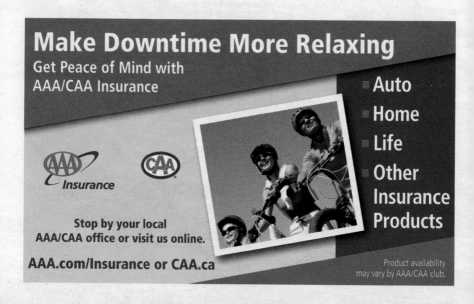

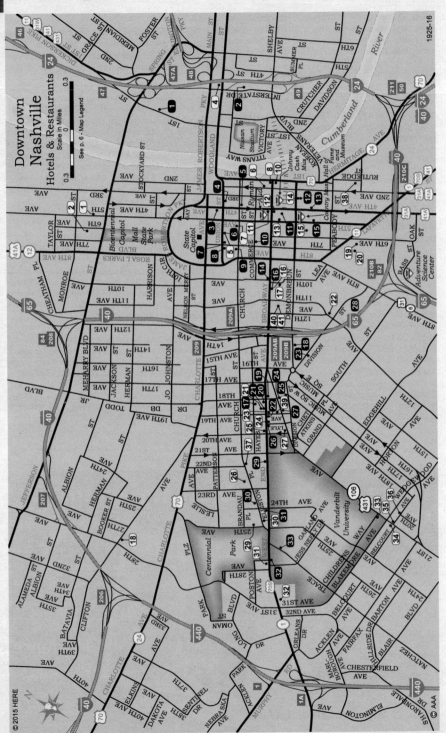

Downtown Nashville
Hotels & Restaurants

See p. 6 • Map Legend

Scale in Miles

1925-16

Downtown Nashville

This index helps you "spot" where approved hotels and restaurants are located on the corresponding detailed maps. Hotel daily rate range is for comparison only. Restaurant price range is a combination of lunch and/or dinner. Turn to the listing page for more detailed rate and price information and consult display ads for special promotions.

DOWNTOWN NASHVILLE

Map Page	Hotels	Diamond Rated	Rate Range	Page
1 p. 196	**Clarion Hotel Nashville Downtown - Stadium** *(See ad p. 208.)*	◈◈◈	$119-$269 SAVE	207
2 p. 196	**Ramada Nashville Downtown**	◈◈	$95-$170 SAVE	214
3 p. 196	**DoubleTree by Hilton Nashville Downtown** *(See ad p. 209.)*	◈◈◈	$199-$399 SAVE	208
4 p. 196	Hotel Indigo-Nashville Downtown	◈◈◈	$199-$469	213
5 p. 196	**Courtyard by Marriott Nashville Downtown**	◈◈◈	$219-$395	208
6 p. 196	**The Hermitage Hotel** *(See ad p. 210.)*	◈◈◈◈◈	Rates not provided SAVE	210
7 p. 196	**Sheraton Nashville Downtown Hotel**	◈◈◈	Rates not provided SAVE	214
8 p. 196	**The Capitol Hotel Downtown, an Ascend Hotel Collection Member** *(See ad p. 206.)*	◈◈	$119-$279 SAVE	207
9 p. 196	Homewood Suites Nashville Downtown	◈◈◈	$209-$299	212
10 p. 196	**Renaissance Nashville Hotel**	◈◈◈◈	$257-$351 SAVE	214
11 p. 196	**Hilton Nashville Downtown** *(See ad p. 211, on inside front cover.)*	◈◈◈◈	Rates not provided SAVE	210
12 p. 196	**Hyatt Place Nashville Downtown**	◈◈◈	$139-$799 SAVE	213
13 p. 196	**Hampton Inn & Suites Downtown Nashville**	◈◈◈	$209-$399 SAVE	209
14 p. 196	**Holiday Inn Express-Nashville Downtown** *(See ad p. 212.)*	◈◈◈	Rates not provided SAVE	212
15 p. 196	Omni Hotel	◈◈◈◈	Rates not provided	214
16 p. 196	**Union Station Hotel - Autograph Collection**	◈◈◈◈	$237-$389 SAVE	215
17 p. 196	Residence Inn by Marriott Nashville West End/Vanderbilt	◈◈◈	$167-$275	214
18 p. 196	Comfort Inn Downtown	◈◈	$100-$400	207
19 p. 196	**Aloft Nashville West End** *(See ad p. 207.)*	◈◈◈	$179-$499 SAVE	206
20 p. 196	SpringHill Suites by Marriott Nashville West End/Vanderbilt	◈◈◈	$153-$252	214
21 p. 196	**Hutton Hotel** *(See ad p. 213.)*	◈◈◈◈	$259-$429 SAVE	213
22 p. 196	Courtyard by Marriott-Vanderbilt West End	◈◈◈	$129-$369	208
23 p. 196	**BEST WESTERN PLUS Music Row**	◈◈◈	$129-$299 SAVE	207
24 p. 196	Hilton Garden Inn Nashville-Vanderbilt	◈◈◈	$139-$399	210
25 p. 196	Home2 Suites by Hilton-Nashville/Vanderbilt	◈◈◈	$149-$399	212
26 p. 196	Hampton Inn Vanderbilt	◈◈◈	$189-$299	210
27 p. 196	Embassy Suites by Hilton Nashville at Vanderbilt	◈◈◈	$199-$409	209
28 p. 196	Fairfield Inn & Suites by Marriott-Nashville Downtown/Gulch	◈◈◈	$202-$332	209
29 p. 196	**Loews Vanderbilt Hotel Nashville**	◈◈◈◈	Rates not provided SAVE	214
30 p. 196	Hampton Inn & Suites Vanderbilt Elliston Place	◈◈◈	$189-$299	209
31 p. 196	Homewood Suites by Hilton Nashville Vanderbilt/West End	◈◈◈	$229-$329	212
32 p. 196	Holiday Inn-Vanderbilt	◈◈◈	Rates not provided	212
33 p. 196	**Nashville Marriott at Vanderbilt University**	◈◈◈	$209-$298 SAVE	214

Map Page	Restaurants	Diamond Rated	Cuisine	Price Range	Page
① p. 196	Germantown Cafe	◆◆◆	New American	$7-$27	216
② p. 196	Monell's Dining & Catering	◆◆	Southern Chicken Comfort Food	$9-$21	217
④ p. 196	Gerst Haus	◆◆	German Sandwiches	$10-$19	216
⑤ p. 196	Capitol Grille	◆◆◆◆	Southern American	$13-$65	215
⑥ p. 196	Wildhorse Saloon	◆◆	American	$10-$23	218
⑦ p. 196	Tazza	◆◆	Italian	$7-$24	217
⑧ p. 196	Hard Rock Cafe	◆◆	American	$9-$30 SAVE	216
⑩ p. 196	Acme Feed & Seed	◆◆	Southern	$9-$22	215
⑪ p. 196	Jacks Bar-B-Que	◆	Barbecue	$5-$22	216
⑫ p. 196	Merchants	◆◆	American	$9-$24	216
⑬ p. 196	The Palm Restaurant (See ad p. 211.)	◆◆◆	American	$13-$52	217
⑭ p. 196	Etch Restaurant	◆◆◆	New American	$10-$38	216
⑮ p. 196	Bob's Steak & Chop House	◆◆◆	Steak	$35-$99	215
⑯ p. 196	Prime 108	◆◆◆	American	$13-$45	217
⑰ p. 196	Flying Saucer Draught Emporium	◆◆	American	$8-$12	216
⑱ p. 196	Swett's Restaurant	◆	American	$8-$12	217
⑲ p. 196	Hot Diggity Dogs	◆	Hot Dogs	$3-$6	216
⑳ p. 196	City Winery Nashville	◆◆	International	$15-$28	215
㉑ p. 196	1808 Grille	◆◆◆	New American	$12-$36	215
㉒ p. 196	**Cantina Laredo**	◆◆	Mexican	$10-$25	215
㉓ p. 196	Midtown Cafe	◆◆◆	Seafood Steak	$13-$37	217
㉔ p. 196	Valentino's Ristorante	◆◆◆	Northern Italian	$13-$48	218
㉕ p. 196	Amerigo, An Italian Restaurant	◆◆◆	Italian	$10-$35	215
㉖ p. 196	Jimmy Kelly's Steak House	◆◆	Steak	$15-$43	216
㉗ p. 196	Noshville - New York Delicatessen	◆◆	Deli Sandwiches	$8-$17	217
㉙ p. 196	Kobe Steaks - A Japanese Restaurant	◆◆	Japanese	$15-$71	216
㉚ p. 196	Rotier's	◆◆	Burgers Steak	$8-$19	217
㉛ p. 196	Hog Heaven	◆	Barbecue	$4-$14	216
㉜ p. 196	Stoney River Steakhouse and Grill	◆◆◆	American	$20-$50	217
㉝ p. 196	Sportsman's Grille In The Village	◆◆	American	$9-$25	217
㉞ p. 196	Provence Breads & Cafe	◆	French	$7-$11	217
㉟ p. 196	Pancake Pantry	◆◆	American	$6-$16	217
㊱ p. 196	Cabana	◆◆	Southern American	$7-$24	215
㊲ p. 196	Elliston Place Soda Shop	◆	Breakfast Sandwiches	$6-$10	216
㊳ p. 196	HUSK	◆◆◆	Southern American	$10-$32	216
㊴ p. 196	Hattie B's Hot Chicken	◆	Southern Chicken	$6-$12	216
㊵ p. 196	Moto Cucina & Enoteca	◆◆◆	Italian	$8-$49	217
㊶ p. 196	Saint Añejo	◆◆	Mexican	$7-$20	217

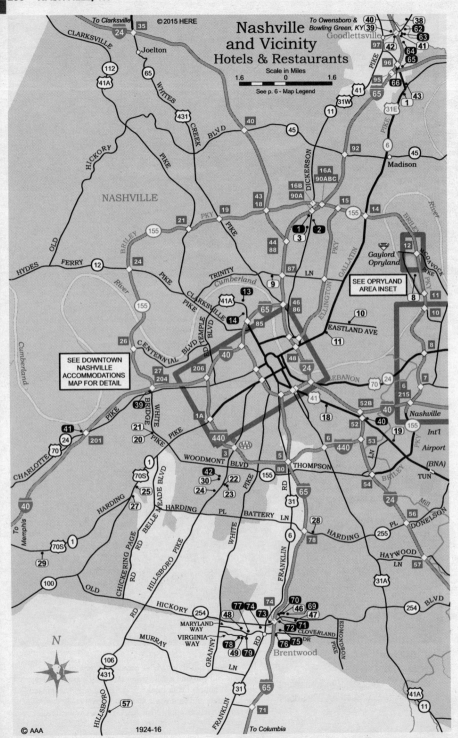

Nashville and Vicinity
Hotels & Restaurants

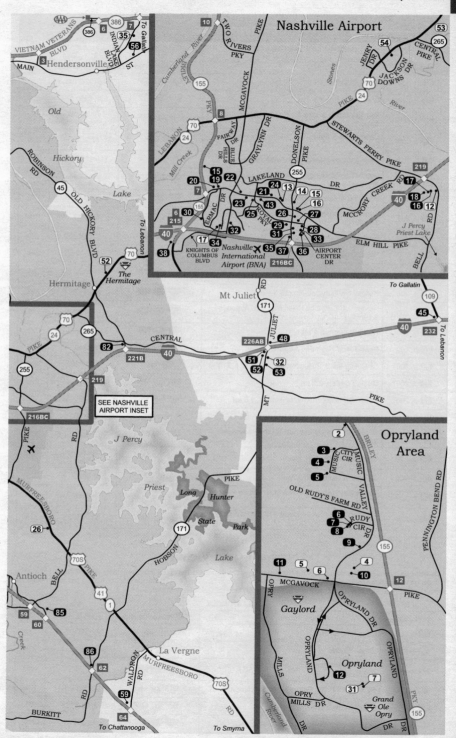

✈ Airport Hotels

Map Page	NASHVILLE INTERNATIONAL (Maximum driving distance from airport: 3.9 mi)	Diamond Rated	Rate Range	Page
17 p. 200	Comfort Suites, 3.7 mi	▼▼▼	$102-$190	218
23 p. 200	**Comfort Suites Airport, 2.4 mi**	▼▼▼	$98-$250 SAVE	218
37 p. 200	**Country Inn & Suites By Carlson, Nashville Airport, 1.3 mi**	▼▼▼	Rates not provided SAVE	218
18 p. 200	Country Inn & Suites By Carlson Nashville Airport East, 3.8 mi	▼▼	$75-$250	218
22 p. 200	**Courtyard by Marriott Nashville Airport, 2.6 mi**	▼▼▼	$99-$269 SAVE	218
15 p. 200	DoubleTree Suites by Hilton Hotel Nashville Airport, 3.9 mi	▼▼	$129-$299	219
31 p. 200	Drury Inn & Suites-Nashville Airport, 1.4 mi	▼▼▼	$100-$199	219
34 p. 200	**Embassy Suites by Hilton Nashville Airport, 3.0 mi**	▼▼▼	$129-$249 SAVE	219
35 p. 200	Hampton Inn & Suites Nashville Airport, 1.3 mi	▼▼▼	$139-$259	220
25 p. 200	Hilton Garden Inn Nashville Airport, 2.2 mi	▼▼▼	$97-$247	221
36 p. 200	**Holiday Inn Express-Airport/Opryland Area, 1.8 mi**	▼▼▼	$99-$249 SAVE	221
20 p. 200	Holiday Inn Opryland-Airport, 3.4 mi	▼▼▼	$119-$299	221
21 p. 200	Homewood Suites by Hilton Nashville Airport, 2.1 mi	▼▼▼	$119-$249	221
38 p. 200	**Hotel Preston, 3.4 mi**	▼▼▼	$119-$299 SAVE	222
27 p. 200	**Hyatt Place Nashville Airport, 2.1 mi**	▼▼▼	$79-$249 SAVE	222
26 p. 200	La Quinta Inn & Suites Nashville-Airport, 1.6 mi	▼▼	$71-$262	222
43 p. 200	**Quality Suites, 2.2 mi**	▼▼▼	$99-$239 SAVE	223
33 p. 200	**Radisson Hotel Nashville Airport, 1.8 mi**	▼▼▼	$99-$299 SAVE	223
29 p. 200	**Red Roof Inn Nashville Airport, 1.5 mi**	▼▼	$50-$130 SAVE	223
19 p. 200	**Residence Inn by Marriott Nashville Airport, 3.4 mi**	▼▼▼	$109-$269 SAVE	223
32 p. 200	**Sheraton Music City Hotel, 2.9 mi**	▼▼▼	Rates not provided SAVE	223
16 p. 200	**Sleep Inn Nashville, 3.7 mi**	▼▼	$85-$125 SAVE	223
28 p. 200	**SpringHill Suites by Marriott Nashville Airport, 1.7 mi**	▼▼▼	$99-$269 SAVE	224
24 p. 200	TownePlace Suites by Marriott Nashville Airport, 1.9 mi	▼▼▼	$159-$299	224

Nashville and Vicinity

This index helps you "spot" where approved hotels and restaurants are located on the corresponding detailed maps. Hotel daily rate range is for comparison only. Restaurant price range is a combination of lunch and/or dinner. Turn to the listing page for more detailed rate and price information and consult display ads for special promotions.

NASHVILLE

Map Page	Hotels	Diamond Rated	Rate Range	Page
1 p. 200	**Days Inn North**	▼▼	$70-$199 SAVE	219
2 p. 200	**Econo Lodge**	▼▼	$46-$133 SAVE	219
3 p. 200	Fairfield Inn & Suites by Marriott Nashville at Opryland	▼▼▼	$101-$177	220
4 p. 200	**BEST WESTERN Suites Near Opryland**	▼▼▼	$100-$200 SAVE	218
5 p. 200	Courtyard by Marriott at Opryland	▼▼▼	$115-$189	218
6 p. 200	Country Inn & Suites By Carlson-Opryland	▼▼▼	$99-$209	218

NASHVILLE (cont'd)

Map Page	Hotels (cont'd)	Diamond Rated	Rate Range	Page
7 p. 200	**Hyatt Place Nashville/Opryland** *(See ad p. 222.)*	◇◇◇	$89-$209 SAVE	222
8 p. 200	Hampton Inn & Suites Nashville at Opryland	◆◆◆	$129-$299	220
9 p. 200	GuestHouse International Inn & Suites	◆◆	$125-$150	220
10 p. 200	The Inn at Opryland, A Gaylord Hotel	◆◆◆	$125-$204	222
11 p. 200	Holiday Inn Express Nashville-Opryland	◆◆◆	$199-$399	221
12 p. 200	**Gaylord Opryland Resort & Convention Center**	◇◇◇	$188-$309 SAVE	220
13 p. 200	SpringHill Suites by Marriott Metro Center	◆◆◆	$125-$329	224
14 p. 200	**Millennium Maxwell House Hotel-Nashville**	◆◆◆	$99-$259 SAVE	223
15 p. 200	DoubleTree Suites by Hilton Hotel Nashville Airport	◆◆◆	$129-$299	219
16 p. 200	**Sleep Inn Nashville**	◇◇	$85-$125 SAVE	223
17 p. 200	Comfort Suites	◆◆◆	$102-$190	218
18 p. 200	Country Inn & Suites By Carlson Nashville Airport East	◆◆	$75-$250	218
19 p. 200	**Residence Inn by Marriott Nashville Airport**	◇◇◇	$109-$269 SAVE	223
20 p. 200	Holiday Inn Opryland-Airport	◆◆◆	$119-$299	221
21 p. 200	Homewood Suites by Hilton Nashville Airport	◆◆◆	$119-$249	221
22 p. 200	**Courtyard by Marriott Nashville Airport**	◇◇◇	$99-$269 SAVE	218
23 p. 200	**Comfort Suites Airport**	◇◇◇	$98-$250 SAVE	218
24 p. 200	TownePlace Suites by Marriott Nashville Airport	◆◆◆	$159-$299	224
25 p. 200	Hilton Garden Inn Nashville Airport	◆◆◆	$97-$247	221
26 p. 200	La Quinta Inn & Suites Nashville-Airport	◆◆	$71-$262	222
27 p. 200	**Hyatt Place Nashville Airport**	◇◇◇	$79-$249 SAVE	222
28 p. 200	**SpringHill Suites by Marriott Nashville Airport**	◇◇◇	$99-$269 SAVE	224
29 p. 200	**Red Roof Inn Nashville Airport**	◇◇	$50-$130 SAVE	223
30 p. 200	Nashville Airport Marriott	◆◆◆	$112-$265	223
31 p. 200	Drury Inn & Suites-Nashville Airport	◆◆◆	$100-$199	219
32 p. 200	**Sheraton Music City Hotel**	◇◇◇	Rates not provided SAVE	223
33 p. 200	**Radisson Hotel Nashville Airport**	◇◇◇	$99-$299 SAVE	223
34 p. 200	**Embassy Suites by Hilton Nashville Airport** *(See ad p. 219.)*	◇◇◇	$129-$249 SAVE	219
35 p. 200	Hampton Inn & Suites Nashville Airport	◆◆◆	$139-$259	220
36 p. 200	**Holiday Inn Express-Airport/Opryland Area**	◇◇◇	$99-$249 SAVE	221
37 p. 200	**Country Inn & Suites By Carlson, Nashville Airport**	◇◇◇	Rates not provided SAVE	218
38 p. 200	**Hotel Preston**	◇◇◇	$119-$299 SAVE	222
39 p. 200	**BEST WESTERN PLUS Belle Meade Inn & Suites**	◇◇◇	$99-$199 SAVE	218
40 p. 200	Holiday Inn Express	◆◆◆	Rates not provided	221
41 p. 200	**Super 8-West**	◇◇	$50-$100 SAVE	224
42 p. 200	Hampton Inn & Suites Green Hills/Nashville	◆◆◆	$179-$329	220
43 p. 200	**Quality Suites**	◇◇◇	$99-$239 SAVE	223

Map Page	Restaurants	Diamond Rated	Cuisine	Price Range	Page
① p. 200	China Cottage	◆◆	Chinese	$6-$28	224
② p. 200	Santa Fe Cattle Co	◆◆	American	$8-$30	226
③ p. 200	Prince's Hot Chicken Shack	◆	Chicken	$5-$22	226
④ p. 200	The Opry Backstage Grill	◆◆◆	Southern American	$7-$30	225
⑤ p. 200	The Nashville Palace	◆◆	American	$4-$10	225
⑥ p. 200	Caney Fork River Valley Grille	◆◆	Southern	$12-$24	224
⑦ p. 200	Old Hickory Steakhouse at Opryland	◆◆◆	Steak	$10-$48	225
⑧ p. 200	Aquarium Restaurant	◆◆◆	Seafood	$11-$37 SAVE	224
⑨ p. 200	Jacks Bar-B-Que	◆	Barbecue	$5-$21	225
⑩ p. 200	Rosepepper Cantina & Mexican Grill	◆◆	Mexican	$9-$24	226
⑪ p. 200	PizzeREAL	◆◆	Pizza	$5-$21	226
⑫ p. 200	Sal's Pizza & Restaurant	◆◆	Italian Pizza	$6-$23	226
⑬ p. 200	Ellendale's Restaurant	◆◆◆	American	$7-$23	225
⑭ p. 200	Bar-B-Cutie	◆	Barbecue	$6-$21	224
⑮ p. 200	Darfon's	◆◆◆	American	$8-$28	225
⑯ p. 200	New Dragon Phoenix Buffet	◆	Chinese	$7-$10	225
⑰ p. 200	**TEN Bar & Grille**	◆◆	American	$8-$40	226
⑱ p. 200	Carol Ann's Home Cooking Cafe	◆	Southern Soul Food	$7-$12	224
⑲ p. 200	**El Chico**	◆◆	Tex-Mex	$7-$15	225
⑳ p. 200	Golden Thai	◆◆	Thai	$6-$19	225
㉑ p. 200	Kebab Gyros	◆	Greek	$6-$13	225
㉒ p. 200	Ginza Japanese Restaurant	◆◆	Japanese	$6-$23	225
㉓ p. 200	Chinatown Restaurant	◆◆	Chinese	$7-$29	224
㉔ p. 200	Noshville-New York Delicatessen	◆◆	Jewish Deli Breakfast	$8-$17	225
㉕ p. 200	Sperry's Restaurant	◆◆	English Seafood Steak	$18-$49	226
㉖ p. 200	H & T Home Cooking	◆◆	Southern Soul Food	$6-$9	225
㉗ p. 200	Sportsman's Grille	◆◆	American	$9-$22	226
㉘ p. 200	Back to Cuba Cafe	◆	Cuban	$7-$13	224
㉙ p. 200	Antonio's of Nashville	◆◆◆	Italian	$11-$30	224
㉛ p. 200	Stax	◆	Burgers	$5-$12	226

LEBANON

Map Page	Hotel	Diamond Rated	Rate Range	Page
(45) p. 200	Sleep Inn & Suites-Lebanon/Nashville	◆◆	$74-$139	128

MOUNT JULIET

Map Page	Hotels	Diamond Rated	Rate Range	Page
(48) p. 200	**Comfort Suites**	◆◆◆	$99-$189 SAVE	174
(51) p. 200	Quality Inn & Suites	◆◆	$70-$120	174
(52) p. 200	Hampton Inn & Suites	◆◆◆	$114-$229	174
(53) p. 200	**Holiday Inn Express Hotel & Suites, Mt. Juliet**	◆◆◆	$114-$179 SAVE	174

Map Page	Restaurant	Diamond Rated	Cuisine	Price Range	Page
32 p. 200	Cori's DogHouse	◆	Hot Dogs Sandwiches	$4-$8	174

HENDERSONVILLE

Map Page	Hotel	Diamond Rated	Rate Range	Page
56 p. 200	**Hyatt Place Nashville - Northeast**	◆◆◆	$79-$209 [SAVE]	104

Map Page	Restaurant	Diamond Rated	Cuisine	Price Range	Page
35 p. 200	Fulin's Asian Cuisine	◆◆◆	Asian	$8-$25	104

LA VERGNE

Map Page	Hotel	Diamond Rated	Rate Range	Page
59 p. 200	Quality Inn & Suites	◆◆	$79-$129	128

GOODLETTSVILLE

Map Page	Hotels	Diamond Rated	Rate Range	Page
62 p. 200	**BEST WESTERN Fairwinds Inn**	◆◆	$70-$300 [SAVE]	95
63 p. 200	Hampton Inn Nashville-Goodlettsville	◆◆◆	$97-$110	95
64 p. 200	**Courtyard by Marriott Nashville Goodlettsville**	◆◆◆	$89-$259 [SAVE]	95
65 p. 200	Country Inn & Suites By Carlson	◆◆◆	$90-$250	95
66 p. 200	**Comfort Suites**	◆◆◆	$100-$150 [SAVE]	95

Map Page	Restaurants	Diamond Rated	Cuisine	Price Range	Page
38 p. 200	Painturo's	◆	Italian Pizza	$5-$22	96
39 p. 200	Buck's Barbeque	◆	Barbecue	$5-$12	95
40 p. 200	Kabuto	◆◆	Japanese Sushi	$8-$32	96
41 p. 200	Chef's Market Catering & Restaurant	◆	American	$9-$16	95
42 p. 200	Pancho Villa Grill	◆◆	Mexican	$6-$23	96
43 p. 200	**El Chico**	◆◆	Tex-Mex	$6-$16	96

BRENTWOOD

Map Page	Hotels	Diamond Rated	Rate Range	Page
69 p. 200	**Four Points by Sheraton Nashville-Brentwood**	◆◆◆	$99-$289 [SAVE]	42
70 p. 200	Holiday Inn Express & Suites Brentwood North-Nashville Area	◆◆◆	$119-$199	42
71 p. 200	**BEST WESTERN Brentwood**	◆◆◆	$109-$149 [SAVE]	42
72 p. 200	**Hyatt Place Nashville/Brentwood** (See ad p. 221.)	◆◆◆	$94-$209 [SAVE]	42
73 p. 200	Hampton Inn-Brentwood	◆◆◆	$119-$289	42
74 p. 200	**Courtyard by Marriott Nashville Brentwood**	◆◆◆	$99-$269 [SAVE]	42
75 p. 200	**Brentwood Suites**	◆◆◆	$99-$199 [SAVE]	42
76 p. 200	**Hilton Brentwood/Nashville Suites**	◆◆◆	$115-$309 [SAVE]	42
77 p. 200	Homewood Suites-Brentwood	◆◆◆	$109-$209	42
78 p. 200	Candlewood Suites	◆◆	Rates not provided	42
79 p. 200	**Residence Inn by Marriott Nashville-Brentwood**	◆◆◆	$109-$269 [SAVE]	43

Map Page	Restaurants	Diamond Rated	Cuisine	Price Range	Page
46 p. 200	Fulin's Asian Cuisine	◆◆◆	Asian	$8-$22	43
47 p. 200	Firebirds Wood Fired Grill	◆◆◆	American	$11-$30	43
48 p. 200	Mere Bulles	◆◆◆	Southern American	$11-$40	43
49 p. 200	Mediterranean Cuisine	◆	Mediterranean	$5-$16	43

HERMITAGE

Map Page	Hotel	Diamond Rated	Rate Range	Page
82 p. 200	**Super 8**	◇◇	$70-$100 SAVE	105

Map Page	Restaurants	Diamond Rated	Cuisine	Price Range	Page
52 p. 200	Hermitage Steakhouse	◇◇	Steak	$17-$76	105
53 p. 200	Sakura Japanese Steak House	◇◇	Japanese	$9-$29	105
54 p. 200	Hermitage House Smorgasbord	◇	Southern American	$11-$15	105

ANTIOCH

Map Page	Hotels	Diamond Rated	Rate Range	Page
85 p. 200	**Hampton Inn-Hickory Hollow**	◇◇◇	$99-$159 SAVE	39
86 p. 200	Rodeway Inn & Suites	◇◇	$80-$176	39

FRANKLIN

Map Page	Restaurant	Diamond Rated	Cuisine	Price Range	Page
57 p. 200	Nashville Pizza Company	◇◇	Pizza	$6-$19	81

DOWNTOWN NASHVILLE
- Restaurants p. 215
- Hotels & Restaurants map & index p. 196

Let Your Voice Be Heard

If your visit to a TourBook-listed property doesn't meet your expectations, tell us about it.

AAA.com/TourBookComments

▼ See AAA listing p. 207 ▼

(See map & index p. 196.)

BEST WESTERN PLUS MUSIC ROW

(615)242-1631

Hotel
$129-$299

 AAA Benefit:
Save 10% or more every day and earn 10% bonus points!

Address: 1407 Division St 37203 **Location:** I-40 exit 209B (Broadway), w at Demonbreun St; 3rd exit at traffic circle; then just e. **Facility:** 102 units. 5 stories, interior corridors. **Amenities:** safes. **Pool(s):** outdoor. **Activities:** exercise room. **Guest Services:** valet and coin laundry. **Featured Amenity:** full hot breakfast.

THE CAPITOL HOTEL DOWNTOWN, AN ASCEND HOTEL COLLECTION MEMBER

(615)254-4311

Hotel
$119-$279

Address: 711 Union St 37219 **Location:** I-40 exit 209A/B (Broadway/Church sts), corner of 7th Ave N, then just n; entrance on 7th Ave N. **Facility:** 100 units. 5 stories, exterior corridors. **Parking:** on-site (fee) and valet. **Amenities:** safes. **Activities:** limited exercise equipment. **Featured Amenity:** breakfast buffet. *(See ad p. 206.)*

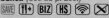

The CAPITOL Hotel
DOWNTOWN NASHVILLE

**Great Location - Downtown Nashville.
Best Value! Walking distance to
entertainment & dining venues.**

CLARION HOTEL NASHVILLE DOWNTOWN - STADIUM

(615)254-1551

Hotel
$119-$269

Address: 211 N 1st St 37213 **Location:** I-24 exit 47, just w on Spring St. Next to Nissan Stadium. **Facility:** 180 units. 9 stories, interior corridors. **Amenities:** *Some:* safes. **Pool(s):** heated indoor. **Activities:** exercise room. **Guest Services:** area transportation. **Featured Amenity:** full hot breakfast. *(See ad p. 208.)*

Clarion Hotel

**Downtown Location
without an Uptown Price!**

COMFORT INN DOWNTOWN

(615)255-9977

Hotel $100-$400 **Address:** 1501 Demonbreun St 37203 **Location:** I-40 exit 209B, just w. Located in a congested area. **Facility:** 153 units. 3 stories, exterior corridors. **Amenities:** safes. **Pool(s):** outdoor. **Activities:** exercise room. **Guest Services:** valet and coin laundry.

Get the App

Stay mobile with maps, travel information and road service on the go.

AAA.com/mobile • CAA.ca/mobile

(See map & index p. 196.)

COURTYARD BY MARRIOTT NASHVILLE DOWNTOWN
(615)256-0900 **5**

Historic Hotel
$219-$395

 **AAA Benefit:** Members save 5% or more!

Address: 170 4th Ave N 37219 **Location:** Corner of Church St; center. **Facility:** At this historic Nashville landmark, guests are greeted by original, ornate gates made of iron and bronze. Step through them to gather and relax under a soaring 30-foot-high ceiling. 192 units. 12 stories, interior corridors. **Parking:** valet and street only. **Activities:** exercise room. **Guest Services:** valet and coin laundry.

COURTYARD BY MARRIOTT-VANDERBILT WEST END
(615)327-9900 **22**

 Hotel $129-$369 **Address:** 1901 West End Ave 37203 **Location:** I-40 exit 209B (Broadway), 1 mi w. **Facility:** 226 units. 4-7 stories, interior corridors. **Parking:** on-site (fee) and valet. **Pool(s):** outdoor. **Activities:** exercise room. **Guest Services:** valet and coin laundry, boarding pass kiosk, area transportation.

AAA Benefit: Members save 5% or more!

DOUBLETREE BY HILTON NASHVILLE DOWNTOWN
(615)244-8200 **3**

Hotel
$199-$399

AAA Benefit: Members save 5% or more!

Address: 315 4th Ave N 37219 **Location:** Corner of Union St and 4th Ave. Located 1 blk from State Capitol. **Facility:** 337 units. 9 stories, interior corridors. **Parking:** valet only. **Terms:** 1-7 night minimum stay, cancellation fee imposed. **Dining:** entertainment. **Pool(s):** heated indoor. **Activities:** exercise room. **Guest Services:** valet laundry, area transportation. (See ad p. 209.)

DOUBLETREE BY HILTON™
NASHVILLE DOWNTOWN

We provide the special comforts and acts of kindness that make the traveler feel human again.

(See map & index p. 196.)

EMBASSY SUITES BY HILTON NASHVILLE AT VANDERBILT
(615)320-8899

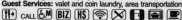 Hotel $199-$409 **Address:** 1811 Broadway 37203 **Location:** I-40 exit 209, 0.5 mi sw. **Facility:** 208 units. 11 stories, interior corridors. **Parking:** on-site (fee) and valet. **Terms:** 1-7 night minimum stay, cancellation fee imposed. **Amenities:** safes. **Activities:** hot tub, exercise room. **Guest Services:** valet and coin laundry, boarding pass kiosk, area transportation.

AAA Benefit: Members save 5% or more!

FAIRFIELD INN & SUITES BY MARRIOTT-NASHVILLE DOWNTOWN/GULCH
(615)690-1740

 Hotel $202-$332 **Address:** 901 Division St 37203 **Location:** I-40 exit 209A, jct 8th Ave S and Division St. Located near a busy train station. **Facility:** 126 units. 8 stories, interior corridors. **Parking:** on-site (fee). **Activities:** hot tub, exercise room. **Guest Services:** valet and coin laundry, area transportation.

AAA Benefit: Members save 5% or more!

HAMPTON INN & SUITES DOWNTOWN NASHVILLE
(615)277-5000

Hotel $209-$399

AAA Benefit: Members save up to 10%!

Address: 310 4th Ave S 37201 **Location:** I-40 exit 210C, 0.6 mi n on 2nd Ave S, then w at Korean Veterans Blvd. **Facility:** 154 units. 6 stories, interior corridors. **Parking:** on-site (fee) and valet. **Terms:** 1-7 night minimum stay, cancellation fee imposed. **Amenities:** video games. **Pool(s):** heated indoor. **Activities:** hot tub, exercise room. **Guest Services:** valet and coin laundry. **Featured Amenity:** breakfast buffet.

HAMPTON INN & SUITES VANDERBILT ELLISTON PLACE
(615)320-6060

Hotel $189-$299 **Address:** 2330 Elliston Pl 37203 **Location:** I-40 exit 209A (Church St), 3.5 mi w. **Facility:** 157 units, some efficiencies. 7 stories, interior corridors. **Terms:** 1-7 night minimum stay, cancellation fee imposed. **Pool(s):** outdoor. **Activities:** exercise room. **Guest Services:** valet and coin laundry.

AAA Benefit: Members save up to 10%!

▼ See AAA listing p. 208 ▼

(See map & index p. 196.)

HAMPTON INN VANDERBILT

(615)329-1144 [26]

 Hotel $189-$299 **Address:** 1919 West End Ave 37203 **Location:** I-40 exit 209B (Broadway), 0.3 mi w. **Facility:** 169 units. 6 stories, interior corridors. **Terms:** 1-7 night minimum stay, cancellation fee imposed. **Pool(s):** outdoor. **Activities:** exercise room. **Guest Services:** valet and coin laundry, area transportation.

AAA Benefit: Members save up to 10%!

HILTON GARDEN INN NASHVILLE-VANDERBILT

(615)369-5900 [24]

Hotel $139-$399 **Address:** 1715 Broadway 37203 **Location:** Corner of 17th Ave S and Broadway; in West End. Next to a regional hospital and college campus. **Facility:** 194 units. 9 stories, interior corridors. **Parking:** on-site (fee) and valet. **Terms:** check-in 4 pm, 1-7 night minimum stay, cancellation fee imposed. **Pool(s):** heated indoor. **Activities:** hot tub, exercise room. **Guest Services:** valet and coin laundry, area transportation.

AAA Benefit: Members save up to 10%!

THE HERMITAGE HOTEL

615/244-3121 [6]

Classic Historic Hotel

Rates not provided

Address: 231 6th Ave N 37219 **Location:** Corner of Union St. **Facility:** The stunning 1910 architecture here has been meticulously restored to its former grandeur. Down-filled duvets and marble bathrooms with glass showers and soaking tubs put units over the top. 122 units. 9 stories, interior corridors. **Terms:** check-in 4 pm. **Amenities:** safes. **Dining:** Capitol Grille, see separate listing. **Activities:** exercise room, massage. **Guest Services:** valet laundry. Affiliated with Preferred Hotels & Resorts. (See ad this page.)

Luxury meets value. Your Hermitage Hotel experience is as unique as you are. Indulge & Enjoy.

HILTON NASHVILLE DOWNTOWN

615/620-1000 [11]

Hotel

Hilton HOTELS & RESORTS

AAA Benefit: Members save 5% or more!

Address: 121 4th Ave S 37201 **Location:** Center. **Facility:** Here you'll enjoy a prime location next to Bridgestone Arena and the Country Music Hall of Fame, and within walking distance of the Tennessee Titans' home, Nissan Stadium. 330 units. 10 stories, interior corridors. **Parking:** on-site (fee) and valet. **Amenities:** safes. **Dining:** 2 restaurants. **Activities:** exercise room, massage. **Guest Services:** valet laundry, rental car service. (See ad p. 211, on inside front cover.)

Rates not provided

HOTELS GET RENOVATIONS.
HILTONS GET MAKEOVERS.

Hilton Nashville Downtown, a AAA Four-Diamond hotel nestled in the heart of "Music City", emerges from a multi-million dollar reinvention. The only all-suites full-service hotel in downtown Nashville unveils chic and modern upgrades to all 330 suites, atrium lobby, grand ballroom and meeting rooms, fitness center and executive lounge. Trattoria Il Mulino, from the iconic Il Mulino New York, opens its latest addition at the Hilton Nashville Downtown.

Call +1 615 620 1000 and book your trip today!
121 4th Avenue South I Nashville, TN | 37201 | nashvilledowntown.hilton.com

©2015 Hilton Worldwide

(See map & index p. 196.)

HOLIDAY INN EXPRESS-NASHVILLE DOWNTOWN
615/244-0150 **14**

Hotel
Rates not provided

Address: 920 Broadway 37203 **Location:** I-40 exit 209A (Church St) westbound; exit 209B (Broadway) eastbound, 0.5 mi e. **Facility:** 287 units. 8 stories, interior corridors. **Parking:** on-site (fee). **Pool(s):** outdoor. **Activities:** exercise room. **Guest Services:** valet and coin laundry, area transportation. **Featured Amenity:** full hot breakfast. *(See ad this page.)*

287 rooms in Downtown Nashville. Minutes from the airport, Music Row & the Entertainment District.

HOLIDAY INN-VANDERBILT
615/327-4707 **32**

Hotel. Rates not provided. **Address:** 2613 West End Ave 37203 **Location:** I-40 exit 209B (Broadway), 1.5 mi w on Broadway. **Facility:** 297 units. 14 stories, interior corridors. **Pool(s):** outdoor. **Activities:** exercise room. **Guest Services:** valet and coin laundry, area transportation.

HOME2 SUITES BY HILTON-NASHVILLE/VANDERBILT
(615)254-2170 **25**

Extended Stay Hotel $149-$399 **Address:** 1800 Division St 37203 **Location:** I-40 exit 209 (Demonbreun St), 0.5 mi w. **Facility:** 119 efficiencies. 7 stories, interior corridors. *Bath:* shower only. **Parking:** on-site (fee). **Terms:** check-in 4 pm, 1-7 night minimum stay, cancellation fee imposed. **Activities:** hot tub, picnic facilities, exercise room. **Guest Services:** valet and coin laundry, area transportation.

AAA Benefit:
Members save up to 10%!

HOMEWOOD SUITES BY HILTON NASHVILLE VANDERBILT/WEST END
(615)340-8000 **31**

Hotel $229-$329 **Address:** 2400 West End Ave 37203 **Location:** I-40 exit 209A (Broadway), 0.7 mi w. **Facility:** 192 efficiencies, some two bedrooms. 7 stories, interior corridors. **Parking:** on-site (fee) and valet. **Terms:** check-in 4 pm, 1-7 night minimum stay, cancellation fee imposed. **Pool(s):** heated indoor. **Activities:** exercise room. **Guest Services:** valet and coin laundry, area transportation.

AAA Benefit:
Members save up to 10%!

HOMEWOOD SUITES NASHVILLE DOWNTOWN
(615)742-5550 **9**

Extended Stay Hotel $209-$299 **Address:** 706 Church St 37203 **Location:** Jct 7th Ave N and Church St. **Facility:** 113 efficiencies. 6 stories, interior corridors. *Bath:* shower only. **Parking:** valet only. **Terms:** 1-7 night minimum stay, cancellation fee imposed. **Activities:** exercise room. **Guest Services:** valet and coin laundry.

AAA Benefit:
Members save up to 10%!

▼ *See AAA listing this page* ▼

Keep your focus safely on the road when driving

(See map & index p. 196.)

HOTEL INDIGO-NASHVILLE DOWNTOWN
(615)891-6000 **4**

▼▼▼ **Historic Hotel** $199-$469 **Address:** 301 Union St 37201 **Location:** I-40 exit 209A (Church St), 0.8 mi e on Charlotte Ave, then just s. **Facility:** In the historic, former American Trust and Nashville Trust buildings, this contemporary property is one of the city's most unique places to stay. Some guest rooms feature original terrazzo floors. 160 units. 14-15 stories, interior corridors. *Bath:* shower only. **Parking:** valet and street only. **Terms:** cancellation fee imposed. **Dining:** entertainment. **Activities:** exercise room. **Guest Services:** valet laundry.

[icons] / SOME UNITS [icons]

HUTTON HOTEL
(615)340-9333 **21**

▼▼▼▼▼ Boutique Contemporary Retro Hotel $259-$429

Address: 1808 West End Ave 37203 **Location:** I-40 W exit 209B (Broadway), 1 mi w. **Facility:** A keen perspective on art, aesthetics, and ecology defines the ambiance here, from award-winning student art to a life-size metal sculpture of a horse to all-bamboo flooring. A memorable stay. 247 units, some two bedrooms. 15 stories, interior corridors. **Parking:** on-site (fee) and valet. **Terms:** cancellation fee imposed. **Amenities:** safes. **Dining:** 1808 Grille, see separate listing. **Activities:** exercise room, massage. **Guest Services:** valet laundry, area transportation. *(See ad this page.)*

[icons] / SOME UNITS [icons]

HYATT PLACE NASHVILLE DOWNTOWN
(615)687-9995 **12**

▼▼▼ Hotel $139-$799

✪ HYATT PLACE®

AAA Benefit: Members save 10%!

Address: 301 3rd Ave S 37201 **Location:** I-40 exit 210C, 0.6 mi n on 2nd Ave S, then w at Korean Veterans Blvd. **Facility:** 255 units. 13 stories, interior corridors. **Parking:** on-site (fee) and valet. **Terms:** cancellation fee imposed. **Dining:** entertainment. **Pool(s):** heated indoor. **Activities:** exercise room. **Guest Services:** valet laundry. **Featured Amenity:** breakfast buffet.

[icons] / SOME UNITS [icons]

AAA.com/ TourBook Comments

Let Your Voice Be Heard

If your visit to a TourBook-listed property doesn't meet your expectations, tell us about it.

AAA.com/TourBookComments

▼ See AAA listing this page ▼

(See map & index p. 196.)

LOEWS VANDERBILT HOTEL NASHVILLE
615/320-1700

Hotel
Rates not provided

Address: 2100 West End Ave 37203 **Location:** I-40 exit 209B (Broadway), 1.3 mi w. **Facility:** A professional and refined staff is always friendly, always ready to make your experience unforgettable at this upscale hotel located near Vanderbilt University. 340 units. 11 stories, interior corridors. **Parking:** on-site (fee) and valet. **Terms:** check-in 4 pm. **Amenities:** safes. **Dining:** 2 restaurants. **Activities:** exercise room, massage. **Guest Services:** valet laundry, rental car service, area transportation.

NASHVILLE MARRIOTT AT VANDERBILT UNIVERSITY
(615)321-1300 🆛

Hotel
$209-$298

AAA Benefit: Members save 5% or more!

Address: 2555 West End Ave 37203 **Location:** I-40 exit 209B (Broadway) eastbound; exit 209A (Church St) westbound, w on Broadway. **Facility:** 307 units. 11 stories, interior corridors. **Parking:** on-site (fee) and valet. **Terms:** check-in 4 pm. **Pool(s):** heated indoor. **Activities:** exercise room. **Guest Services:** valet and coin laundry, area transportation.

OMNI HOTEL
615/782-5300 🆕

Contemporary Hotel. Rates not provided. Address: 250 5th Ave S 37203 **Location:** I-40 exit 210C, just n to 2nd Ave, then w; enter from Korean Veterans Blvd, between 4th and 5th aves. Adjacent to the Country Music Hall of Fame. **Facility:** "An urban elegance with a vintage touch" is more than evident at Music City's newest upscale hotel in the heart of downtown and convenient to just about all of the major attractions. 800 units. 21 stories, interior corridors. **Parking:** on-site (fee) and valet. **Terms:** check-in 4 pm. **Amenities:** video games, safes. **Dining:** 4 restaurants, nightclub, entertainment. **Pool(s):** heated outdoor. **Activities:** sauna, hot tub. **Guest Services:** coin laundry, boarding pass kiosk, area transportation.

RAMADA NASHVILLE DOWNTOWN (615)244-6690 🄴

Hotel
$95-$170

Address: 303 Interstate Dr 37213 **Location:** I-24 exit 49 (Shelby St), 0.4 mi w, then just n. Adjacent to Nissan Stadium. **Facility:** 120 units. 4 stories, interior corridors. **Parking:** on-site (fee). **Amenities:** safes. **Pool(s):** heated indoor. **Activities:** picnic facilities, exercise room. **Guest Services:** valet and coin laundry. **Featured Amenity:** full hot breakfast.

RENAISSANCE NASHVILLE HOTEL
(615)255-8400 🔟

Hotel
$257-$351

AAA Benefit: Members save 5% or more!

Address: 611 Commerce St 37203 **Location:** Center. Adjacent to Nashville Convention Center. **Facility:** Standing tall in a prime location one block off Broadway, crisp and clean rooms are merely a backdrop compared to the enviable views offered by many rooms. From here, downtown is quite walkable. 673 units. 25 stories, interior corridors. **Parking:** on-site (fee) and valet. **Terms:** check-in 4 pm. **Amenities:** safes. **Dining:** 2 restaurants. **Pool(s):** heated indoor. **Activities:** hot tub, exercise room. **Guest Services:** valet laundry, boarding pass kiosk, area transportation.

RESIDENCE INN BY MARRIOTT NASHVILLE WEST END/VANDERBILT
(615)988-9920 🇻

Extended Stay Hotel $167-$275 **Address:** 1801 Hayes St 37203 **Location:** I-40 exit 209A westbound; exit 209B eastbound, 0.5 mi w. Near Vanderbilt University Medical Center. **Facility:** 100 units, some two bedrooms, efficiencies and kitchens. 9 stories, interior corridors. **Parking:** on-site (fee) and valet. **Pool(s):** heated indoor. **Activities:** exercise room. **Guest Services:** valet and coin laundry, area transportation.

AAA Benefit: Members save 5% or more!

SHERATON NASHVILLE DOWNTOWN HOTEL
615/259-2000 🄯

Hotel
Rates not provided

AAA Benefit: Members save up to 15%, plus Starwood Preferred Guest® benefits!

Address: 623 Union St 37219 **Location:** Corner of Union and 7th Ave N. **Facility:** 482 units. 28 stories, interior corridors. **Parking:** on-site (fee) and valet. **Amenities:** safes. **Pool(s):** heated indoor. **Activities:** exercise room. **Guest Services:** valet laundry, area transportation.

SPRINGHILL SUITES BY MARRIOTT NASHVILLE WEST END/VANDERBILT
(615)988-9930 🄴

Hotel $153-$252 **Address:** 1800 West End Ave 37203 **Location:** I-40 exit 209A westbound; exit 209B eastbound, 0.5 mi w. Near Vanderbilt University Medical Center. **Facility:** 100 units. 9 stories, interior corridors. **Parking:** on-site (fee) and valet. **Pool(s):** heated indoor. **Activities:** exercise room. **Guest Services:** valet and coin laundry, boarding pass kiosk, area transportation.

AAA Benefit: Members save 5% or more!

(See map & index p. 196.)

UNION STATION HOTEL - AUTOGRAPH COLLECTION

(615)726-1001 **16**

Historic Hotel
$237-$389

AUTOGRAPH COLLECTION HOTELS

AAA Benefit: Members save 5% or more!

Address: 1001 Broadway 37203 **Location:** I-40 exit 209A (Church St), just ne; corner of 10th Ave. **Facility:** In a restored train station dating from 1900, this exquisite hotel has a barrel-vaulted lobby ceiling with original Luminous Prism stained glass. 125 units. 7 stories, interior corridors. **Parking:** valet only. **Amenities:** safes. **Dining:** Prime 108, see separate listing. **Activities:** exercise room. **Guest Services:** valet laundry.

[SAVE] [❄] [🛎] [Y] CALL [&M] [BIZ] [📶] [✉] [🐾] [▭] / SOME UNITS [SHS]

WHERE TO EAT

1808 GRILLE 615/340-0012 **21**

🔻🔻🔻 New American. Fine Dining. $12-$36 **AAA Inspector Notes:** Enjoy an elegant yet casual dining experience inside the art-filled Hutton Hotel. Field-to-table creations feature locally-sourced ingredients on a seasonally-changing menu, prepared with a Tennessee twist. A comfortable lounge within the dining room encourages a lingering stay, long remembered. **Features:** full bar, Sunday brunch, happy hour. **Reservations:** suggested. **Address:** 1808 W End Ave 37203 **Location:** I-40 W exit 209B (Broadway), 1 mi w; in Hutton Hotel. **Parking:** valet and street only.

[🍴] [B] [L] [D] CALL [&M]

ACME FEED & SEED 615/915-0888 **10**

🔻🔻 Southern. Gastropub. $9-$22 **AAA Inspector Notes:** *Historic.* This place is huge and very popular. Upon arrival, you will be given a paper menu and then asked to stand in line. Grab a table, and your meal—or vittles, as it's called in these parts—will be brought to you. Music memorabilia lines the walls of this former feed and seed store. The menu offers tasty reinvented Southern cuisine such as beer belly tacos, gourmet fried green tomatoes and savory shrimp and grits. **Features:** full bar, Sunday brunch. **Address:** 101 Broadway 37201 **Location:** Downtown; corner of Broadway/US 70 and 1st Ave N/Hermitage Ave; across from Cumberland Riverfront. **Parking:** on-site (fee) and street. [L] [D] CALL [&M]

AMERIGO, AN ITALIAN RESTAURANT 615/320-1740 **25**

🔻🔻🔻 Italian. Fine Dining. $10-$35 **AAA Inspector Notes:** This trendy eatery serves a delicious artichoke cheese dip, for starters. Fresh, homemade entrées include chicken Tuscany served in a red wine sauce over angel hair pasta, and cedar plank-roasted pork chops with pineapple glaze. Among the seasonal menu selections you'll find locally sourced meats and produce. Lunch specials are offered daily. **Features:** full bar, early bird specials, happy hour. **Reservations:** suggested. **Address:** 1920 West End Ave 37203 **Location:** I-40 exit 209B (Broadway), 3 mi w, then 0.5 mi w.

[L] [D] CALL [&M]

BAILEY'S SPORTS GRILLE 615/254-5452

🔻🔻 American. Casual Dining. $7-$17 **AAA Inspector Notes:** A classic pub decor of dark wood paneling and ceramic steins--with a modern American bar, where huge TV screens are tuned to sports in every possible spot, including the restrooms. You'll find the same mixing cultures evident on the menu; burgers, pizzas, and chicken wings sit beside fish 'n' chips, tortilla soup, fresh-baked pretzels, nachos, baby back ribs, and Texas-style brisket. **Features:** full bar, patio dining, happy hour. **Address:** 408 Broadway 37203 **Location:** Center. **Parking:** street only. [L] [D] [LATE] [❌]

Request roadside assistance in a click —

online or using the AAA or CAA apps

BOB'S STEAK & CHOP HOUSE 615/761-3707 **15**

🔻🔻🔻 Steak. Casual Dining. $35-$99 **AAA Inspector Notes:** At this popular, award-winning steakhouse you'll dine in a refined yet casual setting, enhanced by mahogany booths and white tablecloths. Texas beef dominates the menu. All entrées are served with the signature, colossal glazed carrot and choice of potato. With the attentive staff working together professionally and promptly, this Texas original delivers a memorable evening. **Features:** full bar, patio dining. **Reservations:** suggested. **Address:** 250 Fifth Ave S 37203 **Location:** Jct Korean Veterans Blvd and 5th Ave; in Omni Hotel. **Parking:** valet only. [D] CALL [&M]

CABANA 615/577-2262 **36**

🔻🔻 Southern American. Casual Dining. $7-$24 **AAA Inspector Notes:** Individual, curtained cabana booths are perfect for families and groups. Watch a game or bring your photos on a USB drive and ask your server to play it on the booth's personal TV. The Southern comfort cuisine includes cornmeal-fried Louisiana alligator; spicy shrimp and cheddar grits; buttermilk-fried chicken breast; and pan-seared duck breast with Newcastle Brown Ale mustard, mac and cheese and Brussels sprouts. Top off your meal with a melt-in-your-mouth Napoleon brownie. **Features:** full bar, patio dining, happy hour. **Reservations:** suggested. **Address:** 1910 Belcourt Ave 37212 **Location:** In Hillsboro Village. **Parking:** on-site and valet.

[D] [LATE] CALL [&M]

CANTINA LAREDO 615/259-9282 **22**

🔻🔻

Mexican
Casual Dining
$10-$25

AAA Inspector Notes: Sophisticated yet relaxed, this eatery features authentic Mexican fare with a creative twist. A great starter is the top-shelf guacamole, which is prepared tableside and primes the palate for the entree. The menu features traditional favorites such as tacos, enchiladas, fajitas, carnitas and chiles rellenos. Also featured are vegetarian and gluten-free dishes. **Features:** full bar, patio dining, Sunday brunch, happy hour. **Reservations:** suggested, weekends. **Address:** 592 12th Ave S 37203 **Location:** I-40 exit 209B (Broadway), just e, then just s. Located in the Gulch neighborhood. **Parking:** on-site (fee) and valet. [L] [D]

Gourmet Mexican food, fresh-squeezed lime margaritas

CAPITOL GRILLE 615/244-3121 **5**

🔻🔻🔻🔻 Southern American. Fine Dining. $13-$65 **AAA Inspector Notes:** In a historic hotel, this dining room has been restored to reflect its original character. Ceiling arches, columns, inset oak panel walls and upscale decorative accents combine with traditional appointments to create an elegant, yet comfortable, setting. The cuisine has a distinct Southern flair, accented by an imaginative combination of fresh local and regional ingredients. With colors, textures and skillful design, courses are artfully presented to stimulate both the eye and the palate. **Features:** full bar, Sunday brunch, happy hour. **Reservations:** suggested. Semiformal attire. **Address:** 231 6th Ave N 37219 **Location:** Corner of Union St; in The Hermitage Hotel. **Parking:** valet and street only. [B] [L] [D]

CITY WINERY NASHVILLE 615/324-1010 **20**

🔻🔻🔻 International. Casual Dining. $15-$28 **AAA Inspector Notes:** One of the latest dining concepts, this spot offers wines made on- and off-site. The chef has created an interesting menu that blends new Southern favorites with Mediterranean-influenced dishes. The servers will smoothly guide you through a menu that includes tempura-fried catfish, brook trout, pork belly and rack of lamb. Great for sharing is the charcuterie, which includes duck confit, chicken liver parfait and bacon-smoked almonds. For those who can't decide there's a five-course chef's menu. **Features:** full bar, patio dining, happy hour. **Reservations:** suggested. **Address:** 609 Lafayette St 37203 **Location:** Between 6th and 7th Ave S. **Parking:** valet only. [D] CALL [&M]

DEMOS' STEAK & SPAGHETTI HOUSE 615/256-4655

🔻🔻 American. Casual Dining. $7-$16 **AAA Inspector Notes:** This family-owned and -operated eatery offers well prepared traditional fare as well as specialties such as Mexican spaghetti. The cuisine is made from scratch. The atmosphere and service are casual and relaxed. **Features:** full bar. **Address:** 300 Commerce St 37201 **Location:** Center. **Parking:** on-site (fee). [L] [D]

(See map & index p. 196.)

ELLISTON PLACE SODA SHOP   615/327-1090 [37]

🔻 Breakfast Sandwiches. Casual Dining. $6-$10 **AAA Inspector Notes:** *Historic.* It would be a mistake if visitors didn't stop here for a burger and handmade shake, malt, or egg cream. For one thing, it's a Nashville institution as it is the city's oldest continuously operated restaurant in its original location. Second, you may recognize the interior from the many music videos it has been featured in. Finally, it's a favorite among Nashvillians, and you never know who might drop in! **Address:** 2111 Elliston Pl 37203 **Location:** Corner of Church St and 21st Ave N, just w; in Midtown. **Parking:** on-site and street.

[B] [L] [D] CALL 🅖M

ETCH RESTAURANT   615/522-0685 [14]

🔻🔻🔻 New American. Fine Dining. $10-$38 **AAA Inspector Notes:** In 2010, Chef Deb Paquette left Nashville as a culinary celebrity. After a few years of traveling, she returned to open this restaurant—a testament to her artistry and innovation. The truffled pea pesto, salted almonds, and feta crema served with the roasted cauliflower make an otherwise benign vegetable a star. Chef Paquette adds complexity to pork tenderloin with her Spanish mountain mushroom sauce, chorizo, and manchego cheese. **Features:** full bar, happy hour. **Address:** 303 Demonbreun St 37201 **Location:** Between 3rd Ave and Almond St. **Parking:** valet only. [L] [D]

FLYING SAUCER DRAUGHT EMPORIUM   615/259-3039 [17]

🔻🔻 American. Gastropub. $8-$12 **AAA Inspector Notes:** In a restored train station warehouse, the restaurant offers light dining on pizza, soups, salads and sandwiches such as the space club and turkey meltdown. The queso fondue, featuring a sampling of their popular soft pretzels, Bratwurst and ham, could be a meal in itself. **Features:** full bar, patio dining, happy hour. **Address:** 111 10th Ave S, Suite 310 37203 **Location:** Broadway at 10th Ave; behind historic train station. **Parking:** on-site (fee) and street. [L] [D] [LATE] 🚭

GERMANTOWN CAFE   615/242-3226 [1]

🔻🔻🔻 New American. Casual Dining. $7-$27 **AAA Inspector Notes:** This friendly neighborhood restaurant and lounge offers a wonderful view of the city skyline, as well as reasonably priced drinks and a great selection of entrées for both lunch and dinner. You might start with the hearty onion soup with a bubbly Swiss cheese crown, move on to a healthy grilled vegetable salad and end with plum pork medallions or oven-roasted lemon- and basil-stuffed chicken breast. **Features:** full bar, Sunday brunch, happy hour. **Address:** 1200 5th Ave N 37208 **Location:** I-24 exit 47, 0.5 mi w on Jefferson St, then just n. **Parking:** valet and street only. [L] [D] CALL 🅖M

GERST HAUS   615/244-8886 [4]

🔻🔻 German Sandwiches. Casual Dining. $10-$19 **AAA Inspector Notes:** A lively atmosphere prevails in the dining room, where you'll savor classic German food along the lines of schweineschnitzel, sauerbraten and the knockwurst or bratwurst dinners. Top off your meal with a slice of Black Forest cake. **Features:** full bar, patio dining. **Address:** 301 Woodland St 37213 **Location:** I-24 exit 48, just w. [L] [D]

HARD ROCK CAFE   615/742-9900 [8]

🔻🔻 American. Casual Dining. $9-$30 **AAA Inspector Notes:** Rock 'n' roll memorabilia decorates the walls of the popular theme restaurant. Live music on the weekends contributes to the bustling atmosphere. On the menu is a wide variety of American cuisine—from burgers and sandwiches to seafood, steaks and pasta. **Features:** full bar, patio dining. **Address:** 100 Broadway 37201 **Location:** Jct Broadway and 1st Ave S. **Parking:** on-site (fee) and valet.

[SAVE] [L] [D] [LATE] CALL 🅖M

HATTIE B'S HOT CHICKEN   615/678-4794 [39]

🔻 Southern Chicken. Quick Serve. $6-$12 **AAA Inspector Notes:** "Hot chicken" seems to be everywhere in the South. One of Midtown's most popular eateries is close to Broadway, West End and Vanderbilt University. The convenient location makes it a favorite lunch spot. If the waiting makes your mouth water and your forehead sweat, the reward is found in the tasty seasoning of as-hot-as-you-like-it chicken, from "No Heat" to "Fire Starter" to "Shut The Cluck Up!" Try the latter only if you dare. **Features:** beer only, patio dining. **Address:** 112 19th Ave S 37203 **Location:** Between 19th and West End; in Midtown. **Parking:** on-site and street. [L] [D]

HOG HEAVEN   615/329-1234 [31]

🔻 Barbecue. Quick Serve. $4-$14 **AAA Inspector Notes:** This place is literally a shack. But don't judge a book by its cover. This humble, rustic Nashville favorite is a well-kept secret. In nice weather, it is nearly impossible to resist taking some real pit barbecue and Southern-style vegetables into Centennial Park to chow down. **Features:** patio dining. **Address:** 115 27th Ave N 37203 **Location:** I-440 exit West End Ave, 3 mi e; across from Centennial Park.

[L] [D] 🐾

HOT DIGGITY DOGS   615/255-3717 [19]

🔻 Hot Dogs. Quick Serve. $3-$6 **AAA Inspector Notes:** The name says it all. Here you'll find hot dogs and Italian beef with all the fixings. Dog styles include Chicago, Boston, Texan, New York, and of course, Nashville-style with slaw. The chili is a savory dish and can be ordered by the bowl or lathered on your dog. They open early, and close late for lunch. **Address:** 614 Ewing Ave 37203 **Location:** Jct Ewing Ave and Lafayette St. [L] 🅐

HUSK   615/256-6565 [38]

🔻🔻🔻 Southern American. Fine Dining. $10-$32 **AAA Inspector Notes:** *Historic.* The staff is neatly dressed in freshly pressed blue jeans, a canvas bib-top apron, and lace-up boots. And that's just the beginning of this farm-to-table experience found just south of downtown. Led by James Beard Award-winning chef Sean Brock, the menu is inspired by what's being delivered by local farmers. What results is an ingredient-driven experience, the chef's vision of "new Southern" cooking, bound by what is authentically Southern. **Features:** full bar, Sunday brunch. **Reservations:** suggested. **Address:** 37 Rutledge St 37210 **Location:** I-40 exit 210C, n on 2nd Ave S; e on Middleton St; then just n. [L] [D]

JACKS BAR-B-QUE   615/254-5715 [11]

🔻 Barbecue. Quick Serve. $5-$22 **AAA Inspector Notes:** Upstaging the city's live entertainment could be a serious offense, but it happens here, and deliciously so. Since 1976, celebrities, locals and tourists alike have been more than willing to stand patiently in line for their turn to get their hands on some of Nashville's best-loved hickory-smoked barbecue. Don't let the long line discourage you—it's that good. Find your way here and taste for yourself. Just look for the flashing neon pigs next to Robert's Western World. **Features:** beer only, patio dining. **Address:** 416 Broadway, Suite A 37203 **Location:** Center. **Parking:** on-site (fee) and street.

[L] [D]

JIMMY KELLY'S STEAK HOUSE   615/329-4349 [26]

🔻🔻 Steak. Fine Dining. $15-$43 **AAA Inspector Notes:** Dark mahogany fixtures inside this old Victorian mansion present a soothing atmosphere. Reward yourself with luscious Châteaubriand, cooked in mushroom wine sauce. Finish with a famous ice ball—ice cream rolled in coconut, almonds and chocolate sauce. **Features:** full bar, happy hour. **Reservations:** suggested. **Address:** 217 Louise Ave 37203 **Location:** I-40 exit 209A (Church St), 1 mi w, then just n; corner of State St. [D]

KOBE STEAKS - A JAPANESE RESTAURANT   615/327-9081 [29]

🔻🔻🔻 Japanese. Casual Dining. $15-$71 **AAA Inspector Notes:** Talented Japanese chefs skillfully grill meals before your eyes, making for an entertaining experience. Start with piping-hot onion soup or a crisp salad, then feast on lobster, chicken, shrimp or juicy steak. **Features:** full bar. **Reservations:** suggested. **Address:** 210 25th Ave N, Suite 100 37203 **Location:** Across from Centennial Park. **Parking:** valet and street only. [D]

MERCHANTS   615/254-1892 [12]

🔻🔻🔻 American. Casual Dining. $9-$24 **AAA Inspector Notes:** *Historic.* This 1870 downtown landmark was originally the location of a pharmacy, a hardware manufacturing business and wholesale drug company before being converted into The Merchant's Hotel in 1892. Past guests include Hank Williams, Patsy Cline and Roy Acuff. Evidence of its history is found everywhere inside the three-story brick structure. Original features include marble counters and Blood Medicine advertisements on the walls. Downstairs (casual) and upstairs (fine) dining differ in style and menu. **Features:** full bar, patio dining. **Reservations:** suggested. **Address:** 401 Broadway 37203 **Location:** Corner of 4th Ave and Broadway; center. **Parking:** valet and street only. [L] [D] [LATE] CALL 🅖M

(See map & index p. 196.)

MIDTOWN CAFE
615/320-7176 (23)

▼▼▼▼ Seafood Steak. Casual Dining. $13-$37 **AAA Inspector Notes:** This candlelit restaurant has the power to kindle a new romance or rekindle an old one. Share a stellar entrée of tender pork medallions draped with a sweet raspberry sauce. Zucchini and yellow squash mixed with rice accompany each meal. **Features:** full bar, happy hour. **Reservations:** suggested. **Address:** 102 19th Ave S 37203 **Location:** I-40 exit 209B (Broadway), 1 mi w to 19th Ave, then just s. ⬛ ⬛ L ⬛ D

MONELL'S DINING & CATERING
615/248-4747 (2)

▼▼ Southern Chicken Comfort Food. Family Dining. $9-$21 **AAA Inspector Notes:** Historic. Perched on a hilltop, this renovated antebellum home boasts several small, intimate dining rooms. They offer different meat choices, depending on the day of the week, but there always is skillet-fried chicken at every meal. Food is served communal style, so diners get to know the person next to them. **Features:** Sunday brunch. **Address:** 1235 6th Ave N 37208 **Location:** 1.5 mi n. **Parking:** street only. B ⬛ L ⬛ D

MOTO CUCINA & ENOTECA
615/736-5305 (40)

▼▼▼▼ Italian. Casual Dining. $8-$49 **AAA Inspector Notes:** Nashville is full of see-and-be-seen restaurants that are also known for their delicious menus. This is such a restaurant. As popular for an after-work drink as much as an intimate dinner, the attentive and poised dining room staff will impress with their care and knowledge, while the menu touts a unique and creative variety. Black spaghetti and blueberry lasagna are popular favorites on this rustic yet modern Italian menu. **Features:** full bar. **Reservations:** suggested. **Address:** 1120 McGavock St 37203 **Location:** Jct Broadway and 12th Ave S, 1 blk s; between 12th Ave S and 11th Ave S; in The Gulch. **Parking:** valet and street only. L ⬛ D ⬛ CALL ♿M

NOSHVILLE - NEW YORK DELICATESSEN
615/329-6674 (27)

▼▼ Deli Sandwiches. Casual Dining. $8-$17 **AAA Inspector Notes:** Popular throughout Nashville, this diner-style deli and eatery offers an extensive menu featuring New York-style sandwiches. Turkey, pastrami, corned beef, roast beef, salami, Reuben, grilled chicken and more are all served on freshly baked breads. You'll also find several appetizing salads. But this inspector's choice is a Monte Cristo and bowl of homemade chicken noodle soup. Finish that off with a thick slice of the rainbow cake and you'll be full for a week. **Features:** full bar. **Address:** 1918 Broadway 37203 **Location:** I-40/65 exit 209A/B (Church St/Broadway), 0.7 mi w; jct 20th Ave S. **Parking:** on-site and street. B ⬛ L ⬛ D ⬛ CALL ♿M

THE PALM RESTAURANT
615/742-7256 (13)

▼▼▼ American. Fine Dining. $13-$52 **AAA Inspector Notes:** This bustling restaurant is noted for Prime, dry-aged steaks and Nova Scotia lobsters. The huge portions are delivered by an attentive staff in an atmosphere that is fun and lively. At the end of the meal, servers present tempting pastries tableside. Caricature-lined walls lend to the feeling that patrons are dining in an art gallery. Even if you bring a big appetite you still may leave with a doggy bag. **Features:** full bar. **Reservations:** suggested. **Address:** 140 5th Ave S 37203 **Location:** Jct 5th Ave S and Broadway St, just s; adjacent to Bridgestone Arena. **Parking:** valet only. *(See ad p. 211.)* L ⬛ D ⬛ CALL ♿M

PANCAKE PANTRY
615/383-9333 (35)

▼▼ American. Casual Dining. $6-$16 **AAA Inspector Notes:** Bring patience, because the food at this breakfast spot is worth the wait. Some days you will see a line wrapped around the building, but luckily it moves pretty fast and there is no wait once you are inside the door. An order of their French toast is a must, especially with the hot cinnamon and maple syrup drizzled on top. They also offer blintzes, a variety of pancakes and a delicious hash brown recipe. Fresh-squeezed orange juice is an added treat. **Address:** 1796 21st Ave S 37212 **Location:** I-65 exit 81, 1.5 mi w on Wedgewood Ave; in Hillsboro Village. **Parking:** street only. B ⬛ L

Visit AAA.com/searchfordiscounts

to save on travel, shopping,

dining and attractions

PRIME 108
615/620-5665 (16)

▼▼▼ American. Fine Dining. $13-$45 **AAA Inspector Notes:** Whether you come here for breakfast, lunch, dinner or weekend brunch, a great dining experience awaits. The beautiful décor incorporates turn-of-the-20th-century design. Locally grown produce, organically grown vegetables and hormone-free beef are used whenever available. The dinner menu's seafood and steaks are prepared to perfection by chef Thomas Cook. **Features:** full bar, Sunday brunch, happy hour. **Reservations:** suggested. **Address:** 1001 Broadway 37203 **Location:** I-40 exit 209A (Church St), just ne; corner of 10th Ave; in Union Station Hotel - Autograph Collection. **Parking:** valet only. B ⬛ L ⬛ D ⬛ CALL ♿M

PROVENCE BREADS & CAFE
615/386-0363 (34)

▼ French. Quick Serve. $7-$11 **AAA Inspector Notes:** For a quick bite, this café's healthful soups, salads and sandwiches are hard to beat. A more extensive menu is offered until 2 pm, but the service style remains casual and quick. **Address:** 1705 21st Ave S 37212 **Location:** I-65 exit 81, 1.5 mi w on Wedgewood Ave; in Hillsboro Village. **Parking:** street only. B ⬛ L ⬛ D

ROTIER'S
615/327-9892 (30)

▼▼ Burgers Steak. Family Dining. $8-$19 **AAA Inspector Notes:** Historic. Stop by this popular local eatery to try one of their famous burgers. You just might rub shoulders with someone famous, too. **Features:** beer only. **Address:** 2413 Elliston Pl 37203 **Location:** I-440 exit 1, 1 mi e on US 70S/SR 1. **Parking:** street only. L ⬛ D ⬛ LATE

SAINT AÑEJO
615/736-5301 (41)

▼▼ Mexican. Casual Dining. $7-$20 **AAA Inspector Notes:** As one of the newest eateries in The Gulch, locals and visitors alike are gathering here to enjoy a broad drink menu full of exotic, fresh and unique flavors, featuring creative Latin mixology and craft margaritas. An oversized indoor/outdoor patio tempts diners to linger after a delicious and memorable meal. It's quickly becoming one of Nashville's favorite places to see and be seen. And it's a great way to enjoy a friendly casual atmosphere while escaping the downtown crowds. **Features:** full bar, patio dining, Sunday brunch. **Address:** 1120 McGavock Rd 37209 **Location:** Jct Broadway and 12th Ave S, 1 blk s; between 12th Ave S and 11th Ave S; in The Gulch. **Parking:** valet and street only. L ⬛ D ⬛ LATE

SPORTSMAN'S GRILLE IN THE VILLAGE
615/320-1633 (33)

▼▼ American. Casual Dining. $9-$25 **AAA Inspector Notes:** Come relax in a rustic lodge-style atmosphere, where you can enjoy generous portions of traditional homemade food. Fresh catfish, hand-packed burgers, cut fries, Prime steaks and chops, charbroiled salmon salad, fillet or chicken Caesar, and barbecue served on Cajun cornbread are among the offerings. **Features:** full bar, patio dining, Sunday brunch, happy hour. **Address:** 1601 21st Ave S 37212 **Location:** 4 mi w from jct Broadway. **Parking:** on-site and street. L ⬛ D ⬛ LATE

STONEY RIVER STEAKHOUSE AND GRILL
615/340-9550 (32)

▼▼▼ American. Casual Dining. $20-$50 **AAA Inspector Notes:** This upscale steakhouse specializes in hand-cut steaks and gourmet entrées, served in a sophisticated atmosphere by professional waiters. Guests can enjoy diverse menu offerings, such as center-cut filets, bone-in rib-eyes or classic New York strip steaks. Not in the mood for beef? The restaurant offers fresh seafood selections, signature salads and house specialties. **Features:** full bar, patio dining, Sunday brunch. **Address:** 3015 West End Ave 37203 **Location:** Midtown. **Parking:** valet and street only. D ⬛ CALL ♿M

SWETT'S RESTAURANT
615/329-4418 (18)

▼ American. Cafeteria. $8-$12 **AAA Inspector Notes:** This long-established, popular family restaurant features home cooking. **Address:** 2725 Clifton Ave 37209 **Location:** 1.5 mi n on 28th St. L ⬛ D

TAZZA
615/742-3223 (7)

▼▼ Italian. Casual Dining. $7-$24 **AAA Inspector Notes:** Offering both take-out and table service, this place is an excellent decision. Delicious, zesty Italian and American fare is matched with friendly, courteous service and an intimate ambiance. Choices include pasta, pizzas, calzones, deli sandwiches, steaks and more. **Address:** 510 Church St 37219 **Location:** Between 5th and 6th aves. **Parking:** on-site (fee) and street. L ⬛ D

(See map & index p. 196.)

VALENTINO'S RISTORANTE   615/327-0148 (24)

▽▽▽▽ Northern Italian. Fine Dining. $13-$48 **AAA Inspector Notes:** White tablecloths, fresh flowers and professional servers set the romantic atmosphere at this cozy restaurant. The pasta Valentino mixes chicken, shrimp, capers, artichokes and wine in a brown sauce, while the seafood risotto is rich and full of a great variety of fresh seafood. **Features:** full bar, happy hour. **Reservations:** required. **Address:** 1907 West End Ave 37203 **Location:** I-40 exit 209B (Broadway), just w. **Parking:** on-site and valet. (D)

WILDHORSE SALOON   615/902-8200 (6)

▽▽▽ American. Casual Dining. $10-$23 **AAA Inspector Notes:** Life-size sculptures of wild horses, humorously dressed in western gear, greet you at the door. Live music beckons all to "Ride up, tie up your horse and mosey on in." On the menu you'll find award-winning barbecue dishes, steaks, salads and fried pickles. Desserts are a mouthwatering delight. Cover charges may apply, even for guests just having dinner, when there is live entertainment. **Features:** full bar. **Address:** 120 2nd Ave N 37201 **Location:** Center. **Parking:** on-site (fee). (L) (D) (LATE) CALL (&M)

NASHVILLE (C-4)

- **Restaurants p. 224**
- **Hotels & Restaurants map & index p. 200**

BEST WESTERN PLUS BELLE MEADE INN & SUITES
    (615)354-1711 (39)

Hotel
$99-$199

AAA Benefit:
Save 10% or more every day and earn 10% bonus points!

Address: 5600 O'Brien Ave 37209 **Location:** I-40 exit 204B, just s. **Facility:** 57 units. 4 stories, interior corridors. **Pool(s):** outdoor. **Activities:** exercise room. **Guest Services:** coin laundry. **Featured Amenity:** full hot breakfast.

SAVE (☂+) CALL (&M) (BIZ) (HS) (📶) (✕) (🛗) (🖼) (💻)

BEST WESTERN SUITES NEAR OPRYLAND
    (615)902-9940 (4)

Hotel
$100-$200

AAA Benefit:
Save 10% or more every day and earn 10% bonus points!

Address: 201 Music City Cir 37214 **Location:** I-40 exit 15B (SR 155/N Briley Pkwy), 5.3 mi n to exit 12 (McGavock Pike), just w, then 0.5 mi n on Music Valley Dr. **Facility:** 100 units. 5 stories, interior corridors. **Terms:** 3 day cancellation notice-fee imposed. **Amenities:** safes. **Pool(s):** outdoor. **Activities:** sauna, exercise room. **Guest Services:** coin laundry, area transportation. **Featured Amenity:** full hot breakfast.

SAVE (☂+) (☂+) CALL (&M) (➰) (BIZ) (📶) (✕) (🛗) (🖼)
(💻) (/SOME UNITS) (HS)

COMFORT SUITES   (615)391-5959 (17)

▽▽▽ Hotel $102-$190 **Address:** 3431 Percy Priest Dr 37214 **Location:** I-40 exit 219 (Stewarts Ferry Pike), just s, then just w. **Facility:** 65 units. 4 stories, interior corridors. **Pool(s):** heated indoor. **Activities:** exercise room. **Guest Services:** valet and coin laundry.

(☂+) (☂+) CALL (&M) (➰) (BIZ) (HS) (📶) (✕) (🛗) (🖼)
(💻)

COMFORT SUITES AIRPORT   (615)391-3919 (23)

Hotel
$98-$250

Address: 2521 Elm Hill Pike 37214 **Location:** I-40 exit 215 (Briley Pkwy N), 1 mi n; exit 7 (Elm Hill Pike), then 1 mi e. **Facility:** 94 units. 4 stories, interior corridors. **Pool(s):** heated indoor. **Activities:** exercise room. **Guest Services:** valet and coin laundry, area transportation. **Featured Amenity:** full hot breakfast.

SAVE (☂+) (☂+) CALL (&M) (➰) (BIZ)
(📶) (✕) (🛗) (🖼) (💻)

COUNTRY INN & SUITES BY CARLSON, NASHVILLE AIRPORT   615/874-8040 (37)

Hotel
Rates not provided

Address: 590 Donelson Pike 37214 **Location:** I-40 exit 216C, just n. **Facility:** 97 units. 6 stories, interior corridors. **Activities:** exercise room. **Guest Services:** coin laundry, area transportation. **Featured Amenity:** full hot breakfast.

SAVE (☂+) (☂+) CALL (&M) (BIZ) (📶)
(✕) (🛗) (🖼) (💻) (/SOME UNITS) (HS)

COUNTRY INN & SUITES BY CARLSON NASHVILLE AIRPORT EAST   (615)277-1099 (18)

▽▽ Hotel $75-$250 **Address:** 3423 Percy Priest Dr 37214 **Location:** I-40 exit 219 (Stewarts Ferry Pike), just se. **Facility:** 62 units. 3 stories, interior corridors. **Terms:** cancellation fee imposed. **Pool(s):** outdoor. **Activities:** exercise room. **Guest Services:** valet and coin laundry.

(☂+) (☂+) CALL (&M) (➰) (BIZ) (📶) (✕) (🛗) (🖼) (💻)

COUNTRY INN & SUITES BY CARLSON-OPRYLAND   (615)316-9944 (6)

▽▽ Hotel $99-$209 **Address:** 210 Rudy Cir 37214 **Location:** I-40 exit 215B (SR 155 N/Briley Pkwy), 5.3 mi n to exit 12 (McGavock Pike), just w, then 0.3 mi n on Music Valley Dr. **Facility:** 53 units. 3 stories, interior corridors. **Terms:** 3 day cancellation notice. **Pool(s):** outdoor. **Guest Services:** coin laundry.

(☂+) CALL (&M) (➰) (BIZ) (📶) (✕) (🛗) (🖼) (💻)

COURTYARD BY MARRIOTT AT OPRYLAND   (615)882-9133 (5)

▽▽▽ Hotel $115-$189 **Address:** 125 Music City Cir 37214 **Location:** I-40 exit 215B (SR 155 N/Briley Pkwy), 5.3 mi n to exit 12 (McGavock Pike), just w to Music Valley Dr, then 0.5 mi n. **Facility:** 94 units. 4 stories, interior corridors. **Pool(s):** heated indoor. **Activities:** hot tub, limited exercise equipment. **Guest Services:** valet and coin laundry, boarding pass kiosk, area transportation.

AAA Benefit:
Members save 5% or more!

(☂+) (☂+) (☂+) CALL (&M) (➰) (BIZ) (📶) (✕) (💻)
(/SOME UNITS) (🛗) (🖼)

COURTYARD BY MARRIOTT NASHVILLE AIRPORT   (615)883-9500 (22)

Hotel
$99-$269

 COURTYARD Marriott **AAA Benefit:**
Members save 5% or more!

Address: 2508 Elm Hill Pike 37214 **Location:** I-40 exit 215B, Briley Pkwy N to exit 7, then just e. **Facility:** 145 units. 4 stories, interior corridors. **Pool(s):** outdoor. **Activities:** exercise room. **Guest Services:** valet and coin laundry, boarding pass kiosk, area transportation.

SAVE (☂+) (☂+) (☂+) CALL (&M) (➰)
(BIZ) (📶) (✕) (🛗) (🖼)
(/SOME UNITS) (🖼)

(See map & index p. 200.)

DAYS INN NORTH

Motel
$70-$199

(615)228-3421

Address: 3312 Dickerson Pike 37207 **Location:** I-65 exit 90A (Dickerson Pike), just s. **Facility:** 44 units. 2 stories (no elevator), exterior corridors. **Terms:** cancellation fee imposed. **Pool(s):** outdoor. **Featured Amenity: continental breakfast.**

ECONO LODGE
Motel
$46-$133

(615)262-9193

Address: 110 Maplewood Trace 37207 **Location:** I-65 exit 90A, 0.5 mi s on Dickerson Pike; corner of Dickerson Pike and Maplewood Trace. Located in a congested area. **Facility:** 38 units. 2 stories (no elevator), exterior corridors. **Pool(s):** outdoor.

DOUBLETREE SUITES BY HILTON HOTEL NASHVILLE AIRPORT
(615)889-8889

Hotel $129-$299 **Address:** 2424 Atrium Way 37214 **Location:** Briley Pkwy exit 7 (Elm Hill Pike), e to Atrium Way, then 0.5 mi n. **Facility:** 138 units. 3 stories, interior corridors. **Terms:** 1-7 night minimum stay, cancellation fee imposed. **Pool(s):** outdoor, heated indoor. **Activities:** exercise room. **Guest Services:** valet and coin laundry, area transportation.

AAA Benefit: Members save 5% or more!

DRURY INN & SUITES-NASHVILLE AIRPORT
(615)902-0400

Hotel $100-$199 **Address:** 555 Donelson Pike 37214 **Location:** I-40 exit 216 (Donelson Pike), just n. **Facility:** 155 units. 6 stories, interior corridors. **Terms:** cancellation fee imposed. **Pool(s):** heated outdoor, heated indoor. **Activities:** hot tub, exercise room. **Guest Services:** valet and coin laundry.

EMBASSY SUITES BY HILTON NASHVILLE AIRPORT
(615)871-0033

Hotel
$129-$249

EMBASSY SUITES by HILTON

AAA Benefit: Members save 5% or more!

Address: 10 Century Blvd 37214 **Location:** I-40 exit 215 northbound to exit 7 (Elm Hill Pike), 0.3 mi e to McGavock Pike, 0.3 mi s to Century Blvd, then 0.3 mi w. Located within a large business park. **Facility:** 296 units. 9 stories, interior corridors. **Terms:** check-in 4 pm, 1-7 night minimum stay, cancellation fee imposed. **Dining:** TEN Bar & Grille, see separate listing. **Pool(s):** heated indoor. **Activities:** game room, exercise room. **Guest Services:** valet and coin laundry, area transportation. *(See ad this page.)*

▼ See AAA listing this page ▼

Ask about AAA/CAA Associate membership
to share the benefits you value

(See map & index p. 200.)

FAIRFIELD INN & SUITES BY MARRIOTT NASHVILLE AT OPRYLAND
(615)872-8939

▼▼▼ **Hotel** $101-$177 **Address:** 211 Music City Cir 37214 **Location:** I-40 exit 215B (SR 155 N/Briley Pkwy), 5.3 mi n to exit 12 (McGavock Pike), just w, then 0.3 mi n on Music Valley Dr. **Facility:** 109 units. 3 stories, interior corridors. **Pool(s):** heated indoor. **Activities:** limited exercise equipment. **Guest Services:** valet and coin laundry, area transportation.

AAA Benefit: Members save 5% or more!

GAYLORD OPRYLAND RESORT & CONVENTION CENTER
(615)889-1000

▼▼▼▼ **Resort Hotel** $188-$309

AAA Benefit: Members save 5% or more!

GAYLORD HOTELS®

Address: 2800 Opryland Dr 37214 **Location:** I-40 exit 215B or I-65 exit 90B; SR 155/Briley Pkwy, exit 11 (Music Valley Dr/McGavock Pike). **Facility:** This sprawling convention resort has something for everyone, all under a huge glass roof. Room décor themes vary in each section, but all have nice upscale touches and well appointed bathrooms. 2882 units. 6 stories, interior corridors. **Parking:** on-site (fee) and valet. **Terms:** 3 day cancellation notice, resort fee. **Amenities:** safes. **Dining:** 10 restaurants, also, Old Hickory Steakhouse at Opryland, see separate listing, entertainment. **Pool(s):** outdoor, heated indoor. **Activities:** sauna, hot tub, steamroom, regulation pool, game room, spa. **Guest Services:** valet laundry, boarding pass kiosk, rental car service, area transportation.

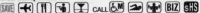

GUESTHOUSE INTERNATIONAL INN & SUITES
(615)885-4030

▼▼ **Hotel** $125-$150 **Address:** 2420 Music Valley Dr 37214 **Location:** I-40 exit 215B (SR 155 N/Briley Pkwy), 5.3 mi n to exit 12 (McGavock Pike), just w, then 0.3 mi n. **Facility:** 184 units. 5 stories, interior corridors. **Pool(s):** heated indoor. **Activities:** hot tub, exercise room. **Guest Services:** coin laundry, area transportation.

HAMPTON INN & SUITES GREEN HILLS/NASHVILLE
(615)777-0001

▼▼▼ **Hotel** $179-$329 **Address:** 2324 Crestmoor Rd 37215 **Location:** I-440 exit 3 (Hillsboro Pike), 0.8 mi s, then 0.5 mi w. **Facility:** 97 units, some efficiencies. 6 stories, interior corridors. **Terms:** 1-7 night minimum stay, cancellation fee imposed. **Pool(s):** outdoor. **Activities:** hot tub, exercise room. **Guest Services:** valet and coin laundry, area transportation.

AAA Benefit: Members save up to 10%!

HAMPTON INN & SUITES NASHVILLE AIRPORT
(615)885-4242

▼▼▼ **Hotel** $139-$259 **Address:** 583 Donelson Pike 37214 **Location:** I-40 exit 216, just n. **Facility:** 111 units. 7 stories, interior corridors. **Terms:** 1-7 night minimum stay, cancellation fee imposed. **Pool(s):** outdoor. **Activities:** exercise room. **Guest Services:** valet and coin laundry, area transportation.

AAA Benefit: Members save up to 10%!

HAMPTON INN & SUITES NASHVILLE AT OPRYLAND
(615)620-2500

▼▼▼ **Hotel** $129-$299 **Address:** 230 Rudy Cir 37214 **Location:** I-40 exit 215B (SR 155 N/Briley Pkwy), 5.3 mi n to exit 12 (McGavock Pike), just w, then 0.3 mi n on Music Valley Dr. **Facility:** 122 units. 5 stories, interior corridors. **Terms:** check-in 4 pm, 1-7 night minimum stay, cancellation fee imposed. **Pool(s):** outdoor. **Activities:** exercise room. **Guest Services:** valet and coin laundry, area transportation.

AAA Benefit: Members save up to 10%!

HAMPTON INN BELLEVUE
(615)662-3133

▼▼▼ **Hotel** $129-$279 **Address:** 7815 Coley Davis Rd 37221 **Location:** I-40 exit 196, just sw. **Facility:** 86 units. 5 stories, interior corridors. **Terms:** 1-7 night minimum stay, cancellation fee imposed. **Pool(s):** outdoor. **Activities:** exercise room. **Guest Services:** valet and coin laundry.

AAA Benefit: Members save up to 10%!

▼ See AAA listing p. 42 ▼

(See map & index p. 200.)

HILTON GARDEN INN NASHVILLE AIRPORT
(615)884-0088 25

▼▼▼ Hotel $97-$247 **Address:** 412 Royal Pkwy 37214 **Location:** I-40 exit 216 North (Donelson Pike), just n to Royal Pkwy, then 0.5 mi w. **Facility:** 110 units. 6 stories, interior corridors. **Terms:** 1-7 night minimum stay, cancellation fee imposed. **Pool(s):** heated indoor. **Activities:** exercise room. **Guest Services:** valet and coin laundry, area transportation.

AAA Benefit: Members save up to 10%!

HOLIDAY INN EXPRESS 615/366-6691 40

▼▼▼ Hotel. Rates not provided. **Address:** 714 Spence Ln 37217 **Location:** I-24 exit 52 southbound; I-40 exit 213 northbound. **Facility:** 87 units. 4 stories, interior corridors. **Pool(s):** heated outdoor. **Activities:** exercise room. **Guest Services:** valet and coin laundry.

HOLIDAY INN EXPRESS-AIRPORT/OPRYLAND AREA
(615)883-1366 36

Hotel
$99-$249

Address: 1111 Airport Center Dr 37214 **Location:** I-40 exit 216C (Donelson Pike N), 1 mi n, then 0.5 mi e. **Facility:** 202 units. 3 stories, interior corridors. **Terms:** cancellation fee imposed. **Pool(s):** outdoor. **Activities:** exercise room. **Guest Services:** valet laundry, area transportation.

HOLIDAY INN EXPRESS NASHVILLE-OPRYLAND
(615)829-7777 11

▼▼▼ Hotel $199-$399 **Address:** 2461 McGavock Pike 37214 **Location:** I-65 exit 90B or I-40 exit 215B (SR 155/N Briley Pkwy); 5.3 mi n to exit 12 (McGavock Pike), 0.8 mi w. **Facility:** 113 units. 5 stories, interior corridors. **Pool(s):** heated indoor. **Activities:** exercise room. **Guest Services:** valet and coin laundry, area transportation.

HOLIDAY INN OPRYLAND-AIRPORT (615)883-9770 20

▼▼▼ Hotel $119-$299 **Address:** 2200 Elm Hill Pike 37214 **Location:** I-40 exit 215B (SR 155/N Briley Pkwy), 0.5 mi n. **Facility:** 383 units. 14 stories, interior corridors. **Terms:** cancellation fee imposed, resort fee. **Dining:** entertainment. **Pool(s):** heated indoor. **Activities:** exercise room. **Guest Services:** valet and coin laundry, area transportation.

HOMEWOOD SUITES BY HILTON NASHVILLE AIRPORT
(615)884-8111 21

▼▼▼ Extended Stay Hotel $119-$249 **Address:** 2640 Elm Hill Pike 37214 **Location:** I-40 exit 216C (Donelson Pike), 0.4 mi n, then just w. **Facility:** 121 efficiencies, some two bedrooms. 3 stories, interior corridors. **Terms:** 1-7 night minimum stay, cancellation fee imposed. **Pool(s):** outdoor. **Activities:** exercise room. **Guest Services:** valet and coin laundry, area transportation.

AAA Benefit: Members save up to 10%!

(See map & index p. 200.)

HOTEL PRESTON
(615)361-5900 **38**

Hotel
$119-$299

Address: 733 Briley Pkwy 37217 **Location:** I-40 exit 215 (SR 155/Briley Pkwy), just s. Located at end of airport runway. **Facility:** 196 units. 11 stories, interior corridors. **Terms:** cancellation fee imposed. **Pool(s):** outdoor. **Activities:** exercise room. **Guest Services:** valet laundry, area transportation.

An artistic, Music City oasis centrally located near the Nashville International Airport.

HYATT PLACE NASHVILLE AIRPORT
(615)493-5200 **27**

Hotel
$79-$249

HYATT PLACE®

AAA Benefit: Members save 10%!

Address: 721 Royal Pkwy 37214 **Location:** I-40 exit 216C (Donelson Pike), just n, then just e. **Facility:** 83 units. 5 stories, interior corridors. **Terms:** cancellation fee imposed. **Pool(s):** outdoor. **Activities:** exercise room. **Guest Services:** valet laundry, area transportation. **Featured Amenity:** breakfast buffet.

HYATT PLACE NASHVILLE/OPRYLAND
(615)872-0422 **7**

Hotel
$89-$209

HYATT PLACE®

AAA Benefit: Members save 10%!

Address: 220 Rudy Cir 37214 **Location:** I-40 exit 215B (SR 155 N/Briley Pkwy), 5.3 mi n to exit 12 (McGavock Pike), just w, then 0.3 mi n on Music Valley Dr. **Facility:** 123 units. 5 stories, interior corridors. **Terms:** cancellation fee imposed. **Amenities:** safes. **Pool(s):** outdoor. **Activities:** exercise room. **Guest Services:** valet laundry, area transportation. **Featured Amenity:** breakfast buffet. *(See ad this page.)*

THE INN AT OPRYLAND, A GAYLORD HOTEL
(615)889-0800 **10**

AAA Benefit: Members save 5% or more!

Hotel $125-$204 **Address:** 2401 Music Valley Dr 37214 **Location:** I-40 exit 215 (SR 155/N Briley Pkwy), just e. **Facility:** 303 units, some two bedrooms. 3 stories, interior/exterior corridors. **Amenities:** *Some:* safes. **Dining:** The Opry Backstage Grill, see separate listing. **Pool(s):** heated indoor. **Activities:** hot tub, exercise room. **Guest Services:** valet laundry, area transportation.

LA QUINTA INN & SUITES NASHVILLE-AIRPORT
(615)885-3100 **26**

Hotel $71-$262 **Address:** 531 Donelson Pike 37214 **Location:** I-40 exit 216C (Donelson Pike), 0.3 mi n. **Facility:** 141 units. 3 stories, interior corridors. **Pool(s):** outdoor. **Activities:** exercise room. **Guest Services:** coin laundry.

▼ See AAA listing this page ▼

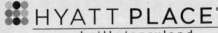

(See map & index p. 200.)

MICROTEL INN & SUITES BY WYNDHAM NASHVILLE
(615)662-0004

Hotel
$62-$90

Address: 100 Coley Davis Ct 37221 **Location:** I-40 exit 196, just se. **Facility:** 71 units. 3 stories, interior corridors. **Pool(s):** outdoor. **Featured Amenity: continental breakfast.**

MILLENNIUM MAXWELL HOUSE HOTEL-NASHVILLE
(615)259-4343 **14**

Hotel
$99-$259

Address: 2025 Rosa L Parks Blvd 37228 **Location:** I-65 exit 85, just n. **Facility:** 287 units. 10 stories, interior corridors. **Terms:** cancellation fee imposed. **Dining:** entertainment. **Pool(s):** outdoor. **Activities:** exercise room. **Guest Services:** valet laundry, area transportation.

NASHVILLE AIRPORT MARRIOTT
(615)889-9300 **30**

▼▼▼ Hotel $112-$265 **Address:** 600 Marriott Dr 37214 **Location:** I-40 exit 215B (SR 155/N Briley Pkwy), 1 mi n to exit 7 (Elm Hill Pike). **Facility:** 392 units. 18 stories, interior corridors.

AAA Benefit: Members save 5% or more!

Terms: check-in 4 pm. **Pool(s):** heated outdoor, heated indoor. **Activities:** hot tub, exercise room. **Guest Services:** valet and coin laundry.

QUALITY SUITES
(615)883-0114 **43**

Hotel
$99-$239

Address: 2615 Elm Hill Pike 37214 **Location:** I-40 exit 216C (Donelson Pike), just n, then just w. **Facility:** 50 units. 3 stories, interior corridors. **Terms:** cancellation fee imposed. **Amenities:** safes. **Guest Services:** coin laundry. **Featured Amenity: full hot breakfast.**

RADISSON HOTEL NASHVILLE AIRPORT
(615)889-9090 **33**

Hotel
$99-$299

Address: 1112 Airport Center Dr 37214 **Location:** I-40 exit 216C (Donelson Pike N), 0.5 mi n, then just e. **Facility:** 180 units. 7 stories, interior corridors. **Terms:** cancellation fee imposed. **Amenities:** Some: safes. **Pool(s):** heated indoor. **Activities:** picnic facilities, exercise room. **Guest Services:** valet laundry, area transportation.

RED ROOF INN NASHVILLE AIRPORT
(615)872-0735 **29**

Motel
$50-$130

Address: 510 Claridge Dr 37214 **Location:** I-40 exit 216C (Donelson Pike), 0.3 mi n. **Facility:** 120 units. 3 stories, exterior corridors. **Amenities:** safes.

RESIDENCE INN BY MARRIOTT NASHVILLE AIRPORT
(615)889-8600 **19**

Extended Stay Hotel
$109-$269

AAA Benefit: Members save 5% or more!

Address: 2300 Elm Hill Pike 37214 **Location:** I-40 exit 215B (SR 155 N/Briley Pkwy), 1.5 mi n. **Facility:** 168 kitchen units. 2 stories (no elevator), exterior corridors. **Terms:** check-in 4 pm. **Pool(s):** outdoor. **Activities:** exercise room. **Guest Services:** valet and coin laundry, area transportation. **Featured Amenity:** breakfast buffet.

SHERATON MUSIC CITY HOTEL
615/885-2200 **32**

Hotel
Rates not provided

AAA Benefit: Members save up to 15%, plus Starwood Preferred Guest® benefits!

Address: 777 McGavock Pike 37214 **Location:** I-40 exit 215B (SR 155 N/Briley Pkwy), 1 mi n to exit 7 (Elm Hill Pike), 0.5 mi e, then s. **Facility:** 410 units. 4 stories, interior corridors. **Pool(s):** outdoor, heated indoor. **Activities:** hot tub, exercise room, massage. **Guest Services:** valet laundry.

SLEEP INN NASHVILLE
(615)882-9220 **16**

Hotel
$85-$125

Address: 3437 Percy Priest Dr 37214 **Location:** I-40 exit 219 (Stewarts Ferry Pike), just s. **Facility:** 59 units. 3 stories, interior corridors. *Bath:* shower only. **Pool(s):** outdoor. **Activities:** limited exercise equipment. **Guest Services:** coin laundry. **Featured Amenity: continental breakfast.**

Ask your AAA/CAA club about travel money and other financial services for travelers

(See map & index p. 200.)

SPRINGHILL SUITES BY MARRIOTT METRO CENTER
(615)244-5474 **13**

◈◈◈ **Hotel $125-$329 Address:** 250 Athens Way 37228 **Location:** I-65 exit 85, 0.4 mi n. **Facility:** 78 units. 3 stories, interior corridors. **Pool(s):** heated outdoor, heated indoor. **Activities:** hot tub, exercise room. **Guest Services:** valet and coin laundry.

AAA Benefit: Members save 5% or more!

CALL ⛓ 🚲 BIZ 📶 ✕ 🔋 📇 🖥

SPRINGHILL SUITES BY MARRIOTT NASHVILLE AIRPORT
(615)884-6111 **28**

◈◈◈ Hotel $99-$269

SPRINGHILL SUITES Marriott

AAA Benefit: Members save 5% or more!

Address: 1100 Airport Center Dr 37214 **Location:** I-40 exit 216 N (Donelson Pike), just n, then just e at Royal Park. **Facility:** 150 units. 6 stories, interior corridors. **Terms:** check-in 4 pm. **Pool(s):** heated indoor. **Activities:** exercise room. **Guest Services:** valet and coin laundry, boarding pass kiosk. **Featured Amenity:** breakfast buffet.

SAVE ♿ ⏶⏷ CALL ⛓ 🚲 BIZ

📶 ✕ 🔋 📇 🖥

SUPER 8-WEST
(615)356-6005 **41**

◈◈ Motel $50-$100

Address: 6924 Charlotte Pike 37209 **Location:** I-40 exit 201B, just n. **Facility:** 55 units. 2 stories (no elevator), exterior corridors. **Guest Services:** coin laundry. **Featured Amenity:** continental breakfast.

SAVE ⏶⏷ 📶 🔋 📇 🖥

/ SOME UNITS 🛎

TOWNEPLACE SUITES BY MARRIOTT NASHVILLE AIRPORT
(615)232-3830 **24**

◈◈◈ **Extended Stay Hotel** $159-$299 **Address:** 2700 Elm Hill Pike 37214 **Location:** I-40 exit 215 (SR 155 N/Briley Pkwy), 1 mi n or exit 7 (Elm Hill Pike), then just e. **Facility:** 101 units, some two bedrooms, efficiencies and kitchens. 4 stories, interior corridors. **Pool(s):** heated indoor. **Activities:** picnic facilities, exercise room. **Guest Services:** valet and coin laundry, area transportation.

AAA Benefit: Members save 5% or more!

♿ ⏶⏷ CALL ⛓ 🚲 BIZ HS 📶 ✕ 🔋 📇

🖥 / SOME UNITS 🛎

ANTONIO'S OF NASHVILLE
615/646-9166 **29**

◈◈◈ Italian. Fine Dining. $11-$30 **AAA Inspector Notes:** Piping-hot bread and olive oil take the edge off your hunger as you peruse a menu lined with savory Italian cuisine. **Features:** full bar, early bird specials. **Reservations:** suggested. **Address:** 7097 Old Harding Pike 37221 **Location:** Just w of jct US 70 S and Old Hickory Blvd. D

AQUARIUM RESTAURANT
615/514-3474 **8**

◈◈◈ Seafood. Casual Dining. $11-$37 **AAA Inspector Notes:** Dine "underwater" around a 200,000-gallon aquarium full of more than 100 species of fish. Appetizers include shrimp, crab dip, crispy calamari and chicken lettuce wraps. Salads of tortilla encrusted shrimp, grilled steak and Thai shrimp make for a great lunch or dinner. The fish selections include grilled Atlantic salmon, Asian sea bass, stuffed flounder and the always popular fish and chips. Meat lovers will enjoy fillet, rib-eye or grilled, fried or spicy Jamaican jerk chicken. **Features:** full bar. **Reservations:** suggested. **Address:** 516 Opry Mills Dr 37214 **Location:** (SR 155/N Briley Pkwy) exit 11; inside Opry Mills Mall. SAVE L D CALL ⛓

BACK TO CUBA CAFE
615/837-6711 **28**

◈ Cuban. Quick Serve. $7-$13 **AAA Inspector Notes:** Wonderful sandwiches of seasoned chicken, pork and steak are heaped on fresh, slightly sweet bread. You'll order at the counter; the food is then promptly delivered to the table. Try the papas rellenas, shrimp enchiladas or one of the numerous stews. For dessert you'll find fresh-baked treats. **Features:** patio dining. **Address:** 4683 Trousdale Dr 37204 **Location:** I-65 exit 78, just e. L D

BAR-B-CUTIE
615/872-0207 **14**

◈ Barbecue. Quick Serve. $6-$21 **AAA Inspector Notes:** This popular locally owned restaurant is where everyone goes to enjoy great-tasting ribs, brisket and chicken, as well as numerous daily specials. A super-friendly staff makes you feel right at home. **Address:** 501 Donelson Pike 37214 **Location:** I-40 exit 216 northbound, 0.8 mi n. L D CALL ⛓

CANEY FORK RIVER VALLEY GRILLE
615/724-1200 **6**

◈◈ Southern. Casual Dining. $12-$24 **AAA Inspector Notes:** The restored front end of an old red pickup truck, wood beams, plank booth seating, an indoor fire pit and a large fish pond grab your attention at this distinctive restaurant. Fried catfish, barbecue platters, wild game and unique dishes like frog legs are just a few of the items offered. In addition, the grouper Reuben, salmon and rib-eye steaks show that this place includes something for everyone. Lunch served Friday-Sunday. **Features:** full bar. **Address:** 2400 Music Valley Dr 37214 **Location:** I-40 exit 215B (SR 155 N/Briley Pkwy), 4 mi n to exit 12 (McGavock Pike), then just w. D CALL ⛓

CAROL ANN'S HOME COOKING CAFE
615/259-2551 **18**

◈ Southern Soul Food. Quick Serve. $7-$12 **AAA Inspector Notes:** Meat-plus-two is the standard ordering procedure at this friendly restaurant featuring a daily changing menu of favorites such as fried chicken, meatloaf, fried pork chops and barbecue ribs. Great sides include fresh, homegrown turnip greens, sweet potatoes, green beans, stewed apples and real mashed potatoes. For dessert you'll find more than 15 varieties of freshly made cakes, plus fruit cobblers and banana pudding. **Features:** full bar, happy hour. **Address:** 407 Murfreesboro Pike 37210 **Location:** I-24 exit 212, 0.3 mi s on Fesslers Ln, then just nw on US 70 S. L D

CHINA COTTAGE
615/865-6854 **1**

◈◈ Chinese. Casual Dining. $6-$28 **AAA Inspector Notes:** Relax in a quiet, genteel atmosphere before indulging in walnut shrimp, Peking duck or crispy beef. **Address:** 1795 N Gallatin Rd 37115 **Location:** I-65 exit 96, 1 mi e, then just s. L D

CHINATOWN RESTAURANT
615/269-3275 **23**

◈◈ Chinese. Family Dining. $7-$29 **AAA Inspector Notes:** Long lines of diners wait for seating in this popular restaurant, known for its casual feel and tasty, traditional dishes, such as sesame chicken. Portions are plentiful. The seafood combination comprises shrimp, scallops and lots of vegetables. **Features:** beer & wine. **Address:** 3900 Hillsboro Rd 37215 **Location:** I-440 exit 3 (Hillsboro Rd), 1 mi s; in Hillsboro Plaza. L D

(See map & index p. 200.)

DARFON'S
615/889-3032 ⑮

▼▼▼ American. Casual Dining. $8-$28 **AAA Inspector Notes:** Dim lighting, a circular bar and wood-topped booths create a trendy mood in this casual restaurant. The varied menu features a spinach-garlic dip with fried pita wedges, a flavorful steak Oscar and tender, grilled zucchini. Several seafood options are available as well. **Features:** full bar, patio dining, Sunday brunch, happy hour. **Address:** 2810 Elm Hill Pike 37214 **Location:** I-40 exit 216C (Donelson Pike), 0.5 mi n. L D CALL ♿M

EL CHICO
615/366-6002 ⑲

**Tex-Mex
Casual Dining
$7-$15**

AAA Inspector Notes: Inside and out, the decor of the popular Mexican restaurant is inviting. The menu features traditional favorites such as enchiladas, tacos, burritos and fajitas. The broad menu also lists a few American classics. **Features:** full bar, patio dining, happy hour. **Address:** 1132 Murfreesboro Rd 37217 **Location:** I-24 exit 52B, 1 mi e. L D CALL ♿M

ELLENDALE'S RESTAURANT
615/884-0171 ⑬

▼▼▼ American. Casual Dining. $7-$23 **AAA Inspector Notes:** Perched on a hilltop, the renovated mansion nurtures a relaxing atmosphere. The menu selection is varied. The Sunday brunch offers a buffet of pastas, breakfast foods and regular lunch menu selections, along with a great variety of mimosas. **Features:** beer & wine, Sunday brunch. **Address:** 2739 Old Elm Hill Pike 37214 **Location:** I-40 exit 216C (Donelson Pike), 1.5 mi n. L D CALL ♿M

GINZA JAPANESE RESTAURANT
615/292-1168 ㉒

▼▼ Japanese. Casual Dining. $6-$23 **AAA Inspector Notes:** An extensive sushi and sashimi bar complements a menu of unusual but fresh and authentic cuisine, including some tempura dishes. Some servers speak limited English, but they are pleasant, polite and eager to please. **Features:** beer only. **Address:** 3900 Hillsboro Plaza, Suite 10 37215 **Location:** I-440 exit 3 (Hillsboro Rd), 1 mi s; in Hillsboro Plaza. L D CALL ♿M

GOLDEN THAI
615/353-9411 ⑳

▼▼ Thai. Casual Dining. $6-$19 **AAA Inspector Notes:** Golden Thai is a casual, low-priced restaurant. The food is made to order, fresh and well seasoned. The coconut soup has explosive flavor that's sure to leave a lasting impression. Traditional Thai floor seating is available, so settle in and enjoy a quiet escape from the city. **Features:** beer & wine. **Address:** 73 White Bridge Rd, Suite 107 37205 **Location:** I-40 exit 204B, 1.5 mi s; in Paddock Place strip mall. L D CALL ♿M

H & T HOME COOKING
615/367-0049 ㉖

▼▼ Southern Soul Food. Family Dining. $6-$9 **AAA Inspector Notes:** In the South, it's meat-plus-three, which includes a choice of daily specials such as meatloaf, Southern fried or baked chicken, catfish, chicken and dressing, salmon croquettes, pork chop and gravy or kielbasa and sauerkraut. Sides include turnip greens, green beans, pinto beans, mashed potatoes, corn on the cob and the kid-favorite macaroni and cheese. For dessert, try the freshly baked peach or blackberry cobbler. **Address:** 2371 Murfreesboro Rd 37217 **Location:** I-24 exit 213A, 0.4 mi e to Murfreesboro Pike, then 6.2 mi se. L D

JACKS BAR-B-QUE
615/228-9888 ⑨

▼ Barbecue. Quick Serve. $5-$21 **AAA Inspector Notes:** This eatery offers up good barbecue including pit-to-plate St. Louis-style ribs, Tennessee pork shoulder and Texas-style beef brisket and smoked sausage. Smoky baked beans, creamy coleslaw and great macaroni and cheese are great sides, while meal-enders could include a slice of sweet chess pie or chocolate fudge pie. **Features:** beer only, patio dining. **Address:** 334 W Trinity Ln 37207 **Location:** I-65 exit 87 (US 431), just s on Brick Church Pike, then 0.3 mi w. L D

JIM 'N NICK'S BAR-B-Q
615/352-5777

▼▼ Barbecue. Casual Dining. $8-$25 **AAA Inspector Notes:** Southern hospitality reigns at Jim 'N Nick's, where diners get neighborly treatment as they dig into huge portions of tasty lean sausage, fresh chili, juicy smoked beef and pork. A slice of sublime homemade pie ends the meal on a high note. **Features:** full bar, patio dining. **Address:** 7004 Charlotte Pike 37209 **Location:** I-40 exit 201, 0.3 mi w. L D CALL ♿M

KEBAB GYROS
615/352-0120 ㉑

▼ Greek. Quick Serve. $6-$13 **AAA Inspector Notes:** Mediterranean flavors infuse vegetarian and meat dishes, including yogurt salad, tabbouleh, hummus and beef or shawarma kebabs. Also offered are many combination platters and desserts such as baklava and rice pudding. **Address:** 73 White Bridge Rd, Unit 1 37205 **Location:** I-40 exit 204, just s; in Paddock Place strip mall. B L D

LOVELESS CAFE
615/646-9700

▼▼ American. Family Dining. $8-$18 **AAA Inspector Notes:** For more than 50 years, guests have flocked to this restaurant for the flaky, fresh-baked biscuits with homemade peach, blackberry and strawberry preserves. Other folks will rave about the pan-fried chicken that has been a staple here for years, as well as the country ham and red-eyed gravy. The few available tables make for long waits that are less painful when the weather is nice and when you visit the different shops located on property. **Address:** 8400 Hwy 100 37221 **Location:** I-40 exit 192, 4 mi se on US 70, then w on SR 100, follow signs. B L D

THE NASHVILLE PALACE
615/889-1540 ⑤

▼▼ American. Casual Dining. $4-$10 **AAA Inspector Notes:** A traditional honky-tonk with entertainment, a dance floor and a casual menu, this place has it all. Live music is strictly of the traditional kind. And like downtown, the walls are plastered with autographed photos, album covers, guitars, posters and sweat-stained outfits once worn on stage. The food is fast and familiar. Service is friendly and hospitable. **Features:** full bar, patio dining, happy hour. **Address:** 2611 McGavock Pike 37214 **Location:** I-40 exit 215B (Briley Pkwy N / SR 155 N), 5.3 mi n to exit 12 (McGavock Pike), 0.6 mi w. L D LATE CALL ♿M ◣

NEW DRAGON PHOENIX BUFFET
615/889-2838 ⑯

▼ Chinese. Casual Dining. $7-$10 **AAA Inspector Notes:** The extensive buffet is lined with favorites such as egg drop and wonton soup, appetizers of fried wonton and steamed dumplings, and entrées of sweet and sour pork, hot and spicy shrimp, beef with Chinese vegetables, as well as several other stir-fry and vegetarian dishes. **Address:** 2828 Elm Hill Pike, Suite 101 37214 **Location:** I-40 exit 216C (Donelson Pike), 0.5 mi n. L D CALL ♿M

NOSHVILLE-NEW YORK DELICATESSEN
615/269-3535 ㉔

▼▼ Jewish Deli Breakfast. Casual Dining. $8-$17 **AAA Inspector Notes:** The extensive menu features New York-style sandwiches of corned beef, pastrami, roast beef and whitefish, which come on freshly baked breads. Also on the menu are filling salads, homemade soups and fresh bagels, plus the yummy desserts that help make this place a Nashville favorite. **Features:** full bar, patio dining. **Address:** 4014 Hillsboro Cir 37215 **Location:** I-440 exit 3 (Hillsboro Rd), 1.7 mi w, then just w. B L CALL ♿M

OLD HICKORY STEAKHOUSE AT OPRYLAND
615/889-1000 ⑦

▼▼▼◆ Steak. Fine Dining. $10-$48 **AAA Inspector Notes:** An Antebellum mansion sets the stage for a delightful meal, served by an attentive professional staff. Tables are set among a tree-shaded courtyard that wraps around a gurgling river. Delicious entrées include hand-cut 1855 Angus steaks, Scottish salmon, lamb and lobster tails. Vegetables are always fresh and are passed around the table just like you do at home. Desserts are generously sized; the dreamy, creamy Baked Alaska can easily be shared with a whole table of ice cream lovers. **Features:** full bar. **Reservations:** suggested. **Address:** 2800 Opryland Dr 37214 **Location:** I-40 exit 215B or I-65 exit 90B; SR 155/Briley Pkwy, exit 11 (Music Valley Dr/McGavock Pike); in Gaylord Opryland Resort & Convention Center. **Parking:** on-site (fee) and valet. D CALL ♿M

THE OPRY BACKSTAGE GRILL
615/889-0800 ④

▼▼▼ Southern American. Casual Dining. $7-$30 **AAA Inspector Notes:** It's obvious the theme at this family-friendly restaurant is country music. Now add a down-home Southern menu and settle in for a knee-slappin' good time. A small stage welcomes singer-songwriters and the occasional singing waiter. **Features:** full bar, patio dining. **Reservations:** suggested, weekends. **Address:** 2401 Music Valley Dr 37212 **Location:** I-40 exit 215 (SR 155/N Briley Pkwy), just e; in The Inn at Opryland, A Gaylord Hotel. L D LATE CALL ♿M

(See map & index p. 200.)

PIZZEREAL   615/226-2206 ⑪

▼▼ Pizza. Casual Dining. $5-$21 **AAA Inspector Notes:** Locally designed artwork decorates the walls of the restaurant, where you can sample delicious Boston-style crusted pizza with many unique toppings. Options include specialty pies, such as the Tuscan garden or spinaci pizzas. A Greek salad makes for a fitting meal complement. **Features:** full bar, patio dining. **Address:** 203 N 11th St 37216 **Location:** I-24 exit 49 (Shelby Ave), 0.5 mi n on S 10th St, just e on Main St, 0.5 mi e on Ordway Pl, just n on 16th St, then just e; in 5 Points/East End. Ⓛ Ⓓ CALL 🅖Ⓜ

PRINCE'S HOT CHICKEN SHACK   615/226-9442 ③

▼ Chicken. Quick Serve. $5-$22 **AAA Inspector Notes:** This local landmark has been serving its special fried chicken for more than 70 years, attracting fans from around the world. Everything is cooked to order, so it takes some time. There are no fancy linens or silverware, but this is the place to go for juicy, crispy-skinned chicken that ranges from hot to blazing spicy. First-timers are smart to start with the mild chicken, which most folks find packs plenty of punch. For dessert, try one of the great homemade pies or cakes. **Address:** 123 Ewing Dr 37207 **Location:** I-65 exit 90A (US 31 W), 0.5 mi s on Dickerson Pike, then just w; in a small strip mall.

Ⓛ Ⓓ LATE

ROSEPEPPER CANTINA & MEXICAN GRILL
615/227-4777 ⑩

▼▼ Mexican. Casual Dining. $9-$24 **AAA Inspector Notes:** Eclectic décor helps define a fun, festive and lively atmosphere. Tasty food is served in huge portions. Tortilla chips are accompanied by a trio of salsas that range from mild to spicy. The sizzling fajitas are good for sharing. **Features:** full bar, patio dining, happy hour. **Address:** 1907 Eastland Ave 37206 **Location:** 2 mi ne on Gallatin Rd, 1.5 mi e. Ⓛ Ⓓ

SAL'S PIZZA & RESTAURANT   615/391-9994 ⑫

▼▼ Italian Pizza. Casual Dining. $6-$23 **AAA Inspector Notes:** Freshly made dough makes for a chewy and wonderful crust, and diners can add on some 20 different toppings. Pasta dishes include spaghetti and tomato sauce, fettuccine Alfredo, manicotti and baked ziti. A lunch buffet is available weekdays for those in a hurry. **Features:** beer only. **Address:** 710 Stewarts Ferry Pike 37214 **Location:** I-40 exit 219 (Stewarts Ferry Pike), just w. Ⓛ Ⓓ

SANTA FE CATTLE CO   615/885-7852 ②

▼▼ American. Casual Dining. $8-$30 **AAA Inspector Notes:** Country boys and city slickers alike can settle amid Southwestern décor to savor juicy, melt-in-your-mouth steaks. Rounding out the vittles is a huge salad with awesome chipotle dressing. Tin pails of peanuts tide guests over as they wait for their main courses, although one should be careful when walking through, as the shells that are abandoned on the floors provide an added rustic element to the surroundings. **Features:** full bar, happy hour. **Address:** 2520 Music Valley Dr 37214 **Location:** I-40 exit 215B (SR 155 N/Briley Pkwy), 5.3 mi n to exit 12 (McGavock Pike), just w to Music Valley Dr, then 0.5 mi n. Ⓛ Ⓓ

SPERRY'S RESTAURANT   615/353-0809 ㉕

▼ English Seafood Steak. Casual Dining. $18-$49 **AAA Inspector Notes:** Enjoying 40 years of business in 2014, this is where everybody goes to celebrate, host out-of-town guests, or when passing through. It's just that special. Favored by locals, it's always a full house, especially during happy hour. Come around often and you might find yourself greeted by name. Warm and welcoming, the atmosphere encourages you to stay and enjoy a perfect steak or scrumptious broiled lobster. The creamy white chocolate cheesecake will send your taste buds soaring. **Features:** full bar, happy hour. **Reservations:** suggested. **Address:** 5109 Harding Rd 37205 **Location:** 7 mi w on US 70 S. Ⓓ

SPORTSMAN'S GRILLE   615/356-6206 ㉗

▼▼ American. Casual Dining. $9-$22 **AAA Inspector Notes:** A local favorite since 1985, the restaurant has a rustic, lodge-style atmosphere, perfect for enjoying generous portions of traditional, homemade food. **Features:** full bar, patio dining, happy hour. **Address:** 5405 Harding Rd 37205 **Location:** Jct US 70/SR 100.

Ⓛ Ⓓ

STAX   615/458-6848 ㉛

▼▼ Burgers. Quick Serve. $5-$12 **AAA Inspector Notes:** A hearty or healthy burger (beef, turkey or veggie) is especially delicious when it's made exactly as you like, which is what you'll get here since the whole concept is that you design your own burger from bun to patty to toppings. A thick milk shake or cold beer will round out a fulfilling meal. **Features:** beer only, patio dining. **Address:** 2800 Opryland Dr 37214 **Location:** I-40 exit 215B or I-65 exit 90B; SR 155/Briley Pkwy exit 11 (Music Valley Dr/McGavock Pike). **Parking:** on-site and valet. Ⓛ Ⓓ CALL 🅖Ⓜ

TEN BAR & GRILLE   615/871-0033 ⑰

American
Casual Dining
$8-$40

AAA Inspector Notes: At times, a hotel lobby restaurant can be overlooked, but don't let that happen next time you stay anywhere near the Century Blvd. business complex. Enjoy delicious Southern-style fare while you dine between tall stone pillars just steps from the airy atrium lobby. Flat-screen TVs ensure you don't miss the news, game or weather. Tasty menu options include freshly ground meatloaf and mashed potatoes, entrée-size salads, brisket chili, chicken and waffles, and bourbon-glazed salmon. **Features:** full bar. **Address:** 10 Century Blvd 37214 **Location:** I-40 exit 215 northbound to exit 7 (Elm Hill Pike), 0.3 mi e to McGavock Pike, 0.3 mi s to Century Blvd, then 0.3 mi w; in Embassy Suites by Hilton Nashville Airport. Ⓛ Ⓓ CALL 🅖Ⓜ

NATCHEZ TRACE PARKWAY (E-2)

The Natchez Trace Parkway angles southwest to northeast for 444 miles across Mississippi, Alabama and Tennessee. The road commemorates the Old Natchez Trace, which began as a Native American footpath leading between the Chickasaw and Choctaw Nations. Later this path became a postal road and pioneer trail. Then known variously as Nashville Road, Natchez Road and Chickasaw Road, it was instrumental in linking the lower Mississippi and southern Ohio river valleys. The parkway extends from Natchez to just south of Nashville.

Wayside exhibits, self-guiding nature trails and interpretive signs highlight locations that tell the history of the parkway. Emerald Mound, said to be the second largest ceremonial mound in the country, is 11 miles northeast of Natchez, on a road about a mile off the parkway at Milepost 10.3. The visitor center in Tupelo, at Milepost 266, shows a 15-minute video and has displays about the Natchez Trace. It is open daily, 8-5. Closed Christmas. There are picnic areas at various points along the route.

For further information contact the Supervisor, Natchez Trace Parkway, 2680 Natchez Trace Pkwy., Tupelo, MS 38804; phone (662) 680-4025 or (800) 305-7417.

Note: Points of interest along the parkway are listed in Milepost order from south to north. Because it is often difficult to reach rangers at the individual sites, the most helpful phone numbers are the two listed above.

MERIWETHER LEWIS SITE is 7.5 mi. e. of Hohenwald, Tenn., at Milepost 385.9 of the 444-mile Natchez Trace Parkway. The 800-acre site is a tribute to the explorer, who, with Capt. William Clark, led the first expedition west across the Rocky Mountains to the Pacific Ocean. Lewis also served as governor of the Upper Louisiana Territory. An interpretive cabin has exhibits that tell the stories of his life and the Natchez Trace.

Within the park are streams, primitive campsites and 7 miles of hiking trails that traverse rolling hills.

In 1809, en route to Washington, D.C. along the Old Trace, Lewis died of gunshot wounds at Grinder's Inn. The cause of death has been debated; some say he was murdered, while most historians believe the wound was self-inflicted. He was buried at the site, and in 1848 the people of Tennessee erected a monument to the explorer that still stands. **Time:** Allow 30 minutes minimum. **Hours:** Grounds daily dawn-dusk. Interpretive cabin hours vary. Closed Christmas. Phone ahead to confirm schedule. **Cost:** Free. **Phone:** (800) 305-7417.

CHICKASAW VILLAGE SITE is n.w. of Tupelo, Miss., between US 78 and SR 6 at Milepost 261.8. The area was the location of a fortified Chickasaw Indian village. Foundation markers and interpretive panels explain the site. An exhibit shelter and audio station tell the story of the Chickasaw; a nature trail identifies some of the plants they used for food and medicine. **Time:** Allow 30 minutes minimum. **Hours:** Daily dawn-dusk. **Cost:** Free. **Phone:** (800) 305-7417.

MOUNT LOCUST is 15 mi. n.e. of Natchez, Miss., at Milepost 15.5. Built in 1779, the inn was a popular stop for travelers on the Natchez Trace in the mid-1800s. It now contains historical exhibits. Rangers give informative talks regarding Mount Locust, the Old Trace and its modern counterpart, the Natchez Trace Parkway. **Time:** Allow 1 hour minimum. **Hours:** Grounds and inn daily 9-4:30. Closed Christmas. **Cost:** Free. **Phone:** (800) 305-7417.

NEWPORT pop. 6,945

BEST WESTERN NEWPORT INN   (423)623-8713

Motel
$70-$170

AAA Benefit: Save 10% or more every day and earn 10% bonus points!

Address: 1015 Cosby Hwy 37821 **Location:** I-40 exit 435, just w. **Facility:** 109 units. 2 stories, exterior corridors. **Pool(s):** heated outdoor. **Activities:** hot tub, limited exercise equipment. **Guest Services:** valet and coin laundry.

CHRISTOPHER PLACE   (423)623-6555

Bed & Breakfast
$150-$330

Address: 1500 Pinnacles Way 37821 **Location:** I-40 exit 435, 2 mi s. on SR 32, 1.7 mi w on English Mountain Rd, then 0.8 mi nw. **Facility:** This quiet, secluded mountaintop estate offers spectacular views of the Great Smoky Mountains and is the perfect setting for a relaxed getaway. The splendid staff offers true Southern hospitality. 10 units. 3 stories, interior/exterior corridors. **Terms:** 2 night minimum stay - seasonal and/or weekends, age restrictions may apply, 14 day cancellation notice-fee imposed. **Pool(s):** heated outdoor. **Activities:** sauna, tennis, trails, exercise room. **Featured Amenity:** full hot breakfast.

COMFORT INN   (423)623-5355

Hotel
$55-$85

Address: 1149 Smokey Mountain Ln 37821 **Location:** I-40 exit 432B, just n. **Facility:** 51 units. 2 stories, interior corridors. **Pool(s):** outdoor. **Activities:** limited exercise equipment. **Guest Services:** coin laundry.

HOLIDAY INN EXPRESS & SUITES   (423)623-2121

Hotel $99-$149 **Address:** 1022 Cosby Hwy 37821 **Location:** I-40 exit 435, just s. **Facility:** 71 units. 4 stories, interior corridors. **Terms:** cancellation fee imposed. **Pool(s):** heated indoor. **Activities:** limited exercise equipment. **Guest Services:** valet and coin laundry.

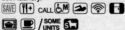

MOTEL 6 #4090   423/623-1850

Motel. Rates not provided. **Address:** 255 Heritage Blvd 37822 **Location:** I-40 exit 435, just n. **Facility:** 66 units, some two bedrooms and kitchens. 3 stories, interior corridors. **Pool(s):** heated outdoor. **Guest Services:** coin laundry.

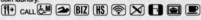

WHERE TO EAT

SAGEBRUSH STEAKHOUSE   423/613-4900

Steak. Casual Dining. $7-$19 **AAA Inspector Notes:** Born from the spirit of Texas cattle drives, the restaurant presents a menu of hearty steaks, prime rib, chicken, seafood and baby back ribs. Yummy desserts merit a splurge. Guests can call ahead to facilitate seating. **Features:** full bar, happy hour. **Address:** 201 Heritage Blvd 37821 **Location:** I-40 exit 435, just ne, then just s.

NORRIS (C-7) pop. 1,491, elev. 1,046'

Norris, founded in conjunction with the building of the Norris Dam, is owned and controlled by the Tennessee Valley Authority (TVA). In 1948 the entire town was sold to a Philadelphia company, which divided the lots and resold them as individual properties. The town and dam are named for Nebraska Sen. George W. Norris, co-sponsor of the bill that established the TVA.

LENOIR MUSEUM is 1 mi. s. of Norris Dam on US 441. The museum is in a wooded area with a small creek. Operated as part of Norris Dam State Park (see Recreation Areas Chart), the "touch museum" displays memorabilia collected from east Tennessee. An unusual mousetrap collection and a restored country store are featured. An 18th-century gristmill and threshing barn operate below the museum. Exhibits include rifles, fossils, pottery, bells, arrowheads, Confederate scrip and Civil War newspapers. **Hours:** Wed.-Sun. 9-5. Closed Thanksgiving and Christmas. **Cost:** Free. **Phone:** (865) 494-9688 or (865) 426-7461.

Turn your road trip dreams into reality with the TripTik® Travel Planner

OAK RIDGE (C-7) pop. 29,330, elev. 868'

A complete city built during World War II for workers of the Clinton Engineer Works (CEW), Oak Ridge is important for its part in the Manhattan Project, which resulted in the production of the first atomic bomb and the invention of the nuclear reactor. Until March 1949 access to the area was restricted, and some installations are still closed to the public. The city is the site of continued energy research, development and production sponsored by both government and private industry.

With a staff of approximately 4,400 researchers, the Oak Ridge National Laboratory (ORNL) performs research for the Department of Energy in areas such as neutron science, high-performance computing, additive manufacturing, new energy resources and national security. Public bus tours departing from the American Museum of Science and Energy *(see attraction listing)* include a tour of the ORNL's Graphite Reactor.

The East Tennessee Technology Park on SR 58 provides a view of the former Oak Ridge Gaseous Diffusion Plant, where uranium was enriched for use as fuel in nuclear reactors and nuclear weapons 1943-85. The plant now serves as a base of operations for the Oak Ridge Environmental Management Program. The Secret City Scenic Excursion Trains depart from the park for narrated tours through once-secret areas of Oak Ridge. Trains are pulled by 1950's era locomotives; phone (865) 241-2140.

In Alvin K. Bissell Park The Secret City Commemorative Walk, at the corner of S. Tulane Avenue and SR 95 (Oak Ridge Turnpike), features bronze plaques that recount the history of Oak Ridge and its World War II-era, top-secret government plants.

The International Friendship Bell, a tribute to Manhattan Project workers and a token of peace from Oak Ridge citizens to Hiroshima victims, stands off Badger Avenue in Bissell Park. Jackson Square Historic Park, a revitalization of the original government town site, contains restored buildings, specialty shops, historic displays and a small botanical garden.

A 2,000-meter flat-water regatta course on the Melton Hill area of the Clinch River is the site of rowing competitions each year. Walking, jogging, skating and bicycling can be enjoyed on a trail skirting Melton Lake.

Counterbalancing the sciences with the performing arts is the Oak Ridge Playhouse in Historic Jackson Square. Founded in 1943, this group recreates Broadway and off-Broadway favorites throughout the year; for schedule and ticket information phone (865) 482-9999.

Oak Ridge Convention and Visitors Bureau: 102 Robertsville Rd., Suite C, Oak Ridge, TN 37830. **Phone:** (865) 482-7821.

AMERICAN MUSEUM OF SCIENCE AND ENERGY is .5 mi. e. of SR 62 at 300 S. Tulane Ave. This museum houses exhibits that focus on the history of the World War II Manhattan Project and the construction of Oak Ridge; uses of fossil fuels and alternative energy sources; and an introduction to basic science and nuclear energy.

The self-guiding tour includes two levels to explore aspects of energy and science through live demonstrations, interactive exhibits, models and audiovisual materials. A 20-minute video presentation covers the history of Oak Ridge. On the grounds, an original flat-top house, one type of housing moved to town during a 1940s-era population boom, reflects period furnishings.

A guided 3-hour bus tour of the U.S. Department of Energy's Oak Ridge Facilities is offered and departs from the museum; stops include the Y-12 New Hope Visitor Center, New Bethel Baptist Church and Cemetery and the Graphite Reactor at the Oak Ridge National Laboratory. A photo ID is required and participants under 10 are not permitted.

Hours: Mon.-Sat. 9-5, Sun. 1-5. Bus tour offered Mon.-Fri. at noon, June-Aug.; reservations must be made in person on the day of the tour and are available on a first-come, first-served basis. Closed Jan. 1, Thanksgiving, Christmas Eve and Christmas. **Cost:** $5; $4 (ages 65+); $3 (ages 6-17). Bus tour included with admission. **Phone:** (865) 576-3200.

CHILDREN'S MUSEUM OF OAK RIDGE, 461 W. Outer Dr., offers hands-on exhibits focusing on art, history and science. Children can explore a life-size, two-story dollhouse, while a simulated rain forest features an observation deck, a waterfall and murals. Three reconstructed Appalachian log cabins, an environmental center and gardens also are onsite. Other galleries highlight model trains, puppets, early Oak Ridge history, the Tennessee River lock system, a tugboat and international cultures. Living Light, a zero-energy solar-powered house, is available for tours on a limited basis.

Time: Allow 1 hour minimum. **Hours:** Tues.-Fri. 9-5, Sat. 10-4, Sun. 1-4 (also Mon. 9-5, June-Aug). Solar-powered house third Sun. of the month 1-4. Holiday schedule varies; phone ahead. **Cost:** $9; $7 (ages 65+); $6 (ages 3-18). **Phone:** (865) 482-1074.

OAK RIDGE ART CENTER is at 201 Badger Ave. The center houses a permanent collection of modern and contemporary prints, paintings and sculpture as well as regional exhibits. Of special note is the Mary and Alden Gomez Painting and Sculpture Collection, which is periodically exhibited. Temporary exhibitions featuring works by national and regional artists also are offered. **Hours:** Tues.-Fri. 9-5, Sat.-Mon. 1-4. **Cost:** Donations. **Phone:** (865) 482-1441.

UNIVERSITY OF TENNESSEE ARBORETUM is 3 mi. s.e. on SR 62. With 250 acres, the arboretum presents more than 800 species of trees, shrubs and flowering plants threaded by more than seven miles of nature trails. Pines, magnolias, azaleas, dogwoods and hollies are some of the major collections. Special groupings feature flora from Asia, Europe and the western United States. Trail guides, displays, brochures and other publications are available at the visitor center. **Hours:** Trails daily 8-dusk. Visitor center Mon.-Fri. 8-noon and 1-4:30. Closed major holidays. **Cost:** Donations. **Phone:** (865) 483-3571.

DOUBLETREE BY HILTON HOTEL OAK RIDGE   (865)481-2468

▼▼▼▼ **Hotel** $84-$159 **Address:** 215 S Illinois Ave 37830 **Location:** 0.3 mi se of SR 95 on SR 62 (Oak Ridge Hwy). **Facility:** 167 units. 5 stories, interior corridors. **Terms:** 7 night minimum stay, cancellation fee imposed. **Pool(s):** heated outdoor, heated indoor. **Activities:** exercise room. **Guest Services:** valet laundry.

AAA Benefit:
Members save 5% or more!

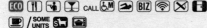

HAMPTON INN   (865)482-7889

▼▼▼ **Hotel** $104-$149 **Address:** 208 S Illinois Ave 37830 **Location:** 0.3 mi se of SR 95 on SR 62 (Oak Ridge Hwy). **Facility:** 60 units. 5 stories, interior corridors. **Terms:** 1-7 night minimum stay, cancellation fee imposed. **Pool(s):** heated indoor. **Activities:** sauna, hot tub, exercise room. **Guest Services:** valet and coin laundry.

AAA Benefit:
Members save up to 10%!

QUALITY INN   (865)483-6809

▼▼ **Hotel** $84-$89 **Address:** 216 S Rutgers Ave 37830 **Location:** Jct SR 95 and 62, 0.9 mi se on SR 62 (Oak Ridge Hwy) to Rutgers Ave, 0.7 mi n. **Facility:** 79 units. 3 stories, interior corridors. **Pool(s):** outdoor. **Activities:** exercise room.

STAYBRIDGE SUITES   865/298-0050

▼▼▼ **Extended Stay Hotel.** Rates not provided. **Address:** 420 S Illinois Ave 37830 **Location:** Jct Lafayette St and SR 62 (Oak Ridge Hwy). **Facility:** 90 efficiencies, some two bedrooms. 5 stories, interior corridors. **Pool(s):** heated indoor. **Activities:** exercise room. **Guest Services:** complimentary and valet laundry.

OCOEE (E-6) elev. 788'

RECREATIONAL ACTIVITIES
White-water Rafting

• **High Country Adventures** is .5 mi. e. of US 411 on US 64. **Hours:** Rafting trips are offered Thurs.-Mon., Memorial Day weekend-Labor Day; Sat.-Sun., early Apr.-day before Memorial Day weekend and day after Labor Day-early Nov. Dates and departure times vary depending on dam control; phone ahead. **Phone:** (423) 338-8634, or (800) 233-8594 for reservations and information.

• **Nantahala Outdoor Center-Ocoee Outpost** is just e. on US 64 from jct. US 411 at Horn's Creek Resort. Kayak trips and a zipline park also are available. **Hours:** Rafting trips are offered daily, Mar.-Oct. Phone ahead to confirm schedule. **Phone:** (828) 488-6900 for information, or (800) 232-7238 for reservations.

OOLTEWAH pop. 687

HAMPTON INN-CHATTANOOGA NORTH   (423)305-6800

▼▼▼▼ **Hotel** $99-$159 **Address:** 6145 Weir Way 37363 **Location:** I-75 exit 11, just e. **Facility:** 115 units. 5 stories, interior corridors. **Terms:** 1-7 night minimum stay, cancellation fee imposed. **Pool(s):** heated indoor. **Activities:** hot tub, limited exercise equipment. **Guest Services:** valet and coin laundry.

AAA Benefit:
Members save up to 10%!

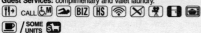

HOLIDAY INN EXPRESS & SUITES OOLTEWAH
SPRINGS-CHATTANOOGA   (423)591-8500

▼▼▼ **Hotel** $99-$159 **Address:** 6274 Artesian Cir 37363 **Location:** I-75 exit 11, just e. **Facility:** 102 units. 4 stories, interior corridors. **Terms:** cancellation fee imposed. **Pool(s):** heated indoor. **Activities:** hot tub, limited exercise equipment. **Guest Services:** valet and coin laundry.

SUPER 8   (423)238-5951

▼▼ **Motel** $50-$81 **Address:** 8934 Lee Hwy 37363 **Location:** I-75 exit 11, just w. **Facility:** 55 units. 1-2 stories (no elevator), exterior corridors.

WHERE TO EAT

EL MATADOR MEXICAN RESTAURANT   423/238-6655

▼▼ Tex-Mex. Casual Dining. $5-$17 **AAA Inspector Notes:** Tex-Mex favorites at this casual eatery include tacos, burritos, enchiladas and fajitas. Friendly servers dish up large portions in a colorful and festive atmosphere. **Features:** full bar, patio dining, happy hour. **Address:** 9203 Lee Hwy 37363 **Location:** I-75 exit 11, 0.3 mi e; in Bi-Lo Shopping Center. L D CALL &M

PARIS (C-3) pop. 10,156, elev. 474'
• Hotels p. 230 • Restaurants p. 230

Paris, named in honor of the French aid received during the American Revolution, was an antebellum trading center for the surrounding plantations. Today the town accommodates dozens of industrial plants and medical facilities. Two edifices are of note: The first is the 60-foot replica of its namesake's most recognizable structure, the Eiffel Tower, at the entrance to Memorial Park. The second is the 1896 Courthouse, the second oldest working courthouse in the state.

As a growing recreational center, Paris profits from its proximity to Paris Landing State Park *(see Recreation Areas Chart)* on Kentucky Lake. More than 5 tons of catfish are the basic ingredient of the World's Biggest Fish Fry, held the last full week in April at the Henry County Fairgrounds. Other activities at this event, which draws more than 100,000 from around the world, include parades, a rodeo, a catfish race, an arts and crafts show and a carnival.

Paris-Henry County Chamber of Commerce: 2508 E. Wood St., Paris, TN 38242. **Phone:** (731) 642-3431.

PARIS-HENRY COUNTY HERITAGE CENTER, 614 N. Poplar St., is housed in an Italian Renaissance Revival mansion built in 1916. The area's history is presented through such items as photographs, uniforms and weapons. **Hours:** Tues.-Fri. 10-4, Sat. 10-2; other dates and times by appointment. Closed Jan. 1-2, Nov. 26-28 and Dec. 24-31. Phone ahead to confirm schedule. **Cost:** Donations. **Phone:** (731) 642-1030.

TENNESSEE NATIONAL WILDLIFE REFUGE is composed of three separate units and is accessible by US 79, US 70, I-40, SR 69 and SR 100. The refuge encompasses 51,358 acres of land and water along Kentucky Lake; the headquarters is at 3006 Dinkins Ln. in Paris.

Established primarily for migratory ducks and geese, the refuge is frequented by more than 300 bird species, including hawks, herons and eagles. Bird-watching, fishing and hunting are popular. **Hours:** Public-use areas open daily 30 minutes before dawn-dusk. **Cost:** Free. **Phone:** (731) 642-2091.

QUALITY INN PARIS   (731)642-2838

▼▼ **Hotel** $75-$140 **Address:** 1510 E Wood St 38242 **Location:** Jct US 641, 2 mi n on US 79. **Facility:** 100 units, some kitchens. 2 stories (no elevator), exterior corridors. **Parking:** winter plug-ins. **Terms:** check-in 4 pm. **Pool(s):** outdoor. **Activities:** picnic facilities, exercise room. **Guest Services:** coin laundry.

⟦🛏⟧ CALL 🔊M ▲ BIZ 🛜 🔌 🍽 💻 / SOME UNITS 🐾

SUPER 8   (731)644-7008

▼▼ **Hotel** $58-$72 **Address:** 1309 E Wood St 38242 **Location:** Jct US 641, 1.5 mi n on US 79. **Facility:** 48 units. 2 stories (no elevator), interior/exterior corridors. **Parking:** winter plug-ins. **Pool(s):** heated indoor. **Activities:** hot tub. **Guest Services:** coin laundry.

⟦🛏⟧ ▲ BIZ 🛜 🔌 🍽 💻 / SOME UNITS 🔋

WHERE TO EAT

ACE'S PIZZA   731/644-0558

▼ Pizza. Casual Dining. $4-$14 **AAA Inspector Notes:** Enjoy freshly prepared pizza, either hand tossed or stuffed, as well as Italian beef sandwiches, Chicago-style hot dogs or huge burgers. Steaks, prime rib and some pasta dishes complete the menu. **Features:** beer only, happy hour. **Address:** 1516 E Wood St 38242 **Location:** Jct US 641, 2.1 mi n on US 79. ⟦L⟧ ⟦D⟧

FRESH MARKET RESTAURANT   731/644-1900

▼▼ American. Casual Dining. $6-$28 **AAA Inspector Notes:** This casual, family-friendly eatery offers a menu with something for everyone, from Alaskan king crab legs to chicken fajitas. House favorites include baby back ribs, prime rib, fried catfish and pork chops. A few Italian influenced entrées appear on the menu, including lasagna, pasta Alfredo and Parmesan chicken. Lighter appetites will enjoy the salads and sandwiches. **Features:** full bar. **Address:** 2255 E Wood St 38242 **Location:** Jct US 641, 3 mi n on US 79. ⟦D⟧

PIGEON FORGE (D-7) pop. 5,875, elev. 1,031'

• Hotels p. 232 • Restaurants p. 234
• Attractions map p. 100
• Hotels & Restaurants map & index p. 84
• Part of Great Smoky Mountains National Park area — see map p. 97

The roots of Pigeon Forge reach back to the late 1700s when travelers from the Carolinas followed the Great Indian Path through the Smoky Mountains to settle here. Isaac Love established an iron forge in 1820 and his son, William, built a tub mill 10 years later.

The "Pigeon" in Pigeon Forge derives from the ill-fated passenger pigeons that fed on the nuts of the beech trees along the banks of the river. The "Forge" came from the forge on the east bank of the river. The town was primarily a farming community until 1940, when the adjacent Great Smoky Mountains National Park, whose headquarters is 10 minutes away, was dedicated.

From early November through February, Pigeon Forge decorates itself with 5 million holiday lights during Winterfest. Also offered are lectures taught by nature experts, seminars and hikes in Great Smoky Mountains National Park, and cowboy performers celebrating the American West.

Pigeon Forge Department of Tourism: 1950 Parkway, P.O. Box 1390, Pigeon Forge, TN 37868. **Phone:** (865) 453-8574 or (800) 251-9100.

Shopping: Shopaholics swear by the factory outlet stores. They include The Shops of Pigeon Forge, Pigeon River Crossings and Pigeon Forge Factory Outlet Mall/Z-Buda Outlet. All are on or near the Parkway off US 441. Those looking for rock 'n' roll souvenirs stop by ⟦SAVE⟧ Hard Rock Cafe, 2050 Parkway.

Shopping can also be found in the area's entertainment complexes. Consider Christmas Place, The Island and Walden's Landing. The Old Mill, still an operational gristmill producing meal and flour daily at 175 Old Mill Ave., houses a complex of shops selling antiques, crafts, candy and gifts, and a general store; phone (865) 428-0771.

COMEDY BARN THEATER is at 2775 Parkway. The theater offers a family-friendly, country variety ensemble in which audience members are encouraged to participate. Barnyard animals, live music and clogging are included in this high-energy comedy show. **Time:** Allow 1 hour, 30 minutes minimum. **Hours:** Shows are offered daily at 5 and 8:15 p.m., May 30-Aug. 8; daily at 8:15 p.m. (with additional performances some Saturdays), rest of year. Phone ahead to confirm schedule. **Cost:** $29.95; $9.95 (ages 2-12). **Phone:** (865) 428-5222 or (800) 295-2844.

⟦GEM⟧ **DOLLY PARTON'S DIXIE STAMPEDE DINNER & SHOW** is 1 mi. n.e. on US 441 at 3849 Parkway. The program includes 32 horses, trick riders, music, comedy, dancers, singers and audience participation themed around a friendly North/South rivalry. It starts with traditional Smoky Mountain music in the nonalcoholic Dixie Belle Saloon.

The main show runs in a 35,000-square-foot arena and includes an aerial act, a 32-horse and rider performance and a four-course feast. A special holiday show, "Christmas at Dixie," runs mid-November through the first week of January. **Time:** Allow 2 hours, 30 minutes minimum. **Hours:** Daily at 6 p.m., mid-Mar. to Dec.; otherwise varies. Phone ahead to confirm schedule. **Cost:** $56-$61; $28-$34 (ages 4-11). Prices vary per show. Reservations are required. **Phone:** (865) 453-4400.

(See map & index p. 84.)

DOLLYWOOD is 1 mi. n.e. off US 441. The 150-acre theme park evokes the homespun fun and traditions of the Smoky Mountains. Conceived and operated by Dolly Parton, the Smoky Mountains family adventure offers craft demonstrations, award-winning entertainment, six seasonal festivals and more than 40 rides and attractions. The Wild Eagle steel wing coaster, the Thunderhead wooden coaster, SkyZip, a coal-fired steam train ride, the FireChaser Express coaster that launches passengers backwards and forwards, various water rides and a large aviary dedicated to eagles are popular.

The Southern Gospel Museum and Hall of Fame recounts the origins of Southern Gospel music and highlights its most influential songwriters and performers. Chasing Rainbows traces Dolly's rise to stardom. Thirty-five live performances take place daily.

Allow a full day. **Hours:** Park open daily 10-10, mid-June to early Aug.; otherwise varies late Mar. to mid-June and early Aug.-Jan. 2. **Cost:** Park $62; $57 (ages 60+); $49 (ages 4-11). SkyZip $39. Combination ticket is available with Dollywood's Splash Country. Prices may vary; phone ahead to confirm admission and schedule. **Parking:** $12. **Phone:** (865) 428-9488 or (800) 365-5996.

DOLLYWOOD'S SPLASH COUNTRY is 1.5 mi. n.e. off US 441 at 1020 Dollywood Ln. The 35-acre water park features speed slides, a four-story water coaster, a 7,500-square-foot leisure pool, three children's activity areas, a lazy river float ride, single and double tube slides, a white-water rafting adventure, corkscrew slides and a 25,000-square-foot wave pool. **Time:** Allow 2 hours minimum. **Hours:** Daily 10-7, mid-June to late July; daily 10-6, late May to mid-June and early to mid-Aug.; Sat.-Sun. 10-6, mid-Aug. through Labor Day. **Cost:** $47; $42 (ages 4-11 and 60+). Combination ticket is available with Dollywood. Prices may vary; phone ahead. **Parking:** $10. **Phone:** (865) 428-9488 or (800) 365-5996.

THE GRAND MAJESTIC THEATER, 2330 Parkway, features music-themed variety shows suitable for all ages. Performances include The Soul of Motown, highlighting the music of soul legends Sam Cooke, Stevie Wonder and Aretha Franklin. The Smith Family Dinner & Show features country, bluegrass and gospel music, comedy routines and celebrity impressions. An optional buffet dinner is served prior to most shows. Holiday shows and several other dinner and non-meal theme shows are presented.

Time: Allow 2 hours minimum. **Hours:** Showtimes vary; phone ahead. Closed Christmas. **Cost:** Smith Family show with dinner $37.95; $14.95 (ages 13-17); $9.95 (ages 0-12); free (one child ages 0-12 with paid adult). Show only $29.95; $9.95 (ages 13-17); $5 (ages 0-12); free (one child ages 0-12 with paid adult). Prices vary for other shows; phone ahead. Reservations are recommended. **Phone:** (865) 774-7777 or (865) 429-8100. 🍴

HATFIELD & MCCOY DINNER SHOW is at 119 Music Rd. The show presents a fictionalized account of one of the most well-known feuds in the country with singing, dancing and joking around elaborate sets and music. During the pre-show, a home-style meal is served.

Time: Allow 2 hours minimum. **Hours:** Shows are given daily at 5 and 8 p.m., mid-Mar. through Jan. 3; Sun.-Fri. at 6 p.m., Jan. 4 through mid-Mar. Additional performances are offered; phone ahead. **Cost:** $54.95; $19.95 (ages 0-11). Reservations are required. **Phone:** (865) 908-7469 or (800) 985-5494. 🍴

MEMORIES THEATRE is at 2141 Parkway. This tribute show features artist impersonations of great performers, both past and present. In addition to Elvis, music legends showcased include Kenny Rogers, Cher, Kenny Chesney, Jerry Lee Lewis, the Blues Brothers and many more, according to a rotating schedule.

Time: Allow 2 hours, 30 minutes minimum. **Hours:** Shows are offered Tues.-Sat. at 7:30 p.m., May-Oct.; Tues. and Thurs.-Sat. at 7:30 p.m., in Apr. and Nov.-Dec.; Sat.-Sun. at 7:30 p.m., in Mar. Closed major holidays. **Cost:** $29; $24.50 (ages 55+); $20 (ages 13-19); $5 (ages 6-12). Prices and schedule may vary; phone ahead. Reservations are recommended. **Phone:** (865) 428-7852 or (800) 325-3078. 🍴

SMOKY MOUNTAIN OPRY, 2046 Parkway, presents a family-friendly variety show featuring dancing, singing, comedy, magic and all sorts of musical styles from Broadway hits to big band classics. Special effects include lasers, aerial acrobatics and pyrotechnics. A Christmas performance is offered. **Hours:** Shows are offered daily at 8 p.m., mid-Feb. to late Oct. (also Wed. at 3, mid-Mar. to late Oct.). Christmas show offered daily at 8 p.m. (also Sun.-Mon. and Fri. at 3), Nov.-Dec. Phone ahead to confirm schedule. **Cost:** $44.95; $19.95 (ages 3-11). **Phone:** (865) 429-7469 or (800) 768-1170.

TITANIC PIGEON FORGE is at 2134 Parkway. The museum strives to tell the story of the *Titanic* in a historically accurate manner, re-creating the vessel's atmosphere with some 20 interactive exhibit galleries. The building is half-scale to the original ship and contains a full-size scale model of the famous grand staircase. Visitors can see hundreds of artifacts from the disaster as well as letters, photographs and other articles on loan from survivors' families.

Time: Allow 2 hours minimum. **Hours:** Open daily. Hours vary; phone ahead to confirm schedule. Closed Christmas. **Cost:** $27; $12.50 (ages 5-12); $70 (family). Reservations are recommended. **Phone:** (800) 381-7670. 💳

WONDERWORKS, 100 Music Rd., has an exterior that makes the building appear to be upside down. It features more than 100 interactive and engaging science-related exhibits, including an earthquake

(See map & index p. 84.)

experience, a space exploration zone, a bubble lab, a 50-foot indoor ropes challenge course and a virtual roller coaster ride. A laser tag maze and an arcade also are available. "The Wonders of Magic" amazes in the evening.

Note: Some activities have height and weight restrictions and may require closed-toe shoes; phone ahead for specific details. **Time:** Allow 3 hours minimum. **Hours:** Daily 9 a.m.-10 p.m. Phone ahead to confirm schedule. **Cost:** $24.99; $16.99 (ages 4-12 and 55+). Combination admission (includes one laser tag game) $27.99; $19.99 (ages 4-12 and 55+). Under age 5 not admitted to laser tag. Wonders of Magic $17.99. **Phone:** (865) 868-1800. ⒯

RECREATIONAL ACTIVITIES
Ziplines
- **Smoky Mountain Ziplines** is at 509 Mill Creek Rd. **Hours:** Open daily (weather permitting). Hours vary; phone ahead. **Phone:** (865) 429-9004.

WINERIES
- **Mountain Valley Vineyards** is on US 441 at 2174 Parkway. **Hours:** Sun.-Thurs. 9-8, Fri.-Sat. 9-9, rest of year. **Phone:** (865) 453-6334 or (866) 453-6334. ⒼⓉ

ACCOMMODATIONS BY WILLOW BROOK LODGE
865/453-5334 ⓳

▼▼ **Motel** $49-$260 **Address:** 3035 Parkway 37863 **Location:** On US 441, between traffic lights 4 and 5. **Facility:** 156 units, some two bedrooms and condominiums. 5 stories, exterior corridors. **Terms:** cancellation fee imposed. **Pool(s):** heated outdoor, heated indoor. **Activities:** hot tub. **Guest Services:** coin laundry.

ALL SEASON SUITES   865/908-3011 ㉖

▼▼ **Hotel.** Rates not provided. **Address:** 239 Dollywood Ln 37863 **Location:** On US 441, just e at traffic light 8. **Facility:** 53 efficiencies, some two bedrooms. 2 stories, interior corridors. **Amenities:** safes. **Pool(s):** heated outdoor. **Activities:** hot tub, game room, exercise room. **Guest Services:** coin laundry.

BEAR CREEK CROSSING BY EDEN CREST VACATION
RENTALS   865/774-0059 ㉓

▼▼ **Vacation Rental Cabin** $100-$2500 **Address:** 652 Wears Valley Rd 37863 **Location:** Jct US 441, 1 mi s on US 321 at traffic light 3. **Facility:** Guests will find this a great way to relax and enjoy nature in the Smoky Mountains. Cabins vary in size, quality and amenities included. 37 cabins. 1-4 stories (no elevator), exterior corridors. **Terms:** off-site registration, check-in 4 pm, 2 night minimum stay - seasonal and/or weekends, 120 day cancellation notice-fee imposed, resort fee. **Pool(s):** outdoor, heated indoor. **Activities:** hot tub, miniature golf. **Guest Services:** complimentary laundry.

BERRY SPRINGS LODGE   (865)908-7935 ❶

▼▼ **Bed & Breakfast** $205-$245 **Address:** 2149 Seaton Springs Rd 37862 **Location:** Jct US 441, 2.3 mi e on Teaster Ln, 2.1 mi ne on Veterans Blvd, 1.6 mi e on Jayell Rd, 0.5 mi s on McCarter Hollow Rd, then just e. **Facility:** The lodge, with its hilltop setting, offers contemporary rooms with sweeping views of the surrounding countryside. Binoculars are provided for guests. 11 units, some cabins. 2 stories (no elevator), interior/exterior corridors. **Terms:** closed 1/1-1/31, 2 night minimum stay - seasonal and/or weekends, 14 day cancellation notice. **Activities:** fishing, bicycles, limited exercise equipment.

BEST WESTERN PLAZA INN   (865)453-5538 ㉗

Hotel
$51-$162

 AAA Benefit: Save 10% or more every day and earn 10% bonus points!

Address: 3755 Parkway 37863 **Location:** On US 441, just s of traffic light 8. **Facility:** 201 units, some efficiencies. 3-5 stories, interior/exterior corridors. **Terms:** check-in 4 pm. **Pool(s):** heated outdoor, heated indoor. **Activities:** hot tub. **Guest Services:** coin laundry.

BEST WESTERN TONI INN   (865)453-9058 ㉙

Motel
$52-$172

 AAA Benefit: Save 10% or more every day and earn 10% bonus points!

Address: 3810 Parkway 37863 **Location:** On US 441, between traffic lights 8 and 10. **Facility:** 115 units. 3 stories, interior/exterior corridors. **Pool(s):** heated outdoor, heated indoor. **Activities:** hot tub. **Guest Services:** coin laundry. **Featured Amenity:** continental breakfast.

BLACK BEAR RIDGE BY EDEN CREST VACATION RENTALS
865/774-0059 ㉒

▼▼▼ **Vacation Rental Cabin.** Rates not provided. **Address:** 652 Wears Valley Rd 37863 **Location:** Jct US 441, 1 mi s on US 321 at traffic light 3. **Facility:** Guests will find this a great way to relax and enjoy nature in the Smoky Mountains. Cabins vary in size, quality and amenities included. 14 cabins, some three bedrooms. 1-3 stories (no elevator), interior corridors. **Terms:** off-site registration, check-in 4 pm. **Pool(s):** outdoor. **Activities:** hot tub. **Guest Services:** complimentary laundry.

CLARION INN PIGEON FORGE   (865)868-5300 ⓯

Hotel
$79-$140

Address: 124 Waldens Main St 37863 **Location:** Jct US 441, just s on US 321, just nw on McGill St, then just ne. **Facility:** 93 units. 6 stories, interior corridors. **Terms:** check-in 4 pm. **Amenities:** safes. **Pool(s):** heated indoor. **Activities:** hot tub, game room, exercise room, spa. **Guest Services:** valet and coin laundry. **Featured Amenity:** full hot breakfast.

COMFORT SUITES PIGEON FORGE   (865)429-3700 ❽

▼▼▼ **Hotel** $89-$250 **Address:** 2423 Teaster Ln 37863 **Location:** Jct US 441, just e at traffic light 2. **Facility:** 76 units. 7 stories, interior corridors. **Terms:** check-in 4 pm. **Pool(s):** outdoor, heated indoor. **Activities:** hot tub, game room, exercise room. **Guest Services:** coin laundry.

COUNTRY CASCADES   865/428-1194 ⓲

▼▼ **Hotel.** Rates not provided. **Address:** 204 Sharon Dr 37863 **Location:** Jct US 441, just w on Wears Valley Rd at traffic light 3, then 0.4 mi s on Florence Dr. **Facility:** 138 units. 7 stories, interior corridors. **Amenities:** safes. **Pool(s):** outdoor, heated indoor. **Activities:** hot tub, limited exercise equipment. **Guest Services:** coin laundry.

(See map & index p. 84.)

ECONO LODGE RIVERSIDE
(865)428-1231 **9**

Hotel
$49-$129

Address: 2440 Parkway 37863 **Location:** On US 441, just n of traffic light 2B. **Facility:** 201 units. 3 stories, exterior corridors. **Terms:** check-in 4 pm. **Pool(s):** heated indoor. **Activities:** hot tub, game room. **Guest Services:** coin laundry. **Featured Amenity:** full hot breakfast.

SAVE [YI+] CALL [&M] [2e] [BIZ] [⊚]
[X] [I] [🛏] [▭] [▱]

HAMPTON INN & SUITES
(865)428-1600 **2**

Hotel $99-$209 **Address:** 2025 Parkway 37863 **Location:** S on US 441, at traffic light 0. **Facility:** 100 units, some efficiencies. 6 stories, interior corridors. **Terms:** check-in 4 pm, 1-7 night minimum stay, cancellation fee imposed. **Pool(s):** heated outdoor. **Activities:** exercise room. **Guest Services:** coin laundry.

AAA Benefit: Members save up to 10%!

[YI+] CALL [&M] [2e] [BIZ] [⊚] [X] [I] [🛏] [▱]
/ SOME UNITS [🐾]

HAMPTON INN PIGEON FORGE
(865)365-1588 **17**

Hotel $99-$239 **Address:** 2497 Teaster Ln 37863 **Location:** S on SR 66 to US 441, just s; at traffic light 2. **Facility:** 122 units. 5 stories, interior corridors. **Terms:** check-in 4 pm, 1-7 night minimum stay, cancellation fee imposed. **Pool(s):** heated outdoor, heated indoor. **Activities:** hot tub, exercise room. **Guest Services:** valet and coin laundry.

AAA Benefit: Members save up to 10%!

[YI+] CALL [&M] [2e] [BIZ] [HS] [⊚] [X] [I] [🛏] [▱]

HOLIDAY INN EXPRESS HOTEL & SUITES
(865)428-8600 **5**

Hotel $69-$189 **Address:** 308 Henderson Chapel Rd 37863 **Location:** Jct US 441, just w at traffic light 1. **Facility:** 105 units. 5 stories, interior corridors. **Terms:** check-in 4 pm, cancellation fee imposed. **Pool(s):** heated indoor. **Activities:** hot tub, game room. **Guest Services:** valet and coin laundry.

[YI+] CALL [&M] [2e] [🛗] [BIZ] [⊚] [X] [I] [🛏] [▱]

HOLIDAY INN HOTEL & CONVENTION CENTER
(865)428-2700 **24**

Hotel $74-$220 **Address:** 3230 Parkway 37863 **Location:** On US 441, between traffic lights 6 and 7. **Facility:** 206 units, some two bedrooms. 5 stories, interior corridors. **Terms:** check-in 4 pm, cancellation fee imposed. **Pool(s):** heated indoor. **Activities:** hot tub, game room, exercise room. **Guest Services:** valet and coin laundry.

[YI] [🛋] CALL [&M] [2e] [BIZ] [HS] [⊚] [X] [I] [🛏]
[▱]

THE INN AT CHRISTMAS PLACE
(865)868-0525 **11**

Classic Resort Hotel
$89-$429

Address: 119 Christmas Tree Ln 37863 **Location:** I-40 exit 407, s on SR 66 to US 441, then just s, at traffic light 2. **Facility:** The Christmas-inspired theme is carried throughout every area of this European-style village lodge. Beautiful holiday décor is incorporated into every guest room. Enjoy Christmas 365 days a year. 145 units, some kitchens. 5 stories, interior corridors. **Terms:** check-in 4 pm, 3 day cancellation notice-fee imposed. **Amenities:** safes. **Pool(s):** heated outdoor, heated indoor. **Activities:** hot tub, game room, exercise room. **Guest Services:** valet and coin laundry.

SAVE [◀] [YI+] CALL [&M] [2e] [BIZ] [HS] [⊚] [X] [I]
[▭] [▱]

THE INN at Christmas Place

Come experience Old World charm and elegance in the Smoky Mountains at The Inn at Christmas Place!

THE INN ON THE RIVER
(865)428-5500 **12**

Hotel $79-$219 **Address:** 2492 Parkway 37863 **Location:** Between traffic lights 2A and 2B. **Facility:** 128 units. 3-4 stories, interior corridors. **Parking:** winter plug-ins. **Terms:** cancellation fee imposed. **Pool(s):** heated outdoor, heated indoor. **Activities:** hot tub.

[YI+] CALL [&M] [2e] [BIZ] [⊚] [X] [I] [▭] [▱] / SOME UNITS [🛏]

LA QUINTA INN & SUITES
(865)908-6633 **13**

Hotel
$64-$268

Address: 125 Community Center Dr 37863 **Location:** Jct US 441, just w at traffic light 2B. **Facility:** 81 units. 5 stories, interior corridors. **Pool(s):** heated indoor. **Activities:** hot tub, exercise room. **Guest Services:** coin laundry. **Featured Amenity:** full hot breakfast.

SAVE [YI+] CALL [&M] [2e] [BIZ] [⊚]
[X] [I] [🛏] [▱] / SOME UNITS [🐾]

MICROTEL INN & SUITES BY WYNDHAM
(865)453-1116 **3**

Hotel $45-$120 **Address:** 2045 Parkway 37863 **Location:** On US 441, just s of traffic light 0. **Facility:** 71 units. 4 stories, interior corridors. **Amenities:** safes. **Pool(s):** outdoor. **Guest Services:** coin laundry.

[YI+] CALL [&M] [2e] [⊚] [X] [I] [🛏] [▱] / SOME UNITS [🐾]

(See map & index p. 84.)

MUSIC ROAD INN (865)429-8803 [7]

▼▼▼ **Hotel** $89-$209 **Address:** 314 Henderson Chapel Rd 37863 **Location:** Jct US 441, just w at traffic light 1. **Facility:** 140 units, some kitchens. 5 stories, interior corridors. **Terms:** check-in 4 pm, 3 day cancellation notice-fee imposed. **Pool(s):** heated outdoor, heated indoor. **Activities:** hot tub, game room, exercise room. **Guest Services:** valet and coin laundry.

MUSIC ROAD RESORT HOTEL & CONVENTION CENTER (865)429-7700 [6]

▼▼▼ Hotel $89-$199

Address: 303 Henderson Chapel Rd 37863 **Location:** Jct US 441, just w at traffic light 1. **Facility:** 163 units, some two bedrooms. 7 stories, interior corridors. **Terms:** check-in 4 pm, 3 day cancellation notice-fee imposed. **Pool(s):** heated outdoor, heated indoor. **Activities:** hot tub, game room, massage. **Guest Services:** valet and coin laundry. **Featured Amenity:** full hot breakfast.

RAMADA PIGEON FORGE NORTH (865)428-0668 [4]

▼▼ Hotel $50-$200

Address: 2193 Parkway 37863 **Location:** On US 441, just n of traffic light 1. **Facility:** 130 units. 3 stories, interior corridors. **Pool(s):** heated indoor. **Activities:** sauna, hot tub, limited exercise equipment. **Guest Services:** valet laundry. **Featured Amenity:** continental breakfast.

RIVERSTONE RESORT & SPA (865)908-0660 [25]

▼▼▼ Vacation Rental Condominium $110-$479

Address: 212 Dollywood Ln 37863 **Location:** Jct US 441, just e at traffic light 8. **Facility:** This luxury condo complex offers upscale décor and floor plans that are incredibly spacious; ranging from one to four bedrooms. The outdoor pool and lazy river are open April through October. 128 condominiums. 6 stories, exterior corridors. **Terms:** check-in 4 pm, 7 day cancellation notice-fee imposed, resort fee. **Pool(s):** outdoor, heated indoor. **Activities:** hot tub, fishing, playground, game room, exercise room, spa. **Guest Services:** complimentary laundry.

SHULAR INN (865)453-2700 [16]

▼ **Hotel** $60-$220 **Address:** 2708 Parkway 37863 **Location:** Between traffic lights 3 and 4. **Facility:** 198 units, some efficiencies. 4-5 stories, interior/exterior corridors. **Terms:** check-in 4 pm, cancellation fee imposed. **Pool(s):** outdoor, heated indoor. **Activities:** sauna, hot tub, limited exercise equipment. **Guest Services:** coin laundry.

SMOKY COVE BY EDEN CREST VACATION RENTALS 865/774-0059 [21]

▼▼▼ Vacation Rental Cabin. Rates not provided. **Address:** 652 Wears Valley Rd 37863 **Location:** Jct US 441, 1 mi s on US 321 at traffic light 3. **Facility:** Guests will find this a great way to relax and enjoy nature in the Smoky Mountains. Cabins vary in size, quality and amenities included. 7 cabins. 1-3 stories, exterior corridors. **Terms:** off-site registration, check-in 4 pm. **Pool(s):** outdoor. **Activities:** hot tub. **Guest Services:** complimentary laundry.

SPRINGHILL SUITES BY MARRIOTT (865)453-4514 [10]

▼▼▼ **Hotel** $83-$194 **Address:** 120 Christmas Tree Ln 37863 **Location:** Jct US 441, just e at traffic light 2. **Facility:** 112 units. 5 stories, interior corridors. **Terms:** check-in 4 pm. **Pool(s):** heated outdoor, heated indoor. **Activities:** hot tub, exercise room. **Guest Services:** valet and coin laundry.

AAA Benefit: Members save 5% or more!

SUPER 8 MOTEL PIGEON FORGE NEAR THE CONVENTION CENTER (865)453-2999 [20]

▼ **Motel** $45-$171 **Address:** 114 Pickel St 37863 **Location:** On US 441, between traffic lights 4 and 5. **Facility:** 75 units. 4 stories, interior corridors. **Pool(s):** heated indoor.

TIMBERS LODGE 865/428-5216 [14]

▼▼ **Motel.** Rates not provided. **Address:** 134 Wears Valley Rd E 37863 **Location:** Jct US 441, just e at traffic light 3. **Facility:** 52 units. 2-3 stories, exterior corridors. **Pool(s):** outdoor.

TWIN MOUNTAIN INN II 865/453-4444 [28]

▼▼ **Hotel.** Rates not provided. **Address:** 3929 S River Rd 37863 **Location:** Jct US 441, just e on Dollywood Ln at traffic light 8, then just s. **Facility:** 50 units. 5 stories, exterior corridors. **Pool(s):** outdoor.

WHERE TO EAT

ALAMO STEAKHOUSE 865/908-9998 [8]

▼▼▼ Steak Seafood Casual Dining $7-$29

AAA Inspector Notes: Pardners check their sidearms at the door before moseying into the Wild West-themed restaurant for some vittles. The house specialty is Black Angus steak grilled over an oak fire. The seafood offerings are plentiful and include baked grouper, salmon and mountain trout, as well as grilled lobster and numerous shrimp dishes. **Features:** full bar. **Address:** 3050 Parkway 37863 **Location:** On US 441, just n of traffic light 5. *Menu on AAA.com*

BENNETT'S PIT BAR-B-QUE 865/429-2200 [6]

▼▼ Barbecue Sandwiches Casual Dining $7-$23

AAA Inspector Notes: Ribs, beef brisket and chicken are smoked over a wood fire to create this casual eatery's popular dishes. Other highlights include wings, burgers and sandwiches. The 40-item soup and salad bar is a meal in itself. At breakfast, the salad bar is converted into a breakfast buffet full of good eats to start the day off right. **Features:** beer only, patio dining. **Address:** 2910 Parkway 37862 **Location:** On US 441, between traffic lights 4 and 5. *Menu on AAA.com*

BIG DADDY'S PIZZERIA 865/429-7171 [7]

▼▼ Pizza Family Dining $9-$22

AAA Inspector Notes: The specialty of the house is hand-tossed pizza baked in a wood-fired brick oven, available in a variety of flavors ranging from the unusual (a Cuban with roast pork, ham, black beans and pickles) to the traditional (Margherita with fresh mozzarella and Roma tomatoes). Build-your-own pies are an option, too. For lighter appetites, the menu offers a few salads and sandwiches. **Features:** beer & wine, patio dining. **Address:** 3053 Parkway 37862 **Location:** On US 441, between traffic lights 4 and 5. *Menu on AAA.com*

(See map & index p. 84.)

BLUE MOOSE BURGERS & WINGS 865/286-0364 2
Wings Burgers. Casual Dining. $6-$10 **AAA Inspector Notes:** Burgers, wings and dogs as well as favorite brews are a great start while watching favorite games on the numerous TVs set up throughout this high energy restaurant. **Features:** beer only, patio dining, happy hour. **Address:** 2430 Teaster Ln 37863 **Location:** US 441, just e of traffic light 2; in Teaster Center.

L D LATE CALL &M

BULLFISH GRILL 865/868-1000 3
American. Casual Dining. $10-$25 **AAA Inspector Notes:** Just as the name implies, it's all about meat, fish, and chicken, too. From its big salads and pastas to its entrées and desserts, there's something on the menu for the whole family. **Features:** full bar, patio dining, Sunday brunch, happy hour. **Address:** 2441 Parkway 37863 **Location:** US 441, just n of traffic light 2B. L D CALL &M

CALHOUN'S ON THE RIVER 865/868-1500
Regional American. Casual Dining. $9-$24 **AAA Inspector Notes:** Wrap yourself in genuine Southern hospitality from the minute you walk in the door. The decor is modern and upscale, and the service fast and friendly. The place has wonderful ribs, but it's hard to go wrong with the white bean chili either. **Features:** full bar. **Address:** 2532 Parkway 37863 **Location:** Between traffic lights 2B and 3; in Walden's Landing Shopping Center.

L D CALL &M

CORKY'S RIBS & BBQ 865/453-7427
Barbecue. Casual Dining. $8-$28 **AAA Inspector Notes:** Diners can feast on hickory-smoked ribs, chicken, brisket and sausages, which are served with all the favorite sides like baked beans, sweet potato fries and slaw. **Features:** beer only. **Address:** 3584 Parkway 37863 **Location:** On US 441, just s of traffic light 7.

L D

HARD ROCK CAFE 865/430-7625 1
American. Casual Dining. $12-$24 **AAA Inspector Notes:** Rock 'n' roll memorabilia decorates the walls of the popular theme restaurant. Live music on the weekends contributes to the bustling atmosphere. On the menu is a wide variety of American cuisine—from burgers and sandwiches to seafood, steaks and pasta. **Features:** full bar. **Address:** 2050 Parkway 37863 **Location:** On US 441, between Wonderworks and Smoky Mountain Opry. **Parking:** on-site (fee).

SAVE L D LATE

HUCK FINN'S RESTAURANT 865/429-3353 13
American. Family Dining. $8-$20 **AAA Inspector Notes:** Good ol' down-home Southern cooking, and lots of it, is what you'll find on the menu. All entrées are served with the traditional trimmings--hushpuppies, coleslaw, hot apples and pickles. Try the house-specialty catfish. And save room for the warm fruit cobbler. **Address:** 3330 Parkway 37863 **Location:** Just s of traffic light 6.

L D

J. T. HANNAH'S KITCHEN 865/428-4200 11
American. Casual Dining. $8-$17 **AAA Inspector Notes:** J.T., a prosperous businessman in the Great Smoky Mountains, operated the largest freight warehouse and stockyards in East Tennessee. Over time, he became a popular restaurateur and the tradition lives on here. The décor is reminiscent of the warehouse roots, while the meats and seafoods continue to be the popular draws. **Features:** full bar. **Address:** 3214 Parkway 37863 **Location:** Just s of traffic light 6. L D CALL &M

MAMA'S FARMHOUSE 865/908-4646 9
Traditional Southern Family Dining $15-$18

AAA Inspector Notes: All-you-can-eat, family-style Southern cookin' sums it up at this farmhouse-style restaurant. A set menu of meats and veggies varies daily, with fried chicken always offered. Biscuits, cornbread and two desserts complete the feast. Kids 5 and under eat free. **Address:** 208 Pickel St 37862 **Location:** On US 441, just w, between traffic lights 4 and 5.

Menu on AAA.com B L D CALL &M

THE OLD MILL RESTAURANT 865/429-3463 12
Southern. Casual Dining. $7-$23 **AAA Inspector Notes:** You won't leave hungry after dining at this rustic eatery adjacent to an old grist mill that still grinds the flour and cornmeal used in many recipes. Every entrée includes a cup of their signature corn chowder, and at dinner the feast also includes a house salad and choice of homemade dessert, like pecan pie or banana pudding. Enjoy Southern fried favorites, plus homey classics like meatloaf, ribs, and chicken and dumplings. **Address:** 164 Old Mill Ave 37863 **Location:** On Jct US 441, just e at traffic light 7.

B L D CALL &M

POYNOR'S POMMES FRITES 865/774-7744 5
German. Quick Serve. $5-$8 **AAA Inspector Notes:** Reminiscent of authentic German street vendors, this quick-serve place has specialty bratwurst, homemade brochen (hard rolls), thick-cut potatoes cooked using the double-fry method (makes for a crunchy exterior and creamy inside) and spaghetti ice cream. There's limited seating, so consider ordering from the grab-n-go menu, then walking around The Island while dunking your fries in a special sauce. **Features:** patio dining. **Address:** 131 The Island Dr, Suite 3107 37863 **Location:** On US 441; between traffic lights 3 and 4, just e. **Parking:** street only.

L D CALL &M

RED ROOSTER PANCAKE HOUSE 865/428-3322 10
Breakfast Sandwiches. Family Dining. $5-$12 **AAA Inspector Notes:** This eatery offers huge portions of innovative breakfast items from a large menu. Friendly servers dish up such items as specialty pancakes, eggs, waffles and burritos. A lunch and kids' menu also are featured. **Address:** 3215 Parkway 37863 **Location:** On US 441, just s of traffic light 6. B L CALL &M

SMOKY MOUNTAIN BREWERY 865/868-1400 4
American. Gastropub. $8-$23 **AAA Inspector Notes:** The dining room affords a view of the brew kettles, where the staff prepare small batches of beer ranging from pilsners to porters. The expansive menu offers wings, burgers, pizzas and calzones. **Features:** full bar, patio dining, happy hour. **Address:** 2530 Parkway 37863 **Location:** Between traffic lights 2B and 3; in Walden's Landing Shopping Center. L D LATE CALL &M

NO WAY JOSE CANTINA & IRON BOAR SALOON 865/429-7779
fyi Not evaluated. This Mexican restaurant dishes up traditional, Baja-inspired favorites. **Address:** 104 Walden's Main St 37863

PINEY FLATS (C-9)

ROCKY MOUNT is s.w. on US 11E to 200 Hyder Hill Rd. The log farmhouse served as the capitol of the Territory of the United States South of the Ohio River when President George Washington appointed William Blount as the territorial governor in 1790. The site was Blount's center for state affairs until a new capitol was built at Knoxville in 1792.

Rocky Mount, built 1770-72, has been restored to its original appearance. Costumed guides portray members of the Cobb family, who first settled in Rocky Mount, and conduct living-history tours explaining the many original furnishings in the main building; they also demonstrate pioneer crafts and skills in the kitchen, weaving cabin, barn and blacksmith shop.

A museum and visitor center depicts the history of eastern Tennessee, with emphasis on the period 1763-92. **Hours:** Guided tours Tues.-Sat. 11-5, early Mar. to mid-Dec.; by appointment rest of year. Closed Labor Day and Thanksgiving. **Cost:** $8; $7 (ages 55+); $5 (ages 5-17). **Phone:** (423) 538-7396 or (888) 538-1791. GT

PINSON (D-2) elev. 380'

PINSON MOUNDS STATE ARCHAEOLOGICAL AREA is n. on US 45, then 2.5 mi. e. to 460 Ozier Rd. The site, used by Native Americans for ceremonial purposes, is considered one of the largest Middle Woodland-period mound groups in the United States. The 1,162-acre area has about 15 mounds, crematory areas, fields and a forest with wildflowers, creeks, trails, picnic areas and a nursery.

A museum, housed in a mound replica, contains park offices, exhibits, an archeological library and a theater. **Time:** Allow 1 hour minimum. **Hours:** Grounds open daily 8-dusk. Museum open Mon.-Sat. 8-4:30, Sun. 1-4:30, Mar.-Sept.; Mon.-Sat. 8-4:30, Sun. 1-5, rest of year. Closed Jan. 1, Easter, Thanksgiving and Christmas. **Cost:** Donations. **Phone:** (731) 988-5614.

PIONEER

COMFORT INN   (423)566-4400

▼▼ **Hotel** $89-$139 **Address:** 335 Howard Baker Hwy 37847 **Location:** I-75 exit 141, just w. **Facility:** 62 units. 2 stories, interior corridors. **Pool(s):** heated outdoor.

PORTLAND pop. 11,480

COMFORT SUITES   (615)325-8887

▼▼▼ **Hotel** $90-$139 **Address:** 9239 Hwy 52 37148 **Location:** I-65 exit 117, just e. **Facility:** 60 units. 3 stories, interior corridors. **Dining:** Brewster's Bar & Grille, see separate listing. **Pool(s):** heated indoor. **Activities:** exercise room. **Guest Services:** coin laundry.

WHERE TO EAT

BREWSTER'S BAR & GRILLE   615/325-8873

▼▼ American. Casual Dining. $7-$16 **AAA Inspector Notes:** This sports bar is a great place to enjoy a good meal while watching favorite sporting events on the overhead TVs. For appetizers, the black-and-tan onion rings or fried green tomatoes are terrific. Move on to low-fat buffalo burgers, roast beef, succulent baby back ribs or roasted chicken. New York-style cheesecake rounds out the meal. The breakfast burger topped with bacon and an egg is hearty and well done. **Features:** full bar, patio dining, happy hour. **Address:** 9239 Hwy 52 37148 **Location:** I-65 exit 117, just e; in Comfort Suites. L D CALL &M

POWELL
• Hotels & Restaurants map & index p. 117

COMFORT INN   (865)938-5500 46

▼▼▼ **Hotel** $84-$149 **Address:** 7585 Barnett Way 37849 **Location:** I-75 exit 112, 0.4 mi e on Emory Rd, then just w. Located past hospital. **Facility:** 69 units. 3 stories, interior corridors. **Pool(s):** heated indoor. **Activities:** hot tub, exercise room. **Guest Services:** valet and coin laundry.

COUNTRY INN & SUITES BY CARLSON   (865)947-7500 47

▼▼▼ **Hotel** $75-$155 **Address:** 7534 Conner Rd 37849 **Location:** I-75 exit 112, just e. **Facility:** 69 units. 3 stories, interior corridors. **Terms:** cancellation fee imposed. **Pool(s):** heated indoor. **Activities:** hot tub, exercise room. **Guest Services:** valet and coin laundry.

HOLIDAY INN EXPRESS   865/938-3800 48

▼▼▼ **Hotel.** Rates not provided. **Address:** 7520 Conner Rd 37849 **Location:** I-75 exit 112, just e. **Facility:** 80 units. 3 stories, interior corridors. **Terms:** check-in 4 pm. **Pool(s):** outdoor. **Activities:** exercise room. **Guest Services:** valet and coin laundry.

SUPER 8 OF POWELL   (865)938-5501 49

▼▼ **Motel** $60-$80 **Address:** 323 E Emory Rd 37849 **Location:** I-75 exit 112, just s. **Facility:** 68 units. 2 stories (no elevator), exterior corridors. **Terms:** cancellation fee imposed. **Amenities:** safes. **Pool(s):** outdoor.

WHERE TO EAT

AUBREY'S   865/938-2724

▼▼ Southern American. Casual Dining. $6-$22 **AAA Inspector Notes:** Diners savor traditional Texas barbecue in a family-friendly atmosphere. On the menu are beef ribs, baby back ribs, chicken, pulled pork, beef brisket, huge hamburgers and some Tex-Mex favorites including Baja fish tacos. **Features:** full bar. **Address:** 7535 Conner Rd 37849 **Location:** I-75 exit 112, just s. L D CALL &M

PULASKI (D-4) pop. 7,870, elev. 699'

COMFORT INN OF PULASKI   (931)424-1600

▼▼▼
Hotel
$125-$190

Address: 1140 W College St 38478 **Location:** On US 64, 1 mi w of jct US 31. **Facility:** 45 units, some efficiencies. 2 stories, interior corridors. **Amenities:** safes. **Pool(s):** outdoor. **Activities:** exercise room. **Guest Services:** valet and coin laundry. **Featured Amenity: full hot breakfast.**

WHERE TO EAT

LEGENDS STEAKHOUSE   931/363-5612

▼▼ Steak. Casual Dining. $7-$28 **AAA Inspector Notes:** In a new location, this popular spot serves great steaks, naturally, but you'll also find seafood, chicken, ribs, burgers and entrée-sized salads. Not having steak tonight? They're pretty famous for their pot roast, though this reviewer recommends the award-winning potato cheese soup. The friendly, down-to-earth staff will take excellent care of you. **Features:** full bar, patio dining, happy hour. **Address:** 1520 W College St 38478 **Location:** US 64 E, 0.4 mi e. L D CALL &M

REEVES DRUG STORE - HOME OF THE 5-CENT COKE
931/363-2561

▼ Sandwiches Deli. Quick Serve. $3-$6 **AAA Inspector Notes:** Stop in to reminisce about the days when a glass of Coke was 5 cents. Guess what...it's still 5 cents here! Enjoy this timeless sandwich shop tucked in the back corner of a busy "general store," where the Deli Girls can mix a fresh milkshake, malt or ice cream float. Juicy burgers, salads and a variety of sandwiches are all made to order; try the bologna or pimiento cheese. Everyone's family here. Join them for breakfast, too. **Address:** 125 N First St 38478 **Location:** On US 31, just n of Madison and N First sts; downtown. **Parking:** street only. B L D

RELIANCE (D-6) elev. 771'

RECREATIONAL ACTIVITIES

White-water Rafting

- **Ocoee Outdoors-Hiwassee Outpost** is 2.6 mi. n.e. to 589 Childers Creek Rd. **Hours:** Hiwassee River trips are offered daily, Memorial Day weekend-Labor Day; Sat.-Sun., Apr.-May and day after Labor Day through Oct. Phone ahead to confirm schedule. **Phone:** (423) 338-2438 or (800) 533-7767.

ROGERSVILLE pop. 4,420

COMFORT INN & SUITES   (423)272-8700

▼▼▼ **Hotel** $80-$110 **Address:** 128 James Richardson Ln 37857 **Location:** US 11 W/SR 1/70, 1.6 mi w, just n. **Facility:** 52 units. 3 stories, interior corridors. **Amenities:** safes. **Pool(s):** heated indoor. **Activities:** hot tub, exercise room. **Guest Services:** valet and coin laundry.

HALE SPRINGS INN   (423)272-5171

▼▼▼ **Country Inn** $125-$165 **Address:** 110 W Main St 37857 **Location:** Jct US 11 W, just s on SR 66/70, then 1 mi e. **Facility:** Originally built in 1824, this completely remodeled Federal-style brick hotel offers spacious rooms with modern appointments and period charm, as well as a casually upscale dining room. 9 units, some two bedrooms. 2 stories, interior corridors. **Terms:** 5 day cancellation notice-fee imposed. **Activities:** massage.

RUGBY (C-6) elev. 1,431'

The town of Rugby owes its origins primarily to Thomas Hughes, an English author and social reformer who established an experimental community in 1880. Hughes, author of "Tom Brown's School Days," worked to improve the lot of the English working class. He also tried to change conditions for the younger sons of gentry, whom English custom excluded from inheritance and whom class pressure limited to such professions as law or medicine. Rugby was intended to provide opportunities for these sons in an agricultural cooperative.

Rugby reached its peak in 1884, but due to harsh weather conditions, a typhoid epidemic and mismanagement, the community began to dwindle. Today Rugby is a small rural community intent on preserving the historic village of its predecessors. River gorges and a forest surround the 20 of the colony's original Victorian buildings that remain.

HISTORIC RUGBY is on Rugby Parkway off SR 52; a visitor center is located at 1331 Rugby Pkwy. Guests may visit four of the colony's buildings. The visitor center contains a large wall mural of 1880s Rugby and a theater where a 22-minute film is shown. Departing from the visitor center, a guided walking tour visits the 1884 Kingstone Lisle; the unchanged 1882 Thomas Hughes Library; the 1906 schoolhouse; and the 1887 Christ Church Episcopal. Four miles of historic trails wind through the grounds.

Time: Allow 2 hours minimum. **Hours:** Hours vary seasonally; phone ahead for schedule. Closed Jan. 1, Thanksgiving, Christmas Eve and Christmas.

Cost: $7; $
K-12). Price
Phone: (423)

HARROW ROAD

Regional American Casual Dining $6-$15

Address: 5545 Rugby Hwy SR 52 3
52 via Farrington Rd; between US 27 and 12

SAVANNAH (D-3) pop. 6,982, elev. 450'

Just 10 miles from Shiloh National Military Park, Savannah's historic district boasts several architecturally striking homes. The oldest edifice is the circa 1830 Cherry Mansion, which served as Gen. Ulysses S. Grant's headquarters prior to the Battle of Shiloh. Other points of interest include a ferry crossing site owned by Alex Haley Sr., the grandfather of "Roots" author Alex Haley, and a portion of the Trail of Tears.

Hardin County Convention & Visitors Bureau: 495 Main St., Savannah, TN 38372. **Phone:** (731) 925-8181 or (800) 552-3866.

Self-guiding tours: A brochure outlining a walking tour of Savannah's historic home district is available at the Tennessee River Museum.

TENNESSEE RIVER MUSEUM is at 495 Main St. Exhibits chronicle prehistoric times, the life of the Mississippian mound builders, the Trail of Tears, the Civil War on the river, the age of steamboats and the Tennessee River today. Items on display include fossils; the Pre-Columbian Shiloh Effigy Pipe; Civil War field artillery, firearms, plates and edged weapons of both armies; objects from the sunken riverboat *City of Florence;* and a section of a mussel boat. A self-guiding tour is available.

Time: Allow 1 hour minimum. **Hours:** Mon.-Sat. 9-5, Sun. 1-5. Closed Easter, Thanksgiving and Christmas. **Cost:** $3; free (ages 0-18). **Phone:** (731) 925-2364 or (800) 552-3866.

DAYS INN OF SAVANNAH   (731)925-5505

▼▼ **Motel** $69-$74 **Address:** 1695 Pickwick Rd 38372 **Location:** Jct US 64, 1.5 mi s on SR 128. **Facility:** 40 units. 1 story, exterior corridors. **Parking:** winter plug-ins. **Amenities:** safes. **Pool(s):** outdoor.

731/645-8880

ddress: 644 Mulberry Ave 38375 **Location:** Jct US 64, just s on US 45. **Facility:** 35 units. 2 stories (no elevator), exterior corridors. **Pool(s):** outdoor. **Featured Amenity:** continental breakfast.

🛜 🖥 🖬 📺 / SOME UNITS 🅢📶

ERVILLE (D-7) pop. 14,807, elev. 903'

Founded in Cherokee territory in 1785, Sevierville (Severe-ville) was named for John Sevier, who later became Tennessee's first governor. Sevier negotiated a treaty with Native Americans who ceded to European settlers the land between the French Broad River and the ridge separating the Little Tennessee and Little rivers.

Douglas Dam, a Tennessee Valley Authority dam 11 miles northeast of town on SR 66, impounds Douglas Lake (see Recreation Areas Chart) on the French Broad River.

Shopping: SAVE Tanger Five Oaks, at 1645 Parkway, has more than 100 outlet stores.

FLOYD GARRETT'S MUSCLE CAR MUSEUM, 320 Winfield Dunn Pkwy., houses American muscle cars from the 1950s, '60s and '70s as well as other distinctive automobiles from the 1940s and '50s. The 90-vehicle collection is worth more than $8 million. **Hours:** Daily 9-6, Apr.-Dec.; 9-5, rest of year. Closed Thanksgiving and Christmas. **Cost:** $11; $5 (ages 8-12). **Phone:** (865) 908-0882.

FORBIDDEN CAVERNS is 14 mi. n.e. on US 411, following signs. The caves were inhabited several thousand years before the first European explored them. From the 1930s to 1943 they were used as a hideaway for making moonshine. The caverns contain a large wall of onyx, natural chimneys, ancient waterfalls and a stream. An audio presentation offers history about the caverns.

Time: Allow 1 hour minimum. **Hours:** Guided 1-hour tours Mon.-Sat. 10-6, Apr.-Nov. Last tour departs 1 hour before closing. Closed Thanksgiving. **Cost:** $14; $8 (ages 5-12). Prices and schedule may vary; phone ahead. **Phone:** (865) 453-5972.

RAINFOREST ADVENTURES, just n.e. of jct. Parkway and Collier Dr. at 109 NASCAR Dr., features more than 600 animals, including cobras, ring-tailed lemurs, parrots, giant tortoises and a pair of cotton-top tamarins. More than 130 species of amphibians, birds, bugs, mammals and reptiles can be viewed. The indoor zoo is home to creatures from various rain forests; staff members conduct educational programs daily. **Time:** Allow 1 hour minimum. **Hours:** Daily 9-5. Closed Christmas. **Cost:** $12.99; $10.99 (ages 55+); $7.99 (ages 3-12). **Phone:** (865) 428-4091.

SMOKY MOUNTAIN DEER FARM AND EXOTIC PETTING ZOO is 6 mi. e. on US 411N (Dolly Parton Pkwy.), then 2 mi. n. on Walnut Grove Pl. to Happy Hollow Ln., following signs. Visitors can safely walk among, feed and pet deer, dromedary camels, kangaroos, pygmy goats and zebras. Also on the grounds are miniature horses, guanacos, Rocky Mountain elk, reindeer, miniature donkeys, emus, watusi and other animals. Pony and horse rides are offered (weather permitting).

Time: Allow 1 hour minimum. **Hours:** Daily 10-5:30 (weather permitting). Last ticket sold at 4. Pony rides are available year-round (weather permitting). Closed Thanksgiving and Christmas. **Cost:** $11.99; $7.99 (ages 3-12); 99c (ages 1-2); 9c (ages 0-1). Pony ride $7.99. One-hour horseback ride $6.99. A child doubling with a parent on one horse $7.99. Other prices vary depending on ride duration. Reservations are required. **Phone:** (865) 428-3337, or (865) 429-2276 for the riding stable. 🅐

SMOKY MOUNTAIN KNIFE WORKS is at 2320 Winfield Dunn Pkwy. Reportedly the world's largest knife showplace, the store includes a museum showcasing primitive knives from Africa and South America as well as an extensive collection of military knives from the Civil War through Vietnam. A section of the store called Trophy Mountain features a large collection of mounted animals in a wilderness setting. **Hours:** Daily 9-9, May-Dec.; Sun.-Thurs. 9-6, Fri.-Sat. 9-8, rest of year. Closed Thanksgiving and Christmas. **Cost:** Free. **Phone:** (865) 453-5871.

GEM **TENNESSEE MUSEUM OF AVIATION** is 2 mi. n.e. of US 441/SR 448 on US 411 N. (Dolly Parton Pkwy.), then s.e. (toward Newport) 1 mi. to 135 Air Museum Way. Housed in a 35,000-square-foot hangar, airworthy vintage and historical aircraft and military vehicles are on display, as are aviation history and technology exhibits, aircraft engines, uniforms and equipment. Visitors may have a chance to witness flight demonstrations.

Time: Allow 1 hour, 30 minutes minimum. **Hours:** Mon.-Sat. 10-6, Sun. 1-6, Mar.-Dec.; otherwise varies. Closed Thanksgiving and Christmas. Phone ahead to confirm schedule. **Cost:** $12.75; $9.75 (ages 60+); $6.75 (ages 6-12). **Phone:** (865) 908-0171 or (866) 286-8738. GT

RECREATIONAL ACTIVITIES
Horseback Riding

• **Five Oaks Riding Stables** is at 1630 Parkway. **Hours:** Horseback rides daily, Apr.-Dec. Phone for schedule rest of year. **Phone:** (865) 774-1800 or (877) 741-8070.

Use travel time to share driving tips and rules of the road with your teens

(See map & index p. 84.)

Ziplines

- **Adventure Park Ziplines** is at 1620 Parkway. **Hours:** Guided 2- to 3-hour tours are offered daily, Apr.-Dec. Phone for schedule rest of year. Reservations are recommended. **Phone:** (865) 453-8644 or (877) 287-6946.
- **Legacy Mountain Ziplines** is at 2431 Upper Middle Creek Rd. **Hours:** Guided 2- to 3-hour tours are offered daily, Mar.-Dec. Phone for schedule rest of year. Reservations are recommended. **Phone:** (865) 312-6232 or (865) 774-3330.

BEST WESTERN GREENBRIER INN
(865)428-1000 **62**

Motel
$50-$120

AAA Benefit: Save 10% or more every day and earn 10% bonus points!

Address: 711 Parkway 37862 **Location:** Jct US 411, 0.7 mi s. **Facility:** 74 units. 3 stories, exterior corridors. **Pool(s):** heated outdoor. **Guest Services:** coin laundry.

BLUE MOUNTAIN MIST COUNTRY INN & COTTAGES
865/428-2335 **68**

Bed & Breakfast. Rates not provided. **Address:** 1811 Pullen Rd 37862 **Location:** Jct US 411, 3.4 mi s on Veterans Blvd, 1.6 mi e on Jayell Rd, then just s. **Facility:** Overlooking a scenic backdrop of farms and mountains, the beautiful Victorian farmhouse features inviting guest rooms furnished with antiques. 17 units, some cottages. 1-2 stories (no elevator), interior/exterior corridors. **Activities:** spa.

CLARION INN WILLOW RIVER
(865)429-7600 **58**

Hotel $92-$155 **Address:** 1990 Winfield Dunn Pkwy 37862 **Location:** I-40 exit 407, 4.4 mi s on SR 66. **Facility:** 88 units. 3 stories, interior corridors. **Amenities:** safes. **Pool(s):** heated outdoor, heated indoor. **Activities:** hot tub, exercise room. **Guest Services:** coin laundry.

COMFORT INN APPLE VALLEY
(865)428-1069 **69**

Hotel
$59-$180

Address: 1850 Parkway 37862 **Location:** On US 441; corner of Apple Valley Rd. **Facility:** 111 units. 3 stories, interior corridors. **Pool(s):** heated outdoor, heated indoor. **Activities:** hot tub. **Guest Services:** coin laundry. *(See ad this page.)*

ECONO LODGE
(865)429-7797 **60**

Motel $39-$139 **Address:** 680 Winfield Dunn Pkwy 37864 **Location:** Jct US 411, 0.7 mi n on SR 66. **Facility:** 80 units. 3 stories, interior corridors. **Pool(s):** outdoor. **Guest Services:** coin laundry.

FAIRFIELD INN & SUITES BY MARRIOTT PIGEON FORGE
(865)429-8300 **67**

Hotel
$48-$139

FAIRFIELD INN & SUITES Marriott

AAA Benefit: Members save 5% or more!

Address: 1650 Parkway US Hwy 441 37862 **Location:** On US 441; across from Tanger Five Oaks Mall. **Facility:** 88 units. 3 stories, interior corridors. **Pool(s):** heated outdoor. **Activities:** exercise room. **Guest Services:** valet and coin laundry. **Featured Amenity:** full hot breakfast.

(See map & index p. 84.)

GOVERNOR'S INN
865/428-1721

Hotel. Rates not provided. **Address:** 121 Nascar Dr 37862 **Location:** Just e on Collier Dr from jct US 441, then just n on Hurley St. **Facility:** 88 units. 3 stories, interior corridors. **Pool(s):** heated outdoor. **Activities:** exercise room. **Guest Services:** valet and coin laundry.

 / SOME UNITS

HAMPTON INN
(865)429-2005

Hotel $119-$179 **Address:** 681 Winfield Dunn Pkwy 37862 **Location:** I-40 exit 407, 7.6 mi s on SR 66; 0.7 mi n of jct US 411. **Facility:** 68 units. 3 stories, interior corridors. **Terms:** 1-7 night minimum stay, cancellation fee imposed. **Pool(s):** heated indoor. **Activities:** hot tub, game room, exercise room. **Guest Services:** valet and coin laundry.

AAA Benefit: Members save up to 10%!

LA QUINTA INN & SUITES SEVIERVILLE/KODAK
(865)933-3339

Hotel $64-$187 **Address:** 2428 Winfield Dunn Pkwy 37764 **Location:** I-40 exit 407, 3.2 mi s on SR 66. **Facility:** 101 units. 4 stories, interior corridors. **Pool(s):** outdoor, heated indoor. **Activities:** hot tub, limited exercise equipment. **Guest Services:** coin laundry.

 / SOME UNITS

OAK TREE LODGE
(865)428-7500

Motel
$50-$125

Address: 1620 Parkway 37862 **Location:** On US 441, 2.4 mi s of jct US 411. **Facility:** 100 units. 3 stories, interior/exterior corridors. **Terms:** cancellation fee imposed. **Pool(s):** heated outdoor, heated indoor.

QUALITY INN & SUITES RIVER SUITES
(865)428-5519

Motel
$60-$139

Address: 860 Winfield Dunn Pkwy 37876 **Location:** Jct US 411, 1.2 mi n on SR 66. **Facility:** 93 units. 3 stories, exterior corridors. **Amenities:** safes. **Pool(s):** outdoor, heated indoor. **Activities:** hot tub. **Guest Services:** coin laundry.

 / SOME UNITS

THE RESORT AT GOVERNOR'S CROSSING
(865)429-0500

Vacation Rental Condominium $109-$249 **Address:** 225 Collier Dr 37862 **Location:** 0.4 mi e of jct US 441. **Facility:** You may be tempted to cook your meals in the full kitchen, but there are so many restaurants nearby. Your little ones will want to spend all their time in the water park pool area. 154 condominiums. 5 stories, interior corridors. **Terms:** check-in 4 pm, 2-3 night minimum stay - seasonal and/or weekends, cancellation fee imposed, resort fee. **Amenities:** *Some:* safes. **Pool(s):** heated outdoor, heated indoor. **Activities:** sauna, hot tub, miniature golf, game room, exercise room. **Guest Services:** complimentary laundry.

SLEEP INN
(865)429-0484

Hotel $45-$150 **Address:** 1020 Parkway 37862 **Location:** On US 441, 1.2 mi s of jct US 411. **Facility:** 70 units. 3 stories, interior corridors. **Terms:** check-in 4 pm, 3 day cancellation notice. **Pool(s):** heated outdoor.

 / SOME UNITS

WHERE TO EAT

APPLEWOOD FARMHOUSE GRILL
865/429-8644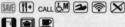

American Family Dining
$9-$17

AAA Inspector Notes: Simple, relaxing décor and basic home-style cooking make this a comfortable place to enjoy a meal. The apple-wood pork loin is smoked and served with apple chutney. Count on attentive service. **Address:** 220 Apple Valley Rd 37862 **Location:** Jct US 441, just w. B L D

APPLEWOOD FARMHOUSE RESTAURANT
865/428-1222

American Family Dining
$8-$18

AAA Inspector Notes: This old farmhouse has a wraparound porch with wooden rocking chairs. Enjoy traditional country food including chicken dumplings, country-fried steak and homemade vegetable soup. **Features:** Sunday brunch. **Address:** 240 Apple Valley Rd 37862 **Location:** Jct US 441, 0.3 mi w. B L D CALL

BIG DADDY'S PIZZERIA
865/908-1123

Pizza Sandwiches Casual Dining
$9-$23

AAA Inspector Notes: The wood-fired brick-dome oven reaches 550 degrees to give the fresh-made pizzas a distinctive texture and crunch. Toppings include the usual pepperoni, sausage, mushrooms and various cheeses. The Big Kahuna is topped with ham, pineapple and goat cheese. Numerous sandwiches and salads also are on the menu. **Features:** beer & wine, patio dining. **Address:** 1820 Parkway 37863 **Location:** Between traffic lights 12.6 and 13. *Menu on AAA.com* L D CALL

BUDDY'S BAR-B-Q
865/428-5001

Barbecue. Quick Serve. $6-$11 **AAA Inspector Notes:** Step up to the counter to order great pit barbecue, including beef, ribs, chicken, chopped pork, or maybe even a sampling of everything. Sides include baked beans, corn on the cob and slaw. Lemon icebox pie makes for a nice end to the feast. **Address:** 705 Winfield Dunn Pkwy 37862 **Location:** Jct US 411, 0.8 mi n on SR 66. L D

THE CHOP HOUSE
865/774-1991

Steak Seafood. Casual Dining. $8-$29 **AAA Inspector Notes:** Friendly servers hustle amid tables with preparations of quality aged meats, fresh seafood, chicken, lamb, pork and pasta. The restaurant is a popular spot for casually upscale dining. **Features:** beer & wine. **Reservations:** suggested. **Address:** 1649 Parkway 37863 **Location:** On US 441, traffic light 13; at Tanger Outlet-Five Oaks Mall. L D

EL PASO MEXICAN RESTAURANT
865/453-6771

Mexican. Casual Dining. $7-$15 **AAA Inspector Notes:** The lengthy menu goes beyond the usual combination plate offerings. You'll find chicken, pork, steak and seafood creations among the chef's specialties. Traditional favorites, such as enchiladas and fajitas, are joined by dishes like grilled pork chops topped with a spicy red sauce, grilled steak in tomatillo sauce, and seafood nachos. Service is friendly, and the cute décor has a south-of-the-border flair. **Features:** full bar. **Address:** 560 Winfield Dunn Pkwy 37876 **Location:** Jct US 411, 1 mi n on SR 66; in small strip mall. L D

(See map & index p. 84.)

FLAPJACK'S PANCAKE CABIN   865/774-5374   (37)

▼ Breakfast. Family Dining. $6-$11 **AAA Inspector Notes:** Settle in to the cozy cabin for a hearty breakfast of waffles, omelets, skillets and heaping portions of pancakes in a variety of flavors, including traditional buttermilk, blueberry, multigrain, and decadent peanut butter and chocolate chip. **Address:** 1016 Parkway 37862 **Location:** On US 441, 1 mi s. (B)

GATTI'S PIZZA   865/428-8817

▼ Pizza. Family Dining. $7-$9 **AAA Inspector Notes:** Diners find great value for the dollar at the casual eatery, where the extensive salad and pizza bar includes a variety of dessert pizzas. **Features:** senior menu. **Address:** 1431 Parkway 37862 **Location:** On US 441; corner of Collier Dr. (L) (D)

GONDOLIER ITALIAN RESTAURANT AND PIZZA
    865/428-8050

▼▼ Italian Pizza. Casual Dining. $6-$16 **AAA Inspector Notes:** In addition to daily specials, diners can select from a tempting variety of calzones and such standards as spaghetti, manicotti and ravioli. Servers are fast and friendly. **Features:** beer only. **Address:** 964 Dolly Parton Pkwy 37862 **Location:** Jct US 441, 1.2 mi e on US 411; in River View Center. (L) (D)

RYAN'S   865/908-9900

▼ American. Cafeteria. $7-$11 **AAA Inspector Notes:** Along with an abundance of hot items such as breaded fried pork chops and golden-brown chicken with an array of vegetables, patrons find a wide choice of salad fixings and desserts. **Features:** senior menu. **Address:** 502 Winfield Dunn Pkwy 37876 **Location:** On SR 66, 0.4 mi n of jct US 411. (L) (D)

THAI BASIL   865/453-9339   (36)

▼▼ Thai. Casual Dining. $8-$17 **AAA Inspector Notes:** Fresh ingredients are used in this restaurant's healthy food, which includes some gluten-free choices. Traditional favorites such as pad thai and tom yum soup can be enjoyed along with numerous daily specials. **Features:** beer only. **Address:** 530 Winfield Dunn Pkwy 37862 **Location:** On SR 66, just n of jct US 411/SR 35 (W Main St/Chapman Hwy); in Sevier Commons Shopping Center. (L) (D) CALL (M)

THAI PALACE   865/365-1350   (38)

▼▼ Thai. Casual Dining. $8-$16 **AAA Inspector Notes:** This family-run restaurant specializes in favorites such as pad thai and tom yum soup, made flavorful by using traditional spices of varying heat levels. **Features:** beer only. **Address:** 1811 Parkway 37862 **Location:** On US 441; just s of Tanger Outlet-Five Oaks Mall.
(L) (D)

SEWANEE (D-5) pop. 2,311, elev. 2,000'

Sewanee: The University of the South, owned by 28 Episcopal dioceses in 12 states, was established in Sewanee in 1857. Although most of the institution's assets were destroyed during the Civil War, the school was rebuilt by 1868 and now boasts a central campus of collegiate Gothic sandstone buildings and expansive lawns surrounded by 10,000 acres of forests, lakes and bluffs.

Green's View, at the end of Green's View Road, looks out over farmlands almost 1,000 feet below. Hiking trails extend along the bluffs into coves containing wildflowers and other plants.

The View from the Cross, at the end of Tennessee Avenue near the campus, is marked by a 40-foot cross, which was erected in memory of area war dead. On the way to the cross, within the School of Theology on Tennessee Avenue, is the Chapel of the Apostles, a soaring modern structure of glass and interlocking wooden beams. The school's Office of Communications can provide further information; phone (931) 598-1000.

ALL SAINTS' CHAPEL is on University Ave. in the center of Sewanee: The University of the South campus. The first phase was begun in 1905. The Episcopal chapel has an interior height of 51 feet and length of 233 feet. Stained-glass windows depict biblical scenes and events in the university's history; memorials and a 5,000-pipe Casavant Freres organ also can be seen.

On the south side of the chapel is 134-foot Shapard Tower, which houses the 56-bell Leonidas Polk Memorial Carillon. A monthly performance schedule is available at the chapel's main entrance. **Hours:** Chapel open daily 8 a.m.-10 p.m. Carillon recitals when classes are in session Tues. and Thurs. at 12:30 and Sun. after services. Hours may vary during special services; phone ahead. **Cost:** Free. **Phone:** (931) 598-1701.

BRESLIN TOWER is at the corner of University and Georgia aves. on the campus of Sewanee: The University of the South. The 1886 clock tower is modeled after the Magdalen Tower at Oxford University in England. Eight change-ringing bells were cast in London by the Whitechapel Bell Foundry, the makers of Big Ben and the Liberty Bell. The largest Breslin bell, known as "The Tenor," weighs 1,255 pounds.

SHELBYVILLE (D-4) pop. 20,335, elev. 771'
• Restaurants p. 242

Synonymous with Shelbyville is the Tennessee walking horse, raised and trained on many farms and stables within a 4-mile radius of town. More than 2,000 of these dignified high-stepping horses perform at the Tennessee Walking Horse National Celebration during late August.

Shelbyville/Bedford County Chamber of Commerce: 100 N. Cannon Blvd., Shelbyville, TN 37160. **Phone:** (931) 684-3482 or (888) 662-2525.

BEST WESTERN CELEBRATION INN & SUITES
    (931)684-2378

▼▼ Hotel $70-$170

AAA Benefit:
Save 10% or more every day and earn 10% bonus points!

Address: 724 Madison St 37160 **Location:** Jct US 231 and 41. **Facility:** 59 units. 2 stories (no elevator), exterior corridors. **Amenities:** safes. **Pool(s):** heated indoor. **Activities:** exercise room. **Guest Services:** valet and coin laundry.

SAVE ⊞ ⊟ BIZ HS 🛜 ✕
🏃 🖥 🖨 🖵 / SOME UNITS 🛏

MICROTEL INN & SUITES BY WYNDHAM   (931)684-8343

▼▼ Hotel $49-$85 **Address:** 1207 N Main St 37160 **Location:** Jct US 231 and 41, 0.9 mi n. Located in a busy commercial area. **Facility:** 62 units. 4 stories, interior corridors. **Pool(s):** outdoor. **Activities:** exercise room. **Guest Services:** coin laundry.

⊞ CALL (M) 🖂 BIZ 🛜 ✕ 🖵
/ SOME UNITS 🛏 ⊟ 🖨

WHERE TO EAT

RAFAEL'S PIZZERIA & ITALIAN RESTAURANT   931/684-9170

▼ Pizza. Quick Serve. $6-$14 **AAA Inspector Notes:** At this no-frills, small town pizza parlor, you'll order at the counter for both dine-in and take-out. Pasta dishes, calzones and subs are available as well as meat entrées and burgers. **Features:** beer only. **Address:** 1200 Madison St 37160 **Location:** Jct US 231 and 41, 1.4 mi e.

L   D   CALL 🅑🅜

SHILOH NATIONAL MILITARY PARK (E-2)

Ten miles southwest of Savannah, the 4,200-acre Shiloh Battlefield preserves the site of the first major Western battle of the Civil War: The Battle of Shiloh, fought April 6-7, 1862. The park contains 156 monuments, more than 200 cannons, a national cemetery and more than 600 historic tablets.

After the fall of Fort Donelson *(see Fort Donelson National Battlefield p. 78)*, Union Gen. Ulysses S. Grant moved his army up the Tennessee River, where he awaited reinforcement. Unannounced, Confederate general Albert Sidney Johnston struck first in a surprise attack that drove Union forces 2 miles toward the river.

The intense battle raged all day, and Johnston was mortally wounded near the Peach Orchard. Grant's reinforcements, the Army of the Ohio commanded by Don Carlos Buell, arrived during the night. The next day the outnumbered Confederates, commanded by Gen. P.G.T. Beauregard, were driven back. In the afternoon they retreated to Corinth, Miss.

More than 109,000 soldiers, most of them inexperienced recruits, battled at this site. After 2 days 23,746 were dead, wounded or missing, making the Battle of Shiloh the bloodiest fight since the war's beginning. It also was a turning point in Union strategy; Grant said afterwards, "I gave up all idea of saving the Union except by complete conquest."

Union dead, originally interred on the battlefield, were subsequently moved to the national cemetery at Pittsburgh Landing. The Confederate dead still lie in mass burial trenches, five of which are marked.

Points of interest on the battlefield are marked, and a 12-mile auto tour has 20 stops with wayside exhibits. Shiloh Indian Mounds National Historic Landmark features several preserved prehistoric mounds.

Also part of the park, Corinth Battlefield's visitor center, Corinth Civil War Interpretive Center, features interactive exhibits and multimedia presentations that examine topics such as slavery, the military importance of railroads and Reconstruction. The center is 23 miles southwest of Shiloh Battlefield in Corinth, Miss.; phone (662) 287-9273.

SHILOH BATTLEFIELD VISITOR CENTER, off SR 22, contains artifacts, exhibits and maps relating to the battle. A 49-minute film is shown every hour. Interpretive programs are conducted Memorial Day-Labor Day. **Time:** Allow 2 hours minimum. **Hours:** Park open daily dawn-dusk. Visitor center open daily 8-5. Closed Jan. 1, Thanksgiving and Christmas. **Cost:** Free. **Phone:** (731) 689-5696.

SMITHVILLE (C-5) pop. 4,530, elev. 1,033'

APPALACHIAN CENTER FOR CRAFT is off I-40 exit 273 to Hwy. 56; continue 6 mi. s. over Center Hill Lake/Caney Fork River, then immediate turn onto Pedigo Ridge Rd. to 1560 Craft Center Dr. This satellite campus of Tennessee Tech University in Cookeville features works by national and regional artists. **Time:** Allow 1 hour minimum. **Hours:** Gallery open Mon.-Sat. 10-6, Sun. noon-5. Closed Jan. 1-2, Easter, Thanksgiving and Dec. 23-31. **Cost:** Free. **Phone:** (615) 597-3051.

SMYRNA (C-4) pop. 39,974, elev. 510'

Smyrna began in 1851 as a way station on the Nashville and Chattanooga Railroad line. The remnants of two forts built to protect the railroad against the Union army are visible at the edge of town.

Rutherford County Chamber of Commerce— Smyrna: 315 S. Lowry St., Smyrna, TN 37167. **Phone:** (615) 355-6565.

SAM DAVIS HOME AND PLANTATION is at 1399 Sam Davis Rd. The restored mid-19th-century frame structure was the residence of the 21-year-old Confederate who chose death rather than a pardon when he refused to identify an informant after being captured behind Union lines. The 160-acre grounds contain outbuildings, slave quarters, period gardens, a family cemetery, visitor center and museum.

Time: Allow 1 hour minimum. **Hours:** Mon.-Sat. 9-5, Sun. 1-4, June-Aug.; Mon.-Sat. 10-4, rest of year. Last tour departs 1 hour before closing. Closed major holidays. **Cost:** Museum, historic house and grounds $12; $10 (ages 65+ and students with ID); $6 (ages 6-12). Museum or house only $8; $6 (ages 65+ and students with ID); $6 (ages 6-12). **Phone:** (615) 459-2341.

COMFORT SUITES SMYRNA   (615)625-9000

▼▼▼ Hotel $110-$165 **Address:** 3001 Highwood Blvd 37167 **Location:** I-24 exit 66A, just e. **Facility:** 64 units. 3 stories, interior corridors. **Pool(s):** heated indoor. **Activities:** hot tub, exercise room. **Guest Services:** coin laundry.

🍴 CALL 🅑🅜 ♨ BIZ HS 🛜 ✕ 🛗 🖼 💷

FAIRFIELD INN & SUITES BY MARRIOTT NASHVILLE-SMYRNA   (615)223-8877

▼▼▼ Hotel $83-$183 **Address:** 810 Expo Dr 37167 **Location:** I-24 exit 66A, just w. **Facility:** 62 units. 3 stories, interior corridors. **Pool(s):** heated indoor. **Activities:** hot tub, exercise room. **Guest Services:** valet and coin laundry.

AAA Benefit: Members save 5% or more!

🍴 CALL 🅑🅜 ♨ BIZ 🛜 ✕ 🛗 🖼 💷

HAMPTON INN & SUITES NASHVILLE-SMYRNA   (615)355-8432

▼▼▼ Hotel $114-$179 **Address:** 2573 Highwood Blvd 37167 **Location:** I-24 exit 66A, just w. **Facility:** 83 units. 3 stories, interior corridors. **Terms:** 1-7 night minimum stay, cancellation fee imposed. **Pool(s):** heated indoor. **Activities:** exercise room. **Guest Services:** valet and coin laundry.

AAA Benefit: Members save up to 10%!

ECO ♦ 🍴 CALL 🅑🅜 ♨ BIZ HS 🛜 🛗 🖼

HILTON GARDEN INN-NASHVILLE/SMYRNA   (615)355-6262

▼▼▼ **Hotel** $114-$179 **Address:** 2631 Highwood Blvd 37167 **Location:** I-24 exit 66A, just w. **Facility:** 112 units. 5 stories, interior corridors. **Terms:** 1-7 night minimum stay, cancellation fee imposed. **Pool(s):** heated indoor. **Activities:** hot tub, miniature golf, exercise room. **Guest Services:** valet and coin laundry.

AAA Benefit:
Members save up to 10%!

ECO ◄ ⊞ ☒ CALL &M 🖘 BIZ 🛜 ✕ 🖥
🖨 ▣

LA QUINTA INN & SUITES   (615)220-8845

▼▼▼ **Hotel** $75-$207 **Address:** 2537 Highwood Blvd 37167 **Location:** I-24 exit 66A, just w. **Facility:** 76 units. 4 stories, interior corridors. **Pool(s):** outdoor. **Activities:** exercise room. **Guest Services:** valet and coin laundry.

◄ ⊞ CALL &M 🖘 BIZ 🛜 ✕ 🖥 🖨 ▣
/ SOME UNITS 🐾

WHERE TO EAT

HICKORY FALLS   615/459-3900

▼▼ ▼▼ American. Casual Dining. $7-$22 **AAA Inspector Notes:** Lining the menu are a variety of entrées, including wood-fired, hickory-grilled steaks, burgers, rotisserie chicken and pork loin. Also available are stuffed mushrooms and spinach dip appetizers, numerous salads and pastas, including rattlesnake chicken or blackened chicken. **Features:** full bar, Sunday brunch, happy hour. **Address:** 999 Industrial Blvd 37167 **Location:** I-24 exit 66B (SR 266 N), 0.5 mi n, then just w; in Colonial Town Park. L D CALL &M

JIM 'N NICK'S BAR-B-Q   615/220-8508

▼▼ ▼▼ Barbecue. Casual Dining. $8-$25 **AAA Inspector Notes:** Southern hospitality reigns at Jim 'N Nick's, where diners get neighborly treatment as they dig into huge portions of tasty lean sausage, fresh chili, juicy smoked beef and pork. A slice of sublime homemade pie ends the meal on a high note. **Features:** full bar. **Address:** 523 Sam Ridley Pkwy W 37167 **Location:** I-24 exit 66, 0.5 mi e. L D

OMNI HUT   615/459-4870

▼▼ ▼▼ Polynesian. Casual Dining. $12-$20 **AAA Inspector Notes:** Arrive early at this cozy restaurant, which tends to fill up fast. Although a Polynesian theme is reflected in the background music and décor, the food is decidedly Chinese, with choices including egg drop soup, crab Rangoon and chicken chow mein. **Reservations:** suggested. **Address:** 618 S Lowry St 37167 **Location:** I-24 exit 70, 1 mi s. D

SODDY-DAISY pop. 12,714

HOMETOWN INN   (423)332-7755

▼▼ ▼▼
Hotel
$55-$85

Address: 222 W Sequoyah Access Rd 37379 **Location:** US 27 exit Sequoyah Rd/Soddy-Daisy, just w. **Facility:** 35 units. 2 stories, interior corridors. **Terms:** 1-3 night minimum stay - seasonal and/or weekends, cancellation fee imposed. **Guest Services:** coin laundry. **Featured Amenity:** continental breakfast.

SAVE CALL &M HS 🛜 🖥 🖨
▣

SOUTHSIDE (C-4) elev. 599'

HISTORIC COLLINSVILLE is at 4711 Weakley Rd. On 40 acres, the log pioneer settlement, which depicts life from the 1830s through the 1870s, encompasses 18 restored buildings appointed with period

furnishings. The 1870s Dogtrot House features the baby tender from the Sterling, Mass., home of Sarah Hale, who wrote "Mary Had a Little Lamb." The Irby-Bumpus Wildlife and Native American Center houses a collection of prehistoric Native American artifacts and local wildlife in lifelike poses.

Time: Allow 1 hour minimum. **Hours:** Thurs.-Sun. 1-5, May 15-Oct. 15. **Cost:** $5; free (ages 0-4). Prices may vary; phone ahead. **Phone:** (931) 648-9141. 🔲

SPRING CITY pop. 1,981

HOWARD JOHNSON HOTEL   (423)365-9191

▼▼ ▼ **Hotel** $90-$110 **Address:** 22500 Rhea County Hwy 37381 **Location:** Jct SR 302, just s on US 27. **Facility:** 42 units. 2 stories (no elevator), interior corridors. **Terms:** cancellation fee imposed. **Activities:** limited exercise equipment. **Guest Services:** coin laundry.

⊞ CALL &M HS 🛜 ✕ 🖥 🖨 ▣

SPRINGFIELD pop. 16,440

HAMPTON INN SPRINGFIELD   (615)384-1166

▼▼ ▼▼ **Hotel** $109-$189 **Address:** 620 22nd Ave E 37172 **Location:** I-24 exit 35, 11.9 mi n on US 431. **Facility:** 59 units. 3 stories, interior corridors. **Terms:** 1-7 night minimum stay, cancellation fee imposed. **Pool(s):** outdoor. **Activities:** exercise room. **Guest Services:** complimentary and valet laundry.

AAA Benefit:
Members save up to 10%!

⊞ CALL &M 🖘 BIZ 🛜 ✕ ▣ / SOME UNITS 🖥 🖨

WHERE TO EAT

DEPOT BAR & GRILL   615/382-8584

▼▼ ▼▼ Steak. Casual Dining. $10-$24 **AAA Inspector Notes:** Built in 1928, the depot has been a grocery store and a liquor store. It's now a popular restaurant. Proximity to a railroad crossing means every now and then a train will roar by. Diners will not be disappointed by the menu and its familiar, comfortably delicious food. This seafood lover highly recommends the salmon spread with baked tortilla chips. My sweet tooth yearns for another piece of chocolate caboose cake, made with three different types of chocolate. **Features:** full bar, patio dining, happy hour. **Reservations:** suggested. **Address:** 1007 S Main St 37172 **Location:** Corner of S Main and 10th sts; downtown. L D CALL &M

TORINO'S GREEK & ITALIAN RESTAURANT   615/384-6548

▼▼ ▼▼ European. Casual Dining. $8-$39 **AAA Inspector Notes:** The casual eatery, established in 1985, prepares a variety of Greek platters, pasta dishes, sandwiches and fresh salads. **Features:** full bar, happy hour. **Address:** 1701 Memorial Blvd 37172 **Location:** 0.7 mi nw of jct US 431/41. L D

SPRING HILL (D-4) pop. 29,036, elev. 734'
• Hotels p. 244 • Restaurants p. 244

RIPPAVILLA PLANTATION is at 5700 Main St. (US 31). This Greek Revival mansion has been carefully restored to its 1860s appearance and is furnished with many of the home's original pieces. Guides explain the architecture and artifacts as well as the effects of the Civil War upon the plantation. An original slave cabin and the restored Freedmen Bureau School are on-site.

Time: Allow 1 hour minimum. **Hours:** Guided tours Mon.-Sat. 9:30-4:30, Sun. 1-4:30, Apr.-Dec.; Tues.-Sat. 10-4, Sun. 1-4, rest of year. Last tour begins 1 hour before closing. Closed Jan. 1, Easter, Memorial Day, July 4, Thanksgiving, Christmas Eve, Christmas and Dec. 31. **Cost:** $10; $8 (ages 62+); $5 (ages 6-12). **Phone:** (931) 486-9037. [GT]

BEST WESTERN SPRING HILL INN & SUITES

(931)486-1234

WWW
Hotel
$129-$149

AAA Benefit: Save 10% or more every day and earn 10% bonus points!

Address: 104 Kedron Pkwy 37174 **Location:** I-65 exit 53, 2 mi w on SR 396 (Saturn Pkwy), then 1 mi n on US 31/Main St. **Facility:** 50 units, some kitchens. 2 stories (no elevator), interior/exterior corridors. **Pool(s):** outdoor. **Activities:** exercise room. **Guest Services:** valet and coin laundry. **Featured Amenity:** continental breakfast.

[SAVE] [⬆] [🏊] [BIZ] [HS] [📶] [🔲]

[📷] [📺]

WHERE TO EAT

FULIN'S ASIAN CUISINE   931/489-9188

WW Asian Sushi. Casual Dining. $8-$29 **AAA Inspector Notes:** Here you can savor a variety of delicious Asian dishes, including ginger lobster, curry seafood Thai casserole, kung pao chicken, egg rolls and more. Have fresh-made sushi or sashimi with your dinner, or enjoy it at the sushi bar. **Features:** full bar, happy hour. **Address:** 1009 Crossings Blvd 37174 **Location:** Jct US 31 and SR 396 (Saturn Pkwy), just n of Main St; in Target Shopping Center.

[L] [D] CALL [🅖M]

PANCHO'S PLACE - MEXICAN RESTAURANTE   931/486-0004

WW Mexican. Casual Dining. $5-$22 **AAA Inspector Notes:** Value, variety and friendly faces are what you'll find at this enjoyable spot serving casual, fresh Mexican meals. There are two locations in Tennessee: Spring Hill and Columbia. **Features:** beer & wine, patio dining. **Address:** 120 Kedron Pkwy 37174 **Location:** I-65 exit 53, 2 mi w on SR 396 (Saturn Pkwy), then 1 mi n on US 31/Main St.

[L] [D] CALL [🅖M]

STONES RIVER NATIONAL BATTLEFIELD (D-4)

In the northwest corner of Murfreesboro on Old Nashville Highway, the 650-acre Stones River National Battlefield occupies a portion of the actual battlefield site. The fiercest fighting during one of the bloodiest battles of the Civil War took place at the Battle of Stones River, fought Dec. 31, 1862, to Jan. 2, 1863. It marked the Union offensive that trisected Confederate territory.

After the Battle of Shiloh *(see Shiloh National Military Park p. 242)* and the fall of Corinth, Miss., the Union army's plan to drive a wedge through Tennessee and Georgia from Nashville was postponed by Confederate general Braxton Bragg's invasion of Kentucky. Following the Battle of Perryville, Bragg withdrew to Chattanooga and moved northwestward to Murfreesboro.

By Dec. 30, Gen. William Rosecrans' Union forces from Nashville faced the Confederates near Stones River. At dawn on the 31st the Confederates struck and, with staggering losses, forced the main Union army back to the Nashville Pike. Jan. 1 was quiet, but the next day the Confederates again made a costly attack; Union artillery stopped their drive. The following day the Confederates withdrew to Tullahoma.

The Battle of Stones River placed Union forces in control of another section of middle Tennessee. One of the nation's oldest intact Civil War monuments and a landmark of the battlefield, the Hazen Brigade Monument, was constructed in 1863 by the survivors of the fight for Hell's Half Acre in the Round Forest, a significant location of the battlefield so named because of the intense fighting there.

Visitors can follow a 45-minute auto tour route or the 4.5-mile paved scenic Stones River Greenway hiking trail, which runs from the McFadden Farm Unit to Fortress Rosecrans. A visitor center offers exhibits as well as an orientation program, a museum and an audio or cellphone tour. Interpretive programs are offered daily, May through October. Battlefield, museum and visitor center open daily 8-5; closed Christmas and Thanksgiving. Free. Phone (615) 893-9501.

STONES RIVER NATIONAL CEMETERY occupies 20 acres of the Stones River National Battlefield in Murfreesboro; a visitor center is across the road from the cemetery. Containing the remains of more than 6,100 Union troops (2,562 of them are unidentified) killed at Stones River and other nearby battlefields, the graveyard was established in 1865. **Hours:** Cemetery and visitor center daily 8-5. Closed Thanksgiving and Christmas. **Cost:** Free. **Phone:** (615) 893-9501.

SWEETWATER (D-6) pop. 5,764, elev. 910'

[GEM] **LOST SEA ADVENTURE** is e. on SR 68, following signs to 140 Lost Sea Rd. This 4.5-acre underground lake, stocked with rainbow trout, is explored by glass-bottom boat. Rock and mineral deposits and cave flowers can be seen in Craighead Caverns. During the Civil War Confederate soldiers mined the caverns for saltpeter, a mineral used in gunpowder. Later, settlers stored food in the 58-degree-Fahrenheit cave. In the 1900s townsfolk created the Cavern Tavern, a natural game room.

Old Sweetwater Village, across from the main entrance of Lost Sea, is a re-creation of an 18th-century village. Log cabins feature a general store, a blacksmith shop, a candy shop and craftsmen demonstrating such traditional skills as glassblowing.

Time: Allow 1 hour minimum. **Hours:** Guided 1-hour cave tours daily 9-7, May-Aug. (also 7-8 p.m., in July); 9-6, Mar.-Apr. and Sept.-Oct.; 9-5, rest of year. Last tour begins 30 minutes before closing. Closed Christmas. **Cost:** $18.95; $9.95 (ages 5-12). **Phone:** (423) 337-6616. [🍴] [🎠]

HOLIDAY INN EXPRESS & SUITES SWEETWATER

423/337-4900

WW Hotel. Rates not provided. **Address:** 1116 New Hwy 68 37874 **Location:** I-75 exit 60, just w. **Facility:** 71 units. 3 stories, interior corridors. **Pool(s):** heated indoor. **Activities:** limited exercise equipment. **Guest Services:** coin laundry.

CALL [🅖M] [🏊] [BIZ] [HS] [📶] [🔲] [📷] [📺] /SOME UNITS [🛏]

QUALITY INN WEST   (423)337-3353

WW Hotel $65-$110 **Address:** 249 New Hwy 68 37874 **Location:** I-75 exit 60, just e. **Facility:** 53 units. 2 stories (no elevator), interior/exterior corridors. **Pool(s):** heated indoor. **Activities:** hot tub, limited exercise equipment. **Guest Services:** coin laundry.

[⬆] [🏊] [BIZ] [📶] [✖] [🔲] [📷] [📺] /SOME UNITS [🛏]

WHERE TO EAT

BRADLEY'S PIT BBQ & GRILL   423/351-7190
◆◆ American. Casual Dining. $5-$20 **AAA Inspector Notes:** Friendly servers dish up plates of hickory-smoked ribs, pulled pork, chicken, fried catfish, sandwiches and steaks at this country-style barbecue eatery. **Features:** beer & wine, patio dining, early bird specials, senior menu. **Address:** 517 New Hwy 68 37874 **Location:** I-75 exit 60, 1.2 mi e. [L] [D] [🛒]

GONDOLIER ITALIAN RESTAURANT AND PIZZA
                                         423/337-5200
◆◆ Italian Pizza. Casual Dining. $5-$18 **AAA Inspector Notes:** In addition to daily specials, diners can select from a tempting variety of calzones and such standards as spaghetti, manicotti and ravioli. Servers are fast and friendly. **Features:** beer & wine. **Address:** 789 New Hwy 68 W 37874 **Location:** Jct US 11, 0.5 mi w on SR 68. [L] [D]

TIPTONVILLE (C-1) pop. 4,464, elev. 296'

Tiptonville lies in Tennessee's northwestern corner, an area shaken during the New Madrid earthquakes 1811-12. A prominent feature left from this period of geologic agitation is 15,000-acre Reelfoot Lake, characterized by large expanses of water lilies and giant cypress trees. As a bird and game refuge, the lake's wilderness supports 54 species of fish and more than 230 species of birds.

Bald eagles make their winter home in the area. Two-hour eagle tours are sponsored by Reelfoot Lake State Park *(see Recreation Areas Chart)* from early January to late February. Tickets and reservations are required; phone (731) 253-9652. During the warmer months, beginning May 1, the state park offers scenic cruises on the lake. Reservations are required for cruises. Reelfoot Lake also is the site of the Reelfoot Arts and Crafts Festival, held the first weekend in October, where more than 300 artisans display their wares.

Nearby is the Marijac Memorial River Park, which offers a scenic overlook of the Mississippi River from benches and picnic areas.

Reelfoot Area Chamber of Commerce: 130 S. Court St., Tiptonville, TN 38079. **Phone:** (731) 253-8144.

TOWNSEND (D-7) pop. 448, elev. 1,036'

• Hotels p. 247 • Restaurants p. 247
• Attractions map p. 100
• Hotels & Restaurants map & index p. 84
• Part of Great Smoky Mountains National Park area — see map p. 97

Townsend folk take their town's nickname seriously. There are no huge hotels, celebrity-chef restaurants, theme parks, outlandish attractions or entertainment strips in the tiny village dubbed "the Peaceful Side of the Smokies," which explains why there is a good measure of tranquility.

On the back doorstep of Great Smoky Mountains National Park *(see place listing p. 97),* Townsend contrasts sharply with touristy Gatlinburg *(see place listing p. 82),* which lies near the park's main entrance on US 441. Although the national park is the main attraction for seekers of recreation and relaxation, visitors have innumerable opportunities in the Townsend area to commune with nature on an intimate level, whether it's tubing on the Little River, exploring the underground passageways of Tuckaleechee Caverns *(see attraction listing),* or gasping at the awesome scenery from atop Foothills Parkway. The park entrance on SR 73 in Townsend is the unofficial gateway to Cades Cove, arguably the most beautiful and most visited place in the Smokies.

Simplicity is the standard when it comes to lodging and food. Choices include creekside campgrounds, hundreds of log cabins and cottages tucked away in secluded valleys and a few updated motels that have stood the test of time. Mealtime options follow suit, with family-owned restaurants serving no-frills country fare such as barbecue and slaw, fried brook trout and fries, or chicken-fried steak with mashed potatoes.

Smoky Mountain Visitors Center: 7906 E. Lamar Alexander Pkwy., Townsend, TN 37882. **Phone:** (865) 448-6134 or (800) 525-6834.

Shopping: A variety of shops on the main drag (E. Lamar Alexander Parkway/US 321 and SR 73) satisfy the casual bargain browser. Dad can set a spell in a rocking chair on the front porch of Apple Valley Farms while Mom peruses the selection of quilts, braided rugs, homemade fudge, mountain-music CDs, local history books and rooster-motif kitchenalia. Dogwood Craft Mall has a couple of rocking chairs for non-shoppers and an assortment of antiques, collectibles and local arts and crafts for those inclined to spend a few bucks on a souvenir. Trillium Cove comprises a collection of gift, garden, home decor and jewelry shops.

If you're in the market for a musical instrument, stop at Wood-N-Strings Dulcimer Shop and watch a master craftsman make dulcimers and banjammers. Musicians host free back-porch pickin' sessions Saturday evenings May to September.

Outdoors enthusiasts can get fishing gear at Little River Outfitters and hiking and camping supplies at The Backcountry.

GREAT SMOKY MOUNTAINS HERITAGE CENTER, 123 Cromwell Dr., re-creates a pioneer village with historic buildings, including cantilever barns, a chapel, a sawmill, a smokehouse and a wheelwright shop. Two galleries display Native American and early settler artifacts dating from 3000 BC to the 1930s. Storytelling, drama, music and teaching events take place in a 500-seat amphitheater. Festivals, concerts and other events are offered year-round. **Time:** Allow 1 hour minimum. **Hours:** Mon.-Sat. 10-5, Sun. noon-5, Apr.-Dec.; Mon.-Sat. 10-5, rest of year. Phone ahead to confirm schedule. **Cost:** $6; $4 (ages 6-17 and 60+). **Phone:** (865) 448-0044.

LITTLE RIVER RAILROAD AND LUMBER COMPANY MUSEUM is at 7747 E. Lamar Alexander Pkwy. (US 321). The museum depicts the growth of Townsend and the history of the 100-year-old Little

(See map & index p. 84.)

River Railroad and Lumber Co. Before ceasing operations in 1939, the company reportedly was one of the largest commercial logging operations in southern Appalachia, constructing more than 150 miles of railroads in the Smoky Mountains and sawing some 500 million board feet of timber.

Time: Allow 30 minutes minimum. **Hours:** Mon.-Sat. 10-5, Sun. 1-5, June-Aug. and in Oct.; Sat. 10-5, Sun. 1-5, Apr.-May and in Sept. and Nov.; by appointment rest of year. **Cost:** Donations. **Phone:** (865) 448-2211.

TUCKALEECHEE CAVERNS is 3 mi. s. of SR 73 (US 321) to 825 Cavern Rd. Although the caverns were known to the Cherokee Indians long before the first settlers arrived, they were not opened for public touring until 1953. For many years, locals congregated in summer near a sinkhole in Dry Valley where temperatures were mysteriously cooler than anywhere else. Two young Townsend boys found an opening near the sinkhole and spent many years crawling around underground. Throughout college they dreamed of creating a tourist attraction and later worked construction jobs in Alaska to earn startup money for their business venture.

The pair spent four years clearing passageways and building concrete walkways by lantern light. One year after the opening, experienced cave explorers discovered a large room the size of a football field with 24-foot stalagmites. Today the Big Room is part of a 1-mile-long lighted walking tour that also includes a 200-foot-high double waterfall and several smaller waterfalls, a clear stream running throughout and such formations as ribbon flowstone, capillary tubes and onyx.

Cavern temperatures remain a chilly 58 F year-round. **Hours:** Daily 10-6, Apr.-Oct.; 10-5, Mar. 15-31 and Nov. 1-15. Last tour begins at closing. **Cost:** $16; $7 (ages 5-11). **Phone:** (865) 448-2274. *(See ad this page.)*

RECREATIONAL ACTIVITIES
Horseback Riding
- **Cades Cove Riding Stables** is in Cades Cove at 10018 Campground Dr. Carriage and hayrides also are available. **Hours:** Horseback and carriage rides daily 9-4:30, early Mar.-May and mid-Aug. to early Dec. Hayrides are given daily at 10, noon and 3, Mar.-Dec. (also at 6 p.m., June 1 to mid-Aug.). Closed Thanksgiving. **Phone:** (865) 448-9009.
- **Davy Crockett Riding Stables** is at 505 Old Cades Cove Rd. **Hours:** Daily 9-5, mid-Mar. to mid-Nov.; by appointment rest of year. **Phone:** (865) 448-6411.

Tubing
- **River Rage Tubing** is at 8307 SR 73. **Hours:** Daily 10-7, Apr.-Sept. (weather permitting). Phone ahead to confirm schedule. **Cost:** Tube, life vest rental and shuttle service $9 (per person, per day). **Phone:** (865) 448-8000. [T]
- **Smoky Mountain River Rat** is at 205 Wears Valley Rd. Kayaking also is available. **Hours:** Daily 10-7, May-Aug. (weather permitting). Hours may vary; phone ahead to confirm schedule. **Phone:** (865) 448-8888.

(See map & index p. 84.)

BEST WESTERN CADES COVE INN

(865)448-9000

Motel
$80-$130

AAA Benefit: Save 10% or more every day and earn 10% bonus points!

Address: 7824 E Lamar Alexander Pkwy 37882 **Location:** Jct SR 73, 0.7 mi s on US 321. **Facility:** 54 units. 2 stories (no elevator), exterior corridors. **Pool(s):** outdoor. **Activities:** exercise room. **Featured Amenity:** full hot breakfast.

HIGHLAND MANOR INN
(865)448-2211

Motel $60-$120 **Address:** 7766 E Lamar Alexander Pkwy 37882 **Location:** Jct SR 73, 0.9 mi s on US 321. **Facility:** 49 units, some kitchens. 2 stories (no elevator), exterior corridors. **Terms:** 3 day cancellation notice-fee imposed. **Pool(s):** outdoor. **Activities:** playground.

WHERE TO EAT

CARRIAGE HOUSE RESTAURANT
865/448-2263

American. Family Dining. $5-$18 **AAA Inspector Notes:** The family-owned restaurant uses a bountiful selection of crisp vegetables to prepare the salad of your choice, along with ample portions of beef, seafood and poultry. Breakfast fare includes all the traditional favorites, including biscuits, omelets and buttermilk pancakes. A small gift shop displays local art and crafts. **Features:** beer only. **Address:** 8310 St Hwy 73 37882 **Location:** Jct US 321, 0.4 mi e.

B | L | D

TRENTON (C-2) pop. 4,264, elev. 315'

Gen. Nathan B. Forrest's 1862 capture of the Union forces in Trenton had little to do with military strategy. Acting as self-appointed scouts, Trenton residents greeted Forrest by waving their hats and handkerchiefs in the direction of the Union troops' hideout. Such subtle hints led the Confederate general to the depot, where he was able to take the Federals by surprise.

Greater Gibson County Area Chamber of Commerce: 200 E. Eaton St., Trenton, TN 38382. **Phone:** (731) 855-0973.

PORCELAIN VEILLEUSE DISPLAY can be seen at City Hall, 309 College St. On display are 526 rare *veilleuse-theieres,* porcelain teapots made primarily in France and Germany in the late 18th and early 19th centuries. The teapots are shaped like animals and people and have candle warmer/night lights within the bases. The city celebrates this collection during the last week in April. **Time:** Allow 1 hour minimum. **Hours:** Mon.-Fri. 9-5. **Cost:** Free. **Phone:** (731) 855-2013.

TULLAHOMA (D-5) pop. 18,655, elev. 1,060'

Tullahoma served as the Confederate winter headquarters under Gen. Braxton Bragg in January 1863, after the bloody and indecisive battle at nearby Stones River *(see Stones River National Battlefield p. 244).* Six months later the town fell to Union forces under Gen. William Rosecrans.

The University of Tennessee Space Institute, a research institution and graduate school for engineers and scientists, conducts advanced studies in aerospace science and technology. The institute is 10 miles southeast on Woods Reservoir.

Tullahoma Area Chamber of Commerce: 135 W. Lincoln St., P.O. Box 1205, Tullahoma, TN 37388. **Phone:** (931) 455-5497.

BEECHCRAFT HERITAGE MUSEUM, 570 Old Shelbyville Hwy., offers several hangars filled with vintage aircraft. Paintings and photographs in the O.A. Beech Gallery and Chapel pay tribute to Olive Ann Beech, who co-founded Beech Aircraft Corp. with her husband, Walter H. Beech.

Displayed in a restored log cabin, the Thaden Collection consists of awards, documents, memorabilia and photographs that relate the life of Louise M. Thaden, one of America's first female pilots. **Time:** Allow 1 hour minimum. **Hours:** Tues.-Sat. 8:30-4:30, Mar.-Nov.; by appointment rest of year. Closed major holidays. **Cost:** $10; $5 (ages 12-17). **Phone:** (931) 455-1974.

GEORGE DICKEL DISTILLERY TOUR is at 1950 Cascade Hollow Rd. Guides relate the history of a whiskey distillery, in operation since 1870. Its time-honored methods of production include using fresh spring water—readily available due to the plant's location on the Cumberland Plateau—and chilling the whiskey prior to the charcoal-mellowing process.

A working post office as well as a visitor center featuring antiques and photos also are on-site. **Time:** Allow 1 hour minimum. **Hours:** Guided tours Tues.-Sat. 9-4:30. Last tour begins 1 hour before closing. Closed major holidays. **Cost:** Free. **Phone:** (931) 857-4110.

BAYMONT INN TULLAHOMA
(931)455-7891

Motel $49-$99 **Address:** 2113 N Jackson St 37388 **Location:** 3 mi n on SR 41A (N Jackson St). **Facility:** 62 units. 2 stories (no elevator), exterior corridors. **Terms:** cancellation fee imposed. **Pool(s):** outdoor. **Activities:** picnic facilities, exercise room.

QUALITY INN
(931)455-4501

Motel $78-$95 **Address:** 1410 N Jackson St 37388 **Location:** 1.1 mi n on SR 41A (N Jackson St). **Facility:** 50 units. 2 stories (no elevator), exterior corridors. **Pool(s):** outdoor.

WHERE TO EAT

EMIL'S BISTRO AND MARKETPLACE
931/461-7070

New American. Casual Dining. $7-$26 **AAA Inspector Notes:** On the fringes of the center of town, this homey café housed in a century-old former residence offers a variety of dining options ranging from light fare to full, hot entrées. The chef, a native of France, takes pride in using the freshest ingredients, applying his European training to American standards. Open for dinner Thursday and Friday evenings. **Features:** beer & wine, patio dining. **Reservations:** suggested. **Address:** 210 E Lincoln St 37388 **Location:** Between Washington and Polk sts; downtown.

UNION CITY (C-2) pop. 10,895

Two railroad tracks—one east-west and the other north-south, running nearby–inspired the city's name. The area also saw minor action during the Civil War. Nowadays Union City acts as the town seat of Obion County and boasts a revitalized downtown and modern amenities.

Obion County Chamber of Commerce: 214 E. Church St., Union City, TN 38261. **Phone:** (731) 885-0211.

DISCOVERY PARK OF AMERICA is at 830 Everett Blvd. This 50-acre indoor-outdoor adventure park engages visitors of all ages with interactive exhibits about history, the military and science. Centered prominently outside is a 100-year-old church, discovered in middle Tennessee and purchased specifically for the park, as well as an 18th-century schoolhouse, a working gristmill, a rail depot with train cars, a replica 1700s public square and a frontier settlement with log cabins.

Ten learning galleries inside the Discovery Center feature everything from a working Gutenberg printing press and the Wright brothers' first airplane to a 22,000-gallon aquarium with sea life and a STEM Landing exhibit featuring a rocket engine and a Blue Angel airplane. Military enthusiasts will want to check out the collection of military vehicles—including a PT-17 Stearman bi-plane suspended from the ceiling—and climb into a Vietnam-War era helicopter.

An indoor playground and a giant slide housed in a 60-foot-tall replica of a human body are kid-friendly favorites. Special exhibits available for an extra fee include an earthquake simulator, a starship theater and a 120-foot viewing tower with a glass elevator and glass floor panels.

Time: Allow 6 hours minimum. **Hours:** Tues.-Sun. 10-5. Closed Jan. 1, Easter, Thanksgiving and Christmas. Phone ahead to confirm schedule. **Cost:** One-day ticket $13.95; $11.95 (ages 65+); $10.95 (ages 4-12). Two-day $19.95; $16.95 (ages 65+); $14.95 (ages 4-12). Special exhibit (Earthquake Simulator, Starship Theater or The Tower) $3.95; combination ticket for all three special exhibits $9.95. **Phone:** (731) 885-5455. [¶] [🏔]

BUCKET'S NEIGHBORHOOD PUB & GRUB   731/885-6646
♥♥ Pizza Burgers. Casual Dining. $7-$19 **AAA Inspector Notes:** This sports bar and grill is a great place to watch your home-town team in action. They're famous for their fresh, creative pizzas. But you'll also find hot and mild wings, gourmet burgers and hearty salads—all of which go down nicely with a cold mug of beer. **Features:** full bar, happy hour. **Address:** 1700 W Reelfoot Ave, Suite 136 38261 **Location:** Jct SR 431, just s on US 51. [L] [D] CALL[ＬＭ]

VONORE (D-7) pop. 1,474, elev. 900'

Since the Tellico Dam was completed in 1979, the development of Vonore has been closely linked with the Tennessee Valley Authority, which now supervises the construction of residential communities and industrial areas on the land surrounding the 16,500-acre reservoir. Spared from Tellico Dam's topographical rearrangement of the area are two attractions of major historical significance.

Fort Loudoun, the first British fort west of the Appalachians, is a mile north of Vonore off US 411. During the French and Indian War the 1756 fort served as England's southwestern outpost. In 1760 the fort was burned by the Cherokees. The fort and its palisades have been reconstructed, and the site includes a powder magazine, blacksmith shop, gun platform and visitor center. *See Recreation Areas Chart.*

Across the Little Tennessee River is Tellico Blockhouse, an American military outpost built on the border of the Cherokee Nation during Tennessee's territorial period. Several important treaty negotiations were conducted with the Cherokee at this site. The blockhouse was later converted into one of the first federally operated trading posts and was a main stop on the stage route between Knoxville and Huntsville, Ala. The fort and blockhouse are open for self-guiding tours.

SEQUOYAH BIRTHPLACE MUSEUM is 1 mi. e. of US 411 at 576 SR 360. The museum honors Sequoyah, the soldier and statesman who created the Cherokee alphabet. Visitors can hear Cherokee myths and legends, examine the Cherokee syllabary, walk a 1.5-mile shoreline trail and learn about the history and culture of the Cherokee.

The Cherokee Memorial holds the remains of 18th-century Cherokees excavated from burial sites in the Little Tennessee Valley. **Time:** Allow 1 hour minimum. **Hours:** Mon.-Sat. 9-5, Sun. noon-5. Closed Jan. 1, Thanksgiving and Christmas. **Cost:** $3; $2.50 (ages 55+); $1.50 (ages 6-12). **Phone:** (423) 884-6246.

GRAND VISTA HOTEL & SUITES   423/884-6200
♥♥ **Hotel.** Rates not provided. **Address:** 117 Grand Vista Dr 37885 **Location:** I-75 exit 72, 14 mi e on SR 72, just e into Tellico West Industrial Park southern entrance, just n onto Deer Crossing, then just nw. **Facility:** 47 units. 2 stories, interior corridors. **Pool(s):** outdoor. **Activities:** limited exercise equipment. **Guest Services:** coin laundry.
CALL[ＬＭ] [🏊] [HS] [📶] [✕] [🍴] [📷] [📼]

WALLAND (D-7) pop. 259, elev. 922'
• **Attractions map p. 100**

RECREATIONAL ACTIVITIES
Horseback Riding
• **Apple Valley Stables** is at 5641 Old Walland Hwy. **Hours:** Reservations are required; phone ahead to confirm schedule. **Phone:** (865) 448-8300 or (888) 785-2708.

WHITE HOUSE (C-4) pop. 10,255, elev. 863'

WHITE HOUSE INN LIBRARY & MUSEUM is at 412 SR 76. Through a wide variety of artifacts and antiques, the museum relates the history of White House. Accessible only via stairs, the second-floor museum is in a replica of the circa 1829 building around which the town grew. A DVD virtual tour can be viewed from a computer in the main-floor library. **Time:** Allow 30 minutes minimum. **Hours:** Mon.-Tues. and Thurs. 9-8, Wed. 9-5, Sat. 9-noon. Closed major holidays. **Cost:** Free. **Phone:** (615) 672-0239.

BEST WESTERN PLUS WHITE HOUSE (615)672-3993

Hotel
$89-$159

 AAA Benefit:
Save 10% or more every day and earn 10% bonus points!

Address: 404 Hester Dr 37188 **Location:** I-65 exit 108, just e, then just s. **Facility:** 71 units. 3 stories, interior corridors. **Pool(s):** heated indoor. **Activities:** hot tub, picnic facilities, exercise room. **Guest Services:** valet and coin laundry. **Featured Amenity:** full hot breakfast.

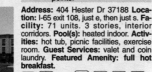

 / SOME UNITS

HOLIDAY INN EXPRESS (615)672-7200

Hotel
$140-$250

Address: 206 Knight Cir 37188 **Location:** I-65 exit 108, just e. **Facility:** 70 units. 3 stories, interior corridors. **Terms:** cancellation fee imposed. **Pool(s):** outdoor. **Activities:** exercise room. **Guest Services:** valet and coin laundry.

 WHERE TO EAT

CHINA SPRING 615/672-3330

 Chinese. Quick Serve. $6-$12 **AAA Inspector Notes:** Guests at this casual spot can sample many different combination plates of beef, chicken, pork, shrimp and veggies as well as wonton soup and egg drop soup. Favorites include the chef's special of sesame chicken as well as the house special featuring scallops, shrimp, chicken, mushrooms and snow peas. **Address:** 301 Richard Wilks Rd 37188 **Location:** I-65 exit 108, just e, then just n. L D CALL

LOS AGAVE'S MEXICAN GRILL 615/672-1122

Mexican. Casual Dining. $5-$12 **AAA Inspector Notes:** This comfortable, popular restaurant dishes up all the favorites, including at least six types of fajitas, wonderful fish tacos and large salads of steak and shrimp as well as a huge burrito California with a choice of steak or grilled chicken. There are more than 100 combinations of lunch and dinner items as well as specialty desserts. **Features:** full bar, patio dining. **Address:** 301 Richard Wilks Rd 37188 **Location:** I-65 exit 108, just e, then just n. L D CALL

WHITES CREEK (C-4) elev. 469'
• Part of Nashville area — see map p. 179

SAVE **FONTANEL MANSION,** 4125 Whites Creek Pike, is the former home of Country Music Hall of Fame member Barbara Mandrell. The 27,000-square-foot log mansion is open for tours and features more than 20 rooms, 13 bathrooms, 5 fireplaces, 2 kitchens, an indoor pool and an indoor shooting range. Decor includes country music memorabilia and photos. Also on the grounds is a 2.5-mile trail for hiking and mountain biking.

Hours: Guided 75-minute tours given daily on the hour 9-3. Tour schedule may vary during special events; phone ahead. Closed Thanksgiving and Christmas. **Cost:** $24; $22 (ages 60+, students and retired military with ID); $14 (ages 7-15); free (ages

0-6 and active military with ID). Reservations are recommended. **Phone:** (615) 724-1600. GT

WHITWELL (D-5) pop. 1,699, elev. 679'

CHILDREN'S HOLOCAUST MEMORIAL AND PAPER CLIP PROJECT is at 1 Butterfly Ln. at Whitwell Middle School. To better grasp the number 6,000,000—the number of Jews exterminated by the Nazis—a middle-school class studying the Holocaust began collecting paper clips, which were worn by Norwegians to protest against Nazi occupation in World War II. A German rail car contains 11 million paper clips, while another 11 million are in a monument honoring the children of Terezin. Other exhibits include historical documents and artifacts.

Time: Allow 45 minutes minimum. **Hours:** Mon.-Fri. 8-3, Aug.-May. During after-school hours, self-guiding audio tours of the rail car are available from Smith Bros. Grocery, 13835 SR 28. **Cost:** Free. **Phone:** (423) 658-5631.

WINCHESTER (D-5) pop. 8,530, elev. 958'

Winchester lies east of Tims Ford Dam and Reservoir, an immense Tennessee Valley Authority project that provided rural electrification in 1970. Since then the project has provided a focus for recreation in Franklin County, of which Winchester is the county seat. Tims Ford State Park *(see Recreation Areas Chart)* covers 10,700 acres and offers varied recreational opportunities. Davy Crockett's farm, Kentuck, once occupied a site south of Winchester near Belvidere.

Franklin County Chamber of Commerce: 44 Chamber Way, P.O. Box 280, Winchester, TN 37398. **Phone:** (931) 967-6788.

FRANKLIN COUNTY OLD JAIL MUSEUM is at 400 Dinah Shore Blvd. N.E. (US 41A). The 1897 brick jailhouse features Native American artifacts, Civil War memorabilia, farm tools, weapons, a display about Winchester native Dinah Shore and a restored jail cell. Visitors can peruse displays about World Wars I and II as well as the Korean, Vietnam and Gulf wars. **Time:** Allow 30 minutes minimum. **Hours:** Tues.-Sat. 10-4, Mar.-Oct. **Cost:** $1. **Phone:** (931) 967-0524.

BEST WESTERN INN (931)967-9444

Motel
$81-$90

 AAA Benefit:
Save 10% or more every day and earn 10% bonus points!

Address: 1602 Dinah Shore Blvd 37398 **Location:** Jct US 41A and 41 Bypass, just w. **Facility:** 51 units, some kitchens. 1-2 stories (no elevator), exterior corridors. **Pool(s):** outdoor. **Activities:** exercise room. **Guest Services:** coin laundry.

   / SOME UNITS

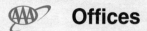 Offices

Main office listings are shown in **BOLD TYPE** and toll-free member service numbers appear in *ITALIC TYPE*.
All are closed Saturdays, Sundays and holidays unless otherwise indicated.
The addresses, phone numbers and hours for any AAA/CAA office are subject to change.
The type of service provided is designated below the name of the city where the office is located:

+ Auto travel services, including books and maps, and on-demand TripTik ® routings.
● Auto travel services, including selected books and maps, and on-demand TripTik ® routings.
■ Books/maps only, no marked maps or on-demand TripTik ® routings.
▲ Travel Agency Services, cruise, tour, air, car and rail reservations; domestic and international hotel reservations; passport photo services; international and domestic travel guides and maps; travel money products; and International Driving Permits. In addition, assistance with travel related insurance products including trip cancellation, travel accident, lost luggage, trip delay and assistance products.
○ Insurance services provided. If only this icon appears, only insurance services are provided at that office.
C Car Care Plus Facility provides car care services.
⊞ Electric vehicle charging station on premises.

AAA NATIONAL OFFICE: 1000 AAA DRIVE, HEATHROW, FLORIDA 32746-5063, (407) 444-7000

TENNESSEE

BRENTWOOD—AUTO CLUB GROUP - SOUTHERN REGION, 1701 MALLORY LN STE 200, 37027. WEEKDAYS (M-F) 9:00-6:00. (615) 376-1601 + ▲ ○

CHATTANOOGA—AUTO CLUB GROUP - SOUTHERN REGION, 2111 GUNBARREL RD, 37421. WEEKDAYS (M-F) 9:00-6:00. (423) 490-2000 + ▲ ○

CORDOVA—AUTO CLUB GROUP - SOUTHERN REGION, 990 N GERMANTOWN PKY #102, 38018. WEEKDAYS (M-F) 9:00-6:00. (901) 751-4577 + ▲ ○

HENDERSONVILLE—AUTO CLUB GROUP - SOUTHERN REGION, 1012 ANDREWS RUN LN #B, 37075. WEEKDAYS (M-F) 9:00-6:00. (615) 264-5480 + ▲ ○

JOHNSON CITY—AUTO CLUB GROUP - SOUTHERN REGION, 3000 PEOPLES ST, 37604. WEEKDAYS (M-F) 8:30-5:30. (423) 928-7671 + ▲ ○

KNOXVILLE—AUTO CLUB GROUP - SOUTHERN REGION, 100 W FIFTH AVE, 37917. WEEKDAYS (M-F) 8:30-5:00. (865) 637-1910, *(800) 234-1222.* + ▲ ○

KNOXVILLE—AUTO CLUB GROUP - SOUTHERN REGION, 110 CAPITAL DR, 37922. WEEKDAYS (M-F) 9:00-6:00. (865) 637-1910 + ▲ ○

MARYVILLE—AUTO CLUB GROUP - SOUTHERN REGION, 715 W LAMAR ALEXANDER PKY, 37801. WEEKDAYS (M-F) 8:30-5:00. (865) 862-9132 + ▲ ○

MURFREESBORO—AUTO CLUB GROUP - SOUTHERN REGION, 1970 OLD FORT PKWY #B, 37129. WEEKDAYS (M-F) 9:00-6:00. (615) 896-5585 + ▲ ○

NASHVILLE—AUTO CLUB GROUP - SOUTHERN REGION, 2501 21ST AVE S #1, 37212. WEEKDAYS (M-F) 9:00-6:00. (615) 297-7700 + ▲ ○

Metric Equivalents Chart

TEMPERATURE

To convert Fahrenheit to Celsius, subtract 32 from the Fahrenheit temperature, multiply by 5 and divide by 9. To convert Celsius to Fahrenheit, multiply by 9, divide by 5 and add 32.

ACRES

1 acre = 0.4 hectare (ha)   1 hectare = 2.47 acres

MILES AND KILOMETERS

Note: A kilometer is approximately 5/8 or 0.6 of a mile. To convert kilometers to miles multiply by 0.6.

Miles/Kilometers		Kilometers/Miles	
15	24.1	30	18.6
20	32.2	35	21.7
25	40.2	40	24.8
30	48.3	45	27.9
35	56.3	50	31.0
40	64.4	55	34.1
45	72.4	60	37.2
50	80.5	65	40.3
55	88.5	70	43.4
60	96.6	75	46.6
65	104.6	80	49.7
70	112.7	85	52.8
75	120.7	90	55.9
80	128.7	95	59.0
85	136.8	100	62.1
90	144.8	105	65.2
95	152.9	110	68.3
100	160.9	115	71.4

LINEAR MEASURE

Customary	Metric
1 inch = 2.54 centimeters	1 centimeter = 0.4 inches
1 foot = 30 centimeters	1 meter = 3.3 feet
1 yard = 0.91 meters	1 meter = 1.09 yards
1 mile = 1.6 kilometers	1 kilometer = .62 miles

LIQUID MEASURE

Customary	Metric
1 fluid ounce = 30 milliliters	1 milliliter = .03 fluid ounces
1 cup = .24 liters	1 liter = 2.1 pints
1 pint = .47 liters	1 liter = 1.06 quarts
1 quart = .95 liters	1 liter = .26 gallons
1 gallon = 3.8 liters	

Celsius ° — Fahrenheit °

Celsius		Fahrenheit
100	BOILING	212
37		100
35		95
32		90
29		85
27		80
24		75
21		70
18		65
16		60
13		55
10		50
7		45
4		40
2		35
0	FREEZING	32
-4		25
-7		20
-9		15
-12		10
-15		5
-18		0
-21		-5
-24		-10
-27		-15

WEIGHT

If You Know:	Multiply By:	To Find:
Ounces	28	Grams
Pounds	0.45	Kilograms
Grams	0.035	Ounces
Kilograms	2.2	Pounds

PRESSURE

Air pressure in automobile tires is expressed in kilopascals. Multiply pound-force per square inch (psi) by 6.89 to find kilopascals (kPa).

24 psi = 165 kPa   28 psi = 193 kPa
26 psi = 179 kPa   30 psi = 207 kPa

GALLONS AND LITERS

Gallons/Liters				Liters/Gallons			
5	19.0	12	45.6	10	2.6	40	10.4
6	22.8	14	53.2	15	3.9	50	13.0
7	26.6	16	60.8	20	5.2	60	15.6
8	30.4	18	68.4	25	6.5	70	18.2
9	34.2	20	76.0	30	7.8	80	20.8
10	38.0	25	95.0	35	9.1	90	23.4

252

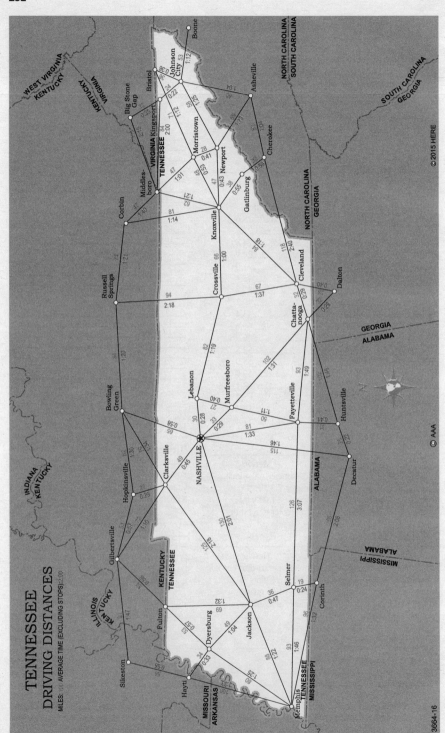

TENNESSEE
DRIVING DISTANCES
MILES: 00 AVERAGE TIME (EXCLUDING STOPS)2:00

Points of Interest Index

Attractions appear at the top of each category
and offer a Great Experience for Members®.

Index Legend

CHILDREN'S ACTIVITIES

EVENTS & FESTIVALS

HISTORIC SITES & EXHIBITS

OUTDOORS & SCIENCE

Photo Credits

Page numbers are in bold type. Picture credit abbreviations are as follows:
- (i) numeric sequence from top to bottom, left to right ■ (AAA) AAA Travel library.

- (Cover) Dollywood, Pigeon Forge / Courtesy of Dollywood
- 2 (i) © Elizabeth Leyden / Alamy
- 2 (ii) Courtesy of the Nashville CVB
- 2 (iii) © Maxine Livingston / Shutterstock.com
- 2 (iv) Courtesy of The Old Mill
- 12 (i) Courtesy of Berry Manor Inn
- 12 (ii) © Chris Dew / Killarney Lodge
- 12 (iii) Courtesy of Hyatt Hotels
- 12 (iv) Courtesy of Montpelier Plantation and Beach
- 12 (v) © Elisa Rolle / Wikimedia Commons
- 12 (vi) Courtesy of The Shores Resort & Spa
- 12 (vii) Courtesy of All Star Vacation Homes
- 12 (viii) Courtesy of Bryce View Lodge
- 12 (ix) Courtesy of Vista Verde Guest Ranch
- 13 Courtesy of Divi Resorts
- 18 (i) © iStockphoto.com / Davel5957
- 18 (ii) © Andrew Soundarajan / Alamy
- 19 © KennStilger47 / Shutterstock.com
- 20 (i) © North Wind Picture Archives / Alamy
- 20 (ii) © Everett Collection Inc. / age fotostock
- 23 (i) © Maxine Livingston / Shutterstock.com
- 23 (ii) © iStockphoto.com / benkrut
- 23 (iii) Courtesy of The Old Mill
- 23 (iv) © Rob Shenk / flickr
- 23 (v) © Bob Delevante / Discovery Park of America

- 24 (i) Courtesy of Hunter Museum of American Art
- 24 (ii) © Van.ike / Wikimedia Commons
- 24 (iii) Courtesy of Dollywood Publicity Department
- 24 (iv) Courtesy of Tennessee Museum of Aviation
- 133 © Elizabeth Leyden / Alamy
- 136 © Martin Norris Travel Photography 2 / Alamy
- 137 © Elizabeth Leyden / Alamy
- 138 Courtesy of Memphis Botanic Garden
- 139 © Ilene MacDonald / Alamy
- 140 © Karen Cowled / Alamy
- 141 © Nikreates / Alamy
- 142 Courtesy of Peabody Memphis
- 143 © ZUMA Press, Inc / Alamy
- 144 © ZUMA Press, Inc / Alamy
- 148 © Elvis Presley Enterprises, Inc.
- 149 © iStockphoto.com / dossyl
- 178 © iStockphoto.com / Sean Pavone
- 181 Courtesy of Gaylord Opryland Resort & Convention Center
- 182 © Brian Jannsen / Alamy
- 183 Courtesy of the Nashville CVB
- 184 © iStockphoto.com / hartcreations
- 185 © Radharc Images / Alamy
- 186 © Martin Thomas Photography / Alamy
- 187 © Brian Jannsen / Alamy
- 188 © Ken Barber / Alamy
- 189 © Ilene MacDonald / Alamy
- 191 © Jon Arnold Images Ltd / Alamy
- 192 © America / Alamy

Let Your Voice Be Heard

We Want To Hear From You

- If a AAA listed establishment doesn't meet your expectations, send us the details so we can look into it.
- Or, if you've got a favorite hotel, restaurant or attraction you'd like us to consider for AAA inspection, send us your recommendation.

Visit us at **AAA.com/TourBookComments**